Tax Administration 2015

COMPARATIVE INFORMATION ON OECD AND OTHER ADVANCED AND EMERGING ECONOMIES

OECD
BETTER POLICIES FOR BETTER LIVES

This work is published under the responsibility of the Secretary-General of the OECD. The opinions expressed and arguments employed herein do not necessarily reflect the official views of OECD member countries.

This document and any map included herein are without prejudice to the status of or sovereignty over any territory, to the delimitation of international frontiers and boundaries and to the name of any territory, city or area.

Please cite this publication as:
OECD (2015), *Tax Administration 2015: Comparative Information on OECD and Other Advanced and Emerging Economies*, OECD Publishing, Paris.
http://dx.doi.org/10.1787/tax_admin-2015-en

ISBN 978-92-64-23231-0 (print)
ISBN 978-92-64-23234-1 (PDF)

Series: Tax Administration
ISSN 2308-7331 (print)
ISSN 2307-7727 (online)

The statistical data for Israel are supplied by and under the responsibility of the relevant Israeli authorities. The use of such data by the OECD is without prejudice to the status of the Golan Heights, East Jerusalem and Israeli settlements in the West Bank under the terms of international law.

Photo credits: Cover © Bruce Rolff/Shutterstock.com

Foreword

Tax Administration 2015 is the sixth edition of the OECD Centre for Tax Policy and Administration's biennial Comparative Information Series. The series' primary purpose is to share information that will facilitate dialogue among tax officials on important tax administration issues, and which may also identify opportunities for ministries of finance and revenue bodies to improve the design and administration of their tax systems.

This edition of the series provides internationally comparative data on aspects of tax systems and their administration in 56 advanced and emerging economies, and includes performance-related data, ratios and trends up to the end of the 2013 fiscal year for the countries concerned.

The comparative series was conceived by Richard Highfield (Senior Adviser, Centre for Tax Policy and Administration) and developed under the auspices of the Forum on Tax Administration. This edition was prepared by Oliver Petzold, Devi Thani and Richard Highfield, with considerable support received from tax officials of the revenue bodies that participated in the compilation of the series.

Tax Administration 2015 is published under the responsibility of the Secretary-General of the OECD.

Table of contents

Foreword 3

Abbreviations and Acronyms 11

Executive summary 15

Introduction 19

Chapter 1. **Institutional arrangements for tax administration** 21

Key points 22
Introduction 23
The revenue body as an institution 26
The extent of revenue body autonomy 31
Scope of responsibilities of the revenue body 34
Special governance arrangements 42
Special institutional arrangements for dealing with taxpayers' complaints 48
Bibliography 54

Chapter 2. **The organisation of revenue bodies** 57

Key points 58
Getting organised to collect taxes 59
Office networks for tax administration 80
Large taxpayer operations 85
Managing the tax affairs of high net worth individuals taxpayers 92
Bibliography 102

Chapter 3. **Selected aspects of strategic management in tax administration** 103

Key points 104
Managing for improved performance 105
Planning and management approaches of revenue bodies 107
Managing and improving taxpayers' compliance 123
Adopting a risk management approach 123
Use of computer-based data matching systems to address non-compliance 135
Bibliography 139

Chapter 4. **Human resource management and tax administration** 141

Key points 142
Introduction 143
Aspects of revenue bodies' HRM strategy 144
Changes in policy in aspects of HRM within revenue bodies 147

Staff metrics: Staff numbers and attrition, age profiles and qualifications 160
Bibliography 167

Chapter 5. **Resources of national revenue bodies** 169

Key points 170
The resources of national revenue bodies 171
Impacts of recent Government decisions on revenue bodies' budgets 171
Overall tax administration expenditure 173
Measures of relative costs of administration 178
International comparisons of administrative expenditure and staffing 183
Third party service delivery of revenue body functions/operations 192

Chapter 6. **Operational performance of revenue bodies** 199

Key points 200
Introduction 201
Tax revenue collections 201
Refunds of taxes 207
Taxpayer service delivery 210
Tax verification activities 217
Tax disputes 223
Tax debts and their collection 228
Bibliography 239

Chapter 7. **The use of online services in tax administration** 241

Key points 242
Provision and use of modern online services in tax administration 243
Enhancing online services: Considerable progress has been made but much more can be done 243
Bibliography 260

Chapter 8. **Tax administration and tax intermediaries** 261

Key points 262
Introduction and context 262
The population and work volumes of tax intermediaries 264
Regulation of tax intermediaries 264
The services and support provided to tax intermediaries 266
Bibliography 277

Chapter 9. **Legislated administrative frameworks for tax administration** 279

Key points 280
Introduction 281
Taxpayers' rights and obligations 282
Access to tax rulings 288
Taxpayer registration and identification numbering systems 290
Collection and assessment of taxes 297
Withholding regimes for other categories of income 301
Use of third party information reporting requirements 304
Administrative review 313
Enforced collection of unpaid taxes 313
Information and access powers 318
Tax offences (including policies to encourage voluntary disclosures) 324
Bibliography 343

Annex A. **Aggregate Tables** . . . 345

Annex B. **Description of formulae used for computation of ratios** . . . 373

Annex C. **Participating revenue bodies** . . . 377

Figures

Figure 2.1 Croatia: Tax Administration . . . 65
Figure 2.2 Latvia's State Revenue Service . . . 65
Figure 2.3 Thailand's Revenue Department . . . 66
Figure 3.1 The compliance risk management framework . . . 123
Figure 5.1 HMRC staffing levels 2005 to 2016 . . . 173
Figure 5.2 Labour force participants/FTE on tax and support functions (OECD countries) . . . 188
Figure 5.3 Labour force participants/FTE on tax and support vis-à-vis tax expenditure/GDP (OECD countries) . . . 188
Figure 5.4 Average FTE usage for key functional groupings (OECD countries) . . . 190
Figure 7.1 The demand management framework . . . 244
Figure 7.2 Maturity model of pre-filling capabilities . . . 255
Figure 7.3 Maturity model of payment methods . . . 257

Tables

Table 1.1 Institutional arrangements for tax administration . . . 29
Table 1.2 Delegated authority of national revenue bodies . . . 32
Table 1.3 Authority delegated to revenue bodies . . . 34
Table 1.4 Social security contributions: Assistance provided by selected revenue bodies . . . 39
Table 1.5 Non-tax roles of revenue bodies reporting such roles . . . 40
Table 1.6 Special body for dealing with taxpayers' complaints . . . 48
Table 2.1 Selected features of the organisational structure of revenue bodies . . . 62
Table 2.2 Features of the organisation structure of selected revenue bodies . . . 63
Table 2.3 Office network for tax administration role-office types by number . . . 83
Table 2.4 Office network for tax administration role-number of staff by office type . . . 84
Table 2.5 Large taxpayer operations: Identification criteria used in 2013 . . . 86
Table 2.6 Large taxpayers: Numbers administered, staff usage and verification results . . . 91
Table 2.7 Revenue bodies with dedicated high net worth individuals dedicated units – operational data for 2012 and 2013 . . . 96
Table 3.1 Selected management practices: business plans, annual reports, surveys . . . 108
Table 3.2 Quantified targets reported by revenue bodies for key areas of performance . . . 110
Table 3.3 Key elements of strategic plans – Australian Tax Office . . . 117
Table 3.4 Key elements of strategic plans – Latvia's State Revenue Service . . . 118
Table 3.5 Key elements of strategic plans – New Zealand Inland Revenue . . . 119
Table 3.6 Key elements of strategic plans – South Africa Revenue Service . . . 120
Table 3.7 Key elements of strategic plans – United Kingdom Revenue and Customs . . . 121
Table 3.8 Key elements of strategic plans – United States Revenue Service . . . 122
Table 3.9 Strategic approach for managing taxpayers' compliance . . . 129
Table 3.10 Managing taxpayers' compliance – Main compliance risks reported for 2014 . . . 130
Table 3.11 Tax gap estimation activities of selected revenue bodies, etc. . . . 132
Table 4.1 Revenue bodies' human resources management (HRM) strategies . . . 145
Table 4.2 Autonomy in staff appointments and measuring staff satisfaction and engagement . . . 151
Table 4.3 Revenue bodies' initiatives to support staff developments . . . 154
Table 4.4 Examples of specific programmes for knowledge capturing . . . 156
Table 4.5 Performance management and remuneration . . . 157
Table 4.6 Staff metrics – arrivals, departures, age profile and academic qualifications . . . 162
Table 4.7 Age profile of revenue body staff in regional groupings . . . 163

Table 4.8 Age profiles and staff with degrees etc., in selected countries 163
Table 5.1 Government downsizing/staff reduction programmes 172
Table 5.2 Salary expenditure/total expenditure for tax administration and support functions 174
Table 5.3 IT and human resource management expenditure (% of all expenditure) 177
Table 5.4 Cost of collection ratios (administrative costs/net revenue collections)/1 181
Table 5.5 Tax administration expenditure/gross domestic product (GDP) 182
Table 5.6 Revenue body staff usage for fiscal year 2013 and related ratios 187
Table 5.7 Staff usage (2013) by major tax functional groupings (% of total usage) 191
Table 5.8 Third party service delivery of tax administration functions 192
Table 5.9 Expenditure on non-tax roles (% of total revenue body expenditure) 194
Table 6.1 Aggregate tax collections (by major tax type) for 2012 and prior years 203
Table 6.2 VAT revenue ratio (VRR) in OECD countries 206
Table 6.3 Revenue collections and refunds (relative shares) 209
Table 6.4 Taxpayer services: Service demand ratios 212
Table 6.5 Service standards and performance in 2013: PIT returns and complaints 214
Table 6.6 Service standards and performance in 2013: VAT refunds and correspondence 215
Table 6.7 Service standards and performance in 2013: In-person and phone inquiries 216
Table 6.8 Examples of responsive service standards and good standards of performance 217
Table 6.9 Verification actions: Value of assessments/total net revenue collections 219
Table 6.10 Verification actions: Number completed for all taxpayer categories 221
Table 6.11 Verification actions: Number completed for large taxpayers 222
Table 6.12 Tax disputes in administrative review: Finalised cases 224
Table 6.13 Tax disputes in administrative review: Unfinalised cases at year-end 226
Table 6.14 Tax debt – year-end aggregates 231
Table 6.15 Tax debts: Debt written off as a share of debt inventory 232
Table 6.16 Tax debts: Movement in tax debt case numbers 233
Table 6.17 Aspects of tax debt collection performance in selected countries 235
Table 7.1 Menu of possible self-service capabilities for enhancing taxpayer services 245
Table 7.2 Strategic priorities for increasing use of online services 247
Table 7.3 Personal income tax returns: Use of electronic filing and pre-filling 251
Table 7.4 Corporate income tax returns: Use of electronic filing and pre-filling 252
Table 7.5 Value added tax (VAT) returns: Use of electronic filing and pre-filling 253
Table 7.6 Tax payment methods available and volume usage (%) in 2013 258
Table 8.1 Tax intermediaries: Laws and regulations, returns prepared, surveys 267
Table 8.2 Menu of possible services to assist tax intermediaries 270
Table 8.3 Examples of on-line services to assist tax intermediaries 273
Table 8.4 Tax administration: Supporting and interacting with tax intermediaries 274
Table 9.1 Taxpayers' rights and selected features of the revenue rulings system 289
Table 9.2 System of taxpayer identifiers used and numbers of registrations – PIT 293
Table 9.3 System of taxpayer identifiers used and number of registrations – CIT and VAT 294
Table 9.4 Use of taxpayer identifiers for information reporting and matching 296
Table 9.5 Personal income tax: Employer withholding, payment and income reporting obligations 302
Table 9.6 Withholding and reporting regimes for income of resident taxpayers 305
Table 9.7 Withholding and reporting regimes for income of non-resident taxpayers 306
Table 9.8 Personal income tax: Assessment system and advance payments (excl. withholdings) . . . 309
Table 9.9 Corporate income tax: Advance payment and annual return filing obligations 310
Table 9.10 Country examples of differentiated tax filing and/or payment regimes 312
Table 9.11 VAT: Payment and return filing obligations 314
Table 9.12 Selected features of tax disputes of assessment or rulings 316
Table 9.13 Enforced tax debt collection powers 320
Table 9.14 Verification of taxpayers' liabilities: information access and search powers of tax officials 322
Table 9.15 Incorrect reporting of tax liabilities – framework for sanctions 325
Table 9.16 Revenue bodies' use of voluntary disclosure 327
Table 9.17 Examples of voluntary disclosure regimes 328
Table A.1 Revenue aggregates: Gross revenue collections for all taxes administered 346

Table A.2 Revenue aggregates: Total refunds of taxes administered, and gross VAT collections and refunds 348
Table A.3 Net revenue collections for all taxes administered by revenue body 350
Table A.4 Aggregate expenditure for all revenue body functions and total expenditure for information technology operations 352
Table A.5 Aggregate expenditure for tax functions and related overheads and human resource management expenditure 354
Table A.6 Total staff usage in 2013 by functional groupings (FTEs) and total salary costs for tax functions and related overheads 356
Table A.7 Value of tax debt outstanding at the year-end: excluding disputed tax debt vs. including disputed tax debt 358
Table A.8 Value of tax debt written off 360
Table A.9 Total amount of debt collected from enforcement actions during the fiscal year and number of year-end debt cases 362
Table A.10 Value of verification actions: For all taxpayers and large taxpayers 364
Table A.11 Service demand volumes for selected services 366
Table A.12 Service demand volumes for selected services 368
Table A.13 General country statistical information: GDP, citizen and labour force populations 370
Table B.1 Description of formulae used for computation of ratios 374
Table C.1 Country details of participating revenue bodies 378

Boxes

Box 1.1 EU Fiscal Blueprints: An overall framework for tax administration 24
Box 1.2 EU Fiscal Blueprints: Structure and administration 25
Box 1.3 Unusual institutional arrangements for national tax system administration 28
Box 1.4 Typical powers of semi-autonomous revenue bodies 33
Box 1.5 The integration of tax and SSC collection 36
Box 2.1 Why is the choice of an organisational model so important? 61
Box 2.2 Cyprus: Developments in institutional and organisational reform 70
Box 2.3 United States: Recent and planned organisational reforms 79
Box 2.4 Examples of large scale office network rationalisation programmes 81
Box 2.5 Portugal's new Large Taxpayer Unit 89
Box 2.6 The state of the world's wealth: Some recent research findings 94
Box 2.7 The United State IRS's Global High Wealth area 96
Box 3.1 Key trends in public sector administration reform 106
Box 3.2 United States IRS: Major trends affecting the IRS – 2014-17 (abbreviated comments extracted from plan) 115
Box 3.3 Austria: The use of horizontal monitoring by the tax administration 131
Box 3.4 United Kingdom HMRC's random audit programmes 135
Box 4.1 United States: Strategy for building a talented, competent and motivated workforce 146
Box 4.2 France: Structure and distribution of human resources 148
Box 4.3 Recruitment practices and policy change 150
Box 4.4 The use of staff surveys to assess staff satisfaction and engagement 152
Box 4.5 Staff development, including engagement with third parties 155
Box 4.6 Italy's performance management system 158
Box 4.7 Unique pay systems of selected revenue bodies 159
Box 5.1 The cost of collection ratio as an indicator of efficiency and/or effectiveness 178
Box 5.2 International comparisons of cost of collection ratios 184
Box 5.3 Categorisation of revenue body operations 189
Box 6.1 Understanding the performance of VAT systems – the VAT revenue ratio (VRR) 204
Box 6.2 Factors that can contribute to a high incidence of tax refunds 208
Box 6.3 Essential features of a modern tax debt collection capability 228
Box 7.1 Argentina's (AFIP) website tools to assist taxpayers 246
Box 7.2 United Kingdom: Building better services for taxpayers 248

Box 7.3 Canada and South Africa: New service offerings 249
Box 8.1 Study into the role of tax intermediaries: The enhanced relationship 263
Box 8.2 The Netherlands: Horizontal monitoring and tax intermediaries. 268
Box 8.3 United Kingdom: HMRC's strategy for administering tax agents. 269
Box 9.1 Illustrative Taxpayers' Charter: Description of taxpayers' rights and obligations. 284
Box 9.2 Ireland: Revenue's Customer Service Charter 286
Box 9.3 United States: Taxpayer Bill of Rights 287
Box 9.4 Japan. New numbering system for tax and social security administration 290
Box 9.5 United Kingdom. Collecting employees' PAYE data in real time 298
Box 9.6 Withholding regimes and self-employment/business income 304

Abbreviations and Acronyms

ACSI	American Customer Satisfaction Index
AE	Agenzia Entrate (Italy's revenue body)
AFIP	Administración Federal Ingresos Publicos (Argentina's revenue body)
AN	Alpha-numeric
ATO	Australian Taxation Office
ATP	Aggressive Tax Planning
BEPS	Base Erosion and Profit Shifting
CFA	Committee on Fiscal Affairs (OECD)
CIT	Corporate income tax
CIAT	Inter-American Center of Tax Administration
CRA	Canada Revenue Agency
CRS	Common Reporting Standard
CTPA	Centre for Tax Policy and Administration (OECD)
DFID	Department for International Development
DGFiP	Directorate Générale des Finances Publiques (France`s Public Finance Administration)
DIAN	Direccion de Impuestos y Aduanas Nationales (Colombia's tax and customs administration)
DPC	Data processing centres
DT	Direct Taxes
DZIT	Department of Zakat and Income Tax (Saudi Arabia)
EA	Enforcement Authority (Sweden)
EC	European Commission
EISS	European Institute of Social Security
EOI	Exchange of Information
ETCB	Estonian Tax and Customs Board
EU	European Union
FDSR	Financial Directorate of the Slovak Republic (Slovakia's revenue body)
FTA	Forum on Tax Administration (OECD)

FTE	Full-time equivalent
FTS	Federal Tax Service (Russian Federation)
GDP	Gross domestic product
GST	Goods and Services Tax
HMRC	Her Majesty's Revenue and Customs (United Kingdom)
HNWI	High Net Wealth Individuals
HRD	Human Resource Development
HRM	Human Resource Management
HST	Harmonised Sales Tax
ICT	Information and communications technology
IGT	Inspector-General of Taxation
IMF	International Monetary Fund
IOTA	Intra-European Organisation of Tax Administrations
IRAS	Inland Revenue Authority of Singapore
IRBM	Inland Revenue Board of Malaysia (the direct taxes administration)
IR	Inland Revenue (New Zealand's revenue body)
IRS	Internal Revenue Service (United States)
IT	Information technology
IVR	Interactive voice response
LB&I	Large Business and International (of the IRS)
LTU	Large Taxpayer Unit
MDMOF	Multiple directorates in Ministry of Finance
MOF	Ministry of Finance
NAFA	National Agency for Fiscal Administration (Romania)
NAO	National Audit Office (United Kingdom)
NRA	National Revenue Agency (Bulgaria)
NRP	National Research Programme
NTA	National Tax Agency (Japan's revenue body)
NTCA	Netherlands Tax and Customs Administration
NTS	National Tax Service (Korea's revenue body)
OCS	Organisational Climate Survey (of IRAS)
OECD	Organisation for Economic Co-operation and Development
OPR	Office of Professional Responsibility
PAYE	Pay-as-you-earn

PIT	Personal income tax
ROS	Revenue On-Line Service (Ireland)
RTI	Real Time Information
RTO	Return Preparer Office
RTPP	Registration of Tax Preparers' Programme
SARS	South Africa Revenue Service
SAT	Servicio de Administración Tributaria (Mexico's tax and customs administration)
SDMOF	Single directorate in Ministry of Finance
SKAT	Denmark's tax and customs administration
SME	Small and medium-sized enterprises
SRS	State Revenue Service (Latvia's revenue and customs body)
SSC	Social security contributions
STA	Swedish Tax Agency
STI	State Tax Inspectorate (Lithuania)
TA	Tax Academy
TAS	Taxpayer Advocate Service (United States)
TAS	Tax Agent Services
TBS	Treasury Board Secretariat
TIGTA	Treasury Inspector General for Tax Administration (United States)
TIN	Taxpayer Identification Number
TO	Taxpayers' Ombudsman
TRP	Tax Return Preparer
USB	Unified semi-autonomous body
USBB	Unified semi-autonomous body with a board
VAT	Value added tax
VDP	Voluntary Disclosure Programme
VERO	Finnish Tax Administration
WB	World Bank

Executive summary

Tax Administration 2015 presents a broad view of tax system administration in 56 countries, drawing attention to many developments and trends in design, management, and performance. Important points to note include:

- Institutional and organisational reforms continue to be a prominent feature of efforts in many countries to improve efficiency and effectiveness. For example:
  - The establishment of revenue institutions with increased autonomy, integrating direct and indirect tax administrations (e.g. Malta) and, in a number of countries (e.g. Portugal, Slovak Republic and Slovenia), aligning tax and customs administration within a single agency.
  - Studies and/or plans to integrate the collection of tax and social security contributions over the medium term (e.g. Greece and Lithuania).
  - Revamped structures with reduced layers of management, consolidation of work processes, and increased centralisation of national management (e.g. Estonia, Finland, and Latvia), substantial streamlining of office networks (e.g. Croatia, Greece, Norway, and Romania), and customer segment-based compliance structures (e.g. Belgium, Czech Republic, Indonesia, Netherlands, and Portugal).
  - The creation of new service delivery centres (e.g. Argentina and Malaysia).

  However, notwithstanding the progress being made there is potential for much more, particularly in some EU member countries.
- The practice of establishing dedicated divisions to manage large corporate taxpayers can be seen in over 85% of revenue bodies. However, the use of similar arrangements for high net worth individual (HNWI) taxpayers, as recommended in previous FTA work, is considerably less widespread, despite evidence of significant growth globally in their numbers and wealth.
- Drawing on recent FTA work, many revenue bodies are using or developing a "co-operative compliance model approach" for their largest taxpayers.
- There are indications that many revenue bodies can improve the transparency of their reporting on service delivery performance.
- A number of themes are noted concerning new revenue body approaches to performance monitoring and evaluation: *(1)* While still confined to a minority of countries, increasing reliance on tax gap estimation methodologies, particularly in respect of the VAT, to gauge overall effectiveness; *(2)* Evaluating levels of revenue body staff engagement against broader public sector performance; and *(3)* The development of new measures for monitoring the use of digital products designed to help taxpayers "self-manage" their tax affairs.

- Chapter 4 draws attention to many of the human resource management challenges that revenue bodies must confront and, in particular, highlights developments and issues concerning staff recruitment, development, measuring engagement, performance management, and ageing workforces.
- Revenue bodies in many countries have mandates to cut their administrative costs as part of fiscal consolidation efforts, for some requiring significant downsising (e.g. Australia, United Kingdom, and United States); the practice of using a variety of third parties to deliver critical administrative functions and support (e.g. IT services) is extensive and appears to be growing.
- Overall, the unweighted measure "average tax/GDP" for OECD countries in fiscal year 2012 rose marginally compared with 2011, and has just about returned to the level existing prior to the global financial crisis.
- Overall VAT performance across OECD countries remains below the levels existing prior to the global financial crisis in 2008, ***notwithstanding efforts in recent years in many countries to increase VAT revenue productivity.***
- Reported performance-related data and computed ratios and trends draw attention to many critical aspects of revenue body performance:
  - Tax refunds represent a significant work stream in many revenue bodies, in particular for OECD countries and for their VAT systems.
  - Some revenue bodies have considerable potential to eliminate and/or shift taxpayer service demand from costly channels (e.g. in-person inquiries) to more efficient channels (e.g. on-line services); many revenue bodies appear to have little data on service demand for their service channels.
  - Verification results vary enormously across countries, and may justify deeper study.
  - For OECD countries over the period 2011 to 2013, average year-end tax debt (including disputed debt) as a share of annual net revenue collections was in the range 22-24%, although these ratios are significantly impacted by abnormally large results for two countries (i.e. Greece and Italy); overall analysis of debt collection was hampered by many gaps in the performance-related data provided by many revenue bodies.
- Considerable efforts are being made to improve the range and quality of online services provided to taxpayers and their representatives over the medium term; commonly reported priority areas were online filing, other new online applications, website enhancements, third party data capture, the use of digital mail products and integrated taxpayer accounts. In addition:
  - Good progress is being made with the use of electronic filing systems, with over 95% of all revenue bodies offering these services; over two-thirds of revenue bodies in OECD countries achieved e-filing usage for over 75% of their PIT, CIT, and VAT client taxpayers in 2013.
  - The use of pre-filling of personal income tax returns continues to evolve; eight revenue bodies (e.g. Denmark) reported that they fully prepare tax returns (or similar documents) for the majority of their PIT taxpayers.
  - Where data were available, substantial progress has been made in recent years in fully automating tax payment collection. However, well over a third of

revenue bodies did not report tax payment volume data suggesting that this aspect of administration may not be receiving adequate attention.

- There would appear to be substantial opportunities for leveraging improved compliance and easing taxpayers' compliance burden when using tax intermediaries. This conclusion draws on observations from revenue bodies' survey responses: *(1)* over 40% reported there are no laws or regulations governing the tax-related work of tax intermediaries; *(2)* over 60% do not regularly survey tax intermediaries on important aspects of tax administration; *(3)* almost 40% do not have formal consultative arrangements for engaging with representatives of tax intermediaries; and *(4)* from a menu of five specialised services for tax intermediaries observed in some countries, only around 25% appear to offer a comprehensive range (i.e. four or more) of such services, and just over 60% reported offering two or less.
- The series concludes with an overview of key elements of the legislated administrative frameworks in place for tax administration, along with a variety of country examples to explain approaches and developments. Among many observations, the series reports that:
    - A number of countries appear to have potential to modify the design of their payment and/or reporting mechanisms (for PIT, CIT, and/or VAT) to obtain a range of benefits (e.g. reduced workloads and cutting costs, easing taxpayers' compliance, and advancing collection of tax revenues); and
    - Voluntary disclosure policies and programmes do not appear to be used widely for achieving tax compliance and bolstering tax revenues. Results from a few countries demonstrate that they can be an effective tool for encouraging taxpayers to report past acts of non-compliance, including in respect of concealed assets and income in offshore bank accounts.

Introduction

The information provided in this edition has been obtained from a survey of revenue bodies in countries covered by the series that was conducted in 2014, and from research of revenue bodies' key corporate documents (e.g. strategic plans and annual performance reports), other OECD tax publications and other sources, conducted by officials of the OECD's Centre for Tax Policy and Administration. Every effort has been made with officials of relevant revenue bodies to validate the information displayed in the series and to note the sources of information used. On advice from a small number of countries, steps have also been taken to correct previously-published data to correct detected errors and/or fill gaps in time series and trend information.

Countries covered by the series

The series covers all OECD countries. As for prior editions, it also includes a selection of non-OECD countries to enrich the nature of the information presented and to benefit a larger number of countries. The criteria used to identify non-OECD countries invited to participate in this edition of the series were:

- Countries that are formal observers or Associates to the CFA (i.e. Argentina, China, India, South Africa, and the Russian Federation) and/or who have applied for OECD membership (i.e. Costa Rica);
- Non-OECD countries that are members of the European Union (i.e. Bulgaria, Croatia, Cyprus[1, 2], Latvia, Lithuania, Malta, and Romania);
- Countries whose revenue body has worked closely with the FTA over recent years (i.e. Colombia, Hong Kong (China), Malaysia, and Singapore);
- A small number of relatively large countries not captured by other criteria but included and to increase the series' geographical coverage (i.e. Morocco and Thailand); and
- G20 countries not captured by the abovementioned criteria (i.e. Brazil, Indonesia, and Saudi Arabia).

The series' content and structure

The series identifies fundamental elements of modern tax administration systems and uses data, analyses and examples to highlight key trends, recent innovations, and examples of good practice and performance measures and indicators. It also includes reasonably comprehensive data and related ratios on resource usage and revenue body performance, in some categories including data for nine years up to fiscal year 2013. Armed with such knowledge, revenue body officials should be better equipped to undertake their own comparative analyses and benchmarking studies, particularly for performance-related aspects and for assessing comparative efficiency.

The publication is structured as follows:

- Chapter 1 describes the institutional arrangements put in place by Governments to conduct national revenue administration operations, including related oversight bodies.
- Chapter 2 outlines the organisational set-ups adopted by revenue bodies and identifies important reforms recently implemented, in course of adoption, or planned.
- Chapter 3 provides brief information on revenue body practices for specific aspects of strategic management, including the management of taxpayers' compliance.
- Chapter 4 provides an overview of human resource management aspects, including recruitment, development, performance management, and remuneration.
- Chapter 5 provides summary data and analyses (covering multiple years) of the resources allocated to revenue bodies to administer national tax laws.
- Chapter 6 sets out summary operational performance data (covering multiple years) for key areas of administration (e.g. revenue collections and refunds, service delivery, verification, disputes, and debt collection).
- Chapter 7 identifies approaches and developments with the provision of modern online services.
- Chapter 8 describes features of revenue bodies' approaches to supporting the work of tax intermediaries.
- Chapter 9 provides an overview of the legal/administrative frameworks in place for tax collection including: taxpayers' rights; provision of rulings; return filing, tax payment and assessment (major taxes); information gathering, enforced debt collection, and sanctions.

The publication concludes with a set of tables containing important historical tax-related data that are used to compute the ratios contained in chapters five and six, and annexes with a summary of individual country/revenue body-related information.

Notes

1. Footnote by Turkey:

   The information in this document with reference to "Cyprus" relates to the southern part of the Island. There is no single authority representing both Turkish and Greek Cypriot people on the Island. Turkey recognises the Turkish Republic of Northern Cyprus (TRNC). Until a lasting and equitable solution is found within the context of United Nations, Turkey shall preserve its position concerning the "Cyprus" issue.

2. Footnote by all the European Union Member states of the OECD and the European Union:

   The Republic of Cyprus is recognised by all members of the United Nations with the exception of Turkey. The information in this document relates to the area under the effective control of the Government of the Republic of Cyprus.

Chapter 1

Institutional arrangements for tax administration

This chapter provides details of the institutional arrangements put in place by governments to conduct national tax administration operations in the 56 countries covered by the series. Topics specifically discussed in some detail include the extent of revenue body autonomy, the collection of social security contributions, the practice of giving revenue bodies "non-tax" related roles, special governance arrangements for tax administration, and the establishment of independent bodies to deal with taxpayers' complaints.

Key points

Institutional arrangements

- The majority of countries (33, almost 60%) have adopted a "unified semi-autonomous" form of institutional setup for the body responsible for the administration of direct and indirect taxes; a formal management/advisory board comprised of external representatives has been established in eleven countries as part of the overall governance framework.
- Other less autonomous forms of institutional setups in place include: *(1)* a single directorate within the ministry of finance (MOF) comprising all relevant functions and responsible for both direct and indirect taxes (12 countries); *(2)* a set of multiple directorates/agencies within the formal structure of the MOF (seven countries); and *(3)* separate direct and indirect tax administrations, generally comprising all relevant functions (two countries).
- Within the EU, both Cyprus and Malta have reform efforts underway to integrate their direct and indirect administrations but this reform challenge is yet to be taken up by Luxembourg.
- Across all surveyed countries, there is a clear dichotomy of approach taken to the collection of social security contributions (SSCs), a major source of tax revenue in many countries. Of the 32 OECD countries with SSC regimes 13 have integrated their collection with tax administration operations while the balance administer their collection through separate social security bodies (although integration has also been foreshadowed as a possible future development, or is being studied, in the Czech Republic, Greece, Portugal, and Slovak Republic). Of the 22 non-OECD countries, seven have integrated SSC and tax collection, while Lithuania and Thailand reported that they also were planning a study, or already had one underway, concerning this aspect of Government revenue collection.
- Thirteen OECD member countries have aligned tax and customs operations within a single agency, including most recently Hungary (2011), Portugal (2012) and Slovakia (2012); in the 22 non-OECD countries, the alignment of tax and customs within a single agency has been adopted in six countries, while legislation has been enacted in Malta to achieve this outcome.
- The national revenue body in the majority of European countries is also responsible for the administration of property taxes (and often, motor vehicle taxes); elsewhere, these taxes are generally administered by revenue bodies of sub-national governments.

Autonomy of revenue bodies

- The degree of autonomy of surveyed revenue bodies varies significantly; the powers least frequently devolved are: *(1)* to design their internal structure (16 countries); *(2)* budget allocation discretion (14 countries); *(3)* to set the levels and mix of staff within overall budget limits (16 countries); and *(4)* to influence/negotiate staff remuneration levels (28 countries).
- Among OECD countries, the overall degree of autonomy appeared relatively limited for revenue bodies in Estonia, Japan, Luxembourg, Portugal and Slovenia, drawing on the information reported by them. For non-OECD countries, revenue bodies in Brazil, Costa Rica, Cyprus, Hong Kong, Indonesia and Saudi Arabia appear to be in similar circumstances.
- There is a concentration of less autonomous forms of institutional setups among EU countries.

Non-tax related functions

- Many revenue bodies reported they have been given additional tasks of a non-taxation nature (e.g. payment of social welfare benefits, the collection of non-tax debts such as child support, and student loans, and administration of aspects of the Government's retirement income policy.

Special tax complaints handling and tax administration oversight bodies

- Governments in ten countries have established independent and dedicated bodies to handle tax administration-related complaints (e.g. a tax ombudsman), while in most other countries dealing with taxpayers' complaints is the responsibility of the Government Ombudsman's Office (or a similar body); two countries (i.e. Australia and United States) have established separate and independent tax administration oversight bodies.

After an introduction, this chapter deals with the following topics:

1. The revenue body as an institution;
2. The extent of revenue body autonomy;
3. The scope of responsibilities of revenue bodies (including non-taxation roles);
4. Special governance arrangements; and
5. Special institutional arrangements for dealing with taxpayers' complaints.

Introduction

In most countries, the tax system is responsible for generating the vast bulk of revenue required to fund public services. Given the range and nature of the laws to be administered, the systems of assessment and self-assessment enacted, and the large numbers of clients, revenue bodies require adequate powers and autonomy to perform in an efficient and effective manner. On the other hand, they must operate and be seen to operate in a fair and impartial manner, and be subject to a range of checks and balances to ensure transparency in their operations and proper accountability for their overall management of the tax system. While this topic has not been the subject of detailed study by the FTA, valuable work has been carried out by other bodies (e.g. European Commission and International Monetary Fund) to define the desirable features and characteristics of the institutional, organisational and operational arrangements appropriate for effective and efficient administration of a country's tax system.

European Commission's Fiscal Blueprints

The European Commission's set of *Fiscal Blueprints*[1] were originally developed to guide EU candidate and member countries in strengthening their revenue bodies.

The blueprints, structured in the form of a diagnostic tool, are organised according to a logical structure in five groups and contain valuable practical guidance for policy makers and revenue officials, expressed in terms of strategic objectives (or "principles"), relative weightings reflecting their perceived importance, and a range of key indicators to help gauge their application in practice. These groups are *(1)* framework, structures and basis; *(2)* human and behavioural issues; *(3)* systems and functioning; *(4)* taxpayer services; and *(5)* support.

The initial group covered by the blueprints – *Framework, structures and basis* – addresses the institutional and organisational arrangements appropriate for effective and efficient tax administration and provides a useful backdrop for the comparative analysis in this series.

Box 1.1 sets out guidance from the blueprints concerning what is termed "the overall framework of a tax administration", a sub-group of the initial blueprint *Framework, structures and basis*. This blueprint emphasises the following desirable features for a national revenue body:

- It is guaranteed an adequate level of autonomy *(ranked of highest importance)*;
- Its obligations are clearly translated into its mission, vision, and objectives;
- It has its own structure and powers for effective *and efficient op*eration;

- It is provided with adequate resources *(ranked of high importance)*;
- It has a stable legal framework; and
- It is accountable for its operations and is subject to control and assessment.

More is said about the autonomy of revenue bodies covered by this series later in this chapter while many of the other matters are dealt with in later chapters.

Box 1.1. **EU Fiscal Blueprints: An overall framework for tax administration**

Strategic objectives	Score (of 100)	Key indicators *(abbreviated for this series)*
1. The tax administration is guaranteed an *adequate level of autonomy*	25	Is autonomy provided for by law? Is there a statutory basis defining to whom the head reports? Is autonomy reflected in its structure and operational responsibilities? Is it able to design and implement its own operational policy?
2. The obligations of the tax administration ***are clearly translated into its mission, vision and objectives***	15	Are its tasks in line with its mission and vision? Does it draw up strategies providing objectives, benchmarks and plans for its operations? Is its mission publicised among taxpayers and other stakeholders, as well as among its personnel?
3. The tax administration has its ***own structure and powers*** allowing for efficient and effective operations	5	Does its structure allow the fulfilment of its tasks and obligations? Does it provide for the decentralisation of responsibilities, so that decisions concerning the taxpayer are made at the most appropriate level?
4. The tax administration is provided with ***adequate resources*** to implement and manage the tax system	20	Is it given sufficient resources and funding to ensure the efficient implementation of its policies and performance of duties? Does its funding result from budget dialogue based on performance agreements? Does its budget planning cycle cover several years, allowing strategic planning and the carryover of funding surpluses?
5. The tax administration is provided with a ***stable legal framework*** ensuring proper administration and enforcement of tax dues	10	Is it responsible for the formulation of laws concerning the assessment, collection and enforcement of taxes (leaving the responsibility for the formulation of other tax laws with the ministry of finance)? Is it provided by law with sufficient powers to efficiently undertake all its statutory responsibilities?
6. The tax administration is ***accountable*** for its operations ***which are subject to control and assessment***	10	Is there a system of internal audit in the tax administration? Is there an independent external institution carrying out the tax administration's audit of operations and assessing its performance?
7. The operations of the tax administration ***are managed and assessed on the basis of the performance management system***	15	Is the tax administration managed in accordance with benchmarks and indicators agreed with the stakeholders while the results of its activities are constantly monitored? Is there a proper reporting system ensuring that performance reports are delivered to the management?

Source: Fiscal Blueprints (European Commission, Taxation and Customs Union) 2007.

Guidance from the blueprints concerning the structural and organisational arrangements for effective and efficient tax administration are set out in some detail in Box 1.2. Succinctly stated, this segment of the blueprints highlights the importance of the following features:

- There is a **unified** body for tax administration responsible for **all** national taxes (direct and indirect) and with **"linkages" to the collection of social contributions (SSC)**, comprised of all the functions necessary for effective and efficient administration of the tax laws.
- The revenue body is **structured primarily on a functional basis,** but also includes divisions/units to identify and manage the key compliance risks and priorities of the main taxpayer groups or segments (e.g. **a dedicated large taxpayer operation overseeing the largest taxpayers).**

Box 1.2. **EU Fiscal Blueprints: Structure and administration**

Strategic objectives	Score (of 100)	Key indicators *(abbreviated for this series)*
1. The tax administration is structured and organised to identify and manage all significant risks and priorities	25	Does it have systems and procedures for a quick identification and response to risks (both fiscal and other)? Is it structured to understand and meet the needs of key taxpayer groups or segments? Is there a large taxpayer unit (LTU) in place, at a national level, to deal with the most important companies? Are there special units with specific skills, offering operational economies of scale (e.g. intelligence, enforced collection)?
2. There is a unified tax administration	15	Is it responsible for all taxes and linked to social contributions? Is it responsible for all fiscal functions (assessment, collection, data processing, audit, taxpayer service and claim investigation) and organised accordingly (i.e. by function)?
3. The tax administration has a robust and adequately resourced headquarters function	15	Does it have a headquarters function able to undertake strategic and operational planning? Can headquarters' departments develop national programmes and provide technical advice and guidance to operational units? Is there a specific department dealing with "think tank studies", the establishment of performance objectives, and the measurement, monitoring and evaluation of field operations?
4. Clear relationship rules are established and agreed upon between the headquarters, regional and local levels	25	Do regional and local managers understand and support the business strategy and are they made responsible for its implementation? Are operational functions in place at central, regional and local levels appropriate and free of duplication or overlapping risks? Have regional and local managers' sufficient flexibility in organising their business? Does the organisational structure allow most decisions concerning taxpayers to be made at the local level?
5. A flexible and reactive allocation of resources	20	Does headquarters have performance indicators to evaluate workload and risks? Are these periodically reviewed and updated? Is the allocation of resources to operational units reviewed and adjusted accordingly?

Source: Fiscal Blueprints (European Commission, Taxation and Customs Union) 2007.

- The revenue body has **a headquarters operation sufficiently resourced and empowered** to carry out all strategic planning tasks, as well as provide guidance, technical advice, and direction and support to operational units.
- There **are clearly defined responsibilities and relationships** at the national, regional and local levels.
- There are **flexible processes in place for resource allocation** at all levels of the organisation.

More is said about the structural and organisational arrangements of revenue bodies covered by this series later in this chapter and, in particular, in Chapter 2.

International Monetary Fund's technical assistance

The guidance provided by the IMF's Fiscal Affairs Department concerning institutional design, autonomy, and structure is largely found in a series of working papers that have been prepared by Fund staff and published over a number of years (e.g. Barrand et al., 2004; Crandall, 2010; and Kidd, 2010) and can be seen in much of the practical advice and recommendations provided to individual countries as part of IMF technical assistance efforts and, for some countries, as part of formal Fund programme requirements.

Concerning institutional design and autonomy, IMF advice has typically recommended the following approaches:

- There is **a unified body responsible for the administration of both direct and indirect taxes, as well as the collection of social security contributions** where these constitute part of Government revenue.
- The revenue body should have **sufficient autonomy**, often described as being "semi-autonomous", in particular concerning aspects of organisation and planning, budget management, performance measurement, and human resource management (e.g. recruitment and staff and career development).
- The body is **organised largely on a functional basis**, but **with a dedicated large taxpayer division** to administer its largest taxpayers.
- The body has **a sufficiently resourced headquarters** to oversee all aspects of its operations, but is not primarily responsible for tax policy matters which are seen to best fall within the province of a dedicated policy function in the MOF.
- There is a **common legal framework for the administration of all taxes**, as opposed to an individual framework for each tax.
- **Office networks** for operational tax administration programmes **should be designed taking account of viable critical mass and economic considerations**, with specialist regional or national centres for some functions.

As will be apparent, both Fund advice and the guidance contained in the EU's Fiscal Blueprints are very much in alignment.

The revenue body as an institution

There have been considerable changes in the organisation of public sector functions over the last decade, in the main seeking to deliver services more effectively to citizens and business and at lower cost to the community at large. A key part of the reforms made has addressed the issue of organisational autonomy. As observed in Crandall (2010):

> [...] there has been a tendency for governments to increase the autonomy of its departments and agencies. The basic principle is that such autonomy can lead to better performance by removing impediments to effective and efficient management while maintaining appropriate accountability and transparency.
>
> Autonomy can mean many things, including independence or even self-government, but in the context of public sector administration it usually refers to ... the degree to which a government department or agency is able to operate independently from government, in terms of legal form and status, funding and udget, and financial, human resources and administrative practices [...]
>
> While the trend toward increased autonomy is clearly a general one for governments, revenue administration has been very much at the forefront of this movement. Many believe there is a compelling case for increased autonomy for revenue administration because it is the source of revenue for the whole of government. It is recognised that the problems addressed by increased autonomy affect the entire government but, it is argued, such problems are felt much more acutely in revenue administration as compared to most other public sector activities, largely on account of the specialised skills needed and because of its revenue-producing role. This "uniqueness" argument may not be as strong as its proponents believe, especially in the context of world-wide public service reform and good governance initiatives.

Activity to reform tax administration by revamping institutional arrangements and increasing revenue body autonomy has been uneven across the countries covered by this series. As a result, there is in 2014 a fairly divergent set of set ups in place.

For the purposes of this series, five categories of institutional setups for conducting tax administration were identified, although in practice there are a number of exceptions (for example, see Box 1.3). These categories were:

- **A single directorate within the ministry of finance (MOF)**: Tax administration functions are the responsibility of a single organisational unit (e.g. a directorate) located within the structure of the MOF (or its equivalent).
- **Multiple directorates within the MOF**: Tax administration functions are the responsibility of multiple organisational units (e.g. directorates) located within the ministry of finance (often sharing necessary support functions such as information technology and human resources);
- **A unified semi-autonomous body**: Tax administration functions, along with support functions (e.g. IT and human resources) are carried out by a unified semi-autonomous body, with the head reporting to a government minister.
- **A unified semi-autonomous body with a management/oversight board**: Tax administration functions, along with necessary support functions (e.g. information technology, human resources) are carried out by a unified semi-autonomous body, the head of which reports to a government minister and oversight body/board of management comprised of external officials.
- **A category of "Other": Other setups not covered by the abovementioned.**

Revenue bodies were requested to specify the category that best matched their current setup and to identify the scope of taxes administered by them (see Table 1.1).

Box 1.3. Unusual institutional arrangements for national tax system administration

Germany: Responsibility for tax administration is largely devolved to regional (i.e. Lander) administrations while a relatively small central body exercises a high level co-ordination role. Customs operations are administered separately (and centrally) while the collection of SSC is also carried out by separate social security agencies.

Italy: Responsibility for tax administration is spread across a number of separate bodies: *(1)* Agenzia delle Entrate (AE) is primarily responsible for tax administration (Direct Taxes, VAT and other tax revenues); as of the 1 December 2012, the AE (due to the incorporation of the Agenzia del Territorio – Real Estate and Land Registry Agency) is also responsible for cadastre, property registers, property valuations, management of the real estate market and advertising. *(2)* Agenzia delle Dogane e dei Monopoli (Customs and Monopolies Agency) is responsible for administering excise duties, VAT on imports and customs duties; as of the 1st December 2012 the Customs Agency merged with the Independent Administration of the State Monopolies. It deals with the sector of public gaming, it constantly verifies the compliance of the licensees and of traders of the gaming sector to the rules and fights against illegal gaming. It also carries out a control activity on production, distribution and sale of manufactured tobacco. In addition, some tax administration functions are not dealt with by the AE directly but are provided by other agencies. Tax fraud work is principally carried out by a separate tax police body (the Guardia di Finanza), while the enforced collection of tax and social contribution debts is carried out by a government-owned body (i.e. Equitalia s.p.a.) and information processing activities by a separate body (i.e. Sogei s.p.a.).

Switzerland: Operational responsibility for the administration of personal income tax and corporate income/profits tax is undertaken by sub-national "cantons" which number 26 across Switzerland, on behalf of the federal government. The VAT is administered centrally by the Federal Tax Administration which also has a number of "national" functions: divisions for Federal Direct Tax, Anticipatory Tax, Stamp Duty, Exchange of Information in Tax Matters, Analysis and Data, Tax Policy and Military Service Exemption Tax.

Source: Tax Administration 2015 survey responses.

As is evident from Table 1.1, 32 of 56 surveyed countries have established a unified semi-autonomous body (or, in the case of China, a separate ministry) responsible for tax administration (and in some cases customs administration) operations, while the balance of countries operate with other (generally less unified and/or autonomous) models[2]. To a large extent, these varied institutional arrangements reflect underlying differences in the political structures and systems of public sector administration in surveyed countries, as well as longstanding historical practice. Key observations from the data provided are set out below:

- All but three surveyed countries have merged the administration of direct and indirect taxes within a single revenue collection body or are in the course of doing so; where this unified approach is not followed, tax administration is carried out by a number of separate directorates/agencies, generally forming part of the internal structure of the Ministry of Finance.

  With reform action underway to establish a unified administration in both Cyprus and Malta, Luxembourg will be the only EU member country yet to modernise this aspect of its institutional set up for tax administration. Of the other surveyed countries, India does not have a national VAT (or equivalent tax), although the matter is under consideration. Malaysia is planning to implement a national GST/VAT

Table 1.1. Institutional arrangements for tax administration

Country	Nature of body*	Major tax types administered by the national revenue body/multiple directorates in 2013						
		PIT	SSC	CIT	VAT	Excises	Real estate	Other taxes: Estate: **E**; Wealth: **W**; Motor vehicle: **M**
OECD countries								
Australia	USB	✓	x	✓	✓	✓	x	-
Austria	SDMOF	✓	x	✓	✓	✓	x	M
Belgium	MDMOF	✓	x	✓	✓	✓	✓	-
Canada	USBB	✓ /1	✓	✓ /1	✓ /1	✓	x	
Chile	USB /1	✓	x /2	✓	✓	✓	✓	E, M /2
Czech Republic	USB	✓	x	✓	✓	x	✓	E, M
Denmark	Other /1	✓	x	✓	✓	✓	✓	E, M
Estonia	SDMOF	✓	✓	✓	✓	✓	✓	M
Finland	USB	✓	✓	✓	✓	x	✓	E
France	SDMOF	✓	x	✓	✓	x	✓	E, W
Germany	Other /1	✓	x	✓	✓	x	✓ /2	E, M /2
Greece	USB	✓	x	✓	✓	✓	✓	E, W, M
Hungary	USB	✓	✓	✓	✓	✓	x	E, M
Iceland	USB	✓	✓	✓	✓	x	x	W, M
Ireland	USB	✓	✓	✓	✓	✓	✓	E, M
Israel	SDMOF	✓	x	✓	✓	✓	✓	M
Italy	Other /1	✓	x	✓	✓	x	x /2	-
Japan	USB	✓	x	✓	✓	✓	x	E, M
Korea	USB	✓	x	✓	✓	✓	✓	E
Luxembourg	MDMOF /1	✓	x	✓	✓	x	x	E, W
Mexico	USBB	✓	x	✓	✓	✓	x	E, W
Netherlands	SDMOF	✓	✓	✓	✓	✓	x	E, M
New Zealand	USB	✓	n.appl.	✓	✓	x	x	-
Norway	USB	✓	✓	✓	✓	x /1	x	E, M /1, W
Poland	MDMOF	✓	x	✓	✓	x	x	E, W
Portugal	SDMOF	✓	x	✓	✓	✓	✓	E, M
Slovak Republic	USB /1	✓	x	✓	✓	✓	x	M
Slovenia	USB	✓	✓	✓	✓	✓ /1	✓	E, W, M
Spain	USB	✓	x	✓	✓	✓	x	W /1, M /1
Sweden	USBB /1	✓	✓	✓	✓	✓	✓	
Switzerland	SDMOF /1	✓	x	✓	✓	x	x	-
Turkey	Other /1	✓	x	✓	✓	✓	✓	E, M
United Kingdom	USBB	✓	✓	✓	✓	✓	✓	E
United States	USBB	✓	✓	✓	n.appl.	✓	x	E
Non-OECD countries								
Argentina	USBB	✓	✓	✓	✓	✓	x	
Brazil	USB	✓	✓	✓	x /1	x	✓ /2	W
Bulgaria	USBB	✓	✓	✓	✓	x	x	
China	Other /1	✓	x	✓	✓	✓		E, M
Colombia	USBB	✓	x	✓	✓	x	x	E, W
Costa Rica	MDMOF	✓	x	✓	✓ /1	✓	✓	M
Croatia	SDMOF	✓	✓	✓	✓	✓	✓	E, M
Cyprus	MDMOF /1	✓	x	✓	✓	✓	✓	-
Hong Kong, China	SDMOF	✓	x	✓	x	x	x	-
India	USBB /1	✓	x	✓	x	x /1	x	W
Indonesia	SDMOF	✓	x	✓	✓	x	✓ /1	-
Latvia	USB	✓	✓	✓	✓	✓	✓	M
Lithuania	USB	✓	x	✓	✓	✓	✓	E
Malaysia	Other /1	✓	x	✓	x	x	✓	-
Malta	MDMOF /1	✓	✓	✓	✓	✓	x	-
Morocco	SDMOF	✓	x	✓	✓	x	✓	M
Romania	USB	✓	✓	✓	✓	✓	x	-
Russia	USB	✓	x	✓	✓	✓	✓	M
Saudi Arabia	SDMOF	x /1	x	✓	x	x	x	-
Singapore	USBB	✓	x	✓	✓	x	✓	E
South Africa	USB	✓	x /1	✓	✓	✓	x	E
Thailand	MDMOF	✓	x	✓	✓	x	x	-

For notes indicated by "/ (number)", see Notes to Tables section at the end of the chapter, p. 52

* **USB:** Unified semi-autonomous body; **USBB:** Unified semi-autonomous body with formal board or advisory group comprised of external officials; **SDMOF**: Single directorate in Ministry of Finance; **MDMOF**: Multiple directorates in MOF.

Source: Survey responses and Secretariat research (e.g. revenue body reports).

system from April 2015 but has foregone the potential benefits of integration with its decision to administer the new tax from its Customs and Excise administration, not the department responsible for Direct Taxes administration. Integration of the GST/VAT, once it is fully established, is likely to be a much more complex and costly undertaking.

- In the 32 OECD member countries that have a separate regime of social security contributions (SSC), 19 countries have them collected by a separate social security agency (or multiple agencies) while the balance of countries have integrated the collection of these revenues with normal tax administration operations; of the 22 non-OECD countries, 18 have a SSC regime and integration has been adopted in seven of these countries.
- Thirty six countries have separate bodies for tax and customs administration; of these, 20 countries have allocated excise administration to the customs body, not the revenue body.
- The national revenue body in the majority of European OECD member countries is also responsible for the collection of real property taxes (and in many, motor vehicle taxes), while in virtually all non-European OECD member countries these taxes are administered by the revenue bodies of sub-national governments.
- Management boards/advisory bodies (with external members) have been established in 11 countries to oversee and/or provide advice on the operation of tax administration.

The practice of establishing a separate unified body for tax administration covering all taxes (and sometimes customs), removed from the formal internal structure of the MOF (or its equivalent) and with a broad range of autonomous powers, mirrors a broader development in public sector administration sometimes described as the "executive agency" model. The model, in a revenue administration context often referred to as the "revenue authority model", has been the subject of a fair amount of external scrutiny on behalf of various national and international organisations (Jenkins, 1994; Taliercio, 2004; Kidd and Crandall, 2006 and 2010; Mann, 2004). The rationale for this model has been described in the following terms (Delay, Devas, and Hubbard, 1998):

The arguments for the executive agency model relate primarily to effectiveness and efficiency: *(1)* as a single purpose agency, it can focus its efforts on the single task; *(2)* as an autonomous organisation, it can manage its affairs in a business-like way, free of political interference in day-to-day operations; and *(3)* freed from the constraints of the civil service system, it can recruit, retain (or dismiss) and motivate staff to a higher level of performance.

It is beyond the scope of this series to explore in detail the pros and cons of this development other than to emphasise a few key points drawn from the cited research:

- Studies made to evaluate the success or otherwise of the "revenue authority" model for tax administration have not been able to draw any firm conclusions as to its overall impacts on revenue body efficiency and effectiveness.
- As noted in a 2005 study report prepared by the United Kingdom's Department for International Development (DFID), and in other reports, on experience with revenue authorities, there are a number of practical issues concerning the quantification of any benefits resulting from the introduction of the model. These include: *(1)* measurement: the difficulty inherent in gauging the impacts, in quantitative terms, of a concept such as autonomy; *(2)* data: limitations with obtaining relevant

data items on pre- and post-implementation basis; and *(3)* attribution/causality: the existence of exogenous factors that make it very difficult to establish causality and thus to attribute any observed benefits to specific initiatives (including the model itself).

- Effective implementation of the model requires various types of support (e.g. good relationships with the MOF, strong leadership by senior management, and human resource policies for achieving good performance and addressing poor performance).
- As noted in the IMF working paper, improved effectiveness and efficiency is likely to flow most directly from an on-going commitment to the reform of structures, systems and processes, in particular, well designed programmes of service and enforcement, the sound allocation of resources, and effective management. Implementation of a new governance structure is, at best, a first step in this direction.
- Many countries that have applied the model see it as a catalyst for reform. As noted in Kidd and Crandall (2006):

  Notwithstanding the lack of demonstrated basis for establishing a revenue authority, there is a strong perception held by those countries that have adopted the revenue authority concept that this particular governance model has made a significant contribution to reform and improved performance.

The extent of revenue body autonomy

Generally speaking, the range of powers given to a national revenue body depends on a variety of factors, including the system of government in place and the state of development of a country's public sector administration practices, as well as the institutional model adopted for tax administration. As already observed, increased autonomy brings with it a prospect of increased efficiency and effectiveness, but it has been difficult in practice to produce clear evidence of such outcomes. As already outlined and indicated in Table 1.1 over half of the OECD countries report they have established semi-autonomous bodies while Table 1.2 provides a summary view of the range and nature of the powers delegated to revenue bodies. Box 1.4 provides examples of the autonomous responsibilities allocated to many revenue bodies.

Based on revenue bodies' survey responses reported in Table 1.2, the areas of *least* flexibility/autonomy observed across countries were: *(1)* the authority to design their own internal organisational structure, including their network of offices (16 countries); *(2)* the authority to re-allocate budgeted funds across operational functions to meet new priorities (14 countries); *(3)* The ability to determine the levels and mix of staff (16 countries); *(4)* The authority to hire and dismiss staff (nine countries); and *(5)* the ability to influence/negotiate staff remuneration levels (in accordance with public sector guidelines) (28 countries).

Among OECD countries, the overall degree of autonomy appeared relatively limited for revenue bodies in Estonia, Japan, Luxembourg, Portugal and Slovenia, drawing on the information reported by them. For non-OECD countries, revenue bodies in Brazil, Costa Rica, Cyprus, Indonesia, and Saudi Arabia appear to be in similar circumstances. For some countries, the survey responses cast doubts on the accuracy of their self-classification as a "unified semi-autonomous body".

Table 1.3 provides a summary of how the distribution of powers/autonomy aligns with the nature of the institutional body reported by surveyed revenue bodies. As will be evident from the data displayed those revenue bodies reporting that they were established

Table 1.2. **Delegated authority of national revenue bodies**

Country	Delegated authority that can be exercised by the revenue body without requiring external approvals /1								
	Make tax rulings	Remit penalties/ interest	Design internal structure	Re-allocate budget	Fix levels/ mix of staff	Set service standards	Influence staff recruitment criteria	Hire and dismiss staff	Negotiate staff pay levels
OECD countries									
Australia	✓	✓	✓	✓	✓	✓	✓	✓	✓
Austria	✓	✓	✓	✓	✓	✓	✓	✓	x
Belgium	✓	✓	✓	x	✓	✓	✓	✓	x
Canada	✓	✓	✓	✓	✓	✓	✓	✓	✓
Chile	✓	✓	✓	✓	x	✓	✓	✓	x
Czech Republic	✓	✓	✓	✓	✓	✓	✓	✓	✓
Denmark	✓	✓	✓	✓	✓	✓	✓	✓	✓
Estonia	✓	✓	✓	✓	x	✓	✓	✓	✓
Finland	✓	✓	✓	✓	✓	✓	✓	✓	✓
France	✓	✓	✓	✓	✓	✓	✓	✓	✓
Germany /2	✓	✓	✓	x	x	✓	✓	✓	x
Greece	✓	✓	✓	✓	x /2	✓	✓	x /2	x
Hungary	✓	✓	x	✓	✓	✓	✓	✓	✓
Iceland	✓	✓	✓	✓	✓	✓	✓	✓	✓
Ireland	✓	✓	✓	✓	✓	✓	✓	✓	x
Israel	✓	✓	✓	✓	✓	✓	✓	✓	x
Italy	✓	✓	✓	✓	✓	✓	✓	✓	x
Japan	✓	✓	x	x	x	✓	✓	✓	x
Korea	✓	✓	x	✓	x	✓	✓	✓	x
Luxembourg	✓	✓ /2	✓	x	x	✓	✓	x	x
Mexico	✓	✓	x	x	✓	✓	✓	✓	✓
Netherlands	✓	✓	✓	✓	✓	✓	✓	✓	✓
New Zealand	✓	✓	✓	✓	✓	✓	✓	✓	✓
Norway	✓	✓	✓	✓	✓	✓	✓	✓	✓
Poland	✓	✓	x	✓	✓	✓	✓	✓	✓
Portugal	✓	✓	x	x	x	✓	✓	x	x
Slovak Republic	✓	✓	✓	✓	✓	✓	✓	✓	✓
Slovenia	✓	x	x	✓	x	✓	✓	✓	x
Spain	✓	✓	✓	✓	✓	✓	✓ /2	✓ /2	✓
Sweden	✓	✓	✓	✓	✓	✓	✓	✓	✓
Switzerland	✓	✓	✓	✓	✓	✓	✓	✓	✓
Turkey	✓	✓	✓	x	x	✓	✓	✓	x
United Kingdom	✓	✓	✓	✓	✓	✓	✓	✓	✓
United States	✓	✓	✓	✓	✓	✓	✓	✓	✓
Non-OECD countries									
Argentina	✓	x	✓	x	✓	✓	✓	✓	✓
Brazil	✓	✓	x	x /2	x /2	✓	✓	x	x /2
Bulgaria	✓	x	✓	✓	✓	✓	✓	✓	✓
China	x	x	✓	✓	✓	✓	✓	✓	x
Colombia	✓	x	x	✓	x	✓	✓	✓	x
Costa Rica	✓	✓	x	x	x	✓	x /2	x /2	x /2
Croatia	✓	✓	✓	✓	✓	✓	✓	✓	x
Cyprus	✓	✓ /2	✓	x	x	✓	x	x	x
Hong Kong, China	✓	x	✓	x	x	✓	✓	✓	x
India	✓	✓	✓	✓	✓	✓	✓	✓	x
Indonesia	✓	✓	x	x	x	✓	x	x	x
Latvia	✓	✓	x	✓	✓	✓	✓	✓	✓
Lithuania	✓	✓	x	✓	✓	✓	x	✓	x
Malaysia	✓	✓	✓	✓	✓	✓	✓	✓	✓
Malta	✓	✓ /2	✓	✓	✓	✓	✓	x	x
Morocco	✓	✓	✓ /2	✓ /2	✓	✓	✓		
Romania	✓	✓	✓	✓	✓	✓	✓	✓	x
Russia	✓	✓	✓	✓	✓	✓	✓	✓	✓
Saudi Arabia	✓	x	x	✓	x	✓	✓	x	x
Singapore	✓	✓	✓	✓	✓	✓	✓	✓	✓
South Africa	✓	✓	✓	✓	✓	✓	✓	✓	✓
Thailand	✓	✓	✓	x	x	✓	✓	✓ /2	x

For notes indicated by "/ (number)", see Notes to Tables section at the end of the chapter, p. 52.
Source: Tax Administration 2015 survey responses.

as semi-autonomous bodies (with or without a board) consistently reported having greater autonomy/freedom than single/multiple directorates within MOF, particularly in relation to the allocation of budgeted funds, fixing the levels and mix of staff, influencing staff recruitment criteria, hiring and dismissing staff, and negotiating remuneration levels etc., as highlighted in blue in the table.

Even with increased autonomy, revenue bodies still must operate within frameworks designed to ensure they remain accountable to wider government and the citizens whom they serve. For some, these frameworks include the establishment of management boards

Box 1.4. Typical powers of semi-autonomous revenue bodies

- ***Budget expenditure management***: Discretion to allocate/adjust budgeted administrative funds across administrative functions to take account of changed circumstances/meet newly emerging priorities. In practice, this discretion should enable a revenue body to use its resources more wisely, obtaining "better value for money spent".
- ***Organisation and planning***: Responsibility for: *(1)* determining the internal organisational structure of the revenue body to conduct tax administration operations, including network size and geographical location of tax offices; and *(2)* formulating the revenue body's strategic and operational plans. Effective exercise of these powers could be expected to enable a revenue body to be more responsive to changed circumstances, contributing to its overall efficiency and effectiveness.
- ***Performance standards***: Discretion to set its own administrative performance standards (e.g. for taxpayer service delivery).
- ***Personnel recruitment, development, and remuneration***: The ability to set academic/technical qualification standards for categories of recruits, and to recruit and dismiss staff, in accordance with public sector policies and procedures; the ability to establish and operate staff training/development programmes; and the ability to negotiate staff remuneration levels in accordance with broader public sector-wide policies and arrangements. In practice, effective use of these powers should enable the revenue body to make more effective use of its human resources.
- ***Information technology***: Authority to administer its own in-house IT systems, or to outsource the provision of such services to private contractors. Given the ubiquity of technology in tax administration, effective use of this responsibility could contribute enormously to overall organisational performance (including responsiveness).
- ***Tax law interpretation***: The authority to provide interpretations, both in the form of public and private rulings, of how tax laws will be interpreted, subject only to review by judicial bodies. The proper exercise of this power in practice can be expected to assist taxpayers by clarifying the application of the law and its administration.
- ***Enforcement***: The authority to exercise, without referral to another body, certain enforcement powers associated with administration of the laws (e.g. to obtain information from taxpayers and third parties and to impose liens over property in respect of unpaid debts). The proper exercise of this power enables revenue bodies to respond quickly to taxpayers' non-compliance.
- ***Penalties and interest***: The authority to impose administrative sanctions (i.e. penalties and interest) for acts of non-compliance and to remit such sanctions in appropriate circumstances. In practice, effective use of this power would afford greater flexibility to the revenue body in its treatment of taxpayers' non-compliance.

Source: OECD CTPA Secretariat.

comprised of external representatives and the existence of external agencies that are tasked to oversee the day-to-day operation of the tax system. Both these areas are covered in more detail later in the chapter and in Chapter 2.

Table 1.3. **Authority delegated to revenue bodies**

	Number of institutions (by institutional category) and areas of delegated authority					
	Single or multiple directorate(s) within MOF		Semi-autonomous body with or without a board		Others (covering a range of setups with widely varying levels of autonomy)	
Nature of authority delegated	Number	% of total (20)	Number	% of total (30)	Number	% of total (6)
To make tax rulings	20	100	31	100	5	83
To remit penalties/interest	18	90	28	90	5	83
To design internal structure	15	75	25	81	6	100
To re-allocate budget as deemed appropriate	13	65	27	87	4	67
To fix levels and mix of staff	11	55	26	84	3	50
To set service standards	20	100	31	100	6	100
To influence staff recruitment criteria	17	85	30	97	6	100
To hire and dismiss staff	13	65	30	97	6	100
To negotiate pay levels	6	30	20	67	2	33

Source: Tax Administration 2015 survey responses.

Scope of responsibilities of the revenue body

A unified body for the collection of direct and indirect taxes

Table 1.1 also provides an overview of the taxes administered by revenue bodies. With few exceptions, Governments in surveyed countries have unified the collection of direct and (most) indirect taxes, establishing a single body for tax administration. The most recent occurrence of unification was the United Kingdom's amalgamation of its Inland Revenue and Customs and Excise Departments into a single organisation – Her Majesty's Revenue and Customs (HMRC) – in April 2005.

As of end 2013, the operation of separate tax bodies among surveyed countries was confined to very small number of countries (i.e. Cyprus, India, Luxembourg, Malta, and Malaysia). However, a number of changes are planned in both Cyprus and Malta that will see major institutional and organisational reform during 2014-15:

- Responding to recommendations of the IMF, ***Cyprus*** has announced plans to integrate its direct and indirect tax departments during 2014 as part of a wide ranging programme of reforms. (Further details are provided in Chapter 2.)
- Following the enactment of relevant legislation in 2012, ***Malta*** is in the course of planning an integrated tax and customs body.

There is one fairly common exception to this more unified approach to administration. As reported in Table 1.1, 20 countries administer the collection of excises through a body other than the main revenue body, in most countries the body responsible for customs administration. Norway reported that its Government has decided to unify all revenue collection responsibilities within its tax administration, entailing a transfer of responsibility for excise administration and the collection of VAT on imports from the customs body, to be in place from 2016.

The collection of social security contributions

Social security contribution (SSC) regimes have been established in the vast majority of countries as a complementary source of government revenue to fund specific government services (e.g. health, unemployment and pensions).[3] As evident from the data in Table 6.1 (Chapter 6), SSC are the largest single source of government revenue in many OECD countries, particularly of those in Europe. However, as indicated in Table 1.1, Governments have taken quite different paths as to how the collection of SSC should be administered.

Of the 31 OECD countries with separate SSC regimes, the majority (19 countries) currently administer their collection through a separate social security agency (or a number of such agencies), rather than through the main tax revenue body. In the other 12 OECD countries, the collection of SSC has been integrated with tax collection. However, notwithstanding the dominance of the separate agency approach to SSC and tax collection, the clear trend over the last two decades has been towards integrating their collection.

Beyond OECD economies, this dichotomy in approach to government revenue collection is also apparent – Cyprus, Malaysia, Singapore and South Africa all administer the collection of SSC via a separate agency, while other countries (i.e. Argentina, Brazil, Bulgaria, China (some provinces only), Croatia, Estonia, Latvia, and Romania) have integrated the collection of SSCs and tax revenue. Elsewhere in Europe, beyond the countries covered by this series, integration is by far the preferred approach, with such arrangements in place in Albania, Macedonia, Moldova, Montenegro, and Serbia.

The rationale for integrating taxes and social security contributions collection

The pros and cons of these fundamentally different approaches to administering government revenue collection have not been studied by the FTA. However, the operation of separate bodies for the collection of taxes and SSC raises some obvious questions concerning their relative efficiency and effectiveness, not to mention the additional compliance burden imposed on taxpayers, particularly businesses, from having to deal with separate collection bodies.

Research by the IMF's Fiscal Affairs Department to identify the reasons why so many countries have chosen to integrate the collection of SSC with tax collection operations over the last decade or so provides some useful insights as to the potential benefits from an integrated approach to tax and SSC collection (see Box 1.5). These considerations are likely to be particularly relevant to developing countries that are contemplating the establishment of SSC regimes or are experiencing difficulties with regimes already in place (in the absence of an integrated approach), and to advanced economies with separate regimes that are looking for opportunities to improve effectiveness and efficiency.

The arguments set out in Box 1.5 raise important considerations for Governments and are supported by the observed experiences of a number of countries that have integrated tax and SSCs collection.

In 2010, researchers (Bakirtzi, Schoukens, and Pieters) working on behalf of the European Institute of Social Security (EISS) examined the approaches and experiences of five countries (i.e. Estonia, Hungary, Italy, Netherlands and United Kingdom) that had undertaken integration activities over the previous 10-15 years[4]. In addition to making many observations they concluded that integration can be a cost-effective and efficient approach, burdens on employers and individuals can be greatly reduced, collection is facilitated by new technologies and the ensuing opportunities for stricter control and enforcement procedures can be expected to result in higher contribution compliance, thereby safeguarding the sustainability of the social security systems. On the other hand, they acknowledged that in practice there are various obstacles and challenges that must be overcome to undertake a successful integration exercise. Proper planning and effective execution of the steps required is clearly critical to realising the potential benefits.

More recently, in a report presented at the 31st General Assembly of the International Social Security Association (ISSA), researchers (Enoff and Ruggia-Frick) presented the findings of their work that examined the merits of the various systems for collecting social contributions. They adopt a more nuanced view on the issue of institutional location, concluding from their analysis that:

> [...] Not any one single factor is overriding in determining effectiveness. Rather it is a combination of several interactive elements which seems to produce the best results.

In their report, they provide a summary description of key elements considered critical to effectiveness: *(1)* governance; *(2)* the age or maturity of the social insurance programme; *(3)* degree of coverage and size and diversity of the labour force; *(4)* process automation and employment of technology; *(5)* co-ordination with outside organisations; *(6)* constant evaluation and adjustment of policies and practices; and *(7)* the social security culture in the country.

Box 1.5. The integration of tax and SSC collection

The main arguments for integration presented in the IMF working paper are as follows:

1. ***Commonality of core processes***: This argument for integration stems from the commonality of the core processes involved in the collection of tax and SSC, including the need to *(1)* identify and register contributors and taxpayers using a unique registration number; *(2)* have systems to collect information in the form of returns from employers and the self-employed, usually based on similar definitions of income; *(3)* for employers, withhold tax and contributions from the income of their employees and pay this to the agencies (usually via the banking system); *(4)* have effective collection systems to follow up those employers who do not file, or do not account for payments; and *(5)* verify the accuracy of the information in returns using modern risk-based audit methods.
2. ***Efficient use of resources:*** Countries that have moved to integrate SSC collection activities into their revenue administrations have often found that the marginal costs of expanding systems used for tax administration to include SSC are relatively minor. This is a particularly important factor to consider for those countries that lack the resources to implement two very similar sets of reforms in different agencies. For example, some countries have integrated the collection of payments as diverse as accident compensation insurance contributions, Medicare contributions, child support contributions, and student loans repayments into the tax administration. While the features of each are very different, the countries in question have seen the value of using the tax administration's core collection capacity to lower collection costs and improve collection rates.

Box 1.5. The integration of tax and SSC collection *(continued)*

3. ***Core competencies of tax and social organisations*:** Over time, tax administrations build core competencies in relation to revenue collection functions. There are countries where tax administrations have been shown to have improved collection levels in relation to social contribution type payments, or been able to do this more efficiently, when they have been transferred from social insurance agencies. Tax administrations, where the sole focus is on revenue collection, develop compliance-based organisational cultures and strongly-aligned processes suited to the assessment and collection of monies. Similarly, social insurance agencies typically build a strong focus on establishing individual entitlements to benefits and efficiently paying them out to recipients. They develop organisational cultures and processes aligned to this role and it is logical to conclude that incorporating the somewhat counter-intuitive responsibility for collections compromises both the collection efficiency and the provision of benefits. Social insurance agencies may have limited success in proceeding beyond a certain level of collection performance.
4. ***Lowering government administration costs:*** Placing responsibility for collections with the tax administration eliminates duplication of core functions that would otherwise occur in the areas of processing, verification, and enforced collection of returns and payments. This can contribute to significantly reducing government administration costs, with: *(1)* fewer staff and economies of scale in human resource management and training, fewer numbers of managers, and common processes for filing and payment and enforcement and data entry data and verification; *(2)* lower infrastructure costs in office accommodation, telecommunications networks, and related functions; and *(3)* elimination of duplicated IT development costs and less risk in system development and maintenance.
5. ***Lowering taxpayer and contributor compliance costs:*** Placing responsibility for collections with the tax administration can also significantly reduce compliance costs for employers, with less paperwork as a result of common forms and record-keeping systems, and a common audit programme covering income, VAT and payroll taxes, and social contributions based on income and payrolls. The increasing use of Internet-based electronic filing and payment systems within the tax administration also lowers taxpayer and contributor compliance costs. This simplification can also improve the accuracy of the calculations made by employers, and therefore compliance levels.

Source: IMF (2004), *Integrating Tax and Social Security Contribution Collections within a Unified Revenue Administration: The Experience of Central and Eastern European Countries*, International Monetary Fund, Washington DC.

Integration developments in course

With considerable pressure on many Governments to improve their budgetary position by improving compliance and cutting costs, it is inevitable that attention will be given to seeking opportunities for rationalising revenue collection processes, including the integration of tax and SSC collection. For this series, a number of countries reported that either such a study was underway or that a decision in principle to integrate had already been made and that preparations were underway:

- ***Czech Republic:*** Plans to re-organise tax administration into a single organisation and to transfer competence to collect SSC from the Czech Social Security Administration and health insurance funds to an integrated revenue agency were first announced in 2009. A new tax organisation was subsequently established in January 2013. However, the integration of tax and SSC collection has been deferred and with the recent election of a new government the matter is still under consideration.

- ***Lithuania*** reported that a study was being prepared to examine the possible consolidation of processes dealing with all Government revenue collection, including a handover of the administration of SSC (currently administered by the State Social Insurance Fund Board) to the revenue body.
- ***Slovak Republic:*** A detailed account of plans to unify the collection of taxes and SSC within a single agency, and the rationale for this, were set out in CIS 2010 (pages 26-27). For this series, officials reported that integration has been delayed and is now not likely to take place until around 2017.
- ***Thailand*** reported that a study was underway.

In addition, authorities in Greece have recently committed to integrating tax and SSC administration by July 2017 following a comprehensive review by the IMF that identified significant weaknesses in existing arrangements for the administration of SSC collection. In preparation for this integration, work will be undertaken in the period up to 2017 to complete the business case, establish a project to lead the work, strengthen collaboration between the SSC administration and the revenue body, implement a central registry of social security contributors and PIT taxpayers, and harmonise the contributions base across the major funds and with the PIT.

Assistance provided by revenue bodies to social security agencies

In those countries where separate arrangements exist for tax and SSC collection, the overlapping nature of the revenue collection responsibilities of the different bodies and their client base presents opportunities for co-operation and mutual assistance. In their survey responses, a number of revenue bodies reported that this occurs in practice in a variety of ways (e.g. through use of common audit programmes, information exchange between agencies, assistance with enforced collection of unpaid SSC, and collaboration to streamline information exchange procedures) – see Table 1.4.

On the other hand, quite a few revenue bodies (e.g. Czech Republic, Germany, Korea, Poland, and Switzerland), including a number where SSC are a substantial source of government revenue, reported that no practical assistance is provided to SSC agencies, raising questions as to the extent of duplicated effort that could be occurring in administering both tax and SSC collection and whether there is potential for increased efficiency and effectiveness from a more collaborative "whole of government" approach to SSC administration.

Non-tax related roles of national revenue bodies

As noted in prior series, many Governments have over the last two decades or so allocated additional roles (hereafter referred to as non-tax related roles) to their revenue bodies, not directly related to the collection of tax revenue. In some cases, these roles have entailed use of a country's tax legislation framework to provide economic benefits to taxpayers (e.g. welfare-type benefits) or to use the tax system to collect non-tax amounts owing to Government (e.g. student loans). In other situations, the role/function has been less directly related to "tax system" administration (e.g. oversight of certain gambling activities). Information concerning the "non-tax" functions of revenue bodies reported for this series is set out in Table 1.5. Countries not mentioned in the table reported no such roles, while resource implications are discussed in Chapter 5.

As will be evident from Table 1.5, the vast majority of revenue bodies reported one or more such roles, and this practice appears to have grown over the last decade. The most common roles

Table 1.4. **Social security contributions: Assistance provided by selected revenue bodies**

Country	SSCs as share of all taxes in 2012 (%)	Revenue body assists SSC agencies	Nature of assistance provided by revenue body				Integrated collection of taxes and SSC	
			Verifies taxpayers' liabilities	Provides details of evasion	Collects SSC debts	Other roles/ actions	Study/ plans underway	Expected timing of integration
OECD countries								
Austria	34.1	✓	✓	✓	x	x	x	
Belgium	32.1	x	x	✓	x	x	x	
Chile	6.5	✓	x /1	x	x	✓ /2	x	
Czech Republic	43.6	x	x	x	x	x	x	
Denmark	1.9	✓	✓	✓	✓	x	x	
France	37.4	✓	x	✓	✓	x	x	
Germany	38.3	x	x	x	x	x	x	
Greece	32.0	✓	x	x	✓	x	✓	2017
Israel	17.1	✓	x	x	x	✓ /1	x	
Italy	30.3	✓ /1	x	x	x	x	x	
Japan	41.6	✓	x	x	✓	x	x	
Korea	24.7	x	x	x	x	x	x	
Luxembourg	29.2	✓	x	✓ /1	x	✓ /2	x	
Mexico	14.9	✓	x	✓	x	x	x	
Poland	37.8	x	x	x	x	x	x	
Portugal	28.3	x	x	x	x	x	x	
Slovak Republic	43.9	✓	✓	✓	x	x	✓	Possibly 2017
Spain	35.8	✓	✓	✓	x	✓	x	
Switzerland	24.9	x	x	x	x	x	x	
Turkey	27.2	x	x	x	x	x	x	
Non-OECD countries								
China	n.a.	✓	✓	✓	✓	x	x	
Colombia	12.4	✓	✓	✓	x	x	x	
Costa Rica	29.7	x	x	x	x	x	x	
Cyprus	25.9	x	x	x	x	x	x	
Lithuania	40.3	✓	✓	✓	✓	x	x /1	
Malaysia	n.a.	x	x	x	x	x	x	
Russia	17.9	x	x	x	x	x	x	
Singapore	n.a.	✓	x	x	x	✓ /1	x	
South Africa	n.a.	x	x	x	x	x	✓	Not known
Thailand	n.a.	x	x	x	x	x	✓	Not known

Note: Table only shows countries with a SSC regime and where revenue body is *not* responsible for SSC collection).

For notes indicated by "/ (number)", see Notes to Tables section at the end of the chapter, p. 53.

Sources: Survey responses, OECD Revenue Statistics (2014), EC, and IMF Article IV Staff Reports.

Table 1.5. **Non-tax roles of revenue bodies reporting such roles**

Country	Nature of non-tax roles administered by revenue body					
	Customs law	Certain benefit payments	Collection of child support	Collection of student loans	Property valuation	Other roles
OECD countries						
Australia	x	✓	x	✓	x	Fuel rebate and grants scheme, Australian Business Register and Superannuation systems
Austria	✓	✓	x	x	✓	Financial Police, regulatory policy tasks (e.g. labour market tasks and compliance controls re Gambling Act)
Belgium	✓	x	✓ /1	x	✓	Aspects of alimony payment and enforced collection
Canada	x	✓	x	✓ /1	✓	National charities programme, other departments debts
Chile	x	x	x	x	✓	Limited role re assessing contributions of self-employed for retirement pensions and occupational accident/ sickness insurance
Czech Republic	x	x	✓	x	x	Supervises lotteries and gambling games.
Denmark	✓	✓	x	x	✓	Agricultural export refund; collection of public debt
Estonia	✓	✓	✓	✓	x	Population register
Finland	x	x	x	x	x /1	
France	x	x	x	x	✓	Public finances, incl. national and local authorities.
Greece	✓	x	x	x	x	/1
Hungary	✓	x	x	✓	x	Collection of member fees for pension funds and supervision of gambling games
Iceland	x	✓	x	x	x	Companies register, supervises accounting rules
Ireland	✓	x	x	x	x	
Israel	✓	✓	x	x	✓	
Italy	x	x	x	x	✓	Management of cadastral services.
Japan	x	x	x	x	x	Administers liquor industry
Korea	x	✓	x	✓	x	
Luxembourg	x	x	x	✓	✓	Administers state property (e.g. contracts, rents etc.).
Mexico	✓	x	x	x	x	Digital Signature Agency for cross-government e-services
Netherlands	✓	✓ /1	x	x	x	
New Zealand	x	✓	✓	✓	x	"KiwiSaver", a voluntary retirement savings scheme
Norway	x	x	x	x	✓	Population register x /1
Portugal	✓	x	x	x	✓	
Slovak Republic	✓ /1	x	x	x	x	
Slovenia	✓ /1	x	x	x	x	Collection of certain non-tax obligations
Spain	✓	✓	x	x	x	
Sweden	x	x	x	x	✓	Population register, public marriage register
United Kingdom	✓	✓	x	✓	✓	Collection of data for Office for National Statistics re overseas trade statistics and Balance of Payments, administration re the Proceeds of Crime Act 2002.
United States	x	✓	x	x	x	
Non-OECD countries						
Argentina	✓	x	x	x	x	
Brazil	✓	x	x	x	x	x
Bulgaria	x	x	x	x	x	Statistical functions, collection of public revenues
Colombia	✓	x	x	x	x	✓ /1
Costa Rica	x	x	x	x	✓	x
Croatia	x	x	x	x	✓ /1	x
Cyprus	x	x	x	x	✓	
Hong Kong, China	x	x	x	x	x	Stamp and betting duties, business registration and hotel accommodation tax legislation.
Indonesia	x	x	x	x	✓ /1	x
Latvia	✓	x	x	x	x	x
Lithuania	x	x	x	x	x	✓ /1
Malaysia	x	x	x	✓	x	Applications for Malaysia's Peoples Aid programme
Romania	✓	x	x	x	x	Some international sanctions involving freezing of assets
Russia	x	x	x	x	x	Bankruptcy procedures, registration of entities, and licensing of gambling activities.
Singapore	x	x	x	x	✓	Regulates property appraisers and implements certain Government pay out schemes (e.g. Wage Credit Scheme)
South Africa	✓	x	x	x	x	

For notes indicated by "/ (number)", see Notes to Tables section at the end of the chapter, p. 53.

Source: Tax Administration 2015 survey responses.

reported are: *(1)* Customs administration (21 revenue bodies); *(2)* Collection of non-tax debts e.g. student loans (eight revenue bodies); *(3)* Payments of benefits under various social/welfare programmes, some of which are integrated with elements of the tax system (12 revenue bodies); *(4)* Administration of collection of child support (i.e. overdue payments from non-custodial parents) (five revenue bodies); and *(5)* Administration of a property valuation function that, for some countries, is linked to the administration of real property taxes (18 revenue bodies).

Customs administration

As of mid-2014, 13 OECD countries (i.e. Austria, Belgium, Denmark, Estonia, Hungary, Ireland, Israel, Mexico, Netherlands, Portugal, Slovak Republic, Slovenia, and Spain) had aligned the administration of tax and customs operations within a single organisation. This practice is also followed by some of the non-OECD countries surveyed (e.g. Argentina, Brazil, Colombia, Latvia, Romania and South Africa), is planned by Malta for its new integrated tax and customs body when fully established, and is fairly common among other countries in South America and in Africa.

The alignment of tax and customs administration within a single agency appears to have its origins in a number of factors, including: *(1)* perceived synergies with customs operations that are responsible for the collection of VAT on imports, a major source of revenue in many developing countries; *(2)* historical factors associated with the separation of direct and indirect taxes administration; and *(3)* efforts to obtain greater economies of scale (e.g. human resource and IT functions).

Countries that have most recently integrated tax and customs operations are all EU members – Hungary (2011), Portugal (2012), the Slovak Republic (2012), and Slovenia (2014). The precise reasons for this recent "surge" in aligning tax and customs operations within a single body have not been identified by the Secretariat.

On the other hand, it is also relevant to point to other examples of institutional reform, some very recent, that reflect a quite different approach.

Customs operations were removed from the Canada Customs and Revenue Agency and placed in a newly established Canada Border Services Agency in 2003. In 2007, shortly after the creation of its new unified tax and customs body (Her Majesty's Revenue and Customs (HMRC), the United Kingdom Government created a new UK Border Agency (now the UK Border Force) which, among other things, entailed the transfer of over 4 800 staff and funding from HMRC to the new body[5]. HMRC, however, continues to retain its role as the United Kingdom's Customs Agency and is responsible for, amongst other things, customs policy, systems and procedures.

Along similar lines to the actions taken in both Canada and the UK, the Australian Government in May 2014 announced its plans to establish an Australian Border Force (ABF) to:

> [...] protect the Australian community from the transnational criminal threat posed by drugs, guns and other illicit imports while facilitating the movement in and out of Australia of legitimate goods, services and people on which our prosperity depends (Australian Government, 2014b).

The ABF will combine the border functions of the Department of Immigration and Border Protection (DIBP) and the Australian Customs and Border Protection Service (ACBPS). The stated purpose of this initiative is to achieve more integrated, strategic and ultimately more effective border operations in critical areas such as investigations, compliance, detention and enforcement – positioning Australia to deal with future as well as current border security challenges (Australian Government, 2014a).

Norway is also planning reforms in this area. In early 2014, the Government announced plans to reform its Customs and Excise Directorate by transferring its major revenue collection responsibilities (i.e. excise duty administration and the collection of VAT on imports) to the Tax Directorate. The reform is to be completed by the beginning of 2016. The stated purpose of this reform is to improve the efficiency of the public sector and the use of community resources. The reform seeks to achieve this by simplifying the focus of the individual agencies, with the Tax Directorate to have overall responsibility for tax revenue collection and a streamlined customs agency strengthened to exploit its strategic position on the border to conduct effective border controls (Norwegian Ministry of Finance, 2014).

Finally, a recently-announced proposal in Kenya aims to separate tax and customs administration, currently under the responsibility of the Kenyan Revenue Authority (KRA). The Kenyan Government's latest Budget Policy Statement released in February 2015 notes that two Bills on re-organisation of the Kenya Revenue Authority into two semi-autonomous but inter-dependent agencies – the Inland Revenue Agency and the Customs and Border Protection Agency – are to be submitted for enactment in 2015. This proposal follows the findings of a Presidential taskforce set up in 2013 that had recommended splitting up the KRA to increase tax efficiency and which had observed that best practice globally pointed to numerous advantages and benefits from integrating aspects of both customs and immigration functions (e.g. improving control over the movement of goods at entry points). At the same time, it noted that the revenue collection role of customs should remain with the main tax collection agency.

Special governance arrangements

Like all government bodies, revenue bodies are ultimately accountable to the citizens they serve. The framework within which this accountability operates varies between countries and is a result of many factors including the institutional arrangements and government structures in place. The following section identifies special/unusual governance mechanisms in place to ensure this accountability is achieved. It focuses on examples of the oversight mechanisms in place in selected revenue bodies. Some approaches for achieving improved accountability for performance are covered in Chapter 3.

Formal management boards and advisory bodies

As indicated in Table 1.1, 11 countries reported that a management/advisory board or council has been interposed between the revenue body and the relevant minister/arm of government to provide a degree of independent advice on the plans and operations of the revenue body and tax administration arrangements in general.[5] In all of the examples cited later in this part, the board's membership includes non-revenue body officials. Also apparent is the fact such arrangements cover a broad cross-section of continents and cultures.

While the specific functions of the boards vary between countries all execute an oversight function and/or would appear to have a role in strategy development and planning, major policy approvals, and the sign-off of formal budgets and business plans and overall performance evaluation. Without exception, board members are not involved in issues concerning the tax affairs of individual taxpayers and do not have access to specific taxpayer information. For some countries where this arrangement has been established, its introduction coincided with the establishment of a new more autonomous body for tax administration (e.g. in Canada and Singapore).

Country examples

Mexico's Governing Board for the SAT

Background	The creation of the Governing Board coincided with the establishment of a new more autonomous revenue and custom body in 1996.
Role	The Board's roles are as follows: *(1)* assist in the development of fiscal policy and customs measures necessary for the development and implementation of the National Development Plan and sectoral programmes; *(2)* provide opinions on draft bills, decrees, resolutions, administrative and general provisions in tax and customs matters; *(3)* approve programmes and budgets of the SAT (*i.e.* the Tax Administration Service); *(4)* approve the basic organisational structure of the SAT; *(5)* consider and approve measures proposed by the chairman of the SAT to improve operational efficiency and taxpayer orientation; *(6)* approve the annual programme of continuous improvement for the SAT, including setting and monitoring targets for increased efficiency and improved taxpayer service delivery (NB: descriptions of measures/performance indicators that must be used are set out in Chapter 3 of this series); and *(7)* analyse proposals for continuous improvement.
Composition	The Board consists of: *(1)* the Secretary of the Ministry of Finance and Public Credit, who will preside; *(2)* three directors selected by the Secretary of Finance from the employees of Finance; and *(3)* three independent directors appointed by the President of the Republic (two of whom must have been nominated by the national meeting of tax officials in the terms of the Fiscal Coordination Law). To be appointed, independent directors must not have held a federal or municipal government appointment in the prior year. Once appointed, they must not engage in tax or customs related-activities that are incompatible with their role and must attend 70% of convened meetings.
Features of its operation	The Board is required to hold regular meetings, one at least every three months, and a quorum requires at least 50% of members. Board decisions are made by majority vote, with the Secretary of Finance, as chair, having a casting vote in the event of a tie.

Source: Decree governing the establishment and operations of the Servicio de Administración Tributaria (SAT), www.sat.gob.mx/informacion_fiscal/normatividad/Documents/LSAT.pdf (Spanish only).

Russia's Public Board of the Federal Tax Service

Background	A Public Board of the Federal Tax Service (FTS) was created in 2009, to enable public scrutiny of the activities of the FTS with a view to furthering its development as a listening body which takes account of public opinion in carrying out its functions.
Role	The Board performs the following tasks: *(1)* Conducting public expert appraisals of projects devised by the FTS; *(2)* Examining tax policy initiatives; *(3)* Participating in the discussion and resolution of matters for which the FTS is responsible; *(4)* Participating in the formulation of proposals for the implementation of measures aimed at the legal and social protection of state civil servants of the FTS; and *(5)* involving members of the public, public associations and representatives of the mass media in matters pertaining to the activities of the FTS.
Composition	Members of the Board include prominent representatives of science and education, leading IT experts, representatives of major media organisations and small, medium-sized and large organisations, and well-known public figures. The Board is chaired by one of its external representatives.
Features of some activities	The Board was involved in the development of the FTS's Conceptual Framework for the Organisation of Work with Taxpayers, and also played an active part in the creation of the Working Group for the Promotion of Tax Awareness, whose objectives are to seek effective ways of increasing public understanding of tax matters and to devise a unified programme of educational measures to be implemented on a nation-wide basis.

Source: Federal Tax Service 2013 Report.

Board of the Inland Revenue Authority of Singapore (IRAS)

Background	The IRAS Board was established in 1992, as part of legislation authorizing the creation of a new statutory authority with autonomy in managing its operations to administer the tax laws.
Role	The Board oversees IRAS and ensures that it carries out its functions competently. The Board meets three times a year to review major corporate policies and approve financial statements, annual budget and major expenditure projects.
Composition	The Board comprises the chairman who is also the Permanent Secretary of the Ministry of Finance, the Commissioner of Inland Revenue, and seven other members (comprising public and private sector representatives).
Features of its operation	The Board operates with two committees. The Audit Committee reviews whether IRAS' accounting and financial policies and internal controls are in place, adequate and adhered to. The Committee works closely with the external auditor, the Auditor-General, in reviewing the financial statements of IRAS, the scope of audit plans and the audit results. The Committee also reviews the annual audit plan of the Internal Audit Branch and the results of its work. The Staff Committee A is the approving authority for key remuneration policies in IRAS as well as key appointments, promotion and remuneration of senior executives in IRAS.

Source: Revenue body's website (March 2014) and survey response.

United Kingdom: The Board of Her Majesty's Revenue and Customs (HMRC)

Background	Legislation to create HMRC in 2005 included provision for the creation of a Board, to be comprised of members of HMRC's internal Executive Committee and (four) non-executive (external) board members. In 2008, HMRC implemented a new governance structure appointing a non-executive Chairman and a new Chief Executive. In 2012, the post of Chairman ceased and was replaced by a Lead Non-Executive Board member appointed to chair the Board. The Lead Non-Executive's role is advisory and is to lead the Board in providing challenge and advice on Departmental performance and its future strategic direction. The Chief Executive and Executive Committee are responsible for running HMRC.
Role	As a non-ministerial department, the role of the Board is critical to the success of HMRC. The Board is in place to advise and challenge the management of HMRC, particularly focusing its attention on the performance of the Department and its future strategic direction. The Board does not have a role in day-to-day operational decision-making, nor in tax policy or individual taxpayer matters. The Non-Executives on the Board bring with them a wealth of experience from a range of backgrounds, including data analytics, human resources, IT, accountancy and the tax profession. Their skills and professional background bring an external perspective to the advice the Board gives to help shape strategy and challenge performance. The Board provides: • **Challenge**: reviewing and challenging the Department's business plan and performance against that plan, with particular reference to agreed strategic priorities; • **Expertise**: providing wider public and private sector expertise to help shape the delivery of strategy and to improve HMRC's performance. They also advise the Chief Executive on senior appointments; • **Strategy**: assuring HMRC's strategic direction is clear and deliverable, taking into account risk and focusing on the long-term success of the Department and value for the taxpayer;

Role (continued)	• **Assurance**: providing the Chief Executive, as Principal Accounting Officer, with assurance that the financial statements are factually accurate, that risk management processes are robust, and that control processes across HMRC are strong and appropriate; and • **Stakeholder views**: reflecting the views of HMRC's external stakeholders; supporting HMRC to develop stakeholder communications plans; and using the cross-government network of Non-Executive directors to bring insight and intelligence to support the Executive Committee to identify challenges and opportunities.
Composition	The Board is chaired by the Lead Non-Executive. Nine Executives currently sit on the Board with 6 Non-Executives.
Features of its operation	The Board meets seven times a year, including a special strategy session in the summer. The Board's committee structure consists of the Board and three supporting committees: *(1)* People, Nominations and Governance; *(2)* Scrutiny; and *(3)* Audit and Risk. Work is delegated to Board committees, where smaller groups of Non-Executives and ExCom members can examine issues in more detail and present their findings to the Board for discussion and conclusion.

Source: HMRC survey response.

United States: Internal Revenue Service's Oversight Board

Background	A nine-member IRS Oversight Board was created by Congress under the IRS Restructuring and Reform Act of 1998.
Role	The Board's responsibility is to oversee the IRS in its administration, management, conduct, direction, and supervision of the execution and application of the internal revenue laws. The Board was created to provide long-term focus and specific expertise in guiding the IRS so it may best serve the public and meet the needs of taxpayers.
Composition	Seven board members are appointed by the President and confirmed by the Senate for five-year terms. These members have professional experience or expertise in key business and tax administration areas. Of the seven, one must be a full-time federal employee or a representative of IRS employees. The Secretary of Treasury and the Commissioner of Internal Revenue are also members of the Board.
Features of its operation	The Board operates much like a corporate board of directors, but is tailored to fit a public sector organisation. The Board provides the IRS with long-term guidance and direction, and applies its private-sector experience and expertise in evaluating the IRS's progress in improving its service. It reviews and approves IRS strategic plans and its budget requests, and evaluates IRS efforts to monitor its own performance. The Board reviews the hiring and compensation of senior IRS officials. It also recommends candidates to the President to serve as IRS commissioner, and can recommend a commissioner's removal. The Board reaches out to a wide variety of stakeholders to understand their views on tax administration and its impact on taxpayers. The Board interacts regularly with external groups that include tax professionals, taxpayer advocacy groups, representatives of state tax departments, IRS advisory committees, IRS employees, the National Treasury Employees Union, and other groups that have an interest in tax administration. The Board also conducts an annual survey of taxpayers' attitudes about compliance and other issues relating to tax administration. The Board regularly meets in sessions and holds at least one public meeting each year. The Board's web site at www.irsoversightboard.treas.gov provides information on the Board's meetings. Following its public meetings, the Board posts its agenda and stakeholder statements on its web site. Press releases describing regular meetings are also available on the web site.

Features of its operation (continued)	The Board publishes an annual report (see www.ustreas.gov/irsob/board-reports.shtml), as well as a report reviewing the progress of IRS's electronic tax filing efforts. The Board may also publish interim reports throughout the year on specific topics, such as the budget. All reports are available on the Board's web site. The Board is also invited to testify before Congress periodically and its testimony is posted on its web site. The Board distributes press releases describing its activities to the media at the end of each of its meetings. Under the law, the Board cannot be involved in specific law enforcement activities, including audits, collection activities, or criminal investigations. It also cannot be involved in specific procurement activities or most personnel matters and it does not develop or formulate tax policy on existing or proposed tax laws.

Source: Oversight Board's website (April 2014).

External/independent oversight of the tax administration system

Governments in Australia and the United States have established specialist bodies independent of the revenue body to report on the workings of the tax administration system. These bodies operate separately and independently of national audit bodies that oversee the workings of all government agencies. In the case of Australia, the specialist body has recently been made responsible for handling individuals' complaints. A brief description of these set-ups is provided below.

Australia: Inspector-General of Taxation

Background	The Inspector-General of Taxation (IGT) was established as an independent statutory agency in 2003.
Role	The IGT's role is to review: *(1)* systems established by the Australian Taxation Office (ATO) to administer the tax laws; and *(2)* systems established by tax laws in relation to administrative matters; for the purpose of reporting and making recommendations to Government on how those systems could be improved. The Act precludes the IGT from reviewing the imposition of taxes and tax rates, and the eligibility criteria for, or levels of, any rebates or grants administered by the ATO. The IGT seeks to improve the administration of the tax laws for the benefit of all taxpayers. Individuals and/or groups of taxpayers, professional associations and businesses are welcome to bring systemic administration issues to the attention of the IGT. The IGT endeavours to address taxpayers' concerns on defective administration while ensuring resources of the agency are directed to those areas of most benefit to taxpayers overall. The overall aim is to identify how to reduce the administrative burden for taxpayers in meeting their tax obligations. In May 2014, the Australian Government announced that the IGT's role would be expanded from 2014-15 to include the function of taxation complaints case handling, previously performed by the Office of the Commonwealth Ombudsman. The purpose of this decision is to enhance the systematic review role of the IGT and to provide taxpayers with a more specialised and focused complaint handling for tax matters.

Features of operation	While a number of Commonwealth Government agencies examine systemic taxation administration matters, the IGT is the only agency with sole responsibility for such reviews. To ensure that reviews undertaken reflect areas of key concern, and to avoid duplication with other agencies, the Inspector-General develops the work programme following consultation with: *(1)* taxpayers and their representatives; *(2)* Ombudsman; *(3)* Auditor-General; *(4)* Commissioner of Taxation; and *(5)* The Secretary of the Commonwealth Treasury. In conducting reviews the IGT may invite submissions and/or request/require the tax officials to provide information and documentation. The Act contains specific provisions on the confidentiality of submissions made to the Inspector-General. On completion of a review the Inspector-General reports directly to Government. All reports are subsequently made available within the timeframe outlined in the Act. The IGT provides an annual report to Parliament.
Examples of studies in 2013-14	*Review into the Australian Taxation Office's compliance approach to individual taxpayers – income tax refund integrity programme (February 2014)*
	Review into aspects of the Australian Taxation Office's use of compliance risk assessment tools (February 2014)

Source: IGT's website (May 2014) and Australian Government Budget 2014-15 (May 2014).

United States: Treasury Inspector General for Tax Administration

Background	The Treasury Inspector General for Tax Administration (TIGTA) was established in January 1999 in accordance with the Internal Revenue Service Restructuring and Reform Act of 1998 (RRA 98). As mandated by RRA 98, TIGTA assumed most of the responsibilities of the IRS" former Inspection Service.
Role	To provide independent oversight of Internal Revenue Service (IRS) activities.
Features of operations	TIGTA consists mainly of auditors and investigators focused on the duties and responsibilities of an Inspector General organisation on matters relating to the IRS. TIGTA is organisationally placed within the Department of the Treasury, but is independent of the Department and all other Treasury offices, including the Treasury Office of the Inspector General (OIG). TIGTA's focus is devoted entirely to tax administration, while Treasury OIG is responsible for overseeing other Treasury bureaus. TIGTA's audit and investigative activities are designed to: *(1)* promote economy, efficiency, and effectiveness in administering the Nation's tax system; *(2)* detect and deter fraud and abuse in IRS programmes and operations; *(3)* protect IRS against external attempts to corrupt or threaten its employees; *(4)* review and make recommendations about existing and proposed legislation and regulations related to IRS and TIGTA programmes and operations; *(5)* prevent fraud, abuse, and deficiencies in IRS programmes and operations; and *(6)* inform the Secretary of the Treasury and Congress of problems and progress made to resolve them.
Examples of studies in 2013-14	*Improvements are needed in documentation and data accuracy for the employment tax study (May 2014)*
	The Internal Revenue Service Should Improve Mainframe Software Asset Management and Reduce Costs (February 2014).
	The Online Payment Agreement Programme Benefits Taxpayers and the Internal Revenue Service, but More Could Be Done to Expand Its Use (September 2013)

Source: Treasury Inspector General for Tax Administration's website (May 2014).

In addition to the Treasury Inspector General in the United States, there is also the Office of Taxpayer Advocate which is responsible for both individual complaints received from taxpayers as well as reporting on systemic issues that arise with the operation of the tax system. More is said on this Office in the following section.

Special institutional arrangements for dealing with taxpayers' complaints

Governments in many countries have established special bodies (e.g. an Ombudsman's Office) to handle individual complaints concerning government agencies (including revenue bodies) in their dealings with citizens and business. In some countries, an agency dedicated to dealing only with tax-related complaints from citizens and business arising from actions/inactions of the revenue body has been established (e.g. an Office of Tax Ombudsman). The primary purpose of such arrangements is to ensure that citizens

Table 1.6. **Special body for dealing with taxpayers' complaints**

(Table only includes countries reporting that a special body exists)

	Special body				
Countries	Exists	Supported by specific legislative framework	Separate from revenue body	Reports on systemic issues	Name of body(ies)
OECD countries					
Australia	✓	✓	✓	✓	Inspector General of Taxation /1
Austria	✓	✓	✓	✓	Tax Ombudsservice
Belgium	✓	✓	✓	✓	Tax Mediator
Canada	✓	✓	✓	✓	Office of Taxpayers' Ombudsman
Czech Republic	✓	✓	✓	x	Public Defender of Rights (generally "Ombudsman")
Denmark	✓	✓	x	✓	Director, Legal Protection /1
Finland	✓	✓	✓	✓	Parliamentary Ombudsman
France	✓	✓	✓	x	Mediator of the Republic, Mediator of MOF /1, Local Mediator
Greece	✓ /1	✓	x	✓	
Hungary	✓	✓	✓	✓	Commissioner for Fundamental Rights; National Authority for Data Protection and Freedom of Information
Iceland	✓	✓	✓	✓	Althing (Parliamentary) Ombudsman
Ireland	✓	✓	✓	✓	Office of the Ombudsman
Israel	✓	x /1	✓	✓	Commissioner of Public Complaints
Italy	✓	✓	✓	x	Tax Ombudsman ("Garante del Contribuente")
Japan	✓	✓	x	✓	Taxpayer Support
Korea	✓	✓	x	✓	Taxpayer Advocate
Luxembourg	✓ /1	✓	✓	✓	Ombudsman
Mexico	✓	✓	✓	✓	Prodecon (Taxpayers Attorney's Office)
Netherlands	✓	✓	✓	✓	National Ombudsman
Norway	✓	✓	✓	✓	Ombudsman
Portugal	✓	✓	✓	✓	Ombudsman
Spain	✓	✓	x	✓	Taxpayers' Counsel (Consejo para la Defensa del Contribuyente)
Turkey	x /1	x	x	x	/1
United Kingdom	✓ /1	✓	✓	✓	Adjudicators Office/ Parliamentary Health Service Ombudsman
United States	✓	✓	✓	✓	Taxpayer Advocate Service /1
Non-OECD countries					
Argentina	✓	✓	x	✓	
Brazil	✓	x /1	✓	✓	Ombud Service of the Ministry of Finance
Bulgaria	✓	✓	✓	✓	National Ombudsman
China	✓	x	x	✓	Taxpayer Rights Protection Division of Taxpayer Service Department
Colombia	✓	✓	✓	✓	Taxpayers' Advocate
Croatia	✓	✓	✓	✓	Independent Sector for Second-Instance Administrative Procedure, Service for Second-Instance Tax Procedure
Cyprus	✓	✓	✓	✓	Ombudsman (DT, VAT)
Hong Kong, China	✓ /1	✓	✓	✓	Office of Ombudsman
India	✓	✓	✓	✓	Ombudsman
Indonesia	✓	✓	✓	✓	Taxation Supervisory Committee
Malaysia	✓ /1	✓	✓	✓	Public Complaints Bureau
Malta	✓	✓	✓	✓	Office of the Ombudsman
South Africa	✓	✓	✓	✓	Office of the Tax Ombud

For notes indicated by "/ (number)", see Notes to Tables section at the end of the chapter, p. 53.

Source: Tax Administration 2015 survey responses.

and businesses have an opportunity to raise matters where they believe they have been treated harshly or unfairly and to have these matters handled independently of the agency to which the matter relates. For this series, revenue bodies were asked to identify: *(1)* whether such a body has been created; *(2)* if so, whether its operations are based on a specific legal framework and set of powers; *(3)* whether it is autonomous from the revenue body; and *(4)* whether it is empowered to report on systemic issues (in addition to dealing with individual complaints of citizens and businesses). In addition, some research was undertaken to identify the nature of the specific arrangements in place in selected countries. A summary of the information provided by revenue bodies is set out in Table 1.6.

Revenue bodies reported a broad mix of arrangements entailing a special body for handling taxpayers' complaints and the key observations are as follows:

- Twenty one revenue bodies reported that taxpayers' complaints are dealt with, along with non-tax complaints, by an independent Office of Ombudsman (or the equivalent) that also reports on systemic issues.
- Ten revenue bodies reported that an autonomous body exists for dealing solely with tax-related complaints (e.g. a "Tax Ombudsman" or "Taxpayers Advocate"), who is also empowered to report on systemic issues.
- Six revenue bodies reported that there was an internal part of their agency for dealing independently with taxpayers' complaints that, with few exceptions, were subject to a specific legal framework.

Country examples

Canada: Taxpayers' Ombudsman

Background	The Office of Taxpayers' Ombudsman (OTO) was established in 2007, coinciding with the establishment of the Taxpayer Bill of Rights (TBR). The first Taxpayers' Ombudsman (TO) was appointed in February 2008.
Role	The mandate of the TO is to assist, advise and inform the Minister of National Revenue about any matter relating to services provided to a taxpayer by the CRA. The TO fulfills this mandate by upholding taxpayer service rights as defined in the TBR and providing an independent and impartial review of unresolved complaints from taxpayers about the service or treatment they have received from the CRA. The TO also makes recommendations directly to the Minister of National Revenue to correct any systemic service issues. The TO's recommendations are not binding. Another important part of its role is raising awareness of taxpayer service rights and the role of the OTO.
Features of operations	The TO will generally only review service complaints made by a taxpayer if they have exhausted all other available service redress mechanisms at the CRA, unless compelling circumstances mandate otherwise. The TO can identify systemic and emerging service-related issues within the CRA to improve service delivery. The TO operates independently and at arm's length from the CRA and reports directly to the Minister of National Revenue.
Recent reports on systemic issues	***Donor Beware:*** *Investigation into the sufficiency of the Canada Revenue Agency's warnings about questionable tax shelter schemes.*
	Getting it Right: *Investigation of service and fairness issues arising from the misallocation of payments by the Canada Revenue Agency.*
Website	www.oto-boc.gc.ca

Source: CRA survey data.

Mexico's Office of Taxpayers' Advocate (Prodecon)

Background	The Office of the Taxpayer Advocate, which commenced operations in September 2011, is a public agency with technical and managerial autonomy that specialises in tax matters, and which provides free, fast and simple advisory services and consulting, advocacy and representation for complaints or claims against acts of the federal tax authorities which contravene the rights of taxpayers. The Office operates independently of the SAT and it is free to make reports on systemic issues requiring attention by the SAT or Government. Its recommendations, however, are not binding on SAT.
Commitments	The **Prodecon** aims to protect the rights and interests of taxpayers, through advice, representation and advocacy, as well as receiving complaints and issuing recommendations on taxation, and other major powers such as the identification of the endemic problems of the tax system, regular meetings with business and professional associations, as well as trustees and organised contributors, to which they must attend the tax authorities in high level, propose corrective measures, interpreting tax rules at the request of the SAT, promote tax culture, and make submissions to the Committee on Finance of the House of Deputies with proposed amendments to the tax rules.
Website	www.prodecon.gob.mx/index.php/home/que-es-prodecon

Source: Taxpayer Advocate's website (October 2014).

South Africa: Office of Tax Ombud

Background	The Office of Tax Ombud was created by sections 14 and 15 of the Tax Administration Act, No. 28 of 2011 (TAAct). This legislation amalgamates, integrates and streamlines the administrative provisions of tax laws so as to decrease the administrative burden and compliance costs borne by taxpayers and the South African Revenue Service (SARS). The Office operates independently of SARS. The Office's operations commenced in October 2013 and it was officially launched in April 2014.
Role	As set out in the Act, the mandate of the Tax Ombud is to review and address any complaint by a taxpayer regarding a service matter, or a procedural or administrative matter arising from the application of the provisions of a tax Act by SARS.
Features of operations	In discharging its mandate, the Tax Ombud's office must review a complaint, and if necessary, resolve it through mediation or conciliation with SARS officials specifically identified to interact with the Tax Ombud's office. The Tax Ombud may only review a complaint after a taxpayer has exhausted SARS' internal complaints resolution mechanisms. Direct access to the Tax Ombud will only be allowed if there are compelling circumstances for doing so. The Tax Ombud reports directly to the Minister of Finance and the Ombud's annual report must be tabled in parliament by the Minister.
Website	www.taxombud.gov.za/about-us.html

Source: Office of the Tax Ombud's website (May 2014).

United States: Taxpayer Advocate Service

Background	The Taxpayer Advocate Service (TAS) was established by the Taxpayer Bill of Rights 2 legislation in 1996, replacing the Office of the Taxpayer Ombudsman.
Role	The TAS is an independent organisation located within the IRS whose employees assist taxpayers who are experiencing economic hardship, who are seeking help in resolving tax problems that have not been resolved through normal channels, or who believe that an IRS system or procedure is not working as it should. The National Taxpayer Advocate heads the programme and each state and campus has at least one local Taxpayer Advocate who is independent of the local IRS office and reports directly to the National Taxpayer Advocate. The goals of the TAS are to protect taxpayers' rights and reduce taxpayer burden.

Features of operations	The Taxpayer Advocate independently represents taxpayers' interests and concerns within the IRS. This is accomplished in two ways: *(1)* Ensuring that taxpayer problems which have not been resolved through normal channels, are handled promptly and fairly; and *(2)* Identifying issues that increase burden or create problems for taxpayers-bringing those issues to the attention of IRS management and making legislative proposals where necessary. In Taxpayer Bill of Rights 2, Congress established the Office of the Taxpayer Advocate and also described its functions: *(1)* To assist taxpayers in resolving problems with the Internal Revenue Service; *(2)* To identify areas in which taxpayers have problems in dealings with the Internal Revenue Service; *(3)* To the extent possible, propose changes in the administrative practices of the IRS to mitigate those identified problems; and *(4)* To identify potential legislative changes which may be appropriate to mitigate such problems. The TAS provides two reports annually to Congress-one setting out its objectives for a fiscal year, the other on its achievements in the fiscal year.
Recent reports on systemic issues	*Toward a more perfect tax system: a taxpayer bill of rights as a framework for effective tax administration (November 2013)*
	The 2013 TAS Annual Report to Congress includes specific segments dealing with: *(1)* The most serious problems facing taxpayers and recommended solutions; *(2)* The ten most litigated tax issues; and *(3)* A range of research studies (*e.g. Analysing Factors in Small Business Compliance* and *Optimising Taxpayer Service Delivery*).
Website	See http://www.irs.gov/Advocate

Source: Taxpayer Advocate Service's website (May 2014).

Notes

1. The fiscal blueprints, originally developed in 1999 and updated in 2007, are described as a set of practical guidelines laying down clear criteria based on EU best practice, against which a tax or fiscal administration is able to measure its own operational capacity. The blueprints are regarded as having broad international application: http://ec.europa.eu/taxation_customs/resources/documents/common/publications/info_docs/taxation/fiscal_blueprint_en.pdf.

2. The term "unified semi-autonomous body" is also intended to encompass the model elsewhere described as the "revenue authority" model seen in some developing countries (e.g. Kenya, Peru, South Africa, and Zambia).

3. The dominant role of such contributions in most of these countries stems directly from the application of the so-called Bismarck model which remains the foundation of the social security system in much of Europe today. The model sees government-provided social security as a special form of insurance, with both benefits and contributions tied to workers' wages. In some countries, the contributions are channelled through separate funds which are kept apart from the central government budget. By contrast, notably in some Scandinavian and English-speaking OECD countries, a substantial part of public spending on social benefits tends to be financed directly out of government general tax revenues although, even in countries following the Bismarck model, social security funds may also show a persistent deficit requiring subsidies from general taxation.

4. The countries selected for this research were: *(1)* countries with a longer standing record with regard to the merger, i.e. the United Kingdom and the Netherlands; *(2)* countries in transition to market economies, such as Hungary and Estonia; and *(3)* countries with a partial merging of collection functions, such as Italy.

5. Border Force is a law enforcement command within the Home Office. Its role is to secure the UK border by carrying out immigration and customs controls for people and goods entering the United Kingdom.

Notes to Tables

Table 1.1. Institutional arrangements for tax administration

/1. **Brazil**: There is no national VAT, but two other taxes: One imposed by each Federal Member-State, the "Imposto sobre a Circulação de Mercadorias e Serviços" (ICMS) and another imposed by each municipality, the "Imposto sobre Serviços" (ISS). At the federal level, there is the "Programa de Integração Social (PIS)", the "Contribuição para o Financiamento da Seguridade Social (Cofins)" and the "Imposto sobre Produtos Industrializados (IPI)". **Canada**: CRA also administers subnational taxes (PIT, CIT and VAT) for most of Canada's ten provinces and three territories. **Chile**: Revenue body (SII) performs all normal tax administration functions except the enforced collection of taxes which is carried out by the Treasury. **China**: Separate body with minister. **Costa Rica**: A General Sales Tax is levied on the sale of all goods and some specific services. **Cyprus, Luxembourg, Malta**: Have separate directorates for Direct Taxes, Indirect Taxes, and/or Customs and Excise. **Denmark:** The Danish tax administration (SKAT) is located under the Ministry of Taxation, along with a number of other tax-related bodies. **Germany**: Multiple organisational units in the ministries of finance in 16 Länder and the Federation are responsible overall. Major taxes are administered by 16 Federal States (Länder) MOFs. In addition the Federal Central Tax Office under the supervision of the Federal MOF performs certain functions. **India**: Department of Revenue includes two Boards, the Central Board of Direct Taxes (CBDT) and the Central Board of Excise and Customs (CBEC), which report to the Finance Minister through the Revenue Secretary, who heads the Revenue Department. Board Members are all officers from Indian Revenue Service. (NB: Only the CBDT is covered by this series.) **Indonesia**: Tax administration administers farm land and forestry property taxes. Land and building tax for rural and urban sectors administered by local (regional) government. **Italy**: There are a number of separate bodies involved in tax administration that are described in the body of chapter text. **Malaysia**: The Inland Revenue Board is a semi-autonomous body with a board administering direct taxes while the Customs and Excise Department administers indirect taxes and is a government department under the Ministry of Finance. **Norway**: The revenue body will administer excises and motor vehicles from 2016. **Saudi Arabia**: The revenue body (DZIT) also administers "zakat", a tax-like duty on commercial activities of Saudi persons. There is no tax on employment income, but other activities of individuals (such as professional and trading activities) are taxable. **Slovak Republic**: The Tax Administration and Customs Administration merged into the newly established Slovak Financial Administration on 1 January 2012. **Slovenia**: In 2014, Tax Administration and Customs Administration merged into the Financial Administration of the Republic of Slovenia. **South Africa**: Collects unemployment insurance fund contributions on behalf of Department of Labour. **Spain**: Wealth tax – This is a regional tax but the revenue body provides some administrative support; Excise duty is collected on certain means of transport. **Sweden**: Swedish Tax Agency with the Advisory Council. **Switzerland**: Direct taxes are administered at sub-national level (by cantons). The Federal Tax Administration supervises the national share of the direct taxes. **Turkey**: The Presidency of Revenue Administration, a semi-autonomous authority, carries out all mainstream tax administration functions excluding tax audits which are carried out by the separate Tax Inspection Board.

/2. **Brazil**: There is a National Federal real property tax, concerning rural land, named "Imposto territorial Rural" (ITR). The taxation of real property located within urban zones is imposed by each Municipality and the tax is called "Imposto Territorial Urbano" (IPTU). **Chile**: Re SSC, the revenue body has a limited role in the assessment of self-employed individuals for contributions for retirement pension and occupational accident and sickness insurance as from 2013. For motor vehicles, the revenue body establishes the tax base for the application of the annual tax on the use of vehicles, levied by municipalities. **Germany**: Lander tax bodies determine property values for real property tax collected by municipalities; the motor vehicle tax was administered by Länder tax bodies by means of an official delegation of powers to them until 30 June 2014. **India**: Only the excise levied by the Central Government, but not the excise levied by State Governments. **Italy:** Revenue body administers a property valuation function which supports the collection of a Unique Municipal Tax, introduced in 2012, levied on the nominal value of (building and lands and paid to municipalities.

Table 1.2. Delegated authority of national revenue bodies

/1. Separate references for countries with multiple revenue bodies.

/2. **Brazil**: The revenue body proposes the levels and combinations of personnel, which are established by the Ministry of Planning; wage negotiations are not directly carried out by the tax administration although it can influence and act as a facilitator along with the competent authorities; to reallocate budget, a decree of the President (for lower values) or legislative authorisation (via Congress) is needed. **Costa Rica**: Directorate

General of the Civil Service Directorate establishes the classification for each job, remuneration and classification for each specialty, as well as the procedures for hiring and dismissal. The Tax Administration follows those provisions on employment. **Cyprus**: Revenue body can only remit the penalty for compromise of offence. **Germany**: Generally, each Lander's MOF can decide on the internal structure. The more important decisions on levels and mix staff are made by State and Federal Parliaments as part of the budget. Each MOF can hire within the limitations provided by its budget and can influence recruitment criteria, but dismissing staff is virtually impossible under German civil service law. Most of the 16 States and the Federal MOF maintain their own IT operations. **Greece:** Minister decides overall numbers while GSPR can re-arrange positions as needed; hiring and firing requires approval of Minister of Finance. **Luxembourg, Malta**: Only penalties. **Morocco**: Concerning structure, only for the network of offices. For funding decisions, the revenue body has very limited power to re-allocate capital budgeted administrative funds to meet new priorities. **Spain**: Recruitment and dismissal of staff must be done under the Spanish Civil Service Law. Dismissal is extremely rare. **Thailand**: Only for non-civil servant staff.

Table 1.4. Social security contributions: Assistance provided by selected revenue bodies

/1. **Chile**: Revenue body has a limited role in the assessment of self-employed individuals for contributions for retirement pension and occupational accident and sickness insurance as from 2013. **Israel:** Automatic transfer of information, reports and information upon request. **Italy**: There is a useful exchange of information and tools between revenue body and National Social Security Institute (INPS); available web services enable INPS to access the tax register information system to verify taxpayers' data with cross referenced verifications. **Lithuania**: There is a study being prepared to examine the possible consolidation of processes the state revenue collection area: a handover of administration of social insurance contributions to State Tax Inspectorate (now administrated by State Social Insurance Fund Board), as well as Customs and Financial Crime Investigation Service. **Luxembourg**: Direct Taxes Department only. **Singapore**: IRAS assists Central Provident Fund Board (which is currently administrating a compulsory social security savings scheme) by transmitting income information about self-employed taxpayers to aid in the computation of the contribution amount payable.

/2. **Chile**: The SII collaborates with: *(1)* the Social Security Institute (IPS), providing information relevant to determine the entitlement to pensions under the "pension solidaria" system; and *(2)* the National Health Fund (FONASA), by providing information on the income of those paying contributions to FONASA to ensure that the benefits granted correspond to their level of income, among others. **Luxembourg**: Indirect Taxes Department only: Exchange of information for i.e. statistical purposes.

Table 1.5. Selected non-tax roles of revenue bodies

/1. **Canada**: CRA collects amounts owed on defaulted Canada Student Loans. **Colombia:** DIAN also administers gambling licenses fees and "development fees" – subsidies to specific activities (e.g. rice and cacao crops, filmmaking, software development) within sectors within the economy, which are collected upon the performance of specific transactions. DIAN also enforces foreign exchange regulations related to international trade operations. **Croatia**: Only for tax purposes. **Finland:** All property valuation is tax-related. **Greece**: Treasury and budget, chemical state laboratory, public property and national legacies. **Indonesia:** Only for farm land and forestry property tax. **Lithuania**: Includes takeover, accounting, safekeeping, realisation, return and write-off of property under the state jurisdiction including forfeited, derelict, inherited property of the state, material evidences, treasures and findings and, since 2012, acceptance of Public Officials' declarations on public and private interests. **Netherlands:** NTCA is responsible for the implementation of income-related schemes, also known as "benefits", which provide for allowances that households may obtain towards the cost of childcare, rent or health care. Over 6 million households receive such benefits at present. **Slovak Republic:** Tax Administration and Customs Administration merged into the Slovak Financial Administration in 2012. **Slovenia**: Tax Administration and Customs Administration merged into the Financial Administration of the Republic of Slovenia in 2014.

Table 1.6. Special body for procedural justice/dealing with tax-related complaints

/1. **Australia:** In May 2014, the Australian Government announced that the Inspector General of Taxation's role would be expanded from 2014-15 to include the function of taxation complaints case handling, previously performed by the Office of the Commonwealth Ombudsman. **Brazil**: The legal framework is being elaborated and it depends on the bill related to the Ombud Service which is pending in the National Congress. **Hong Kong, Luxembourg**: Information relates to office of Government Ombudsman (or equivalent title). **Denmark**: The role of the previous Citizen Ambassador has been merged with that of the Director for Legal Protection. **France**: Mediator of the Republic is competent for all issues between citizens and public service (not only tax administration); Mediator of the Ministry of Finances is competent for issues between taxpayers and all MOF departments including tax administration; taxpayers may also refer to mediators at local level (who are part of tax administration). **Greece:** Committee operated under former Directorate of Economic Inspection until end of June 2014, but now operates within newly established General Secretary of Public Revenue. **Israel:** The Internal Auditor also serves in the capacity of Ombudsman and operates according to the professional standards of internal auditors. **Malaysia:** The body receives complaints against public services and is regulated by circulars issued by the Prime Minister's Department. **Turkey**: A Taxpayer Feedback System was piloted in 2012 as part of an EU-funded project. It collected feedback in terms of suggestions, problems and praise. However, the project was discontinued in the light of deficiencies in its design. The system is to be re-established by the Revenue Administration. **United Kingdom**: HMRC operates a complaints process based on 2 internal tiers, an independent tier (tier 3 – the Adjudicator) and then the Parliamentary and Health Service Ombudsman (generally tier 4). **United States**: The TAS safeguards procedural justice and deals with taxpayers' complaints. TAS is headed by the National Taxpayer Advocate who is appointed by the Secretary of the Treasury. TAS is embedded within the IRS, but operates independently.

Bibliography

Australian Government (2014a), *A stronger border – establishment of an Australian Border Force,* Minister for Immigration and Border Protection, Canberra.

Australian Government (2014b), *2014-15 Budget, Budget Paper No.2*, Canberra.

Barrand, P., G. Harrison and S. Ross (2004), *Integrating Tax and Social Security Contribution Collections within a Unified Revenue Administration: The Experience of Central and Eastern European Countries*, IMF, Washington.

Bakirtzi, E. and K.U. Leuven (2010), *Merging the Administrations of Social Security Contribution and Taxation*, European Institute of Social Security, Leuven.

Crandall, W. (2010), *Revenue Administration: Autonomy in Tax Administration and the Revenue Authority Model*, IMF, Washington, pp. 1-4.

Delay, Devas, and Hubbard (1998), *The Reform of Revenue Administration: A Study for the Department for International Development (DFID),* The School of Public Policy, University of Birmingham, p. 39.

DFID (2005), *Revenue Authorities and Taxation in Sub-Saharan Africa: A Concise Review of Recent Literature from the Investment, Competition and Enabling Environment Team*, Department for International Development, London.

Enoff, L.D and R. Ruggia-Frick (2013), *Innovations in contribution collection and compliance*, Summary Report for World Social Security Forum, ISSA, Geneva.

European Commission (2007), *Fiscal Blueprints – A Path to a Robust, Modern and Efficient Tax Administration*, Luxembourg: Office for Official Publications of the European Commission, pp. 13-20.

IMF (2014), *GREECE: Fifth Review under the Extended Arrangement under the Extended Fund Facility, and Request for Waiver of Non-observance of Performance Criterion and Rephasing of Access*; Staff Report, International Monetary Fund. Washington.

Kidd, M. (2010), *Revenue Administration: Functionally Organized Administration*, IMF, Washington.

Kidd, M. and W. Crandall (2010), *Revenue Administration: A Toolkit for Implementing a Revenue Authority,* IMF, Washington.

Kidd, M. and W. Crandall (2006), *Revenue Authorities: Issues and Problems in Evaluating their Success*, IMF, Washington, p. 12.

Mann, A. (2004), *Are Semi-Autonomous Revenue Authorities the Answer to Tax Administration Problems in Developing Countries?* USAID, Washington.

Norwegian Ministry of Finance (2014), *Transfer of Data from the Customs and Excise Tax Administration,* MOF Mission Letter (14/1686 SL ACST/KR), Oslo.

Republic of Kenya Executive Office of President (2013), *Report of the Presidential Taskforce on Parastatal Reforms,* October 2013, Nairobi, page 94.

Republic of Kenya National Treasury (2015), *2015 Budget Policy Statement (Draft)*, February, Nairobi, page 6.

Taliercio, R. (2004), *Designing for Performance: The Semi-Autonomous Revenue Authority Model in Africa and South America,* World Bank, Washington.

World Bank (2010), *Integration of Revenue Administration: A Comparative Study of International Research*, World Bank, Washington.

Chapter 2

The organisation of revenue bodies

This chapter describes aspects of the organisational arrangements of surveyed revenue bodies, and includes a fairly comprehensive summary of recent and planned reforms to improve the efficiency and effectiveness of tax system administration. It also includes a brief outline of organisational and operational arrangements put in place to manage large corporate taxpayers and high net worth individuals.

Key points

Organisational structures/features

- Many revenue bodies have undergone, or have underway, major organisational reform efforts to achieve improved outcomes, in particular substantial cost reductions. Important reform themes observed from country survey responses include institutional reform, increased responsibilities for revenue bodies), increasing application of customer segment approaches (incl. large taxpayer units), reducing layers of management allied with shifts towards a more centralised form of management, major office network rationalisation, and shared services approaches involving multiple government agencies.
- The "function" criterion continues to be significant in the design of revenue bodies' structures but around two-thirds reported a design based on a broad mix of criterion – a "hybrid" structure.
- The vast majority of revenue bodies have concentrated their information processing work in a small number of sites and maintain in-house tax fraud investigation and enforced tax debt collection functions.
- While the majority of revenue bodies reported the operation of a full in-house IT function, around 20% rely significantly on outsourced arrangements or other parts of government for their IT support.

Office networks and resource allocation

- While all revenue bodies operate with office networks which are geographical and hierarchical, many have created centralised operations (e.g. phone call centres, data processing centres, and large taxpayer offices) to increase efficiency and effectiveness.
- Prior editions of this series have drawn attention to the abnormally large (and expensive!) office networks that have historically characterised the tax administration landscape of many surveyed countries, especially many in Europe. On a positive note, it can be reported that some of the countries concerned have taken up this reform challenge and significantly scaled down their office networks (e.g. in Croatia, Denmark, Greece, and Norway). However, this reform challenge still remains for many (e.g. Belgium, Czech Republic, France, Luxembourg, and Poland) and should constitute a key part of reform efforts in coming years in order to significantly reduce operating costs and improve efficiency.
- Across surveyed bodies, there is an enormous variation in the relative size of revenue bodies' headquarters function, reflecting a variety of factors (e.g. a more centralised approach to the national management of tax administration operations and large in-house IT functions).

Large taxpayer units

- The vast majority (around 85%) of surveyed revenue bodies have established dedicated units responsible for administering their largest taxpayers; however, these units vary significantly in the scale of their operations – a product of the varying (and sometimes quite complex) criteria used to identify relevant taxpayers – and in the scope and range of their responsibilities.

High net worth individuals

- Despite evidence of significant growth in the numbers and wealth of high net worth individual taxpayers over recent years, relatively few revenue bodies have established specialist units to oversee their administration, as recommended by the FTA in its 2009 study.

Getting organised to collect taxes

Organisational structures of revenue bodies and their evolution

Over the last two decades or so, the organisational structure of many revenue bodies has been the subject of major reform aimed at improving operational efficiency and effectiveness and the delivery of services to taxpayers. By and large, these reform efforts have mirrored a broader trend in the evolution of the structure of revenue bodies, moving initially from a structure based primarily on "tax type" criterion to one based on "functional" criterion. For many revenue bodies, steps have also been taken to structure their compliance (i.e. service and verification) functions on the basis of "taxpayer segment", at least so far as large taxpayers are concerned, while a few bodies apply the "taxpayer segment" approach more broadly. A description of some of the factors relevant to this evolution is set out below:

- *The "type of tax" organisational model:* The earliest organisational model employed by tax administrators was based principally on "type of tax" criterion. Applying this model, separate multi-functional departments were responsible for each tax and were largely self-sufficient and independent of each other. While serving its original objectives, this model was eventually seen to have a number of shortcomings, including:
    - Inefficiencies and excessive costs, largely as a result of its inherent duplication of operational functions across different taxes;
    - Burdensome on those taxpayers with multiple tax dealings, requiring them to deal with different departments on similar issues (e.g. debts);
    - Complications and additional costs, both to revenue bodies and taxpayers, in co-ordinating compliance actions across different taxes;
    - Inconsistent treatment of taxpayers (e.g. service delivery, debt, and audit);
    - Inflexible use of staff whose skills (and often entire careers) were largely confined to a particular tax; and
    - Excessively fragmented management of the tax system, complicating organisational planning and co-ordination.

To address these and other shortcomings, many revenue bodies saw merit in restructuring their operations, adopting a model based on "functional" principles:

- *The "functional" organisational model:* With the functional model, work and staff are organised largely within functional groupings (e.g. registration, information processing, audit, collection, etc.) and work across taxes. This approach to organising work permits greater standardisation of work processes across taxes, thereby simplifying computerisation and arrangements for taxpayers, and can improve efficiency. Compared to the "tax type" model, the functional model has come to be seen as offering many advantages and its adoption has led to many developments that improve tax administration performance (e.g. single points of access for tax inquiries, unified taxpayer registration, common policies/approaches to tax accounting, and better management of tax audit and debt collection functions.) However, some revenue bodies have taken the view that this model is not optimal for the delivery of compliance programmes across all segments of taxpayers given their differing characteristics and behaviours and attitudes to tax compliance.

- *The "taxpayer segment" organisational model*: A further development among a small number of countries (e.g. Australia and United States) has been to organise service and enforcement functions principally around "segments of taxpayers" (e.g. large businesses, SME, and individuals). The rationale for organising these functions around taxpayer segments is that each group of taxpayers has different characteristics and tax compliance behaviours and, as a result, presents different tax risks that require a more tailored treatment approach. In order to manage these risks effectively, the revenue body needs to develop and implement treatment strategies that are appropriate to the unique characteristics and compliance issues presented by each group of taxpayers. Revenue bodies also need a structured approach to researching and understanding what these compliance issues are. Proponents of the "taxpayer segment" type of structure contend that grouping key functional activities within a unified and dedicated management structure increases the prospects of improving overall compliance levels. While application of the "taxpayer segment" model is still in its early stages of use, many countries have partially applied this approach by creating dedicated large taxpayer divisions/units.

With the move to organising some revenue body functions by "taxpayer segments" today's modern revenue bodies are typically structured according to a mix of "functional", "taxpayer segment" and "tax" criteria, a hybrid form of structure.

Why organisational structure is important

International organisations promoting reform of tax administration have consistently drawn attention to the importance of revenue bodies having a coherent organisational structure for the administration of national taxes. As observed in Box 1.2 in Chapter 1, the EC's Fiscal Blueprints establish two strategic objectives dealing directly with organisational structure: *(1)* the tax administration is structured and organised to identify and manage all significant risks and priorities; and *(2)* there is a unified tax administration. In relation to these objectives, the blueprints draw attention to a range of indicators, including:

- Is it (the revenue body) structured to understand and meet the needs of key taxpayer groups or segments?
- Is there a large taxpayer unit (LTU) in place, at a national level, to deal with the most important companies?
- Are there special units with specific skills, offering operational economies of scale (e.g. intelligence, enforced collection)?
- Is it responsible for all taxes and linked to social contributions?
- Is it responsible for all fiscal functions (assessment, collection, data processing, audit, taxpayer service and claim investigation) and organised accordingly (i.e. by function)?
- Are there special units with specific skills, offering operational economies of scale (e.g. intelligence, enforced collection)?

These indicators all point to the preference for a body structured primarily on a functional basis, with divisions to deal with key taxpayer segments (e.g. large).

Similar views concerning the importance of structure are advanced by IMF Fiscal Affairs officials, drawing on extensive experience in tax reform projects – see Box 2.1.

Box 2.1. Why is the choice of an organisational model so important?

In recent years, organisation structures have become increasingly important in both the private and public sectors. Concerns have been raised related to accountability, responsibility and transparency within organisations – for example, what are their legal authorities and powers? what oversight mechanisms exist? what kind of flexibilities are available to address modern management problems? Governments are seeking ways to improve operational results while increasing transparency and accountability within their departments and agencies. The organisation structure of the tax administration is a key component in these efforts.

The organisation structure of tax organisations has evolved considerably over time. From organisation structures based on type of tax, to those based on function (the subject of this note) to those based on the type of taxpayer (small, medium or large), economies of different sizes and at different stages of development have attempted different kinds of organisational reform. Many tax administration organisations are actually a combination of these structural categories.

An effective organisation is the basic platform from which all other procedural reforms are launched and maintained. Without the right organisation structure in place, revenue administrations cannot operate effectively and their revenue collection efforts will be sub-optimal. Where function-based organisations have not been implemented, the extensive procedural and operational reforms needed to support modernisation would likely be ineffective.

Source: Revenue Administration: Functionally Organised Tax Administration, IMF, 2010.

Table 2.1 highlights a number of high level structural features of revenue bodies in all countries covered by this series. As will be evident from the information reported, there are significant variations in the organisational structures of revenue bodies from country to country. However, there appears to be a substantial reliance on the "functional" model of organisation – 12 of 56 revenue bodies indicated that the functional model has been adopted as the primary criterion for structuring their tax administration operations, while another 35 reported that a broad mix of criteria, including "function", are applied in practice. As will also be apparent from Table 2.1, 48 revenue bodies have complemented their largely functional structure with a dedicated division (in a few cases limited to audit-related tasks) to administer the tax affairs of their largest taxpayers. Other important observations are:

- The vast majority of revenue bodies (43 of 56 countries) operate some form of dedicated processing centres (e.g. for processing of tax returns and payments).
- Over 80% of revenue bodies reported the operation of a dedicated large taxpayer unit (LTU) to manage taxpayers' tax affairs, including Portugal who reported the creation of a new unit in 2012 (see comments later in this chapter). Countries reporting they did not have such an operation in the main are relatively small, still applying technical assessment methods (as opposed to self-assessment principles) and/or operate with separate direct and indirect tax operations (e.g. Cyprus, Luxembourg, and Malta).
- Less than a third of revenue bodies operate dedicated units to manage the tax affairs of high net worth individuals, notwithstanding data pointing to significant growth in the population of wealthy taxpayers and growing evidence of the increased concentration of wealth. (Further comments on this aspect are provided later in this chapter);

Table 2.1. Selected features of the organisational structure of revenue bodies

Country	Main criteria for structure: **T**: tax type, **F**: function, **TP**: taxpayer	Selected features of revenue bodies' internal organisational structure						
		High net worth individuals	Large taxpayer division/ unit	Dedicated processing centres	Debt collection function	Tax fraud function	Dedicated disputes function	Full in-house IT function
OECD countries								
Australia	All	✓	✓	✓	✓	✓	✓	✓
Austria	All	x	✓	x	✓	✓	✓	x /1
Belgium	All	x	✓	✓	✓	✓	x	✓
Canada	F	✓ /1	✓	✓	✓	✓	✓	✓ /2
Chile	All	✓ /1	✓	✓	x /1	✓	✓	✓
Czech Republic	T, F	x	✓	✓ /1	✓	✓	✓	✓
Denmark	All	x	✓	✓	✓	✓	✓	x
Estonia	All	x	x	✓	✓	✓	✓	✓
Finland	All	x	✓	✓	✓	✓	✓	x /1
France	TP	✓ /1	✓	✓	✓	✓	✓	✓
Germany	All	x	✓	✓	✓	✓	✓	✓
Greece	All	✓ /1	✓	✓	✓	✓	✓	✓
Hungary	All	x	✓	✓	✓	✓	✓ /1	✓
Iceland	All	x	x	x	x	✓	✓	x
Ireland	TP	✓	✓	✓	✓	✓	x /1	✓
Israel	All	x	✓	✓	✓	✓	✓ /1	✓
Italy	All	x	✓	✓	x	✓ /1	✓	x /2
Japan	All	✓	✓	✓	✓	✓	✓	✓
Korea	All	x	x /1	x	x /2	x /2	✓	✓
Luxembourg	F, T	x	x	✓	✓	✓	✓	x
Mexico	F, TP	x	✓	✓	✓	✓	✓	✓ /1
Netherlands	F, TP	x /1	✓	✓	✓	✓	x	✓
New Zealand	All	✓	✓	✓	✓	✓	✓	✓
Norway	All	x	✓	✓	✓	✓	✓	✓
Poland	All	x	✓	✓	✓	✓	✓	✓
Portugal	All	✓ /1	✓	✓	✓	✓	✓	✓
Slovak Republic	F	x	✓ /1	x	✓	✓	✓	x
Slovenia	All	x	✓	✓	✓	✓	x	✓
Spain	All	✓ /1	✓	✓	✓	✓	x /2	✓
Sweden	All	x	✓	x	x	✓	x	✓
Switzerland	F, T	x	x	✓	x	✓	✓	✓
Turkey	F	x	✓	✓	x	✓	✓	✓
United Kingdom	All	✓	✓	✓	✓	✓	✓	x
United States	TP	✓	✓	✓	✓	✓	✓	✓
Non-OECD countries								
Argentina	All	✓	✓	✓	✓	✓	✓	✓
Brazil	F /1	✓	✓	x	✓	✓	✓	✓
Bulgaria	F	x	✓	x	✓	✓	✓	✓
China	All	x	✓	✓	✓	✓	✓	✓
Colombia	F	x	✓	✓	✓	x	✓	✓
Costa Rica	F	✓	✓	x	✓	✓	✓	✓
Croatia	All	x	✓	✓	✓	✓	x	✓
Cyprus	T	x	x /1	✓	✓	x	✓	x
Hong Kong, China	All	x	x	✓	✓	✓	✓	✓
India	F	x	✓	✓	✓	✓	✓	✓
Indonesia	All	✓	✓	✓	✓	✓	✓	✓
Latvia	F	x	✓	x	✓	✓	✓	✓
Lithuania	F	x	✓	✓	✓	x	✓	✓ /1
Malaysia	F	✓ /1	✓	✓	✓	✓	✓	✓
Malta	All	x	x	✓	✓	✓	✓	x
Morocco	F, TP	x	✓	x	✓	✓	✓	✓
Romania	F, T	✓	✓	✓	✓	✓	✓	✓
Russia	All	x	✓	x	✓	x	✓	✓
Saudi Arabia	F	x	✓	x	✓	✓	✓	✓
Singapore	F, T	x	✓ /1	✓	✓	✓	x	✓
South Africa	All	✓	✓	✓	✓	✓	✓	✓
Thailand	F, TP	x	✓	x	x	✓	✓	✓

For notes indicated by "/ (number)", see Notes to Tables section at the end of the chapter, p. 98.

Source: Tax Administration 2015 survey responses.

- All but 9 revenue bodies have a dedicated in-house debt collection function. Survey responses and related research identified some unusual arrangements for enforced tax debt collection in four countries, where the conduct of much/most of this work is undertaken outside the revenue body:

  Chile reported that enforced tax debt collection is the responsibility of the Treasury that also collects other government debts, while in ***Iceland*** the Customs Agency is responsible for tax debt collection. In ***Sweden***, enforced tax debt collection is the responsibility of a separate government body – the Enforcement Authority (EA) – that, until 2006, was part of the Tax Agency; the EA operates as an independent authority and general debt collection body. Finally, in ***Italy***, enforced tax debt recovery is the responsibility of a government body – Equitalia Spa – jointly-owned by the revenue body and the Social Security Institute.

- The great majority of revenue bodies in OECD countries maintain a dedicated division responsible for the investigation of serious cases of tax fraud/evasion.

- Organisational arrangements for the provision of information technology support vary significantly across revenue bodies, ranging from comprehensive in-house IT operations (e.g. United States), centralised IT operations within the MOF that are shared across a number of government bodies (e.g. Austria), to partially or fully outsourced arrangements involving private sector bodies (e.g. Australia, Denmark, Latvia, Mexico, and United Kingdom). A recent development reported by Canada describes the creation of a new government department – Shared Services Canada – to provide IT support to multiple government agencies (including the CRA), that aims to lower costs and streamline operations.

Country examples of high level organisational arrangements

Prior editions of the series have provided examples of the high level organisational structure of national revenue bodies' headquarters and identified a number of themes and similarities across sub-groupings of these countries. These are summarised in Table 2.2. In this series, examples are provided from three revenue bodies (i.e. Croatia, Latvia and Thailand) and categorised within the previously observed groupings – see Figures 2.1 to 2.3 (NB: the figures are derived from published materials of the revenue bodies concerned).

Table 2.2. **Features of the organisation structure of selected revenue bodies**

Design themes observed in revenue bodies' organisational structures	Series edition	Country examples
Taxpayer segment: This model is *characterised by a number of "taxpayer segment" divisions* responsible for compliance activities (service and verification) for taxpayers in each segment. There are also some functional units (*e.g.* for operations, client contact and debt) supporting the work of all segments. For the United States, the model replaced a more functionally-oriented setup for the delivery of service and enforcement activities, which was overseen by a formal layer of management and co-ordination at the regional level. This regional management layer was removed with the new structure.	2008	Australia and United States (Figures 1 and 9)
	2013	Finland (Figure 2.3

Table 2.2. **Features of the organisation structure of selected revenue bodies** *(continued)*

Design themes observed in revenue bodies' organisational structures	Series edition	Country examples
Function: The organisational models depicted for these revenue bodies *reflect the more traditional model of a functionally-organised body* with, for most, a formal layer of regional management. For New Zealand, there is also a tax policy function, an arrangement generally not seen in other OECD countries.	2008	Canada, Chile, Korea (Figures 2, 3 and 5)
	2010	Hungary, Japan and New Zealand (Figures 6, 7 and 9)
	2013	Czech Republic, Italy, Russia, Sweden, Turkey (Figures 2.2, 2.5, 2.7, 2.9, 2.11)
	2015	Croatia, Thailand (Figures 2.1 and 2.3)
Function (also with customs administration): The models shown for these revenue bodies are *based largely on functional criteria, and also reflect the integration of customs operations*, as well as a layer of regional management overseeing local operations. As noted in Chapter 1, a number of countries have aligned tax and customs operations within a single agency. The Brazilian, Spanish, Irish, Mexican and South African models also show a customer segment operation for large taxpayers.	2008	Estonia, Spain (Figures 4 and 7)
	2010	Argentina, Austria, Israel, Mexico (Figures 3, 4, 8 and 10)
	2013	Brazil, Ireland, Netherlands, South Africa (Figures 2.1, 2.4, 2.6 and 2.10)
	2015	Latvia (Figure 2.2)
Function (within the MOF): This model is *a less autonomous set-up where tax administration functions are grouped together under common management within the formal structure of the Ministry of Finance (MOF).* A feature of this model is that support functions such as finance, human resources and information technology are shared with other MOF operational arms.	2010	France (Figure 5)
Other approaches: The UK model reflects the evolution of HMRC's internal structure following the merger in 2005 of the former separate direct and indirect tax administrations to create an integrated revenue and customs body. The model, driven in part by an objective of establishing clearer lines of accountability, is based on a matrix style of management where both "functional" and "tax type" considerations are given emphasis. The Singaporean model bears some similarities with its function and tax type configuration, although not responsible for customs.	2008	United Kingdom (Figure 8)
	2013	Singapore (Figure 2.8)

Source: 2013 series: From page 63 at www.oecd.org/ctp/administration/tax-administration-series.htm.

Figure 2.1. **Croatia: Tax Administration**

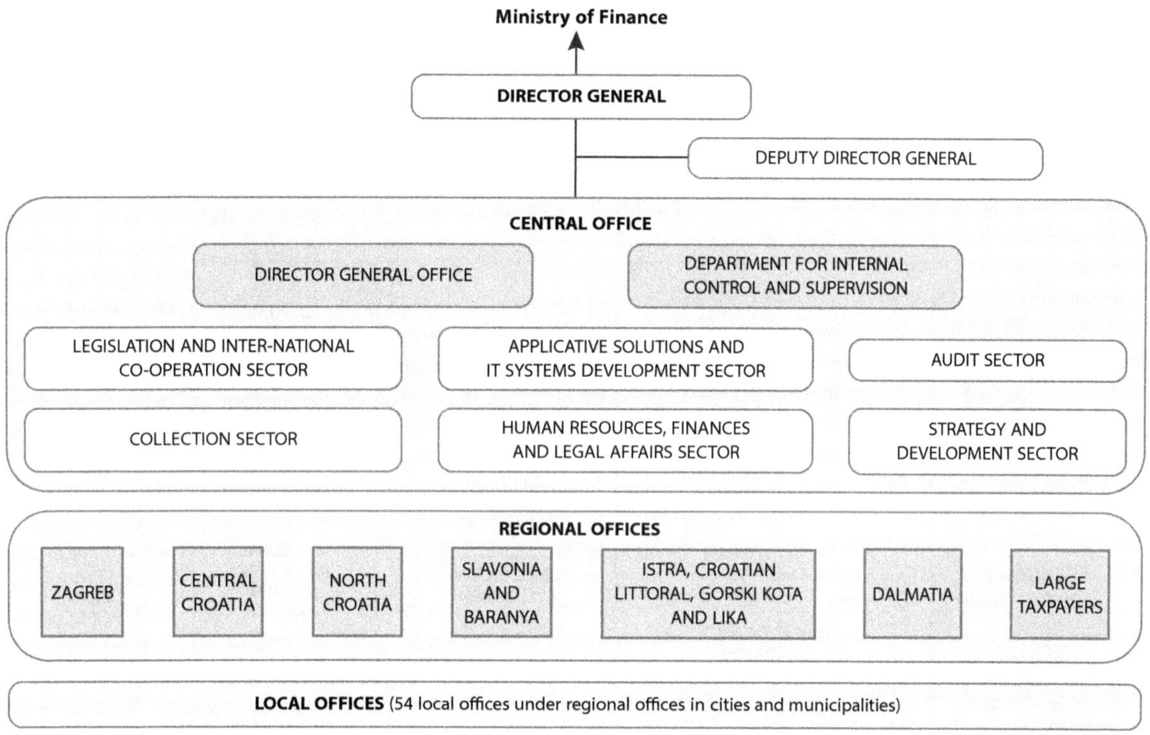

Source: Revenue body survey response (March 2015).

Figure 2.2. **Latvia's State Revenue Service**

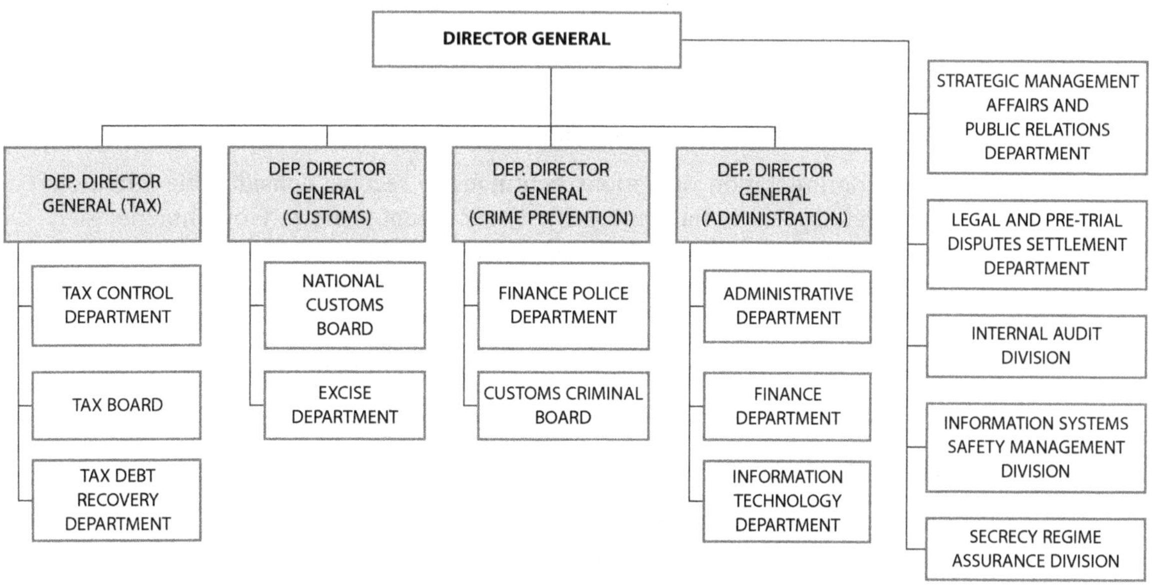

Source: SRS 2012 Annual Report.

Figure 2.3. **Thailand's Revenue Department**

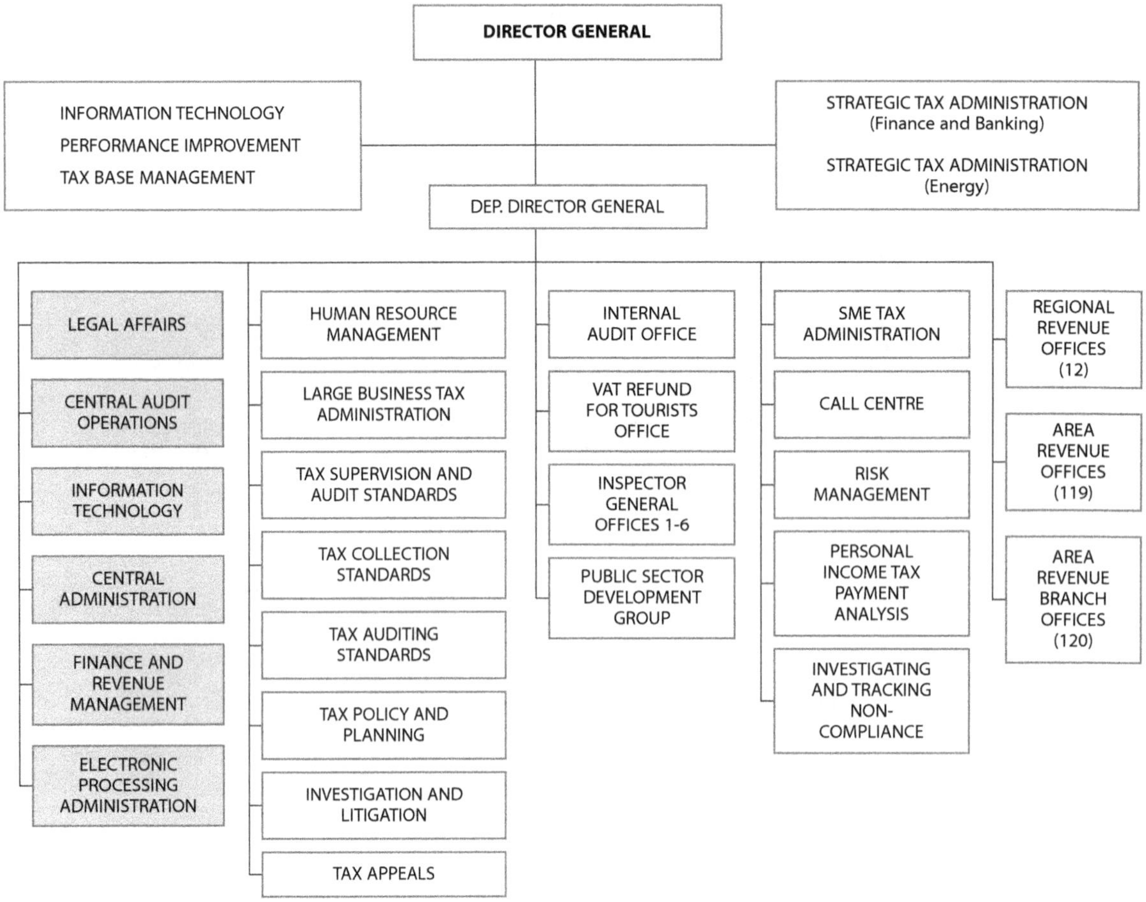

Source: Revenue Department's 2013 Annual Report.

Reorganising for improved performance

Reforming tax administration operations continues to receive considerable attention in many countries and appears to have intensified over recent years as Governments give mandates for reform efforts to improve efficiency and cut costs. For this series, revenue bodies reported a large variety of reform activity, much of it falling into the following categories:

1. Institutional re-organisation, including the allocation of new roles and functions.
2. Consolidation of office networks to achieve greater economies of scale.
3. Eliminating administrative duplication.
4. Major business process redesign, underpinned by better use of ICT.
5. Strengthening management capability to address fiscal fraud.
6. Implementing "whole of government" service delivery approaches.

For this series, revenue bodies were requested to provide brief details of major "organisational" reforms recently implemented or in course of development. This was supplemented by research of reports and studies made by other international organisations. The key reforms identified are briefly summarised below:

- ***Argentina*** reported that consistent with its overall strategic approach, taxpayer assistance is a priority objective, and that the importance of taking actions that facilitate the building of good relationships between citizens and the tax administration is recognised. To this end, it has established a model of mobile institutional assistance that enables AFIP to increase its presence in populous areas and has created two mobile units to deliver taxpayer services.

- ***Australia*** reported that its new leadership team is driving a transformation programme that seeks to "reinvent" the ATO in order to achieve its vision of being known for contemporary services, expertise and integrity. This includes transforming how clients and staff experience the tax and superannuation systems and will be underpinned by significant cultural change. The programme challenges thinking around concepts such as compliance and participation, and managing the pressures of being a useful and sustainable large public service organisation. (More details of the transformation programme are set out in Chapter 3.) Other reforms recently implemented include abolition of the Australian Valuation Office (previously under the ATO), the closure of 10 regional (shop front) sites from 31 October 2014, and transfer of responsibility for individual taxpayer complaints from the Australian Ombudsman Office to the Office of Inspector General of Taxation.

- ***Austria*** reported a series of reforms, continuing the Government's and revenue body's previously reported focus on tackling fraud. On 1 July 2013 the Financial Police became economically independent in terms of human resources and now operates with its headquarter in Vienna and branches in every tax office. The data, information and preparation centre is part of the Financial Police and responsible for database research and analysis as well as for providing information to national and international authorities. For further details, see https://english.bmf.gv.at/combating-fraud/Financial-Police.html and https://english.bmf.gv.at/e-government/financial-police-online.html. Co-ordinators for combating fraud have been established in each tax office and are experts for dealing with fraud cases and their functions including the collection of information on fraud-related matters, sharing this information within the tax office and within the network of combating fraud co-ordinators in all tax offices, and acting as experts for co-operation with other bodies engaged in combatting the different aspects of fraud.

  In a further phase of structural change, the Tax Investigation Unit and the Tax Office for duties, transfer taxes and games of chance, both previously organised on a regional and local level, have been implemented as units with nationwide competences.

  From January 2014, the former Independent Finance Tribunal became a court (i.e. the Federal Financial Court) with nationwide responsibility for all appeals against tax matters.

- ***Belgium*** reported a number of developments, concerning both institutional and organisation aspects for Government revenue collection. Since 1970, Belgium has undergone a process of regionalisation whereby it has gradually become a federal state. Regions have their own taxing powers and this enables them to establish some regional taxes (in areas such as water, and waste). Some taxes formerly collected on behalf of the State (e.g. property tax, inheritance tax, certain registration rights, or road tax) have been transferred over time to regions meaning that they are now competent to change the tax rate, the tax base and exemptions in respect of these regional taxes. The Federal Government (specifically, the Federal Public Service Finance) continues to service these regional taxes, unless a region decides to provide this service itself. To date, some regions have already taken over the service of some regional taxes. The personal income tax has meanwhile become a joint tax – a national tax in respect of which each region is authorised to levy an additional surcharge and implement reductions and tax increases related to substantive competence of the Regions. The federal government continues to service the personal income tax. In 2014, this process of regionalisation entails a further transfer of some responsibilities and staff from the Federal level to the regions.

Officials also reported developments concerning the organisation of the Federal Public Services Finance, specifically dealing with tax administration:

- *General Administration of Taxation:* Establishment of tax administration for target groups (i.e. individuals, SME and large enterprises) is underway.
- *General Administration for Tax Collection and Recovery (GACR):* Changes have been made to the structure and competence of the GACR, till recently only competent for the collection and recovery of income taxes and VAT. Concerning structure, 14 Regional Recovery Centres now provide leadership to the tax recovery offices within their jurisdiction. Later in 2014 the "single collector" principle will be implemented by merging the current recovery offices into polyvalent recovery teams within the regional centres. A single Perception Centre, with national competence, collects the different taxes, rights and duties. The Special Recovery Centre will deal with specific types of recovery, including the mutual assistance in the field of recovery; recovery focused on payment evasion and recovery of debts resulting from organised fiscal fraud. Concerning competencies, since March 2014, the services responsible for the collection and recovery of non-fiscal debts (alimony, fines, unduly paid benefits, etc.) were integrated within the GACR.

The aim of these reforms is to create synergies by having one collection and recovery authority dealing with all claims and debts. At the same time, a centrally defined strategy will be implemented across Belgium and the collection and recovery services will be open to regional differences. It should also improve effectiveness and efficiency, which will ultimately lead to savings for the government and debtors.

- The ***Bulgarian*** National Revenue Agency (NRA) reported that **a** Fiscal Control' Directorate has been established within the NRA Headquarters. Preparations for its launch were made in 2013 and it became operational in January 2014. The main purpose of this directorate is to perform fiscal control on the transportation of goods of high fiscal risk. The introduction of this fiscal control is aimed at preventing non-payment of VAT, corporate taxes and personal income tax. Subject to fiscal control is the transportation of goods of high fiscal risk on the entire territory of Bulgaria, irrespective of the place of goods delivery/unloading – on Bulgarian territory, the territory of another EU Member State or the territory of a third country, i.e. the fiscal control includes the intra-Community acquisitions, the intra-Community supplies, the transit of goods through Bulgaria from one EU Member State to another Member State, and the in-country supplies. No fiscal control is applied on the goods subject to the customs regime.

- ***Canada*** reported that the Offshore Compliance Division (OCD) has been established to implement certain offshore non-compliance Budget 2013 measures and to deliver related programmes and activities. Specifically, measures announced in Budget 2013 included: launching an offshore paid informant programme (Offshore Tax Informant Programme); mandatory reporting of international electronic funds transfers over CAD 10 000 to the CRA by certain financial intermediaries; enhanced reporting requirements for Canadian taxpayers with foreign properties or assets, and; streamlining the judicial process that provides the CRA authorisation to obtain information from third parties such as banks. Budget 2013 also provided for an investment of CAD 30 million over five years in support of these measures.

  The OCD is a dedicated unit within the Compliance Programs Branch (CPB) reporting directly to the Assistant Commissioner. It is comprised of 25 employees within Headquarters and 45 field employees that form specialised audit teams located in three Tax Services Offices across the country.

  The OCD's key areas of responsibility include: *(1)* developing and managing the Electronic Funds Transfer (EFT) reporting system to generate business intelligence; *(2)* leading the Offshore Tax Informant Programme and co-ordinating all related activities; *(3)* utilising all available sources of business intelligence, including information received through Exchange of Information (EOI) from the CRA's international partners, to identify and select high risk cases for compliance action; *(4)* providing technical expertise to dedicated audit resources addressing offshore non-compliance; and *(5)* working with domestic and international partners to identify emerging trends and issues related to offshore non-compliance.

- ***China's*** State Administration of Taxation (SAT) reported that since 2012, in accordance with the Central Government requirement to deepen reforms of administrative systems, it has been advancing organisational changes of tax authorities to accelerate their functional transformation and institutional improvement. To accommodate the demand of a "one-level tax investigation" and a specialised tax administration on large businesses, the reform focuses on the following aspects: *(1)* optimising the assignment of working responsibilities, organisational structure and staffing; *(2)* streamlining superior-subordinate relationship; *(3)* promoting high level tax authorities to assume more significant functions. The aim of the reform is to establish a flat tax organisational system, scientifically designed functions and efficient management, which adapts to the reforms of tax system and administration, as well as the taxpayer service optimisation. Through these reforms, human resources within the tax system are expected to be more centralised, and tax administration resources should be allocated to better accord with the distributional status of tax revenue sources. In addition, they are expected to further improve taxpayer's service and tax compliance.

- ***Costa Rica***, which has applied to become a member of the OECD, reported that over the last two decades it has progressively followed and adjusted to best international practices with regards to the structure of its tax administration operations. In 1998, a major reform programme entailed transition to a mixed functional structure which focusses on a traditional functional structure and national specialised units for complex functions, according to the type of taxpayers (e.g. large corporates and high net worth individuals) or their high impact on the revenue body's goals. In 2012, a new Tax Fraud Investigation and Repression Sub-division was created, while 2013 saw the establishment of a Tax Control Council within the revenue body. Work is currently underway to create a modern call centre operation.

- ***Croatia*** reported a number of recently-introduced tax administration reforms, part of its on-going modernisation programme that is being supported by the World Bank. In January 2012, a Large Taxpayers Office (LTO) was established, with its main office in Zagreb, and supported by three local offices in other Croatian regional centres. The LTO provides specific services for around 680 large taxpayers in the whole of Croatia as well as a dedicated audit function with specialist staff (for transfer pricing, thin capitalisation, etc).

  Following the passing of a new Tax Administration Act (December 2014), the structure of regional and local offices has been rationalised, and a new network structure came into force from January 2015. With this new structure, there are now six regional offices (previously 20), and the LTO as a separate office, with the number of local offices being reduced from 124 to 54. Each regional office is competent for all taxpayers within its defined region, while both regional and local offices will be similarly structured (on a functional basis) and staffed (according to workloads). In addition, the new arrangements provide for reductions in the number of manager positions, although no overall reductions of staff, and increased staff mobility between offices. Officials reported that the objectives of these changes are to improve efficiency and operational processes, enhance managerial oversight from the centre, and to achieve greater consistency in the quality of services delivered to taxpayers.

- ***Cyprus*** reported that major institutional and organisation reforms are underway, the details of which are set out in Box 2.2, drawing on the formal memorandum of policies agreed between the Cypriot government and the IMF.

Box 2.2. Cyprus: Developments in institutional and organisational reform

Integrating VAT and Inland Revenue services: In early January 2014, the government approved the reform plan outlining the organisational design of a new integrated tax department and the implementation timeline (see diagram below). In a first step, by the end of April, the authorities will submit to parliament a new enabling law providing for the transfer of powers and operations from the existing separate tax agencies to the new integrated tax department. Subsequently, a new senior management team will be appointed to take charge of the two agencies under the new transitional structure with the reform planned to be fully implemented by March 2016.

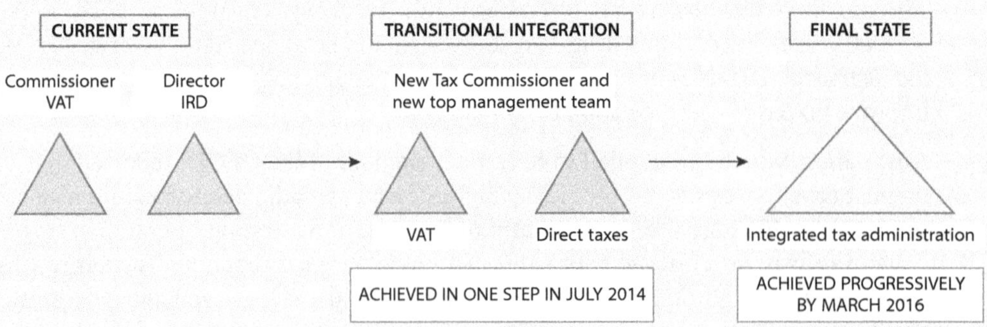

By the end of 2014, it is planned to establish an integrated unit for large taxpayers – which account for the largest share of revenues – in the new department.

Source: Third Review under the Extended Arrangement etc. Staff Report, IMF April 2014.

- ***Czech Republic*** officials reported the establishment, effective January 2013, of the Financial Administration of the Czech Republic, newly consisting of the previous General Financial Directorate, the Appellate Financial Directorate 14 Tax Offices in regions and the Specialised Tax Office (for large taxpayers).
- ***Denmark*** reported that to clarify tasks and responsibilities the central body of the Danish Ministry of Taxation (known as the "Koncerncenter") was re-organised on 1 January 2013. The "Koncerncenter was split into two bodies – a Department of Taxation focusing on legislation, tax policy and assisting the minister and a Central Customs and Tax Administration (SKAT) with responsibility for customs and tax administration. Following the split of "the Koncerncenter" the Central Customs and Tax Administration was re-organised on 1 April 2013. As part of this re-organisation, the regional structure was abolished, and all tasks were organised in six nationwide divisions (i.e. Customer Service (3 000 staff), Compliance (2 000 staff), Debt Collection (1 300), Economy and Controlling (450 staff), Information Technology (200 staff), and Human Relations/Group functions (400 staff). The purpose of the reform was to promote effective management, strong academic environments and efficiency improvement. It is anticipated that the reforms will permit gradual staff reductions while simultaneously improving efficiency and the uniformity and quality of the services offered to Danish taxpayers.

  In addition to SKAT, there is an independent Tax Appeals Agency and an independent Gambling Authority within the Ministry of Taxation.
- ***Estonia***'s Tax and Customs Board (ETCB) reported that prior to 2012 extensive structural reform in the ETCB had last been undertaken in 2008. In 2012, in order to be able to pay better salaries to keep the best officials, restructuring was undertaken and the only positions retained were those essential to carry out the ETCB's mission.

  As part of its restructuring, the ETCB abolished traditional regional tax and customs offices and instead created competence centres for each area of work. This kind of management model requires less co-ordination and is more cost efficient from the viewpoint of distributing work according to the real workload, experience, and competence levels of staff. Among other things, these reforms resulted in organisational downsizing by some 14%. With the economy now improving, there are more positions emerging which in turn creates competition with the private sector.

  In 2012, an Information Technology Centre was created in the MOF, consolidating IT budgets, operations and support for all MOF activities, including for tax and customs administration.
- ***Finland*** noted that following a major reorganisation completed at the end of 2011, the focus continues on strengthening the national units and reducing the number of regional tax offices. The aim of the national units is to distribute work in a more flexible manner, ensure uniformity of taxation and establish a closer connection between steering, development and operations. In the national units, taxation tasks are either distributed around the country or centralised nationally. At the same time, regional offices can be reduced as customers increasingly carry out most of their tax affairs using online and telephone services. For the future, operations will be concentrated in growth centres, where skilled labour is readily available and, from customers' viewpoint, there is the advantage of greater knowledge and expertise.
- ***France*** reported since January 2013 (five years after the merger of the General Tax and the Public Accounting Directorates), a new organisational chart of the DGFiP

headquarters has been progressively introduced to meet upcoming challenges under the best possible conditions. It also seeks to further integrate aspects of the two former directorates. Among the changes implemented, the Public Relations and Communication Office joined the Director General's office, while senior management has been unified through the appointment of a single Deputy Director General. Moreover, two highly specialised units have been set up to deal with international tax cases and to develop data-mining tools. A dedicated customer service unit has also been set up.

- ***Greece:*** Officials reported that a major programme of reform/re-organisation has been implemented, including the following elements:
  - To improve the efficiency of tax administration and ensure its increased autonomy, while providing accountability mechanisms and transparency, the Ministry of Finance has established a new General Secretariat of Public Revenue (GSPR), abolishing the former General Secretariat of Tax and Customs Affairs;
  - A new organisational structure has been developed and was implemented in Q3 of 2014;
  - Audit operations have been restructured and a formal Large Taxpayer Unit has been established;
  - The network of tax offices is being rationalised and has been scaled down from 241 (end of 2011) to some 118 (as of January 2014).
  - A transfer of responsibilities and personnel of the General Secretariat of Information Systems (GSIS) and the Special Agency against Financial Crime to the GSPR became effective in July 2013.
- ***Hungary:*** As noted in the prior series, the National Tax and Customs Administration (NTCA) commenced operations 1 January 2011, resulting from the merger of two predecessor organisations (i.e. the Hungarian Tax and Financial Control Administration and Customs and Finance Guard). The purpose of the integration was to achieve higher standards for the collection of revenues, and improvements in the quality of efficiency, transparency and cost-effectiveness of both tax and customs administration, which can only be realised in an environment guided by uniform principles and rules.

  From the outset, there was limited internal re-organisation as a key objective was to ensure stable and efficient organisational operation from the outset, noting the many challenges associated with merging two sets of traditions, structure, culture and personnel. During 2012 and 2013, numerous organisational adjustments were made to help achieve the goals of integration.
- ***Indonesian*** authorities reported that in 2012 the Minister of Finance established an Oil and Gas Tax Office to oversee the administration of companies operating in the oil and gas sectors. Action was also taken to unify and streamline the Foreign Enterprise and Individual (Badora) Tax Office, which administers the tax affairs of foreign enterprises and individual taxpayers, to handle all tax matters for such taxpayers.
- ***India*'s** Central Board of Direct Taxes indicated that ongoing restructuring of the organisation according to changing needs and functional requirement is being

carried out, aimed at upgrading responsibilities, functional modifications, adopting a systems-based approach, and manpower and capacity augmentations.

- ***Ireland*** reported that Revenue has reduced its overall staffing numbers by 13% since 2008 in accordance with the Government's Employment Control Framework (ECF). Its ECF target for 2014 is 5 748.

  Since January 2012, as a direct result of Revenue's investment in delivering high quality electronic services, simplification initiatives, business process improvements and outsourcing, it has mitigated the effect of these reductions and redeployed over 300 staff to core areas such as debt management and compliance interventions. The transfer of human resource, pension and payroll functions to shared services centres and the introduction of additional working hours in 2013 in line with the public service reform agenda also provided opportunities to continue service delivery with reduced resources.

  Revenue continues to manage its staff numbers target by addressing critical skills gaps, identifying new and emerging skills needs, building internal capacity through training and targeted recruitment and succession planning.

- ***Israel*** noted that it has a number of major projects underway. These include work to make greater use of technology in many areas (e.g. processing of real estate transactions, cross-checking of VAT invoices) and streamlining related tax return reporting obligations of taxpayers (e.g. concerning the reporting of annual accounts by corporations), a special focus on the use of fictitious invoicing, building a new system for administering withholding processes, and simplifying the annual reporting obligations of small businesses.

  A number of service-related reforms are also being implemented. New service centres were established in field offices in 2013 to serve as a "front desk" for submitting documents and offer initial service to taxpayers. Currently this service is available in some of the local offices. A plan to expand the service centre network coverage is scheduled for 2015 and will include areas where no tax office exists. The existing call centre gives telephone services for a number of subjects. Wider telephone assistance through the call centre is planned to address all telephone service demands at one point of contact in view of taxpayers' needs and to limit the need for in-office assistance.

- ***Italy*** reported that in December 2012 the Real Estate and Land Registry Agency (Agenzia del Territorio) was integrated into the revenue body. This reform is part of a wider programme of review of all Government expenditure with the aim to reduce overall costs and improve efficiency.

  The integration has a number of specific objectives: *(1)* to enhance customer services and improve tax compliance – *citizens now have a unique reference point for all matters related to property taxation*; *(2)* to strengthen actions to tackle tax evasion – *the revenue body is now able to manage in an integrated way the database for all properties*; *(3)* to build economies of scale in carrying out indirect support activities and management – *by eliminating duplicate roles in personnel management, administration and accountability, ICT, internal control and security, communication, strategic governance and planning.* Implementation of the reform is still in progress and is expected to be completed by the end of 2015, and cut at least 363 managerial offices.

Furthermore, as a part of the spending review, the Revenue Agency is progressively closing 58 smaller territorial offices in 2014. (Territorial offices deal with taxpayer services and mass controls). The purpose of this reform is to reduce accommodation costs as well as provide for a more rational distribution of personnel assigned to nearby larger offices.

- ***Latvia*** noted that further refinements were made in 2012 to the SRS structure, continuing the programme of organisational enhancement reported in prior series. In April 2012, the Tax Control Department was reorganised by including the Customs Audit Department. In addition, steps were taken to strengthen executive management, establishing four positions of Deputy Director General directly subordinated to Director General of the SRS: Deputy Director General in Tax Area, also serving as Director of Tax Control Department, Deputy Director General in Customs Area, also serving as Director of National Customs Board, Deputy Director General in the Area of Crime Prevention, serving also as Director of Finance Police Department, and Deputy Director General in Administrative Area. In December 2012 the Large Taxpayers Department was included into the Tax Department as a client service centre integrating at the Tax Department all processes related to client service.
- ***Lithuania*** indicated that a study was being prepared to examine the possible consolidation of processes dealing with Government revenue collection, including a handover of SSC administration (now performed by the State Social Insurance Fund Board), as well as Customs and the Financial Crime Investigation Service.
- ***Malaysia*** reported that its headquarters had been restructured, and now includes a Dispute Resolution Department, a Special Task Department (Investigation), and divisions for Intelligence, Risk Management, Petroleum and Development and Facility Management. The objectives of the restructure are to strengthen operations, simplify and expedite appeal processes and expedite reporting and decision-making. In addition, 10 new Revenue Service Centres (RSC) were opened in 2012 and 2013. IRBM took part in opening counters at six Urban Transformation Centre (i.e. public amenities centres established by the government for the urban community) together with other government agencies. The objectives are to provide services to the taxpayer and to improve operational efficiency in revenue collection.
- ***Malta*** reported that the Office of Commissioner for Revenue (CFR) was established early in 2012. The primary objective for the establishment of this Office was to merge the Revenue Departments of the Ministry for Finance into one organisation to provide better services to taxpayers, resulting in less bureaucracy as per Government policy, and to collect tax revenue more efficiently and effectively. Whilst the CFR has a mandate to merge the Inland Revenue Department (IRD), Value Added Tax Department (VAT), Tax Compliance Unit (TCU) and the Customs Department (CUST), the first phase of the merger is to focus on IRD, VAT and the TCU given that the nature of the work at the Customs Department is highly specific and not within the general trading activity of VAT and Income Tax. Merging of the tax audit and investigation arms commenced in 2014 and further action concerning other functions will take place in late-2014. In addition, steps are being taken in 2014 to harmonise the legal framework for tax administration (e.g. penalties).

Officials also reported that the overall merger is taking place over an extended period given the organisational cultural differences that must be handled sensitively and to ensure that the changes do not disrupt tax revenue flows.

- ***Mexico*** reported a number of changes in its organisation in July 2012. A new General Administration (i.e. Foreign Trade Audits with six Regional Offices) was created to improve operational efficiency. Other organisational changes included functions re-assignment between the General Administration of Planning and the General Administration of Taxpayer Services, and consolidation of human resources functions with the Central Administration of Fiscal Training etc.
- As foreshadowed in TA2013, the ***Netherlands*** Tax and Customs Administration (NTCA) reported it has re-organised its Taxes Division. Previously, this division was organised into 13 regions. The previous structure was replaced by a new organisational model in support of a subject-oriented approach. Four segments were created: *(1)* Private Taxpayers; *(2)* SMEs; *(3)* Large Enterprises; and *(4)* a department for mainstream production processes (e.g. processing of taxpayers' returns). Also six central staff departments have been set up. By placing final responsibility for all segments and departments in the hands of a single national director at deputy commissioner level and introducing a clearer separation of responsibilities between planning and implementation, the strength of management has been increased.
- ***New Zealand***'s IR noted a number of developments concerning its senior management structure and governance arrangements, along with a number of initiatives involving collaboration with other government agencies.

  In late 2012, IR reviewed its senior management structure and approach to governance. The review established a new Executive Leadership Team (ELT) with nine second-tier managers reporting direct to the Commissioner. The new structure includes changes to the responsibilities of some deputy commissioners, new deputy commissioner roles and adds three chief officer roles to the ELT. The ELT took up its role in February 2013. It provides greater focus on delivering IR's services for customers and ensures that the leadership required to drive its change programme over the next few years is in place. Reporting lines in the new structure were aligned progressively during the first half of 2013. IR has also recently created three new governance boards: *(1)* a Strategy Board, which focuses on longer-term organisational strategy development including environmental scanning, strategic planning, and resourcing implications; *(2)* an Investment Board to focus on investment-related decisions for Inland Revenue; and *(3)* a Business Performance Board to focus on shorter-term financial and business performance, resource management, and operational and financial planning. The new governance boards are expected to significantly strengthen the quality of IR's governance and decision-making, particularly as it increases the pace of change.

  IR is also increasingly working with other government agencies to make the public sector more effective and provide better services. It is contributing to the Government's Better Public Services results, sharing information with other agencies to improve performance, and sharing service delivery and facilities. These efforts include: *(1)* helping design the future "one-stop online shop" for business, a shared online "front door" that integrates all information, government-to-business transactions and online services provided by the public and private sectors; *(2)* supporting the introduction of a New Zealand Business Number, which is a key enabler for delivering integrated services for business across government; and *(3)* helping create an integrated New Zealand business register.

- ***Norway*** reported that its office network rationalisation programme commenced in January 2011 with the objective of reducing its network of local offices by over half (i.e. from 225 to 110) in 2013 has been successfully completed. In addition, as described in Chapter 1 work commenced in the first half of 2014 to carry out the transfer of responsibility for excise duty administration and the collection of VAT on imports from the Customs and Excise Directorate to the Tax Directorate. This work, which is to be completed by January 2016, aims to support Government goals for improving the efficiency of the public sector and is one of a number of projects being implemented to achieve this outcome.

- ***Poland*** reported that a range of measures had been initiated to strengthen administration and to reinforce its public perception as a professional, modern and friendly administration. These have include actions to: *(1)* consolidate various ancillary processes in tax administration and adjust structures to adopt the products of the e-Taxes Programme [e-Podatki]; and *(2)* establish a system of service and support for taxpayers through the implementation of new solutions or improvement of existing ones in three areas – tax information (management of tax knowledge), working standards of Tax Administration while rendering services for taxpayers (organisation of a front office), and support of taxpayers in individual matters (handling of an individual matter).

- ***Portugal*** noted that since the January 2012, a new body has been operating, named Autoridade Tributária e Aduaneira (AT), resulting from the merger of the former Tax Directorate, Customs Directorate and Directorate for Tax and Customs' Information technology. A reorganisation of the structure and functions, and an integration of the human resources were all implemented in 2012, with the key objective of creating a more efficient and effective tax and customs administration. Organisational restructuring included the creation of a Large Taxpayers Unit and the establishment of a working group to deal with High Net Wealth Individuals. Other reforms are in course of implementation, including a major rationalisation/ reduction of local and regional tax offices.

  In April 2014, the IMF reported (IMF, 2014a) that recent steps by authorities to curb tax evasion and improve compliance included hiring approximately 1 000 new tax auditors and making the Compliance Risk Management Unit fully operational from February 2014. Next steps involve AT's plan to establish a dedicated Taxpayer Services Department, with the goal of unifying most taxpayer services and improving the relationship between taxpayers and the tax administration.

- As reported in TA2013, ***Romania's*** Government in 2012 gave in principle agreement in 2012 to a multi-year tax administration reform programme to be funded with a loan from the World Bank (WB). The loan for the programme was finalised in 2013 and reform activities commenced, drawing on recommendations of prior technical assistance by the IMF, EC and WB. The project is expected to extend over five to six years. As reported by NAFA officials, the reform will focus on fighting tax evasion, reducing the administrative burden on taxpayers, and increasing collection efficiency. The restructuring process will seek to minimise direct contact with taxpayers, providing taxpayer service through the use of a robust self-service website, through an accessible call centre, and other means. Reduced physical contact also minimises opportunities for corrupt behaviour.

Once the project objectives are realised, NAFA staff will be properly trained and distributed across the organisation, with a focus on staff re-assignment to key areas such as audit and debt collection. More information on NAFA's reform programme can be found in a report for the loan programme (World Bank, 2013).

In line with programme's broad objectives, a number of reforms have recently been introduced. In September 2013, NAFA created eight regional directorates (previously 42) and intends in scaling down its network of local offices, moving from 215 in 2013 to around 47 by 2015. It has also organised its data processing centre and call centres directly under its national headquarters. It has also reorganised its criminal investigation and anti-fraud activities and, in the process, reallocated around 1 700 staff to prevention and control activities while also increasing resources in the Bucharest Region to combat fraud.

In 2013, NAFA reorganised its fiscal investigation and anti-fraud activities by creating a new internal anti-fraud division, named Anti-fiscal Fraud General Directorate (DGAF). The main purpose of DGAF is to prevent and firmly fight the acts and deeds of tax evasion as well as fiscal and customs fraud. For the development of the new directorate's administrative capacity around 2 000 positions were earmarked for prevention and control activities, out of which about 20% perform their activity under the exclusive authority of the Prosecutor's Office, offering specialised technical support to the Prosecutor in carrying out criminal investigations, in cases concerning economic and financial crimes. At a national level, DGAF carries out its activity through a central structure and 8 regional anti-fiscal fraud directorates having as main attributions: current and thematic fiscal control, traffic control, fraud investigation, risk analysis and selection of important fraud cases, methodology and antifraud procedures establishment, administrative co-operation and information exchange within EU member states, inter-institutional co-operation with specialised bodies of other ministries and specialised institutions such as: the Prosecutor's office, Romanian Intelligence Service (SRI), National Anticorruption Directorate (DNA), Directorate for Investigating Organised Crime and Terrorism.

- ***Saudi Arabia's*** revenue body, the Department of Zakat[1] and Income Tax (DZIT), has been implementing a major computerisation project that should radically improve all its operational aspects. The main objectives of the project are to improve operational efficiency and taxpayer service delivery.
- ***Singapore*** reported that it had set up an International Tax Affairs and Relations (ITAR) Branch in September 2013. The Branch maintains strategic oversight of IRAS' international engagement framework and programmes. It drives international engagement efforts to advance Singapore's interest on the international tax front and advises the Government on international tax matters. It manages the Exchange of Information (EOI) function and is the liaison office for all international engagements. The ITAR Branch complements the existing Tax Policy and International Tax Division that provides technical advice in the formulation of tax policies and fair application of tax laws, reviews tax policies, initiates tax rules changes and safeguards Singapore's economic interest through tax treaty negotiations and resolution of international tax issues.
- ***Slovakia*** advised that the Customs Directorate of the Slovak Republic and the Tax Directorate of the Slovak Republic were merged into the Financial Directorate of the Slovak Republic (FDSR) on 1 January 2012, the first stage of its UNITAS programme. At present, the Slovak Financial Administration consists of the FDSR,

8 Tax Offices with branches and contact places in the seats of the higher territorial units, one Office for the Large Taxpayers, 8 Customs Offices in the seats of the higher territorial units, one Customs Office in Michalovce, all with branches and stations, and one Criminal Office. Establishing of the FDSR has unified some of the processes at the central level (e.g. the organisation of the tax and customs revenues collection was unified). During 2013, systematic support was provided to these unified processes with the aim to reach objectives of the UNITAS programme – enhanced effectiveness of the financial administration, reduced administrative costs, and improvement of customer-orientated attitude to the taxpayer.

In addition, action has been taken to enlarge the scope of its large taxpayer operations. Until 2012, the Large Taxpayer Office (LTO) administered the largest taxpayers located in Bratislava and its surroundings. Since 2013, its scope has been enlarged to encompass all of the Slovak Republic. LTO's head office is situated in Bratislava and it performs various functions: audit (5 auditing departments across Slovakia), compliance, collection, enforcement, taxpayer's services, avoidance, evasion and others (e.g. IT services, public relations, register), also with methodological guidance provided by the FDSR).

- ***Slovenia*** reported on a number of developments. In October 2012, the Tax Administration initiated an upgrading of its tax information system to improve internal work processes as well as automating some of the obligations of taxpayers. Previously, taxpayers paid every duty to a special payment sub-account, which caused unnecessary administrative work and costs for taxpayers. The project of simplification for payment of taxes and other obligatory duties has considerably decreased the number of payment sub-accounts and it has replaced them with suspense tax sub-accounts according to types of general government revenues. Centralisation of tax accountancy has resulted in changes in the enforcement field. A new system for reminding tax debtors in writing and via the telephone has been introduced as well as the whole enforcement process is integrated into the upgraded information system. This work is performed centrally, while tasks resulting from the issue of reminders are performed from local offices. All strategic decisions in connection with pre-enforcement procedures and subsequent enforcement action are made centrally and recorded within the system on the basis of business rules. Local office staff perform operational enforcement tasks.

  On 1 July 2013, the territorial organisation of tax offices was transformed, with local offices converted to tax desks and services offered to taxpayers reduced to two days per week. This rationalisation has permitted it to direct more staff resources onto control work.

  Following the passage of legislation (the Finance Administration Act) a new agency – Finance Administration of the Republic of Slovenia – came into effect on 1 August 2014, merging the operations of the previously separate Slovene Tax and Customs Administrations. The Government has estimated that due to expected new circumstances, which have occurred with the entry of Croatia into the EU, and due to the increased effectiveness at collection of obligatory duties and increased rationality in organisation of units, which are competent for collection of public revenues, it is rational that both administrations are united as a uniform finance administration. In this way the new authority will also provide uniform, effective and fast realisation of tasks, equal treatment of all taxpayers, reduction of costs, equal availability of tax services and even burden of work on all employees.

- ***Spain*** reported that an International Taxation Office was created within the Tax Auditing Department of the Spanish Tax Agency on 1 April 2013. This Office is a new specialised unit in charge of centralised planning and providing uniform criterion in international taxation affairs. It has an appraisals unit and, in some cases, it can also perform audits. The Office is based in Madrid and staffed with 50 officials, with its priorities being international related-party operations and application of the arms-length principle as well as transfer pricing issues of multinational corporations, and correct taxation in Spain of non-residents′ incomes. It also co-ordinates simultaneous controls with other Tax Administrations. The objective of the new office is to strengthen the Tax Agency's resources to fight against international tax fraud, in line with the directives of the OECD and EU.

  As a result of the Government's plan for the rationalisation of structures across the whole Spanish Public Administration, some organisational changes have been made. Some regional and local offices have been merged and, as a result, the number of regional offices has been reduced from 51 to 39 and the number of local offices from 239 to 227.

- The ***United States*** reported a series of organisational reforms recently implemented or in course of development (see Box 2.3).

Box 2.3. United States: Recent and planned organisational reforms

Large Business and International: The Large Business and International (LB&I) Operating Division implemented several organisational changes in 2012. The reorganisation of the LB&I large business industry units into clearer geographical sections was effective October 2012. At that time, LB&I also transferred all of its employment tax specialists to a combined unit in the Small Business and Self-Employed Operating Division. Also during 2012, LB&I added a unit specialising in Transfer Pricing Operations as part of the realignment of its international functions into a single international unit. LB&I also realigned its foreign payments audit oversight activities in 2012 and created the Foreign Payments Practice (FPP). FPP is an integrated withholding tax programme within LB&I. Further, LB&I has developed a knowledge management network for international issues through the use of International Practice Networks ("IPNs"). IPNs are designed to provide examination teams the technical advice they need to manage their cases efficiently, consistently and with a high degree of technical proficiency, as well as to foster effective collaboration and the sharing of knowledge and expertise across LB&I and Chief Counsel.

Small Business/Self Employed: Examination Function: In October 2013, the IRS realigned its SB/SE Examination Area operations to balance the Areas' geographic configurations with their taxpayer base. The previous Collection and Examination Area alignments were originally established 10 years ago, but population and economic changes over the last decade had created an imbalance.

Small Business/Self Employed: Collection Function: In addition to the three separate existing Collection organisations, the Internal Revenue Service (IRS) created a new Collection organisation that officially launched in fiscal year 2012. The primary goal of the new organisation is to focus on development and communication of the unified vision, policies, strategies, governance and work plans for all of the collection organisations. This would facilitate the three pre-existing organisations' ability to increase focus and resources on collection programme execution while transferring strategic and oversight related activities to the newly created organisation for a more cohesive business approach.

Box 2.3. **United States: Recent and planned organisational reforms** *(continued)*

Tax Exempt/Government Entities: Determination Process: To receive tax-exempt status an organisation must apply to the IRS for a determination seeking IRS recognition for tax-exempt status. The IRS's Tax Exempt and Government Entities (TE/GE) division is streamlining this process and simplifying the information requested from a majority of applicants in order to improve customer service and reduce taxpayer burden. While staff levels will remain consistent with historical levels, the mix of staff is changing to allow the majority of applications to undergo a quick review through a new application form for tax exemption. Additionally, streamlined application processing is being implemented for other application streams, including for those applications requiring additional review.

Office of Professional Responsibility: For changes introduced for this relatively new IRS division, see Chapter 8.

Enterprise Re-alignment of IRS Compliance Functions: IRS underwent a realignment of its taxpayer compliance operations in November 2014. Although the basic work streams are not changing under the re-alignment, post-refund audits and all collection activities now align under a new Small Business/Self Employed (SB/SE) collection function, and pre-refund compliance activities, along with Earned Income and ID Theft verification activities, align under the Wage and Investment (W&I) Division. The objective of the realignment is to streamline accountability and responsibility for all IRS compliance operations, to increase efficiency and reduce redundancy, and to better identify emerging compliance issues.

Source: IRS survey response.

Office networks for tax administration

Considerable changes have occurred over recent decades in the design and size of office networks for national tax administration, generally resulting from technological advances and Government drives for increased efficiency and cost reductions.

That was then… this is now

Traditionally, office networks of national revenue bodies in many countries were comprised of large numbers of regional and/or local offices to carry out the full range of functions required for administration of tax laws. Factors driving the need for such networks included the large numbers of taxpayers to be administered, their geographical spread and the general objective of providing services that were reasonably accessible to the majority of citizens and businesses who needed them. Also relevant in the past, but one might reasonably think much less so in 2014, was a country's political structure, a factor that appears to explain some of the exceptionally large networks still seen today in a number of European countries.

Over recent decades, a number of developments have led to significant changes in both the size and nature of revenue bodies' office networks in many countries:

- ***Technology-driven changes in information processing work:*** The advent of new technologies has enabled many revenue bodies to concentrate some routine/seasonal functions (e.g. the processing of tax returns and payments) into larger dedicated processing centres, centralising much of this work. In addition, the development of new payment methods via the Internet or the outsourcing of tax payment collection to financial bodies has led to major reductions in the payment processing workloads of many revenue bodies.

- ***Technology-driven changes enabling enhanced service delivery:*** Driven by objectives to improve both the efficiency and quality of taxpayer services, many revenue bodies have taken steps to make more effective use of the various service delivery channels available to them (e.g. phone, walk-in offices, and Internet) for delivering services to taxpayers. This has included the use of dedicated call centres to replace/reduce the need for in-person inquiry services and/or distributed phone inquiry services, the introduction of more efficient tax payment methods (e.g. direct debits and on-line payment via the Internet), the use of e-filing to reduce paper returns, and use of the Internet to provide comprehensive information, guides and forms for taxpayers.
- ***Developments based on "whole of government" approaches:*** The delivery of some government services on a "whole of government" basis has, in some countries, seen the emergence of government shop-fronts delivering basic tax-related services that were previously delivered via local offices.
- ***Government mandates for increased efficiency:*** Aware of the potential opportunities for streamlining, Governments in many countries have become more active in seeking reductions in costs through office consolidation programmes and finding alternate ways of delivering necessary services required by taxpayers. As a result, office networks in many countries have been reconfigured into a smaller number of larger offices to achieve "economies of scale" and to facilitate operational management. In some countries, management structures and lines of reporting have been streamlined, involving for some the elimination of a regional layer of management.

Examples of large scale office network rationalisation programmes

Over recent years, a number of revenue bodies have responded to the need for greater efficiency and effectiveness by rationalising their office networks. A number of examples are described in Box 2.4.

Box 2.4. **Examples of large scale office network rationalisation programmes**

Austria: Since 2004, the office network of the Directorate General for Taxes and Customs has been reshaped to achieve increased efficiency. Previously comprised of 7 regional directorates and 81 tax offices, the new network implemented from 2004 now sees five regional management areas, 40 tax offices, and one Large Trader Division).

Croatia: Tax officials reported that as part of its modernisation reform programme the office network has been restructured. The number of regional offices has been reduced from 20 to 6, while the local office network more than halved – from 124 to 54.

Denmark: In 2005, the central and municipal tax administration bodies merged thereby creating a country-wide unified tax administration, moving from a situation where each of the 275 municipalities had their own separate office. Since then the tax administration has been further restructured. In 2013 the regional structure was abolished, and all tasks were organised in 6 nationwide divisions (i.e. Customer Service, Compliance, Debt Collection, Economy and Controlling, Information Technology and Human Relations) located in 29 nationwide branches. The purpose of the reform was to promote effective management, strong academic environments and efficiency improvement. It is anticipated that the reforms will permit gradual staff reductions while simultaneously improving efficiency and the uniformity and quality of the services offered to Danish taxpayers.

Box 2.4. **Examples of large scale office network rationalisation programmes** *(continued)*

Greece: A major institutional and organisational reform programme has seen the office network scaled down by around 60% – from 241 offices as of the end of 2011 to 118 at the beginning of 2014.

Norway: A rationalisation programme implemented over recent years has seen the local office network significantly scaled down – from 225 in 2011 to 108 in 2014.

Romania: Reform efforts currently being planned include attention being given to the scale of Romania's current network of regional and local offices. NAFA's structure now includes 8 (previously 42) regional offices and 215 (previously 221) local offices. Steps are being taken to consolidate to 47 local tax offices by 2015.

Sources: Survey responses.

The overall position in early 2014

Tables 2.3 and 2.4 display data on the make-up of the office networks used for tax administration in surveyed countries and the staffing numbers at each level of the network. Some of the more noteworthy observations and common features apparent from the data provided are set out below:

- Office networks in quite a few countries, particularly within Europe, are relatively larger in comparison with the set up in many other countries. For some countries, this results from their responsibilities for administering taxes on real property and/or motor vehicles and/or historical practice. Revenue bodies in some of these countries (e.g. Greece and Portugal) have signalled their intention to significantly reduce the size of their networks while others have already taken steps to do so.
- Around 60 per cent of revenue bodies have established dedicated information processing centres for bulk information processing work.

  There appears to have been a significant increase in the overall numbers of revenue bodies using dedicated (telephony) call centre operations for handling taxpayers' inquiries and providing information, and outwards-bound inquiry work. However, based on the responses received, countries in Central and South America generally appear to make fairly limited use of such capabilities, while the same also applies in large populous countries such as India, Japan, Russia, and Turkey.
- Across surveyed bodies, there is enormous variation in the relative size of the headquarters (HQ) function, and the definition of "headquarters" varies significantly from country to country.[2] The practice of maintaining large HQ operations (i.e. aggregate staffing in excess of 15% of total staffing) can be seen in countries across many continents – Canada, Costa Rica, Cyprus, Finland, Hungary, Lithuania, Luxembourg, Malaysia, Mexico, Netherlands, New Zealand, Portugal, Saudi Arabia, Slovenia, South Africa, and Sweden. This reflects a variety of factors, for example, a more centralised approach to the national management of tax administration operations, large in-house IT functions, and the fact that, in some of these countries, headquarters functions may include elements of technical support to field operations, and for certain programmes, carry out operational work.

Table 2.3. **Office network for tax administration role-office types by number**

Country	Revenue bodies' office network for tax administration (number of operational units at end 2013)					
	Headquarters	Regional offices	Local/branch offices	National data processing centres	Call centres	Other offices
OECD countries						
Australia	1	17 /1	11	-	10	5
Austria	1	5	40	-	-	-
Belgium	1	35	3 153	5	15	1 /1
Canada	1	5	39	8 /1	10 /1	-
Chile	1	19	47	1	1	-
Czech Republic	1	15	201	-	-	1 /1
Denmark /1	0 /1	0	28	-	1	-
Estonia	1	-	15	-	1	-
Finland	1	-	37	1	2	-
France	1	110	1 283	9	14	6 /1
Germany	17 /1	12	546	12	34 /2	16
Greece	1	2	118	2	2	-
Hungary	1	25	50	1	8	2 /1
Iceland	1	8	-	-	1	-
Ireland	1	7	74	-	-	6
Israel	1	-	80 /1	1	1	-
Italy	1	34	213	3	7	-
Japan	1	12	518	-	-	33
Korea	1	6	111	1	1	2 /1
Luxembourg	2	-	84 /1	4	-	-
Mexico	1	6	67	2	3	49 /1
Netherlands	1 /1	14	-	1	1	4
New Zealand	1	-	17	3	6	-
Norway	1	5	108 /1	1	1	1 /2
Poland	1	32	400	1	4	-
Portugal	1	36	367	-	80 /1	-
Slovak Republic	1	17 /1	153 /1	-	1	2
Slovenia	1	16	-	-	4	41 /1
Spain	1 /1	56 /2	227 /2	2	2 /2	1
Sweden	1	8	63	1	1	/1
Switzerland	1	-	-	-	-	-
Turkey	1	70	1 063	2	2	52
United Kingdom	1				19 (in 2011)	362
United States /1	1	139	119	28 /2	19	-
Non-OECD countries						
Argentina	1	38	272	1	1	5
Brazil	1	10	558 /1	- /2	-	-
Bulgaria	1	6	23	-	1	-
China	1	71 /1	6 667 /2	-	68	-
Colombia	1	43	6	1	-	22
Costa Rica	1	4	11	-	- /1	-
Croatia	1	20	124	- /1	1	1 /2
Cyprus	2	15 /1	-	5 /2	-	1 /2
Hong Kong, China	1	-	-	-	-	-
India	1	18	500	1 /1	5	-
Indonesia	1	31	538	4	1	-
Latvia	1	-	32	-	1	-
Lithuania	1	10	-	1	1	1
Malaysia	1	12	77 /1	1	2	-
Malta	3 /1	1	-	-	1	1
Morocco	1	15	72	1	1	-
Romania	1	8	215	1 /1	1 /1	-
Russia	1	84	910	1	6	19 /1
Saudi Arabia	1		13	-	-	-
Singapore	1	-	-	-	-	-
South Africa /1	1	29	47	7	7	55
Thailand	1	12	968	1	1	-

For notes indicated by "/ (number)", see Notes to Tables section at the end of the chapter, p. 99.
Source: Tax Administration 2015 survey responses.

Table 2.4. **Office network for tax administration role-number of staff by office type**

Country	Revenue bodies' office network for tax administration (x number of staff in 2013 [FTEs])						
	Headquarters	Regional offices	Local/branch offices	National data processing centres	Call centres	Other offices	All offices – TOTAL
OECD countries							
Australia	2 927	16 189	80	-	1 010	42	20 248
Austria	217	205	7 062	-	-	-	7 484
Belgium	982	222	18 091	84	107	83	19 568
Canada	8 897	121	20 053	6 823	2 278	-	38 172 /1
Chile	857	2 500	800	34	4	-	4 195
Czech Republic	899	1 809	12 114	-	-	209	15 031
Denmark /1	/1	-	-	-	395	6 476	6 871
Estonia	983	-	-	-	-	-	983
Finland	838	-	4 056	49	129	-	5 072
France	1 771	9 211	50 367	2 485	571	2 559	66 964 /1
Germany	1 236	5 179	100 584	2 727	n.a.	749	110 494
Greece	2 200	n.a		n.a	n.a	n.a	11 500
Hungary	1 639	3 848	15 089	1 183	251 /1	723	22 482 /1
Iceland	124	105	-	-	11	-	240
Ireland	706	109	4 475	-	-	455	5 745
Israel	937	-	4 638	376	84	-	6 035 /1
Italy	1 957	3 732	33 010	480	635	-	39 814
Japan	787	11 439	42 830	-	-	800	56 194
Korea	702	4 161	13 617	156	114	91	18 841
Luxembourg	153 /1	-	762 /1	69 /1	-	-	984 /1
Mexico	7 742	508	20 681	15 /1	20 /1	7 444	36 410
Netherlands	3 865 /1	15 412	-	1 171	425	-	20 873
New Zealand /1	1 030	-	1 515	329	558	-	3 432
Norway	304	---------------4 252-------------		870 /1	325	47	5 798
Poland	181	9 085	39 027	94	171	-	48 558
Portugal	1 972	4 057	5 312	-	156 /1	-	11 341
Slovak Republic	1 446	7 415	4 107	-	56	435	9 296
Slovenia	386	1 976	-	-	-	-	2 362
Spain	3 416	-----------22 815------------		/1	/1	/1	26 231 /2
Sweden	2 051	------------8 520------------		/1	/1	-	10 571
Switzerland	965	-	-	-	-	-	965
Turkey	1 041	10 134	40 060	-	134	-	51 369
United Kingdom	1 600	-	40 676	2 777	19 392	375	64 820 /1
United States	4 072	10 896	43 444	11 164	17 401	-	86 977
Non-OECD countries							
Argentina	2 962	8 097	7 274	93	91	3 640	22 157 /1
Brazil	1 537	1 570	21 438 /1	-	80	-	24 625
Bulgaria	814	--------------6 838------------		-	28	-	7 680
China	800	11 000	740 700	-	3 500		756 000
Colombia	752	3 959	180	30	-	323	5 244
Costa Rica	237	29	695	-	-	-	961
Croatia	287	1460	2347	-	8	112	4214
Cyprus	168 /1	601	-	5	-	8	782 /1
Hong Kong, China	2 826	-	-	-	-	-	2 826
India	n.a.	n.a.	n.a.	n.a.	n.a.	n.a.	41 357
Indonesia	3 910	3 137	24 863	246	117	-	32 273
Latvia	3 484	-	801	-	27	-	4 312
Lithuania	1 295	2 181	-	58 /1	72 /1	53 /1	3 476
Malaysia	2 169	309	7 975	509	87	-	11 049
Malta	711	17	-	-	15	2	728
Morocco	561	2 966	1 020	174	14	-	4 735
Romania	2 459	4 924	17 085	7	6	-	24 481
Russia	1 117	3 431	133 157	165	143	18 013	156 026
Saudi Arabia	537	-	1061	-	-	-	1 598
Singapore	1 870	-	-	-	-	-	1 870
South Africa /1	3 428	2 981	1 841	1 166	2 091	3 194 /1	14 701
Thailand	2 490	1 696	18 978	226	119	-	23 509

For notes indicated by "/ (number)", see Notes to Tables section at the end of the chapter, p. 100.

Source: Tax Administration 2015 survey responses.

Large taxpayer operations

As noted earlier in the chapter, the vast majority of revenue bodies have established dedicated units – hereafter referred to as Large Taxpayer Units (LTUs)-to manage some/all aspects of the tax affairs of their largest taxpayers.[3] Croatia and Portugal (see Box 2.5) are examples of two countries that have recently established such units. Further background on this development and its rationale are set out below.

The common characteristics of large taxpayers

Large taxpayers are very different from other categories of taxpayers and present certain significant risks to effective tax administration. Many revenue bodies have recognised that managing these risks requires strategies and approaches appropriate to the unique characteristics and compliance behaviour of these taxpayers. Key characteristics of the large business segment identified from prior FTA work include:

- *Concentration of revenue:* A small number of large taxpayers typically are responsible for the bulk of tax revenue collected by a revenue body. This concentration of tax revenue payments results from the size of these taxpayers and the range of taxes they are responsible for, including as withholding agents for their employees and the collection of value added taxes.
- *Complexity of their business and tax dealings:* Revenue bodies typically describe large taxpayers as complex for a variety of reasons, including: *(1)* they have multiple operating entities and/or diverse business interests; *(2)* there is high volume of transactions in day-to-day business activities; *(3)* a large number of employees; *(4)* they have international dealings, often involving cross-border transactions with related parties; *(5)* some operate in industries that present unique tax issues (e.g. mining and banking); *(6)* many are widely spread in geographical terms; *(6)* some taxpayers' affairs raise complex tax law issues; and *(7)* there are complex financing and tax planning arrangements.
- *Major tax compliance risks: M*any of these taxpayers present major tax compliance risks due to various factors, for example: *(1)* significant offshore activities; *(2)* policies and strategies to minimise tax liabilities; *(3)* large portion of tax assessments result from audit activity of large taxpayers; and *(4)* growing/significant differences between financial accounting profits and the profits computed for tax purposes.
- *Use of professional/dedicated tax advice: M*any large businesses engage professional advisers to handle their tax planning etc., while others maintain their own in-house tax advisers.
- *Status: G*enerally, most large businesses are publicly-listed corporate companies, and also include multinationals and some private groups, and they have a high profile in the business-media.

For these sorts of reasons, many revenue bodies have established dedicated LTUs, supported by highly skilled and expert staff to manage all/most aspects of the tax affairs of their largest taxpayers. Across surveyed revenue bodies, these organisational units are likely to have different names and the scope and nature of their activities may vary but most have been established to improve the revenue body's capability to manage and improve the compliance of this important segment of taxpayers.

Criteria used by revenue bodies to identify large businesses

Most revenue bodies have established clear and fairly specific criteria for identifying their large taxpayers – see Table 2.5 – and for some countries these are reflected in tax procedure law.

As will be evident from Table 2.5, the criteria used to define taxpayers as "large businesses" and to place them under the responsibility of the large business unit typically include one or more of the following: *(1)* size of annual turnover or gross sales; *(2)* size of total assets; *(3)* aggregate amount of tax paid per annum across all taxes; *(4)* businesses operating in economic sectors important to the country concerned (e.g. banking, insurance, mining, and oil); *(5)* businesses with significant international business activities and/or which are foreign-controlled; *(6)* the number of employees; and/or *(7)* a combination, sometimes quite complex, of the abovementioned criterion. It is also evident that some revenue bodies place emphasis on the management of corporate groups and related affiliates to ensure that a "whole of taxpayer" focus is brought to the tasks of identifying and treating compliance risks. Finally, some revenue bodies (e.g. Argentina, Ireland, Spain, and South Africa) have placed responsibility for the administration of "high net-worth" individuals (HNWIs) under the control of their LTU, recognising that many of the taxpayers concerned have direct links with the large corporate taxpayers also under its control.

Table 2.5. **Large taxpayer operations: Identification criteria used in 2013**

Countries	Criteria applied by individual revenue bodies to identify large corporate taxpayers
OECD countries	
Australia	Turnover over AUD 250 m
Austria	Turnover over EUR 9.68 m
Belgium	*(1)* Groups of (associated) companies that are obliged to publish consolidated annual accounts (which include at least one large taxpayer); *(2)* Taxpayers belonging to a specific economic sector: in general, financial sector (banks, insurance companies, companies listed on the stock exchange, etc.); *(3)* Size: If a taxpayer exceed at least two of the following criteria: *(i)* turnover : EUR 7.3m; *(ii)* value of assets : EUR 3.65m; and (4) number of employees: 50. If the number of employees exceeds 100, the taxpayer will also be considered large taxpayers; (5) VAT Units which include at least one large taxpayer.
Canada	*(1)* Income tax: Gross annual revenue over CAD 250 m; *(2)* Indirect taxes (GST/HST): Gross annual revenue over CAD 100 m /1
Chile	Turnover equal to or higher than 90 000 UTA, during each of the last three commercial years; taxable capital equal or higher than 110 000 UTA, during each of the last three tax years; and other criteria. (NB: UTA=Unidad Tributaria Anual (i.e. Annual Tax Unit, equal to 12 times the Monthly Tax Unit of December, indexed to inflation) (as per SII Resolution 109 of 2013).
Czech Republic	*(1)* taxable year turnover > CZK 2 billion; *(2)* bank or bank branch; *(3)* insurance company or branch; *(4)* reinsurance company or branch; *(5)* each member of a group (according to the VAT Act), if at least one member is one of the above mentioned entities; *(6)* any legal or natural entity appointed by the General Financial Directorate
Denmark	Groups with total turnover over DKK 3 billion; companies with over 250 staff
Estonia	(The ETCB does not have a dedicated Large Taxpayer Division.)
Finland	Turnover over EUR 50 m. Threshold applies to an individual company or group of companies.
France	Turnover over EUR 400 m (exclusive of VAT or gross assets) and related companies (directly or indirectly by more than 50%)
Germany	Most regional "Lander" administrations have a large taxpayer audit function; industry criteria applied are *(1)* Trading: turnover over EUR 7.3 m or profit over EUR 280 000; *(2)* Manufacturing: turnover over EUR 4.3 m or profit over EUR 250 000; *(3)* Freelancers: turnover over EUR 4.7 m or profit over EUR 580 000; *(4)* Financial Institutions: actual net worth over EUR 140 m or profit over EUR 560 000; *(5)* Insurance companies: insurance premium revenues over EUR 30 m; *(6)* Agricultural and silvi-cultural companies: economic value on the basis of land over EUR 230 000 or profit over EUR 125 000; *(7)* Other enterprises: turnover over EUR 5.6 m or profit over EUR 330 000.
Greece	Turnover over EUR 20 m (in 2012); all banks, insurance and other companies listed on Stock Exchange where turnover over EUR 10 million, and all taxpayers regardless of size which carry out cross-border transactions with associated enterprises, as decreed.

Table 2.5. **Large taxpayer operations: Identification criteria used in 2013** *(continued)*

Countries	Criteria applied by individual revenue bodies to identify large corporate taxpayers
Hungary	Taxpayers are classified by size of their average customer value (i.e. average tax capacity) calculated for a reference period. Large taxpayers are classified in category 1 priority taxpayers (defined in line with the limit determined in the decree of the Ministry for National Economy). This category also includes banks and insurance companies operating as joint-stock companies. Taxpayers located in Budapest and in Pest county as well as the banks and insurance companies operating as joint-stock companies are overseen by the Large Taxpayers Directorate. The cases of non-Budapest and non-Pest county-based taxpayers are overseen by designated audit divisions at local tax directorates.
Iceland	n.a. (The revenue administration does not have a dedicated Large Taxpayer Division.)
Ireland	*(a)* Corporations with a turnover exceeding EUR 162 m or tax payments over EUR 16 m, *(b)* semi-state commercial organisations, *(c)* financial services sector, and *(d)* relatively large scale enterprises in certain sectors.
Israel	Turnover and certain business industries are automatically defined as "large" taxpayers (e.g. banks, insurance, and energy)
Italy	Turnover exceeds EUR 100 m
Japan	Corporations with over Y 100 m in capital
Korea	n.a. (NTS does not have a dedicated Large Taxpayer Division.)
Luxembourg	n.a. (There is no dedicated Large Taxpayer Division for direct and indirect taxes administration.)
Mexico	Gross revenue over 645 m pesos; financial institutions; companies reporting consolidated results; foreign governments, international organisations, diplomats; federal centralised public administration; state-owned oil companies; federal social security agencies; non-residents; all matters related to the international tax regime (e.g. transfer pricing, thin capitalisation)
Netherlands	Criteria are: *(1)* listed company at the (Amsterdam) stock exchange and/or *(2)* standard weighted fiscal worth exceeding EUR 25 m and/or; *(3)* foreign parent and own standard weighted fiscal worth exceeding EUR 12.5 m ; and/or *(4)* at least 5 foreign subsidiaries and own standard weighted fiscal worth exceeding EUR 12.5 m; and/or; *(5)* all non-profit organisations standard weighted fiscal worth exceeding EUR 37.5 m; and/or *(6)* all companies in the financial industry (banks, insurance), the oil and gas industry (upstream and downstream) and in the energy-supply industry; and *(7)* other taxpayers(who may be covered under the supervision concept for very large taxpayers if complex issues exist, or a taxpayer is viewed a high-profile case or with certain degree of financial risk.
New Zealand	Large enterprise customers have a gross turnover exceeding NZD 100 m, or are operating in specialist industries or subject to specialised tax laws.
Norway	From 2015, the large taxpayer segment is defined as taxpayers with turnover / assets over NOK 1 bn, whereas taxpayers with turnover/ assets over NOK 3 bn are assessed at the Large Taxpayer Office).
Portugal	Non-financial companies with turnover over EUR 200 m; insurance companies, credit institutions and other financial entities with turnover over EUR 100 m; companies with tax payments over EUR 20 m; companies related to those that have been selected based on the above criteria (e.g. controlled companies and parent companies)
Poland	Criteria are capital tax groups, banks, insurance establishments, units providing public trade of securities and provisions on investment funds, units operating as pension funds, branches or agencies of a foreign company, and companies that raised annual net revenue of at least 5 million in the previous year, participate directly or indirectly in the management of companies located abroad or control thereof or have a share in their capital, managed directly or indirectly by a non-resident, or where a non-resident has a minimum of 5% of the votes at a meeting of shareholders or at a general meeting, and as a resident jointly participate directly or indirectly in the management of a domestic entity and foreign entity, or control or have at the same time a share in the capital of such entities.
Slovak Republic	Companies with turnover exceeding EUR 40 m; banks and branches of foreign banks; insurance companies and branches of foreign insurance companies; reinsurance companies and branches of foreign reinsurance companies
Slovenia	Companies with turnover over EUR 50 m; banks; savings banks; insurance companies; companies, which organise classic permanent games of chance and special games of chance; stock exchanges bourse brokerage companies; investment companies; management companies; pension companies; central securities clearing corporations.
Spain	***Assigned automatically:*** Turnover over EUR 100 m, large corporate groups, major banks and insurance, and those third party reporters providing over 10 000 records. ***Assigned by Head of the Service for Planning and Institutional Relations (following a proposal of the Head of the Large taxpayers Office)***: Partners highly related to other legal entities assigned to the Large Taxpayers Central Office or that manage complex economic transactions.
Sweden	Groups with over 800 employees, companies with annual payroll over SEK 50 m, companies supervised by Swedish Financial Supervisory Authority
Switzerland	n.a. (Federal VAT administration does not have a dedicated Large Taxpayer Division.)
Turkey	Taxpayers whose yearly revenue, total assets or equity exceed certain thresholds which are revised every year. Also, irrespective of these criteria, taxpayers who operate in the financial sector (e.g. banks, insurance companies and brokers) are considered large taxpayers.

Table 2.5. **Large taxpayer operations: Identification criteria used in 2013** *(continued)*

Countries	Criteria applied by individual revenue bodies to identify large corporate taxpayers
United Kingdom	Turnover over GBP 600 m /1
United States	Corporations, subchapter S corporations and partnerships with assets over USD 10 m. Large Business and International's "LB&I" is also responsible for all foreign corporations and certain foreign partnerships; US persons residing abroad, in a US territory or involved in cross-border activities and investment; and Non-US citizens that have a US filing requirement.
Non-OECD countries	
Argentina	Mix of tax assessed, tax paid, annual sales, VAT debt, economic sector and number of employees
Brazil	General criteria are: gross income over BRL 120m; amount of debts stated in the Federal Tax Debts and Credits Statements (DCTF) over BRL 12m; payroll based on the Collection Form for the Employment Security Fund and Information to Social Security (GFIP) over BRL 21 m; or social security debts over BRL 7 m
Bulgaria	*(1)* Taxable persons meeting at least one of the following criteria: a) revenues of over BGN 3 m; b) taxes refunded of over BGN 2 m; *(2)* Companies in the industries of banking or insurance.
China	Cross-regional business, complex tax issues, or certain scale of tax revenue
Colombia	Largest taxpayers representing 60% of total taxes paid (CIT, VAT, and withholding) in the previous tax year, no debts with DIAN, and existing since more than 3 years
Costa Rica	Annual average for the last three tax periods: *(1)* taxes equal or above CRC 250 m; *(2)* income equal or above CRC 40 bn; and *(3)* total assets equal or above CRC 40 bn. Also, if an economic group meets the conditions all taxpayers within the group can be classified as "large taxpayers" even if the conditions are not met individually by the taxpayer. The same applies for economic groups in which one or more taxpayers are considered as large taxpayers.
Croatia	One of the following conditions has to be met: *(1)* revenue equal or above HRK 150 m; *(2)* business activity of a) insurance, leasing and telecommunications with revenue above HRK 15 m, or b) banks, regardless of the amount of revenue; *(3)* large projects where the expected revenue exceeds HRK 150 m and to which a significant number of taxpayers (e.g. subcontractors) can be associated to.
Cyprus	Tax revenue and size of business (VAT taxpayers only) /1
Hong Kong, China	n.a. (There is no dedicated Large Taxpayer Division.)
India	All taxpayers assessed in five major cities who have paid excise of over Rs 50 million, service tax over Rs 50 million or advance corporate income tax over Rs 100 million.
Indonesia	Weighted average of tax payment (80%) and turnover (20%) for last three fiscal years, and DGT discretion
Latvia	*(i)* annual net turnover or total amount of VAT transaction value above LVL 3 million; *(ii)* taxes paid above LVL 250 000; *(iii)* state or municipality budget-funded institutions with annual amount of taxes paid above LVL 3 million; *(iv)* credit institutions, insurance companies, taxpayers dealing with the organisation of gambling and lotteries
Lithuania	Turnover over LTL 60 m; number of employees exceeds 10; finance and insurance
Malaysia	Specific sectors
Malta	n.a. (There is no dedicated Large Taxpayer Division.)
Morocco	Turnover equal or over MAD 50 m
Romania	From 2014; *(1)* Base criteria, named "aggregated value criteria", are derived from the aggregation of 2 indicators: *(1)* the amount of owed fiscal obligations declared by the taxpayer – 50%; ii) total income from operating activities – 50%; *(2)* Specific criteria: national bank, banking, insurance and other financial institutions; and *(3)* financial investment entities: Taxpayers who commit to make investments exceeding EUR 10 million
Russia	Profits over RUB 20 bn; Federal taxes over RUB 1 bn a year; Rendering services in the sphere of communication and logistics in amounts over RUB 300 m; Rendering services in the sphere of insurance and banking which pay federal taxes over RUB 300 m; Assets with overall value of RUB 20 bn; or Entity with more than 100 employees
Saudi Arabia	*(1)* Significant industries/activities (e.g. oil, banks, etc), *(2)* equity over SR 100 m; and *(3)* gross income over SR 100 m
Singapore	*(1)* Corporate income tax: Net tax assessed, turnover, complexity; *(2)* GST: Annual GST supplies over SGD 100 m
South Africa	Groups with turnover over ZAR 1 bn; groups engaged in mining and financial services with turnover over ZAR 250 m; entities part of MNE with turnover over ZAR 250 m
Thailand	Turnover of THB 2 bn and above

For notes indicated by "/ (number)", see Notes to Tables section at the end of the chapter, p. 100.

Source: Tax Administration 2015 survey responses.

Box 2.5. Portugal's new Large Taxpayer Unit

As foreshadowed in TA2013, Portuguese authorities have taken steps to establish a fully-fledged Large Taxpayer Unit (LTU) that came into existence from January 2012. This reform is one of many undertaken in Portugal over recent years to mobilise revenues, streamline tax administration and increase efficiency. For this series, Portuguese authorities provided specific information on the establishment and work of its LTU that is briefly summarised below:

Legislative authorisation

Legislation introduced *(1)* establishes criteria for selection of taxpayers to be allocated to LTU; *(2)* confers competence on the Director-General of the revenue body to define which taxpayers will relate with the tax administration through a client relationship manager; and *(3)* adapts the fiscal codes and related legislation in order to assign responsibility to the LTU concerning the competences related to procedures with respect to taxpayers followed by the LTU.

Basic approach and coverage

The LTU's approach is to be at direct contact with large companies in order to get a clear understanding of their specific needs, to better support them and develop open and transparent working relationships thus improving tax compliance. The LTU is responsible for dealing on a range of tax issues with more than nine hundred businesses (306 entities which meet the LTU key criteria and 618 related companies). In 2013, these companies represented just on 44% of total revenue collections (across all taxes and taxpayers).

Tax compliance risk management

Portuguese authorities reported that under the risk assessment system devised for large taxpayers (chart below), determining an overall risk rating involves assessing businesses against seven criteria and twenty four indicators:

1. ***Governance:*** Co-operation, transparency, level of litigation, and tax planning.
2. ***Organisation and structure:*** Well defined or complex and diverse structure, large number of associates/ subsidiaries, major acquisitions or disposals.
3. ***Business deals*:** Transfer pricing transactions supported by documented TP policy or TP agreement.
4. ***Information and internal control systems:*** Consistency and stability of information systems, reliability of outputs, appropriate tax accounting arrangements – tax liabilities correctly calculated.
5. ***Tax management:*** Evidence of capability and willingness to manage their own tax compliance risk.
6. ***Tax contribution*** (24 indicators): *(1) Compliance in corporate income tax*: Tax return on sales; corporate income tax on sales; *(2) Compliance in VAT:* level of VAT paid on taxable transactions; relation between VAT paid and gross added value; and *(3) Economic and financial performance*: equity to asset ratio; return on equity; productivity; increase in gross added value; increase in sales.
7. ***Tax debts.***

Portugal: Risk assessment of large taxpayers

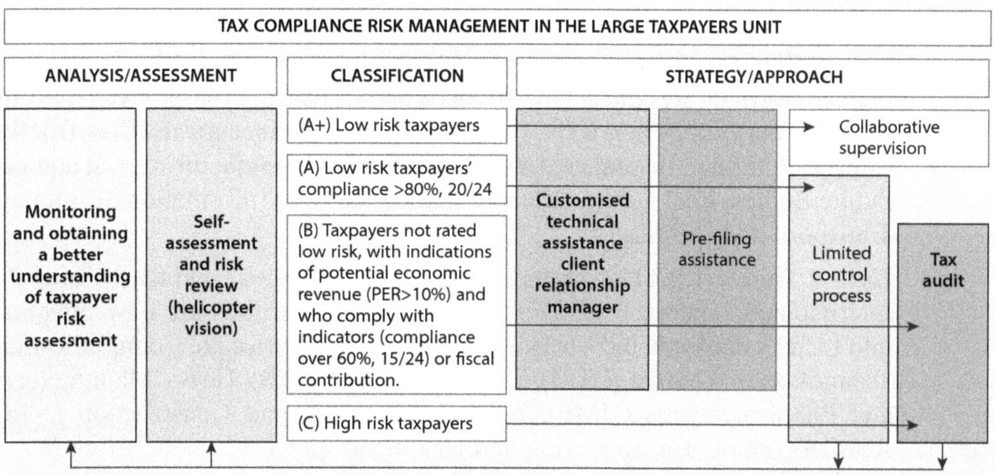

Source: Survey response.

Common and/or important features of large taxpayer units

Prior work by the FTA has identified a number of fairly common and/or important features concerning the organisation and management of LTU:

- An LTU's responsibilities tend to cover both direct and indirect taxes, enabling a "whole of taxpayer" focus to be given to administering taxpayers' affairs.
- Business units typically provide both service and verification functions; reflecting this and the significant revenue and compliance risks they are responsible for, considerable resources are devoted to large taxpayer administration in many countries (e.g. Argentina, Australia, Canada, Indonesia, Italy, Japan, Mexico, Netherlands, Poland, Russia, South Africa, Spain, Thailand, Turkey, United Kingdom, and United States – see Table 2.6).
- Use of an "account manager" concept to provide designated large businesses with a nominated contact point for interactions with the revenue body.
- Increasing emphasis on the use of co-operative compliance strategies (see Chapter 3 for more information on this development).
- In addition to tax and accounting skills, the inclusion of specialist teams/expertise for support in areas such as industry knowledge, economics, international tax issues and computer-based examination techniques. To optimise performance, considerable emphasis is given to the development of industry knowledge through the use of industry-based teams and experts for key sectors of each country's economy, as is evident from the examples below:
  - ***Ireland:*** Revenue's Large Case Division is sector-based where case managers develop knowledge of how a sector works and build technical sectoral capability. The sector-based focus covers: Alcohol, Tobacco and Multiples; Betting, Food and Media; Financial Services Banking; Financial Services Insurance and Investment Funds; Financial Services Pensions; Information, Communication and Technology; Healthcare and General Manufacturing; Construction, Property, Mining and Energy; Motors, Oils and Transport; as well as specific areas dealing with Anti-Avoidance, High Wealth Individuals and Professionals from the largest accountancy and legal practices.
  - ***Russia:*** There are nine industry-focused inter-regional inspectorates for major taxpayers covering oil, gas, power, metallurgy, communications, transport, engineering, banks and finance, and processing industries and contraction and trade.
  - ***United Kingdom:*** Compliance operations are organised into 17 industry-based sectors: Agriculture and Food, Alcohol and Tobacco, Automotive, Banking, Business Services, Chemicals, Healthcare and Pharmaceuticals, Construction, General Retailing, Insurance, Leisure and Media, Manufacturing, Oil and Gas, Public Bodies, Real Estate, Telecommunications and Information Technology, Transport, and Utilities.
  - ***United States:*** LB&I is organised along six domestic industries and four International functions. LB&I's field specialist functions are now integrated into LB&I's domestic industries. The domestic industries are Communications, Technology and Media (CTM), Financial Services (FS), Heavy Manufacturing and Pharmaceuticals (HMP), Natural Resources and Construction (NRC), Retailers, Food, Transportation and Healthcare (RFTH), Global High Wealth (GHW). The international arm consists of an Assistant Deputy Commissioner, International (ADCI), International Individual Compliance (IIC), International Business Compliance (IBC), and Transfer Pricing Operations (TPO).

Table 2.6. **Large taxpayers: Numbers administered, staff usage and verification results**

Countries	No. of entities administered in 2013	Staff (FTEs)	Verification programme results			
			Number of completed actions		Value of assessments (millions in local currency)	
			2012	2013	2012	2013
OECD countries						
Australia	24 000 /1	1 280	12 405	8 425	2 391	2 353
Austria	9 340	455	4 907	4 535	1 279	823
Belgium	18 011 /1	55	n.a.	n.a.	n.a.	n.a.
Canada	*(1)* 24 000 /1, *(2)* 14 256	*(1)* 556, *(2)* 307	2 125	2 761	3 687	4 210
Chile	1 515	191	833	790	275 251	104 178
Czech Republic	1 452	458	n.a.	174	n.a.	3 462
Denmark	2 000 (in 150 groups)	260	563	383	17 765	22 915
Finland	4 400	156	205	163	44	45
France	37 418	295	5 539	5 849	7 206	6 258
Germany	n.a.	n.a.	41 365	41 746	14 643	13 430
Greece	n.a	105	551	914	299	312
Hungary	1 313	382	3 077	2 994	112 305	140 495
Ireland	8 000 (in 630 groups)	213	1 528 /1	1 994	83	111
Israel	10 155	77 /1	n.a.	n.a.	n.a.	n.a.
Italy	3 200	500	382 /1	361 /1	10 818	7 649
Japan	29 705	2 352	3 357	2 910	94 108	101 086
Mexico	16 685	1 275	1 152	988	59 963	80 858
Netherlands	2 000 /1	700	13 200	10 300	n.a.	n.a.
New Zealand	16 700	177 (E)	586	593	340	638
Norway	4 400 /1	55	n.a.	n.a.	n.a.	n.a.
Poland	71 806	2 417	208 344	196 161	913	1 142
Portugal	924	179	2 037	2 320	677	353
Slovak Republic	626	112	521	1 028	11	8
Slovenia	660	71	248	500	23	15
Spain	3 049	829 /1	n.a.	n.a.	n.a.	n.a.
Sweden	18 713	362	n.a.	n.a.	n.a.	n.a.
Turkey	16 996	813	2 038	3 676	n.a.	n.a.
United Kingdom	800 groups /1	1 185 /1	1 759	1 352	5 000	5 300
United States	250 496 /1	5 111	16 652	15 449	9 705	13 230
Non-OECD countries						
Argentina	897	532 (incl. HNWI)	15 870	20 500	5 590	6 015
Brazil	11 982	154 (E)	2 168	2 647	86 626	152 508
Bulgaria	1 002	164	1 450	1 113	65	22
China	45 144, 45 groups	3 515	13	17	203 000	171 718
Colombia	8 524	279	6 120	2 397	379 693	310 416
Costa Rica	468	63	664	631	16 728	5 909
Croatia	680	112	n.a.	96	n.a.	464
Cyprus	200	11	15	19	19 (b)	4(b)
India	n.a.	n.a.	n.a.	n.a.	n.a.	n.a.
Indonesia	2 730	529	730	2 130	11 147 000	10 242 000
Latvia	1 247	82	536	687	25	76
Lithuania	568	53	1 107	667	22	38
Malaysia	n.a.	n.a	n.a.	n.a.	n.a.	n.a.
Morocco	3 632	40	199	127	2 679	3 374
Romania	1 940	225	1 336	1 073	944	2 559
Russia	16 833	2 717	n.a.	n.a.	95 918	119 288
Saudi Arabia	2 563	94	269	258	3 213	4 198
Singapore	*(1)* 1 600, *(2)* 1 741	*(1)* 53, *(2)* 25	n.a.	n.a.	n.a.	n.a.
South Africa	6 097	570	75	187	43	316
Thailand	2 753	547	n.a.	n.a.	n.a.	n.a.

Note: This table only includes revenue bodies that reported the establishment and operation of a Large Taxpayer Unit.

For notes indicated by "/ (number)", see Notes to Tables section at the end of the chapter, p. 100.

Source: Tax Administration 2015 survey responses.

- As evident from data in Tables 2.6 and 6.8 (Chapter 6), verification checks constitute a major element of an LTU's activities in many countries, often resulting in a high degree of taxpayer coverage and significant tax adjustments.

Managing the tax affairs of high net worth individuals taxpayers

High net worth individuals (HNWIs) are another segment of taxpayers that has drawn the attention of a number of revenue bodies and major banking corporations specialising in wealth management. The FTA's 2009 report *Engaging with High Net Worth Individuals* drew attention to the challenges posed to revenue bodies from this segment of taxpayers, in particular those set out below:

- The HNWI segment consists of high wealth and high income individuals and is of particular interest for revenue bodies because of the: *(1)* complexity of these taxpayers' tax and private affairs and the large numbers of entities many are likely to control; *(2)* amounts of tax revenue at stake; *(3)* the opportunity to undertake aggressive tax planning; and *(4)* impact on the overall integrity of the tax system.
- To improve compliance, revenue bodies could consider changing the structure of their operations to more effectively focus resources, for example, through the creation of a dedicated HNWI unit and to include a focus on the activities of HNWI-related activities.
- Greater international co-operation, at both a strategic and an operational level, would improve the sharing of information and expertise between revenue bodies, particularly on cross-border changes.

Drawing on these conclusions, the study made a number of recommendations, including that revenue bodies could improve the compliance of HNWIs by:

1. Gaining a greater understanding of the risks posed by the HNWI segment by: *(1)* looking at the types of aggressive tax planning (ATP) schemes in the marketplace, the suppliers of ATP, and the HNWIs motivation; and *(2)* developing a strong commercial awareness of the broader concerns of HNWIs, including privacy, wealth preservation and their ability to pass wealth to future generations.
2. Building an effective capability to manage tax risks by establishing an appropriate structure in revenue bodies to deal with HNWIs and focusing resources by: *(1)* creating dedicated units which are adequately staffed by experienced officials; and *(2)* establishing a framework for dialogue between senior revenue officials, HNWIs and their advisers.
3. Improving international co-operation, including the use of regular meetings between heads of HNWI units and other specialists within revenue bodies.
4. Creating an appropriate legislative framework targeted at specific aggressive tax planning risks by taking a holistic approach to focus their strategies.

Dedicated HNWI organisational units and their staff resources

In recommending that revenue bodies set up dedicated organisational units where this was not already the case, the FTA's study made a number of observations as to their rationale that are re-stated below (from page 42 of the study report):

> It is important that tax administrations have regular and continued interaction with the HNWI segment and their advisers on issues such as planning, compliance

and service. This can increase the tax administration's understanding of not only specific taxpayers but also its broader understanding of the HNWI population. It will also help the HNWI segment and their advisers gain an understanding of the tax administration. A tax administration will most effectively gather information on the HNWI segment where it tasks certain parts of its organisation with doing so.

The way in which resources are focussed on the HNWI segment can take a number of forms. The most prevalent is that of a dedicated unit. Advisers clearly stated in the consultation process that this was also their preferred method of dealing with the tax administration in relation to their HNWI clients. Such a unit will typically take responsibility for those taxes that have a direct impact on the HNWI's personal tax liabilities. In some countries the coverage extends further to dealing with associated investment and business entities such as trusts, controlled investment companies and other operating entities, and the unit may also take responsibility for family members to enable the administration to take a wider view of the HNWI.

A dedicated unit is not a goal in itself but is a delivery vehicle that serves several functions: it sends a clear message to the non-compliant HNWI that he or she faces a real risk of being pursued by the tax administration which may in turn reduce aggressive behaviour and improve voluntary compliance; it enables a tax administration to match the level of expertise and knowledge of the HNWI's advisers in addition to developing the commercial awareness of tax administration staff; and it also allows for the concentration of skills, targeted training, the retention of knowledge and thus an improvement over time of the understanding of the HNWI population. A dedicated unit can be monitored, and further improved, more easily than when resources are spread.

Emerging trends in the growth and wealth of HNWIs

The FTA's May 2009 report on HNWIs observed that this taxpayer segment should be of interest to revenue bodies given the complexity of their affairs and the tax revenue potentially at stake from any non-compliance. However, it did not attempt to quantify the possible scale of this risk or to provide data on the likely population or wealth of HNWI taxpayers across member countries.

As for previous editions of this series, research was carried out of external sources to identify trends in the growth and wealth of HNWIs, based on definitions used by the organisations concerned. A useful source of information found on this matter is the report produced by Capgemini and RBC Wealth Management and published under the title *World Wealth Report*.[4] The 2014 edition of the report is the source of data used in the series and some of its key findings and observations are set out in Box 2.6. Importantly:

- Overall, significant growth in both the numbers and wealth of HNWIs across all regions with the exception of Latin America
- Significant growth in the estimated numbers of HNWIs for a fair number of countries covered by this series – in particular, the United States, Japan, Germany, China, United Kingdom, Switzerland, Italy, South Korea, Netherlands, Spain, Saudi Arabia, and Norway.

Other research sources (i.e. Crédit Suisse's Global Wealth Report 2013) provide additional perspectives on the growth and distribution of wealth, including for HNWIs, although using different classifying criteria and data sources.

Taken as a whole, the findings of the abovementioned research, assuming their general accuracy, lend support to the findings of the FTA's 2009 study and the need for revenue bodies to be vigilant in respect of this segment of taxpayers.

Box 2.6. The state of the world's wealth: Some recent research findings

The authors of the *World Wealth Report* define HNWIs as individuals with investable wealth in excess of USD 1 million, while a threshold of USD 30 million is applied to define the category "ultra-HNWIs". Some key findings from their 2014 research are set out hereunder:

Key findings (overall)

- **HNWI ranks expanded by nearly two million individuals in 2013, marking a 15% growth rate and the second largest increase since 2000.** North America and Asia-Pacific continued to lead the way, with Japan's HNWI population witnessing significant growth.
- **HNWI wealth grew by almost 14% to reach a second-consecutive record high of USD 52.62 trillion in 2013, building on a strong five-year trend.** Over the past five years, HNWI wealth globally increased by nearly USD 20 trillion, USD 2 trillion more than the total HNWI wealth in all of Asia-Pacific, the Middle East, and Africa.
- **Ultra-HNWI population and wealth growth in 2013 outperformed other wealth bands in all regions except Latin America.** The slow growth in Latin America, which holds the largest percentage of ultra-HNWI wealth (32.9%), constrained the global figure in 2013 and also over the last five years.
- **Three clear HNWI performance clusters have emerged among the top 25 markets since the crisis in 2008, with the above-average growth country cluster representing a diverse mix of markets.** Oil-rich Norway and Kuwait, the financial centres of Hong Kong and Singapore, and the emerging economic powerhouses of China, India, Russia, and Taiwan comprise the above-average growth cluster. Latin America and the Eurozone, meanwhile, have lagged.
- **HNWI wealth is expected to reach another record of USD 64.3 trillion by 2016, representing 22% growth over 2013 and almost USD 12 trillion in new HNWI wealth.** Growth is expected to be driven by robust expansion in most regions, though Asia-Pacific will lead the way with 9.8%. Asia-Pacific is still expected to have the largest HNWI population by 2014 and the most wealth by 2015.
- While numbering only 128 000 world-wide (and 0.9% of HNWIs), **ultra-HNWIs account for more than one-third (34.6%) of global HNWI wealth**; mid-tier millionaires with USD 5-30 million of assets number 1.2 million (9% of HNWI population) and 22.3% of wealth. The largest group by far and with assets of USD 1-5 million, numbering around 12.4 million and making up 90.1% of the total) hold 43.1 % of global wealth.

Box 2.6. **The state of the world's wealth: Some recent research findings** *(continued)*

Key findings (individual countries)

The data below identifies the top 25 individual countries according to estimated numbers of HNWIs in 2013. Also displayed is the estimated growth in numbers that occurred between 2012 and 2013.

Top 25 HNWI Population Ranking, 2013

Country	No. of HNWIs (000's)	% growth over 2012	Country	No. of HNWIs (000's)	% growth over 2012
United States	4 006	16.6	Spain	161	11.6
Japan	2 327	22.3	Russia	160	4.3
Germany	1 130	11.4	India	156	2.0
China	758	17.8	Saudi Arabia	151	16.4
United Kingdom	527	13.4	Mexico	130	-1.2
France	472	9.7	Kuwait	125	21.2
Switzerland	330	16.8	Hong Kong	124	9.4
Canada	320	7.2	Norway	120	11.4
Australia	219	5.8	Taiwan	112	17.4
Italy	203	15.6	Argentina	109	7.5
South Korea	176	10.3	Austria	108	9.4
Netherlands	173	16.5	Singapore	105	4.5
Brazil	172	4.1			

Source: Capgemini Financial Services Analysis, 2014 (as published in World Wealth Report 2014).

The approaches of revenue bodies in 2014

For the purpose of this series participating countries were surveyed on whether any special steps had been taken to create dedicated HNWI units, what resources were being devoted to the administration of HNWI taxpayers, the criteria used to identify HNWIs and related entities and the numbers of HNWIs being administered, and the results of related verification activities.

Information concerning the operation of dedicated units to administer HNWIs, as viewed from the survey, is set out in Table 2.7. The key observations and findings are:

- While there are some indications of increased attention being given to this segment, relatively few revenue bodies have established dedicated units to oversee the tax affairs of HNWIs, a surprising outcome given the very significant growth in the estimated numbers and wealth of these taxpayers, as indicated by external studies. Some background to the US IRS's rationale and approach to its management of high-wealth taxpayers is set out in Box 2.7.
- For those revenue bodies with dedicated HNWI units, the scale of these units varies significantly in terms of the numbers of HNWIs administered and the resources used, suggesting substantial differences in the roles and range of functions carried

out by the respective units and the intensity of related verification activities; a number of countries reported that their HNWI segment taxpayers are administered within their large taxpayer units.

- Resource usage data suggest relatively sizeable operations in Australia, Greece, Indonesia, United Kingdom, and United States.
- The criteria used by revenue bodies to identify their HNWI taxpayers tend to focus primarily on estimated wealth/asset levels of the taxpayers concerned.
- Not all revenue bodies with dedicated units reported verification outputs meaning there is insufficient information for any level of comparison.

Given the indications of growth in recent years in the numbers and wealthy individuals referenced in Box 2.6 and the relatively small number of revenue bodies reporting they have dedicated units to deal with such taxpayers (however defined at the individual country level), there would seem a case for most revenue bodies to consider whether they have the appropriate organisational and management arrangements in place to ensure that this segment of taxpayers receives the appropriate level of scrutiny to detect and deter non-compliance.

Box 2.7. The United State IRS's Global High Wealth area

The LB&I global high-wealth (GHW) industry area began operations in November 2009 and was formed to take a holistic approach in examining high-wealth individuals. An individual Form 1040 is at the centre of each GHW audit, and GHW employs an enterprise approach to its audits, considering the relationship and compliance risk inherent in all entities connected to the high-wealth individual. The enterprise approach is necessary because examinations on a return-by-return or year-by-year basis fall short of providing a complete picture of the tax compliance of individuals and the enterprises they control.

Source: IRS survey response.

Table 2.7. **Revenue bodies with dedicated high net worth individuals dedicated units – operational data for 2012 and 2013**

Country	Criteria applied to identify HNWI taxpayers	No. of taxpayers administered in 2013	Staff (FTEs) used in 2013	Verification programme results: Number of completed actions 2012	2013	Value of assessments (in millions in local currency) 2012	2013
OECD countries							
Australia	Individuals with net wealth over AUD 30 m	2 600	300	505	731	889	1 091
Canada	Individuals who either alone or together with related parties control a net worth of at least CAD 50 m. Entities owned by HNWIs that are already identified as part of the Large Files programme are excluded from the HNWI initiative usually performed by Aggressive Tax Planning auditors.	630 groups (Est) /1	50 /2	(HNWI workload was conducted within the Large Business Audit Division during the 2012 and 2013 operational period, the results of which are included in overall large taxpayer figures. The HNWI workload is now conducted in the Aggressive Tax Planning programme.)			
France	(see Footnote 1 for Table 2.1)						

Table 2.7. **Revenue bodies with dedicated high net worth individuals dedicated units – operational data for 2012 and 2013** *(continued)*

Country	Criteria applied to identify HNWI taxpayers	No. of taxpayers administered in 2013	Staff (FTEs) used in 2013	Verification programme results: Number of completed actions 2012	Number of completed actions 2013	Value of assessments (in millions in local currency) 2012	Value of assessments (in millions in local currency) 2013
Greece	/1	n.a	125	495	454	22	73
Ireland	Individuals with assets over EUR 50 m and non-residents with substantial economic interests in Ireland	496 /1	21	196	344	0.1 /2	0.5
Japan	*(Confidential)*	252	64	4 572	4 120	12 000	10 100
New Zealand	Taxpayers with complex tax affairs. Usually with assets over NZD 50 m. Most have over 30 entities associated with them.	194	9 (est.)	17	18	50 /2	90 /2
Portugal	Income over EUR 5 m and wealth over EUR 25 m	191	3	n.a	n.a	n.a	n.a
Spain /1	***Assigned by decision of Head of the Service for Planning and Institutional Relations (following a proposal of the Head of the Large taxpayers Office)***: Income over EUR 1 m or personal assets over EUR 10 m, or individuals/ partners related to other large taxpayers or who manage complex economic transactions.	212	/1	n.a	n.a	n.a	n.a
United Kingdom	Assets over GBP 20 m	6 100	375	1 389	1 822	200	222
United States	Individuals with tens of millions of USD of assets or income /1	n/a	119	n.a	n.a	n.a	n.a
Non-OECD countries							
Argentina	Mix of assets and securities, tax paid, annual sales, VAT debt, economic sector and no. of employees	1 143	(With large taxpayers)	2 034	3 440	326	523
Brazil	The specific criteria are not made public	4 428	34	188	275	898	1 791
Indonesia	Weighted average of tax payment (80%) and income (20%) for last three fiscal years, and DGT discretion	1 509	132	51	307	138	616
Malaysia	Individuals with statutory income equal or over MYR 1 m, assets equal or over MYR 5 m, or both together equal or over MYR 5 m	36 /1	13	(Separate results data not available.)			
Romania	Individuals who control over EUR 20 m in wealth or with annual reported income over EUR 3 m	433	30	(Separate results data not available.)			
South Africa	Gross income over ZAR 7 m and / or unencumbered assets over ZAR 75 m in respect of individuals linked to large corporate taxpayers	468	10	?	?	?	?

For notes indicated by "/ (number)", see Notes to Tables section at the end of the chapter, p. 101.

Source: Tax Administration 2015 survey responses.

Notes

1. The "Zakat" is a levy applied at a flat rate of 2.5% on the net worth (not net income) of Saudi natural persons, wholly Saudi owned companies, and Saudi partners in joint ventures (except for rain-fed agricultural products and irrigated agricultural products for which the rate is 10% and 5% respectively).

2. For this series, a reasonably broad definition is taken of what constitutes "headquarters functions"; that is, it includes all functions that support national planning and operations, including the national executive and programme policy development and management, as well as all support functions such as information technology operations, human resource management, public relations, security, finance, and internal audit.

3. Both the FTA report and this series use the term "High Net Worth Individuals" (HNWIs) to refer to individuals at the top of the wealth or income scale. The term is used broadly and thus includes both high wealth and high income individuals. However, it is recognised that there are segments within this broad definition that display different characteristics and may, therefore, require different administrative responses from revenue bodies.

4. For their purposes, the authors use a proprietary methodology which defines HNWIs as those individuals having investable assets of USD 1 million or more. For "ultra-HNWIs", the investable assets criterion is set at USD 30 million. Details of the methodology are elaborated in the author's report.

Notes to Tables

Table 2.1. Selected features of the organisational structure of revenue bodies

/1. **Austria:** Federal Computing Centre of Austria acts as e-Government partner of the public administration and is the IT service provider for Austrian public administration. **Brazil:** There are also specialised offices based on taxpayer segment criteria, such as: large taxpayers, HNWI, and Financial Institutions. **Canada:** HNWI workload is conducted within the Aggressive Tax Planning programme. **Chile:** Re HNWI, this is a new function created in October 2014 within the Auditing Division, in charge of monitoring HNWI and company directors. Re enforced debt collection, primary responsibility rests with Treasury. **Cyprus**: For VAT only. **Czech Republic**: Except for Real Estate Transfer Tax. **Finland:** IT operations are largely outsourced. **France**: The tax administration does not have a specific service to manage HNWI taxpayers' situation – it is done by local services. Its HNWI Unit called DNVSF (National Directorate of Fiscal Situation Audits) is exclusively dedicated to audits and shared between regular HNWIs' and "Top HNWIs". **Greece: A** HNWI Audit Centre has operated to deal exclusively with HNWI taxpayers since around mid-2013; a Directorate for Dispute Resolution was established early in 2014. **Hungary:** Several organisational units of the NTCA are responsible for this task. **Ireland:** Revenue does not have a dedicated unit in charge of appeals disputes, although does have an Appeals function. Customers may lodge complaints at their local office, submit their case for internal or external review and/or make an appeal under statutory provisions (via the Appeals Commissioners, Ombudsman's Office or the Equality Tribunal). **Israel**: A dedicated unit exists only for real estate taxation within the regional offices of some major districts. **Italy:** The Revenue Agency has a Central Anti-fraud Unit for: *(1)* analysis of widespread fraud in tax and development of law enforcement strategies, tax avoidance and resulting operational methods; *(2)* co-ordination and monitoring of control activities linked to widespread fraud and conducted in the territory; and *(3)* conducting investigations and audits at national level on major fraud; however, the Financial Police (Guardia di Finanza) by virtue of its primary role of economic and financial police plays the central role in dealing with serious criminal tax evasion cases, under direction of Prosecutor Offices. To tackle international tax fraud, tax evasion and tax avoidance the Central Assessment Directorate works the Central Office on Combating International Tax Illicit (U.C.I.F.I.) – with tasks of direction and co-ordination of the fight of international tax evasion, with the assistance of the Finance Police.

One of several tasks the office is involved is the identification of the phenomena of illicit transfer or holding financial and economic activities abroad or residence transferred abroad in order to receive a favourable taxation and to lead to unlawful evasion of tax; the office defines the strategies to combat international fiscal illicit and the related operative methodologies; and it carries out controls and investigations on the major relevant and dangerous phenomena. **Korea**: Large taxpayer unit at regional level only. **Lithuania:** Separate IT department provides all internal services and systems support, while all systems development is carried out by external companies. **Malaysia:** Special Units in branches to handle tax cases related to HNWIs and VIP/Staff. **Mexico**: The General Administration of Communications and Information Technologies is responsible for IT-functions. Some of the software and system developments are outsourced. **Netherlands**: A dedicated cross-segment team was established in 2014, tasked with developing an integrated HNWI compliance strategy for the NTCA. **Portgual**: A working group has been created to deal with HNWI. **Singapore**: There are separate large taxpayer departments for Corporate Tax and Goods and Services Tax. **Slovak Republic:** There is one Large Taxpayer Office in Bratislava for all the Slovak Republic territory. **Spain**: HNWI taxpayers can be assigned to the Large Taxpayers Central Office under certain circumstances by the Head of the Service for Planning and Institutional Relations; other wealthy taxpayers are managed by provincial offices or, where appropriate, regional offices.

/2. **Canada:** Although a portion of information technology services are provided by Shared services Canada, the CRA has an information technology branch responsible for business application systems and infrastructure. **Italy:** IT services are delivered by an IT company (Sogei) fully owned by the Ministry of the Economy and Finance. A dedicated Unit in the Revenue Agency manages relations with Sogei. **Korea**: Debt collection unit at regional level only (only for large taxpayers); there is a Forensic and Anti-tax Evasion Office at the regional level. **Spain:** The Tax Appeals Courts (central and regional level) are part of the Ministry of Finance and Public Administration, independent of the Tax Agency.

Table 2.3. Office network for tax administration – office types by number (end of 2013)

/1. **Australia: Ten** regional offices are to be closed by 31 October 2014. **Belgium**: Contact centre (2 temporary sections during peak season). **Brazil**: 544 Federal Revenue Offices and 14 Federal Revenue Judgement Offices. **Canada:** One regional data processing centre is co-located within a local office; one call centre is co-located within a data centre and one other is co-located within a local office. **China**: Regional offices include offices of provincial level and offices of municipality directly under the central government. **Costa Rica**: The Tax Administration's call centre started operations in February 2014 and is still under development. Currently, it is only working for one of the local offices. **Croatia**: The national data processing centre is outsourced and part of the "Information Systems and Information Technologies Support Agency". **Cyprus:** There are separate departments/offices at all levels for direct and indirect taxes. **Czech Republic:** Appellate Financial Directorate. **Denmark:** SKAT is headed by a Director General. It has 29 nationwide branches (including one call centre) and the 29 branches are organised in 6 nationwide divisions, each headed by a Deputy Director General. SKAT has no formal headquarters, with traditional HQ functions such as administrative policy development, process design, financial management, IT and national oversight embedded in the 6 nationwide divisions. **France:** These offices include the Large Business Directorate, National and International Tax Audit Directorate, National Tax Investigations Directorate, National Tax Situation Tax Audit Directorate, National Directorate for State Property Operations and the Directorate for Residents Abroad and General Services. **Germany:** There are 16 decentralised Lander administrations. **Hungary:** Criminal Affairs Directorate General, Institute for Training, Healthcare and Culture. **India**: There are also 36 Regional Computer Centres. **Israel**: Local offices exist separately for IT/VAT and Excise/Real Estate/Investigations. **Korea**: National Tax Officials Training Institute and NTS Liquors License Aid Centre. **Luxembourg:** There are separate departments/offices at all levels for direct and indirect taxes. For 2015, it is expected that the number of local offices dealing with indirect taxes (40 offices) will be reduced without impact on general staffing levels. **Malta:** Taxes are administered by three separate departments that are to be integrated into one organisation over the next 2 to 3 years. **Malaysia:** Comprised of 36 assessment branches, 17 investigation branches and 24 revenue service centres (stamp duty and counter services in sub-urban/rural areas). **Mexico**: These are customs offices. **Netherlands:** Headquarters is the Directorate General; Taxes Division is led by a dedicated head office. The Centre for Professional Education and Communication, Fiscal Investigation and Information Service, Facility Management Unit and IT-departments are labelled under "other offices". **Norway:** Following an office reduction project the network was reduced from 225 offices (at beginning of 2011) to 108 in 2013. **Portugal**: Data for call centres are also included in aggregates for headquarters and regional and local offices. **Romania**: Data processing centres and call centres are organised under national headquarters. **Russia**: This includes, interregional inspectorates for large taxpayers, federal districts and on transfer pricing. **Slovak Republic**: Regional offices are settled in the seats of the Higher Territorial Units and the local offices are the organisational units of these regional offices (the tax and the customs branches). They are settled in different cities than seats of Higher Territorial Units; **Slovenia**: On

1 July 2013, the territorial organisation of tax offices of the Slovenian Tax Organisation changed as a result of which local branches of regional tax offices were transformed into tax desks (41), which perform their activities on dis-located locations. **South Africa:** Data includes customs operations. **Spain:** Office of the Director General, 11 Departments, Large Taxpayer Office, National Office for Fraud Investigation, International Taxation Office. **Sweden:** There are 103 service offices in co-operation with a few other state agencies. **United States**: The breakdown and number of offices is based on the number of "Fund Centres." This is not the same as physical facilities (of which there are 634); often several business units have "offices" in the same building but with different Fund Centres; conversely, some Business Units assign many physical locations to a single Fund Center. Each Business Unit has a different level of detail by "office" represented. Therefore, the breakdown provided is an approximate estimate only.

/2. **Brazil**: The tax administration does not have its own data processing centres, the service is provided by a public enterprise (Federal Service of Data Processing – Serpro). **China**: Local offices include offices of municipal level and offices of district level and county level directed by provincial offices; **Croatia:** Office for large taxpayers. **Cyprus:** There are 5 data processing centres, using self-employed staff, for direct taxes administration. The "other" office is the Valuation of Immovable Property Office. **Germany**: 28 call centres are located in 1 (Hesse) of the 16 Länder. **Norway:** Petroleum Taxation Office. **Spain:** There are 17 regional offices, 39 provincial offices, 192 local tax offices, and 31 customs and excise local offices; calls centres are supported by a basic information service that is partly outsourced to external companies, and reinforced during campaign periods. **United States**: Includes both the IRS's central computing centre and the large tax return submission centres.

Table 2.4. Office network for tax administration – office types by number of staff (end of 2013)

/1. **Argentina:** Staffing aggregates include all customs and social security staff. For SSC functions, AFIP administers the collection and tax examination of SSC within its Social Security General Directorate. **Brazil:** 20 638 in Federal Revenue Offices and 800 in Federal Revenue Judgement Offices. **Canada:** Reflects tax-administration related employees (excludes Benefits Programmes). **Cyprus**: Staff usage figures cover both direct and indirect taxes, administered separately. **Denmark:** See comment for Table 2.3. **France**: The aggregate corresponds to staff that are used only for tax functions; the entire DGFIP, dealing with other functions is 76 175 FTEs. **Hungary:** Aggregate data includes Customs operations; data for call centres are also included in aggregates for headquarters and regional offices where they are located; **Israel:** Staff aggregates include Customs. The data does not include students working temporarily in part-time jobs. In 2013, around 420 student FTEs were employed. **Lithuania**: These aggregates are included in HQ aggregate. **Luxembourg**: Staff usage figures are not expressed in full-time equivalent. They cover both direct and indirect taxes, administered separately**;** **Mexico**: National processing and call centre operations are outsourced-numbers shown are SAT's supervisors. **Netherlands**: Aggregate amount includes staff at the Centre for Professional Education and Communication (373 FTEs); Fiscal Investigation and Information Service (986 FTEs); Facility Management Unit (804 FTEs); IT departments (1 529 FTEs) which are not defined as headquarters in the Netherlands. **New Zealand**: Staff aggregates estimated on the basis of a 65/35% allocation between tax and non-tax activity. **Norway**: Excludes services and administrative staff. **Portugal**: Data for call centres are included in aggregates for headquarters and regional and local offices. **South Africa**: Data aggregates include customs operations; other offices FTEs are principally customs operations. **Spain**: National processing centre staff in headquarters data. **Sweden**: Staff FTEs of one data processing centre (722) in head office data and staff FTEs of one call centre (ca. 400) in regional/local office data. **United Kingdom**: In addition to staff in table categories, there is an additional 258 FTE in non-office accommodation (stores/garages).

/2. **Spain:** Includes customs staff (3 829 FTE) that deal with tax issues (e.g. VAT on imports, excises).

Table 2.5. Large taxpayer operations: Identification criteria used in 2013

/1. **Canada:** The Indirect Taxes (GST/HST) category includes: GST/HST registrants, excluding the Municipalities, Universities, Schools, and Hospitals (MUSH sector), with annual revenue in excess of CAD 100 million; Companies controlled by those large registrants; and Complex non-resident registrants. **Cyprus**: It is expected that the Large Taxpayer Unit will cover both direct taxes and VAT from 1 January 2015. **United Kingdom**: From April 2014, a number of factors will be used to identify large groups including turnover, number of employees and number of entities. As a result the number of groups administered will increase to 2 000. Number of staff will also increase to 2 014;

Table 2.6. Large taxpayers: Number administered, staff usage and verification results

/1. **Australia:** Around 1 250 economic groups encompassing 24 000 entities. **Belgium:** In 2013 only one pilot office in Brussels is managing the large taxpayers located in the Brussels-Capital Region and the large

Taxpayers belonging to a specific economic sector of the whole country. **Canada**: The Income Tax category includes approx. 1 100 large business entities 24 000 controlled entities. **Ireland**: Only for the period May to December 2012. **Israel:** Includes all staff functions in one dedicated large taxpayer office (including support functions) and only operational staff in the dedicated units of two other, mixed, offices. **Netherlands:** There are about 9 000 large businesses of which 2 000 are considered very large taxpayers. Figures refer only to very large taxpayers. **Norway:** About 75 large corporate groups (with about 2 600 companies); in addition, 570 companies in the shipping sector, 133 companies in the energy sector, 248 companies under the CFC regime and some other companies. **Spain**: Resources also include administration of designated large personal taxpayers/HNWIs. **United States**: Number reported is the number of returns filed in 2012 by Corporations (USD 10 m to USD 250 m)-48 059; Corporations (USD 250 m and over)-14 288; Foreign Corporations (USD 10 m and over)-3 247; Partnerships (large business)-144 743; and S Corps (USD 10 m and over)-40 159.

Table 2.7. Revenue bodies with dedicated high net worth individuals' organisational units – Operational data for 2012 and 2013

/1. **Canada**: A current estimate of HWNIs identified is around 630 groups which may include more than one individual. The number of HNWI audited during a particular year is not published. **France**: See notes to Table 2.1. **Greece:** All taxpayers, regardless of income level and nature of income that satisfy following criteria: *(a)* total value of real property exceeds EUR 2 million after 01/2009; *(b)* annual cost of living exceeds EUR 150 000 for 2012; *(3)* expenditure on real estate etc. over EUR 400 000 (2012) and EUR 500 000 (2013); *(4)* with offshore remittances of over EUR 50 000 in 2009-13; *(5)* prescribed foreign persons; and *(6)* other cases entrusted to Interregional Audit Centres (as per Ministerial decision). **Ireland**: 496 HNWIs and Partnerships. **Malaysia**: In 2013, a special task force was set up at the headquarters level consisting of Tax Compliance Department, Intelligence Division and Special Action Department to monitor HNWIs with 13 personnel. 36 HNWIs were monitored and administered by this taskforce in 2013. The 2012 figure (4272 HNWIs excluding VIPS/staff) was based on the 1st criteria only. IRBM also decentralised the VIP/staff unit (previously handling HNWIs) to various branches. **Spain**: Designated HNWIs are administered from within the Large Corporate Taxpayers Division; staff FTEs included in data for Large Corporate Division taxpayers. **United States**: Through the GHW unit within LB&I, the IRS focuses compliance expertise on high income/ high wealth individuals and the enterprises they control. The IRS is in the process of developing a model to define high wealth taxpayers. Note that the majority of IRS data and definition is focused on taxpayer income rather than overall wealth, since the United States does not tax wealth.

/2. **Canada**: The HNWI workload is conducted within the Aggressive Tax Planning programme. **Ireland:** Results for 2012 cover only part of year (from May 2012). **New Zealand**: Amount shown is total value of discrepancies determined, including adjustments for loss reductions and imputation credits.

Bibliography

Capgemini and RBC Wealth Management (2014), *World Wealth Report 2014,* Cap Gemini and RBC Wealth Management.

Credit Suisse (2011), *Global Wealth Report 2011,* Credit Suisse Research Institute, Zurich.

IMF (2014a), *Portugal: Eleventh Review under the Extended Arrangement and Request for Waivers of Applicability of End-March Performance Criteria,* Staff Report, Country Report No. 14/102, International Monetary Fund, Washington.

IMF (2014b), *Romania: First and Second Reviews Under the Stand-By Arrangement and Request for Waiver of Non-observance of a Performance Criterion, Modification of Program Conditionality, and Re-phasing of the Availability Dates of Purchases,* Staff Report, Country Report No. 14/87, International Monetary Fund, Washington.

Kidd, M. (2010), *Revenue Administration: Functionally Organized Administration*, IMF, Washington.

Latvian State Revenue Service (2013), *Annual Report 2012 of the State Revenue Service,* Riga.

OECD (2009), *Engaging with High Net Worth Individuals on Tax Compliance*, OECD Publishing, available at http://dx.doi.org/10.1787/9789264068872-en.

Revenue Department of Thailand (2013), *Annual Report 2012,* Bangkok.

World Bank (2013), *Project Appraisal Document on a Proposed Loan to Romania for a Revenue Administration Modernisation Project*, Washington.

Chapter 3

Selected aspects of strategic management in tax administration

This chapter describes key aspects of revenue bodies' practices for the preparation and publication of strategic plans, and the use of targets and service standards in tax administration. It selectively draws on a sample of revenue bodies' strategic plans covering the medium term out to 2018 to highlight goals, priorities, and key strategies. It concludes with a section on strategic approaches for improving taxpayers' compliance, including a snapshot of work undertaken by the Forum on Tax Administration, and revenue body practice concerning the use of risk management techniques, tax gap research and the random audits programmes.

Key points

Planning and management approaches of revenue bodies

- Just over 60% of revenue bodies reported that there were formal quantified targets set for 2014, with the focal areas being; *(1)* reductions in aggregate tax debt (16 countries); *(2)* improved taxpayer satisfaction (19 countries); and/or *(3)* reductions in administrative expenditure (13 countries).
- The practice of setting formal standards for service delivery was reported by 27 of the 34 OECD revenue bodies surveyed, and by 18 of the 22 non-OECD revenue bodies; however, this observation needs to be treated with a degree of caution as the number of revenue bodies reporting examples of service delivery standards for some of the more routine and voluminous areas of service (e.g. processing returns with refund claims and answering taxpayers' letters and phone inquiries) was considerably less.
- The number of revenue bodies reporting service delivery performance achieved against the standards set by them is disturbingly low, with just on 50% reporting that this practice is followed.
- Viewed across all of the aspects surveyed, there would seem considerable potential to improve related management practices, including the transparency of tax administration (e.g. by publishing plans, performance reports, and/or results of taxpayer surveys), in at least ten surveyed revenue bodies, including seven in OECD countries – Germany, Iceland, Israel, Luxembourg, Slovenia, Switzerland.

Revenue bodies' strategic plans

- Compared to plans reviewed in prior editions, a number of themes appear to be emerging in relation to approaches to performance monitoring and evaluation. First, there appears to be an increased reliance on tax gap estimation methodologies to better inform revenue bodies of their effectiveness. Second, concerning staff engagement revenue bodies in advanced economies appear to be increasingly evaluating their performance against broader public sector trends in staff engagement rather than assessing their own internal performance over time. Third, in line with the emphasis being given to making far greater use of digital technologies to help taxpayers to "self-manage" their tax affairs, new performance measures are emerging.

Managing and improving tax compliance

- Over 90% of revenue bodies reported having a formal process for identifying, assessing, and prioritising their key tax compliance risks; from a tax compliance risk menu of 9 risk categories, the risks most frequently identified were corporate profit shifting/ transfer pricing (37 countries); VAT fraud (36); non-compliance from hidden economy activities (37); other tax avoidance schemes (32); and unpaid tax debts (31)
- Building on the FTA's 2013 study, many revenue bodies are using, testing, or planning to use a co-operative compliance model approach for their largest taxpayers.
- There appears to be a tendency for increased attention by revenue bodies to undertake tax gap measurement exercises for all or their major taxes.
- Just over 50% of revenue bodies reported use of random audit programmes for risk profiling and/or compliance research/ tax gap measurement purposes.
- Nine countries, including a surprising seven OECD countries (i.e. Czech Republic, Italy, Japan, Luxembourg, Poland, Slovak Republic, and Switzerland), reported that they do not administer computer-based income data matching systems for managing taxpayers' compliance.
- Reflecting concerns for the incidence of VAT non-compliance, a relatively large number of revenue bodies, including many in European and Latin/South American countries reported they were using systems to process bulk VAT invoice data for risk profiling and detection purposes.

This chapter provides a brief description of revenue body practices concerning the aspects of planning (e.g. strategic business plans and performance reports, the use of targets, service standards, and surveys of taxpayers), against the background of a number of important trends in public sector management and accountability. It then addresses aspects of revenue bodies' strategic approaches for improving taxpayers' compliance. For both topics, the chapter draws on specific country examples identified in survey responses and/or from OECD Secretariat research to illustrate particular developments, approaches, practices and other information that may be of interest to revenue bodies and other readers.

Managing for improved performance

Developments in the management of public sector agencies

There have been enormous changes in the management of public sector agencies over the last two decades. As outlined in Box 3.1 (OECD, 2005), these changes have included a commitment to open government and increased accountability,[1] more formalised planning approaches (both at the strategic and operational levels), a much increased focus on performance (e.g. performance management and budgeting systems), institutional and organisational restructuring, the use of market-based mechanisms, and modernising employee management arrangements, bringing them more into line with what is seen in the private sector.

Revenue bodies have not been immune to these reform drivers, as evidenced by:

- The increasing practice of preparing and publishing formal strategic business plans, many containing outcomes-focused performance targets and indicators for key goals and objectives;
- The emergence of customer/service charters setting out the nature and standards of service taxpayers can expect;
- The use in some countries of annual performance contracts between the revenue body and the MOF;
- Increased exposure to oversight and review by external bodies (e.g. national audit bodies, ombudsman);
- The preparation and publication of detailed annual performance reports, for some with performance reporting aligned with planned goals and objectives;
- A more structured and systematic approach to the allocation of resources, monitoring resource usage, and evaluating performance;
- Institutional and organisational restructuring designed to drive change and improve efficiency of government operations (as described in Chapters 1 and 2 of this series);
- The use of third party service approaches and user pays mechanisms;
- The introduction of modern human resource management approaches (e.g. contracts, performance pay and management approaches).

And the drive for reforms must inevitably be dynamic in nature. As emphasised in the referenced OECD publication the public sector, and by implication, its constituent agencies face the need to continuously adapt to the challenges of their ever-changing environments:

> Governments must adapt to constantly changing societies. It is not a matter of one-off "reform" but of having a whole-of-government public management policy capability

that enables governments to make adjustments with the total system in mind. Effective public management policies need clear problem diagnosis and outcome evaluation.

Citizens' expectations and demands of governments are growing, not diminishing: they expect openness, higher levels of service quality delivery, solutions to more complex problems, and the maintenance of existing social entitlements. Reforms to the public sector in the past 20 years have significantly improved efficiency, but governments of OECD countries now face a major challenge in finding new efficiency gains that will enable them to fund these growing demands on 21st century government. For the next 20 years, policy makers face hard political choices. Since most governments cannot increase their share of the economy, in some countries this will put pressure on entitlement programmes. These new demands on builders of public management systems will require leadership from officials with enhanced individual technical, managerial and political capacities who think and plan collectively and who can work well with other actors.

Box 3.1. **Key trends in public sector administration reform**

In the past 20 years, governments have made major changes to the way they manage the public sector. Most OECD public administrations have become more efficient, more transparent and customer oriented, more flexible, and more focused on performance. However, public administrative arrangements are inextricably linked to fundamental institutions of public governance. Reformers need to be aware of the possible effects of reforms on wider governance values.

Lessons learnt from key public policy levers

- ***Open government:*** Across OECD member countries, governments are becoming more open and more transparent, accessible and consultative. This phenomenon has found expression through new legislation and institutions and a wide array of policy measures. Today 90% of OECD countries have a Freedom of Information Act and an Ombudsman Office and over 50% have customer service standards.
- ***Enhancing public sector performance:*** Governments have become much more performance focused. The performance movement has increased formalised planning, reporting and control across many governments. Most OECD countries have introduced performance management and budgeting. In 2005, 72% included non-financial performance data in their budget documentation. Thus information available to managers and policy makers has both increased and improved.
- ***Modernising accountability and control:*** How governments keep control over large and complex operations has changed over the past 15 years because of technological innovations, changes in the size and structure of government, and the introduction of performance budgeting and management. The main trends in control across OECD countries are the move from *ex ante* to *ex post* control, and the development of stronger processes of internal control. In practice there is a move from the inefficient but relative certainty of checking the regularity and legality of individual transactions to the more efficient but relative uncertainty of verifying the proper operation of systems. The challenge is to maintain control in systems that are more delegated, with more autonomous agencies and third-party providers.

Box 3.1. **Key trends in public sector administration reform** *(continued)*

- ***Reallocation and restructuring:*** The need for government to set outer limits for expenditure and to reallocate within those limits has changed national budgeting from a support function to the primary vehicle for strategic management. The budget process is also frequently used as a vehicle for wider managerial reform. The ability to change organisational structures is essential for a modern government. However, structural change – either the dismantling of existing organisations or the creation of new ones – should not be undertaken lightly. Dismantling organisations can lead to a loss of continuity, of institutional memory and of long-term capacity. The proliferation of more or less autonomous arm's-length public bodies makes collective action and co-ordination difficult. Governments should understand the structural strengths and weaknesses of their existing systems and build on their strengths.
- ***The use of market-type mechanisms:*** Market-type mechanisms of various kinds have become more common across OECD member countries, although there are marked country differences in their use. These mechanisms have the potential to produce significant efficiency gains. The decision to use market-type mechanisms needs, however, to be made on a case-by-case basis, and the specific design of these instruments is critical to their successful application. It remains important to protect key governance principles, not to confuse private gain and public interest or to obscure public responsibility or accountability. Governments must protect their freedom for future action if priorities change.
- ***Modernising public employment:*** The nature of public employment in OECD countries has evolved significantly. In many countries the employment arrangements of public servants have become more like those of the private sector by altering the legal status and employment conditions. Individualised employment policies have become increasingly common; these include the introduction of contracts and performance-related pay, the latter now being implemented in two-thirds of OECD countries.

The implementation of these policies tends to make a collective culture more difficult to achieve. Early reformers underestimated the complexity of introducing private sector techniques into the public service. Staying with traditional public employment arrangements, however, is not a feasible option for most countries.

Source: Modernising Government: The Way Forward, OECD (2005).

Planning and management approaches of revenue bodies

For the purpose of this series, revenue bodies were asked to answer a number of general questions concerning aspects of their planning processes (e.g. setting of goals and targets, preparation of a strategic plan and/or annual performance reports). Survey responses were supplemented by research of publicly-available strategic plans and annual performance report documents of a representative sample of revenue bodies to identify any common approaches, the key tax issues being addressed, shed some light on emerging practices in the setting of high level goals and objectives, targets and related performance measures, and to gain some insights as to the degree of transparency of revenue bodies in their planning processes and performance reporting.

A summary of revenue bodies' responses is provided in Tables 3.1 and 3.2. The key observations and findings from the responses and related research are as follows:

- With few exceptions, all revenue bodies reported that they prepare a multi-year business plan, although the number indicating that such plans were made public was less than 80%; the majority of revenue bodies not disclosing their plans were the less autonomous forms of institutions described in Chapter 1.

Table 3.1. **Selected management practices: business plans, annual reports, surveys**

	Selected management practices of revenue body								
	Business plan		Annual report		Service delivery standards			Surveys of taxpayers	
Country	Prepared	Made public	Prepared	Made public	Set	Made public	Results published	Citizens	Business
OECD countries									
Australia	✓	✓	✓	✓	✓	✓	✓	✓	✓
Austria	✓	x	✓	✓	✓	✓	✓	✓	✓
Belgium	✓ /1	✓	✓	✓	✓	x	x	x	x
Canada	✓	✓ /1	✓	✓	✓	✓	✓	✓	✓
Chile	✓	x	✓	✓ /1	✓	✓	x	✓ /2	✓ /2
Czech Republic	✓	✓	✓	✓	x	x	x	✓	✓
Denmark	✓	✓	✓	✓	x	x	x	✓	✓
Estonia	x	x	✓ /1	✓ /1	✓	✓	✓	✓	✓
Finland	✓	✓	✓	✓	✓	✓	✓	✓	✓
France	✓	✓	✓	✓	✓	✓	✓	✓	✓
Germany	x	x	x	x	x	x	x	✓	✓
Greece	✓	✓	✓	✓	✓	x	✓	x	x
Hungary	✓	✓	✓	✓	✓	✓	✓	x	x
Iceland	✓	x	✓	✓	x	x	x	x	x
Ireland	✓	✓	✓	✓	✓	✓	✓	✓	✓
Israel	✓	x	✓	✓ /1	x	x	x	x	x
Italy	✓	✓	✓	✓	✓	✓	x	✓	✓
Japan	x	x	✓	✓	✓	✓	✓	✓	✓
Korea	✓	✓	✓	✓	✓	✓	x	✓ /1	✓ /1
Luxembourg	x	x	✓	✓	x	x	x	x	x
Mexico	✓	✓	✓	✓	✓	✓	✓	✓	✓
Netherlands	✓	x /1	✓	✓ /2	✓	✓ /2	✓ /2	✓	✓
New Zealand	✓	✓	✓	✓	✓	✓	✓	✓	✓
Norway	✓	✓	✓	✓	✓	✓	✓	✓	✓
Poland	✓	✓	✓	✓	✓	✓	x	✓	✓
Portugal	✓	✓	✓	✓	✓	✓	✓	✓	✓
Slovak Republic	✓	✓	✓	✓	✓	✓	✓	x	x
Slovenia	✓	x	✓	✓	x	x	x	x	x
Spain	✓	✓	✓	✓	✓	✓	✓	✓ /1	✓
Sweden	✓	✓	✓	✓	✓	x	x	✓	✓
Switzerland	✓	x	✓	x	✓	x	x	✓ /1	✓
Turkey	✓	x	✓	✓	✓	✓	✓	✓ /1	✓ /1
United Kingdom	✓	✓	✓	✓	✓	✓	✓	✓	✓
United States	✓	✓	✓	✓	✓	✓	✓	✓	✓
Non-OECD countries									
Argentina	✓ /1	✓	✓	✓ /2	✓	✓	x	✓	✓
Brazil	✓ /1	✓	✓	✓	✓	✓ /2	✓	✓	✓
Bulgaria	✓	✓ /1	✓	✓	✓	✓	x	✓	✓
China	✓	x	✓	✓	✓	✓	✓	✓	✓
Colombia	✓	✓	✓	✓	✓	✓	✓	✓	✓
Costa Rica	✓	x	✓	x	✓	x	x	x	x
Croatia	✓	✓	✓	✓ /1	x /2	x /2	x	✓	✓
Cyprus	✓	x	✓	✓ /1	✓	✓	x	x	x
Hong Kong, China	✓	✓	✓	✓	✓	✓	✓	✓	✓
India	✓	✓	✓	✓	✓	✓	✓	✓	✓
Indonesia	✓	✓	✓	✓	✓	✓	x	✓	✓
Latvia	✓	✓	✓	✓	✓	✓	x	✓	✓
Lithuania	✓	✓	✓	x /1	✓	✓	✓	✓	✓
Malaysia	✓ /1	✓	✓	✓	✓	✓	✓	✓	✓
Malta	✓	✓	✓	✓	✓	✓	x	x	x
Morocco	✓	x	✓	✓	✓	✓ /1	x	✓ /2	✓ /2
Romania	✓	✓	✓	✓	✓	✓	✓	✓	✓
Russia	✓ /1	✓	✓ /1	✓ /2	✓	✓	x	✓	✓
Saudi Arabia	x	x	✓	✓	x /1	x	x	✓	✓
Singapore	✓	x	✓	✓	✓	✓	✓	✓	✓
South Africa	✓	✓	✓	✓	✓	✓	x	x	x
Thailand	✓	✓	✓	✓	✓	✓	✓	✓	✓

For notes indicated by "/ (number)", see Notes to Tables section at the end of the chapter, p. 137.
Source: Tax Administration 2015 survey responses.

- Just over 60% of revenue bodies reported that there were formal quantified targets set for 2014 in one or more of the following areas:
  - Reductions in aggregate tax debt (17 countries);
  - Reductions in tax gap (four countries);
  - Improved taxpayer satisfaction (19 countries);
  - Reductions in administrative burden (8 countries); and
  - Reductions in administrative expenditure (13 countries).
- Details of specific targets reported by revenue bodies are summarised in Table 3.2. In comparison with prior series, the practice of setting high level targets (and reporting performance against them) appears to be growing, possibly in part as a result of increased pressures from Government for improved performance and increased external scrutiny.
- Understanding taxpayers' satisfaction with services and their overall perceptions of revenue bodies' administration was the most commonly identified targeted area and its importance is apparent from the published comments and reports of revenue bodies, for example, Latvia and New Zealand:

  > To my mind, one of the most essential indicators in performance evaluation of any institution or company is the judgment of the customers regarding the performance of the institution or company and the quality of services rendered to them (Latvian State Revenue Service, 2013).

  > Ensuring that our customers are satisfied with our services contributes to voluntary compliance. In 2013–14, 79% of customers thought we made it easy to get it right, and 82% of our customers were confident that we were fair (New Zealand Inland Revenue, 2014).
- The practice of preparing an annual performance report was reported by over 90% of revenue bodies; in a few cases involving the less autonomous forms of institutional setups (e.g. Estonia and Netherlands), performance related information is reported via reports of the MOF, in some cases that are formally made to the Government; while not the subject of detailed analysis, the

  Secretariat's research over many years suggests there are considerable variations in the scope and nature of information disclosed in annual performance reports, with some failing to disclose important information on aspects of tax administration (e.g. "outcome-focused" measures, service delivery performance, and the incidence of tax debts).
- The practice of setting formal standards for service delivery was reported by 26 of the 34 OECD revenue bodies surveyed, and by 18 of the 22 non-OECD revenue bodies; however, this observation needs to be treated with a degree of caution as the number of revenue bodies reporting examples of service delivery standards for some of the more routine and voluminous areas of service (e.g. processing returns with refund claims and answering taxpayers' letters and phone inquiries) was considerably less.

  Further information on the more commonly used service standards and the levels of performance achieved is provided in Chapter 6.

Table 3.2. **Quantified targets reported by revenue bodies for key areas of performance**

1. Tax debt reduction

Description of targets reported	Country
Recovery of unpaid debts – goal of 83% (i.e. % of amounts paid after due date compared to amounts not paid on time).	Argentina
Rate of collected debt/ newly established debt (2014) exceeds corresponding ratio for 2013	Bulgaria
Target (2014): A reduction in the collectable debt for other areas than tax and tariffs. The target is to achieve a debt collection percentage of 110.	Denmark
Reduction in debt of 15-20 million euros per annum	Estonia
A number of voluntary payment targets are set that indirectly relate to reducing the incidence of tax debt, e.g. *(1)* for individuals, 98.5% of liabilities raised in 2014 are collected in 2014; and *(2)* for business, 98% of taxes due are collected by the due date (NB: rates do not apply to amounts collected after tax audits).	France
Based on a formula for the financial year; for 2014, target is to collect INR 610 180 million of opening arrears debt + 30% of the current debt raised during the financial year	India
35% reduction in aggregate tax debt outstanding	Indonesia
Annual target of 25% reduction of the largest outstanding debts set for the local Income Tax offices. For VAT, target depends on the number of employees in the office; targets range from 0.81% of the office debt per employee to 3.24%.	Israel
Reductions in aggregate end-of-year debt: *(1)* 2014 – minus 12% of prior year debt; *(2)* 2015 – minus 8% of previous year debt: *(3)* 2016 – minus 2% of prior year debt.	Latvia
Reduction of aggregate tax debt by 25% per year	Lithuania
Reduce total tax debt at beginning of year by 56.2%	Malaysia
Reduction of 17.8% of the total tax debt	Mexico
10% of outstanding amounts to be recovered	Morocco
Tax arrears not to exceed 2.5-3.0% of total tax receipts	Netherlands
Debt reduction target of 1.05-1.1 billion euros was set for 2013	Portugal
SARS aims to reduce the debt to revenue ratio to 6% by 2019	South Africa
Remaining aggregate end-of-year debt should not exceed 16 442 million baht by the end of 2014	Thailand

2. Tax gap reduction

Description of targets reported	Country
Seeking to achieve a reduction of 0.5% per year	Estonia
Target (2012 and beyond): To ensure that the tax gap does not exceed 2% of estimated total tax potential. Taxes included in this definition are: PIT, and CIT and VAT for companies with 250 or less employees. Moonlighting (shadow economy) activities are also excluded.)	Denmark
Measures initiated to increase enforcement and quantified targets in terms of expected revenue set for each measure. However, a measurable goal is not set. Improvements in tax compliance are included in state budget in total; a goal of 2 billion NIS was noted in the state budget as the expected target from both improved compliance and increased collection.	Israel
Tax gaps are being estimated in 2014 for VAT, labour taxes and excise. Targets will be set from 2015	Latvia

3. Improved taxpayer satisfaction

Description of targets reported	Country
Customer satisfaction with services of Integrated Social Security System (SIPA) reaches target of 7.4, based on polls. Complaints management: target of 85% resolution rate for complaints and suggestions received by Citizen Assistance Programme	Argentina
Acknowledging baseline from 2012 survey, target is to achieve an average score on quality of services that is 76% (where 0 = no approval or satisfaction and 100 = fully satisfied with service quality	Austria
As measured by survey in respect of revenue body's performance: *(1)* average assessment of overall competency (target 4.4); *(2)* average assessment of service quality (target 4.3); and *(3)* average assessment of front office organisation and services (target 4.3), all measured on a scale of 2 to 6. Targets generally increased every next year.	Bulgaria

Table 3.2. **Quantified targets reported by revenue bodies for key areas of performance** *(continued)*

Description of targets reported	Country
Level of satisfaction with revenue body's services is 6, measured on a scale ranging from 1 (poor) to 8 (excellent).	Brazil
Opinion concerning the contribution of the revenue body to the economic and social development of Brazil is 6, measured against a scale ranging from 1 (poor) to 8 (excellent).	
Revenue body uses annual survey to establish a "net satisfaction rate". Goal in 2014 is to achieve score of 59, and a minimum of 59.5 (2015 to 2020)	Chile
Level of satisfaction with SAT reported by surveyed taxpayers reaches 80%	China
Targets (2013 and beyond): To maintain a 3.8 target for both businesses' and individuals satisfaction Measured (separately) on a scale of 1 to 5 where 1 is low satisfaction and 5 is high satisfaction.	Denmark
DGFIP uses the « Marianne » quality indicator programme that is used across the public sector: This programme covers quality indicators such as the proportion of mail being handled within 15 working days, e-mails being handled within 5 working days, phone calls being answered after 5 rings or less, requests regarding quality of service being handled within 15 working. The target for 2014 is 75% (86.8% achieved in 2013).	France
Increased taxpayer satisfaction level from 3.9 to 4.2 (as per 2014-19 MOF transformation plan)	Indonesia
Taxpayer satisfaction with the online return filing and tax payment system: target of 60%	Japan
Taxpayer satisfaction with filing assistance on the NTA website: target of 80%	Japan
Client satisfaction levels to be achieved – 8.4 points (out of 10) in 2014; and 8.5 points (out of 10) in 2016.	Latvia
Customer satisfaction level of 9.1 (out of 10 [fully satisfied]) to be achieved in 2014	Lithuania
Minimum % of customers who are satisfied with the quality of *(1)* phone and correspondence contacts (target 85%); and *(2)* online services (target: 90%)	New Zealand
Minimum % of customers who are confident IRD takes action to ensure people receive their proper social support entitlements (target 70%)	
75% of surveyed taxpayers perceive the revenue body as fair	Norway
Achieve taxpayer satisfaction level rating of 96% for 2014	Mexico
Taxpayer satisfaction level with online services, as surveyed, achieve or exceed targets for 2014: 72% (good) and 78% (good and very good).	Portugal
70% of taxpayers are satisfied with the service provided	Turkey
75.8% of customers say HMRC is "straightforward to deal with" by March 2015	United Kingdom
The IRS uses the American Customer Satisfaction Index (ACSI) which is a national indicator of customer satisfaction with the quality of products and services available to consumers in the United States. ACSI scores range between a low of 0 and a high of 100. Over 55 Federal government agencies have used the ACSI to measure citizen satisfaction of more than 110 services and programmes. The IRS long term ACSI goal is 75 for income tax filed by FY 2017.	United States

4. Compliance burden reduction

Description of targets reported	Country
ATO share of AUD 1 billion savings required from across Government.	Australia
Government programme requires implementation of specific initiatives rather than achieving specific amounts of reduced burden.	Austria
Overall government target to reduce burden (including tax related burden) by 20% (2010 to 2014); achievement of 13% by the end of 2013.	Bulgaria
As part of the Government of Canada's Red Tape Reduction Action Plan, the CRA has completed several initiatives and has plans to put in place more initiatives to reduce compliance burden, based on priorities identified by small and medium businesses.	Canada
90% of corporate income tax returns to be received by e-filing.	Colombia
Private individuals – 5% reduction by 2015; Businesses – 5% reduction by 2015.	Netherlands
Government target to reduce overall administrative burden (including tax-related burden) by NOK 10 billion by the end of 2015.	Norway
Reduce annual costs of compliant businesses in complying with tax obligations by GBP 250 million by March 2015, against a 2011 baseline.	United Kingdom

Table 3.2. **Quantified targets reported by revenue bodies for key areas of performance** *(continued)*

5. Operating costs reductions

Description of targets reported	Country
Fixed % efficiency dividend – annual funding reduction of total administrative budget	Australia
Staffing levels fixed for next 3 years	Bulgaria
Measures announced in the 2012 and 2013 federal budgets, when fully implemented, will result in the CRA realising efficiencies of CAD 313.7 million annually. The Federal Budget 2013 also announced that departments would realise savings of 5% on public service travel, on an ongoing basis, with the CRA's contribution being CAD 2.1 million.	Canada
Seeking to achieve an operating cost/ overall revenue collection ratio of 0.90 in 2014.	France
1.3% reduction required in 2014. (*NB: Office resource reduction encouragement:* 50% of annual reduction to be given to office staff and designated for cultural or educational enrichment programmes.	Israel
The targeted cost to collect one euro: 2014 – 0.0216 euro; 2015 – 0.0210; 2016 – 0.0210.	Latvia
Target of 5% operating expenditure reduction compared with 2013 budgeted amount.	Mexico
Reduce cost to achieve savings of 400 million euros per annum from 2016.	Netherlands
9% reduction to be achieved in 2014.	Slovenia
Budget reductions for 2014 require IRS to reduce FTEs to 84 268, compared to 89 857 in 2013.	United States
Reduction in operating expenditure of 15% from 2010 to 2015.	Iceland
Reduce operating expenditure/ staffing by 5% per year.	Thailand
Make GBP 1.2 billion of savings over period 2010-11 to 2015-16, with some savings being re-invested into tackling non-compliance; make 5% sustainable cost savings in 2015/16.	United Kingdom

Source: Tax Administration 2015 survey responses.

- The numbers of revenue bodies reporting their service delivery performance against the standards set by them is disturbingly low, with just on 50% of revenue bodies reporting that this practice is followed (generally at the same level across both OECD and non-OECD countries); included in these results are five OECD revenue bodies (i.e. Belgium, Iceland, Israel, Luxembourg, and Slovenia) that reported that they have no established set of service standards and do not conduct surveys of citizens to gauge their satisfaction with the services delivered and/or competence of tax administration in general.

  On a positive note, a number of examples can be cited of revenue bodies that commit positively to both having a comprehensive range of service standards and being transparent in their reporting of the performance achieved by them, including the Canada Revenue Agency:

  > Canadians' confidence in the integrity of the tax system is essential to the CRA's success. Meeting our service standards shows that we are answering the needs of taxpayers and benefit recipients. Our service standards tell citizens what level of performance they can reasonably expect from the CRA under normal circumstances. We review our standards and targets every year and update them as needed (Canada Revenue Agency, 2014).

  Concerning the gathering of customer feedback, many revenue bodies are known to conduct periodic surveys or use some other methods. For example, Estonia reported that it constantly collects customers' feedback to gauge their satisfaction with the services delivered and competence of administration. It administers a "Promoter Index" method as a survey tool, a flexible web-based feedback system that helps to identify taxpayers' needs and expectations and to respond to them in a prompt manner.

A lack of commitment to providing good standards of service, along with questions of transparency concerning revenue body performance, should be of concern in tax administration environments generally characterised by complex tax systems and significant tax compliance issues. The matter is one that may be worthy of more detailed exploration by the FTA with a view to providing practical guidance and encouragement for this important aspect of tax administration.

- Around three-quarters of all revenue bodies reported that they conduct regular surveys of taxpayers (i.e. both citizens and businesses) to gauge their views and perceptions of service delivery quality and the overall standard of administration; the approach taken in relation to surveying tax intermediaries is discussed in Chapter 8.
- Viewed across all of the aspects surveyed, there would seem considerable potential to improve related management practices, particularly concerning the transparency of tax administration (e.g. by publishing plans, performance reporting, and results of taxpayer surveys) in at least ten surveyed revenue bodies, including six in OECD member countries – Germany, Iceland, Israel, Luxembourg, Slovenia, Switzerland.

Revenue bodies' strategic plans and statements

Research carried out for this series over many years has found that most revenue bodies prepare a strategic plan (or documents with a similar name and purpose) covering a medium term period of three to four years. While such documents can vary in their level of detail they generally aim to set out key directions and priorities, and organisational goals and objectives for the target period, against the background of a stated organisational mission/mandate, vision for the future and set of values. In some cases, objective targets are established that can be used to gauge overall progress towards the goals set. Well prepared, such documents can be a valuable tool for communicating with both internal and external audiences and fostering commitment, as reflected in the comments of the IRS Commissioner in his organisation's strategic plan for the period 2014-2107:

> In my experience, a large organisation like the IRS depends on strategic plans to prioritise goals and effectively manage its resources. I'm pleased to present the 2014-2017 IRS Strategic Plan and lay out the agency's primary goals and objectives for the next four years. The plan reflects the contributions of every part of the IRS, and it provides clear direction of where we will focus in the years ahead (IRS, 2014).

Prior editions of this series have set out extracts of the strategic plans of selected revenue bodies to highlight the major strategies being adopted, and aspects of the approaches being followed in relation to performance management. For this series, a similar approach has been adopted. Extracts of key elements of the published strategic/business plans of a sample of revenue bodies (i.e. Australia, Latvia, New Zealand, South Africa, United Kingdom, and the United States) are set out in the following sections. These examples have been drawn from a cross-section of countries to highlight common themes (e.g. mission, vision, and goals), the high level strategies that are being been adopted and measures of success being used to gauge progress towards established goals. From the plans examined, a few points can be made:

- Officially-published strategic plans tend to provide a clear and relatively brief articulation of revenue body mission, vision, values, and strategic goals and related objectives and, for many, key measures of performance.

- Statements of mission, in addition to a revenue body's role/mandate, frequently emphasise the broader societal role and benefits of a well-functioning tax (and, for some, customs) system.
- Expressions of a revenue body's values (i.e. norms of behaviour) typically include integrity, professionalism, mutual respect/trust, and fairness/procedural justice; some also emphasise aspirations of improved performance through continuous improvement and/or innovation.
- A few revenue bodies (e.g. United States and South Africa) include in their plans a brief description of the major environmental factors or context that have shaped/ influenced their strategy decisions.

  The latest plan of the United States' IRS provides a particularly informative account of such factors and while a number may be peculiar to its own context others are likely to have wider relevance – see Box 3.2.

  In its plan (pages 13-14), SARS draws attention to a range of critical environmental factors, including:

  - Prevailing negative domestic and global economic conditions that are expected to put its compliance and revenue targets at risk;
  - Developments in the global tax environment, including the OECD's Base Erosion and Profit Shifting (BEPS) Initiative, and adoption of the Common Reporting Standard for automatic exchanges of information;
  - The illicit economy, especially illicit cigarette and tobacco, that poses threats to economic growth, tax revenue and legal formal businesses;
  - Concerns for the incidence of corruption in the public sector at large and the threat this poses to voluntary tax compliance; and
  - A potential widening of SARS' mandate as it is required to support critical government efforts to increase employment opportunities, improve conditions for small businesses and help improve government performance across the whole of government.
- Formal strategic goals tend to be relatively few in number and, in relation to tax administration, tend to focus on improving taxpayers' compliance, improved service delivery/customer experience, and strengthening internal capabilities; contrasted to observations in prior series, it appears that much greater attention is being given to improving operational efficiency and productivity. (This matter is discussed further in Chapter 5.)
- Key measures of success/performance for each goal and related objectives are, in most cases, quantified for out-years in order to gauge progress and are both "outcome" and "output" related; concerning the measurement of "outcomes", measures/indicators (and their trends) used by these revenue bodies include:
  - Measures of taxpayers' satisfaction with the services provided and overall perceptions of revenue body administration and their trend over time;
  - Rates of taxpayers' compliance achieved (e.g. for filing, reporting and payment for the major taxes), and their trend over time;
  - Increased use of self-service channels;

  - Cost efficiency: the ratio of costs to net revenue over time;
  - Reductions in compliance/administrative burden; and
  - Perceptions of employee engagement/satisfaction, measured by staff surveys, and their trend over time.

- Compared to plans reviewed in prior series, a number of themes appear to be emerging in relation to performance evaluation and reporting.

Box 3.2. United States IRS: Major trends affecting the IRS – 2014-17 (abbreviated comments extracted from plan)

- **Effectively executing our mission in a challenging environment:** IRS faces challenges with respect to our budget, human capital and overall complexity of our mission responsibilities. We intend to raise awareness of these elements of our environment in order to proactively mitigate them before they become operational issues impacting our ability to fulfil our core mission.
- **Evolving scope and increasing complexity of tax administration:** In recent years, the IRS has been tested by the volume and complexity of changes to the Tax Code [...] These legislative changes often must be implemented within limited timelines that strain resources and impose disruptions in workload planning [...] By strategically allocating our resources, ensuring our IT systems are agile and providing our workforce with necessary training and support, we will continue to be highly responsive to changes in the Tax Code throughout the coming years.
- **Expanding global tax environment and changing business models:** Emerging technology opens new markets to businesses and facilitates access to new customers and geographies. This presents a dual challenge for the IRS, keeping up with increasing international business activity and changing business models. Moreover, the evolution and proliferation of virtual commerce has expanded the exchange of goods, services and currencies – real and virtual – across jurisdictions, further complicating tax administration. Businesses with US tax obligations are increasingly adopting more complex incorporation structures, shifting away from C-corporations and moving towards flow-through entities, such as partnerships and S-corporations. As a result, we must tailor our services to ensure that we help these businesses understand and meet their tax filing obligations.
- **Increasing occurrence of refund fraud and identity theft:** Since 2010, the IRS has seen a significant increase in both refund fraud schemes and identity theft [...] Assuring the accuracy of refunds and the security of taxpayer data remain our priorities going forward. We are committed to stopping this threat to tax administration, protecting our government's revenue and safeguarding the identity of all taxpayers.
- **Meeting taxpayer's expectations to digitally interact in a secure manner:** The growth of the Internet over the past decade has changed consumer expectations as they become increasingly more accustomed to using the web for anything from ordering phone service to conducting transactions with financial institutions using traditional online and mobile devices. More and more, customers show a preference for internet-based service before trying other service channels such as phones, paper or in-person [...] Looking forward, we are committed to expanding our portfolio of digital service offerings to meet customer expectations while continuing to keep taxpayer data secure. Our investment in innovative technology is key to accelerating the move to a "web first" organisation that provides the electronic services that taxpayers desire, the tools that employees deserve and the mission-critical security that the IRS needs.

Box 3.2. **United States IRS: Major trends affecting the IRS – 2014-17 (abbreviated comments extracted from plan)** *(continued)*

- **Growing use of the tax community in tax preparation:** The tax community has had a significant impact on tax administration in recent years [...] the IRS must continue to acknowledge the expanding importance of tax professionals and the broader tax community. We must serve them effectively and ensure they adhere to professional standards that advance efficient administration of the tax system
- **Sustaining a skilled and talented workforce:** As tax administration becomes increasingly complex and the demand for varied taxpayer services increases, we are continually challenged with the task of maintaining a workforce with diverse, advanced skill sets. An additional challenge is that a considerable percentage of our workforce is currently eligible for retirement. The entire leadership team must actively engage with employees during these difficult times, providing them the support they need to effectively fulfil their duties.
- **Demographic trends and projections:** Demographic projections signal the US population is becoming increasingly more diverse, with implications for both the talent-pool from which the IRS draws as well as the needs and expectations of taxpayers [...] We need to prepare for these changes well in advance if we are to continue providing the highest level of service for all taxpayers.

Source: IRS Strategic Plan 2014-2017.

First, while still confined to a minority of countries there appears to be an increased reliance on tax gap estimation methodologies, particularly in respect of the VAT, to better inform revenue bodies of their effectiveness; this is likely to have resulted in part from pressures by Governments to make revenue bodies more accountable for their performance and to improve the transparency of tax administration performance.

Second, concerning staff engagement revenue bodies in advanced economies appear to be increasingly evaluating their performance against broader public sector trends in staff engagement rather than assessing their own internal performance over time.

Third, with considerable emphasis being given to making far greater use of digital technologies with a particular objective on helping taxpayers to "self-manage" their tax affairs, new performance measures are emerging. Tables 3.3 to 3.8 provide examples of this direction, including some novel examples of new performance measures reported by the US IRS:

- **Service Interactions Available Electronically:** % of e-services available to the taxpayer on IRS.gov relative to the most frequent services provided to the taxpayer across all channels.
- **Service Interactions Processed Electronically:** % of electronic interactions conducted by taxpayers relative to total number of service interactions conducted across all channels.
- **Software Currency:** Monitors % of Commercial off the Shelf software products in use in IRS that are within one version of current release.

Table 3.3. **Key elements of strategic plans – Australian Tax Office**

<table>
<tr><td rowspan="3">What we want to achieve</td><td>MISSION: We contribute to the economic and social wellbeing of Australians by fostering willing participation in our tax and superannuation systems.</td></tr>
<tr><td>VISION: We are a leading tax and superannuation administration known for our contemporary service, expertise and integrity.</td></tr>
<tr><td>VALUES: We are impartial, committed to service, accountable, respectful and ethical.</td></tr>
<tr><td>Our strategic intent</td><td>We want the ATO to be relevant and valuable to the Australian community for the long term – trusted and respected here and internationally and considered a leading organisation by all stakeholders.

To the extent we can influence and control, we will aim to make the tax and superannuation systems and our administration fair, efficient and sustainable – where tax and superannuation are recognised and valued as a necessary part of our community in Australia.</td></tr>
<tr><td rowspan="4">Our goals</td><td>Easy for people to participate – We will design and operate the tax and superannuation systems for the majority of taxpayers who do the right thing, rather than for the few who don't.</td></tr>
<tr><td>Contemporary and tailored service – People expect convenient and accessible service in their dealings with a contemporary service organisation.</td></tr>
<tr><td>Purposeful and respectful relationships – To succeed in the future, we must have a greater connection with, and understanding of, the community, government and stakeholders and their needs and expectations.</td></tr>
<tr><td>Professional and productive organisation – Delivering our change agenda and business improvements is about backing our words with actions. This is about leading and managing well, and mobilising and motivating our people.</td></tr>
<tr><td>Our strategies</td><td>• Build a culture that embodies our values and transforms the client experience
• Simplify interactions, maximising automation and reducing costs
• Connect with the community and other agencies in meaningful ways
• Influence policy and law design for more certain outcomes
• Use data in a smarter way to improve decisions, services and compliance
• Reshape the workforce to optimise capability and performance</td></tr>
<tr><td rowspan="2">Measuring our success</td><td>The ATO's outcome to deliver to government is: Confidence in the administration of aspects of Australia's taxation and superannuation systems through helping people understand their rights and obligations, improving ease of compliance and access to benefits, and managing non-compliance with the law.</td></tr>
<tr><td>The way we measure our performance against this outcome includes the following measures:
• Community and key stakeholders engagement and satisfaction with ATO performance
• Number of customer service interactions delivered through our multi-channel environment
• Proportion of businesses and individuals registered in the system
• Proportion of businesses and individuals that lodge on time
• Proportion of liabilities paid on time by value for each of the major tax revenue types
• Adjusted average cost to individual taxpayers of managing their tax affairs
• Net cost to collect $100
• Earlier resolution of disputed cases
• Ratio of collectable debt to net tax collections
• GST gap as a proportion of GST revenue
• Operating within budget
• Employee engagement compared to previous years and other large Australian Public Service organisations.</td></tr>
</table>

Source: ATO Corporate Plan 2014-18 and survey response.

Table 3.4. **Key elements of strategic plans – Latvia's State Revenue Service**

Mission	Fair administration of tax and customs matters for the protection of society and entrepreneurship.				
Values	**Integrity, Professionalism, Responsibility, and Loyalty**				
Strategic objectives *(Strategy also describes a range of tasks to achieve each objective)*	To act in accordance with the behaviour necessary for the compliance of taxpayers and customs clients in order to ensure the collection of public budget revenues and effective protection of the financial interests of the EU.				
	To ensure society's protection, security and safety by performing effective customs control measures.				
	To prevent criminal State revenue and customs offences by decreasing tax fraud and smuggling.				
	To increase the efficiency and effectiveness of using the SRS's resources.				
Strategic performance indicators *(Year-by-year targets vs actual 2013 performance)*	**Specific indicators**	**Values of performance indicators**			
		2013	**2014**	**2015**	**2016**
		Actual	*Forecast*		
	1. Execution of SRS's administered budget revenue plan (%)	104.5	100	100	100
	2. Changes of the collected amount of the SRS's administered budget revenue in comparison with the previous year (%)	+5.5	+3.9	+4.2	+3.3
	3. Tax revenue as a share GDP (%)	29.3	30	31	33
	4. Changes to tax gap (%) for VAT, PIT and excises (NB: Indicators to be set after evaluations in 2014)	X	X	X	X
	5. Shadow economy (%)	25.5	25	24.5	24
	6. Indicators of WB's Doing Business Series:				
	• Time necessary to calculate and pay taxes (hours per year);	264	250	190	170
	• Time necessary to register for VAT (days)	10	9	9	8
	• Customs clearance and technical control (days):				
	Export	1	1	1	1
	Import	2	2	2	2
	7. Share of illegal excise goods market (%) for cigarettes, alcohol and fuel (NB: Awaiting development of measurement methodology)	X	X	X	X
	8. Percentage of favourable court decisions for the SRS ((%) weighted average (tax disputes, administrative violations and forced execution and other dispute cases)	83.1	84.8	85	85
	9. Customer satisfaction level (from survey results) – fully satisfied and rather satisfied (points in 10 point system) for each of tax and customs	- (8.41/ 2012)	8.41	-	8.5
	10. Personnel satisfaction level (from survey) – fully satisfied and rather satisfied (%)	- (80.9/ 2012)	80	80	80
	11. Cost of one collected euro, in total SRS (euro)	0.0192	0.0216	0.0210	0.0210

Source: State Revenue Service Business Strategy 2014-2016.

Table 3.5. **Key elements of strategic plans – New Zealand Inland Revenue**

What we are here for	We contribute to the economic and social well-being of New Zealand by collecting and distributing money		
What we want to be	A world-class revenue organisation recognised for service and excellence		
Strategic intentions	To help achieve *IR for the future*, we will focus on three main areas: *(1)* implementing our transformation change agenda; *(2)* contributing to government policy and priorities; and *(3)* delivering and improving our core business, including enhancing the customer experience. We will work in these three linked areas concurrently, balancing our need to deliver today and transform for tomorrow.		
Contributing to government priorities	We have a responsibility as a government agency to contribute to the Government's priorities. These are to: *(1)* responsibly manage the Government's finances; *(2)* build a more competitive and productive economy; *(3)* deliver better public services within tight fiscal constraints; and *(4)* rebuild Canterbury. We will also continue to participate in a range of all-of-government activities, and collaborate with other agencies to reduce costs and improve efficiency and effectiveness.		
Delivering and improving our core business	**Improve the customer experience:** We want customer interactions with us to be as convenient and easy as possible. We will continue to do this by enhancing and expanding our services.		
	Improve compliance: A key aspect of our core business is helping to maximise voluntary compliance. We assist customers who are willing to meet their compliance obligations but are unaware or uncertain how to do so. Influencing voluntary compliance, targeting inadvertent non-complaisance by providing information, assistance and tools, and detecting and deterring deliberate non-compliance are part of our core activities.		
	Improve business efficiency: We will continue to increase the value for money we deliver through improving our processes, strengthening our capital asset management, maintaining our ICT environment and reducing property overheads.		
Measuring our performance *(2018 Targets vs 2013 performance)*	**IMPACT INDICATORS**	**TARGET**	**LATEST**
	More customers self-manage:		
	• % of customers aware of their obligations and entitlements increases	85%	82%
	• % of customers who find it easy to comply increases	80%	79%
	More customers register and report accurate information when required:		
	• % of returns filed without errors increases	88%	85%
	• % of applications submitted without errors increases	90%	83%
	• % of correct student loan deductions for New Zealand-based borrowers is maintained	98%	99%
	• Employer registrations follow an appropriate trend	n/a	
	• GST assessed to consumer spending follows an appropriate trend	n/a	
	More customers claim their correct entitlements:		
	• % of accurate Working for Families Tax Credits payments increases	70%	67% (12)
	• % of child support assessments collected increases	75%	73%
	• Working for Families Tax Credits registrations follow an appropriate trend	n/a	
	• Donation rebates claimed follow an appropriate trend	n/a	
	More customers pay and file information on time:		
	• % returns filed on time is maintained	83%	83% (12)
	• % payments made by customers on time is maintained	86%	86% (12)
	• % child support assessments paid on time increases	68%	64%

Source: New Zealand Inland Revenue (2014), *Statement of Intent 2014-18*, Wellington.

Table 3.6. **Key elements of strategic plans – South Africa Revenue Service**

Our mission	To optimise revenue yield, facilitate trade and enlist new tax contributors by promoting awareness of the obligation to comply with South African tax and customs laws, and to provide quality and responsive service to the public.		
Our vision	To become an innovative revenue and customs agency that enhances economic growth and social development, and supports our integration into the global economy in a way that benefits all South Africans.		
Our values	Mutual respect and trust, equity and fairness, integrity and honesty, transparency and openness, and courtesy and commitment		
Core outcomes sought	OUTCOME 1: Increased Customs Compliance		
	OUTCOME 2: Increased Tax Compliance		
	OUTCOME 3: Increased Ease and Fairness of Doing Business with SARS		
	OUTCOME 4: Increased Cost Effectiveness, Internal Efficiency and Institutional Respectability		
Over-arching strategic shifts to achieve the four core outcomes	Moving from targeting eligible taxpayers to building the reality of fiscal citizenship among all South Africans		
	Moving from a gatekeeper to a risk management approach		
	Moving from entity and product approach to integrated economic view		
	Moving from uniform service offering to differentiated service offering		
	Moving from manual to automated/digital/self service		
	Moving from isolated departmental view of SARS efficiency to a whole of government view		
	Move from high administrative burden due to multiple registrations, multiple channels and manual forms to reduced administrative burden through, for example, single registration, integrated channels and dynamic forms		
	Move from people performing below potential due to non-standardised internal processes, no value alignment and low skill/low value-add to people performing at their peak through, for example, values alignment and high skill/high value-adding activities		
Outcome measures *(2019 targets against current baselines)* *(NB : customs measures and targets omitted in interests of space)*	**MEASURES**	**TARGET**	**BASELINE**
	OUTCOME 2: Increased Tax Compliance		
	Total revenue	As agreed	ZAR 728 bn
	Debt book as a % of total revenue	6.0%	9.18%
	% PIT filing compliance	92.5%	91.5%
	% Audit coverage of registered taxpayers	12.5%	10.6%
	% In-depth audit coverage of registered taxpayers	0.085%	0.26%
	OUTCOME 3:		
	% Uptake in electronic filing for all tax products	99%	96.2%
	Average processing turnaround time for PIT returns (days)	30mins	0.16
	Average processing turnaround time for CIT returns (days)	<1	0.47
	Average processing turnaround time for VAT refunds (days)	21	32.1
	% VAT refunds processed in 14 days	77	69.6
	OUTCOME 4:		
	Employee engagement %	65.2	64.1
	Leadership effectiveness index %	88	85.3
	Employment equity: demographics %	72	71.3
	Employment equity: gender on management level %	49	40.6
	Employment equity: disability %	2.3	1.99
	Treasury allocation to revenue % (*i.e.* cost of collection/revenue)	1 to 1.2	0.98

Source: SARS (2014), *SARS Strategic Plan 2014-2019*, South African Revenue Service, Pretoria.

Table 3.7. **Key elements of strategic plans – United Kingdom Revenue and Customs**

Our purpose	• We make sure that the money is available to fund the UK's public services. • We also help families and individuals with targeted financial support.
Our vision	We will close the tax gap, our customers will feel that the tax system is simple for them and even handed, and we will be seen as a highly professional and efficient organisation.
Our way	We understand our customers and their needs, make it easy for our customers to get it right, believe that most of our customers are honest, treat everyone with respect, are passionate in helping those who need it and relentless in pursuing those who bend or break the rules, recognise that we have privileged access to information and we will protect it, behave professionally and with integrity, do our own jobs well and take pride in helping our colleagues to succeed, develop the skills and tools we need to do our jobs well, and drive continuous improvement in everything we do.
Our plans – goals and strategies	**Maximise Revenues**: Includes specific initiatives and actions to *(1)* Make better use of data and automation; *(2)* Add capacity to tackle debt, error and fraud; *(3)* Crack down on tax evasion; *(4)* Close down tax avoidance; *(5)* Catch organised criminals; and *(6)* Enforce the rules.
	Improve the service that we give our customers: Deliver new digital services focusing on *(1)* PAYE Online; *(2)* Digital self-service; *(3)* Your tax account; *(4)* Agents Online Self-Service, *(5)* All customer segments and *(7)* All customers needing additional support.
	Make sustainable cost savings: Includes specific initiatives and actions to *(1)* reduce costs for customers; and *(2)* reduce our own internal costs
Measuring success	**Maximise revenues**: A key measure of success is the additional tax revenue we bring in through our compliance and enforcement activity. • We plan to deliver additional compliance revenues of GBP 24.5 billion in 2014-15 and GBP 26.3 billion in 2015-16; we will aim to reduce losses through error and fraud in the tax credits system towards 5.5 per cent of finalised tax credit entitlement by 2014-15, down from 7.3 per cent in 2011-12.
	Improve the service that we give our customers: In 2014-15 we plan to: • Work towards our aspiration of handling 90 % of calls across all of our helplines, achieving a consistent level of at least 80 % in 2014-15; handle 80 per cent of correspondence within 15 working days and 95 % within 40 working days, with at least 90 % passing quality standards. For our benefits and credits customers we will continue to: • Handle all new claims and changes of circumstances for UK customers within 22 days; handle all new claims and changes of circumstances for international customers within 92 days. By March 2015, 75.8 per cent of our customers will find it straightforward to deal with us.
	Make sustainable cost savings: • We will make sustainable cost savings of GBP 198 million in 2014-15 and a further GBP 205 million in 2015-16; we will also deliver business cost reductions totalling GBP 250 million by March 2015, as part of a wider improvement in business customer experience.
	What this means for our people: We plan to: • Improve employee engagement over the next two years by continuing to work towards our ambition of achieving the Civil Service benchmark of 58 per cent; improve engagement among the Senior Civil Service by achieving an engagement score of 72 per cent in 2014-15 and 75 per cent in 2015-16. • Close the capability gap for the change leadership priority with an increase of 21 per cent in 2014-15, and 15 per cent in 2015-16; increase the percentage of staff who feel they have the skills required to do their job to 85 per cent in 2014-15 and 91 per cent in 2015-16. • Reduce the average working days lost per employee to seven in 2014-15 and 6.5 in 2015-16.

Sources: HMRC (2012), *Business Plan 2012-15*, United Kingdom Her Majesty's Revenue and Customs, London.

Table 3.8. **Key elements of strategic plans – United States Revenue Service**

Mission	Provide America's taxpayers top-quality service by helping them to understand and meet their tax responsibilities and enforce the law with integrity and fairness to all.		
Vision	We will uphold the integrity of our nation's tax system and preserve the public trust through our talented workforce, innovative technology and collaborative partnerships.		
Values	Honesty and Integrity, Respect, Continuous Improvement, Inclusion, Openness and Collaboration, and Personal Accountability.		
Strategic foundation	Invest in our workforce and the foundational capabilities necessary to achieve our mission and deliver high performance for taxpayers and stakeholders.		
Strategic goals	Deliver high quality and timely service to reduce taxpayer burden and encourage voluntary compliance.		
	Effectively enforce the law to ensure compliance with tax responsibilities and combat fraud.		
Goals and measures *(2017 targets v current measure)*	**MEASURES**	**TARGET (2017)**	**LATEST**
	Voluntary Compliance Rate: Measures amount of tax paid voluntarily and in a timely manner.	86%	83% (2011)
	American Customer Satisfaction Index (ACSI): Monitors overall individual taxpayer satisfaction with tax filing processes	75%	72%(2013)
	Enforcement Satisfaction Score: % of taxpayers contacted as part of IRS compliance efforts who feel the process was satisfactory.	75%	72% (2013)
	Employee Engagement: Measures employee engagement based on annual survey and index developed by IRS to compare itself with other large agencies.	Top quartile	Ranked 8/15 (2013)
	Service Satisfaction Score: Measures satisfaction of those taxpayers who contacted IRS seeking assistance.	94%	91% (2013)
	E-file Rate – Individuals: % of individuals returns filed electronically	90%	83% (2013)
	End to end: Tracks availability of software and system components of critical IRS systems.	99%	99% (2014)
	E-file Rate – Business Returns: % of business returns filed electronically	50%	40% (2013)
	Service Interactions Available Electronically: % of e-services available to the taxpayer on IRS.gov relative to the most frequent services provided to the taxpayer across all channels.	75%	50% (2014)
	Service Interactions Processed Electronically: % of electronic interactions conducted by taxpayers relative to total number of service interactions conducted across all channels.	50%	23% (2014)
	Software Currency: Monitors % of Commercial off-the-shelf software products in use in IRS that are within one version of current release.	85%	75% (2014)
	Portal Availability: Measures availability and response time of IRS.gov	100%	100%

Source: IRS (2014), *IRS Strategic Plan 2014-17*, United States Internal Revenue Service, Washington, DC.

Managing and improving taxpayers' compliance

As evident from the extracts of selected revenue bodies' plans, achieving improved taxpayers' compliance is very much the underpinning rationale for a revenue body's existence. Since its creation in 2002, the FTA has provided a substantial amount of practical guidance on the features of an effective strategic approach for improving taxpayers' compliance, drawing on leading revenue body practices.

Adopting a risk management approach

Traditionally, revenue bodies utilised a compliance strategy based on deterrence through the use of audits and penalties. Gradually, a more holistic view emerged entailing the use of more multi-faceted approaches and a focus on understanding risks. The FTA report *Compliance Risk Management: Managing and Improving Tax Compliance* (OECD, 2004) described how a risk management framework could help revenue bodies to prioritise risks and choose appropriate risk treatments – see Figure 3.1. At the heart of that framework is the analysis of the underlying drivers of taxpayer behaviour. Effective treatment strategies can only be identified once those drivers are properly understood.

Figure 3.1. **The compliance risk management framework**

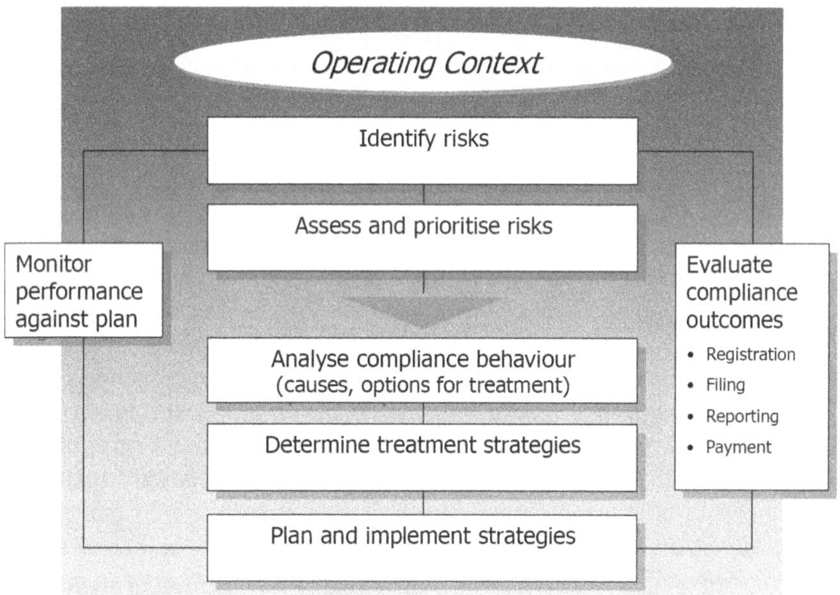

Source: Compliance Risk Management: Managing and Improving Tax Compliance (2004), OECD.

Through greater understanding of the environmental context, it was suggested that use of the model would enable revenue bodies to assess and determine which risks/taxpayer behaviours it can or cannot influence, and to consider and prioritise which risk treatments were required.

Recognising the influences on taxpayers' compliance behaviour

A compliance strategy relying on diverse treatments not only requires the means to measure the effectiveness; it also requires a capability to choose the right form of treatment in the right circumstances. As explained, doing so depends on being able to understand what drives taxpayer behaviour. The FTA note *Understanding and Influencing Taxpayers' Compliance Behaviour* (OECD, 2010b) describes the most important drivers of individual taxpayers' compliance behaviour. These were grouped into five categories (economy, norms, deterrence, opportunity and fairness) and discussed on the basis of revenue body experience and academic literature. The note acknowledged the limitations of standard economic models as predictors of behaviour. It also emphasised that the five categories of drivers should not be looked at in isolation, as in practice they interact in complex ways to generate sometimes unpredictable outcomes.

In more recent years, the FTA has devoted considerable effort into exploring and describing the elements of an approach to tax administration that focuses very much on creating an environment of support and co-operation between the revenue body, taxpayers and other key stakeholders to achieve greater voluntary tax compliance.

The central importance that understanding taxpayer behaviour now plays in modern tax compliance risk management naturally drives revenue bodies towards increasing the engagement and involvement of taxpayers. This recognises that taxpayers are not a homogeneous group and that effective interventions are responsive to the diversity of their attitudes to tax compliance and the underlying reasons for those attitudes. Armed with the understanding that engagement and involvement provides, revenue bodies are better equipped to design treatments that are more effective and long-lasting. This is as true of taxpayers exhibiting a desire not to comply, as it is of those who are willing to do the right thing.

Seeking compliance through increased co-operation and transparency

In 2008, the FTA published the *Study into the Role of Tax Intermediaries* (OECD, 2008b). The study addressed the topic of aggressive tax planning and analysed the tripartite relationship between revenue bodies, taxpayers and tax intermediaries. The report concluded that there was significant scope to influence the "demand side" of aggressive tax planning arrangements in relation to large corporate taxpayers. These taxpayers and revenue bodies were encouraged to engage in a relationship based on co-operation and trust. The study spelt out how more co-operative relationships between taxpayers and revenue bodies could be established and described a conceptual framework for these relationships, and coined an expression for them – the enhanced relationship. It also recommended that revenue bodies should look to establish a tax environment in which trust and co-operation can develop so that enhanced relationships with large corporate taxpayers and tax advisers can be established.

The 2008 study described two pillars as the basis for enhanced relationships between large corporate taxpayers and revenue bodies:

- In dealings with taxpayers, revenue bodies should demonstrate understanding based on commercial awareness, impartiality, proportionality, openness through disclosure and transparency, and responsiveness; and
- In dealings with revenue bodies, taxpayers should provide disclosure and transparency.

Following the 2008 study, the FTA undertook further studies dealing with enhanced relationships with banks and with high net worth individuals. Further work was completed in 2012-13 to take account of revenue bodies' experiences since the 2008 study. This work, titled *Co-operative Compliance: A Framework* (OECD, 2013a) found that while the two pillars were still valid, significant new issues had emerged as these approaches had matured and become more widespread. One of these was the development of compliance risk management strategies by revenue bodies that focus on effectively influencing and improving taxpayer compliance behaviour. This work noted that the development of co-operative relationships with large businesses was embedded in these strategies. In addition, tax control frameworks had emerged as a key tool to disclosure and transparency. The term "enhanced relationship" also raised questions about the nature of the approach and to some gave rise to connotations of inequality in tax treatment. In short, large corporate taxpayers and revenue bodies, while they are satisfied that the principles on which the approach is based remain sound, were concerned that the name "enhanced relationship" had given rise to misunderstandings and in some cases suspicion that the concept violated important principles, such as equality before the law.

Accordingly, the report addressed the substance of those concerns and, based on a consensus view of countries participating in the work, coined the term "co-operative compliance" to describe the concept more accurately as it not only describes the process of co-operation but also demonstrates its goal as part of the revenue body's compliance risk management strategy: compliance leading to payment of the right amount of tax at the right time. As noted by the study's sponsoring Commissioner, Peter Veld of the Netherlands Tax and Customs Administration (OECD, 2013a):

> Since the Forum on Tax Administration (FTA) first discussed the concept of the "enhanced relationship" in the 2008 Study, many more countries have developed approaches based on the principle that businesses that are prepared to be fully transparent can expect certainty about their tax position in return. This report distils these experiences into a model of co-operative compliance. This builds on the original thinking but spells out more clearly how the model delivers better compliance, effectiveness and efficiency.

Prevention is better than cure – achieving compliance "right from the start"

Involving taxpayers and engaging them in dialogue is strongly linked to the perception of procedural fairness of the treatment of the revenue body. The FTA note *Right from the Start: Influencing the Compliance Environment for Small and Medium-sized Enterprises* (OECD, 2012) put the risk management approach and the acquired knowledge together into a holistic approach with the purpose of creating situations in which compliance is achieved for SME taxpayers "right from the start". It gives a practical framework, expressed in terms of four dimensions, for revenue bodies to generate value (to themselves, taxpayers and society) by exploring systematic and coherent strategies to create an environment that influences compliance processes and behaviours before the actual reporting takes place. The four dimensions are:

- Acting in real time and up-front, so that problems are prevented or addressed when they occur;
- Focusing on end-to-end processes rather than just focusing on the revenue body processes and try to make the processes of the taxpayer fit into them;
- Making it easy to comply (and difficult not to); and
- Actively involving and engaging taxpayers, their representatives and other stakeholders, in order to achieve a better understanding of the taxpayer's perspective and to co-operate with third parties.

There have been two further detailed studies to promote further thinking and development of these approaches. The FTA study *Together for Better Outcomes* (OECD, 2013b) explores how engaging and involving SME taxpayers and stakeholders can contribute to improved outcomes and reduced costs. It also identifies a range of other benefits, including fairer competition, reduced compliance burdens, and improved trust. By fostering greater trust between SMEs and revenue bodies this approach can create a virtuous circle that encourages still higher levels of voluntary compliance. The study provides a conceptual framework, a review of experience, and tools and guidance to assist revenue bodies. The study concludes that while there is substantial experience to build on, there also is potential for more systematic, far-reaching and potentially transformative approaches.

In October 2014, the FTA completed and published the report *Tax compliance by design* (OECD, 2014). The report takes an "end-to-end" perspective on the tax revenue collection process of SME taxpayers and focuses on the opportunities for achieving improved compliance at the point taxpayers' tax liabilities are determined by leveraging developments in technology. As noted in the report's executive summary:

> "Tax compliance by design" recognises that most SMEs want to be compliant. Historically, poor systems and a poor understanding of the tax system have been major causes of non-compliance. However, technology is changing the way SMEs operate. As the costs of software have fallen and the emergence of the "cloud" has enabled new ways of delivering technology, SMEs have gained access to new and sophisticated systems for managing their businesses. Most SMEs now use technology in some form to help them keep track of their business and to improve effectiveness. Information and payments are increasingly becoming digital. There is rapid growth of new payment systems using mobile devices. The use of electronic invoices is increasing. Electronic cash registers are used for handling cash transactions. A number of cheap and simple-to-use on-line accounting systems are available [...].
>
> The study discusses two basic approaches to achieving tax compliance by design – the ***"secured chain approach"*** and the ***"centralised data approach"***.
>
> The idea behind the ***"secured chain approach"*** is to create a secured flow of information from the capture of business transactions to the final determination of the correct amount of tax being paid. The role of the revenue body is mainly to act as a facilitator of needed features in the environment in order to make sure that the flow of information from the taxpayer is secure enough. This reduces the need for the revenue body to handle all of the data by itself and it reduces the need for doing post-filing audits.
>
> The idea behind the ***"centralised data approach"*** is to make sure that the revenue body itself can capture as many business transactions from the source as possible in order to determine the right amount of tax to be paid with minimum information from the taxpayer. The role of the revenue body is more about managing the whole process, handling and transforming all information by itself so the need for the taxpayer to provide information on his own transactions is significantly reduced.

Together, both approaches show that there are a range of possibilities to create or support an environment conducive to tax compliance and reduced compliance burden. The report includes country examples to demonstrate the respective concepts.

Monitoring and evaluation of compliance risk management strategies

The focus on risk management also draws attention to the need to measure the effects, or outcomes, of interventions, both at the aggregate level and in respect of individual interventions. In short, results in terms of improved taxpayers' compliance cannot be judged by measuring outputs such as the number and value of completed audits, the amounts of tax debt collected, or educational activities; measures that are more "outcomes-focused" are necessary.

A key element of the recommended compliance risk management process (Figure 3.1) was a compliance measurement framework that would provide revenue bodies with a range of compliance indicators that could be used to monitor and evaluate the impacts of their compliance activities, both at the aggregate level and in respect of specific risk treatments strategies. Such a framework would enable a continual cycle of review and refinement. This issue was addressed initially in the FTA's report *Monitoring Taxpayers' Compliance: A Practical Guide Based on Revenue Body Experience* (OECD, 2008a). The report promoted the idea that revenue bodies should have in place a compliance monitoring framework at the aggregate/macro level that should include a set of measures and indicators for the major risk types (i.e. registration, filing on time, payment on time and correct reporting) across each of the major taxes administered. Consistent with this recommended approach, the report also acknowledged that a number of revenue bodies had taken steps to produce periodic estimates of the tax gap for their major taxes to improve their understanding of the likely scale and composition of non-compliance and its trend over time.

Further work in this area, but with a shift in focus to individual risk treatment strategies, was undertaken in 2010/11 and 2013/14. The note *Evaluating the effectiveness of compliance risk treatment strategies* (OECD, 2010b) set out a practical methodology for conducting outcome evaluations of compliance risk treatment strategies in priority areas. The note drew on innovative work undertaken by the ATO and was supplemented with further assistance from a number of other revenue bodies that had been intensifying their efforts to better understand the impacts of their compliance programme activities. After outlining a number of important concepts and issues that are often raised in an evaluation context (e.g. output/outcome programme model and attribution), the guidance note introduced and elaborated a four phase compliance effectiveness methodology for use with specific risk treatment strategies.

In October 2014, the FTA published the report *Measures of tax compliance outcomes: A practical guide* (OECD, 2014). Noting the pace of change and more recent developments concerning how tax compliance can be managed and influenced the report begins by explaining key terms and context concerning the measurement of outcomes, presents some guiding principles drawing on the experience of revenue bodies, and then presents a comprehensive stock take of practical approaches for measuring whether the right revenues are coming in, that taxpayers are complying voluntarily and that the community has confidence that tax is administered fairly. The report concludes with a segment discussing the challenge of choosing the "right" set of outcome measures for a revenue body and shares lessons learnt by revenue bodies on implementing outcome measures. Comments made by HMRC's Second Permanent Secretary Edward Troup, the report's sponsoring Commissioner, draw attention to the dynamics of the environment in which revenue bodies should address this matter:

> As our approach evolves we need to develop measures to demonstrate our successes and improve our performance. In recent years, measuring the effectiveness of innovative compliance interventions has been a challenge across the FTA. This

report does not prescribe a set solution because the development of measures is an ongoing process rather than a one-off effort. Instead, it builds on revenue bodies' experiences, facilitated by the unique international forum the FTA provides, to offer practical guidance on principles, approaches and implementation for compliance measures. By sharing best practice across revenue bodies, we make faster and surer progress on this and other challenges (OECD, 2014).

Managing taxpayers' compliance in 2014

This context provides a useful backdrop to understanding, in fairly high level terms, contemporary approaches of many revenue bodies for managing taxpayers' compliance, as gleaned from their survey responses.

For this series, revenue bodies were asked small number of questions dealing with: *(1)* the use of formal compliance risk management and, where used, the five key areas of tax compliance risk identified for 2014; *(2)* co-operative compliance approaches; *(3)* the use of tax gap estimation methodologies and random audit programmes; and *(4)* the use of technology for systematic third party data matching for for income tax and VAT administration purposes respectively. Survey responses were supplemented by research of published documents of a number of revenue bodies to provide additional insights. A summary of revenue bodies' responses is provided in Tables 3.9 and 3.10. The key findings and observations are as follows:

Compliance risk identification, assessment, and prioritisation

- The vast majority (53 of 56 revenue bodies) reported that they have a formal process for identifying, assessing and prioritising their compliance risks areas (e.g. profit shifting, VAT fraud, and tax debts) as part of their planning.
- From a risk menu comprised of nine risk categories, the five categories most frequently reported by revenue bodies as key priorities were:
  - Corporate profit shifting/ transfer pricing (37 countries).
  - VAT fraud (36 countries).
  - Economic activities in the hidden economy (37 countries).
  - Other tax avoidance schemes (32 countries).
  - Unpaid tax debts (31 countries).
- The very high priority being given to address corporate profit shifting/transfer pricing risks is in line with the G20's support for co-ordinated international actions (e.g. the measures contained in Base Erosion and Profit Shifting (BEPS) programme) and is reflected in the published corporate strategies of many revenue bodies, including the Canada Revenue Agency (CRA, 2014):

  To deter non-compliance, we are taking a strong stance against international tax evasion and aggressive tax avoidance, implementing a number of measures announced in Economic Action Plan 2013. These included the Offshore Tax Informant Program, new reporting requirements for international electronic fund transfers, a streamlined process for obtaining third party information, and expanded reporting requirements for taxpayers with foreign income or property. We have also continued to increase the number of auditors working on international files in 2013-2014, to ensure we have the on-the-ground capacity to get the job done.

Table 3.9. **Strategic approach for managing taxpayers' compliance**

Country	Formal risk management process is used	Tax gap estimates for some/ all taxes: Required by MOF	Research carried out	Results made public	Random audits for some/all taxes	Co-operative compliance model used or planned for large taxpayers	Computer-based systems: Matching income reports	VAT invoices
OECD countries								
Australia	✓	x	✓/1	✓/1	x /1	✓	✓	x
Austria	✓	x	x	n.a	✓	✓	✓	x
Belgium	✓	✓	✓	x	-	-	-	-
Canada	✓	x	x	n.a	✓	✓	✓	x
Chile	✓	x	✓	✓	x	x	✓	✓
Czech Republic	✓	✓	x	x	x	x	x	x
Denmark	✓	✓	✓	✓	✓	✓	✓	✓
Estonia	✓	✓	✓	✓/1	✓	x	✓	x
Finland	✓	✓/1	✓/1	✓/1	✓/1	✓ (pilot project)	✓	✓
France	✓	✓	x	n.a	✓	✓	✓	
Germany	✓	x	x	n.a	✓	x	✓	x
Greece	✓	-	-	-	-	-	-	-
Hungary	✓	x	x	x	✓	x /1	✓	✓
Iceland	✓	x	x	n.a	✓	x	✓	✓
Ireland	✓	x	x	n.a	✓	✓	✓	✓
Israel	✓	x	x	n.a	✓	✓/1	✓	✓
Italy	✓/1	x	x	n.a	x	✓	x	x
Japan	✓	x	x	n.a	✓	x	x	x
Korea	✓	x	x	x	x	✓	✓	✓
Luxembourg /1	✓	x	✓	✓	✓	x	x	✓
Mexico	✓	✓	✓	✓	x	✓	✓	✓
Netherlands	✓	x	x	n.a	✓	✓	✓	x
New Zealand	✓	x	x	n.a	x	✓	✓	x
Norway	✓	x	✓	x	✓	✓	✓	✓
Poland	✓	✓	✓	x	x	✓	x	x
Portugal	✓	x	✓	x	x	✓	✓	✓
Slovak Republic	✓	x	✓/1	✓	x	✓	x	✓
Slovenia	✓	x	✓	✓	x	✓	✓	✓
Spain	✓	x	x /1	n.a	x	✓	✓	✓
Sweden	✓	x	✓	✓	x	✓	✓	✓
Switzerland	✓ (for VAT)	x	✓	x	✓	✓	x	x
Turkey	✓	✓	✓	x	✓		✓	✓
United Kingdom	✓	✓	✓	✓	✓	✓	✓	x
United States	✓	x	✓	✓	✓	✓	✓	n.a
Non-OECD								
Argentina	x	x	✓	✓	-	-	✓ (as per Table 7.1)	
Brazil	✓	x	x	n.a	✓	x	✓	✓
Bulgaria	✓	x	✓	x	✓	✓	✓	✓
China	✓	x	✓	x	-	✓	✓	✓
Colombia	✓	x	✓	✓	✓	x	✓	✓
Costa Rica	✓	x	x /1	x /1	x	x	✓	✓/1
Croatia	✓	✓	✓	x	✓	✓	✓	x
Cyprus	x	x	x	n.a	✓	x	x	x
Hong Kong, China	✓	x	x	n.a	✓	x	✓	x
India	✓	x	x	n.a	✓	x	✓	n.a
Indonesia	✓	x	x	n.a	x	x /1	✓	✓
Latvia	✓	x	✓	x	x	x	✓	✓
Lithuania	✓	x	✓	x	✓/1	✓	✓	x
Malaysia	✓	x	x	n.a	✓	x	✓	n.a
Malta	✓	x	x	n.a	✓	x	✓	x
Morocco	x /1	x /1	x /1	n.a	x	✓/1	✓	x
Romania	✓	x	x /1	n.a	x	x	✓	x
Russia	✓	x	x	n.a	x	✓/1	✓	✓
Saudi Arabia	✓	x	x	n.a	x	x	✓	n.a.
Singapore	✓	x	x	n.a	✓	✓	✓	✓
South Africa	✓	x	x	n.a		✓	✓	x /1
Thailand	✓	x	✓	x	x	✓	x	x

For notes indicated by "/ (number)", see Notes to Tables section at the end of the chapter, p. 138.
Source: Tax Administration 2015 survey responses.

Table 3.10. **Managing taxpayers' compliance – Main compliance risks reported for 2014**

Country	Compliance risks – five main tax compliance risk areas identified and assessed by revenue body for 2014								
	Profit shifting /transfer pricing	Other tax avoidance schemes	VAT fraud	Other tax fraud	Hidden economy	Evasion – illegal activities	Other evasion	Unpaid tax debts	Non-filing of returns
OECD countries									
Australia	✓	✓	✓	✓	✓				
Austria	✓	✓	✓			✓		✓	
Belgium	✓	✓	✓				✓	✓	✓
Canada /1	✓	✓	✓		✓			✓	
Chile		✓	✓	✓	✓		✓		✓
Czech Republic			✓	✓	✓	✓			✓
Denmark	✓		✓		✓	✓	✓	✓	✓
Estonia			✓	✓	✓	✓	✓		
Finland	✓		✓	✓	✓			✓	
France	✓		✓		✓	✓			✓
Germany	✓		✓		✓	✓			✓
Greece	✓		✓		✓			✓	✓
Hungary	✓	✓	✓	✓	✓	✓	✓	✓	✓
Iceland	✓	✓	✓						✓
Ireland	/1	/1	/1	/1	/1	/1	/1	/1	/1
Israel	✓		✓		✓	✓			✓ /1
Italy	-	-	-	-	-	-	-	-	-
Japan	-	-	-	-	-	-	-	-	-
Korea	✓	✓	✓		✓			✓	
Luxembourg /1			✓					✓	✓
Mexico		✓	✓	✓				✓	✓
Netherlands	/1	/1	/1	/1	/1	/1	/1	/1	/1
New Zealand	✓	✓		✓	✓			✓	
Norway	✓	✓	✓	✓	✓	✓	-	-	✓
Poland	✓	✓	✓	✓	✓	✓		✓	✓
Portugal	✓	✓	✓	✓	✓				
Slovak Republic		✓	✓	✓				✓	✓
Slovenia	✓	✓	✓		✓			✓	✓
Spain	✓	✓	✓		✓			✓	
Sweden	✓	✓	✓		✓	✓			
Switzerland /1			✓		✓		✓	✓	
Turkey			✓	✓			✓		✓
United Kingdom	✓	✓		✓	✓			✓	
United States		✓		✓		✓		✓	✓
Non-OECD countries									
Argentina	-	-	-	-	-	-	-	-	-
Brazil	✓	✓		✓	✓			✓	
Bulgaria /1	✓		✓		✓		✓		
China	✓	✓	✓					✓	✓
Colombia	✓	✓	✓					✓	✓
Costa Rica				✓	✓	✓		✓	✓
Croatia	✓		✓		✓			✓	✓
Cyprus	✓		✓		✓			✓	✓
Hong Kong, China	✓	✓					✓	✓	✓
India	✓				✓		✓	✓	✓
Indonesia	✓	✓	✓					✓	✓
Latvia		✓	✓		✓			✓	✓
Lithuania		✓	✓	✓	✓	✓			
Malaysia	✓	✓			✓			✓	✓
Malta			✓	✓		✓		✓	✓
Morocco /1	-	-	-	-	-	-	-	-	-
Romania	✓	✓	✓	✓	✓				
Russia	✓	✓	✓	✓	✓				
Saudi Arabia	✓				✓	✓		✓	✓
Singapore /1	✓	✓	✓	✓	✓				
South Africa	✓ /1	✓ /1		✓ /1	✓ /1				
Thailand	✓	✓	✓		✓			✓	

For notes indicated by "/ (number)", see Notes to Tables section at the end of the chapter, p. 138.
Source: Tax Administration 2015 survey responses.

The use of co-operative compliance approaches

- Over 30 revenue bodies, including those in France, Hungary and Russia, reported that they are using, testing, or planning to use a co-operative compliance approach (sometimes referred to as "horizontal monitoring") for their largest taxpayers – see Austrian example in Box 3.3.

Box 3.3. Austria: The use of horizontal monitoring by the tax administration

Following the international example, large companies also have the opportunity to request supervision on an advisory basis in partnership with the Austrian tax and customs administration. The Horizontal Monitoring (HM) pilot project was started for this purpose in November 2011. Representatives from the Austrian Economic Chamber, Federation of Austrian Industries, Austrian Chamber of Public Accountants and Tax Advisers and the University of Vienna were involved in development of the project.

HM uses a tax control framework that is based on risk analysis and maintained on a co-operative, partnership basis. Cooperative development of the tax control system is the focus of regular meetings during the ongoing HM process. One of the key objectives of HM, namely timely and legally accurate collection of taxes, can be best pursued in this fashion. In 2013, the number of participating companies increased to 15. These are currently at a variety of different stages in the HM process. Six of the companies have already signed the "Declaration for Participation in the HM Project". For companies, participation in HM increases planning and legal security and reduces compliance costs. In addition to timely and legally accurate tax collection, the tax and customs administration expects that it will be able to shift personnel to risk areas over the medium term.

Source: Annual Report 2013 of the Austrian Tax and Customs Administration.

The use of tax gap estimation methodologies

The use of tax gap estimation methodologies is a relatively contentious issue among tax administrators internationally with some (i.e. opponents) questioning their accuracy, reliability and overall value to management of the tax system, while others (i.e. proponents) argue that, properly designed and conducted, they can provide useful information that assists both internal and external stakeholders in a variety of ways, notwithstanding their limitations.

Although still confined to a minority of countries covered by the series, interest in the use of tax gap measures, particularly in respect of the VAT, has grown considerably in recent years as Governments, tax administrators and others have sought to quantify the extent of revenue leakage from countries' tax systems and/or to better understand the overall impacts of revenue bodies' compliance improvement activities. Also contributing to this increased interest has been a series of major tax gap studies initiated by the EC into members' VAT systems and a number of innovative research efforts and approaches employed by some national revenue bodies (e.g. the United Kingdom HMRC and the Danish Tax and Customs Administration). Work of the FTA has also drawn attention to the potential value of tax gap measures (in an overall strategic sense rather than to monitor operational performance) to promote better understanding of the workings of a country's tax system and the effectiveness of its administration.

For this series, revenue bodies were asked a limited range of questions concerning the use of tax gap methodologies and to provide any additional information concerning specific related initiatives deemed to be relevant. The Secretariat also undertook some limited research to identify the status of work in this area and a brief summary is set out in Table 3.11. Drawing on all of the information obtained, the following observations can be made:

- Around 20% of revenue bodies (11 of 56) reported they are required by their MOF to provide periodic estimates of the tax gap for some/all of the major taxes administered.
- Around 43% of surveyed revenue bodies (24 of 56), including those with a formal mandate to do so, reported they undertake research to produce estimates of the aggregate tax gap for some/all of their major taxes.
- Relatively few revenue bodies (13 of 56 surveyed) reported that the results of their tax gap estimation research are made public.

Table 3.11. **Tax gap estimation activities of selected revenue bodies, etc.**

Country	Description of activities
Australia	**Historically**, the ATO was not a proponent of tax gap measurement, given concerns for the accuracy and reliability of the underlying methodologies, the costs of random audit activities, and doubts as to their value in a compliance management context. However, over more recent years work has been undertaken to explore their value in relation to Australia's VAT and Luxury Car Tax. These estimates were published in its 2011-12, 2012-13, and 2013-14 annual reports. Following a detailed study in 2013-14 of tax gap measurement methodologies and their use by a number of countries, the ATO announced in August 2014 its intention to take a phased approach to expanding the scope of its tax gap research to include all the major taxes it administers, including income taxes.
Chile	The Internal Revenue Service of Chile (SII) has carried out measurements of the tax gap dating back to 1980. The gap rates have been mainly estimated for VAT, the major source of Chile's tax revenue. The methodology for the estimation of the tax gap relies on data from National Accounts, published by Chile's Central Bank. The results of SII's research are published annually.
Denmark	The Danish Tax and Customs Administration (SKAT) has for a number of years carried out a compliance measurement programme for its major taxes. Historically, the programme has been used to gather an extensive array of data on aspects of taxpayer compliance (e.g. the nature and magnitude of taxpayers' errors and regional/local compliance patterns), in order to help refocus and redesign its compliance strategies. Reports of its findings are made public. For this series, SKAT reported that it is required by the Government/ MOF to keep the tax gap at ≤ 2% of estimated tax potential (for PIT, CIT and VAT but excluding large corporates (over 250 employees for VAT and CIT) and moonlighting (shadow economy) activities). SKAT reported that it measures the income tax and VAT gap for individuals and SME's on a biannual basis using a comprehensive programme of random audits.
Estonia	The ETCB produces an annual Strategic Base Analysis where taxes and risks as well as tax gaps are calculated and analysed. In 2013-14, it undertook work with the IMF, applying its Revenue Administration Gap Analysis Programme VAT gap estimation methodology to Estonia for the period 2007–12 to assist authorities better understand their VAT system performance. The methodology employs a top-down approach for estimating the potential VAT base, using statistical data on value-added generated in each sector. There are two main components to this methodology for estimating the VAT compliance gap: *(1)* estimate the potential net VAT collections for a given period, and *(2)* determine the accrued net VAT collections for that period. The difference between the two values is the compliance gap. The study was part of work to better understand the key sources of VAT revenue leakage, a particular cause of concern in recent years. A copy of the IMF's technical assistance report on the topic can be found at www.imf.org/external/pubs/cat/longres.aspx?sk=41578.0.
European Commission (EC)	Concerned for the incidence of VAT revenue leakage across the EU, the EC engaged external consultants in both 2007 and 2012 to undertake a comprehensive study of the VAT tax gap for EU member states. The EC's most study report of 2013 provides reasonably detailed information and explanations on estimated VAT gaps for a period of up to ten years (to 2011) for all 27 EU members, except Cyprus. This study report can be found at http://ec.europa.eu/taxation_customs/resources/documents/common/publications/studies/vat-gap.pdf. An updated report, yet to be studied in detail by the FTA Secretariat cover years up to 2012 and provides some revision of previously reported information.

Table 3.11. **Tax gap estimation activities of selected revenue bodies, etc.** *(continued)*

Country	Description of activities
Finland	Following a Government direction, the Finnish Tax Administration (VERO) launched a project in 2013 to develop indicators for gauging the tax gap, in co-operation with the National Board of Customs, the Ministry of Finance, Statistics Finland, and the Government Institute of Economic Research. As reported in VERO's 2013 annual report, in its first year the project focused on drawing up a more accurate definition of the tax gap, getting acquainted with international practices and testing methods by which audit results could be applied more generally. Based on the analysis completed and relying on methods developed by the IMF, an assessment of the tax gap will be launched in 2014, commencing with VAT.
Korea	The National Tax Service reported in its survey response that it intends undertaking tax gap research for its major taxes. Its 2014 business plan sets out its intention to commence gap measurement research in respect of income taxes.
Latvia	For this edition of the series, Latvia's State Revenue Service reported that tax studies were being undertaken in 2014 for VAT, labour taxes and excises.
Lithuania	The State Tax Inspectorate (STI) reported that it uses both direct and indirect methods for evaluation of both the shadow economy and tax gap. Surveys for evaluation of the shadow economy are made periodically (generally involving independent research bodies; drawing on this research, the STI undertakes an evaluation of the tax gap. In addition, the STI uses indirect methods of shadow and tax gap evaluation (e.g. calculations using household consumption data).
Mexico	The SAT is required by law to deliver two studies each year into the incidence of tax evasion. These studies are typically carried out by external researches (i.e. academic institutions). In 2013, two studies were completed: (1) a study to produce global estimates of non-compliance for the major taxes; and (2) a study to identify the main determinants influencing attitudes towards compliance or non-compliance (evasion) in the payment of taxes in Mexico.
Slovak Republic	Concerned about a decline in VAT revenue, the MOF (with IMF assistance) has been carrying out gap analysis research of Slovakia's VAT system (initially for 2008-12).
Slovenia	For this edition, the revenue body reported that the Government's Statistical Office calculates the VAT tax gap for the purpose of monitoring the effectiveness of VAT collection. The estimates calculated are made public.
Sweden	The Swedish Tax Agency (STA) conducts tax gap research studies periodically to derive estimates of the tax gap, including its key constituents that are summarised in a "tax gap map". Officials have reported that the main reason for preparing the "tax gap map" is to construct a simple and pedagogic overview of the tax gap to facilitate internal and external communication and to identify areas where deeper knowledge is required. The STA's most recent study report *The Development of the Tax Gap in Sweden in 2007-12*, published in early 2014 follows an assignment given by the Swedish Government to produce a new tax gap map, quantify the tax gap, and describe how the gap had changed between 2007 and 2012. The report can be found at www.skatteverket.se/download/18.15532c7b1442f256baeae28/1395223863657/The+development+of+the+tax+gap+in+Sweden+2007-12.pdf.
United Kingdom	HMRC has over the last decade published regular assessments of the tax gap, primarily in the area of indirect taxes (VAT and Excise). In 2009, it published a comprehensive assessment of the tax gap for all taxes administered, based on what are described as "top-down" and "bottom-up" measurement approaches, which was published in conjunction with the UK Chancellor's Pre-budget report. This research has continued and HMRC now publishes regular updates of its tax gap estimates for all taxes, in line with its strategic goal "to close the tax gap". In late 2013, the IMF conduct a review of HMRC's tax gap analysis programme and provides advice and guidance on further improving it. Details of HMRC's most recent gap research published in October 2014 can be found at https://www.gov.uk/government/uploads/system/uploads/attachment_data/file/364009/4382_Measuring_Tax_Gaps_2014_IW_v4B_accessible_20141014.pdf.
United States	IRS administers the National Research Programme (NRP) to develop comprehensive tax gap updates for 2001 and subsequent years. The IRS's latest series of tax gap estimates was published in January 2012 in respect of the 2006 fiscal year and a rolling programme of further studies is underway to update the 2006 estimates. The results of the NRP are published on the IRS's website: www.irs.gov/uac/The-Tax-Gap.

Source: Secretariat research and survey responses.

The use of random audit programmes

Random audit programmes have been used by revenue bodies for many years for a variety of purposes: *(1)* to develop/refine audit risk profiling systems; *(2)* to assist in the development of tax gap estimates; *(3)* to monitor compliance in specific areas of the tax system; *(4)* as a general deterrent to non-compliance; and *(5)* as a source of data to support legislative changes. Notwithstanding the useful information they can provide, some revenue bodies are reluctant to use such programmes given concerns for the additional compliance costs they impose on compliant taxpayers and the revenue foregone from deploying audit staff away from more revenue productive work.

Drawing on the survey responses and related research the key findings and observations are as follows:

- Over half of surveyed revenue bodies (29 of 56) reported the use of, or intention to use, random audit programmes for some of the taxes administered.
- Details of the random audit programmes of a small number of revenue bodies, obtained from survey responses and/or other published materials, are briefly described below to provide additional insights:
  - ***Canada:*** The CRA runs a Research Audit Programme to obtain information on the compliance of the small and medium enterprise taxpayer population. Files are selected randomly using statistical sampling methodologies rather than based on an evaluation of risk in order to produce statistically valid and unbiased results. In particular, the objectives of the research programme are to measure the non-compliance rates by industry as a basis for monitoring compliance trends over time; and to provide information to validate and refine the CRA's risk assessment systems in order to improve file selection and target audit resources more effectively. Historically, aggregate results have been published but the information produced is not used for tax gap measurement purposes.
  - ***Hungary:*** A Random Based Selection System (VAK-system) has been operating since 2001, entailing some 5% of post-tax audits that are selected on the basis of a stratified sample. Conclusions of general taxpayer behaviour are drawn by exploring the data of the stratified sample. Test results of VAK can be used to calculate the portion of concealed tax detectable by tax authority means and provide information for the measurement of the selective efficiency.
  - ***Ireland:*** Revenue conducts a random audit programme each year on a sample of cases drawn from a population of taxpayers (largely self-employed and investor-type taxpayers). The primary purpose of the programme is to ensure that no self-assessed taxpayer is exempt (or believes himself or herself exempt) from the possibility of being audited. The programme is also designed to measure and track compliance with tax legislation and to provide feedback and insight on new trends and compliance issues within the tax system, thereby informing Revenue's compliance strategy. Aggregate results are published but the findings are not used for tax gap estimation purposes.
  - ***United Kingdom:*** HMRC undertakes on-going research to produce aggregate tax gap estimates for all its major taxes. The detailed findings and descriptions of the methodologies used are prepared in accordance with the Code of Practice for Official Statistics. In addition to publishing annually the results of its tax gap research HMRC also makes public the detail of the methodology its uses to derive its estimates. The information in Box 3.4 has been extracted directly from its published report and provides further details concerning its random audit programme.

Box 3.4. United Kingdom HMRC's random audit programmes

Random enquiry programmes allow HMRC to estimate the extent of under-declaration of liabilities arising from the submission of incorrect returns. Each return selected is subject to a full enquiry involving a complete examination of books and records. Under certain circumstances, a full enquiry may not take place if the return can be verified through third party information.

There are three direct tax random enquiry programmes which are used to produce tax gap estimates. They cover: *(1)* Self-assessment individuals and small partnerships; *(2)* Small and medium-sized employers; and *(3)* Corporation tax for small and medium-sized businesses. In its latest cycle of research for the 2011-12 income year, the sample sizes applied were: *(1)* 2 599 taxpayers; *(2)* 819 taxpayers; and *(3)* 567 taxpayers respectively.

To produce population estimates for total tax gaps from the samples, the average tax gap estimates from random enquiries are multiplied by the number of taxpayers in the population. Adjustments are made for cases selected but "dropped" – that is, no enquiry is made because the return satisfies the criteria for not taking up an enquiry.

Source: Measuring Tax Gaps 2014 Edition, Methodological Annex.

With the increasing emphasis being given by many revenue bodies to strengthen their knowledge of the nature and causes of tax non-compliance and the concomitant interest in developing more sophisticated automated risk profiling approaches, it would appear that random audits will continue to be used fairly widely, notwithstanding related cost considerations.

Use of computer-based data matching systems to address non-compliance

Income tax administration

As described more fully in Chapter 9, the income tax laws of many countries include reporting requirements on third parties such as employers (re employment income), financial institutions (re interest income) and public companies (re dividends) to provide revenue bodies with an extensive source of information that can be used to verify taxpayers' compliance with the tax laws.

With use of technology rapidly increasing across the business population over the last decade or so, the opportunity for many of them to provide timely reporting to revenue bodies at minimal compliance costs has increased enormously. At the same time, many revenue bodies have become more innovative in their uses of such information not only using the information reported to detect instances of non-compliance but also to prepare pre-filled tax returns (or similar documents) that can be sent to taxpayers for their verification. Using third party data in this way reduces taxpayers' compliance burden and reduces the errors that might otherwise arise. The use of prefilling is discussed in Chapter 7.

The administrative tasks associated with receiving and accurately processing large volumes of third party reports with tax reports is not a straightforward undertaking and revenue bodies generally have had to develop their capabilities in this area over a considerable period of time.

Specific challenges that can and have arisen include: *(1)* developing standards for the accurate reporting by third parties of third party reports using electronic media; *(2)* ensuring timely reporting compliance by third parties; *(3)* achieving high rates of accuracy in matching taxpayer identities contained in third party reports with revenue body records; *(4)* once taxpayer matches are achieved, using the third party data to identify potential "at risk" cases; *(5)* dealing with large numbers of "at risk" cases identified in a cost effective way; and *(6)* finding cost effective means for using "unmatched" third party reports.

> "We matched more than 650 million transactions against information we hold that helped to identify where individuals and businesses may not have reported all of their income. Around 480 000 income tax reviews and audits were conducted as a result of data-matching activities."
> — ATO Annual Report 2013-14, page 57

These challenges will be brought into further focus with the adoption by many countries of the Common Reporting Standard (CRS) for automatic exchanges of third party reporting that are expected to commence in 2017. This standard, which relates to the reporting of financial account information of non-residents between participating countries, is expected to entail many millions of transactions that will need to be systematically processed by revenue bodies to detect and deter tax non-compliance.

VAT administration

Rapid growth in the use by business of modern accounting systems, including for invoicing purposes, has also opened up new opportunities for revenue bodies to enhance the administration of their VAT systems. While not the subject of detailed study by the FTA, countries such as Chile, Korea, Mexico, and Portugal are known to have developed applications for the mass processing of VAT invoice data, to assist in the detection of non-compliance. Chile, a country that relies to a very large degree on its VAT as a source of tax revenue, has also developed a number of innovative strategies for assisting very small taxpayers manage their VAT administration that are described briefly in the recent FTA report *Tax compliance by design.*

For this series revenue bodies were asked whether they administer computer-based information processing systems for: *(1)* matching large volumes of third party income reports to check income tax compliance and for other income tax administration purposes (e.g. prefilling of tax returns); and *(2)* processing bulk VAT invoice data to check compliance by businesses with VAT obligations.

Income matching programmes

Nine countries, including 7 OECD countries (i.e. Czech Republic, Italy, Japan, Luxembourg, Poland, Slovak Republic, and Switzerland) reported that they do not administer such systems for managing taxpayers' compliance. The precise reasons why such systems are not used has not been explored but may be explained, in part, by policy-related factors. For example, in some countries interest and dividend income is not assessable in the hands of residents or it may be subject to final withholding tax at source meaning that there is no obligation to report it in annual tax returns. In both situations, there is no need for revenue bodies to capture and process income-related reports.

Bulk processing of VAT invoice data

Twenty five countries reported they were using systems to process VAT invoice data in some way to assist them manage VAT compliance. The practice appears particularly popular in Central and South American countries and its adoption has grown over recent years among some EU countries in the aftermath of the findings the EC-commissioned VAT gap studies.

Note

1. *Modernising Government* describes "open government" as embodying the following characteristics: *(1) transparency*: that its actions, and the individuals responsible for those actions, will be exposed to public scrutiny and challenge; *(2) accessibility*: that its services and information on its activities will be readily accessible; and *(3) responsiveness*: that it will be responsive to new ideas, demands and needs.

Notes to Tables

Table 3.1. Selected management practices: business plans, annual reports, surveys

/1. **Argentina:** AFIP produced and published in 2011 its Strategic Plan 2011-15 detailing its institutional mandates (mission, vision and values) and the strategic objectives defined in long term. **Belgium**: There is an integrated management plan for multi-year period 2012-17; a new plan will be prepared in 2015. **Brazil**: The RFB developed software that registers the strategic objectives, goals and results indicators. In addition, a management information centre with control over all RFB areas, including strategic management, was created. **Bulgaria:** Only the 5 year business plan of the NRA is published. **Canada**: The Corporate Business Plan is a confidential document. Only the Summary of the Corporate Business Plan is published and made available to the public. **Chile**: The SII does not publish an annual report; however, relevant information is made public in the Annual Public Account. Information published includes data re taxpayer population, amounts of tax collected, tax gap estimates, human resources of the tax administration, e-services offered, etc. **Croatia:** The annual report is submitted to the Ministry of Finance which publishes a consolidated report for the Ministry as a whole. **Cyprus:** Only collections are published by Direct Tax Department. Results of Direct Tax and VAT Departments are published in the General Auditors Report. **Estonia:** Annual performance report: the performance results of ETCB are incorporated into the annual report of Ministry of Finance and it is published on the website of ETCB; ETCB does not prepare separate annual report since 2008. **Israel**: Partial publication but does not include data. **Korea**: On an irregular basis. **Lithuania:** STI annual report is not made public because STI is not a separate holder of assignments since 2011. **Malaysia**: The IRBM Corporate Plan 2012-15 was published in 2012. It is a revised version of the existing corporate plan and outlines the strategies in the management of IT, revenue and organisational risk as well as optimum use of resources, co-operation networking and human capital development for the period 2012 to 2015. **Morocco**: Partial publication. **Netherlands**: The State Secretary for Finance reports on future strategies for the NTCA as well as performance targets as part of Annual Budget. **Russia**: A plan of activities for the FTS for each calendar year is approved by the MOF and published on the FTS's website. **Saudi Arabia**: Done informally through website and weekly newspapers where views and comments are received and responded to through workshops and seminars. **Spain:** The Institute for Fiscal Studies (part of MOF) carries out an annual Public Opinion Survey on tax matters, including tax administration. The Tax Agency also uses a public poll on e-services for PIT. **Switzerland**: Federal cantons are in charge of contact with citizens and conduct their own surveys. The Federal Tax Administration conducts surveys of VAT taxpayers. **Turkey**: Surveys are applied to all taxpayers as whole, not separately.

/2. **Argentina:** The final Report of the Annual Management Plan is prepared by AFIP and submitted for the approval of an Advisory Council formed by representatives of different public institutions. **Brazil**: The Federal Revenue publishes data related to the services provided to taxpayers via monthly reports and a Citizen Service Charter (both published on the internet). **Chile:** Surveys required by law introduced in 2010 that establishes an economic incentive to improve service quality based on an annual survey that measures a quality indicator (or net satisfaction rate) for both individual and business taxpayers; there are annual targets to be met to achieve the economic incentive. **Croatia:** Apart from the standards that are regulated within the national tax law, the tax administration does not have a formal set of service delivery standards for all of its services, but a "Catalogue and standards to the taxpayers" is currently being prepared and will be made public. **Morocco**: Every three years. **Netherlands**: Reports are made available to Parliament twice every year. **Russia:** Report on the results and main activities (DROND) of the FTS of Russia for the medium term is sent to the Russian Ministry of Finance annually and published as part of Russian Ministry of Finance's DROND on the MOF website.

Table 3.9. Strategic approach for managing taxpayers' compliance

/1 **Australia:** Research to date has been in respect of indirect taxes but is to be extended to direct taxes over the next two years. As the new estimates are developed a decision will be made by the ATO on the benefits of including them in their published effectiveness measures. The ATO is giving consideration to introducing a random audit programme. Central to their decision to proceed will be the ability to design a programme which can sufficiently minimise any additional regulatory burden on taxpayers as well as administrative and opportunity costs to the ATO. **Costa Rica:** Tax gap estimation is within the competency of the General Directorate of Fiscal Matters in the MOF, while some studies regarding tax evasion have been published by the Comptroller General; VAT invoice data are partially available (i.e. for transactions made with debit and credit cards. **Estonia:** The ETCB produces an annual Strategic Base Analysis where taxes and risks as well as tax gaps are calculated and analysed. This is one of the inputs for strategic planning for the following period. The results are made public only partially according to need. **Finland:** The Tax Administration is required to provide tax gap estimates in 2014; research associated with this requirement will be supported by random audits conducted on a small scale from 2014. **Hungary:** A Horizontal Monitoring Committee was established in 2013 and it is currently examining the possibility of introducing a co-operative compliance-based model. **Israel:** Applied only for certain sectors and executed through headquarters, not the Large Taxpayer Office. **Italy:** Process described as only for sector studies concerning non-filed returns or returns filed with anomalous data (and not for large taxpayers). **Lithuania:** A random audit programme to test VAT compliance commenced in 2014 in response to recommendations from its MOF. **Luxembourg:** There are separate direct and indirect tax administrations; only the Indirect Tax Administration uses a risk assessment process, conducts random audits, and estimates tax gap (VAT only). **Morocco:** The tax administration is currently implementing a formal process for identifying, assessing and prioritising its key compliance risks areas. This project began in 2013. Concerning the use of co-operative compliance approaches, the tax administration has adopted an enhanced programme of categorisation which is a new approach for managing compliance of enterprises. **Romania:** Gap estimation work will be undertaken as part of NAFA's reform programme (RAMP); **Russia:** FTS reported that pilot project was launched in 2012 with certain large taxpayers who agreed to participate; taxpayers concluded agreements with FTS to a form of "horizontal monitoring", as seen in the Netherlands, which seeks to broaden information exchange and improve tax compliance. The results of the pilot programme will determine if it is to be extended. **Slovak Republic:** Tax gap analysis concerning Slovakia's VAT is undertaken by the MOF. **Spain:** A comparison is made with National Accounts data each year. **South Africa:** SARS does not yet reconcile detailed VAT invoices to match input and output credits, although this is part of SARS longer term strategy.

Table 3.10. Managing taxpayers' compliance – main compliance risks for 2014

/1 **Bulgaria:** Revenue body also identified SSC non-compliance as a high risk area. **Canada:** other tax avoidance includes offshore non-compliance while hidden economy includes non-filing. **Ireland:** Revenue identifies and addresses compliance risk across all the sectors listed in the menu. It does not prioritise one area over another and resources are deployed commensurate with the risks identified in each of these sectors. **Israel:** There is no general reporting requirement. However, the risk of non-reporting by those who are so required has been identified. A special commission is working on expanding the reporting requirement to specific populations and also an intelligence project examines profiling risks and produces additional individuals required to report. For example, quantitative parameters are applied concerning ownership of luxury assets, excessive travel etc. **Luxembourg:** Risk areas concern VAT only. **Morocco:** The tax administration is currently implementing a formal process for identifying, assessing and prioritising its key compliance risks areas. This project began in 2013. **Netherlands**: NTCA applies Compliance Risk Management which is a systematic process in which a tax administration makes deliberate choices on which treatment instruments could be used to effectively stimulate compliance and prevent non-compliance, based on the knowledge of all taxpayers (behaviour) and related to the available capacity. **South Africa:** SARS introduced its first SARS Compliance Programme for the five year period 2012/13 – 2016/17. The following seven broad priority areas have been identified: *(1)* Wealthy South Africans and their associated trusts; *(2)* Large business and transfer pricing; *(3)* Construction industry; *(4)* Illicit cigarettes; *(5)* Undervaluation of imports in the clothing and textile industry; *(6)* Tax practitioners and trade intermediaries; and *(7)* Small businesses. **Switzerland:** All risk categories relate only to VAT administration and it also reported risks in particular industrial sectors in its top five risk areas. **Singapore:** IRAS also identified compliance risks arising from excessive and incorrect expense claims in its top five risk areas.

Bibliography

ATO (2014a), *ATO Corporate Plan 2014-18*, Australian Taxation Office, Canberra.

ATO (2014b), *Annual Report 2013-14*, Australian Taxation Office Canberra.

Austrian Federal Ministry of Finance (2014), *Annual Report 2013 of the Austrian Tax and Customs Administration*, Vienna.

CRA (2014), *Annual Report 2013-14*, Canada Revenue Agency, Ottawa.

Castro H.J.F et al. (2013), *Study of Global Tax Evasion (commissioned by Mexico's SAT)*, Monterey Institute of Technology and Higher Studies, Mexico City.

Centre for Social and Economic Research (2013), *Study to Quantify and Analyse the VAT Gap in the EU-27 Member States: Final Report*, Report produced for the European Commission, The Hague.

HMRC (2014a), *Business Plan 2014-16,* United Kingdom Her Majesty's Revenue and Customs, London.

HMRC (2014b), *Measuring Tax Gaps 2014 Edition,* United Kingdom Her Majesty's Revenue and Customs, London.

HMRC (2014c), *Measuring Tax Gaps, 2014 Edition, Methodological Annex,* United Kingdom Her Majesty's Revenue and Customs, London.

HMRC (2012), *Business Plan 2012-15,* United Kingdom Her Majesty's Revenue and Customs, London.

IMF (2014), *Republic of Estonia: Technical Assistance Report-Revenue Administration Gap Analysis Program-The Value-Added Tax Gap,* International Monetary Fund, Washington.

IRS (2014), *IRS Strategic Plan 2014-17,* United States Internal Revenue Service, Washington, DC.

Latvian State Revenue Service, *State Revenue Service Business Strategy 2014-2016,* Riga.

New Zealand Inland Revenue Department (2014), *Statement of Intent 2014-18.* Wellington.

OECD (2014), *Tax compliance by design*, OECD Publishing, Paris, http://dx.doi.org/10.1787/9789264223219-en.

OECD (2013a), *Co-operative Compliance: A Framework*, OECD Publishing, Paris, http://dx.doi.org/10.1787/9789264200852-en.

OECD (2013b), *Together for Better Outcomes,* OECD Publishing, Paris, http://dx.doi.org/10.1787/9789264200838-en.

OECD (2012), *Right from the Start: Influencing the Compliance Environment for Small and Medium-sized Enterprises* OECD Publishing, Paris, www.oecd.org/site/ctpfta/49428016.pdf (accessed on 13 March 2015).

OECD (2010a), *Evaluating the effectiveness of compliance risk treatment strategies,* OECD Publishing, Paris, www.oecd.org/tax/administration/46274278.pdf (accessed on 13 March 2015).

OECD (2010b), *Understanding and Influencing Taxpayers' Compliance Behaviour*, OECD Publishing, Paris, www.oecd.org/tax/administration/46274793.pdf (accessed on 13 March 2015).

OECD (2008a), *Monitoring Taxpayers' Compliance: A Practical Guide Based on Revenue Body Experience,* OECD Publishing, Paris, www.oecd.org/tax/administration/40947920.pdf (accessed on 13 March 2015).

OECD (2008b), *Study into the Role of Tax Intermediaries,* OECD Publishing, Paris, http://dx.doi.org/10.1787/9789264041813-en.

OECD (2005), *Modernising Government: The Way Forward*, OECD Publishing, Paris, http://dx.doi.org/10.1787/9789264010505-en.

OECD (2004), *Compliance Risk Management: Managing and Improving Tax Compliance,* OECD Publishing, Paris, www.oecd.org/dataoecd/44/19/33818656.pdf.

SARS (2014), *SARS Strategic Plan 2014-2019,* South African Revenue Service, Pretoria.

Chapter 4

Human resource management and tax administration

This chapter outlines aspects of revenue bodies' approaches to human resources management (HRM), including overall strategy, recruitment and appointment and related autonomy, measuring staff engagement, staff development, and performance management and remuneration. It provides examples of specific approaches and initiatives being deployed by revenue bodies to improve overall organisational performance and staff well-being. It concludes with a section on selected staff metrics (e.g. age profiles and qualifications).

Key points

Aspects of Human Resources Management Strategy

- The vast majority (88%) of revenue bodies reported having a formal HRM strategy, with around the same proportion (93%) having conducted assessments of current and future skills and capability needs, and having plans in place to meet these needs.
- Just under two-thirds of revenue bodies have major changes planned or underway in their policies in one or more of the areas of recruitment, training, performance or rewards; many revenue bodies (43%) have plans for significant changes to policies regarding training and development.
- Most revenue bodies periodically survey staff on their levels of satisfaction, engagement and motivation. Almost all of these share survey results with staff and most (84%) also consult with staff when considering responses to survey findings.

Staff Recruitment, Appointment and Development

- With a few notable exceptions in OECD countries, most revenue bodies have a fair degree of autonomy for managing staff recruitment, although for most this is subject to budgetary limits set by government or Ministry of Finance; some revenue bodies are subject to Government staff recruitment freezes to cut costs.
- Most revenue bodies (93%) are able to recruit staff and make appointments based on clearly defined qualification and experience criteria.
- Most revenue bodies reported they have staff development initiatives to increase commercial awareness (63%) and risk management capability (89%); around two-thirds (68%) of revenue bodies undertaking staff development to increase commercial awareness use external networks for this purpose.

Performance Management and Remuneration

- Most revenue bodies (82%) have performance management systems in place, although a fair proportion of these (20%) do not set objectives for each member of staff at the start of the performance period; the vast majority of revenue bodies (92%) review the performance of each staff member at least annually.
- Most revenue bodies (80%) have staff remuneration levels tied directly or broadly to wider public sector pay scales, with the balance having their own unique arrangements. Over two-thirds reported they have some flexibility to reward good performance.

Overall staffing levels and attrition

- The majority of revenue bodies (60%) experienced net reductions in staffing during 2013, with relatively large net reductions seen in Canada, Greece, United Kingdom and United States.
- Attrition rates varied considerably, ranging from 0.9% (Malaysia) to 13% (Mexico) but were concentrated towards the lower end of this range.

Age profiles and educational qualifications

- There are significant variations in the age profiles of revenue bodies' staff when viewed across different geographical groupings, with considerably older workforces seen in Nordic countries, other European countries (e.g. Belgium, Ireland, Italy, Netherlands, Portugal, and Spain) and Colombia.
- There is a particularly high correlation between those revenue bodies reporting both a relatively high proportion of staff with academic qualifications and a workforce that is predominantly comprised of staff under 50 years of age (e.g. in Chile, Korea, Latvia, Russia, Thailand, and Turkey).

Introduction

The investments made by revenue bodies in employing staff, including their recruitment, remuneration, and development, are by far the single largest component of total operating budgets, and for some exceed 80% of their total annual operating budget (Chapter 5 refers). Competent, professional, and productive staff are also an essential enabler for revenue bodies to carry out their basic mandate. For these reasons, how this investment is managed is a critical issue for all revenue bodies.

Recent years have seen an increasing number of revenue bodies reducing and/or reshaping their workforces to meet newly emerging priorities. At the same time, all revenue bodies generally face an environment with a changing risk picture, increasing work volumes and growing law complexity, and rising community expectations. Technological advances, affecting both revenue bodies and their clients, are also having a major impact. All of these factors heighten the need for revenue bodies to have human resource management strategies in place that will enable them to meet their current and future challenges, as indicated in the following quote:

> As tax administration becomes increasingly complex and the demand for varied taxpayer services increases, we are continually challenged with the task of maintaining a workforce with diverse, advanced skill sets. An additional challenge is that a considerable percentage of our workforce is currently eligible for retirement. By 2016, 41% of IRS front-line managers and 61% of IRS executives will be retirement eligible. These employees possess valuable experience, knowledge and skills that we will need to replenish. Properly executing succession planning and implementing knowledge management solutions, while attracting and retaining the next generation of IRS employees, is critical to our long-term success. To ensure taxpayers and the tax community continue to view our workforce as highly competent, we must identify and close skill gaps, develop employees' skill sets, provide career advancement opportunities and grow our future leaders to be prepared for tomorrow (IRS Strategic Plan 2014-17, page 8).

This chapter broadly follows the structure outlined in the chapter of the EC's Fiscal Blueprints (also described in Chapter 1) dealing with human resource management (HRM). The EC's blueprint sets out a framework to promote:

> [...] the development of human resources management strategy, policies, systems and procedures that support the achievement of the tax administration's objectives and the development of members of staff through structured training and professional development

The blueprints also set out the key components of a modern and efficient HRM function under the following broad headings:

- ***Strategy:*** Development of human resource management strategy, policies and systems which fully support the tax administration's business strategy
- ***Autonomy:*** The revenue body is empowered to make decisions about matters such as recruitment, retention, performance management, promotion, career progression, training and development, dismissal and retirement.
- ***Policies and practices:*** Human resource policies and practices that motivate, support, and protect employees.
- ***Training and development strategy:*** A long-term training and development strategy for employees endorsed at top management level.

- ***Structure and systems:*** An organisational structure and systems to support the delivery of employee training and development needs.

This chapter highlights some aspects of HRM strategies and major policy changes implemented by revenue bodies drawing on survey responses, annual reports and other sources. It seeks to present a summary picture of the state of play and provide examples and references that may assist revenue bodies as they assess their current situation and lay out directions for the future. The overall aim is to: a) gather insights on key elements of revenue bodies' human resources management practices and priorities; b) highlight selected examples of good practice described in revenue body publications; and c) identify opportunities for revenue bodies to consider when reviewing aspects of their HRM performance. Also included are staff metrics covering overall staff numbers, recruitment, rates of attrition, age profile and qualifications.

Aspects of revenue bodies' HRM strategy

Revenue bodies were asked a few basic questions relating to key elements of their approach to HRM, for example: *(1)* Does the revenue body have a formal human resources management strategy/plan? *(2)* Does it assess current and future staff skills and capability needs, and does it have a plan for filling identified gaps? *(3)* Does it have formal targets for increasing staff capabilities? They were also surveyed on whether they are planning major changes in key areas of policy in relation to human resources management: recruitment, training and development, performance management, rewards and remuneration, and plans for dealing with anticipated staff or capability increases or reductions. A summary of responses is provided in Table 4.1, while some observations on the responses and related research are set out below:

- The vast majority of revenue bodies (88%) reported having a formal HRM strategy or plan covering some, if not all, of their activities and many now report against aspects of this in their annual performance reports, with a broad range of topics covered including recruitment, staff satisfaction and development, performance management, remuneration and staff metrics. Box 4.1 sets out some relevant perspectives of the United States Internal Revenue Service on identified challenges, priorities, and strategies drawn from its Strategic Plan for 2014-17 (IRS, 2014).
- Some revenue bodies are in the process of renewing their formal HRM strategies. For example, the Canada Revenue Agency launched a policy renewal and simplification project in 2013 to reduce the overall number of human resource corporate policy instruments, making them more accessible and understandable for employees and managers. This project seeks to strengthen and improve human resources programmes particularly in the areas of planning, recruitment and performance management. Mexico has implemented new human resource policies to comply with its new SAT Strategy Map, new tax reforms and capability increase.
- A large majority of surveyed revenue bodies (93%) have conducted assessments of their current and future skills and capability needs, and have developed plans to fill any gaps in such needs.
- A large majority (82%) reported assessing staff capabilities and having targets for increasing staff capability, including the following examples:
    - France reported that an assessment of the skills of current staff members is carried out during an annual assessment interview and includes an assessment

Table 4.1. Revenue bodies' human resources management (HRM) strategies

	Aspects of HRM strategy			Major policy changes implemented or planned for				
Country	Formal strategy exists	Capabilities assessed and plans for filling gaps	Formal targets for increasing capabilities	Recruitment	Training and development	Performance management	Rewards (incl. wages and bonuses)	Increasing/ reducing staff
OECD countries								
Australia	✓	✓	✓	x	x	x	x	✓/1
Austria	✓	✓	✓	x	x	x	x	x
Belgium	✓	✓	✓	✓	✓	✓	✓	✓
Canada	✓	✓	✓	✓	✓	✓	✓	✓
Chile	✓	✓	✓	✓	x	x	x	✓
Czech Republic	✓	✓	✓	x	x	✓	x	✓
Denmark	✓	✓	x	x	✓/1	x	✓	✓/2
Estonia	✓	✓	✓	x	x	✓	✓	x
Finland	✓	✓	✓	x	x	✓	✓	x
France	✓	✓	✓	✓	✓	✓	✓	✓
Germany	✓	✓	x	x	x	x	x	x
Greece	✓	✓	x	✓	x	✓	✓	✓
Hungary	✓	✓	✓	x	✓	x	x	x
Iceland	✓	✓	x	x	x	x	x	x
Ireland	✓	✓	✓	x	x	x	x	✓
Israel	✓	✓	✓	✓	✓	✓	✓	✓
Italy	✓	✓	x	✓/1	✓	✓	✓	x
Japan	✓	✓	✓	x	x	x	x	x
Korea	✓	✓	✓	x	x	x	x	x
Luxembourg	x/1	✓	✓	x	x	x	x	x
Mexico	✓	✓	✓	✓	✓	✓	x	✓
Netherlands	✓	✓	✓	✓	✓	x	x	✓
New Zealand	✓	✓	✓	x	x	x	x	x
Norway	✓	✓	✓	x	x	x	x	x
Poland	✓	✓	✓	x	x	x	x	x
Portugal	✓	✓	✓	✓/1	✓	x	x	x
Slovak Republic	x	✓	✓	x	✓	x	x	x
Slovenia	x	x	x	x	x	x	x	x
Spain	✓	✓	✓	✓/1	x	x	x	x
Sweden	✓	✓	x	x	x	x	x	x
Switzerland	✓	✓	✓	✓	✓/1	x	x	✓
Turkey	✓	✓	✓	✓	✓	x	x	x
United Kingdom	✓	✓	✓	x	x	x	x	x
United States	✓	✓	✓	x	x	✓	x	x
Non-OECD								
Argentina	✓	✓	✓	✓/1	✓	✓	✓	x
Brazil	✓	✓	✓	x	✓	x	✓/1	✓
Bulgaria	✓	x	✓	x	✓	x	x	x
China	✓	✓	✓	x	✓	✓	x	x
Colombia	✓	✓	✓	x	x	x	x	✓
Costa Rica	x/1	x	x	✓	✓	✓	✓	x
Croatia	✓	x	x	x	✓	✓	x	x
Cyprus	✓	✓	✓	x	x	x	x	x
Hong Kong, China	✓	✓	x	x	x	x	x	x
India	✓	✓	✓	✓	✓	✓	✓	✓
Indonesia	✓	✓	✓	x	x	x	x	x
Latvia	✓	✓	✓	x	x	x	x	x
Lithuania	x	✓	✓	x	x	x	x	x
Malaysia	✓	✓	✓	✓	✓	✓	✓	✓
Malta	✓	✓	✓	✓	✓	✓	✓	✓/1
Morocco	✓	✓	✓	✓	✓	✓	✓	✓
Romania	x	✓	✓	✓	✓	✓	x	✓
Russia	✓	✓	✓	x	x	x	x	x
Saudi Arabia	x	✓	✓	✓	✓	✓	✓	✓
Singapore	✓	✓/1	✓	x	x	x	x	x
South Africa	✓	✓	✓	x/1	x/1	x/1	x/1	x/1
Thailand	✓	✓	✓	✓	x	x	x	x

For notes indicated by "/ (number)", see Notes to Tables section at the end of the chapter, p. 164.
Source: Tax Administration 2015 survey responses.

of training needs. The assessment of skills of future staff members has been introduced recently and includes the identification of professional skills. The national training plan is updated each year to fill identified gaps. Attendance by staff members to training is monitored on a regular basis and monitored through reporting covering various indicators (e.g. number of staff members which have not undertaken some training for 3 years and more, ratio of staff members (excluding managers) who have undertaken some training and ratio of middle-level managers who have undertaken some training when taking up their new position.)

- Malaysia's IRBM reported that its uses a Talent Management System which comprises Training Needs Analysis Modules to analyse gaps in competencies. Based on reports acquired from the system staff are sent to various training and development courses to close gaps. IRBM has set a key performance indicator for staff competencies: 60% of IRBM staff must attend 56 hours of formal training/learning session annually.

- There appears a strong inverse correlation between those countries who are not targeting increasing staff capability and those who are not planning or undertaking major changes in policy in areas of recruitment, training, performance or reward and remuneration i.e. those countries who are not planning or undertaking significant changes in these policy areas are most likely not targeting staff capability increases, with the exception of Denmark, Italy, Costa Rica and Croatia.
- Statistically, OECD and non-OECD revenue bodies move towards each other in these aspects of HRM strategy. Around three-quarters (74%) of OECD countries responded positively across all categories in this basket of indicators while the same is true for a two-thirds (68%) of non-OECD countries. In the previous edition this used to be 68% of the OECD revenue bodies and 39% of the non-OECD revenue bodies respectively.

Box 4.1. United States: Strategy for building a talented, competent and motivated workforce

The IRS's strategic plan for 2014-17 (briefly referenced in Chapter 3) sets out a number of goals, objectives and strategies to establish a strategic foundation for organisational experience. Investing in the IRS's workforce is the primary area to be addressed, as described below:

Objective: Be the best place to work in government by building a highly talented, diverse workforce and cultivating an inclusive and collaborative environment.

Context, current situation and directions: The IRS' employees are our greatest asset. Our highly-skilled workforce and strong culture enable us to overcome challenges and meet the growing demands of taxpayers. Over the past two years, we initiated a streamlined hiring process to increase hiring efficiency and centralised recruitment efforts to ensure that IRS' hiring needs are met. We also developed an IRS leadership coaching programme, redesigned the Career Management Resource Centre, expanded the use of leadership readiness programmes and implemented 39 workforce initiatives to improve existing IRS programmes.

Box 4.1. **United States: Strategy for building a talented, competent and motivated workforce** *(continued)*

It is imperative for the IRS to continue building a high performing workforce. To that end, we will continue to recruit and hire top talent, further streamlining the hiring process to best meet our workforce needs. Training will be provided to ensure our employees have the requisite skills to do their jobs efficiently and effectively. We will engage them to improve performance, promote an inclusive and collaborative culture and proactively resolve work-place conflict. We will also provide career development and job rotation opportunities to continue the development of future leaders for the IRS. Finally, we will improve succession planning and better harness the vast knowledge of our employees.

Strategies

- Assess workforce needs and simplify the hiring and on boarding process to attract highly-skilled and diverse talent.
- Foster a collaborative and inclusive environment that values engagement and generates innovation through diverse ideas and experiences.
- Establish knowledge management practices that capture enterprise-wide expertise, disseminate best practices and promote knowledge sharing across divisions.
- Promote career progression and rotation opportunities that share knowledge, retain talent, accelerate advancement of top performers and build future leaders.
- Empower employees with the tools and training to further develop skill proficiency and improve business performance.

Measuring progress

The IRS will measure employee engagement based on questions from the Office of Personnel Management's annual survey and an index developed by the IRS to compare itself to other large Federal agencies with 20 000 or more civilian employees. In 2013, the IRS ranked 8 of 15 large agencies; for 2017, its goal is to be in the top quartile.

Source: United States IRS Strategic Plan 2014-17, www.irs.gov/pub/irs-pdf/p3744.pdf.

Changes in policy in aspects of HRM within revenue bodies

Less than two-thirds of revenue bodies (64%) reported that they have major policy changes planned or underway in at least one of the following key HRM areas: recruitment, training and development, performance management, rewards and remuneration, and increasing or reducing staff (see Table 4.1). More than three-quarters of these (75%) are planning changes in two or more of these major areas. All areas are more or less equally affected ranging from training (43%) followed by recruitment and performance management (both 39%), staffing (38%), and rewards and remuneration (29%). Examples are included in the dedicated sections.

In the current budgetary climate it is perhaps not surprising that revenue bodies have less freedom in the area of reward and remuneration, although more innovation in terms of non-monetary rewards might help revenue bodies overcome other HRM challenges. Some examples of rewards and non-monetary rewards are included in the section on reward and remuneration.

Almost 60% of surveyed revenue bodies experienced (sometimes quite significant) reductions in headcount over the last year while only about a third expanded their workforce. Some revenue bodies reported large budget reductions or other staff policy changes over recent years or planned for the coming years, for example:

- In Australia, organisational change is required to make necessary savings/ reductions across the ATO as handed down by Government in the Budget Response Programme; approximately 3 000 staff left the ATO in 2014 as a result of this programme.
- Ireland's Revenue reported that a centrally negotiated National Agreement for the Public Service has created an incentive for staff to retire before mid-2016. This development means that Revenue will experience staff losses at an accelerated pace before this deadline. Revenue has undertaken targeted recruitment, redeployment and training to prepare for the anticipated loss of knowledge and experience.

Staff are the single biggest cost for all revenue bodies. Reductions in budgets therefore have a significant impact on numbers of staff revenue bodies are able to maintain. To be able to achieve objectives in times of an often increasing scope of responsibility combined with reductions in budgets and staffing levels, an increase in both organisational and individual capability is likely to be required.

Changes in headcount also constitute a major HRM challenge in itself. There are several elements to this. If the reductions are over and above what can be achieved through expected staff turnover, the revenue body needs, as a first step, to manage both the uncertainties and practical aspects related to this in accordance with the values of the organisation. For example, Brazil is mapping job positions with professional profiles, in order to enhance the geographical and functional distribution of staff and to bring individual expectations in line with institutional objectives to deal with the changes in number or staff. Significant reductions will also often require careful knowledge management and possibly involve training and/or redeployment of remaining staff. These challenges calls for a systematic approach, as described in an example from France – Box 4.2.

Box 4.2. **France: Structure and distribution of human resources**

France's DGFiP's human resources are allocated to it under the national budget. It is subject to two limits: *(1)* a limit on the total number of jobs; and *(2)* a limit on its total payroll. In this context, the paid workforce is currently composed of 112 000 agents, for a total payroll of EUR 7.1 billion (85% of its total budget). Within these limits, DGFiP may structure its employment levels as wished. This structure is currently as follows:

- 29% of category A jobs (management, expertise – including tax audit – designing and steering staff);
- 40% of category B jobs (supervisory and operating staff); and
- 31% of category C jobs (task completing staff).

Changes in the workforce reflect a sharp decline as the number of officers fell by nearly 30% in 12 years. Correspondingly, the overall performance maintains a satisfactory level, the intervention rate tax on still getting better (1.02% in 2011, 0.88% in 2013). Productivity has therefore increased significantly in the DGFiP, thereby contributing to putting more stress on the workforce.

Box 4.2. **France: Structure and distribution of human resources** *(continued)*

Distribution of the human resources

The merger in 2008 of the General Directorate of Taxation and the General Directorate of Public Accounts to form the DGFiP (General Directorate of Public Finances) has allowed it to benefit from an extensive network that offers high accessibility to all its audiences (professionals, individuals, and public authorities). It allows its officers to consider a career in a particularly diverse range of professions.

A mobility system that is largely based on staff preferences: Given the large volume of the officials involved (112 000) and the historically high number of facilities (over 3 000 currently), a periodic mobility scheme, centrally managed and locally refined, has been developed to allow a balanced distribution of human resources.

Basically, the scheme relies on periodically mapping all jobs (by job type and geographical location) with the expression of the mobility wishes of public servants, either when first taking up their post after recruitment or as part of a personal project of geographical and / or functional mobility. This map identifies the location and the jobs, itemising them by blocks of occupations. Mapping is updated annually to take into account both job adjustments (on a downward trend) and evolution of the workload in the various network components of DGFiP. It aims at ensuring a balance between the different assignments, with regard to workloads, productivity and efficiency respectively obtained in the various business segments, in line with government priorities.

This rather flexible system allows each officer to find a balance between work and family life, to organise its career path according to its expectations and curiosity for other functions, or, on the contrary, to pursue a path on various occupations within the same skill block (e.g. tax audit).

A clear framework to fill the positions at stake: At the senior management's level, evolution wishes are also collected, but appointments result from the implementation of customised career paths and the composition of harmonious management teams. These executives are therefore appointed by the Minister on proposal of the Director of Public Finances and placed on the most appropriate job in light of their career. At this level, high-ranking civil servants who do not belong to DGFiP are also recruited ("tour extérieur" in French) and enrich the structure with their experience gained from other functions.

In addition, some specific executive or officer jobs, which technicality and sensitivity are proven, are assigned under special arrangements. These jobs account for about 15% of the mapping. This centralised allocation scheme is then refined locally, the territorial directors being in charge of assigning a specific job to each designated officer in relation with the local organising method implemented. These procedures for allocating jobs generally work well and provide a good balance between personal expectations and public service requirements.

Source: DGFiP, *CIAT Technical Conference, October 6 to 9, 2014, Santiago de Compostela, Spain.*

Staff recruitment and appointment

Governments in most countries give some level of autonomy to their revenue body for determining: the numbers and types of staff to be hired; the skills and qualifications required for specific jobs; the duration and types of employment contracts; and the location of staff. However, most revenue bodies have autonomy governed by laws or budgetary constraints determined at governmental level, and there is wide variation in the extent of the autonomy. For example, in Spain the Tax Agency has a generic autonomy in making decisions about staff matters. However, the number and skills of staff is co-ordinated with the Ministry of Finance. And in France the conditions and requirements of the types of skills and academic qualifications are determined by ministerial decree. Revenue bodies report most autonomy in location of staff (88%), followed by skills and qualifications (77%) followed by duration of contract (71%) and finally number and types of staff to be hired (66%) – see Table 4.2.

In the previous edition the importance of having high quality recruitment processes allowing critical skills and new talent to be brought in when and where it is needed was recognised. In more than 50% of the revenue bodies the number of external recruitments in fiscal year 2013 exceeded the number of external recruitments in fiscal year 2011 which illustrates the importance of this aspect. A number of revenue bodies reported initiatives in this area – see Box 4.3.

Box 4.3. Recruitment practices and policy change

Argentina: A new System for Personnel Recruitment has been implemented that includes technical/ psycho-technical tests, language tests and physical examinations (prior to admission) and to pass an intensive training course to be admitted into the organisation.

Belgium: During 2014 – 2016 new departments will be created and existing departments will be grouped together. More specific profiles will be recruited with more specific job descriptions. Unlike in the past, newly recruited staff will have the possibility to choose a specific tax administration or a specific function within the administration.

France: On 12 March 2012 DGFIP adopted new legislation (law no. 2012-347) regarding the nomination of temporary/non-statutory agents as statutory officials and also involved communication action vis-à-vis relevant members of staff fulfilling the requirements.

Romania: Until late 2013, the budgetary constraints prevented the Romanian revenue body (NAFA) to make decisions on staff recruitment. As part of a reform several memoranda were adopted, authorising NAFA to hire staff in areas considered important. In general, NAFA employs staff on a permanent basis. At the moment of recruitment the geographical location of the newly recruited is clearly established, resulting in limited autonomy in making decisions about the geographical location after recruitment. With respect to geographical location, NAFA has some legal constrains e.g. the power of decision about temporary change of staff location is limited to 6 months/year and for periods over 6 months, the staff consent is mandatory.

Source: Tax Administration 2015 survey responses.

Most surveyed revenue bodies (93%) reported that they are able to recruit staff and make appointments based on clearly defined qualification and experience criteria. A number of revenue bodies reported that whilst requirements are not published, they are assessed prior to any recruitment exercise and used to inform the recruitment process.

Some countries have separate recruitment agencies or other mechanisms to manage recruitment for all of the public sector. For example in Israel nearly all employees will be recruited through a professional recruitment services and all positions, including less professional, will require a tender which is a national requirements.

Table 4.2. **Autonomy in staff appointments and measuring staff satisfaction and engagement**

	Autonomy and flexibility exists for recruitment decisions concerning					Staff satisfaction, engagement and motivation		
Country	No./ type of staff	Skill types and qualifications	Duration of contracts	Geographical location	Appointments on merit	Periodic surveys	Results shared	Staff consulted
OECD countries								
Australia	✓	✓	✓	✓	✓	✓	✓	✓
Austria	x	✓	✓	✓	✓	✓	✓	✓
Belgium	✓	✓	x	x	✓	✓	✓	✓
Canada	✓	✓	✓	✓	✓	✓	✓	✓
Chile	✓	✓	✓	✓	✓	✓	✓	✓
Czech Republic	✓	✓	✓	✓	✓	✓	✓	✓
Denmark	✓	✓	✓	✓	x	✓	✓	✓
Estonia	✓	✓	✓	✓	✓	✓	✓	✓
Finland	✓	✓	✓	✓	✓	✓	✓	✓
France	x /1	x	x /1	✓ /1	x	✓	✓	✓
Germany	✓	x /1	✓	✓	x	✓	✓	✓
Greece	✓	✓	x	✓	✓	x	x	x
Hungary	x /1	x	✓	✓	✓	✓ /2	✓	x
Iceland	✓	✓	✓	✓	✓	✓	✓	✓
Ireland	✓	✓	✓	✓	✓	✓	✓	✓
Israel	x	✓	✓	✓	✓	✓	✓	✓
Italy	✓	✓	✓	✓	✓	✓ /1	✓	x
Japan	x	x	x	x	✓	✓	✓	✓
Korea	✓	x	✓	✓	✓	✓	✓	✓
Luxembourg	✓ /1	✓	✓	✓	✓	✓	✓	✓
Mexico	x /1	✓	✓	✓	✓	✓	✓	✓
Netherlands	✓	✓	✓	✓	✓	✓	✓	✓
New Zealand	✓	✓	✓	✓	✓	✓	✓	✓
Norway	✓	✓	✓	✓	✓	✓	✓	✓
Poland	x	✓	✓	✓	✓	✓	✓	✓
Portugal	✓	✓	x /1	✓	✓	x	x	x
Slovak Republic	✓	✓	✓	✓	✓	x	x	x
Slovenia	x /1	✓	✓	✓	✓	✓ /2	✓	✓
Spain	x	x	x	✓	✓	x	x	x
Sweden	✓	✓	✓	✓	✓ /1	✓	✓	✓
Switzerland	x	✓	✓	x	✓	✓	✓	✓
Turkey	✓	✓	✓	✓	✓	✓	✓	✓
United Kingdom	✓	✓	✓	✓	✓	✓	✓	✓
United States	✓	✓	✓	✓	✓	✓	✓	✓
Non-OECD countries								
Argentina	✓	✓	✓	✓	✓	✓	✓	✓
Brazil	x	✓	x	✓	✓	✓	✓	x
Bulgaria	✓	x	✓	✓	✓	✓	✓	✓
China	x	x	x	✓	✓	✓	✓	✓
Colombia	x /1	x	x	✓	✓	✓	✓	✓
Costa Rica	✓	x	x	✓	✓	✓	✓ /1	✓ /1
Croatia	x /1	✓	✓	✓	✓	✓	x	x
Cyprus	x	x	x	x	✓ /1	x	n.a.	n.a.
Hong Kong, China	✓	✓	✓	n.a.	✓	x	x	x
India	x	✓	x/✓ /1	x/✓ /1	✓	x	x	x
Indonesia	x	x	x	x	x	✓	x	x
Latvia	✓	✓	✓	✓	✓	✓	✓	x
Lithuania	✓	✓	x	✓	✓	x	x	x
Malaysia	✓	✓	✓	✓	✓	✓	✓	✓
Malta	✓	✓	✓	✓	✓ /1	x	x	x
Morocco	✓	✓	n.a.	✓	✓	x	x	x
Romania	✓	✓	✓	✓	✓	✓ /1	x	x
Russia	x	x	✓	✓	✓	x	x	x
Saudi Arabia	✓	✓	x	✓	✓	x	x	x
Singapore	✓	✓	✓	n.a.	✓	✓	✓	✓
South Africa	✓	✓	✓	✓	✓	✓	✓	✓
Thailand	x /1	✓	x	✓	✓	✓	✓	✓

For notes indicated by "/ (number)", see Notes to Tables section at the end of the chapter, p. 164.
Source: TAS survey responses.

Staff satisfaction and engagement

Revenue bodies were asked a number of questions relating to key elements of their approach to staff satisfaction and engagement, specifically whether: *(1)* they periodically survey staff on their attitudes, perceptions and workplace satisfaction, and staff engagement and motivation; *(2)* the results of any such surveys and assessments shared with staff; and *(3)* staff are consulted in developing and implementing actions plans in response to such survey and assessment findings. High performing organisations tend to score highly in staff engagement, satisfaction and motivation, sharing the results of surveys of these areas with staff, and involving them in the selection, design and implementation of changes determined to be needed. It is a recognised leading employer practice to conduct regular surveys to gather employee perceptions concerning the workplace and human resource management to better inform decision making in these areas – refer examples in Box 4.4. It is important to note that

Box 4.4. **The use of staff surveys to assess staff satisfaction and engagement**

Canada

The CRA participates in the Public Service Employee Survey (PSES). The PSES is a survey of all federal public servants that has been conducted every three years since 1999. The survey measures employees' opinions on their leadership, workforce and work environment. The PSES is conducted by Statistics Canada on behalf of the Office of the Chief Human Resources Officer, Treasury Board of Canada Secretariat.

Surveys such as the PSES help identify opportunities to strengthen people management, promote innovation in the workplace and improve workforce productivity. By evaluating aspects of their workplace, public service employees have a direct impact on organisational planning by helping identify what is needed to improve the effectiveness of the public service in achieving excellence in service to Canadians. The CRA ensures that results are shared and discussed with all employees through employee engagement sessions. These sessions are held to discuss the results, identify key areas for attention, and develop concrete and achievable action plans to improve the workplace and strengthen people management in our organisation.

Finland

The Finnish Tax Administration Agency conducts an annual survey of staff satisfaction (that is also employed more widely across central government agencies) that covers a broad range of areas (e.g. supervisors, work content and challenges, pay, self-improvement, workplace atmosphere and co-operation, physical environment and flow of information). Results are discussed with staff and trend results are published in the annual report, along with a comparison with the average performance across central agencies. Results over the last four years show an improving trend and performance marginally ahead of the average of central agencies.

Singapore

The Organisational Climate Survey (OCS) is one means through which IRAS measures the effectiveness of the overall employee engagement process and identifies ways to enhance it. IRAS analyses the results of each OCS and formulate organisational, divisional or branch action plans to address the gaps identified. The OCS results and related outcomes are communicated to staff at a divisional/branch level. Besides OCS, IRAS monitors staff feedback from various channels such as exit interviews with resigning staff and staff focus groups. IRAS monitors the results from these channels and incorporate them in the review of engagement mechanisms.

Sources: Survey responses from Canada and Singapore, and 2013 annual report of the Finnish Tax Administration.

everyone has a role to play in this – it is not just the responsibility of the senior leadership. Most revenue bodies (97%) conduct periodic surveys of staff satisfaction, although the frequency of surveys varies from twice per year to once every two or three years. Almost all (93%) of those revenue bodies who survey staff also share survey results with staff and most (84%) also consult with staff when considering responses to survey findings.

Staff development

Most revenue bodies reported they are undertaking staff development in the areas of commercial awareness (63%) and/or risk management (89%) – see Table 4.3. More than two-thirds (71%) of the 35 revenue bodies that are undertaking staff development in the area of commercial awareness utilise networks with external organisations including legal and accounting firms, at least in part to help develop commercial awareness skills of their staff. Two thirds (64%) of revenue bodies partner with educational establishments for training purposes and almost the majority (45%) of revenue bodies engage with other external parties to develop commercial awareness of their staff – see Box 4.5. Among the obvious benefits of these arrangements is that they contribute to raising the professional standing of the tax profession. This is in line with the overall tendency in some OECD countries to further professionalise the public sector through increased access to university-accredited training for public service professions.

The enhancement of risk management skills of staff has been a priority for many revenue bodies. For instance, Hungary has, since many years, a multilevel risk analysis training programme to support the development of the skills of professionals (managers and administrators alike). In Romania the NAFA has put in place sound risk management procedures and training courses in risk management and commercial awareness are being developed and put in place.

Taxpayers adopt varying attitudes in their interaction with revenue bodies. Revenue bodies will be more effective in treating compliance issues when understanding what influences and drives specific taxpayer behaviour. For that reason, the majority of revenue bodies (61%) have introduced initiatives for developing behavioural science skills of staff. For instance, the ATO offers 20 formal courses that have a learning outcome related to building expertise in understanding behaviours of taxpayers, focusing on client service, interviewing, negotiation, dispute management and advanced dispute resolution and behavioural economics. It also has courses that focus on enabling staff to be resilient in difficult taxpayer relationships. Hungary is developing professional and behavioural competencies such as decisive action, negotiation technique, ethical behaviour, professionalism) by training programmes, which may directly or indirectly have a positive impact on taxpayer behaviour.

Reduced resources and increased complexity of tax law requires an adequate share of information and training within the revenue body. Additionally, numerous revenue bodies have to deal with important outflow of employees due to retirement in the very near future and knowledge management to ensure technical expertise and leadership capacity is becoming particularly valuable. Knowledge transfer is a key strategy for addressing these challenges. Table 4.4 sets out some examples of knowledge management initiatives by various revenue bodies, for example through mentoring (e.g. Canada and Malaysia), and by capturing and transferring knowledge of senior/retiring employees (e.g. United States and Colombia).

Table 4.3. **Revenue bodies' initiatives to support staff developments**

Country	Formal partnerships with education bodies re tax studies	Networks with externals to develop commercial awareness	Other initiatives to develop commercial awareness	Initiatives to enhance staff skills on risk management	Initiatives to apply behavioural sciences to treat compliance issues	Programme for knowledge capture/ transfer from senior staff near retirement
OECD countries						
Australia	✓	✓	✓	✓	✓	x
Austria	x	x	x	✓	x	x
Belgium	✓	x	x	✓	✓	✓
Canada	x /1	✓	✓	✓	✓	✓
Chile	✓	✓	✓	✓	✓	x
Czech Republic	✓	x	✓	✓	x	x
Denmark	✓	x	x	✓	✓	x
Estonia	✓	x	✓	✓	✓	✓
Finland	✓	✓	✓	✓	x	x
France	✓	✓	x	✓	x	✓ /1
Germany	x	✓	x	x	x	x
Greece	x	x	x	✓	x	✓
Hungary	✓	x	x	✓	✓	✓ /1
Iceland	x	x	x	x	x	✓
Ireland	✓	✓	✓	✓	✓	✓
Israel	✓	x	x	✓	x	x
Italy	✓	✓	x	✓	✓ /1	x
Japan	✓	✓	x	✓	x	x
Korea	✓	✓	✓	✓	✓	x
Luxembourg	x	x	x	✓ /1	x	x
Mexico	✓ /1	✓	✓	✓	✓	x
Netherlands	✓	✓	✓	✓	✓	✓
New Zealand	✓	x	✓	✓	✓	x
Norway	✓	✓	✓	✓	✓	x
Poland	✓	x	x	✓	✓	✓
Portugal	x /1	x	x	x	x	✓
Slovak Republic	x	x	x	✓	✓	x
Slovenia	✓	✓	x	✓	✓	x
Spain	✓ /1	x	x	✓	x	x
Sweden	x	x	x	✓	✓	✓ /1
Switzerland	✓	✓	✓	✓	✓	x
Turkey	✓	✓	✓	✓	✓	✓
United Kingdom	✓	✓	✓	✓	✓	✓
United States	✓	✓	✓	✓	✓	✓
Non-OECD countries						
Argentina	✓	✓	✓	✓	✓	x
Brazil	✓ /1	x	x	✓	✓	x
Bulgaria	✓	x	✓	✓	x	✓
China	✓	x	x	✓	✓	✓
Colombia	✓	✓	✓	✓	✓	✓
Costa Rica	x	x	x	✓	✓	x
Croatia	x	x	x	x	x	x
Cyprus	x /1	x	✓	✓	x	x
Hong Kong, China	✓	✓	✓	✓	✓	✓
India	✓	✓	✓	✓	x	x /1
Indonesia	✓	x	✓	✓	✓	✓
Latvia	✓	✓	✓	✓	✓	✓
Lithuania	x	x	x	x	x	x
Malaysia	✓	✓	x	✓	x	✓
Malta	x	x	✓ /1	✓ /2	x	✓ /1
Morocco	✓	x	x	✓	x	✓
Romania	x	x	x	✓	✓	x
Russia	x	x	✓	✓	✓	x
Saudi Arabia	✓	✓	✓	✓	✓	✓
Singapore	✓	✓	✓	✓	✓	✓
South Africa	x	x	x	✓	x	✓ /1
Thailand	x	x	x	x	x	x

For notes indicated by "/ (number)", see Notes to Tables section at the end of the chapter, p. 165.

Source: Tax Administration 2015 survey responses.

Box 4.5. Staff development, including engagement with third parties

Australia

The ATO has informal relationships with large scale industries to build technical skills and commercial awareness. Additionally, the ATO engages with many industries through attendance at industry and professional conferences and external learning events. It also has regular contact with external organisations to discuss learning opportunities to the ATO. For example, the ATO has built a Learning and Development Community of Practice with several government and private organisations in Melbourne, Australia. The ATO also engages external providers and subject matter experts for specific learning needs such as a quarterly tax update series provided by the Certified Practising Accountants Society, one of the professional bodies in Australia, with a special focus on real case studies. The ATO has also instituted an Expert Speaker series that brings specialists in from the private sector to make presentations on specialist tax topics and management topics.

The ATO has a range of internal and externally facilitated formal courses that build capability around tax effective activities of business, financial instruments, oil, gas and resource industry and employer obligations. In addition, the ATO also use external conferences to build commercial awareness in a wide range of client industries and professions. The ATO has a focus on private industry and public sector secondments designed to enhance capability. This has the potential to apply to a diverse range of technical and specialist roles where exposure to external operating environments would be beneficial.

The ATO has developed a Dispute Management Curriculum that provides a range of foundation, intermediate and advanced level courses to address learning needs with respect to; prevention of disputes, recognising emerging disputes, managing conflict situations, client relationship management, negotiation and influencing skills, facilitation and understanding alternative dispute resolution.

Italy

The Revenue Agency is strengthening the link between educational projects and strategies of the organisation by promoting the use of IT-network learning-oriented methodologies (e.g. e-learning, e-meeting and community of practices). The medium term objective is to transform the trainers into architects of learning processes capable of developing dynamic continuous learning environments while preserving a systemic vision. In line with this vision, the Training Plan 2013-2015 includes two significant actions: *(1)* strengthen the synergies between the training and the internal communication and staff development; and *(2)* educate the staff, especially the newly hired personnel, to be balanced, moderate and integral in the judgement of taxpayers. For these purposes behavioural modules have been included in the technical-fiscal courses to build the bases for a trustful relation with taxpayers to improve tax compliance.

The Training Plan 2013-2015 introduced important innovations in the management training. Top of the priorities are interventions suited for managers and staff with managerial-responsibility positions so called Key-figures. For these staff the training is related and connected to the professional development. The connection between training and development is important as well for the staff working for the achievement of strategic objectives. In January 2013 four new training and development paths were introduced which pointed out on the managerial role aligning knowledge, competences and working methods. Staff involved will be: front office staff, staff for medium-size companies' tax audits, co-ordinators of front office area and human resources co-ordinators.

The Revenue Agency has been carrying out a variety of training projects that aim to create and strengthen the confidence of taxpayers in the tax administration. These initiatives have involved all new recruits, front-office personnel and auditor functionaries, all up totalling 8 400 participants.

Box 4.5. **Staff development, including engagement with third parties** *(continued)*

Singapore

The Tax Academy (TA) was set up to raise the professional competency of the tax community in Singapore. The TA has established connections with local and international partners that include academic and research institutions (such as Nanyang Technological University, Vienna University of Economics and Business, Leiden International Tax Centre), professional bodies (such as CPA Australia, ICPAS). A Master Tax Specialist (MTS) Programme under the Specialist Development Framework is designed to deepen Accredited Tax Specialists' knowledge in specific areas of taxation to broaden their understanding of related non-tax issues on a specific subject matter such as regulatory rules, corporate structures, etc. (development of a "T-shaped" specialist). Trainees have to complete three training milestones – training, research and experiential training – to be certified as a MTS.

Source: Tax Administration 2015 survey responses.

Table 4.4. **Examples of specific programmes for knowledge capturing**

Country	Description
Canada	The CRA has a Knowledge Management Framework in place and has built an online Knowledge Transfer Compendium for employees that highlights knowledge transfer best practices from across the organisation such as coaching, mentoring, job shadowing, establishment of learning paths.
Colombia	Colombia established a programme to capture and transfer knowledge of senior officials to younger generations through learning communities organised according to the expertise and interests of the participants.
Ireland	Revenue's succession planning programme consists of early identification of potential exits via workforce planning analysis and a process of localised documentation of knowledge/ procedures and the coaching of replacements.
Malaysia	The training and development programme includes a Temporary International Placement (TRIP) Programme, a CEO's Incubators programme, and affiliations with Government Agencies which are specialised in top management training e.g. Razak School of Government (RSOG). And a Mentor Mentee Programme and an On The Job Training has been established.
Singapore	IRAS has established an Accredited Tax Specialist (ATS) Scheme which aims at driving behaviour change in competency development and knowledge sharing in IRAS. Besides encouraging ATSs to continue to upgrade their technical knowledge, the ATS scheme was also designed to encourage knowledge sharing by the tax specialists as ATSs have to be involved in learning and sharing activities in order to maintain their status. To incentivise the ATSs to participate in maintenance activities, ATSs who meet the requirements are rewarded with an ATS allowance. The ATS Scheme is driven by the Specialist Development Committee (chaired by Deputy Commissioner level).
United States	The IRS is in the early stages of implementing a formal knowledge management programme and is establishing templates for capturing the knowledge of retiring employees. The IRS has conducted knowledge capture interviews with senior officials that are recorded and made available online.

Source: Tax Administration 2015 survey responses.

Performance management

Over 80% of revenue bodies reported that they have performance management systems in place, although a fifth of these (20%) do not set individual objectives for each staff member at the start of the performance period – see Table 4.5. A number of revenue bodies underscored the importance of relating individual objectives and behaviours to the overall objectives and values of the organisation.

Table 4.5. **Performance management and remuneration**

Country	Performance management				Remuneration			
	System in place for all staff	All staff have development plan	All staff have measurable objectives	Performance evaluated each year	Pay levels tied directly to public sector	Pay levels tied broadly to public sector	Body has its own unique pay system	Flexibility exists to reward good performance
OECD countries								
Australia	✓	✓	✓	✓	x	✓/1	x	✓
Austria	✓	✓	✓	✓	✓	✓	x	✓
Belgium	✓	✓	✓	✓	✓	x	✓	✓
Canada	✓	✓	✓	✓	x	✓	x	✓
Chile	✓	✓	✓	✓	x	x	✓	✓
Czech Republic	✓	x	✓	✓	✓	x	x	✓
Denmark	✓	✓	x	✓	✓	x	✓	x
Estonia	x /1	✓	✓	✓	x /2	✓	✓	✓
Finland	✓ /1	✓	x	✓	x	x	✓	✓
France	✓	x	x	✓	✓ /1	x	✓	✓
Germany	✓	x	✓ /1	✓ /1	✓	x	x	✓ /2
Greece	x	x	x /1	✓	✓	x	x	x
Hungary	✓	x	✓	✓	x	✓	✓	✓ /1
Iceland	x	x	x	✓	✓	✓	x	✓
Ireland	✓	✓	✓	✓	✓	x	x	x
Israel	✓	x	✓	✓	x	✓	x	✓
Italy	x	x	x	x	✓	✓	x	✓
Japan	✓	✓	✓	✓	x	✓	x	✓
Korea	✓	✓	✓	✓	✓	✓	x	✓
Luxembourg	✓ /1	x	x	✓	✓	x	x	x
Mexico	✓	x	x /1	✓	✓	x	x	x
Netherlands	✓	x	x	✓	✓	x	x	✓
New Zealand	✓	✓	✓	✓	x /1	x /1	✓	✓
Norway	✓	✓	✓	✓	✓	✓	x	x
Poland	✓	✓	✓	x	✓	x	x	✓
Portugal	✓	✓	✓	✓	✓	x	✓	✓
Slovak Republic	✓	x	x	x	✓	✓	x	✓
Slovenia	x	✓	✓	✓	✓	x	x	x
Spain	✓	✓ /1	✓	✓	✓	x	x	✓ /1
Sweden	✓ /1	✓	x	✓	x	x	✓	✓
Switzerland	✓	✓	✓	✓	x	✓	x	✓ /1
Turkey	✓	✓	✓	✓	✓	x	x	x
United Kingdom	✓	✓	✓	✓	x	✓	x	✓
United States	✓	x	✓	✓	✓	✓	✓	✓
Non-OECD countries								
Argentina	n.a.	n.a.	n.a.	✓	x	x	✓ /1	✓ /2
Brazil	✓ /1	x	x	✓ /2	✓	x	✓ /3	x /3
Bulgaria	✓	✓	✓	✓	✓	✓	✓	✓
China	x	x	x	✓	x	x	x	x
Colombia	✓	✓	✓	✓	x	x	✓ /1	✓
Costa Rica	✓ /1	x	✓ /1	✓	✓	x	x	x
Croatia	✓ /1	x	✓	✓	x	x	✓	x
Cyprus	x	x /1	x /2	✓ /3	✓	x	x	x
Hong Kong, China	✓	x	✓	✓	✓	x	x	x
India	✓	x	✓	✓	✓	✓	x	x/✓ /1
Indonesia	✓	x	✓	✓	✓	x	x	x
Latvia	✓	✓	✓	✓	✓	x	x	x
Lithuania	✓	✓	✓	✓	✓	✓	x	x
Malaysia	✓	✓	✓	✓	x	✓	x	x
Malta	✓ /1	✓	✓	✓	✓	✓	x	✓ /2
Morocco	x	x	x	x	✓	x	x	✓
Romania	✓	x	✓	✓	✓ /1	x	✓	x
Russia	✓	✓	✓	✓	x	x	✓	✓
Saudi Arabia	x	x	x	✓	✓	x	x	x
Singapore	✓	✓	✓	✓	x	x	✓	✓
South Africa	✓	x /1	✓	✓	x	x	✓ /2	✓
Thailand	✓	✓	✓	✓	✓	x	x	✓

For notes indicated by "/ (number)", see Notes to Tables section at the end of the chapter, p. 166.
Source: Tax Administration 2015 survey responses.

A large majority of surveyed revenue bodies (92%) reported that they review the performance of each staff member at least annually while an additional revenue body only reviews annually the performance of staff with management responsibility. These performance reviews can be based on any combination of individual objectives, objectives set for a particular team or unit, and overall objectives and values, and the performance review is frequently linked to rewards and remuneration as well as personal development plans. Normally the performance review is carried out by the closest manager, often in dialogue with the individual staff member concerned, but a small number of revenue bodies also reported the use of so-called "360 degree" assessment systems (where an individual's performance is assessed based on input from a wide selection of people with whom the individual interact professionally).

Portugal's revenue body indicated that the performance management system used is applied by the whole public administration. The Integrated System for Management and Performance Evaluation applies to the performance of all civil servants, managers and public departments. This system enables a distinction to be made between public departments' achievements, performance evaluation and benchmarking, and to assess civil servants' performance linked to merit and not based on career antiquity. The performance system is applied to all Public Administration and comprehends all departments and staff, including middle management and local office managers. The performance system works in cascade and links the performance of the organisation, with the performance of departments (including regional and local offices) and with the performance of staff. Performance evaluation has implications on career evolution and on rewards. Each staff member has a personal development plan and clear measurable objectives and indicators.

Italy also provided a description of its performance management system introduced in 2001, a summary of which is set out in Box 4.6.

Box 4.6. Italy's performance management system

The performance management system known as SIRIO (an acronym for the Integrated System of Results, Indicators and Objectives) is used to assess individual performance on an annual basis. It takes into account the evaluation of results (achievement of the assigned targets) and organisational competencies (individual qualities).

Within this system a capability/competency model describes the following knowledge and abilities required of executives/managers (of which there were 1 284 managerial positions in 2013): *(1)* Cognitive competencies such as analytical thinking and developing and spreading knowledge; *(2)* Achievement competencies such as initiative and achievement orientation; *(3)* Relationship competencies such as persuasiveness, orientation to others and flexibility; *(4)* Leadership such as team leadership, empowerment and developing others, and assertiveness; and *(5)* Self-control such as self-confidence, integrity and coherence.

Officers in charge of organisational and responsibility functions (some 3 420 officials in 2013) are evaluated based on a tailored competency framework, which is largely similar to the competency model for manager and middle management, and takes into account: *(1)* Cognitive dynamism such as analytical and conceptual thinking; *(2)* Reliability such as integrity and passion for work; *(3)* Achievements such as taking initiatives, achievement orientation and developing and transferring knowledge; *(4)* Relationship dynamism such as with orientation to others, teamwork and flexibility; and *(5)* Leadership such as team building capacity and influencing people.

Source: Survey response.

Rewards and remuneration

Over two-thirds of revenue bodies (67%) reported having their staff remuneration levels tied directly or broadly to wider public sector pay scales, while almost one-third reported that they have their own unique pay system – see examples in Box 4.10. Almost two-thirds of revenue bodies (63%) reported having some flexibility to reward good performance. The nature of the reward mechanisms in place varies greatly and includes individual or collective salaries, flexibility to adjust salary scales, promotions, individual or collective bonuses, and non-monetary rewards – see Table 4.5.

In some countries (e.g. Portugal and Slovak Republic), remuneration schemes are set out in specific law or acts. In Hungary, a fixed remuneration system is applied to all state administrative bodies, including the revenue body. However, the revenue body has its own table of remuneration to modify salaries in a positive and a negative direction.

Pay systems are often characterised by performance requirements such as actual performance, experience, complexity of tasks and responsibilities, job title, working conditions and outstanding results (e.g. Croatia, Hungary and Sweden). The Finnish salary system, for example, includes 16 requirement levels. Examples of remuneration systems from two other revenue bodies are set out in Box 4.7, in the case of Singapore revealing an administration with considerable autonomy and flexibility in designing its own remuneration arrangements.

Box 4.7. Unique pay systems of selected revenue bodies

Singapore

IRAS, an autonomous revenue authority, has its own scheme of service and a set of salary pay grades which are benchmarked to the jobs market. A performance-based remuneration system (PARS) that ties rewards to performance has been adopted. Performance bonus and salary increments are given in addition to monthly salaries to recognise good performance and motivate staff to continue their good performance. Under PARS, better performing staff are rewarded with higher performance bonuses and increments. The bonus payments corresponding to each performance grade are transparent, so staff could see the differentiated payments and be motivated to strive for better performance, thus reinforcing superior performance.

The Organisation Bonus framework helps to strengthen the linkage between organisation bonus and business needs, and make it more transparent to all staff. Key Performance Indicators (KPI) are selected as the payment criteria for the Organisation Bonus framework. The KPIs covers the critical areas of the business and affects all branches. All staff are familiar with the KPIs and they are able to relate and influence the outcomes. The number of KPIs met will determine the amount of Organisation Bonus that IRAS can pay to staff, providing a direct linkage between staff performance and organisation performance;

United States

The IRS has a Payband System that spans several grades of the General Schedule for employees in one of the three following categories of IRS supervisory/managerial positions: Senior Managers (SM) are first-level supervisory/managerial positions that report directly to a member of the Senior Executive Service (SES); Department Managers (DM) are second-level supervisory/managerial positions located in the Campuses: and Frontline Managers (FM) are supervisory/managerial positions not covered under the SM or DM pay band.

Source: Tax Administration 2015 survey responses.

Many revenue bodies (e.g. Australia, Bulgaria, Germany, France, Hungary, Japan, South Africa, Sweden and Switzerland) reported having some flexibility to adjust salaries to reward good performance, and often the basic salary is subject to review in connection with the annual performance review. Some revenue bodies (e.g. Australia) reported advancement in the pay scale being conditional on performance being rated at least satisfactory, while others (e.g. France) reported that advancement in the pay scale can be accelerated to reward excellent performance. In some countries, individual bonuses are limited to senior staff or staff with special responsibilities for instance in Canada for executives, managers and senior HR practitioners, in France for senior executives and staff working in headquarters, in Italy officers with organisational positions, and in Portugal for customs staff.

Overall, there appears to be a clear tendency to have a larger proportion of the salary for senior staff tied to performance. There is great variation with respect to the frequency with which individual bonuses are paid ranging from a monthly over a quarterly and six-monthly to an annual basis. In Spain, a bonus is paid monthly and re-evaluated at the end of the year taking into account annual objectives set out.

A number of revenue bodies (e.g. France and Italy) reported having collective bonuses based on the performance of the organisation as a whole. Similarly, the Chilean revenue body indicated that it has bonuses tied to collective goals as well as individual performance. In Argentina, the collective bonus is proportionate to the amount of taxes collected by the revenue body. In Finland, the salary system specifies 16 different requirement levels. A person's total salary is formed by her/his task requirement level and an assessment of his/her personal level of performance. While not regarded as a bonus system per se, the personal level of performance can be up to a maximum of 48% of the total salary.

Experience with non-monetary rewards appears quite limited. In TA2013, the United States IRS reported the use of time off (i.e. paid leave as bonus) and framed certificates signed by the Commissioner or the Division Commissioner. Portugal reported a remuneration bonus in the form of a productivity allowance in nature. On this background, it is possible that many other revenue bodies could make more use of non-monetary rewards and consider their potential value also from a change management perspective. Non-monetary rewards reinforce the intrinsic motivation and have the additional benefit of being less sensitive to budget constraints.

Staff metrics: Staff numbers and attrition, age profiles and qualifications

The survey sought limited quantitative data concerning staffing levels, numbers of recruits and departures, staff age profiles and educational qualifications – see Table 4.6 and the comments that follow.

Staff turnover/attrition rate

The measure "staff turnover or attrition" refers to the rate at which employees leave an organisation during a defined period (normally a year). It is computed as:

Staff attrition (%) = number of staff departures / average staffing level (where the average staffing level equals opening staff numbers + end-of-year staff numbers / 2) × 100

Generally speaking, a high attrition rate will reflect an unusual volume of movements of staff out of an organisation resulting from a variety of abnormal factors For example, downsizing policies and/or lack of recruitment, demographics (e.g. an aged workforce), and staff dissatisfaction).

Attrition rates computed for revenue bodies cover a very broad range, with exceptionally low rates (i.e. under 2%) seen in Chile (1.9%), Germany (1.0%), and Malaysia (0.9%) and exceptionally high levels (i.e. over 12%) in Mexico (13.0%) and New Zealand (12.7%) – see Table 4.6. However, attrition rates are clustered towards the lower end of the range indicated, with more than two-thirds (68%) having a rate less than half the maximum observed. The relatively low rates of attrition are most likely the outcome of the difficult economic circumstances prevailing in many countries, resulting in less external job opportunities for revenue body staff, while revenue bodies themselves have significantly cut back staff recruitment in the face of expenditure cutbacks.

Closely related to the measure of "attrition rate" is the "rate of staff churn" (i.e. the total impact of both new recruits and departures as a percentage of total average staff). Across the total surveyed population the average rate of churn observed was 10%, with 10 countries displaying average churn of 15% or more and very high levels observed for Mexico (27%), New Zealand (27%) and Russia (30%). Accepting that this may include quite significant numbers of temporary staff such high rates of churn can, nevertheless, impose a significant workload and the management and human resources effort needed to provide effective support for large movements of staff inwards and outwards should not be underestimated. As well as external churn, revenue bodies must also manage internal churn – dealing with those staff who change jobs, get promoted, take career breaks or secondments etc., another significant, but here unquantified, demand on their HRM capacity and processes.

Age profiles of revenue body staffing

Drawing on the data in Tables 4.6 and 4.7 (with the latter displaying regional groupings), there are significant variations between the age profiles of revenue bodies' staff when viewed across different geographical groupings, no doubt resulting from a complex mix of cultural, economic, and sociological factors (e.g. economic maturity, recruitment, remuneration, and retirement policies, and rates of morbidity) and suggesting substantial differences in relative levels of experience of revenue body officials across the different groupings. For example:

- Revenue body staff are older in Nordic countries where, on average, around 50% are aged 50 and older (including Denmark [56%], Finland [57%] and Iceland [53%]) and in some other European countries (e.g. Belgium [54%], Ireland [51%], Italy [55%], Netherlands [56%], Portugal [56%] and Spain [56%]; elsewhere, only Colombia shows a relatively older workforce [61%]).
- By way of contrast, staff are considerably younger on average in Eastern European countries, Asian countries, Russia, Saudi Arabia and South Africa.

Qualifications

The section on staff development identified an apparent tendency of revenue bodies beginning to partner with universities to provide externally accredited training. Such a tendency would be in line with the overall trend in some OECD countries to further professionalise the public sector through increased access to university-accredited training. The proportion of staff with university or degree-level qualifications varies significantly, with less than 25% of staff qualified at equivalent to degree level in four revenue bodies, 25-49% in 16 revenue bodies, 50-74% in 18 revenue bodies and over 75% in 12 revenue

Table 4.6. **Staff metrics – arrivals, departures, age profile and academic qualifications**

	Staffing indicators				Age profile (%)				
Country	No. at start of FY2013	Recruited in FY2013	Departures in FY 2013	Attrition rate %	Under 30 years	30-49 years	50-59 years	Over 59 years	% with degree
OECD countries									
Australia	22 048	754	1 101	5.0	12.0	51.0	30.0	7.0	47
Austria	7 594	167	277	3.7	7.0	47.0	45.0	1.0	54
Belgium	24 708	948	1 777	7.3	6.9	39.5	48.6	5.0	27
Canada	35 082 /1	115	1 612	4.7	4.0	50.9	36.9	8.3	n.a.
Chile	4 230	45	80	1.9	6.1	60.8	21.6	11.5	75
Czech Republic	14 804	1 184	957	6.4	6.9	51.6	34.0	7.5	40
Denmark	7 325	260	705	9.9	3.0	41.0	40.0	16.0	22
Estonia	1 546	112	123	8.0	16.2	49.0	26.3	8.5	62
Finland	5 322	214	379	7.2	5.6	37.2	38.9	18.3	44
France	115 411 /1	1 879	n.a.	n.a.	4.0	48.0	42.0	6.0	n.a.
Germany	110 382	1 092	1 156	1.0	13.8	44.3	33.3	8.6	52
Greece	n.a.	193	1 252		2.0	47.0	51.0		46
Hungary	22 966	1 347	1 386	6.0	17.4	61.9	19.4	1.3	61
Iceland	259	16	23	9.0	7.0	39.0	27.0	26.0	54
Ireland	5 745	60	149	2.6	2.6	46.7	45.7	5.0	43
Israel	5 983	209	169	2.8	12.0	48.0	27.0	13.0	38
Italy	41 035	83	935	0.8	1.0	45.0	45.0	10.0	41
Japan	56 194	758	1 829	3.2	n.a.	n.a.	n.a.	n.a.	n.a.
Korea	18 841	1 574	584	3.0	3.0	74.0	22.0	1.0	82
Luxembourg	985	31	32	3.3	11.8 /1	67.6 /1	19.7 /1	0.9 /1	5 est.
Mexico	36 189	4 971	4 707	13.0	22.3	58.6	15.5	3.6	60
Netherlands	28 107 /1	1 528 /1	778 /1	2.7	5.0	39.3	37.5	18.2	28
New Zealand	5 452 /1	801	697	12.7	18.0	51.0	22.0	9.0	30 est.
Norway	6 359	264	374	5.9	4.0	49.0	33.0	14.0	50 est.
Poland	48 818	1 152	1 482	3.0	7.0	63.0	26.0	4.0	88
Portugal /1	11 566	115	340	3.0	0.7	43.6	49.3	6.4	46
Slovak Republic	8 923	761	383	4.2	11.0	62.0	25.0	2.0	68
Slovenia	2 354	8	64	2.8	0.0	86.0	12.0	2.0	60
Spain	26 962	383	980	3.7	0.8	43.0	48.5	7.7	39 /1
Sweden	9 849 /1	483	769	7.9	8.2	47.6	26.9	16.9	62
Switzerland	1 078	74	55	5.1	8.0	57.0	28.0	7.0	66
Turkey	46 334	6 442	1 407	2.9	18.9	61.7	18.3	1.1	77
United Kingdom	74 983	2 535	4 799	6.5	10.3	49.2	34.4	6.1	26
United States	97 942 /1	7 351 /1	11 165 /1	11.6	5.7	42.7	38.1	13.5	45
Non-OECD countries									
Argentina	22 346	321	510	2.3	3.4	57.5	31.0	8.1	52
Brazil	24 625	952	1 373	5.6	8.9	43.9	36.3	10.9	77
Bulgaria	7 693	488	445	5.8	8.7	59.7	27.6	4.0	81
China	756 000	18 000	18 000	2.4	9.6	71.6	18.8	0	62
Colombia	8 709	211	597	7.0	2.6	18.2	22.2	38.4	n.a.
Costa Rica	969	66	36	3.7	14.3	54.2	28.4	3.1	79
Croatia	4 227 /1	87	136	3.2	2.0	53.0	34.0	10.0	46
Cyprus	827	6	45	5.6	1.0	60.0	34.0	5.0	55
Hong Kong, China	2 757	147	98	3.5	10.0	50.6	39.4	0.0	27
India	41 357	n.a.	n.a.	n.a.	n.a.	n.a.	n.a.	n.a.	n.a.
Indonesia	31 325	1 795	777	2.4	33.0	56.0	11.0	0	52
Latvia	4 312	311	284	6.6	14	56	19	11	94
Lithuania	3 296	278	289	8.8	10.8	44.4	36.4	8.4	81
Malaysia	10 658	173	98	0.9	15.0	64.0	21.0	0.0	51
Malta	751	27	43	5.8	n.a.	n.a.	n.a.	n.a.	14
Morocco	4 935	152	200	4.1	18.0	51.0	31.0	0.0	20
Romania	25 461	1 452 /1	2 432	9.7	3.1	67.9	25.9	3.1	88
Russia	132 917	25 359	15 768	11.4	27.0	56.0	16.0	3.0	93
Saudi Arabia	1 507	91	50	3.3	22	69	9	0.0	56
Singapore	1 870	163	135	7.2	23.1	53.1	20.3	3.5	55
South Africa	14 701	369	934	6.5	25.3 /1	54.1 /1	20.5 /1	0.1 /1	n.a.
Thailand	22 695	1 042	608	2.7	10.5	65.0	24.5	0	80

For notes indicated by "/ (number)", see Notes to Tables section at the end of the chapter, p. 167.
Source: Tax Administration 2015 survey responses.

bodies. The average (unweighted) for the 50 revenue bodies able to report this information was 54%, marginally above the average computed in the prior series (51%). Encouragingly, there was a particularly high correlation between those revenue bodies reporting both a relatively high proportion of staff with academic qualifications and a workforce that was predominantly under 50 years of age (see Table 4.8).

Table 4.7. **Age profile of revenue body staff in regional groupings**

Regional groupings of revenue bodies	Percentage of staff by age bands			
	<30 years	30-49 years	50-59 years	Over 60 years
North America (3)	9	48	33	10
South America (5)	6	47	31	14
Europe (25)	8	49	36	7
Nordic countries (5)	4	43	37	16
Russia (1)	27	56	14	3
Middle East/Africa (4)	20	59	20	1
Asia (7)	10	71	19	<1
Pacific (2)	13	51	29	7
OECD countries (32)	9	50	34	7
Non-OECD countries (20)	12	67	20	1

Note: Data reflects information in Table 4.5 for all countries except Greece, India, Japan and Malta.
Source: Survey responses (aggregated by regional groupings).

Table 4.8. **Age profiles and staff with degrees etc., in selected countries**

Country	Percentage of staff by age bands			% with degree or equivalent qualification
	<30 years	30-49 years	total < 50 years	
Chile	6	61	67	75
Korea	3	74	77	82
Poland	7	63	70	88
Turkey	19	62	81	77
Brazil	9	44	53	77
Bulgaria	9	60	69	81
Costa Rica	14	54	68	79
Latvia	14	56	70	94
Lithuania	11	44	55	81
Romania	3	68	71	88
Russia	27	56	83	93
Thailand	10	65	75	80

Source: Tax Administration 2015 survey responses.

A number of revenue bodies make explicit reference in their annual reports and/or business plans to their strategies and plans to increase overall internal qualification levels, either as a general aim or targeting specific skills. The series will continue to monitor overall tendencies and specific initiatives in this area.

Notes to Tables

Table 4.1. Revenue bodies' human resource management strategies

/1. **Argentina:** A new system of recruitment has been implemented that includes technical/psycho-technical tests, language testing and physical examinations (prior to hiring), and a requirement to pass an intensive training course to be admitted to the AFIP. **Australia:** The staff enterprise agreement is currently being negotiated, which may result in changes to some policies such as staffing policy. **Brazil:** Two types of rewards are at the planning/implementation stage: *(1)* Border compensation – in process of legal regulation (i.e. financial compensation for staff who work in border areas, including other public services such as the Federal Police, the Federal Highway Police, agricultural and labour inspectors; and *(2)* a bonus linked to institutional efficiency – a proposition sent by the tax Administration to higher authorities – related to the attainment of strategic institutional results. To this end, a set of institutional strategic indicators was proposed to compose the Index of Institutional Efficiency. **Costa Rica:** The Tax Administration is part of an enhancement and development of human resources pilot plan. **Denmark:** The current organisation of SKAT into business areas encompasses centralisation of competence development, i.e. planning, prioritisation and execution as well as funding of all competence development in SKAT in now based in business area HR in a single division. **Italy:** The Agency has employed 8 500 new graduates since 2003 as candidates for ongoing employment. Candidates' induction into the Agency entails four phases: *(1)* Technical – professional test; *(2)* Aptitude test – to verify their aptitudes and skills required for the professional profile; *(3)* Apprenticeship – candidates must also serve an apprenticeship period of a maximum of six months in the Revenue Agency's offices. They must demonstrate the ability to apply knowledge in the solution of operational problems and organisational behaviours; and *(4)* Final oral examination/interview, based on an evaluation of professional preparation, aptitudes and motivations. There is a blended learning: classroom training, training on the job and e-learning. At the end of the apprenticeship period the Head of the Unit assess the candidate's performance. **Luxembourg:** Separate recruitment department for the entire public sector; **Malta:** With the merger of the direct and indirect tax departments, IRD is currently conducting a capacity building exercise in order to identify those areas that can be merged, e.g. Tax Compliance/Audits. A call for applications will be issued in order to increase the number of Tax Compliance Unit (TCU) staff. **Portugal:** The enactment of a draft legal act concerning permanent staff regulation of customs and tax officers introducing significant amendments to careers, recruitment and training is pending and depends on negotiations with the labour unions as well as Government approval. **Singapore:** The manpower planning cycle is integrated with the IRAS Strategic Management Process, allowing IRAS to better plan and manage organisation-wide manpower requirements and resources. **South Africa:** Policy reviews are to be made in all these areas in 2014/15. **Spain:** The General Rationalisation Programme for the whole Public Sector includes staffing reduction plans but excludes staff devoted to the fight against fraud. **Switzerland:** Due to a future reorganisation and the introduction of new IT systems the skills required of staff are expected to slightly move to more qualified areas. Development and training plans must therefore be put in place.

/2. **Denmark:** A combined competence and resource control system is planned to handle the coming years major changes in staff composition and to better prepared for a higher degree of project work.

Table 4.2. Autonomy etc., in recruitment, and staff satisfaction and engagement

/1. **Colombia:** The numbers and types of staff to be hired are defined by decree of the national government, the types of skills and academic qualifications required for specific jobs are indicated by resolution of the institution, all employment contracts are subject to an annual evaluation; **Costa Rica:** The first survey concerning workplace satisfaction was circulated to the Ministry of Finance's staff on April, 2014. **Croatia:** Regarding the employment of new staff, the number of people who can be hired on an annual basis is limited according the Plan of admission to the civil service, which is administered by the Ministry of Public Administration. The Decision of the Croatian Government to ban the recruitment of new civil servants and employees of government agencies, professional services and offices of the Croatian Government is still in force (entered into force in 2009). The Tax Administration can recruit 1 new member of staff only if two members leave the employment, but with the approval of the Ministry of Public Administration. **Cyprus:** Procedure of publishing and appointment done by the Public Service Commission, its decisions being based on recommendations of Directors of Tax Departments. **France:** In France the type of staff is based on existing categories (and some internal rules) and technical specificities (e.g. technical, IT, cadastre) and the number of staff and the duration of contracts are determined by law (i.e. finance bill). The geographical assignment of staff is approved by the relevant joint body (administration and union representatives), but there are exceptions for specific departments or positions. **Germany:** The requirements for some functions are regulated by law. Apart from that, a general trend towards greater flexibility is discernible. **Hungary:** The authorised number of personnel of the NTCA is determined by Government Decree. **India:** Organisation has certain limited autonomy within the budgetary limits and sanctioned strength of manpower to optimise performance; **Italy:** The Revenue body carried out a research in late-2013 with the Sapienza University of Rome to study interpersonal relations, the management of communication technologies and the participation to operational decisional processes inside the Agency. The research used an online questionnaire to all staff, except to managers and the results are still being processed. **Luxembourg:** Tax administrations can propose the number and type of staff to be hired, but final decision by the separate recruitment department. **Malta:** Appointments based on merit applies to all three Tax Authorities. In the case of VAT, this is only done for the position of Inspectors within the VAT Department. The skills and academic qualifications of clerks and other positions are determined by the Ministry for Finance. **Mexico:** It is necessary to request the authorisation to modify the number and type of staff to an external government agency (i.e. Secretaría de la Función Pública); **Portugal:** The rules regarding recruitment are laid down by law and applicable to all public administration. Therefore, the duration of contracts is legally determined; **Romania:** A specific component of yearly evaluation form is dedicated to employee's observations. An instrument for the evaluation of staff satisfaction has been established. Moreover, a formal Advisory Committee is in place, with the possibility to perform surveys and assessments about workplace satisfaction. The yearly staff training and developing plan is analysed and undersigned by the Advisory Committee; **Slovenia:** Number and types of staff which will be hired is determined by Ministry of Finance and Government; **Sweden:** In accordance with the Swedish constitution; **Thailand:** For non-civil servant position the Revenue Department has autonomy in making decision all of the above matters.

/2. **Hungary:** Surveys are conducted for some NTCA bodies, with the results shared only with managerial staff. **Slovenia:** Surveys are not periodical and systematic.

Table 4.3. Revenue bodies' initiatives to support staff development

/1. **Brazil:** The Tax Administration has a partnership with the School of Finance Administration (ESAF), a permanent capacity building programme (Corporate Education Programme) and also an initial training programme for the first year of professional activity of tax inspectors (Professional Training Programme); **Canada:** The CRA is currently in discussions with Chartered Professional Accountants (CPA) Canada, the organisation that represents Canada's accounting profession. Progress is being made with regards to having CPA Canada recognise audit work toward the experience component for professional certification. **Cyprus:** The Tax departments co-operate with the Cyprus Academy of Public Administration. **France:** Initial training very much relies on the recourse to some senior staff members (explicitly laid down in the ministerial decree on initial training for new staff members). **Hungary:** Experienced and professional staff generally transfer their knowledge through educational assistance to younger officers. **India:** Experience sharing is undertaken formally as part of structured training activities as well as informally within functional teams, where more experienced personnel share their skills and expertise with junior incumbents. **Italy:** In 2012, the Revenue Agency carried out various training projects with the aim to create and consolidate a relation of confidence with taxpayers. In particular there have been set up training initiatives in technical-fiscal and behavioural field which in-depth the topics of tax compliance, authoritative power and relation with the taxpayer (both in the phase of cross-examination and in the customer's services).The sharing of fiscal knowledge and communicative and relational effective behaviours allows a better and speeder way to give information to taxpayers. These initiatives involved all the new recruited, the front-office personnel and auditor functionaries for a total of 8.400 participants. **Luxembourg:** Only for staff in Indirect Taxes. **Malta:** Only for the Customs Department. **Mexico:** The SAT has established and implemented training programmes with legal and accounting organisations as well as universities, in order to support and enhance the development of the staff based on skills/competencies required for both strategic and critical processes. SAT has established a network with the Mexican Institute of Public Accountants to professionalise our staff. **Portugal:** Formal arrangements/partnerships with universities and/or other educational bodies have not been established yet, however is very common for revenue body officials (namely senior officials) to be invited by universities and other recognised educational bodies to join their training programmes in order to provide training on taxation-related subjects. **Spain:** The Tax Agency channels its advanced training programmes on tax matters through the Institute for Fiscals Studies (IFS) within MOF. The IFS has signed many agreements with universities and educational bodies. **South Africa:** Some spend the last year in the Academy developing curriculum and/or training other employees. **Sweden:** Facilitating knowledge transfer is primarily a managerial responsibility, and sharing knowledge is part of our code of conduct/co-worker policy.

/2. **Malta:** Only for the VAT and Customs Department.

Table 4.5. Performance management and remuneration

/1. **Argentina:** There are two separate Collective Labour Agreements, one for the customs officials and the other for the tax/social security officials, in force since 1992 and 1991, respectively. In addition to specific updates made in recent years, in January 2008, several aspects of the two agreements were changed symmetrically (Rights, Obligations, Duties and Prohibitions; Employment Relationship, Salary, Labor Day, Incompatibilities, Compensation and Benefits, Leaves, Union Recognition, etc.). **Australia:** The ATO has some degree of flexibility within the relatively fixed remuneration system to reward good performance. Pay rates and salary advancement arrangements are negotiated under the terms of the Fair Work Act 2011 and in accordance with the Australian Government Public Sector Bargaining Policy. Work is assigned to employees in line with APS-wide job classification levels. **Brazil:** Institutional and individual competencies have been mapped since 2011. Staff can voluntary evaluate their own competencies and they can be evaluated by their supervisor. The results obtained allow the identification of competency gaps for the design of local, regional and national capacity building plans. **Colombia:** Staff pay levels are decreed by the central government and discriminated based on the categories/scales of employment. **Costa Rica:** Partially. Not every procedure has been assigned with management indicators. The revenue body is currently working on a pilot project to assess productivity. **Croatia:** The performance evaluation system of officers and other employees is regulated by the Civil Servants Act and in the Regulation on the procedures and criteria of evaluation of civil servants. **Cyprus:** The development plan addresses the needs of employees at large, not individually. **Estonia:** There is a performance management system for key positions which comprise approximately 17% of staff.

Finland: Performance targets are set on an "office" level, not as personal objectives. **France:** Wages and salaries of public servants are defined by Article 20 of Law 83-634 (July, 13th of 1983) about rights and obligations of civil servants. They include among others the index-related salary and the compensation set by various laws. Amount of wages depend on individual wage is determined according to the body the agent belongs to and the scale's level he achieved. The individual wage of each civil servant is determined by the body he belongs to. A gross index is associated to each body and scale's level. This index allows the calculation of gross and net wages. **Germany:** The system differs from one federal state to another. **Greece:** The revenue body uses measurable objectives for managers and auditors. **Hungary:** A fixed remuneration system is applied in state administrative bodies, with remuneration depending on the level of qualification and the number of years of service. The salary system of the NTCA is set according to this rule but it has an own table of remuneration. The Law on the NTCA provides the option to modify the salary of the employee both in a positive and a negative direction based on the evaluation of their professional work, and a possibility to establish a personal salary. **India:** There is limited flexibility within the relatively fixed remuneration system to incentivise performance. **Luxembourg:** Indirect taxes: the objectives are fixed for each different tax. AED has to deal with or for each tax office/department, but not for each staff member; **Malta:** Only for the Direct Tax Authority (Revenue Body) and Customs Department; **Mexico:** All staff members in core areas have measurable objectives, but not all staff members in support administrative units have them. **New Zealand:** Pay scales for non-manager positions are bargained with unions. Pay scales for managers are decided by IR. Both the discussions with unions and IR's consideration of manager pay scales are informed by a range of external factors, including public sector pay scales. **Romania:** Since 2011 the revenue body is using incentives (linked to 2010 medium monthly value) as part of the total salary. This incentive is unique (for fiscal administration only) and was imposed at national level by law. It consists in supplementary amount introduced in total salary. The system is not flexible or negotiable and was established in direct correlation with the importance of the staff position within the organisation. **South Africa:** Performance development plans (PDP) are setup and approved via an electronic system to which all staff have access and are able to log their own plans. PDP are therefore created based on development objective identified. **Sweden:** The salary system in combination with the systematic dialogue between manager and employee is a very powerful performance management system. **Switzerland:** The remuneration system is defined for all administrative federal offices, combined with salary ranges which are determined by each function.

/2. **Argentina:** There is a variable remuneration called "Account of Hierarchy". This account consists of a 0.70 of the total amount of AFIP's tax collection. To the corresponding monthly total amount, firstly 24% is withdrawn as employer's social security contributions; to the amount obtained, 5% is withdrawn for the payment of an incentive for the effective provision of the service and the remainder is divided into two subsections: a) general part and b) selective part, which is according to the employee's performance evaluation and determines the amount to be received. **Brazil:** The annual performance evaluation of the Tax Inspector career is carried out for staff who participate in the career progression. It excludes those who are ending their careers, and also those in overhead functions and who work at the Internal Affairs' Office. Regarding administrative staff, an annual performance evaluation is carried out intended to have an effect on salary bonuses. **Cyprus:** Only staff in Audit Sections and Training have clear measurable objectives. **Estonia:** Public sector pay scales ceased to exist in April 2013. **France:** Objectives are set for all staff members but are only measurable for some of them. **Germany:** The system differs from one federal state to another. **Malta:** Applies only to Direct Tax Authority (Revenue Body) and Customs Department. **South Africa:** SARS has statutory independence to set its own human resources practices separately from the public/civil service.

/3. **Brazil**: The Tax Inspector career comprises the position of Tax Analyst or Tax Inspector in the Federal Revenue of Brazil (RFB). The pay scales of these functions are different from other administrative staff. Out of the total of current staff in the RFB, 76% are in the Tax Inspector career stream and are remunerated through a single salary share, with the receiving of any other advantage vetoed. Administrative staff are regularly evaluated, having merit as one of the evaluation criteria, which reflects on their remuneration. **Cyprus:** Performance evaluation is not connected directly to employees' results.

Table 4.6. Staffing metrics

/1. **Canada:** Number of staff employed excludes term employees and students. **Croatia:** Officers and employees hired on full-time basis. **France:** people with the DGFIP status and those having the headquarters status. **Luxembourg:** Only for indirect taxes. **New Zealand:** Data is for all staff, tax and non-tax. Numbers given are actual headcount rather than sum of FTE. Numbers given includes all permanent and fixed term staff. **Netherlands:** in FTE. **Portugal:** The average age of the staff is 49 years old. The increasing aging of the workforce is partly due to the freezing of new admissions and the raising of the legal retirement age. **Romania:** The large number of newly recruited staff and number of staff who left the revenue body are the direct consequence of the large structural reform in 2013. **South Africa:** Actual age categories used are: Less than 32; 33-45; 46-64; and over 64. **Spain:** Only 39% of the staff needs compulsory a degree to occupy their post but most of the staff is indeed graduated. **Sweden:** FTEs. **United States:** A large number (17 575 [18%]) of IRS staffing (97 942) are seasonal staff, those seasonal employees that for the most part support specific tax season requirements. A majority of the yearly hiring (i.e. 4 216 of 7 351) employees recruited represent the normal yearly hiring requirements for the seasonal staff. Because of the fluctuation with seasonal staff, 3 852 of 11 165 employees who left the IRS in FY2013 separated after their seasonal rotation.

Bibliography

DGFiP (2014), *The optimization of human resources management in the tax administrations,* General Directorate of Public Finances *CIAT Technical Conference,* October 2014, Santiago de Compostela, Spain.

EC (2007), *Fiscal Blueprints – A Path to a Robust, Modern and Efficient Tax Administration*, Luxembourg: Office for Official Publications of the European Commission, Brussels, pp. 13-20.

Finnish Tax Administration (2014), *Annual Report 2013,* Helsinki.

IRS (2014), *IRS Strategic Plan 2014-17,* United States Internal Revenue Service, Washington, DC.

Chapter 5

Resources of national revenue bodies

This chapter provides summary operational and trend-related data (for some data items for up to nine years) and related analyses concerning the resources used for tax administration in surveyed revenue bodies and, where applicable, other revenue body roles. It also includes some brief comments concerning the use of third parties to provide critical services and support to revenue bodies for the administration of tax laws.

Key points

Government mandates to cut costs of operations

- Revenue bodies in many countries have mandates to cut their administrative costs as part of fiscal consolidation efforts, for some requiring significant downsizing (e.g. Australia and United Kingdom).

Aggregate salary and IT costs

- Aggregate salary costs as a share of aggregate administrative costs vary widely across revenue bodies, generally within a band ranging from 50% to 90%; this outcome appears to result from a variety of factors (e.g. the extent of outsourcing and IT investments, and the treatment of accommodation costs).
- Viewed over a seven year period (2007-13), aggregate salary costs as a share of aggregate administrative costs for OECD countries have averaged around 72%.
- IT-related costs (both salary and other administrative costs) are a significant component of the overall expenditure budget of many revenue bodies; across all revenue bodies, total IT-related costs were reported by 16 revenue bodies as exceeding 15.0% in 2013 (including 6 that reported over 20%) of total administrative expenditure.
- Revenue bodies reporting consistently high levels of IT expenditure (as a share of total expenditure) tend to perform highly across a series of performance-related measures reported in other parts of this series (e.g. e-filing (Tables 7.3 to 7.5), e-payment (Table 7.6), average staffing (Table 5.6), total administrative costs/GDP (Table 5.5), total costs/net revenue (Table 5.4), and debt levels (Table 6.14).

Expenditure and staffing-related ratios

- Cost of collection ratios that have traditional been used internationally to draw conclusions on relative efficiency and effectiveness vary widely across surveyed revenue bodies, significantly influenced by structural and other factors unrelated to relative efficiency and effectiveness. For this reason they needed to be interpreted with considerable care and used only as a pointer to further inquiry.
- A statistically significant upwards movement in the ratio occurred in 2009 for the majority of revenue bodies, in the aftermath of the global financial crisis in 2008 that led to a serious deterioration in tax revenues in many countries; the trend for many countries from 2010 to 2013 shows a consistently declining ratio as the tax revenue bases of countries recovered following the global financial crisis and/or taking account of government expenditure reduction programmes.
- The computed ratios for tax-related expenditure as a proportion of GDP vary significantly but there is a concentration of revenue bodies with a ratio in the region of 0.15% to 0.25% of GDP for most/all of the period covered; a few revenue bodies consistently show a ratio in excess of 0.3% which may be due to efficiency-related factors.
- Staffing ratios (e.g. number of citizens or labour force members/FTE) vary enormously across OECD countries due to structural and efficiency-related factors.
- There are significant variations in the relative distribution of staff resources across key functional groups, more than likely resulting from a complex mix of factors, and point to the need for substantial care when interpreting the data in a comparative way.

Third party delivery of tax administration-related activities

- Revenue bodies use a large variety of third parties for the delivery and support of tax administration operations, including the provision of IT services, the collection of tax payments, the answering of (simple) inquiries, for the provision of HR administrative support services, and to collect tax debts.

The resources of national revenue bodies

The overall level of resources devoted to tax system administration is an important and topical issue for many governments, their revenue bodies, and external observers. All governments have limits on the funds at their disposal for public sector administration (including for revenue bodies) and many are actively seeking to reduce public sector costs. For their part, revenue bodies must decide how to make optimal use of the funds allocated to them to administer the laws in the most efficient and effective manner. As noted earlier in this series, most revenue bodies have some flexibility in deciding how their available funding is used for carrying out their responsibilities. Where this flexibility exists, resource allocation can be a critical part of planning, enabling resource shifts to be made to meet newly emerging priorities.

This chapter provides a relatively detailed account of the aggregate resource allocations made to revenue bodies to carry out their mandate, an array of comparative analyses and trend data, and some insights on expected developments in staffing, in particular for those revenue bodies where Government decisions have been taken to improve efficiency and/or downsize operations. Various ratios are presented as some of these are used regularly in international comparisons of tax administration systems.

Given the "comparative" nature of this series, every effort has been made to validate the accuracy of the information reported by revenue bodies and used in the series, and for some countries this has entailed revisions of historical data and ratios published in previous editions of this series that have now been revised. Recognising that some revenue bodies also perform various "non-tax roles", steps have also been taken with the assistance of participating revenue bodies to quantify their resource impact and to exclude them from relevant tabulations in order to present tabulations and ratios etc., that prepared on a comparable basis (or as near to as practicable). For the reasons outlined, considerable care should be taken when interpreting this information presented and in drawing any conclusions as to the relative efficiency and effectiveness of the individual revenue bodies identified.

Impacts of recent Government decisions on revenue bodies' budgets

At the time of planning the preparation of this edition, it was known that governments in many countries were taking steps to reduce their public sector wage costs, in some cases by fairly significant amounts. As large employers, revenue bodies are prime targets for such expenditure reduction efforts and, depending on their scale, these may present significant challenges for maintaining service delivery standards and compliance programmes, not to mention a myriad of staff management issues. The survey accordingly sought brief details of any major "downsizing"/expenditure reduction policies that were in place to gain some insight as to their scale and how they were being realised. A brief summary of the responses is set out in Table 5.1.

Of particular note, a number of revenue bodies in surveyed countries are subject to significant downsizing mandates that will impact in 2014 and beyond, for example:

- ***Australia:*** Around 3 000 staff in 2014 (of a total of 20 200 in 2013).
- ***Finland:*** Over 200 FTEs in each of 2014 and 2015 (of a total of 5 100 FTEs in 2013), continuing a downwards trend observed in prior series that has seen reductions between 2007 and 2013 of around 14%.

Table 5.1. **Government downsizing/staff reduction programmes**

(Table only includes revenue bodies from countries reporting that specific reductions are required)

Country	Scale of required reductions and related timeframes
OECD countries	
Australia	By 30 June 2014, a reduction of 900 staff; and by 31 October 2014, a further reduction of 2 100 staff.
Belgium	A range of changes are to be made that will entail the transfer of staff from the Federal level to the Regions
Canada	Measures announced in the 2012 and 2013 federal budgets, when fully implemented, will result in the CRA realising efficiencies of CAD 313.7 million annually. The Federal Budget 2013 also announced that departments would realise savings of 5% on public service travel, on an ongoing basis, with the CRA's contribution being CAD 2.1 million.
Denmark	Progressive declines in total budget expected, from around DKK 5.1 billion (2013) to DKK 4.5 billion (2017)
Finland	Reductions of 4.4% required in both 2014 and 2015, and around 2% after 2015.
France	The Finance Bill for 2014 requires a net decrease of the DGFIP's overall staffing (around 60% of which is devoted to tax administration) by 1 988 FTEs. The following measures have been taken to limit the impact of this staff reduction in local services: *(1)* In terms of staff reductions headquarters will proportionally contribute more than local services; *(2)* a higher contribution to staff cuts has been requested from management services and other services which are not in direct contact with taxpayers; and *(3)* in order to limit the compression on the lowest category of staff, the proportion of the upper category regularly increases in order to reach an equivalent level compared to other categories. An equivalent proportion for each management level will be involved in this compression policy this year. In parallel, additional staff allocation has been granted to services in charge of the fight against tax fraud. In 2014, 50 additional jobs have been allocated to tax audit.
Germany	Some Länder (i.e. regional government) have long term goals along these lines, however with a different focus.
Ireland	Revenue staff numbers have been reduced since 2008 in line with the current Government policy to reduce public sector numbers. Revenue's Employment Control Framework (ECF) figure for 2014 is 5 748. Current staff levels are in line with the ECF.
Israel	Reduction of 1.3% in 2014 (none in prior year)
Italy	With the integration of the Real Estate and Land Registry into the main revenue body, managerial posts in the support areas of administration, personnel management, internal control and communications have been rationalised and provided for savings of 363 managerial posts.
Mexico	5% expenditure reduction is expected to impact staffing costs
Netherlands	NTCA has to achieve savings of 400 million euros per annum by 2016; it has chosen not to reduce staff but to reduce the number of buildings and to concentrate work streams.
New Zealand	No specific reductions prescribed but strong Government focus on expenditure rationalisation and increased efficiency applies to all agencies. Government's focus is on "Better Public Services" through cross-government collaboration and optimising internal processes and it has set a cap on the size of core government administration across the public service.
Portugal	Government wide programme to terminate employment of less qualified staff by mutual agreement from 2013 – 33 lost from revenue body at the end of 2013.
Slovenia	Government requires 1% reduction of employees per year in public sector. Revenue body will achieve it share by natural attrition.
Spain	General rationalisation programme for the whole of the public sector that includes reduction of staff plans, but excludes staff devoted to dealing with fraud.
United Kingdom	GBP 1.2 billion savings over the period 2010-11 to 2015-16, with some of this being reinvested back into tackling non-compliance. Staff reduction of around 14 000 over this period, reaching around 52 000 FTEs by the end of March 2016.
United States	Budget reductions for 2014 require IRS to reduce FTEs to 84 268, compared to 89 857 in 2013.
Non-OECD countries	
Cyprus	Nothing specific reported for revenue body, but Government decision to reduce public sector staffing by 4 500 by 2016.
Romania	No specific cuts but major restructuring project commenced to minimise direct contact with the taxpayer, providing taxpayer service through the use of a robust self-service website, through an accessible call centre, and other means. Once the project will be completed, NAFA staff will be properly trained and distributed across the organisation, with a focus on staff re-assignment to key areas such as audit and debt collection. (extract from NAFA modernisation project presentation)
Russia	A programme for downsizing was announced in 2011. The initial plan was to reduce tax administration staff by 20 %, from 172 490 to 137 563. This staff reduction was initiated due to major reforms in technology for date capture, document dispatch and data processing operations in the FTS. By the end of the programme that was set for the 2013 year FTS had managed to reduce staff by 10%.

Source: Tax Administration 2015 survey responses.

- ***Russia:*** A staffing reduction target of 20%, equivalent to around 35 000 FTE was set in 2011; by the end of 2013, roughly 10% of the reduction had been achieved.
- ***United States:*** A reduction of over 5 000 FTEs in 2014, compared to use of almost 90 000 FTEs in 2013.
- ***United Kingdom:*** At the end of March 2013, staffing of around 63 000 FTEs and to be reduced to around 52 000 by March 2016, continuing a significant downwards trend that has been occurring over the last 8 years and with more still to come – see Figure 5.1.

Figure 5.1. **HMRC staffing levels 2005 to 2016**

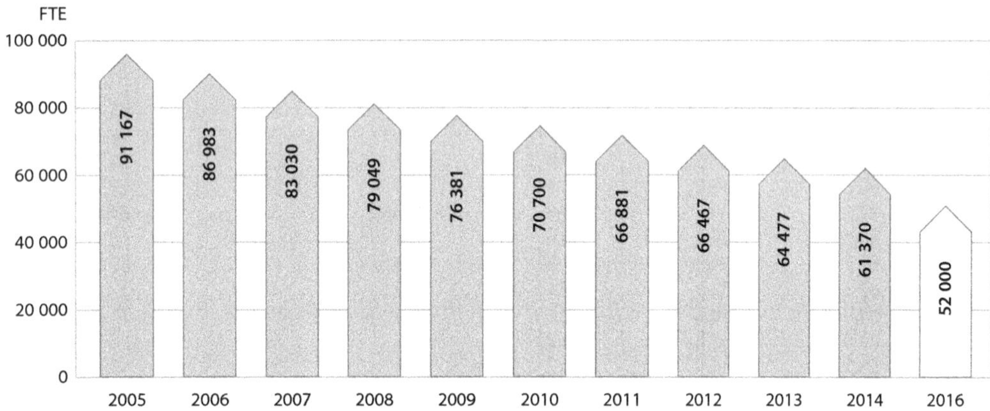

Note: Historic years adjusted for UK Border Agency and Serious and Organised Crime Agency departures.

Source: United Kingdom HMRC Business Plan 2014-16.

Overall tax administration expenditure

This section focuses on the aggregate level of expenditure of revenue bodies (for all categories of expenditure) to carry out their tax and other mandated responsibilities. For comparison purposes, efforts have been made to separately identify the resources used (and costs of) tax and non-tax related functions. A number of ratios are used to make comparisons across surveyed bodies countries – where relevant, any known abnormal factors influencing the ratios for individual countries are also identified.

Separate expenditure information is also provided in respect of information technology (IT) operations and human resource management (HRM), *covering both tax and non-tax responsibilities*. For these areas of revenue bodies' operations, the survey sought data concerning: *(1) Information technology operations:* Actual or estimated costs of providing *all* information technology support for administrative operations; and *(2) Human resource management functions:* Actual or estimated costs of providing *all* human resource management support functions (e.g. personnel, payroll, recruitment, learning and development) for administrative operations.

Aggregate Tables A.4 to A.6 (refer Annex A of this series) set out a variety of expenditure/resource usage data, for some categories covering up to nine years (2005 to 2013), including aggregate data reported by revenue bodies in prior series. Table 5.2 sets out relative aggregate salary expenditure data for all years to display trends, while Table 5.3

Table 5.2. **Salary expenditure/total expenditure for tax administration and support functions**

Country	Salary expenditure/total expenditure for all tax administration and support functions (%)						
	2007	2008	2009	2010	2011	2012	2013
OECD countries							
Australia	71.3	59.6	62.3	62.1	63.1	64.8	62.5
Austria	82.2	63.2	67.5	80.0	80.3	82.8	83.8
Belgium	81.7	81.9	81.7	82.9	81.4	80.1	79.6
Canada	77.0	77.2	78.9	76.7	77.8	77.7	76.3
Chile	78.1	78.4	80.3	81.8	83.3	83.3	86.3
Czech Republic	78.7	60.3	59.8	81.7	72.1	n.a.	n.a.
Denmark	68.5	n.a.	n.a.	n.a.	n.a.	62.9	60.9
Estonia	75.9	76.5	77.3	78.4	76.5	77.3 /1	76.0 /1
Finland	65.2	64.9	64.4	65.6	64.5	64.1	64.8
France	79.1	81.3	81.1	81.5	80.8	79.3	79.9
Germany	83.3	83.7	82.3	81.3	81.6	81.3	79.2
Greece	n.a.	n.a.	n.a.	n.a.	n.a.	n.a.	n.a.
Hungary	80.0	61.6	71.4	48.5	51.7 /1	57.9 /1	52.4 /1
Iceland	n.a.	53.6	52.7	65.6	69.4	68.6	68.9
Ireland /1	71.5	68.5	71.7	72.6	74.9	74.3	73.3
Israel	n.a.	87.5	87.9	68.2	68.3	59.7	60.9
Italy /1	69.5	56.5	56.4	54.4	55.6	57.1	58.5
Japan	81.1	80.7	80.8	80.5	80.7	81.4	81.0
Korea	66.5	64.0	63.6	61.9	64.4	68.1	68.2
Luxembourg	81.5	80.0	81.3	83.3	82.1	82.8	81.0
Mexico	82.5	82.4	83.1	88.9	85.2	82.1	78.1
Netherlands	64.0	65.5	67.1	70.6	72.0	74.8	73.2
New Zealand	63.0	62.5	64.3	59.9	59.2	55.3	55.0
Norway /1	63.1	64.0	65.2	66.4	68.5	67.2	67.3
Poland	71.8	71.7	72.8	80.4	81.7	68.9	68.7
Portugal	79.4	79.0	81.0	81.9	80.3	86.2	82.9
Slovak Republic	49.6	n.a.	n.a.	50.9	44.8	72.2	68.7
Slovenia	68.5	68.4	68.3	65.7	66.3	64.0	64.9
Spain	67.1	68.5	73.1	71.7	72.2	71.4	72.8
Sweden /1	69.6	65.3	69.0	69.5	68.4	70.5	70.1
Switzerland	90.6	90.6	89.4	94.0	92.6	81.9	81.9
Turkey	68.4	67.6	66.1	71.2	71.7	67.4	68.3
United Kingdom	61.2	58.8	55.2	54.4	57.1	58.8	58.0
United States	71.5	70.4	71.5	71.6	72.9	73.3	73.7
OECD ave. (unw.)	72.9	70.8	71.9	72.0	71.9	71.8	71.2
Non-OECD countries							
Argentina	94.2	94.7	95.3	95.8	96.9	95.9	95.2
Brazil /1	n.a.	n.a.	n.a.	60.1	59.8	69.3	69.3
Bulgaria	76.0	76.6	85.1	81.7	80.6	83.3	82.9
China	n.a.	n.a.	n.a.	n.a.	n.a.	n.a.	n.a.
Colombia	n.a.	n.a.	n.a.	76.4	75.8	74.3	69.6
Costa Rica	-----Not covered by the series for these years-----					68.8	74.3
Croatia	-----Not covered by the series for these years-----					57.3	57.2
Cyprus	n.a.	n.a.	78.1	81.4	81.8	82.5	81.2
Hong Kong, China	n.a.	n.a.	n.a.	86.6	88.9	88.0	86.4
India	n.a.	57.5	65.5	66.0	61.3	57.7	58.6
Indonesia	n.a.	31.7	37.3	65.0	50.5	31.1	31.5
Latvia	61.5	72.4	68.9	58.6	65.6	68.1	68.6
Lithuania	68.6	73.1	77.8	79.9	78.9	76.8	79.0
Malaysia	67.3	51.2	39.2	79.2	82.4	75.4	78.4
Malta	66.7	66.7	60.0	65.7	75.3	70.0	65.0
Morocco	-----Not covered by the series for these years-----					n.a.	n.a.
Romania /1	76.5	85.9	97.1	n.a.	n.a.	75.1	84.8
Russia	n.a.	66.5	68.2	74.4	71.8	66.6	69.3
Saudi Arabia	82.8	80.9	79.2	n.a.	n.a.	n.a.	n.a.
Singapore	58.2	58.9	55.0	52.8	55.3	56.7	54.0
South Africa /1	60.6	61.8	57.7	n.a.	n.a.	66.9	66.9
Thailand	-----Not covered by the series for these years-----					63.5	62.8

For notes indicated by "/ (number)", see Notes to Tables section at the end of the chapter, p. 196.
Source: Tax Administration 2015 survey responses.

displays relative total expenditure attributable to the use of IT (2009 to 2013), and HRM expenditure (2010 to 2013). The key observations are as follows:

Aggregate salary expenditure

- Aggregate salary costs vary widely, falling within a band of 50-90% of aggregate administrative costs for the vast majority of revenue bodies.
- Viewed over a seven year period (2007-13), aggregate salary costs as a share of total administrative costs for OECD countries have averaged around 72%.
- The factors that result in some revenue bodies reporting relatively high aggregate salary costs (e.g. Argentina, Chile, Hong Kong, Portugal, and Romania) have not been individually identified; however, general experience points to a number of possibly contributing factors, including the non-attribution of accommodation and/or IT services that are funded by other arms of Government and relatively low IT investments.
- The factors that lead to revenue bodies reporting relatively low aggregate salary costs (for example, by Hungary, Malta, New Zealand, Singapore and United Kingdom) have not been individually identified but these may result from a range of factors including the significant use of third party service approaches (e.g. the provision of IT infrastructure and related support and the collection of tax payments) as seen in many countries – see Table 5.8 – and full charging of accommodation costs, including costs of unused accommodation resulting from staff downsizing.

Information technology (IT) expenditure

- Reported IT-related costs also vary enormously in their relative magnitude which may result from a variety of factors (e.g. low real investment in IT, sharing of IT costs with other parts of MOF, and errors and inconsistency across revenue bodies in properly classifying IT-related expenditure for this survey) – see Tables 5.3 and A.4.
- Notwithstanding the wide variation, IT-related costs (i.e. salary and other administrative costs) are a significant component of the overall expenditure budget of many revenue bodies; across all revenue bodies, total IT-related costs were reported by 16 revenue bodies as exceeding 15% of total expenditure in 2013 (with 6 reporting amounts in excess of 20%).
- Viewed over the five year period (2009-13), average IT costs for all OECD revenue bodies countries are reported fairly consistently at around 11-12% of total revenue body expenditure; for non-OECD countries, the average investment in IT appears to be much lower although there are some notable exceptions (e.g. Brazil, Croatia, Latvia, and Singapore).
- Of the 13 revenue bodies (in both OECD and non-OECD countries) reporting IT expenditure over 15% in three or more years of the five year period covered by the series generally perform favourably across a series of performance-related measures reported in other parts of this series (i.e. e-filing [Tables 7.3 to 7.5], e-payment [Table 7.6], total administrative costs/GDP [Table 5.5], and total costs/net revenue [Table 5.4], and average staffing [Table 5.6]).[1] (See summary of measures overleaf.)

Country	Efficiency-related indicators				
	Overall e-filing rates (for PIT, CIT, and VAT)*	Electronic payment rates*	Average staffing ratio*	Total costs/ GDP**	Costs/ net revenue**
Australia	✓✓	✓✓	✓	✓	✓
Austria	✓✓	✓✓	✓	✓	✓✓
Brazil	✓✓	✓	✓✓	✓	✓
Denmark	✓✓	n.a.	x	x	✓✓
Finland	✓	✓✓	✓	✓	✓
Iceland	✓✓	n.a.	✓✓	✓	n.a
Netherlands	✓✓	✓✓	x	xx	✓
New Zealand	✓	✓✓	✓✓	✓	✓
Norway	✓✓	✓✓	x	✓	✓✓
Singapore	✓✓	✓✓	✓✓	✓✓	✓✓
Sweden	✓✓	✓✓	✓	✓	✓✓
United Kingdom	✓✓	✓✓	✓	x	✓✓
United States	✓	✓	✓✓	✓✓	✓✓

Ratings: * ✓✓ above average ✓ average **x** below average **xx** well below average

** ✓✓ very favourable ✓ favourable **x** unfavourable **xx** very unfavourable

- Revenue bodies in OECD countries appear to be making far greater investments in their use of IT, relatively speaking, compared to non-OECD countries; from the data in Table 5.3, it will be seen that 11/34 OECD (roughly one-third) made IT investments over 15% in three or more years of the five year period covered by the series while for non-OECD countries the corresponding number was two of twenty-two.
- There are five revenue bodies in OECD countries with relatively high investments in staffing and relatively low reported investments in IT that, with minor exceptions, perform below average in a range of efficiency-related indicators covered by the series (i.e. size of office network (Table 2.4), overall e-filing take-up rates (Tables 7.3 to 7.5), average staffing levels (Table 5.6), total administrative costs/GDP (Table 5.5), and total costs/net revenue (Table 5.4).[2]

Country	% of total costs in 2013		Efficiency related indicators				
	Salary	IT	Size of office network**	Overall e-filing rates (for PIT, CIT and VAT)*	Average staffing ratio*	Total costs/ GDP**	Costs/ net revenue**
Belgium	79.6	4.5	xx	✓✓	xx	xx	✓
France	79.9	2.9	xx	✓	x	✓	✓
Germany	79.2	6.8	xx	x	xx	x	x
Luxembourg	81.0	4.8	xx	xx	xx	x	✓
Poland	68.7	1.0	xx	xx	xx	x	x

Ratings: * ✓✓ above average ✓ average **x** below average **xx** well below average

** ✓✓ very favourable ✓ favourable **x** unfavourable **xx** very unfavourable

Table 5.3. **IT and human resource management expenditure (% of all expenditure)**

	Total IT expenditure / total revenue body expenditure %					Total HRM costs / total expenditure %			
Country	2009	2010	2011	2012	2013	2010	2011	2012	2013
OECD countries									
Australia	22.9	21.7	21.5	21.1	21.2	5.3	6.0	4.7	4.2
Austria	10.4	13.5	15.4	27.6	26.8	5.0	5.0	5.0	5.2
Belgium	7.8	6.4	6.1	5.3	4.5	n.a.	n.a.	2.2	2.1
Canada	12.6	11.3	10.5	10.5	11.1	1.9	1.9	1.5	1.6
Chile	5.2	5.6	5.7	7.4	5.3	3.2	3.4	4.1	3.7
Czech Republic	13.7	3.4	20.4	16.4	14.9	0.5	0.5	0.6	0.6
Denmark	16.2	14.5	14.8	16.5	16.9	2.1	1.9	2.3	2.4
Estonia	11.5	11.5	15.8	/1	/1	1.5	2.6	1.3 /2	1.0 /2
Finland	20.0	n.a.	27.5	27.8	26.8	n.a.	n.a.	n.a.	n.a.
France	4.2	3.6	3.6	3.2	2.9	n.a.	n.a.	2.5	2.5
Germany	6.4	6.5	6.5	6.9	6.8	1.3	1.3	1.4	1.6
Greece	n.a.	n.a.	n.a.	n.a.	n.a.	n.a.	n.a.	n.a.	n.a.
Hungary	12.0	4.8	5.2	6.1	6.5	1.6	2.9	2.0	2.0
Iceland	30.4	16.4	16.8	16.1	16.7	n.a.	n.a.	n.a.	n.a.
Ireland /1	n.a.	13.6	10.2	11.8	12.7	1.3	1.4	1.4	1.3
Israel	8.8	5.0	5.2	2.4	2.9	1.3	1.2	1.6	1.4
Italy	4.9	4.6	5.2	4.8	4.9	3.8	3.9	3.8	4.3
Japan	8.3	8.5	8.6	7.1	6.9	0.0	0.0	0.0	0.0
Korea	7.6	8.8	7.1	7.7	6.6	0.7	0.7	0.7	0.7
Luxembourg /1	5.5	2.2	3.7	3.3	4.8	n.a.	n.a.	n.a.	n.a.
Mexico	3.9	4.1	4.1	4.0	4.0	1.2	1.0	0.9	0.8
Netherlands	18.1	16.2	14.2	14.9	15.5	2.5	1.9	2.1	2.2
New Zealand	19.2	24.5	22.5	18.8	18.3	1.5	1.6	1.5	1.8
Norway	21.0	21.9	20.8	24.9	27.0	2.2	2.3	1.2	1.2
Poland	2.8	1.4	1.6	0.9	1.0	0.1	0.4	0.3	0.2
Portugal	2.4	1.4	1.2	1.6	2.0	n.a.	n.a.	0.5	0.5
Slovak Republic	n.a.	8.6	15.5	11.7	17.9	0.9	0.8	1.7	1.7
Slovenia	n.a.	n.a.	n.a.	13.0	10.6	n.a.	n.a.	n.a.	n.a.
Spain /1	4.6	5.7	5.6	11.2 /1	10.8 /1	n.a.	n.a.	8.6	8.5
Sweden	19.5	16.8	17.7	17.0	19.5	n.a.	n.a.	n.a.	n.a.
Switzerland	8.9	2.0	2.6	1.3	3.3 /1	0.8	0.9	1.0	1.0
Turkey	3.6	0.8	2.2	1.9	3.6	n.a.	n.a.	n.a.	n.a.
United Kingdom	21.2	20.3	22.8	20.0	21.3	1.7	1.6	1.4	1.2
United States	14.9	15.4	15.0	15.2 /1	17.4 /1	2.0	1.8	1.7	1.5
OECD ave. (unw.)	11.6	9.7	11.1	10.9	11.3	1.8	2.0	2.1	2.0
Non-OECD countries									
Argentina /1	0.7	0.6	0.8	0.8	1.1	0.04	0.1	0.05	0.05
Brazil	n.a.	16.2	15.5	15.5	16.0	n.a.	n.a.	n.a.	n.a.
Bulgaria	n.a.	0.6	2.4	2.9	2.9	1.0	1.1	0.3	0.9
China	n.a.	n.a.	n.a.	1.9	1.9	n.a.	n.a.	n.a.	n.a.
Colombia	n.a.	3.4	3.5	6.7	5.3	1.1	1.3	n.a.	n.a.
Costa Rica	– Not covered by series in these years –			2.8	3.9	Not covered by series		n.a.	n.a.
Croatia	– Not covered by series in these years –			12.9	16.0	Not covered by series		0.4	0.4
Cyprus	n.a.	2.3	3.0	4.3	7.9	0.7	1.1	0.7	0.9
Hong Kong, China	n.a.	9.1	9.6	9.6	10.0	1.2	1.3	1.1	1.1
India	n.a.	7.0	7.1	10.3	12.0	0.1	0.3	0.6	1.0
Indonesia	n.a.	n.a.	n.a.	2.8	2.7	n.a.	n.a.	0.6	0.4
Latvia	14.8	13.3	9.8	13.5	16.0	5.4	4.8	1.5	1.2
Lithuania	6.7	7.3	7.8	9.8	9.3	1.1	0.9	0.9	0.9
Malaysia	27.5	5.9	2.4	3.0	1.9	2.7	3.0	3.8	3.5
Malta /1	7.9	0.2	0.2	0.1	0.2	0.6	0.6	0.8	0.8
Morocco	– Not covered by series in these years –			n.a.	n.a.	Not covered by series		n.a.	n.a.
Romania	n.a.	n.a.	2.7	8.8	2.8	n.a.	n.a.	0.0	0.0
Russia	5.7	5.9	6.9	7.4	7.4	1.8	1.8	1.9	2.0
Saudi Arabia	6.7	n.a.	n.a.	n.a.	n.a.	n.a.	n.a.	n.a.	n.a.
Singapore	33.8	40.4	39.4	36.6	39.6	1.6	1.8	1.8	1.7
South Africa	4.8	n.a.	n.a.	n.a.	n.a.	n.a.	n.a.	n.a.	n.a.
Thailand	– Not covered by series in these years –			1.3	0.3	Not covered by series		2.3	2.2

For notes indicated by "/ (number)", see Notes to Tables section at the end of the chapter, p. 196.
Source: Tax Administration 2015 survey responses.

Human resource management expenditure

As relatively large employers, revenue bodies must invest fair amounts in their HRM support functions. For survey purposes, revenue bodies were asked to quantify the actual or estimated costs of providing all human resource management support functions (e.g. personnel, payroll, recruitment, learning and development) for administrative operations (incl. non-tax roles).

Table 5.3 sets out the level of expenditure for HRM functions as a proportion of all revenue body expenditure for the period 2010 to 2013 – the data should be interpreted with care owing to the possibility of misinterpretation/inconsistencies in its compilation. The key observations are:

- Data reported by 41 (of 56) revenue bodies revealed an average expenditure of around 2% on HRM functions, but there were a number of countries reporting substantially higher amounts-Australia (4-5%), Austria (around 5%), Chile (around 4%), Italy (around 4%), Malaysia (3-4%) and Spain (8.5%).
- Revenue bodies reporting a relatively high amount of HRM expenditure generally reported major changes underway or planned concerning a mix of recruitment, training, performance management and/or rewards related reforms (see Table 4.1 of Chapter 4).

Measures of relative costs of administration

The cost of collection ratio

It has become a fairly common practice for revenue bodies to compute and publish (e.g. in their annual reports) a "cost of collection" ratio as a surrogate measure of the efficiency/effectiveness of their administration. (Countries that follow this practice include Australia, Japan, Korea, New Zealand, Singapore, Slovenia, South Africa, United Kingdom, and United States.) The ratio is computed by comparing the annual costs of administration incurred by a revenue body, with the total revenue collected (after refunds) over the course of a fiscal year, and is often expressed as a percentage or as the cost of collecting 100 units of revenue. Most revenue bodies tend to publish the ratio for a number of years and, all other things being equal, changes in the ratio over time should reflect movements in relative efficiency and/or effectiveness. This arises from the fact that the ratio is derived from a comparison of inputs (i.e. administrative costs) to outputs (i.e. tax revenue collections); initiatives that reduce relative costs (i.e. improve efficiency) or improve compliance and revenue (i.e. improve effectiveness) will impact on the ratio. In practice, however, there are a number of factors that may influence the cost/revenue relationship, but which have nothing to do with relative efficiency or effectiveness. Examples of such factors are elaborated in Box 5.1. Clearly, any analysis of movements in the trend of the ratio over time should pay regard to such factors.

Box 5.1. The cost of collection ratio as an indicator of efficiency and/or effectiveness

Observed over time, a downward trend in the "cost of collection" ratio can constitute evidence of a reduction in relative costs (i.e. improved efficiency) and/or improved tax compliance (i.e. improved effectiveness). However, experience has also shown that there are many factors that can influence the ratio which are not related to changes in a revenue authority's efficiency and/or effectiveness:

Box 5.1. **The cost of collection ratio as an indicator of efficiency and/or effectiveness** *(continued)*

- **Changes in tax rates***:* The legislated rates of tax are an important factor in determining the cost/revenue relationship. In theory, a policy decision to increase the overall tax burden should, all other things being equal, improve the ratio by a corresponding amount, but this has nothing to do with improved operational efficiency or effectiveness.
- **Macroeconomic changes***:* Abnormal changes in rates of economic growth etc. or inflation over time are likely to impact on the overall revenue collected by the tax administration and the cost/revenue relationship. This is especially likely to occur in countries that are prone to considerable volatility in the movement of such indicators.
- **Abnormal expenditure of the revenue authority***:* From time to time, a tax authority may be required to undertake an abnormal level of investment (e.g. the building of a new information technology infrastructure, acquisition of more expensive new accommodation). Such investments are likely to increase overall operating costs over the medium term, and short of off-setting efficiencies, will impact on the cost/revenue relationship. The introduction of new taxes may also present additional up front administrative costs that initially impact on the cost/revenue ratio, but which are dissipated over time. (The use of accrual accounting may reduce the impact of these expenditures on the cost/revenue relationship.)
- **Changes in the scope of taxes collected by a revenue body***:* From time to time, governments decide to shift responsibility for the collection of particular taxes from one agency to another. For example, in Bulgaria, responsibility for the collection of most social contributions was moved from social security bodies to the newly formed National Revenue Authority in 2006.

As the "cost of collection" ratio takes account of total revenue collections, there has been a tendency by some observers to use it as an indicator of effectiveness. However, its usefulness in this regard is limited for one fundamental reason. The difference between the amount of tax actually collected and the maximum potential revenue is commonly referred to in tax literature as the "tax gap". Put another way, the amount of revenue collected compared with the maximum potential revenue, expressed as a percentage, is the overall level of compliance or effectiveness achieved by the tax administration. All other things being equal, initiatives that improve compliance with the laws (i.e. improve effectiveness) will impact on the cost/revenue relationship. ***However, because the cost/revenue ratio ignores the revenue potential of the tax system, its value as an indicator of effectiveness is extremely limited.*** This is particularly relevant in the context of international comparisons – countries with similar cost/revenue ratios can be poles apart in terms of their relative effectiveness.

Source: OECD CTPA Secretariat.

A summary of computed cost of collection ratios covering an extended (nine year) timeframe to highlight trends for surveyed revenue bodies is provided in Table 5.4. These ratios have been computed using data reported by revenue bodies for this and prior editions of the series. For a few countries, the ratios for years up to 2011 reported in prior editions have been revised to correct errors in source data advised by the countries concerned. *The final column of the table draws attention to various factors unrelated to the efficiency and effectiveness of the revenue body, that for the countries concerned affect one or more elements of the ratio's computation (*i.e. *expenditure and revenue) and which hinder* *direct comparability across the population of countries included in the table.* Important observations from the information reported are as follows:

- Cost of collection ratios vary widely across revenue bodies, significantly influenced by structural and other factors unrelated to relative efficiency, of the kind described throughout this series (e.g. a country's legislated tax burden and range of the taxes collected).
- A statistically significant upwards movement in the ratio occurred in 2009 for the majority of revenue bodies, in the aftermath of the global financial crisis in 2008 that led to a serious deterioration in tax revenues in many countries – examples here include Belgium, Canada, Chile, Czech Republic, France, Ireland, Japan, Latvia, Lithuania, Portugal, Russia, Spain and the United States.
- The trend for many countries from 2010 to 2013 shows a consistently declining ratio as the tax revenue bases of countries recovered following the global financial crisis and/or taking account of government expenditure reduction efforts (e.g. Australia, Austria, Argentina, Brazil, Bulgaria, Canada, Colombia, Ireland, Lithuania, Portugal, United Kingdom and United States).
- For a few revenue bodies, there has been significant downwards movement in the ratio as a result of "structural" factors (e.g. responsibilities involving the collection of new revenue streams such SSC) and for some downsizing/efficiency improvement programmes (e.g. United Kingdom).

Taken as a whole, the data presented emphasise the need for considerable care when undertaking cross-country comparisons of the cost of collection ratio in the context of assessments of relative efficiency in order to avoid erroneous conclusions. (This matter is discussed in further detail later in this chapter.)

Ratio of administrative expenditure to GDP

The relative size and trend of a revenue body's tax-related administrative expenditure over time can also be viewed by way of comparison with a country's aggregate GDP (as is the practice for observing aggregate tax burdens over a number of years). In other words, what proportion of a country's resources (expressed in terms of GDP) is expended by Government each year to administer tax laws?

Such a comparison removes the impact of changes in the legislated tax burden and economic factors that are inherent in the "cost of collection" ratio, and is particularly relevant in times of austerity when Government budgets are under strain. However, the ratio and its trend can be influenced by some abnormal factors (e.g. major new investments in technology, costs associated with implementing a new tax) that also need to be recognised. Computations of this ratio are set out in Table 5.4, with the key observations as follows:

- The ratios for tax-related expenditure as a proportion of GDP vary significantly but there is a concentration (around one-third) of revenue bodies with a ratio between 0.15-0.25 percent of GDP for much of the period reported.
- Very high ratios (i.e. greater than 0.30% of GDP) are consistently displayed for three revenue bodies (i.e. Belgium, Hungary and the Netherlands).
- Relatively low ratios (i.e. less than 0.10%) are consistently displayed for revenue bodies in nine countries (i.e. Colombia, India, Indonesia, Korea, Mexico, Saudi Arabia, Singapore, Thailand and United States); with two exceptions (i.e. Korea and United States), these are all countries with relatively low tax burdens.

Table 5.4. **Cost of collection ratios (administrative costs/net revenue collections) /1**

Country	Administrative costs for tax administration/net revenue collected % /2									Variation	Significant factors affecting comparability between countries' computed ratios
	2005	2006	2007	2008	2009	2010	2011	2012	2013	2013-08	
OECD countries											
Australia	1.04	0.99	0.93	0.95	1.00	1.05	0.99	0.98	0.93	-0.01	
Austria	0.66	0.66	0.64	0.79	0.85	0.70	0.66	0.68	0.67	-0.12	SSC not included
Belgium	1.43	1.57	1.39	1.27	1.40	1.29	1.36	1.23	1.17	-0.10	SSC not included
Canada	1.32	1.32	1.22	1.13	1.31	1.36	1.31	1.24	1.15	0.02	
Chile	0.69	0.63	0.60	0.67	0.91	0.77	0.68	0.67	0.66	-0.01	Costs exclude debt collection function
Czech Republic	1.29	1.38	n.a.	1.18	1.46	1.27	1.34	1.34	1.31	0.13	SSC and excises not included
Denmark	0.69	n.a.	0.61	0.64	0.67	n.a.	n.a.	0.56	0.48	-0.16	
Estonia /3	1.02	0.88	0.86	0.38	0.40	0.35	0.34	0.37	0.40	0.02	Costs exclude all IT support that is provided by MOF
Finland	0.78	0.79	0.77	0.80	0.88	0.84	0.80	0.79	0.75	-0.05	Excises not included
France	1.08	1.28	0.96	1.17	1.31	1.25	1.20	1.19	1.11	-0.06	SSC and excises not included
Germany	1.66	1.55	1.38	1.36	1.46	1.50	1.40	1.34	1.35	-0.01	SSC and excises not included
Greece	n.a.	n.a.	n.a.	n.a.	n.a.	n.a.	n.a.	n.a.	n.a.	n.a.	
Hungary	0.99	1.11	1.15	1.17	1.20	1.20	1.12	1.13	1.15	-0.02	
Iceland	n.a.	n.a.	n.a.	n.a.	n.a.	0.62	0.60	n.a.	n.a.	n.a.	Excises not included; Costs exclude debt collection
Ireland	0.82	0.78	0.79	0.95	1.08	1.26	1.14	0.87	0.85	-0.10	Costs include customs
Israel	n.a.	n.a.	n.a.	0.74	0.79	0.75	0.68	0.94	0.94	0.20	SSC not included
Italy	n.a.	n.a.	n.a.	1.08 /3	1.20 /3	0.89 /3	0.83 /3	0.89 /3	1.05 /3	-0.03	Ratio not comparable with others: see note
Japan	1.65	1.52	1.50	1.49	1.71	1.93	1.75	1.84	1.74	0.26	SSC not included
Korea	0.80	0.78	0.70	0.79	0.84	0.81	0.76	0.70	0.74	-0.05	SSC not included
Luxembourg	n.a.	n.a.	1.17	1.01	1.13	0.85	0.85	0.95	0.93	-0.08	SSC and excises not included
Mexico	1.01	0.89	0.81	0.75	0.84	0.71	0.70	0.70	0.69	-0.06	SSC not included
Netherlands	1.36	1.14	1.12	0.99	1.11	1.02	0.97	0.94	0.95	-0.04	
New Zealand	0.76	0.71	0.75	0.76	0.88	0.81	0.89	0.92	0.85	0.09	Excises not included
Norway	n.a.	0.58	0.53	0.54	0.50	0.56	0.55	0.43	0.41	-0.13	Excises not included
Poland	1.94	1.75	1.42	1.59	1.72	1.91	1.69	1.55	1.60	0.01	SSC and excises not included
Portugal	1.34	1.22	1.18	1.27	1.57	1.55	1.37	0.94	0.99	-0.28	SSC not included
Slovak Republic	2.20	2.49	2.41	n.a.	n.a.	3.06	3.04	1.36	1.43	n.a.	SSC not included
Slovenia	0.95	0.97	0.84	0.81	0.90	0.96	0.93	0.91	0.89	0.08	Excises not included
Spain	0.74	0.68	0.64	0.82	0.97	0.88	0.86	0.66	0.67	-0.15	SSC not included, costs include customs (2010-11)
Sweden	n.a.	n.a.	n.a.	0.39	0.40	0.41	0.40	0.39	0.39	0.00	Costs exclude debt collection
Switzerland	n.a.	n.a.	n.a.	0.45	0.46	0.37	0.38	0.30	0.29	-0.16	Ratio is not comparable. For VAT administration only.
Turkey	0.87	0.84	0.83	0.85	0.93	0.78	0.76	0.78	0.64	-0.21	SSC not included
United Kingdom	1.10	1.09	1.11	0.90	0.91	0.98	0.83	0.74	0.73	-0.17	
United States /3	0.52	0.48	0.45	0.49	0.61	0.66	0.62	0.56	0.47	-0.02	
Non-OECD countries											
Argentina	0.89	1.01	1.08	0.93	1.14	1.32	1.25	0.97	0.95	0.02	
Brazil	– Data not collected for these years –					1.02	0.91	0.88	0.80	n.a.	Costs include Customs
Bulgaria	3.19	1.69	1.13	1.18	1.20	1.41	1.34	1.31	1.25	0.08	Excises not included
China	n.a.	n.a.	n.a.	n.a.	n.a.	n.a.	n.a.	n.a.	n.a.	n.a.	
Colombia	Data not collected for these years					0.93	0.68	0.49	0.56	n.a.	SSC not included
Costa Rica	----- Data not collected for these years -----							1.34	1.19	n.a.	
Croatia	----- Data not collected for these years -----							0.80	0.80	n.a.	
Cyprus	n.a.	n.a.	n.a.	0.78	0.94	1.25	1.23	1.14	1.16	0.38	SSC and excises not included; cost data pre-2010 incomplete
Hong Kong, China	n.a.	n.a.	n.a.	n.a.	n.a.	0.85	0.75	0.65	0.66	n.a.	Excises not included
India	n.a.	n.a.	n.a.	0.76	0.75	0.61	0.55	0.59	0.57	-0.19	Data for direct taxes only
Indonesia	n.a.	n.a.	n.a.	0.64	0.58	0.48	0.55	0.60	0.56	-0.08	Excises not included
Latvia	1.24	1.20	1.13	1.13	1.14	0.80	0.79	1.03	1.06	-0.07	
Lithuania	1.40	1.23	1.14	1.06	1.18	1.06	0.98	0.90	0.81	-0.24	SSC not included
Malaysia	1.20	1.14	1.29	1.04	1.41	0.78	0.70	0.82	1.00	-0.04	Data for direct taxes only
Malta	n.a.	n.a.	n.a.	n.a.	n.a.	1.12	1.00	0.95	0.95	n.a.	Costs include customs administration
Morocco	----- Data not collected for these years -----							n.a.	n.a.	n.a.	
Romania	n.a.	n.a.	n.a.	0.81	0.72	0.50	0.87	1.24	1.21	0.40	Costs include customs from 2012
Russia	n.a.	n.a.	n.a.	1.16	1.39	1.10	0.90	0.79	0.81	-0.35	
Saudi Arabia	n.a.	n.a.	n.a.	1.06	1.26	1.38	1.57	1.56	1.62	0.56	Very limited range of taxes in place
Singapore	1.02	0.93	0.83	0.77	0.81	0.89	0.87	0.78	0.79	0.02	SSC and excises not included
South Africa	1.19	1.21	1.02	0.97	1.03	1.15	1.08	1.09	1.05	0.08	Costs include Customs, net revenue collection includes SSC
Thailand	----- Data not collected for these years -----							0.73	0.71	n.a.	

For notes indicated by "/ (number)", see Notes to Tables section at the end of the chapter, p. 196.

Source: Tax Administration 2015 survey responses.

Table 5.5. **Tax administration expenditure/gross domestic product (GDP) /1**

Country	Administrative costs for tax administration/gross domestic product (at market prices) % /2									Variation	Significant factors affecting comparability between countries' ratios
	2005	2006	2007	2008	2009	2010	2011	2012	2013	2013-08	
OECD countries											
Australia	0.240	0.231	0.213	0.217	0.211	0.206	0.193	0.198	0.191	-0.026	
Austria	0.144	0.143	0.141	0.187	0.189	0.156	0.150	0.156	0.157	-0.030	
Belgium	0.374	0.402	0.332	0.335	0.344	0.322	0.336	0.314	0.304	-0.032	
Canada	0.224	0.223	0.210	0.205	0.235	0.225	0.222	0.222	0.209	0.004	
Chile	0.109	0.100	0.105	0.116	0.125	0.120	0.117	0.117	0.110	-0.006	Costs exclude debt collection
Czech Republic	0.203	0.202	0.188	0.179	0.195	0.179	0.189	0.196	0.197	0.019	
Denmark	0.358	0.296	0.286	0.288	0.299	n.a.	n.a.	0.248	0.226	-0.062	
Estonia	0.275	0.236	0.235	0.120	0.119	0.113	0.105	0.126	0.139	0.018	Excludes IT costs
Finland	0.201	0.199	0.192	0.200	0.215	0.204	0.198	0.198	0.197	-0.003	
France	0.256	0.244	0.232	0.224	0.230	0.224	0.219	0.198	0.191	-0.033	
Germany	0.292	0.287	0.272	0.270	0.284	0.283	0.273	0.269	0.275	0.005	
Greece	n.a.	n.a.	n.a.	n.a.	n.a.	n.a.	n.a.	n.a.	n.a.	n.a.	
Hungary	0.299	0.335	0.397	0.392	0.398	0.421	0.379	0.410	0.423	0.030	
Iceland	n.a.	n.a.	n.a.	0.074	0.077	0.163	0.157	0.152	0.148	0.075	Costs exclude debt collection
Ireland	0.237	0.237	0.236	0.269	0.284	0.254	0.241	0.232	0.240	-0.029	Costs include customs
Israel	n.a.	n.a.	n.a.	0.172	0.168	0.143	0.137	0.170	0.180	0.007	
Italy /3	0.307	0.296	0.284	0.185	0.198	0.147	0.139	0.152	0.188	0.002	Some major costs not included
Japan	0.139	0.138	0.137	0.141	0.149	0.143	0.142	0.152	0.148	0.007	
Korea	0.106	0.106	0.104	0.112	0.113	0.106	0.103	0.098	0.099	-0.014	
Luxembourg	0.238	0.224	0.216	0.227	0.256	0.229	0.228	0.231	0.233	0.006	
Mexico	0.083	0.077	0.073	0.073	0.076	0.069	0.068	0.068	0.070	-0.002	
Netherlands	0.395	0.385	0.367	0.326	0.339	0.328	0.309	0.307	0.322	-0.004	
New Zealand	0.198	0.198	0.198	0.210	0.226	0.187	0.201	0.214	0.202	-0.008	
Norway	0.187	0.177	0.169	0.157	0.177	0.170	0.162	0.135	0.132	-0.025	
Poland	0.306	0.289	0.277	0.236	0.228	0.273	0.247	0.217	0.213	-0.023	
Portugal	0.250	0.241	0.238	0.240	0.260	0.258	0.247	0.197	0.226	-0.014	
Slovak Republic	0.213	0.193	0.172	n.a.	n.a.	0.176	0.181	0.162	0.182	n.a.	
Slovenia	0.313	0.329	0.266	0.263	0.285	0.296	0.288	0.283	0.269	0.005	
Spain	0.131	0.127	0.126	0.130	0.134	0.135	0.133	0.108	0.110	-0.020	Costs include customs(2010-11)
Sweden	0.183	0.184	0.188	0.182	0.184	0.175	0.174	0.167	0.164	-0.018	Costs exclude debt collection
Switzerland	0.030	0.029	0.028	0.028	0.029	0.023	0.023	0.024	0.024	-0.004	VAT administration only
Turkey	0.161	0.152	0.151	0.149	0.169	0.149	0.149	0.154	0.134	-0.016	
United Kingdom	0.329	0.334	0.334	0.279	0.287	0.265	0.234	0.223	0.213	-0.066	
United States	0.079	0.077	0.074	0.077	0.081	0.083	0.080	0.074	0.069	-0.008	
Non-OECD countries											
Argentina	0.162	0.180	0.204	0.205	0.248	0.260	0.257	0.262	0.269	0.064	
Brazil	n.a.	n.a.	n.a.	n.a.	n.a.	0.206	0.196	0.188	0.175	n.a.	Costs include customs
Bulgaria	0.338	0.244	0.215	0.223	0.237	0.238	0.227	0.223	0.218	-0.005	
China	n.a.	n.a.	n.a.	n.a.	n.a.	n.a.	n.a.	0.130	0.121	n.a.	
Colombia	n.a.	n.a.	n.a.	n.a.	n.a.	0.072	0.060	0.069	0.080	n.a.	
Costa Rica	--------- Data not collected for these years ---------							0.114	0.105	n.a.	
Croatia	--------- Data not collected for these years ---------							0.263	0.258	n.a.	
Cyprus	n.a.	n.a.	n.a.	0.181	0.190	0.247	0.246	0.223	0.228	0.048	
Hong Kong, China	n.a.	n.a.	n.a.	n.a.	n.a.	0.059	0.056	0.056	0.057	n.a.	
India	n.a.	n.a.	n.a.	0.042	0.043	0.034	0.029	0.029	0.028	-0.014	Direct taxes only
Indonesia	n.a.	n.a.	n.a.	0.064	0.053	0.041	0.050	0.061	0.057	-0.007	
Latvia	0.345	0.342	0.328	0.338	0.339	0.227	0.224	0.303	0.312	-0.026	
Lithuania	0.272	0.248	0.228	0.219	0.211	0.171	0.155	0.144	0.135	-0.084	
Malaysia	0.118	0.117	0.135	0.111	0.153	0.078	0.081	0.102	0.122	0.011	Costs exclude indirect taxes
Malta	0.472	0.447	0.376	n.a.	n.a.	0.379	0.339	0.314	0.322	n.a.	Costs include customs adminisration
Morocco	--------- Data not collected for these years ---------							n.a.	n.a.	n.a.	
Romania	0.188	0.212	0.251	0.224	0.193	0.123	0.223	0.355	0.333	0.110	Costs include customs
Russia	n.a.	n.a.	n.a.	0.224	0.226	0.182	0.156	0.139	0.138	-0.086	
Saudi Arabia	0.009	0.010	0.010	0.008	0.011	0.011	0.013	0.013	0.015	0.006	Limited range of taxes in place
Singapore	0.086	0.078	0.070	0.082	0.086	0.083	0.088	0.083	0.088	0.006	
South Africa	0.274	0.291	0.256	0.249	0.270	0.263	0.253	0.262	0.257	0.008	Costs include customs
Thailand	--------- Data not collected for these years ---------							0.087	0.087	n.a.	

For notes indicated by "/ (number)", see Notes to Tables section at the end of the chapter, p. 196.

Sources: Survey responses, OECD Statistical Database, Eurostat and World Bank Statistics.

- A consistent downwards trend in relative administrative costs can be observed for a small number of countries (e.g. Australia, Denmark, France, India, Lithuania, Mexico, Netherlands, Norway, Poland, Russia, Spain, Sweden and United Kingdom).
- Within-country comparisons of this ratio over time may be suitable for drawing assessments of relative efficiency over time, although the indicator is susceptible to periodic revisions of GDP made by statistical bodies.
- As for the cost of collection ratio already discussed, cross-country comparisons of this ratio in the context of assessments of relative efficiency need to be undertaken with considerable care to avoid ill-founded conclusions.

International comparisons of administrative expenditure and staffing

Cost of collection ratios

Given the many similarities in the taxes administered by federal revenue bodies from country to country, there has been a natural tendency by observers to make cross-country comparisons of "cost of collection" ratios and draw conclusions on revenue body efficiency and effectiveness. However, experience shows that such comparisons are difficult to carry out in a consistent fashion given a range of variables to be taken into account – see Box 5.2. The most significant factors to be taken account of that are not related to efficiency and effectiveness are: *(1)* variations in the size of the legislated tax burden; and *(2)* the range and nature of taxes administered, in particular whether the revenue body is responsible for the collection of social security contributions.

Many of the factors referred to can be seen from the data in Table 5.3:

- For many surveyed countries (particularly a number in Europe) social security contributions, which in many countries constitute a significant revenue stream, are collected by a separate agency and therefore their costs and the revenue collected are excluded from the calculation used to compute the ratio – see information below which illustrates this particular aspect:

	Countries (by level of tax/ GDP in 2012)*		
Cost of collection ratio in 2013	20-30%	30-40%	Over 40%
Less than 0.60		Malta	Denmark, Sweden
0.61-0.80		Croatia, Spain*, United Kingdom	Austria*, Finland
0.81-1.00	Lithuania*	Estonia, Ireland, Luxembourg*, Netherlands, Portugal*, Slovenia	
1.20	Latvia	Cyprus*, France*, Hungary	Belgium*, Italy*
1.20-1.40	Romania	Czech Republic*, Germany*, Bulgaria	
Over 1.41		Poland*, Slovak Republic*	

* For these countries, SSC are collected by separate agencies, not the revenue body.

- The inability of some revenue bodies (i.e. Ireland, Mexico (prior to 2005), South Africa and Spain) to exclude the costs of non-tax functions (e.g. customs) from the cost base used to calculate the ratio.
- There are substantial differences in the statutory tax burden (and hence the potential tax revenue base) across surveyed countries (ranging from below 20% to almost 50% of GDP) that influences what is collected in practice, and hence the computed ratio.

- Unusual institutional arrangements exist in some countries (e.g. Italy for tax fraud functions, Chile and Sweden for tax debt collection functions) that see some mainstream tax administration-related functions performed by a body separate from the main revenue body; as a result, the cost data used to compute the ratio for these bodies understates the real costs of tax administration, and hence the computed ratio.

For these sorts of reasons, international comparisons of both ratios need to be made with care and take account of any of the abnormal factors highlighted, as well as other differences in approaches to tax administration highlighted in this series.

Box 5.2. International comparisons of cost of collection ratios

Analytical work undertaken in conducting comparisons of cost of collection ratios has revealed that there are many factors to explain the marked variations in the ratio observed from country to country. The more significant factors are described below:

- **Differences in tax rates and structure***:* Rates of tax and the actual structure of taxes all will have a bearing on aggregate revenue and, to a lesser extent, cost considerations. For example, comparisons of the ratio involving high-taxing countries (e.g. those where tax burdens regularly exceed 40% of GDP) and low-taxing countries (e.g. those where tax burdens are less than 20%) are hardly realistic given their widely varying tax burdens.
- **Differences in the range and nature of taxes administered by federal revenue authorities***:* There are a number of differences that can arise here. In some countries, more than one major tax authority may operate at the national level (e.g. as in India, Cyprus and Malta), or taxes at the federal level are predominantly of a direct tax nature, while indirect taxes are administered largely by separate regional/state authorities (e.g. the United States). In other countries, one national authority will collect taxes for all levels of government, i.e. federal, regional and local governments (a number of EU countries).
- **Collection of social insurance contributions, etc.:** As described earlier in this series, there are significant variations from country to country in the collection of social security contributions. A few countries (e.g. Australia, New Zealand) do not have separate regimes of mandatory social contributions, while others make separate provision for them and have them collected by the main tax revenue collection agency. Some countries have them collected by a separate government agency. Given that social contributions are a major source of tax revenue for many countries, the inclusion/exclusion of social contributions in the revenue base for "cost of collection" calculation purposes can have a significant bearing on the computed ratio.
- **Differences in the range of functions undertaken***:* The range of functions undertaken by revenue bodies can vary from country to country. For example, in some countries the revenue body is also responsible for carrying out activities not directly related to tax administration (e.g. administration of customs laws, the administration of certain welfare benefits), while in others some tax-related functions are not carried out by the revenue body (e.g. enforced debt collection). Ideally, these sorts of differences should be allowed for in any cross-country comparisons undertaken of relative aggregate costs and related ratios.

Box 5.2. **International comparisons of cost of collection ratios** *(continued)*

- **Lack of a common measurement methodology:** There is no universally accepted methodology for the measurement of administrative costs. Revenue bodies that publish a cost of collection ratio generally do not reveal precise details of the measurement approach adopted for their calculations. In relation to administrative costs, the treatment of employee pension costs, accommodation costs, interest paid on overpaid taxes, the use of cash and non-cash methods (e.g. by means of a float) to recompense financial institutions for collecting tax payments, and capital equipment purchases are some of the potentially significant areas where the measurement approaches adopted may vary. The ratio is also influenced by the selection of the revenue base i.e. "gross" or "net" (i.e. after refunds) revenue collections figure for its computation. For example, the US Internal Revenue Service (IRS), which has one of the lowest reported costs of collection ratios for any national revenue body, and the Irish Office of the Revenue Commissioners, both use "gross" revenue as the basis of their reported computation, while most other authorities use a "net" figure. As a result, for both countries the reported ratio is around 10-12 % lower than if it were computed on a "net" revenue basis. For this series, calculations are made on the basis of "net revenue" collections.

Source: OECD CTPA Secretariat.

Relative staffing levels of revenue bodies

A summary of the staff usage (expressed as FTEs) by national revenue bodies is set out in Table 5.6. To the extent possible and to allow cross-country comparisons, efforts have been made to exclude staffing related non-tax related roles. In order to reflect a degree of relativity, aggregate staff levels have been compared with overall official country population and labour force data to compute two ratios: *(1)* the number of citizens per one full-time staff member: and *(2)* the number of labour force participants per full-time staff member. Figure 5.2 displays the computed ratio for all OECD countries while Figure 5.3 displays a comparison with the ratio "tax administrative expenditure/GDP" discussed earlier in the chapter.

Comparisons of this nature are naturally subject to some of the qualifications referred to concerning "cost of collection" ratios – in addition to efficiency considerations, exogenous factors such as the range of taxes administered (e.g. social contributions, motor vehicle and property taxes) and the performance of non-tax related roles (where these cannot be isolated) all impact on the magnitude of the reported ratio. For some countries, demographic features (e.g. country age profile and rate of unemployment) are also likely to be relevant. Revenue bodies in a number of countries (e.g. United Kingdom) also have major restructuring programmes underway, some of which project significant staffing reductions over the coming years. To assist readers, known abnormal factors influencing the reported ratios are identified.

Concerning OECD countries, it will be evident that the greatest level of consistency occurs in relation to the ratio based on country labour forces (i.e. the number of labour force participants/one revenue body staff member [FTE]):

- Seven revenue bodies (i.e. Belgium, Czech Republic, Germany, Hungary, Luxembourg, Poland, Slovak Republic) have a ratio less than 400; drawing on data presented elsewhere in this series, tax administration in these countries tends to be is characterised by one or more of the following:

- Relatively large office networks (see Table 2.4);
- Outdated institutional/organisational arrangements (Table 1.1);
- Relatively low investments in IT (see Table 5.3), although in the case of the Czech Republic this has been bolstered in recent years, while for Luxembourg the full costs are unable to be quantified as they are shared with other parts of MOF via a separate IT department); and/or
- Low overall take up (i.e. PIT, CIT, and VAT in aggregate) of e-filing (Tables 7.3 to 7.5), with the exception of Belgium.

- Ten revenue bodies have a ratio between 401-600 labour force members/FTE.
- Eight revenue bodies have a ratio in the range 601-800.
- Nine revenue bodies have a ratio over 800 (with six "outliers" (i.e. Chile, Japan, Korea, Mexico, Switzerland and the United States) where the ratio exceeds 1 000):
  - For ***Chile*** (1 998:1), the staffing data provided do not include the full range of normal tax administration functions (e.g. debt collection) and as a result its ratio is not directly comparable with others.
  - In the case of ***Japan,*** where the ratio is 1 170:1, staffing levels of the revenue body (i.e. the NTA) have remained in the region of 50 000 to 56 000 for the last 50 years, reflecting decisions both to keep staff resources roughly constant and, importantly, to minimise workloads. Compared to other countries, administrative workloads have been kept relatively low with the assistance of, among other things; special tax system design features (e.g. high thresholds for various reporting and payment obligations, less frequent tax payment obligations and extensive use of tax withholding). (Further information on some of these features can be found in Chapter 9.) Also relevant is the collection of social security contributions by a separate agency.
  - ***Korea*** (a ratio of 1 373:1) also makes extensive use of tax system design features that minimise workloads, in comparison with arrangements seen in other countries. For example, there is substantial use of final withholding systems for the bulk of employee taxpayers (employers withhold monthly, calculate employees' tax liability and clear the balance off at the end of year), withholding at source arrangements for dividend and interest income and certain payments for independent services, and biannual reporting and payment arrangements for VAT liabilities. Social contributions are also collected by a separate agency.
  - With annual tax collections equivalent to around 20% of GDP, ***Mexico's*** tax system (ratio of 2 038:1) is of a considerably smaller scale than most other OECD countries. Its tax system arrangements are characterised by substantial use of final withholding system arrangements for employee taxpayers (with quite limited registration of personal taxpayers [equivalent to around to 20 % of the official labour force]), and a relatively small population of registered business taxpayers.
  - The very high ratio for ***Switzerland*** (i.e. 5 049:1) results from the fact that the Federal Tax Administration is responsible only for VAT administration, with both personal and corporate income taxes administered at the sub-national level by separate agencies in each canton, the costs of which are not accounted for in this series. For this reason, the ratio largely reflects the resources required for VAT administration, thus making it incomparable with all other national revenue bodies.

Table 5.6. **Revenue body staff usage for fiscal year 2013 and related ratios /1**

	Staff usage aggregates (FTEs) /2			Staff usage ratios		
Country	All revenue body functions	Tax and related support functions	% FTEs for tax and support functions	Citizens/ FTEs on tax and support functions	Labour force/ FTEs on tax and support functions	Factors affecting comparability of countries' computed ratios (i.e. ratios in columns 5 and 6)
OECD countries						
Australia	20 248	17 477	86.3	1 323	699	
Austria	7 521	7 484	99.5	1 132	587	
Belgium	22 232	19 485	87.6	573	254	
Canada	39 521	38 172	96.6	921	501	
Chile	4 195	4 195	100.0	4 186	1 998	FTEs exclude debt collection
Czech Republic	15 031	14 272	95.0	736	372	
Denmark	6 802	5 861	86.2	955	493	
Estonia	1 549	983	63.5	1 343	692	
Finland	5 072	5 072	100.0	1 071	528	
France	114 417	66 964	58.5	979	427	
Germany	110 494	110 494	100.0	743	387	
Greece	11 500	8 000	69.6	1 383	621	
Hungary	22 482	17 870	79.5	555	246	
Iceland	240	240	100.0	1 333	750	FTEs exclude debt collection
Ireland	5 745	5 745	100.0	799	376	FTEs include customs
Israel	6 035	5 104	84.6	1 579	721	
Italy /2	39 814	31 706	79.6	1 914	805	
Japan	56 194	56 194	100.0	2 265	1 170	
Korea	18 841	18 841	100.0	2 665	1 373	
Luxembourg /2	984	984	100.0	549	254	
Mexico	36 410	25 457	69.9	4 651	2 038	
Netherlands	28 313	20 873	73.7	804	429	
New Zealand	5 282	3 433	65.0	1 302	705	
Norway	6 962	6 733	96.7	754	401	
Poland	48 821	47 593	97.5	809	365	
Portugal	11 341	10 066	88.8	1 065	535	
Slovak Republic	9 296	6 813	73.3	796	399	
Slovenia	2 365	2 365	100.0	871	427	
Spain	26 231	22 402	85.4	2 081	1 035	
Sweden	9 705	7 877	81.2	1 214	650	FTEs exclude debt collection
Switzerland	965	925	95.9	8 692	5 049	Data for VAT administration only
Turkey	51 369	51 046	99.4	1 490	548	
United Kingdom	63 843	53 205	83.3	1 176	605	
United States	86 977	86 977	100.0	3 635	1 802	No major indirect tax
Non-OECD countries						
Argentina	22 157	16 901	76.3	2 452	1 130	
Brazil	24 625	24 625	100.0	8 136	4 163	FTEs include customs
Bulgaria	7 680	7 672	99.9	949	439	
China	756 000	n.a.	n.a.	n.a.	n.a.	
Colombia	9 095	5 244	57.7	9 215	4 491	
Costa Rica	961	961	100.0	5 070	2 300	
Croatia	4 212	4 187	99.4	1 017	401	
Cyprus	782	774	99.0	1 124	556	
Hong Kong, China	2 826	2 588	91.6	2 790	1 491	
India	41 357	41 357	100.0	30 276	11 636	Data for direct taxes only
Indonesia	32 273	32 273	100.0	7 742	3 724	
Latvia	4 312	3 091	71.7	654	327	
Lithuania	3 476	3 476	100.0	854	423	
Malaysia	11 049	9 005	81.5	3 299	1 488	Data for direct taxes only
Malta	750	736	98.1	571	258	FTEs include customs
Morocco	4 735	4 735	100.0	6 971	2 541	
Romania	24 481	22 043	90.0	908	453	
Russia	128 977	128 977	100.0	1 113	586	
Saudi Arabia	1 589	1 589	100.0	18 143	7 149	Very limited range of taxes
Singapore /2	1 898	1 898	100.0	2 845	1 128	
South Africa	14 701	11 864	80.7	4 466	1 665	
Thailand	23 129	23 129	100.0	2 897	1 706	

For notes indicated by "/ (number)", see Notes to Tables section at the end of the chapter, p. 196.

Sources: Survey responses, OECD Statistical Database, Eurostat, World Bank, International Labour Organization.

- In the case of the ***United States*** (where the ratio is 1 802:1), a meaningful comparison of relative staffing levels with other surveyed countries is complicated by the absence of a national VAT (or a similar tax), as is the case in all other OECD countries. A further consideration is that, unlike most other surveyed countries, there are separate income taxes and retail sales taxes levied at the state level in the United States that are administered separately by state revenue agencies, not by the IRS. (A more valid comparison would require account being taken of the staff required by these agencies, which is beyond the scope of this series.) For these reasons, the computed ratio for the IRS – and this observation applies also to its computed "cost of collection" ratio – is not really comparable with that of revenue bodies in any other OECD country.

For revenue bodies in non-OECD surveyed countries, the computed ratio reflects an even greater divergent pattern, ranging from 258:1 to over 11 000:1. The full range of factors that might explain this disparity has not been identified, although in the case of the EU member countries included the following aspects are likely to be characterised by one or more of the following factors: *(1)* relatively large office networks (see Table 2.4); *(2)* outdated institutional/organisational arrangements (Table 1.1); *(3)* relatively low investments in IT (see Table 5.3); and/or *(4)* low overall take up of e-filing (Tables 7.3 to 7.5).

Figure 5.2. **Labour force participants/FTE on tax and support functions (OECD countries)**

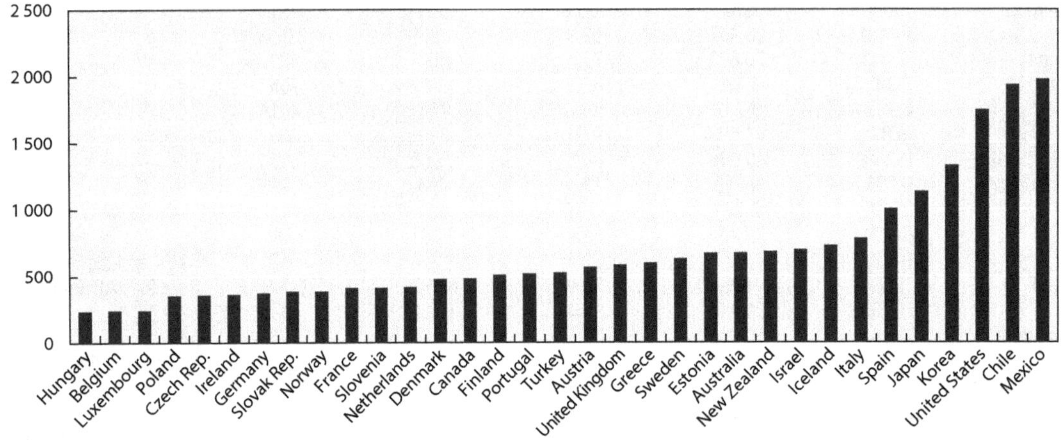

Figure 5.3. **Labour force participants/FTE on tax and support vis-à-vis tax expenditure/GDP (OECD countries)**

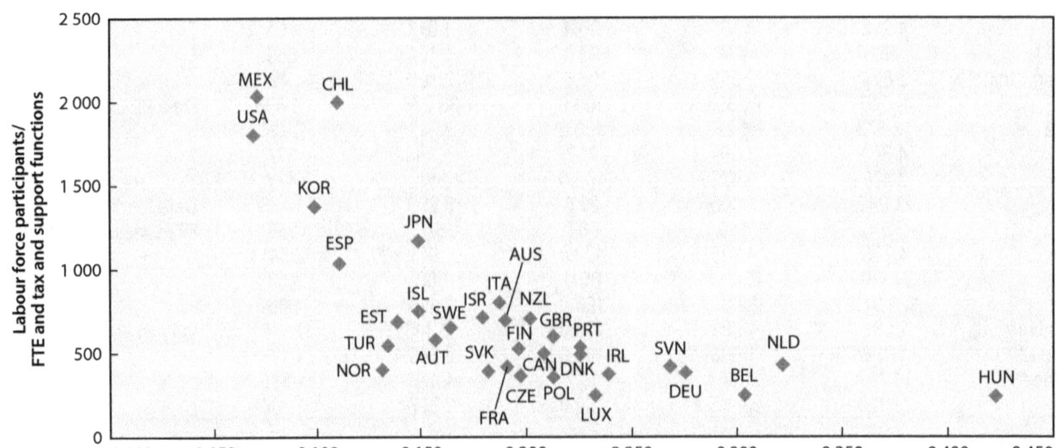

Allocation of staff resources by functional groupings

Given the similarity in the taxes administered across surveyed countries, an obvious area of comparison concerns how revenue bodies allocate their total staff resources across the range of tax administration and support functions that must be undertaken to achieve organisational objectives. For this purpose, revenue bodies were requested to indicate the allocation of aggregate staff resources (in FTE terms) for tax administration purposes across six "functional groupings" that are described in Box 5.3. Table 5.6 provides an indication of the data gathered for just over 90% of surveyed revenue bodies on resource allocation (i.e. % of FTE by functional groups) in 2013. Given definitional issues, and the possibility of some inconsistencies in data compilation, the information presented needs to be interpreted with care.

Box 5.3. **Categorisation of revenue body operations**

For survey purposes, the following definitions were used:

A. ***Taxpayer account management***: Staff used (in FTEs) for all functions associated with maintaining taxpayers' records (e.g. registration, data processing, taxpayer accounting, filing, withholding tax administration, storage etc.)

B. ***Audit, investigation and other verification-related/compliance improvement functions:*** Staff used (in FTEs) for all functions associated with verifying (either through field visits, office interviews or in writing) the information contained in taxpayers' returns for all taxes administered, and specific "upfront" compliance improvement programmes (e.g. inspections and other record reviews)

C. ***Tax debt collection and related functions:*** Staff used (in FTEs) for all functions associated recovering unpaid taxes and outstanding tax returns etc.

D. ***Other tax operations:*** Staff used (in FTEs) for all other tax functions not covered by categories A, B, and C (e.g. disputes and complaints, taxpayer services (e.g. call centres).

E. ***Support: human resources:*** Staff used (in FTEs) for support functions associated with personnel, recruitment, and staff training and development-related services and work.

F. ***Support: other functions:*** Staff used (in FTEs) for all other support functions such as executive, corporate planning, public relations and communications, information technology services, accommodation, supply, security, internal assurance, public relations and finance functions.

Drawing on the information in Table 5.6, the key observations are as follows:

- Within most functional groupings there are some extreme "outlier" ratios reported that are perhaps best ignored for the purpose of detailed analysis as they are likely to result from limitations in available data, unusual organisational setups, and/or misinterpretation of the series requirements. Figure 5.4 displays the "average" allocations observed across functional groupings for OECD countries.
- ***Client account management functions:*** Significantly for this grouping, over one-third of revenue bodies (20) reported staff usage exceeding 30% of aggregate staff, including 11 where the ratio exceeded 40%. Of this latter group, seven reported IT expenditure less than 10% of total expenditure (or were unable to quantify the amount of IT expenditure incurred).

Figure 5.4. **Average FTE usage for key functional groupings (OECD countries)**

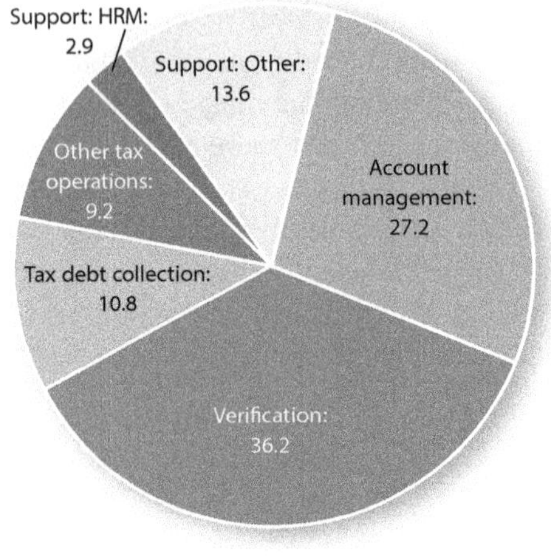

- ***Audit, investigation and other verification activities:*** Survey responses for this category varied significantly ranging from around 9% to over 65%. Overall, around 50% of surveyed revenue bodies reported usage in excess of 30%, although the concentration was much larger among OECD countries (around two-thirds) compared to non-OECD revenue bodies (around a third).

  Six revenue bodies reported allocations to audit etc., exceeding 50% (i.e. Austria, Estonia, Iceland, Japan, Slovenia, and Singapore).

- ***Enforced debt collection and related functions:*** Usage reported for this functional grouping ranged from a low 0% (in Chile and Sweden where this work is primarily the responsibility of a separate body) to almost 34% (Romania); significantly, around half of revenue bodies reported total usage exceeding 10% of aggregate staff, and in 14 countries the proportion exceeded 15% indicating the relative importance of this function in these offices.

  Based on data in Tables 5.6 and 6.13, debt collection resources appear relatively low having regard to the reported incidence of debt in some revenue bodies:

Measure	Czech Republic	Slovak Republic	Bulgaria	Croatia	Latvia	Malta
% staff on debt collection 2013	5.8	4.2	9.8	8.6	8.1	4.9
Tax debt /net revenue (2013)	18.1	33.0	15.3	35.3 (incl. disputed debt)	29.5 (incl. disputed debt)	22.1

- ***Corporate overhead functions (including IT support and human resources):*** Usage reported for this grouping also varied enormously, suggesting some inconsistency in how these functions are viewed and quantified. Against an average across OECD countries of around 16.5%, seven revenue bodies (i.e. Chile, Colombia, Indonesia, Israel, Poland, Spain, and Sweden) reported an unusually high proportion (i.e. over 25%) of total staffing, the reasons for which have not been fully identified, although in the case of Spain it has been established that all IT applications and related software and tools (including the administration's Internet-based electronic office) are developed in-house, while support is also provided for customs administration.

Table 5.7. **Staff usage (2013) by major tax functional groupings (% of total usage)**

Country	Total FTEs for all tax functions and support	Total staff usage on major tax functions as a share of total usage/1					
		Account management	Verification (incl. audit)	Tax debt collection	Other tax operations	Support: Human resources	Support: Other functions
OECD countries							
Australia	17 477	17.5	35.0	9.8	16.5	6.0	15.2
Austria	7 484	11.4	63.7	10.4	8.7	0.0	5.9
Belgium	19 485	n.a.	n.a.	n.a.	n.a.	n.a.	n.a.
Canada	38 172	25.3	28.9	20.0	7.7	3.5	14.6
Chile /2	4 195	19.9	40.4	0.0	1.4	3.5	34.8
Czech Republic	14 272	60.2	19.0	5.8	15.1	0.0	0.0
Denmark	5 861	26.7	40.7	8.2	2.3	2.3	19.8
Estonia	983	1.0	67.0	10.1	10.1	0.6	11.2
Finland	5 072	38.3	38.9	9.5	2.5	2.0	8.9
France	66 964	43.3	15.3	10.1	12.3	18.9	0.0
Germany	110 494	39.5	39.6	6.8	9.5	3.6	0.9
Greece	8 000	56.3	25.0	10.0	3.8	2.5	2.5
Hungary	17 870	24.0	36.3	15.3	1.1	1.6	21.8
Iceland /2	240	6.7	65.4	0.0	10.0	0.8	17.1
Ireland /2	5 745	26.9	30.7	14.3	8.6	0.9	18.6
Israel	5 104	12.9	40.3	16.6	3.6	4.2	22.4
Italy /2	31 706	35.8	38.4	2.8	8.9	4.6	6.0
Japan /2	56 194	0.0	63.3	21.2	2.3	0.7	12.4
Korea /2	18 841	58.0	24.0	1.0	9.3	0.6	7.1
Luxembourg /2	984	22.2	42.1	17.1	12.3	2.3	4.0
Mexico	25 457	15.9	35.2	23.4	7.9	5.1	12.5
Netherlands	20 873	26.4	41.8	7.4	2.0	6.6	15.7
New Zealand	3 433	37.4	22.4	9.4	6.4	2.0	22.5
Norway	6 733	6.2	41.6	12.4	10.9	2.0	27.0
Poland	47 593	18.6	24.8	12.1	17.8	0.8	25.8
Portugal	10 066	53.0	16.8	18.8	2.5	2.1	6.7
Slovak Republic	6 813	40.3	22.9	4.2	8.9	1.8	22.0
Slovenia	2 365	6.2	57.6	18.5	3.5	1.4	12.9
Spain	22 402	32.1 /2	22.6	19.7	0.0	7.8 /3	17.8 /3
Sweden /2	7 877	0.0	32.5	0.0	36.1	0.0	31.5
Switzerland	925	9.2	25.4	7.9	56.4	1.1	0.0
Turkey	51 046	60.1	19.9	8.1	0.3	3.4	8.4
United Kingdom	53 205	33.4	42.7	12.0	3.6	1.8	6.5
United States	86 977	33.2	34.0	14.4	1.6	1.5	15.2
OECD ave. (unw.)		27.2	36.2	10.8	9.2	2.9	13.6
Non-OECD countries							
Argentina	16 901	19.8	36.1	7.2	12.1	2.1	22.7
Brazil /2	24 625	20.2	19.7	20.8	25.3	2.2	11.8
Bulgaria	7 672	25.3	42.0	9.8	9.4	1.3	12.1
China	n.a.	n.a.	n.a.	n.a.	n.a.	n.a.	n.a.
Colombia	5 244	8.9	28.0	17.1	20.0	2.8	23.1
Costa Rica	961	n.a.	n.a.	n.a.	n.a.	n.a.	n.a.
Croatia	4 187	56.0	19.8	8.6	8.5	4.7	2.4
Cyprus	774	23.3	36.7	11.8	12.7	1.0	14.6
Hong Kong, China	2 588	58.8	9.3	17.2	2.0	0.1	12.5
India	41 357	n.a.	n.a.	n.a.	n.a.	n.a.	n.a.
Indonesia	32 273	20.8	14.0	2.0	2.1	9.2	51.9
Latvia	3 091	46.5	25.9	8.1	2.0	1.3	16.1
Lithuania	3 476	38.8	28.7	6.7	14.3	0.9	10.5
Malaysia	9 005	9.1	37.9	23.6	15.1	2.0	12.2
Malta	736	14.3	12.9	4.9	60.9	1.5	6.1
Morocco	4 735	59.3	10.7	12.7	0.0	2.3	15.0
Romania	22 043	17.8	22.5	34.1	11.3	0.9	13.5
Russia	128 977	7.4	47.1	8.7	16.9	2.0	17.9
Saudi Arabia	1 589	16.6	35.9	10.2	12.5	18.4	6.4
Singapore /2	1 898	8.7	52.2	11.1	9.7	1.6	16.8
South Africa	11 864	49.3	16.6	9.3	8.6	2.5	13.7
Thailand	23 129	n.a.	n.a.	n.a.	n.a.	n.a.	n.a.

For notes indicated by "/ (number)", see Notes to Tables section at the end of the chapter, p. 197.

Source: Tax Administration 2015 survey responses.

There are many management-related factors (beyond misclassification and data errors) that may explain some of the observed variations in functional staffing allocations: *(1)* the use of administrative assessment versus self-assessment approaches; *(2)* the degree of automation of routine tax administration; *(3)* the use centralised versus decentralised functions; *(4)* the degree of reliance placed on outsourcing (e.g. for IT support); *(5)* poor management practices that see excessive resources devoted to overhead functions; *(6)* tax system design features that impact routine workloads (e.g. payment and filing frequency, VAT registration thresholds); and *(7)* the nature and size of the revenue body's office network. These are all considerations that are covered by this series. The widely-ranging ratios reported for the various functional groupings point to the need for careful analysis in conducting comparisons in this area.

Third party service delivery of revenue body functions/operations

"Third party service delivery", described as "outsourcing" in prior editions of this series, refers to the use of other parties to deliver services required for the conduct of tax administration operations. It includes the engagement of (or "outsourcing" to) private sector bodies, such as financial institutions to collect tax payments or private firms to provide information technology support, as well as the delivery of revenue body function by other parts of government using a "shared services" delivery approach, or by way of a separate arrangement between a revenue body and some other government body. Generally speaking, the choice to use a third party service delivery approach is driven by an objective to increase cost efficiency/cut costs through eliminating duplication of efforts

Table 5.8. **Third party service delivery of tax administration functions**

	Revenue bodies that use these bodies for some/all of the functions specified	
Function/task	Private sector enterprises	Another government body
Receipt/collection of tax payments (e.g. via a bank or post office)	Argentina, Austria, Brazil, Bulgaria, Canada, Chile, Colombia, Costa Rica, Croatia, Cyprus, Finland, Greece, India, Ireland, Israel, Italy, Japan, Korea, Latvia, Lithuania, Malaysia, Mexico, New Zealand, Norway, Portugal, Russia, Singapore, Slovenia, Spain, Sweden, Thailand, Turkey, United Kingdom, United States	Argentina, Australia, Croatia, Hong Kong, Iceland, Italy, Latvia, Malta, Morocco, Poland, Slovakia, Turkey
Answering taxpayers inquiries (e.g. via call centre-type operations, shop fronts)	Australia, Brazil, Chile, Colombia, India, Ireland, Malta, Mexico, New Zealand, Slovakia, Spain, United States	China, Costa Rica, Italy, New Zealand, Norway, Poland, Slovakia, Turkey
Data processing (e.g. for capturing of information from tax returns etc.)	Costa Rica, Cyprus, Finland, Israel, Mexico, Norway, Russia, Thailand	Brazil, Croatia, Germany, Italy, Malta, Norway, Poland, Turkey
Collecting tax debts (e.g. using private debt collection bodies)	Australia, Brazil, Ireland, Israel, Netherlands, United Kingdom	Brazil, Costa Rica, Croatia, Iceland, Italy, Korea, Malta, Norway, Poland, Turkey
Information technology services	Australia, Brazil, Bulgaria, Chile, China, Colombia, Croatia, Cyprus, Czech Republic, Denmark, Finland, Iceland, India, Israel, Japan, Latvia, Malaysia, Mexico, New Zealand, Norway, Russia, Singapore, Spain /1, Thailand, United Kingdom	Australia, Austria, Bulgaria, Canada, Costa Rica, Croatia, Cyprus, Estonia, Finland, Germany, Greece, Italy, Luxembourg, Malta, Norway, Poland, Switzerland, Turkey
Personnel and/or staff recruitment functions	Australia, Colombia, Israel, New Zealand, United Kingdom	Belgium, Brazil, Costa Rica, Cyprus, Finland, Greece, Ireland, Italy, Japan, Luxembourg Malta, Norway, Poland, Turkey
Other functions	Australia /1, Canada /1, Cyprus, Latvia, Malta /1, Singapore /1	Australia /1, Canada, Cyprus, Israel /1, Latvia, Saudi Arabia /1

Source: Tax Administration 2015 survey responses.

and/or by achieving economies of scale. For this series, revenue bodies were asked to indicate whether specific tax administration functions/tasks were delivered by third parties. Table 5.8 summarises revenue bodies' responses while some important observations are set out hereunder:

- The more commonly reported tasks that are outsourced to the private sector are the collection of tax payments (e.g. by banks and other financial institutions) and the provision of information technology support.
- Some of the more unusual arrangements reported with third parties were:
  - ***Collecting tax payments:*** In Japan, tax payment services are provided in convenience stores. The US IRS reported use of a "lock box" facility requiring some balance due taxpayers to send their voucher and payment to a designated location (a lockbox bank) provided by a network of financial institutions.
  - ***Taxpayer inquiries:*** Australia reported that a share of its inbound telephony inquiries are answered by outsourced call centres; in New Zealand, limited use is made of outside or other Government call centres in peak periods, while Spain also uses external service providers for basic inquiries. In the United States, the National Telecommuting Institute (NTI) receives and responds to orders for tax material from taxpayers.
  - ***Enforced tax debt collection:*** Australia reported that generally the enforced collection of debts up to AUD 75 000 are able to be outsourced to private debt collection agencies; the United Kingdom also reported some use of debt collection agencies; the Netherlands reported it has a pilot project underway involving a private firm issuing letters for the collection of low value/high volume tax debts.
  - ***IT infrastructure support:*** Shared Services Canada, a federal agency, provides IT infrastructure services for 43 federal agencies including the CRA. Cyprus also reported use of IT services provided by a separate Government IT department.
  - ***Provision of corporate support services:*** Finland reported there is a service known as "Palkeet" that provides "whole of government" administration of financial and human resource services; the United Kingdom uses external contractors for occupational health assessments.
  - ***Other:*** In Canada, Revenue Quebec, a provincial tax administration, is responsible for federal VAT administration in Quebec, not the CRA.

With increasing Government attention on driving public sector bodies to become more efficient, in particular larger service delivery agencies such as revenue bodies, it seems inevitable that the use of third party service delivery approaches will continue to grow in coming years.

The non-tax roles of national revenue bodies

Reference was made in Chapter 1 to the practice of Governments allocating "non-tax related roles" to revenue bodies and the rationale for doing this (see Table 1.6). To demonstrate the significance of this development, Table 5.9 provides data on the estimated proportion of each revenue body's budget expenditure attributable to non-tax functions for 2005 to 2011 (where available).

Table 5.9. **Expenditure on non-tax roles (% of total revenue body expenditure) /1**

Country	Non-tax expenditure (as % of total revenue body expenditure)							Main non-tax role(s) performed by revenue body (where known)
	2007	2008	2009	2010	2011	2012	2013	
OECD countries								
Australia	11	15	12	13	16	15	16	Superannuation/retirement
Austria	n.a.	23	24	18	20	18	17	Customs, welfare, labour market laws
Belgium	28	29	30	33	35	34	37	Customs, property valuation
Canada	15	16	17	16	15	15	14	Welfare/benefits
Czech Republic	6	5	5	5	5	5	5	
Denmark	13	10	10	n.a.	n.a.	18	17	Customs, welfare
Estonia	n.a.	56	56	56	55	42 /2	38 /2	Customs, welfare
France	42	41	40	40	40	46	46	Public accounting functions, land register, property valuation
Greece	n.a.	n.a.	n.a.	n.a.	n.a.	n.a.	n.a.	Customs – not quantified
Hungary	0	14	13	0	26	24	24	Customs
Iceland	n.a.	n.a.	n.a.	n.a.	n.a.	n.a.	n.a.	Benefits – not quantified
Ireland	n.a.	n.a.	n.a.	n.a.	n.a.	n.a.	n.a.	Customs – not quantified
Israel	n.a.	11	11	21	21	11	10	Customs
Italy	n.a.	20	17	18	17	13	13	Property valuation
Korea	n.a.	n.a.	n.a.	n.a.	n.a.	n.a.	n.a.	Benefits – not quantified
Luxembourg	n.a.	n.a.	n.a.	n.a.	n.a.	n.a.	n.a.	Property valuation – not quantified
Mexico	14	15	21	19	20	19	19	Customs
Netherlands	20	28	28	29	29	30	30	Customs, benefits
New Zealand	31	36	35	38	35	33	30	Welfare/benefits
Norway	4	2	2	6	4	19	20	Property valuation, population register
Portugal	10	10	10	10	10	37	36	Customs, property valuation
Slovak Republic	3	n.a.	n.a.	n.a.	3	42	42	Customs
Spain	n.a.	14	15	n.a.	n.a.	14	14	Customs
Sweden	15	9	9	15	17	20	20	Population register
Switzerland	n.a.	6	5	11	10	5	6	
Turkey	n.a.	n.a.	n.a.	n.a.	n.a.	13	14	
United Kingdom	n.a.	n.a.	4	4	4	4	4	
United States	n.a.	n.a.	n.a.	n.a.	n.a.	n.a.	n.a.	Benefits – not quantified
Non-OECD countries								
Argentina	n.a.	51	51	51	49	49	48	Customs
Brazil	n.a.	n.a.	n.a.	n.a.	n.a.	n.a.	n.a.	Customs – not quantified
China	n.a.	n.a.	n.a.	n.a.	n.a.	17	16	
Colombia	n.a.	n.a.	n.a.	45	45	42	42	Customs
Croatia	n.a.	n.a.	n.a.	n.a.	n.a.	n.a.	n.a.	Property valuation – not quantified
Cyprus	n.a.	n.a.	n.a.	n.a.	n.a.	1	1	Property valuation
Hong Kong, China	n.a.	n.a.	n.a.	9	10	9	10	Business registration
India	n.a.	n.a.	n.a.	2	2	2	2	
Indonesia	n.a.	n.a.	n.a.	n.a.	n.a.	n.a.	n.a.	Property valuation – not quantified
Latvia	n.a.	22	17	52	48	47	46	Customs
Malaysia	n.a.	20	10	38	36	40	37	
Romania	n.a.	n.a.	n.a.	20	15	n.a.	n.a.	Customs – not quantified
Russia	n.a.	15	15	13	14	15	15	
Singapore	n.a.	n.a.	n.a.	n.a.	n.a.	n.a.	n.a.	Property valuation – not quantified
South Africa	n.a.	n.a.	n.a.	n.a.	n.a.	n.a.	n.a.	Customs – not quantified

Source: Tax Administration 2015 survey responses.

The key observations are as follows:

- Rates of expenditure on non-tax functions appear relatively constant over the period 2007 to 2013, suggesting little further recent movement in this practice.
- Responsibility for customs administration is the predominant source of non-tax expenditure in many countries (e.g. Argentina, Austria, Colombia, Denmark, Estonia, Hungary, Latvia, Mexico, Netherlands, and Romania) although the amounts/proportions reported vary considerably – from 14 to almost 50% – for reasons that have not been identified.
- In the case of countries such as Canada and New Zealand, responsibility for Government welfare/benefit-related responsibilities appear to be the primary influencing factor, and in the case of New Zealand are a significant element of overall expenditure (at 30%).

Notes

1. The individual country ratings indicated on p. 176 are based on the definitions set out hereunder:

	Ratings			
	✓✓ Above average	✓ Average	x Below average	xx Well below average
Indicator	✓✓ Very favourable	✓ Favourable	x Unfavourable	xx Very unfavourable
Overall e-filing rates (for PIT, CIT, and VAT) for latest year (Tables 7.3-7.5)	Average 75% across major taxes	Average 50-75%	Average 25-50%	Average below 25%
Fully electronic payment rate in latest year (Table 7.6)	70% or more	Between 50-70%	Between 25-50%	Less than 25%
Average labour force/ FTE ratio in latest year (Table 5.6)	Ratio above 700	Ratio between 501-700	Ratio between 400-500	Ratio below 400
Total administrative costs/ GDP ratio over last five years (Table 5.5)	Generally below 0.15%	Generally between 0.15-0.20%	Generally between 0.20-30%	Generally over 0.30%
Administrative costs/ net revenue over last five years (Table 5.4)	Generally below 0.75%	Generally between 0.75-1.00%	Generally between 1.00-1.25	Generally over 1.25%
Size of office network -relative to country's demographics (Table 2.3)	Relatively small	Medium size	Relatively large	Relatively very large

2. The observation concerning Luxembourg is subject to two qualifications. Officials report that not all IT costs have been quantified, with a major part of such costs being shared with other parts of MOF through support by a separate IT department. Concerning the take-up of e-filing services, while overall performance is poor, reasonable progress has been made in recent years with VAT e-filing, achieving take-up of 50% in 2013.

Notes to Tables

Table 5.2. Salary expenditure/total expenditure-tax administration

/1. **Brazil, Ireland, Romania and South Africa:** Expenditure data includes customs. **Estonia**: Total expenditure excludes IT costs. **Hungary**: Data of the National Tax and Customs Administration, after the merger of two predecessor organisations: Tax and Financial Control Administration and Customs and Finance Guard. **Italy**: Total expenditure data for 2010-13 relate only to revenue body; some prior year data may include other bodies involved with tax work (e.g. Equitalia). **Norway**: Wages do not include employers' contribution to pension plans (8% of wage amount) which is contributed outside the budget of the Norwegian Tax Administrations budget. **Sweden**: Expenditure data (and related ratios) exclude costs of independent Enforcement Agency staff that conducts enforced debt collection activities.

Table 5.3. IT and human resource management expenditure (% of all expenditure)

/1. **Argentina**: Ratio to total cost including customs; IT expenditure includes hardware and software equipment as well as all kind of services and technical assistance on this matter. **Estonia**: In 2012, the Ministry of Finance established an Information Technology Centre (ITCMF). As a result, the ETCB IT budget has moved to ITCMF. **Ireland**: Expenditure for IT related operations does not include employee costs. **Luxembourg**: Major part of IT- and HRM-related costs not quantified as shared with other parts of MOF in separate departments. **Malta**: IT expenditure only for direct tax authority. **Spain**: 2012 and 2013 IT costs include wages of the IT Department (2 063 people). **Switzerland**: Increase from 2012 to 2013 as a result of mayor IT projects and reorganisation to the IT department. **United States**: IT-related operations do not include Business Systems Modernisation investments.

/2. **Estonia**: Total expenditure excludes IT costs.

Table 5.4. Cost of collection ratios (administrative costs/net revenue collections)

/1. Observations and conclusions based on the information in this table should pay close regard to the comments in the related text in this chapter.

/2. The year-by-year data is compiled from surveys conducted among revenue bodies around every two years. For TA 2014, some prior year data items and related ratios (reported in previous editions of CIS) were revised to take account of new data provided by a few revenue bodies or to correct errors detected in the data originally used for these calculations.

/3. **Estonia**: Ratios for 2005 to 2007 include customs operations but not for subsequent years. **Italy:** The computed ratios for these years significantly understate the true ratio as they do not take account of expenditure incurred on tax-related work carried out by other agencies (e.g. tax fraud work of the Guardia di Finanza and enforced debt collection undertaken by Equitalia spa) that have not been quantified. **United States**: Ratios indicated vary from IRS-published ratios owing to use of "net" and not "gross" revenue collections as the denominator.

Table 5.5. Tax Administration expenditure/gross domestic product (GDP)

/1. Observations and conclusions based on the information in this table should pay close regard to the comments in the related text in this chapter.

/2. The year-by-year data is compiled from current and prior surveys conducted among revenue bodies. For TA 2015, some prior year data items and related ratios (reported in previous editions of this series) were revised to take account of new data provided by a few revenue bodies or to correct errors detected in the data originally used for these calculations.

/3. **Italy**: Calculations up to 2009 based on cost data provided for tax related functions of revenue body (Agenzia Entrate), tax-related work of separate tax police body (Guardia di Finanza), and separate tax debt collection function (Equitalia); data not provided for subsequent years.

Table 5.6. Revenue body staff usage and related ratios

/1. Use of the information in the table should pay close regard to the comments in this chapter.

/2. **All countries**: The definition of the number of person-days that constitute one person year (one full time equivalent [FTE]) varies from country to country; for the purpose of this tabulation and related analysis no attempt has been made to apply a standard definition in order to arrive at a more consistently based summary of aggregate FTEs/revenue body. **Italy:** Data refers to Revenue Agency only and excludes Equitalia (debt collection), Guardia di Finanza (tax fraud work) and Sogie (data processing). **Luxembourg**: Staff usage figures not expressed in FTE. **Singapore**: Staff strength at 31 March 2013.

Table 5.7. Staff usage (2013) by major tax function groupings (% of total usage)

/1. The data on distribution of resources should be treated with caution owing to differences in interpretation between countries on the functional split used and organisational arrangements in place.

/2. **Brazil and Ireland**: Data includes Customs. **Chile, Iceland and Sweden**: Data exclude tax debt collection functions; **Italy**: Data for revenue body agency only and excludes Equitalia (debt collection), Guardia di Finanza (tax fraud work) and Sogie (data processing). **Japan**: Inseparable from the audit, investigation and other verification function and debt collection function. **Korea**: Staff in taxpayer account management and verification functions are also engaged in the work of debt collection and there is no dedicated unit for debt collection. **Luxembourg**: Staff usage figures not expressed in FTE. **Singapore**: Staff strength at 31 March 2013. **Spain**: Account management staff also do some verification functions (massive and desk controls).

/3. **Spain**: Staff also supports Customs Department.

Table 5.8. Third party service delivery of tax administration functions

/1. **Australia:** Includes outsourcing of mail and publication distribution, while certain categories of litigation must be outsourced to Australian Government Solicitor. **Canada**: Tax and information returns records retrieval and storage operated by a private sector company as of January 2014. **Israel**: Printing services; **Malta**: Applies only in the case of VAT where the functions include printing, issuing, distributing and storage of receipt books. **Saudi Arabia**: DZIT has contracted the Saudi Post to make express mail delivery to taxpayers. **Singapore**: Civil legal proceedings against recalcitrant taxpayers for not paying their outstanding taxes are outsourced to a law firm to provide legal services/advice relating to suits for tax, bankruptcy and winding-up proceedings. Private liquidators are appointed to manage cases for winding-up. **Spain**: Most of the IT services are developed and provided internally by the IT Department.

Table 5.9. Expenditure on non-tax roles (% of total revenue body expenditure)

/1. Table only shows countries that reported one or more non-tax roles for 2012/13.

/2. **Estonia**: Total expenditure excludes IT costs.

Chapter 6

Operational performance of revenue bodies

This chapter provides a comparative overview of reported operational data and related ratios and their trend concerning the performance of surveyed revenue bodies. The main subject areas covered are: (1) *revenue collections;* (2) *tax refunds;* (3) *taxpayer services;* (4) *verification activities;* (5) *dispute resolution; and* (6) *the collection of unpaid tax debts.*

Key points

Tax revenue collections

- Overall, the unweighted measure "average tax/GDP" for OECD countries in fiscal year 2012 rose marginally compared with 2011, and has just about returned to the level existing prior to the global financial crisis.
- Overall VAT performance across OECD countries remains below the levels existing prior to the global financial crisis in 2008, ***notwithstanding efforts in recent years in many countries to increase VAT revenue productivity.***

Refunds of taxes

- The incidence of aggregate tax refunds varies markedly between countries, reflecting a range of tax system design and other factors, with significant implications for respective revenue body workloads.
- In overall terms for OECD countries, the proportion of tax being refunded to taxpayers appears to have fallen to around the level observed prior to the onset of the global financial crisis (i.e. around 20-22%); for non-OECD countries, the overall incidence of refunds is substantially lower overall.

Delivery of services to taxpayers

- The volume data reported, when presented in a relative and comparative context, suggest that many revenue bodies have considerable potential to eliminate and/or shift service demand from costly channels (e.g. in-person inquiries) to more cost efficient service channels (e.g. online services).
- Many revenue bodies appear to not have sufficient data (and knowledge) of the service demand for some of their more costly service channels (e.g. in-person inquiries and phone calls)
- The practice of applying standards for key areas of service delivery and monitoring the performance achieved remains a relatively immature practice among revenue bodies.
- For some areas of service delivery, the standards applied (and levels of service achieved) vary significantly across revenue bodies (e.g. processing VAT refunds); however, it is possible to identify many examples of "responsive standards" and "high standards of performance".

Tax verification activities

- The aggregate value of verification results (as a % of annual net revenue collections) varies significantly but represents less than 4% of annual net revenue collections for around 60% of revenue bodies; 20 revenue bodies reported results less than 2%, 14 reported an amount in the range 2-4%, while 15 revenue bodies reported results over 4% (including four over 8% (i.e. Brazil, Hungary, Italy, and Mexico).

Collection of tax debts

- The overall incidence of year-end aggregate tax debts (including disputed debt) in OECD countries rose marginally in the years 2011 to 2013-from around 22% to just over 24% of net annual revenue collections – although the computed ratios are significantly impacted by two abnormal "outlier" results.
- For OECD countries where data are provided (i.e.19), the incidence of disputed tax debt as a share of the overall debt inventory averages around one-third of total debt inventories.
- Viewed over the three years 2011 to 2013, the overall incidence of tax debts (excluding disputed debts) in OECD countries was fairly stable at around 21 percent of net annual revenue collections, although the computed ratios are significantly impacted by the two abnormal "outlier" results. Generally speaking, many countries were unable to report fairly basic information In respect of their debt collection activities, suggesting possible major weaknesses in their systems of performance measurement and monitoring.

Introduction

This chapter provides an overview of reported operational data and related trends concerning the performance of revenue bodies. The subject areas covered are: *(1)* revenue collections; *(2)* tax refunds; *(3)* taxpayer services; *(4)* verification activities; *(5)* dispute resolution; and *(6)* the collection of unpaid taxes.

Given the "comparative" nature of this series, every effort has been made to ensure that a common understanding has been applied by surveyed revenue bodies in interpreting the various terms used (e.g. "verification", "tax disputes", and "tax arrears") for gathering operations-related data. Furthermore, steps have been taken to validate the data and computations provided and in some cases this has included revisions of fiscal years' data and ratios reported in previous editions.

For the reasons outlined in this chapter and elsewhere in this series, considerable care should be taken when interpreting this information and in drawing any conclusions as to the relative efficiency and effectiveness of the individual revenue bodies identified. In particular, reference should be made to other parts of the series (e.g. data related to the scope of taxes collected, institutional and organisational arrangements, and resource allocations) to identify factors that may explain what appear to be "unusual outcomes" reported in this chapter.

Tax revenue collections

The end-product of the work of revenue bodies is the net amount of revenue collected (after refunds are paid) which can be credited to Government revenue accounts. This section provides information on the aggregate net tax revenues of surveyed countries *for all levels of Government*, often expressed in terms of a country's "tax burden". Generally speaking, the major share of these revenues is collected by the revenue bodies included in this series, although the exact proportion varies significantly from country to country given a variety of factors (e.g. institutional design issues as discussed in Chapter 1). For this series, the chapter also provides a brief account of the performance of VAT systems in OECD countries, viewed through the OECD's measure "VAT revenue ratio (VRR)" and its trend.

The OECD generally seeks to publish internationally comparable data on the tax revenues of OECD countries for all levels of government. The term "taxes" is confined to compulsory, unrequited payments to government. Taxes are unrequited in the sense that benefits provided by government to taxpayers are not normally in proportion to their payments. It is important to recognise that the tax ratios published by the OECD depend just as much on the denominator (GDP) as the numerator (tax revenue), and that the denominator is subject to revision for a variety of reasons. Readers are directed to

Note: The OECD maintains an extensive tax database and publishes a large array of comparative reports on the design and performance of tax systems. Readers interested in finding out more on these particular aspects are directed to the following sources:

- ***Tax revenue performance***
- ***Rates of taxes, thresholds, etc.***
  www.oecd.org/ctp/taxpolicyanalysis/oecdtaxdatabase.htm#A_RevenueStatistics
- ***Trends and developments concerning consumption taxes***
  www.oecd.org/ctp/consumptiontax/oecdconsumptiontaxtrendspublications.htm

the OECD publication *Revenue Statistics 1965-2013, 2014 edition* for more information concerning the impact of GDP revisions on reported tax ratios in member countries.

Table 6.1 provides official aggregate country tax revenues (for each major tax type and *in total covering all levels of government*) for OECD countries as a percentage of gross domestic product (GDP) for fiscal year 2012, along with aggregate tax/GDP data for the prior two years (OECD, 2014a). Data for other countries have been obtained from the sources indicated. Important observations from the information in Table 6.1 are as follows:

- Tax burden ratios vary enormously between surveyed countries, and within and across OECD and non-OECD categories; for fiscal year 2012, eight countries in the European region – Austria, Belgium, Denmark, Finland, France, Italy, Norway and Sweden – had tax/GDP ratios exceeding 40%. In contrast, total tax revenue in 10 other surveyed countries/regions (i.e. China, Colombia, Hong Kong (China), India, Indonesia, Malaysia, Mexico, Saudi Arabia, Singapore, and Thailand) were less than 20% of GDP; just on 40% of surveyed countries had an aggregate tax burden between 30-40% of GDP.
- Overall, the unweighted measure "average tax/GDP" in fiscal year 2012 in OECD countries (33.7%) grew marginally compared to 2011 (33.4%) although a number of countries registered substantially greater growth.
- Social contributions, which are not collected by the main revenue body in many OECD countries, are a significant source of tax revenue and are the predominant source of tax revenue in almost two-thirds of OECD countries, and almost half of non-OECD surveyed countries.
- The variations in aggregate tax burdens evident from Table 6.1 have a number of implications from a tax administration viewpoint, particularly in the context of international comparisons. The significant variations in tax burden ratios coupled with variations in the mix of direct and indirect taxes mean that there can be quite different administrative workloads and compliance issues from country to country.

Aggregate Tables A.1 to A.3 in Annex A set out aggregates for the nine year period (2005 to 2013) of gross revenues, tax refunds, and net tax revenues *reported by revenue bodies* for this and prior series. Unlike the data in Table 6.1 which includes *all levels of Government*, these data represent the taxes collected by revenue bodies in this series and are used to compute various ratios for comparative purposes.

VAT system performance

The performance of VAT systems in many countries has come under increased scrutiny in recent years as Governments seek to improve their budgetary position. This issue has been of particular concern within the European Union where a number of studies undertaken to estimate the aggregate tax gap for the VAT and its trend over time in member countries have pointed to findings suggesting substantial revenue leakage in many countries. These studies are referenced briefly in Chapter 3.

Box 6.1 sets out an explanation of the VAT revenue ratio (VRR) that has been developed by the OECD to assist in the analysis of the performance of VAT systems and their trend over time (OECD, 2012a). As will be evident from the explanation provided, the ratio is impacted by both policy design choices that reduce the amount of VAT revenue that would otherwise be collected and administrative weaknesses and limitations that result in a portion of the legal tax base going uncollected. In the studies prepared for the EC these two factors are described as the VAT "policy gap" and the "compliance gap" respectively.

Table 6.1. **Aggregate tax collections (by major tax type) for 2012 and prior years**

	Taxes collected (Tax/GDP%) for fiscal year 2012						All taxes (Tax/GDP %)	
Country	PIT	SSC	CIT	VAT	Excises	All taxes	2011	2010
OECD countries								
Australia	10.7	n.a.	5.2	3.3	1.7	27.3	26.3	25.6
Austria	9.5	14.2	2.2	7.8	2.3	41.7	41.0	40.9
Belgium	12.2	14.1	3.0	6.9	2.0	44.0	42.9	42.4
Canada	11.2	4.8	2.9	4.2	1.3	30.7	30.4	30.5
Chile	8.3	1.4	in PIT	8.1	1.5	21.4	21.2	19.5
Czech Republic	3.6	14.7	3.3	7.1	3.7	33.8	33.4	32.5
Denmark	23.9	0.9	3.0	9.7	4.0	47.2	46.6	46.5
Estonia	5.3	11.3	1.4	8.6	4.5	32.1	31.9	33.2
Finland	12.6	12.7	2.1	9.0	3.8	42.8	42.0	40.8
France	7.9	16.5	2.5	6.8	2.3	44.0	42.9	41.6
Germany	9.3	13.9	1.8	7.1	2.4	36.5	35.7	35.0
Greece	7.0	10.8	1.1	7.1	3.6	33.7	32.5	31.1
Hungary	5.3	12.6	1.3	9.1	3.6	38.5	36.9	37.6
Iceland	13.2	3.7	1.9	8.1	3.0	35.3	34.5	33.3
Ireland	9.1	4.2	2.3	5.9	2.8	27.3	26.7	26.8
Israel	5.5	5.1	2.7	7.3	1.7	29.6	30.9	30.6
Italy	11.6	13.0	2.8	5.9	2.3	42.7	41.4	41.5
Japan	5.5	12.3	3.7	2.7	1.8	29.5	28.6	27.6
Korea	3.7	6.1	3.7	4.3	2.1	24.8	24.0	23.2
Luxembourg	8.4	11.3	5.2	7.0	3.5	38.5	37.5	38.0
Mexico	5.2	2.9	(in PIT)	3.7	0.6	19.6	19.5	18.5
Netherlands	7.3	15.0	1.9	6.5	2.6	36.3	35.9	36.1
New Zealand	12.4	n.a.	4.7	9.9	0.9	33.0	31.4	31.0
Norway	9.9	9.6	10.5	7.7	2.7	42.3	42.7	42.6
Poland	4.5	12.1	2.1	7.1	4.0	32.1	31.8	31.3
Portugal	5.8	8.8	2.7	8.2	2.8	31.2	32.0	30.0
Slovak Republic	2.6	12.3	2.4	6.0	2.7	28.1	28.3	27.7
Slovenia	5.7	14.9	1.2	8.0	4.5	36.5	36.3	36.7
Spain	7.2	11.5	2.0	5.3	2.0	32.1	31.2	31.4
Sweden	11.9	10.0	2.6	8.9	2.4	42.3	42.3	43.1
Switzerland	8.5	6.7	2.8	3.5	1.3	26.9	27.0	26.5
Turkey	4.0	7.5	2.0	5.8	5.1	27.6	27.8	26.2
United Kingdom	9.1	6.3	2.7	6.9	2.8	33.0	33.6	32.8
United States	9.2	5.4	2.5	0.0	1.0	24.4	24.0	23.7
OECD ave. (unw.)	8.6	9.0	2.9	6.6	2.6	33.7	33.3	32.8
Non-OECD countries								
Argentina	2.5	8.3	3.8	8.7	1.9	37.3	34.6	33.5
Brazil	7.3	9.7	in PIT	8.5	0.1	36.3	34.9	33.2
Bulgaria	3.0	7.2	1.9	9.4	5.1	27.9	27.3	27.5
China		---------- 4.9 ----------		---------- 9.6 ----------		19.4	19.0	18.2
Colombia	6.6	2.4	in PIT	5.5	0.8	19.6	18.8	18.0
Costa Rica	3.9	6.2	in PIT	5.0	2.8	21.0	21.0	20.5
Croatia	3.7	11.5	2.0	12.3	3.4	35.7	35.3	36.4
Cyprus	4.0	9.1	6.3	8.9	3.4	35.3	35.3	35.6
Hong Kong, China		---------- 9.1 ----------		---------- 5.1 ----------		14.2	13.6	12.8
India	n.a.	n.a.	n.a.	n.a.	n.a.	16.1	16.1	15.2
Indonesia		----------5.6----------		4.1	1.2	11.9	11.8	11.6
Latvia	5.7	8.4	1.6	7.1	3.2	27.9	27.6	27.2
Lithuania	3.5	11.0	1.3	7.7	2.9	27.2	27.4	28.5
Malaysia	2.4	n.a.	n.a.	n.a.	n.a.	16.1	15.3	13.7
Malta	6.7	6.0	6.3	7.8	3.0	33.6	33.0	32.2
Morocco		---------- 9.3 ----------		---------- 12.0 ----------		24.0	23.0	22.7
Romania	3.5	8.8	2.2	8.5	3.5	28.3	28.4	26.8
Russia	3.6	6.2	3.8	5.7	1.3	34.7	35.1	31.8
Saudi Arabia		0.5		n.a.	n.a.	1.3	1.1	1.1
Singapore	n.a.	n.a.	n.a.	n.a.	n.a.	13.7	12.9	12.7
South Africa	8.0	n.a.	4.9	6.1	n.a.	23.7	23.0	22.4
Thailand		---------- 7.8 ----------		---------- 7.9 ----------		16.9	16.9	15.8

Sources: Revenue Statistics (OECD, 2014), Revenue Statistics in Latin America (OECD, 2014); Taxation Trends in the European Union (2014); South African Revenue Service; Morocco Tax Administration and IMF Article IV Consultations: Staff Reports.

Box 6.1. Understanding the performance of VAT systems – the VAT revenue ratio (VRR)

Precise measurement of VAT performance is not easy. It has traditionally been measured by the "efficiency ratio", defined as the ratio of VAT revenues to GDP divided by the standard rate (expressed as a percentage). Although the efficiency ratio is widely used as a diagnostic tool in evaluating VATs, its limitations are significant. In particular, the measure suffers from a fundamental weakness: a "perfect" efficiency ratio of 100 per cent could be achieved by a product-type VAT levied at a uniform rate. However, this is misleading since the norm is a consumption-type VAT. This difficulty is addressed by taking household consumption as a reference of the potential tax base rather than production (Ebrill, Keen, Bodin and Summers, 2001).

From this perspective, a VAT system should be considered, in absolute terms, "efficient" when it covers the whole of the potential tax base at a single rate and where all the tax due is collected by the tax administration. The VAT Revenue Ratio (VRR) is intended to be such a measure of "efficiency" or "performance". It builds on a concept developed initially by the IMF (the "C-efficiency ratio").

What does the VRR measure?

The VRR measures the difference between the VAT revenue actually collected and what would theoretically be raised if VAT was applied at the standard rate to the entire potential tax base in a "pure" VAT regime and all revenue was collected. The "standard" rate means the rate normally applicable to the tax base, unless otherwise varied by legislation. Legislation can (and almost all countries do) provide that lower (or higher) rates are applicable to a defined list of products. Almost all OECD countries (except Chile, Israel and Japan) apply lower VAT rates in addition to the standard rate. None of them applies higher VAT rates.

The potential VAT base includes all supplies of goods, services and intangibles made for consideration (or deemed to be made for consideration) by businesses or any other entity acting as a business (e.g. individuals, government entities providing supplies for direct consideration, etc.). In other words, the tax base corresponds to the expenditure made to obtain goods, services and intangibles. In practice, only transactions (sales) or deemed transactions (e.g. barter) are taxed under VAT and not consumption as such. For example, public goods provided by government, like defence (for which no user fee is possible, even in theory), do not belong to the tax base, as there is no direct payment in exchange for them. Under a "pure" VAT regime", all supplies made for consideration should be taxed at the standard rate, without any reduced rate, exemptions or specific tax relief. In practice, no country applies such a "pure VAT regime".

Interpretation of the VRR

In theory, the closer the VAT system of a country is to the "pure" VAT regime, the closer its VRR is to 1. A lower value reflects such factors as the effects of reduced rates, exemptions or a failure to collect all tax due. A VRR above 1 is possible in theory where almost all the tax base is covered by the standard rate and a number of exemptions without right to deduction apply so that the cascading effect of the exemption (see below) provides additional revenue for the government that exceeds the cost of the exemption. A VRR close to 1 is taken as an indicator of a VAT bearing uniformly on a broad base with effective tax collection. However, the interpretation of the measure should be made with caution. In practice, the VRR rarely equals 1. A number of complex – and sometimes contradictory – factors may influence the results. These include:

- Tax compliance never reaches 100 per cent.
- In many countries, a wide range of goods and services are subject to reduced rates of VAT.

Box 6.1. Understanding the performance of VAT systems – the VAT revenue ratio (VRR) *(continued)*

- Some goods and services are usually exempt from VAT (e.g. healthcare, education, financial services). Such exemption may reduce tax revenue (when exemption applies to goods and services directly supplied to final consumers (e.g. healthcare) or may increase revenue when exemption occurs early in the supply chain (e.g. financial services made to businesses) and the revenue arising from the cascading effect exceeds the potential tax arising from regular taxation.
- Some distortions may be created by the place of taxation rules applicable to international trade (e.g. services taxed in the country where the supplier is established while its consumers reside abroad).
- Very small traders are exempt from VAT collection in many countries (registration/ collection thresholds) to minimise their compliance costs and revenue bodies' administrative costs, but reducing VAT revenue.
- Public sector bodies are generally exempt from or outside the scope of VAT in most countries, meaning they cannot deduct their input VAT. However, countries have created various mechanisms that, depending on their nature, can have positive or negative impacts on computed VRRs.
- The evolution of consumption patterns may also affect tax revenue. For example, when the share of consumption of necessities (taxed at a lower rate) increases within the consumption basket of households (e.g. as a result of an economic crisis).

Source: OECD Consumption Tax Trends 2012 and 2014.

Table 6.2 provides a summary of the VRRs computed for OECD countries up to 2012 (OECD, 2014b).

The computed ratios reveal a variety of trends warranting comment and, for some countries, raise a number of concerns:

- Computed VRRs across OECD countries vary widely and can be explained by two factors: *(1)* vastly different policy choices across Governments for reliance on VAT as a source of revenue that, for many, entail extensive use of reduced rates and/or exemptions that result in a relatively large "VAT policy gap"; and *(2)* high levels of non-compliance in some countries resulting in relatively large "compliance gaps".
- Overall VAT performance across OECD countries remains below the levels existing prior to the global financial crisis in 2008, ***notwithstanding efforts in recent years in many countries to bolster VAT revenue productivity.***
- A significant downwards trend (i.e. by 0.10 or more from 2006-12) is observed in six countries (i.e. Estonia, Iceland, Ireland, Slovak Republic, Slovenia, and Spain).
- The VRR displayed for Luxembourg (exceeding the theoretical maximum of one and having grown consistently since the late 1990s) is attributed to the liberalisation of financial services and the boom in e-commerce, market factors that in combination with their specific VAT treatment (i.e. allowing Luxembourg to get VAT revenue from exported e-commerce and financial supplies) within the EU have bolstered VAT revenues and, as a result, the computed VRR for the years shown in the table.

Table 6.2. **VAT revenue ratio (VRR) in OECD countries**

Country	Standard VAT rate 2012	VAT revenue ratio 2000	2005	2006	2007	2008	2009	2010	2011	2012	Difference 2006-12
OECD countries											
Australia	10.0	n.appl.	0.56	0.54	0.54	0.49	0.51	0.50	0.48	0.47	-0.07
Austria	20.0	0.61	0.59	0.57	0.58	0.59	0.58	0.58	0.58	0.59	0.02
Belgium	21.0	0.50	0.50	0.52	0.51	0.48	0.47	0.48	0.48	0.48	-0.04
Canada	5.0	0.50	0.50	0.47	0.51	0.51	0.49	0.49	0.48	0.48	0.01
Chile	19.0	0.64	0.67	0.64	0.67	0.70	0.59	0.62	0.63	0.64	0.00
Czech Republic	20.0	0.42	0.56	0.53	0.54	0.57	0.55	0.53	0.55	0.57	0.05
Denmark	25.0	0.60	0.63	0.65	0.65	0.62	0.59	0.58	0.59	0.59	-0.06
Estonia	20.0	0.72	0.76	0.81	0.80	0.67	0.73	0.67	0.68	0.70	-0.11
Finland	23.0	0.61	0.60	0.61	0.60	0.58	0.56	0.55	0.56	0.56	-0.05
France	19.6	0.50	0.52	0.51	0.51	0.50	0.47	0.47	0.48	0.48	-0.03
Germany	19.0	0.60	0.54	0.56	0.54	0.55	0.55	0.54	0.55	0.55	-0.01
Greece	23.0	0.49	0.46	0.46	0.48	0.46	0.39	0.45	0.38	0.37	-0.08
Hungary	27.0	0.52	0.48	0.55	0.59	0.57	0.62	0.53	0.52	0.52	-0.03
Iceland	25.5	0.59	0.61	0.64	0.59	0.52	0.45	0.44	0.44	0.45	-0.19
Ireland	23.0	0.62	0.66	0.67	0.63	0.55	0.47	0.49	0.47	0.45	-0.22
Israel	16.0	0.62	0.62	0.62	0.66	0.65	0.65	0.65	0.65	0.64	0.01
Italy	21.0	0.43	0.39	0.41	0.41	0.39	0.36	0.40	0.40	0.38	-0.03
Japan	5.0	0.68	0.71	0.70	0.69	0.67	0.67	0.69	0.69	0.69	-0.01
Korea	10.0	0.59	0.64	0.63	0.63	0.63	0.65	0.67	0.67	0.69	0.06
Luxembourg	15.0	0.76	0.90	0.89	0.94	0.97	0.97	0.99	1.05	1.13	0.24
Mexico	16.0	0.28	0.30	0.33	0.33	0.34	0.30	0.32	0.31	0.31	-0.02
Netherlands	19.0	0.57	0.59	0.58	0.59	0.57	0.52	0.55	0.53	0.53	-0.05
New Zealand	15.0	0.99	1.03	1.04	0.96	0.98	0.99	1.12	0.95	0.96	-0.08
Norway	25.0	0.67	0.57	0.61	0.63	0.57	0.54	0.56	0.56	0.57	-0.04
Poland	23.0	0.42	0.46	0.50	0.52	0.49	0.45	0.47	0.47	0.42	-0.07
Portugal	23.0	0.60	0.56	0.51	0.51	0.49	0.43	0.48	0.45	0.47	-0.04
Slovak Republic	20.0	0.44	0.60	0.57	0.53	0.53	0.47	0.46	0.49	0.43	-0.13
Slovenia	20.0	0.67	0.66	0.68	0.69	0.68	0.59	0.59	0.60	0.58	-0.10
Spain	18.0	0.52	0.57	0.57	0.53	0.43	0.32	0.46	0.39	0.41	-0.16
Sweden	25.0	0.52	0.55	0.56	0.57	0.58	0.57	0.59	0.58	0.56	0.00
Switzerland	8.0	0.74	0.72	0.74	0.73	0.74	0.70	0.72	0.71	0.71	-0.03
Turkey	18.0	0.45	0.38	0.39	0.36	0.35	0.34	0.39	0.43	0.40	0.01
United Kingdom	20.0	0.47	0.46	0.46	0.46	0.44	0.44	0.44	0.44	0.44	-0.02
OECD ave. (unw.)	18.7	0.57	0.59	0.59	0.59	0.57	0.54	0.56	0.55	0.55	-0.04

Source: Table 3.A3.1. Consumption Tax Trends: VAT/GST and excise rates, trends and policy issues (December 2014).

Refunds of taxes

A topic given relatively little attention in describing national tax systems and the work of revenue bodies is the incidence of tax refunds, and issues associated with their associated workload and costs for revenue bodies and taxpayers to settle.

Given the underlying design of the major taxes administered (i.e. PIT, CIT and VAT) some element of over-payment by a proportion of taxpayers is unavoidable. However, as discussed in this section the overall incidence of tax refunds (measured as a share of gross revenues) for many countries is higher than perhaps generally recognised and varies significantly across countries. Related to this, the relatively high incidence of tax refunds for some taxes (e.g. VAT) raises a number of important tax system management issues of concern to taxpayers, policy-makers and revenue bodies.

Excess tax payments represent a cost to taxpayers in terms of "the time value of money", which is particularly critical to businesses that are operating with tight margins where cash flow is paramount. Any delays in refunding legitimately overpaid taxes may therefore result in significant "costs" to taxpayers, particularly where there are inadequate provisions in tax laws for the payment of interest to taxpayers in respect of delayed refunds. Another important consideration is that tax regimes with a high incidence of tax refunds are particularly attractive to fraudsters (especially via organised criminal attacks) and for this reason can present a significant and growing risk to revenue bodies that necessitates effective risk-based approaches for identifying potentially fraudulent refund claims.

Drawing on research by the Secretariat, there are many factors that can influence the incidence of refunds for each of the major taxes administered – see Box 6.2 – and these can be observed to varying degrees across countries in this series.

Concerning VAT systems, the combination of factors that result in a relatively high incidence of taxes to be refunded to taxpayers, coupled with a requirement to pay interest on delayed refunds creates an element of conflict for most revenue bodies that must be carefully managed.

On the one hand, revenue bodies must be alert to potentially excessive refund claims, taking steps have effective risk profiling techniques to detect such claims before they are processed. On the other hand, they are under pressure to process legitimate refund claims expeditiously so as to not unduly impact the cash flow of businesses seeking refunds. These considerations have prompted international and regional tax organisations to give attention to this matter with a view to providing "best practice" guidance, particularly for revenue bodies in developing and transitional economies, for example (IMF, 2005).

Table 6.3 displays ratios for seven years reflecting the overall incidence of tax refunds in each fiscal year, acknowledging that workloads associated with refunding overpaid taxes can be significant for many revenue bodies. The table also displays data on the incidence of VAT refunds for both 2012 and 2013. The key observations from the tabulation are as follows:

All refunds

- The overall incidence of tax refunds in 2013 (for 44 of 56 revenue bodies) varies significantly, resulting from various tax system design factors of the kind described in Box 6.2:
  - Five revenue bodies reported in excess of 30% (i.e. Bulgaria, Mexico Poland, Slovak Republic, and Switzerland);

  - Eight revenue bodies (all OECD) reported between 20-30%;
  - Nineteen revenue bodies reported an amount between 10-20%; and
  - Twelve revenue bodies reported aggregate refunds < 10%.

- In overall terms for OECD countries, the proportion of tax being refunded to taxpayers appears to have fallen in 2012 and 2013 to around the level observed prior to the onset of the global financial crisis (i.e. around 20-22%).
- For non-OECD countries, the overall incidence of refunds is substantially lower than observed in OECD countries, except in the case of Bulgaria.
- Leaving aside the negative impacts of global financial crisis on tax revenues in 2009 and 2010, an upwards trend in the overall incidence of refunds is observed for Mexico; on the other hand, a fair downwards trend can be observed for the Slovak Republic.

Box 6.2. **Factors that can contribute to a high incidence of tax refunds**

Personal income tax

- Employee withholding schedules (where the non-cumulative approach is used) that are calibrated to marginally "over-withhold" taxes from employees' wages, pending the settlement of liabilities in end-of-year tax returns;
- Tax system design features that result in various tax benefits being delivered to taxpayers via the end-of-year tax return assessment process;
- The use of flat rate (creditable) withholding mechanisms for investment income (e.g. interest) that result in "overpayment" of taxes for lower income taxpayers (that must be refunded with the filing of a tax return);
- Design features of the system for making advance payments of tax that result in more tax being paid than the finally assessed amount;
- Taxpayers under-reporting income and/or over-claiming deductions and other entitlements in the end-of-tax return process to inflate their refund entitlements.

Corporate income tax

- Reversals of relatively large assessments following the resolution of taxpayers' disputes; and
- Design features of the system for making advance payments of tax that result in more tax being paid than the finally assessed amount.

Value added tax

- Features of a country's economy (e.g. the extent of value added of export industries, the proportion of taxable and zero-rated sales in the economy);
- Design features of the VAT system, particularly the extent of zero-rating and use of multiple rates; and
- Inflated VAT refund claims that go undetected, including those resulting from fraudulent schemes designed to exploit weaknesses in VAT refund controls.

Source: OECD CTPA Secretariat.

Table 6.3. **Revenue collections and refunds (relative shares)**

Country	Total refunds of tax/ gross revenue collections (%)							VAT refunds/gross VAT collection (%)		VAT refunds/total refunds of tax (%)	
	2007	2008	2009	2010	2011	2012	2013	2012	2013	2012	2013
OECD countries											
Australia	20.1	20.8	24.2	25.0	24.4	23.5	23.8	53.8	54.0	58.1	58.2
Austria	n.a.	n.a.	n.a.	n.a.	n.a.	16.5	15.7	32.3	32.3	81.9	84.4
Belgium	n.a.	20.3	22.5	n.a.	n.a.	19.8	19.1	32.4	31.8	56.2	54.8
Canada	21.6	19.9	23.5	23.3	22.9	22.2	22.1	53.4	54.2	49.2	50.6
Chile	29.3	26.0	36.3	21.5	19.3	24.4	24.2	35.6	35.0	79.5	83.2
Czech Republic	n.a.	30.1	29.3	29.4	31.2	31.1	29.9	48.9	46.1	100.0	100.0
Denmark	n.a.	n.a.	n.a.	n.a.	n.a.	24.9	24.4	57.8	58.4	89.3	89.8
Estonia	28.9	18.3	28.4	17.8	19.2	18.2	17.4	43.6	43.5	88.5	91.0
Finland	21.7	24.0	22.7	22.4	23.1	23.2	21.5	46.0	43.4	73.5	74.5
France	8.3	13.9	18.7	16.9	15.9	18.5	17.0	26.2	25.3	64.8	66.0
Germany	n.a.	n.a.	n.a.	n.a.	n.a.	n.a.	n.a.	n.a.	n.a.	n.a.	n.a.
Greece	5.4	7.1	9.9	10.9	10.7	6.7	7.3	9.6	13.8	41.4	51.1
Hungary	17.0	16.6	16.6	18.2	20.1	19.4	18.3	39.5	40.5	73.2	79.8
Iceland	n.a.	n.a.	n.a.	n.a.	n.a.	n.a.	n.a.	43.1	40.6	n.a.	n.a.
Ireland	13.9	15.3	16.1	32.9	29.3	12.7	11.3	21.9	21.9	44.7	49.4
Israel	n.a.	16.2	16.3	18.3	15.8	19.6	18.9	74.2	77.3	74.0	70.2
Italy	n.a.	13.1	14.2	14.0	12.7	13.7	15.5	21.9	25.7	48.3	49.2
Japan	12.6	13.7	16.2	19.3	14.7	13.8	13.2	25.7	25.0	50.9	50.2
Korea	18.9	23.6	22.9	23.2	24.9	23.9	24.9	47.7	48.5	84.1	83.4
Luxembourg /1	n.a.	10.5	11.2	8.5	9.0	10.0	9.0	27.5	24.5	100.0	100.0
Mexico	24.6	25.4	28.3	27.0	29.4	31.0	34.1	34.6	39.6	45.3	43.2
Netherlands	n.a.	n.a.	n.a.	n.a.	n.a.	n.a.	n.a.	n.a.	n.a.	n.a.	n.a.
New Zealand	16.6	18.0	18.4	18.0	19.9	20.4	17.9	44.8	41.5	84.6	84.7
Norway	n.a.	n.a.	n.a.	n.a.	n.a.	n.a.	n.a.	53.9	51.9	n.a.	n.a.
Poland	n.a.	27.3	28.7	27.0	27.6	29.1	30.6	38.7	41.2	83.1	83.7
Portugal	16.1	17.1	20.8	19.8	20.0	18.7	17.5	26.1	27.8	59.7	62.3
Slovak Republic	61.5	63.0	60.9	64.4	66.0	49.2	46.0	59.8	55.8	78.3	76.6
Slovenia	n.a.	n.a.	n.a.	n.a.	n.a.	n.a.	n.a.	46.3	43.7	n.a.	n.a.
Spain	18.1	23.7	29.7	23.7	22.9	20.8	23.2	32.0	33.5	53.7	51.3
Sweden	n.a.	n.a.	n.a.	n.a.	n.a.	n.a.	n.a.	43.4	n.a.	n.a.	n.a.
Switzerland	n.a.	48.5	44.1	45.9	44.2	36.9	35.5	31.0	31.0	36.0	37.5
Turkey	10.7	11.5	12.2	10.7	10.8	12.1	11.3	n.a.	n.a.	n.a.	n.a.
United Kingdom	13.3	14.5	15.4	17.1	18.6	16.5	16.5	41.6	42.0	75.7	78.0
United States	11.0	15.5	18.7	19.9	17.2	14.8	12.8	-----------------No VAT in place-----------			
OECD ave. (unw.)	19.5	21.3	23.3	23.0	22.8	21.1	20.7	39.8	39.6	68.2	69.4
Non-OECD countries											
Argentina	4.3	3.0	2.0	1.9	1.8	0.6	0.9	1.3	1.1	56.4	33.7
Brazil	n.a.	n.a.	n.a.	4.5	4.4	5.8	4.2	3.1	5.4	15.8	30.4
Bulgaria	28.0	31.0	24.9	28.3	29.5	31.2	31.6	63.4	62.8	98.2	96.9
China	n.a.	10.1	10.3	n.a.	n.a.	n.a.	n.a.	n.a.	n.a.	n.a.	n.a.
Colombia	n.a.	n.a.	n.a.	10.5	8.1	5.8	4.6	6.5	5.2	52.0	43.7
Costa Rica	-------Not included in the series in these years-----					n.a.	n.a.	n.a.	n.a.	n.a.	n.a.
Croatia	-------Not included in the series in these years-----					12.0	11.2	24.6	23.0	90.8	90.5
Cyprus	5.8	4.1	6.1	5.1	4.9	5.5	7.2	9.9	13.5	83.7	87.0
Hong Kong, China	n.a.	n.a.	n.a.	6.7	6.0	4.1	5.0	-----------------No VAT in place-----------			
India	n.a.	11.8	13.2	14.6	16.5	16.0	12.6	-----------------No VAT in place-----------			
Indonesia	n.a.	6.1	5.6	6.2	5.9	6.0	6.9	9.4	9.3	62.0	55.6
Latvia	n.a.	11.7	15.7	14.6	16.0	14.7	14.7	37.6	37.4	85.6	84.7
Lithuania	18.2	14.8	13.9	14.3	14.9	15.5	15.0	31.0	27.3	87.8	88.8
Malaysia	7.2	9.4	12.2	8.1	6.4	6.4	6.6	-----------------No VAT in place-----------			
Malta	n.a.	7.2	6.2	6.6	7.4	7.9	7.4	17.6	16.7	63.2	61.9
Morocco	-------Not included in the series in these years-----					5.4	4.8	15.7	15.0	75.8	84.2
Romania	n.a.	7.6	7.3	7.7	8.9	6.2	6.8	12.8	14.0	75.7	74.4
Russia	n.a.	n.a.	n.a.	n.a.	n.a.	n.a.	n.a.	44.4	48.0	n.a.	n.a.
Saudi Arabia	n.a.	0.0	0.0	n.a.	n.a.	n.a.	n.a.	-----------------No VAT in place-----------			
Singapore	n.a.	n.a.	n.a.	n.a.	n.a.	n.a.	n.a.	n.a.	n.a.	n.a.	n.a.
South Africa	15.5	16.2	18.5	19.0	16.3	17.9	17.3	40.7	39.2	79.7	80.1
Thailand	-------Not included in the series in these years-----					16.4	16.4	33.6	33.6	83.3	81.2

For notes indicated by "/ (number)", see Notes to Tables section at the end of the chapter, p. 236.

Source: Tax Administration 2015 survey responses.

VAT refunds

- The overall incidence of VAT refunds in 2013 (using data for 45 of 51 revenue bodies administering a VAT) is substantially higher than the "all tax refunds" category, indicating the predominance of VAT as a source of tax refunds:
  - Seven revenue bodies reported VAT refunds exceeding 50% of gross VAT revenue (i.e. Australia, Bulgaria, Canada, Denmark, Israel, Norway, and Slovak Republic) for both 2012 and 2013;
  - Eleven revenue bodies reported between 40-50%;
  - Nine revenue bodies reported an amount between 30-40%; and
  - Eighteen revenue bodies reported aggregate refunds < 30%.

  While for many of these countries the incidence of VAT refunds can largely be attributed to a relatively high volume of exports, the data nevertheless highlights the importance of revenue bodies having systematic processes in place for granting timely VAT refunds to compliant taxpayers, as well as robust compliance checks for the detection of fraudulent VAT registrations and refund claims (ideally before refunds are paid to claimants).
- Over 20% of revenue bodies were unable to quantify the value of refunds, suggesting a possible gap in their performance monitoring arrangements.

Taxpayer service delivery

The provision of a comprehensive array of services for taxpayers and their representatives is an important component of the work of revenue bodies given the size of their client base, and the range and complexity of the taxes administered. However, revenue bodies face many competing demands. With limits on the resources that they can devote across the full range of their responsibilities, careful choices must be made as to how those resources are to be allocated to achieve the optimal mix of outcomes. As part of this, consideration must also be given to ensuring that service demands are satisfied in the most economical way, meaning the revenue bodies require both a detailed understanding of their service demand volumes and the costs of the various channels used for satisfying such demand.

In 2012, the FTA undertook a study – *Working smarter in revenue administration – Using demand management strategies to meet service delivery goals* – with the purpose of identifying the demand management processes revenue bodies had in place, and the steps they took to understand the root causes of service demand and how that knowledge was applied to either reduce demand or shift it to more cost efficient channels. Among other things, the study drew attention to weaknesses in the governance arrangements for managing service demand in many revenue bodies and encouraged them to do more to improve their understanding of their service demand workloads and the root causes of that demand. More is said on this topic in Chapter 7.

Managing service demand-service volumes

As for the prior series, the survey sought volume data on the main service demand categories of revenue bodies. Aggregate data obtained from survey responses for this and the prior series are set out in Tables A11 and A12, while Table 6.4 sets out various ratios computed to place the data in a comparative context. The key observations and findings are as follows:

In-person inquiries

- Many revenue bodies (over 40%) were unable to quantify the level of demand for this service channel in 2012 and 2013, suggesting possible weaknesses in their knowledge of this service channel and ability to improve its efficiency.
- For revenue bodies where data are available, there are significant variations in the relative levels of in-person inquiries received, ranging from less than one inquiry per 100 citizens (Canada) to over 160 inquiries per 100 citizens (Portugal).
- Using the benchmark ratio "inquiries made/100 citizens" for the 2012 and 2013 fiscal years, revenue bodies in France, Hungary, Portugal, Spain, and Sweden have an unusually high incidence of "in-person inquiries" in comparison with other revenue bodies; all of these revenue bodies have relatively large office networks, having regard to their respective demographic factors.
- Many revenue bodies with relatively high "in-person inquiry" volumes have relatively low "phone telephony" volumes and/or offer in-person payment services, suggesting potential for efficiency gains from increasing use of telephony and Internet services and modern payment services respectively – examples of revenue bodies in this category include Estonia, France, Hungary, and Portugal.
- The Canada Revenue Agency has the lowest rate of service demand for this channel, the result of concerted efforts over a number of years to reduce the costs of in-person services and recently resulting in the closure of payment and inquiry counters, as described in OECD (2012).
- On a positive note, and as described in Chapter 2, a fair number of revenue bodies are taking steps to significantly scale back the size of their office networks, a measure that might reasonably be expected to lead to significant reductions in their volumes of "in-person inquiries".

Telephony inquiries answered

- A large number of revenue bodies reported "telephony inquiries" volume information; while these data also show a significant variation in the relative level of calls answered by revenue body staff – using the benchmark "calls answered per 100 citizens" for both 2012 and 2013 – these variations in rates may in part be explicable by differences in roles and the range of taxes administered by the revenue bodies concerned, for example: *(1)* some revenue bodies (e.g. Canada, New Zealand, and Netherlands) have significant non-tax functions (e.g. the administration of welfare-related responsibilities); and *(2)* some revenue bodies administer a broader array of taxes (e.g. taxes on real property and motor vehicles).
- A number of revenue bodies with a low ratio of "telephony inquiries" per 100 citizens also have relatively large office networks and relatively small or no call centre operations, suggesting possible potential to make greater use of phone service channels.

Telephony inquiries (handled by IVR)

- Significant IVR volumes were reported by over 25% of revenue bodies (see Table A.12); on the other hand, responses from almost 60% of revenue bodies' suggest that such technology is not used for taxpayer service delivery purposes; compared to TA2013, significantly increased usage was reported by Australia, Colombia, Poland, Portugal, United Kingdom and United States.

Table 6.4. **Taxpayer services: Service demand ratios**

(Table only includes revenue bodies that reported volumes of in-person inquiries received and/or phone inquiries answered.)

Country	In-person inquiries: No. dealt with per 100 citizens				Phone inquiries (excl. IVR/1): No. answered per 100 citizens				Factors that may be unduly influencing ratios*
	2010	2011	2012	2013	2010	2011	2012	2013	
OECD countries									
Australia	2.95	2.42	2.14	1.90	39.90	41.90	44.45	41.07	R
Austria	n.a.	n.a.	n.a. /2	n.a. /2	n.a.	42.20	54.57	57.85	N
Belgium	n.a. /2	n.a. /2	n.a. /2	n.a. /2	6.50	5.80	6.11	5.65	N
Canada	0.70	0.70	0.74	0.44	48.10	51.00	49.28	47.04	
Chile	13.72	14.17	15.71	15.30	4.90	4.87	4.97	4.45	N
Denmark	7.30	7.10	6.98	4.56 /2	n.a.	n.a.	48.48	49.46	
Estonia	23.80	22.30	15.33	12.37	18.50	19.20	16.92	16.54	
Finland	n.a.	n.a.	23.76	19.71	17.40	19.80	32.90	38.31	N
France /2	24.20	28.50	28.23	27.36	5.20	4.90	n.a.	n.a.	N
Greece	n.a.	n.a.	n.a.	n.a.	n.a.	n.a.	n.a.	6.15	
Hungary	23.50	25.00	26.00	23.86	7.80	7.50	n.a.	n.a.	N
Iceland	13.30	23.30	n.a.	n.a.	43.00	43.00	n.a.	n.a.	
Ireland	19.30	18.00	16.78	14.64	38.10	38.60	32.70	53.16	N
Israel	n.a.	n.a.	n.a.	n.a.	n.a.	n.a.	7.59 /2	7.94 /2	
Italy	16.10	17.10	15.65	15.91	3.30	3.30	n.a.	n.a.	N
Japan	3.30	2.90	3.04	3.07	4.00	4.00	4.16	3.94	N
Korea	n.a.	n.a.	n.a.	n.a.	n.a.	n.a.	3.00	2.99	N
Mexico	8.30	9.50	8.75	7.08	4.40	4.10	3.58	3.04	
Netherlands	5.30	5.90	4.80	2.93 /2	83.20	85.00	84.73	86.41	R
New Zealand	4.50	4.50	4.51	4.47	90.90	84.10	79.01	73.83	R
Norway	n.a.	n.a.	n.a.	n.a.	44.50	40.60	35.06	35.43	N
Poland	n.a.	n.a.	n.a.	n.a.	n.a.	n.a.	4.18	4.39	N
Portugal	141.00 /2	122.60 /2	152.24 /2	163.25 /2	6.70	9.20	11.42	15.86	N, P
Slovak Republic	n.a.	n.a.	n.a.	n.a.	n.a.	n.a.	n.a.	1.02	N
Spain	n.a.	n.a.	28.59	41.36	13.00	12.40	13.34	12.55	N, R
Sweden	14.90	16.00	20.01	23.01	47.80	46.80	17.02	14.23	N
Switzerland	n.a.	n.a.	n.a.	n.a.	25.60	25.60	n.a.	n.a.	
Turkey	n.a.	n.a.	n.a.	n.a.	0.40	0.70	n.a.	n.a.	N
United Kingdom	5.00	5.20	4.24 /2	3.20 /2	43.90	38.20	34.33	34.55	N
United States	2.10	2.10	2.18	2.06	11.90	11.10	9.81	9.53	
Non-OECD countries									
Argentina	n.a.	n.a.	n.a.	n.a.	< 1.00	< 1.00	0.78	0.99	N
Brazil	10.40	10.30	10.29	9.99	1.10	1.30	1.02	0.42	N
Bulgaria	n.a.	n.a.	n.a.	n.a.	n.a.	n.a.	3.14	3.71	
China	n.a.	n.a.	n.a.	n.a.	n.a.	n.a.	1.06	1.20	
Colombia	7.20	6.90	n.a.	n.a.	n.a.	n.a.	1.57	2.40	N
Costa Rica			1.25	1.34			1.87 /2	1.85 /2	N
Croatia			n.a.	n.a.			1.64	1.88	
Hong Kong, China	3.20	2.90	3.06	3.19	0.43	0.42	0.56	0.42	
India	n.a.	n.a.	n.a.	n.a.	n.a.	n.a.	0.09	0.17	
Indonesia			n.a.	n.a.			0.13	0.18	
Latvia	22.40	26.60	20.59	9.90 /2	5.70	10.50	19.61	19.80	
Lithuania	5.60	3.20 /2	n.a. /2	n.a. /2	22.60	20.60	21.67	22.56	
Malaysia	< 1.00	< 1.00	8.49	9.11	1.70	1.80	1.47	0.91	N, P
Malta	11.50	11.00	11.90	10.24	25.50	17.00	16.67	16.67	
Romania	n.a.	n.a.	n.a.	n.a.	n.a.	n.a.	5.72	4.90	N
Saudi Arabia	n.a.	n.a.	0.74	0.87	n.a.	n.a.	n.a.	n.a.	
Singapore	3.60	2.80	1.91	1.86	19.20	19.10	18.71	18.15	
South Africa	n.a.	n.a.	12.17	15.80	10.10	11.10	10.67	9.64	N
Thailand			n.a.	n.a.			0.93	0.98	N, P

* Legend: **P**: receives in-person payments; **R**: as significant non-tax roles; **N**: has relatively large office network given demographic factors.

Source: Tax Administrati*on 2015 survey responses.*

Written (paper) correspondence

- Volume data for this channel are restricted to less than half surveyed countries and show wide variation in absolute terms, with volumes generally skewed to relatively small amounts (i.e. under 200 000 per annum); relatively significant usage (expressed in millions) was reported for 2013 by Australia (5.8), United Kingdom (18.3), and United States (20.8).

Written (email) correspondence

- Volume data for this channel showed wide variation in absolute terms, but volumes generally are skewed to relatively small amounts (i.e. under 200 000 per annum); significant usage was reported for 2013 by Argentina (390 000), Denmark (440 000), France (710 000), India (2 760 000), Mexico (1 700 000), New Zealand (800 000), Sweden (370 000), United States (5 760 000).

Are you being served? The use of service delivery standards

In a "taxpayer service delivery" context, quality has many dimensions (e.g. timeliness, accuracy of advice, and ease of access to information) and an exhaustive study of the approaches and performance of revenue bodies in this regard is beyond the scope of this series. For comparative purposes, this series focuses on a few of the more mainstream (and voluminous) areas of service provided by revenue bodies – the volumes of "service demand" work received, the standards that have been set for "timeliness", and the level of performance achieved in relation to those standards.

Tables 6.5 to 6.7 provide information for six specific areas of service delivered by revenue bodies – the actual performance standard used in practice and the level of performance achieved in 2013. The areas of service covered by the survey are: *(1)* processing PIT returns with refunds; *(2)* resolving taxpayers' complaints; *(3)* processing VAT returns with refunds; *(4)* sending a substantive response to a written letter on a routine matter; *(5)* dealing with in-person enquiries; and *(6)* answering taxpayers' telephone inquiries. The key findings and observations are as follows:

- The practice of establishing service standards and measuring the performance achieved against them remains a relatively immature practice across surveyed revenue bodies, with less than half having a comprehensive set of standards for all/ most of the areas of service delivery identified.
- For the areas of service surveyed, standards most frequently existed for the processing of VAT refunds and written inquiries, answering telephone inquiries, and handling taxpayers' complaints; standards were less frequently reported for the processing of income tax returns.
- For some areas of service delivery, the standards applied (and levels of service achieved) vary quite significantly (e.g. processing of VAT refunds).
- Survey data from a number of countries reveal examples of what might be deemed "highly responsive" standards and outstanding levels of service performance (see Table 6.8).

Table 6.5. **Service standards and performance in 2013: PIT returns and complaints**

(Countries only shown where an administrative standard is applied in practice and actual performance is reported)

	Processing PIT returns		Resolving taxpayers complaints	
Country	Standard set for processing in 2013	Result	Standard set for processing in 2013	Result
OECD countries				
Australia	Paper: 80% processed in 42 days E-filed: 94% in 12 days	90% 97%	85% resolved in 21 days	95%
Austria	Process within an average of 24 days (both paper and e-filed returns)	18.5 days	100% within 14 days	n.a.
Canada	Paper: 100% in average of 4-6 weeks E-filed: 100% in average of two weeks	4.3 weeks 1.6 weeks	80% acknowledged within two business days/ 80% resolved within 30 business days	92% / 94.3%
Chile	Varies /1	100%	-	-
Denmark	100% processed in six weeks	99%	100% within 90 days	88.4%
Estonia	E-filed: 5 working days (unless inquiry needed)	100%	Within 30 working days	n.a.
France	-	-	96.5% of complaints processed in one month /1	96.56%
Greece	-	-	Resolving 80% of the arising issues concerning inbound calls	80%
Ireland	E-filed: 100% in five work days	77%	Processed in 20 work days	84%
Israel	Within 90 days (legal requirement)	73% /1	Interim reply within 14 days	n.a.
Italy	80% till tax year 2011	77.25%	100% within 20 days	93.51%
Japan	95% in six weeks	96.3%	90% to have trouble shooting in three days	87.9%
Korea	100% in 30 days from the closing day of return period	n.a.	-	-
Luxembourg	-	-	Within three months	95%
Mexico	E-filed: 100% in 40 days for *(1)* large taxpayers and *(2)* regular taxpayers, and in 5 days for *(3)* individuals	*(1)* 86.7% *(2)* 95.3% *(3)* 98.6%	-	-
Netherlands	98-100% filed before 1 April paid by 1 July	99.9%	98-100% resolved in six weeks	98%
New Zealand	85% within 6 weeks	86.2%	-	-
Norway	-	-	90% within three months	91.1%
Poland	All in three months	100%	-	-
Portugal	-	-	Resolve within 14-18 days	11 days
Spain	Average time of processing: 32 days	n.a.	Average time of processing: 32 days	n.a.
Switzerland	-	-	For VAT: resolve within 30 days of receipt	99.9%
United Kingdom	-	-	80% resolved within 15 work days	58.4%
United States	100% in 40 days /1	99%	Initial action *(1)* and initial contact *(2)* for economic burden cases in three days, five days for others /2	*(1)* 97.2%, *(2)* 95.7%
Non-OECD countries				
Argentina	-	-	Resolve 85% of complaints registered	82%
Brazil	-	-	Answer within 30 days	98%
Hong Kong, China	Assess 96% within nine months	98.2%	Interim reply: 99% in seven days Substantive reply: 99% in 15 days	100% 100%
India	All returns to be processed in less than 180 days.	121 days average	All taxpayers' complaints to be resolved in 60 days.	60 days average
Lithuania	100% processed before 31 July where filed before 1 May	99.9%	-	-
Malaysia	Paper: Process 70% within 90 days of filing. E-filed: Process 70% within 30 days of filing	98% 98.9%	70% cases resolved within 60 days	100%
Malta	100% within six months	90%	80% within five work days and 100% within 20 days	80%
Singapore	Process 100% of refund in 30 days	100%	Paper: six work days; other: four work days	Average of 3.08 days
South Africa	Process in less than 1 working day	0.16 working days	-	-

For notes indicated by "/ (number)", see Notes to Tables section at the end of the chapter, p. 236.

Source: Tax Administration 2015 survey responses.

Table 6.6. **Service standards and performance in 2013: VAT refunds and correspondence**

(Countries only shown where an administrative standard is applied in practice and actual performance is reported)

Country	Processing VAT returns with refunds		Sending substantive reply to written correspondence	
	Standard set for processing in 2013	Result	Standard set for processing in 2013	Result
OECD countries				
Australia	92% in 14 days (e-filed), 85% in 14 days (paper)	100%, 98%	85% in 28 days	92%
Austria	Process within an average of 25 days	18.2 days	Within eight weeks (two weeks for wage tax)	n.a
Canada	95% in 30 calendar days /1	93.8%	-	-
Chile	95% of refund requests made by Reverse Charge Regime taxpayers, processed within the established period /1	97.1%	-	-
Denmark	100% processed in two weeks	99%	Basic email-80% in 5 days; other decisions-90% in 90 days	79%; 88.4%
Estonia	5 working days	100%	five work days	n.a.
Finland	3.6 days	3.8 days	100% in two days (Internet inquiries)	88%
France	80% processed in less than 30 days	89.7%	75% processed in 15 work days /1	90.7%
Hungary	-	-	30 work days	98%
Ireland	100% processed in 5 working days (e-returns)	100%	50% in 10 working days, 85% in 20 working days and 100% in 30 working days	68%, 85%, 93%
Israel	Within 90 days	n.a.	Initial response within 14 days (as per law)	n.a.
Italy	80% till tax year 2011 and 30% tax year 2012	98.53% / 31.83%	80 000 emails	104 646 emails
Korea	90% in 20 days	92.5%	-	-
Luxembourg	Legal delay	Achieved	Within three months	Achieved
Mexico	E-filed: 100% in 40 days for *(1)* large taxpayers and *(2)* regular taxpayers, and in 10, 15 or 20 days for *(3)* certified enterprises	*(1)* 91.5% *(2)* 92.1% *(3)* 73.4%	20 days according to the provisions of the law	65.9% on time
New Zealand	95% within four weeks	97.7%	75% within three weeks	76.6%
Norway	100% within 21 days /1	n.a.	Preliminary answer within 15 working days	n.a.
Poland	Standard time is 60 days /1	100%		
Portugal	25 to 30 days	29.5 days	70 to 85 days	77.8 days
Spain	Average time of processing: 32 days	n.a.	-	-
Switzerland	Within 30 days of receipt	99.9%	For VAT: within 30 days of receipt	90%
United Kingdom	-	-	80% within 15 working days and 95% within 40 working days	85% / 97%
United States	n.appl.	-	Routine letters; *(1)* Interim response in 30 days, and *(2)* Final response in 45 days	*(1)* 100%, *(2)* 55 days
Non-OECD countries				
Cyprus	-	-	All within 30 days	n.a.
Hong Kong, China	n.appl.	-	***Simple:*** 95% in 7 working days, 99% in 9 working days; ***Technical***: 98% in 21 working days, 99% in 42 working days	99.9% 99.9%
Lithuania	Refunds in 30 days of receipt of required documents	7.6 days (ave.)	100% responded to in 20 work days	99.8%
Malaysia	-	-	Within 3 working days	100%
Malta	-	-	80% within five work days and 100% within 20 days	80%
Morocco	100% within three months	57%	-	-
Singapore	95% in one month	98.1%	80% in 15 work days	92.3%
South Africa	21 working days	31.7 days /1	75% within 21 days	75.1%

For notes indicated by "/ (number)", see Notes to Tables section at the end of the chapter, p. 237.

Source: Tax Administration 2015 survey responses.

Table 6.7. **Service standards and performance in 2013: In-person and phone inquiries**

(Countries only shown where an administrative standard is applied in practice)

Country	Dealing with in-person inquiries at tax offices: Standard set for processing in 2013	Dealing with in-person inquiries at tax offices: Result	Answering telephone inquiries: Standard set for processing in 2013	Answering telephone inquiries: Result
OECD countries				
Australia	90% in 15 min.	96%	80% in five minutes (general public), 90% in two minutes (tax agent)	81%, 91%
Austria	Immediately /1	-	Wait time of one minute maximum	37.64 secs
Canada	- /1	-	80% in two minutes for both individuals and business inquiries /2	82%, 82%
Chile	-	-	80%	59%
Denmark	-	-	Achieve satisfaction of 3.8 (scale 1/5)	3.9
Estonia	Within 10 min.	n.a.	Average waiting time of 25 secs.	15.48 secs
Finland	-	-	70% in 60 secs	59%
France	-	-	60% of calls answered in five rings	67%
Greece	-	-	30% of inbound calls in less than six minutes	Average 5.5 mins
Hungary	Waiting time should not exceed 25 mins	6.6 mins	General information system (TCC): 95% of calls made are answered / Client information system (ÜCC): 90% of calls made are answered	99.4% / 95.4%
Ireland	-	-	PAYE: 50% in 30 secs, 85% in 3 min, and 100% in 5 min.; Other: As for PAYE	/1
Israel	-	-	3 mins (for call centres only)	4.08 mins
Italy	-	-	1 900 000	2 252 235
Japan	85% satisfaction rate with service	87%	*(1)* 95% satisfaction rate with service *(2)* 95% receive counselling in 15 min.	*(1)* 94.5% *(2)* 99%
Luxembourg	Appointments by mutual agreement	-	Immediate answer if the question is simple /1	95%
Mexico	-	-	Answer 80% of calls in an average of 22 secs	88%
New Zealand	-	-	*(1)* 70% in 1 min. on priority queue, and *(2)* 70 % in 4 mins. on general queue	*(1)* 64.3%, *(2)* 78.3%
Norway	-	-	Average waiting time max. 6 mins	6.2 mins
Portugal	Average wait time 21 to 24 mins	21.48 mins	Answer 70% to 80% of calls received	72.1%
Turkey	Satisfaction target of 90%	98%	*(1)* Receive 400 000 telephone inquiries *(2)* Answer 80% in 30 seconds	*(1)* 463 630 *(2)* 43.25%
United Kingdom	-	-	Handling 90% of calls	79.4%
United States	-	-	*(1)* 70% level of service; *(2)* average speed of answer within 899 secs	*(1)* 60.5% *(2)* 1 058 secs
Non-OECD countries				
Argentina	-	-	Answering 75%	71%
Brazil	Average waiting time of maximum 15 minutes	10 mins 42 secs	Average waiting time of maximum 3 minutes 50 seconds	3 mins 23 secs
Bulgaria	-	-	Answering 95%	95%
China	-	-	Through rate for incoming calls: 75%-80%	80%
Colombia	-	-	Answering 90%	78%
Hong Kong, China	Peak times: 95% in 10 minutes Other times: 99% in 10 minutes	99.6% 100%	May and June: 85% in 3 minutes, 90% in 4 minutes, Other months: 90% in 3 minutes, 95% in 4 minutes	90.2, 99.1 93.9, 99.1
Indonesia	-	-	Answering 72%	84.3%
Lithuania	-	-	Answering 80%	72%
Malaysia	Waiting time not more than 15 minutes	100%	Answer 80% of calls that went through before the third ring	95%
Malta	-	-	Average wait time of 1 minute	100%
Singapore	80% in 20 minutes	88.7%	Non-peak period: 85% in 1 minute Peak period: 70% in 1 minute	84% 81%
South Africa	-	-	82% first contact resolution	84%

For notes indicated by "/ (number)", see Notes to Tables section at the end of the chapter, p. 237.

Source: Tax Administration 2015 survey responses.

Table 6.8. **Examples of responsive service standards and good standards of performance**

Area of service	Country	Standard set	Performance in 2013
Processing PIT returns with refunds	Estonia	e-filed: 100% in five work days (unless inquiry needed)	100%
	Canada	e-filed: 100% in average of two weeks	1.6 weeks
Resolving taxpayers complaints	Portugal	Resolve (all) within 14-18 days	11 days
	Singapore	Finalise paper-based complaints in six work days, others in four work days	Average of 3.08 work days
Processing VAT returns with refunds	Ireland	e-filed: 100% processed in five days	100%
	Estonia	All in five working days	100%
Replying to written correspondence	Hong Kong	***Simple:*** 95% in seven work days, 99% in nine work days; ***Technical***: 98% in 21 work days, 99% in 42 work days	99.9% for both categories
	Ireland	50% in 10 work days, 85% in 20 work days and 100% in 30 working days	68%, 85%, 93%
	Lithuania	100% responded to in 20 work days	99.8%
Dealing with in-person inquiries	Hong Kong	Peak: 95% in 10 min; other times: 99% in 10 min	99.6%, 100%
	Japan	85% satisfaction rate with service	87%
Answering telephone inquiries	Austria	Wait time of one minute maximum	37.64 secs (aver.)
	Canada	80% in two minutes (both individuals and businesses)	82%, 82%

Tax verification activities

As discussed in Chapter 5, tax audit and verification activities represent a major investment of revenue body resources in surveyed countries. Based on the data in Table 5.7 in Chapter 5, around 40% of surveyed revenue bodies reported that over 30% of staff resources (FTEs) are devoted to tax audit, investigation, and other verification-related activities. For this reason alone, the resources used for these activities and the contribution they make to revenue collections and overall taxpayers' compliance are of considerable interest to all revenue bodies.

For the purposes of this and prior series, "verification activities" are defined as comprising all of the activities typically undertaken by revenue bodies to check whether taxpayers have properly reported their tax liabilities in the returns filed by them. The primary verification activity undertaken by revenue bodies is usually described by the term "tax audit" (including field, desk, or correspondence audits) or "tax control". Less frequently used terms are "examinations", "investigations", and "enquiries". It is also known that across revenue bodies "audit" activities vary in their scope and intensity, and indeed in the precise nature of actions taken by officials that are deemed to constitute an "audit". Revenue bodies also carry out various other activities (e.g. in-depth fraud investigations, income/document matching checks, phone inquiries, computer-based edit and mathematical checks, and inspections of books and records) that can result in changes to taxpayers' reported liabilities. For this series, the information provided aims to reflect all forms of the verification activity undertaken by revenue bodies. *It does not aim to include work, and resultant taxes and penalties, associated with returns filed by taxpayers after follow-up non-filing enforcement related actions.*

Table A10 located at the end of this series sets out aggregates over a 9 year period (2005 to 2013) of the total value of assessments results from all verification activities (and for large taxpayers) reported by revenue bodies for this and prior series. Tables 6.9 to 6.11 give an indication of the scale of tax audit and related verification activities, in terms of the value of assessments resulting from such actions and the numbers of actions taken/ taxpayers reviewed. The key observations are as follows:

All taxpayer categories

- The aggregate value of revenue bodies' verification results (i.e. assessed tax and penalties) as a share of net revenue collections for 2013 vary widely:
  - Four reported results over 8% (i.e. Brazil, Hungary, Italy, and Mexico);
  - Eleven reported results in the range 4 to 8%;
  - Fourteen reported results in the range 2 to 4%;
  - Twenty reported results less than 2% net revenue collections; and
  - Seven revenue bodies did not report any results for verification activities.
- For both Brazil and Italy, the amounts reported were equivalent to just over 17% of annual net revenue collections; not surprisingly, both revenue bodies also report an unusually large inventory of disputed tax debt (see Table 6.14).
- Viewed over a five year period ending in 2013 where relevant data were available, a small number of revenue bodies (including Chile, Cyprus, France, Indonesia, Mexico, Poland, Slovenia, and Spain) reported generally consistent increases in the aggregate value of their verification outputs.
- Reported verification outputs (i.e. numbers of completed actions) across countries vary enormously, even after account is taken of relevant taxpayer population data. There was insufficient information available to fully understand the reasons for these variations but possible influencing factors include differences in: *(1)* the use/ non-use of assessment versus self-assessment procedures; *(2)* the scale of third party information checking programmes, and local audit policies (e.g. the mix of audit types carried out).
- Consistent and fairly significant increases in the numbers of completed verification actions over the period covered can be identified for only four revenue bodies (i.e. Argentina, Canada, and Malaysia) while for many others the reported volumes over the years covered fluctuate widely suggesting deliberate policy choices, possible changes to the interpretation given to "verification activities" and/or errors or inconsistency in data compilation

Large taxpayers

- Verification results for large taxpayers figured prominently in the results reported by many revenue bodies; of the 38 revenue bodies that reported results for large taxpayers, 13 indicated that the value of tax assessments for these taxpayers exceeded one-third of overall verification activities in 2013.
- Seven revenue bodies in OECD countries reporting the existence of a dedicated unit to monitor the tax affairs of large taxpayers failed to report the results of verification activities (i.e. Belgium, Israel, Netherlands, Norway, Spain, Sweden, and Turkey), raising questions as to the comprehensiveness of the arrangements in place for monitoring the compliance of these taxpayers.

Table 6.9. **Verification actions: Value of assessments/total net revenue collections**

	All taxpayers							Large taxpayers						
	Value of completed actions/net tax collections (%)							Value of completed actions/net tax collections (%)						
Country	2007	2008	2009	2010	2011	2012	2013	2007	2008	2009	2010	2011	2012	2013
OECD countries														
Australia	2.8	3.0	3.1	3.7	3.8	3.8	3.9	1.0	1.2	0.8	1.3	0.9	0.8	0.8
Austria	3.3	3.2	2.3	2.4	3.1	3.0	2.5	1.9	2.0	0.9	1.0	1.7	1.8	1.1
Belgium	n.a.	n.a.	7.9	8.9	9.4	n.a.	n.a.	n.a.	n.a.	n.a.	n.a.	n.a.	n.a.	n.a.
Canada	3.2	3.1	3.2	3.9	3.3	3.0	3.1	1.2	1.6	1.2	1.5	1.2	1.1	1.2
Chile	1.1	1.8	2.2	3.6	3.8	4.3	4.0	0.2	0.2	0.1	0.7	0.8	1.2	0.5
Czech Republic	n.a.	1.7	1.8	2.5	2.5	2.6	1.8	n.a.	n.a.	n.a.	n.a.	n.a.	n.a.	0.6
Denmark	n.a.	n.a.	n.a.	2.9	1.9	3.3	3.3	n.a.	n.a.	n.a.	0.4	0.4	2.1	2.6
Estonia	n.a.	0.9	2.0	1.3	1.0	0.8	0.8	n.a.	n.a.	n.a.	n.a.	n.a.	n.a.	n.a.
Finland	0.6	4.4	5.2	1.0	0.8	0.8	0.7	n.a.	n.a.	n.a.	n.a.	n.a.	0.1	0.1
France	2.2	2.5	2.9	4.5	4.4	5.5	4.9	0.6	0.8	1.0	1.6	1.6	2.1	1.7
Germany	3.8	3.8	4.4	3.7	3.5	n.a.	n.a.	2.7	2.7	3.2	2.5	2.4	2.6	2.3
Greece	5.6	5.6	6.3	8.5	6.8	4.8	3.5	4.1	3.6	2.9	5.0	4.8	0.6	0.7
Hungary	6.6	8.6	8.9	8.7	7.6	8.0	9.1	0.6	0.9	1.0	1.2	1.1	1.1	1.3
Iceland	n.a.	n.a.	n.a.	n.a.	n.a.	n.a.	n.a.	n.a.	n.a.	n.a.	n.a.	n.a.	n.a.	n.a.
Ireland	1.3	1.2	1.6	1.5	1.5	1.1	1.2	0.4	0.3	0.4	0.3	0.3	0.2	0.2
Israel	n.a.	3.4	4.2	3.4	3.5	6.8	7.8	n.a.	0.4	0.6	n.a.	n.a.	n.a.	n.a.
Italy	n.a.	13.4	17.0	20.3	23.1	20.5	17.7	n.a.	1.0	2.1	3.6	4.5	3.9	2.7
Japan	1.8	1.6	1.6	2.0	1.5	1.3	1.1	0.5	0.4	0.3	0.6	0.3	0.2	0.2
Korea	3.6	n.a.	n.a.	n.a.	n.a.	3.6	n.a.	n.a.	n.a.	n.a.	n.a.	n.a.	n.a.	n.a.
Luxembourg /1	1.7	0.6	0.9	0.6	0.6	0.6	0.7	n.a.	n.a.	n.a.	n.a.	n.a.	n.a.	n.a.
Mexico	5.1	5.3	6.8	7.6	7.2	6.4	8.9	2.9	3.2	4.1	4.6	4.3	4.0	4.9
Netherlands	n.a.	n.a.	n.a.	n.a.	n.a.	n.a.	n.a.	n.a.	n.a.	n.a.	n.a.	n.a.	n.a.	n.a.
New Zealand	2.1	2.8	2.6	6.2	3.1	2.4	2.3	0.7	1.4	1.2	4.6	1.6	0.7	1.2
Norway	0.7	n.a.	n.a.	n.a.	n.a.	3.2	2.0	n.a.	n.a.	n.a.	n.a.	n.a.	n.a.	n.a.
Poland	0.2	0.7	0.8	0.9	1.0	1.1	1.5	0.0	0.2	0.2	0.3	0.3	0.4	0.5
Portugal	5.0	4.9	9.0	6.8	5.5	5.6	4.1	1.6	1.2	2.5	1.7	1.4	1.9	0.9
Slovak Republic	6.4	8.1	9.6	14.7	17.2	6.2	6.4	0.1	1.2	0.1	0.4	0.05	0.1	0.1
Slovenia	0.8	1.2	1.6	2.4	2.6	2.5	3.3	n.a.	0.1	0.04	n.a.	n.a.	0.2	0.1
Spain	2.9	3.7	4.9	5.3	5.7	6.8	6.5	n.a.	n.a.	0.7	n.a.	n.a.	n.a.	n.a.

Table 6.9. **Verification actions: Value of assessments/total net revenue collections** *(continued)*

	All taxpayers							Large taxpayers						
	Value of completed actions/net tax collections (%)							Value of completed actions/net tax collections (%)						
Country	2007	2008	2009	2010	2011	2012	2013	2007	2008	2009	2010	2011	2012	2013
Sweden	n.a.	0.6	0.4	0.5	0.3	n.a.	n.a.	n.a.	n.a.	n.a.	n.a.	n.a.	n.a.	n.a.
Switzerland	n.a.	0.3	0.5	0.2	0.2	0.2	0.2	n.a.	n.a.	n.a.	n.a.	n.a.	n.a.	n.a.
Turkey	7.8	6.7	8.1	n.a.	n.a.	4.8	8.5	4.5	3.6	4.6	n.a.	n.a.	n.a.	n.a.
United Kingdom	2.1	n.a.	n.a.	4.1	3.2	4.0	4.4	1.0	n.a.	n.a.	1.8	1.8	1.1	1.1
United States	2.2	2.5	3.1	3.1	3.1	2.2	2.0	0.4	0.7	0.6	0.8	0.7	0.5	0.5
Non-OECD countries														
Argentina	2.5	2.4	2.7	2.5	2.5	1.4	1.3	n.a.	1.9	1.9	1.8	1.8	0.8	0.6
Brazil	n.a.	n.a.	n.a.	11.4	11.5	11.7	17.2	n.a.	n.a.	n.a.	7.2	8.3	9.3	14.5
Bulgaria	2.1	2.0	2.2	1.6	2.2	2.7	1.3	0.8	0.4	0.6	0.3	0.7	0.5	0.2
China	n.a.	0.1	0.2	n.a.	n.a.	n.a.	n.a.	n.a.	n.a.	n.a.	n.a.	n.a.	n.a.	n.a.
Colombia	n.a.	n.a.	n.a.	1.1	0.9	0.7	0.7	n.a.	n.a.	n.a.	0.5	0.5	0.4	0.3
Costa Rica	-------- Not covered by the series for these years --------					n.a.	n.a.	-------- Not covered by the series for these years --------					0.9	0.3
Croatia	-------- Not covered by the series for these years --------					1.5	1.4	-------- Not covered by the series for these years --------					n.a.	0.4
Cyprus	7.0	1.0	1.3	6.2	6.3	7.5	6.3	n.a.	n.a.	n.a.	n.a.	n.a.	0.5	0.1
Hong Kong, China	n.a.	n.a.	n.a.	2.1	2.7	3.4	1.9	n.a.	n.a.	n.a.	n.a.	n.a.	n.a.	n.a.
India	n.a.	n.a.	n.a.	0.04	0.1	n.a.	n.a.	n.a.	n.a.	n.a.	n.a.	n.a.	n.a.	n.a.
Indonesia	n.a.	2.1	2.4	3.0	2.4	3.1	4.2	n.a.	n.a.	0.2	n.a.	n.a.	1.3	1.1
Latvia	2.0	2.9	4.1	4.6	5.6	4.2	4.2	0.04	0.02	0.3	n.a.	1.3	0.5	1.6
Lithuania	0.9	1.1	2.9	2.0	1.6	1.8	1.6	n.a.	0.1	0.3	0.01	0.2	0.1	0.2
Malaysia	4.7	2.1	3.9	3.6	2.6	1.5	3.1	0.4	n.a.	n.a.	n.a.	n.a.	n.a.	n.a.
Malta	n.a.	n.a.	n.a.	1.1	0.7	1.2	1.6	n.a.	n.a.	n.a.	n.a.	n.a.	n.a.	n.a.
Morocco	-------- Not covered by the series for these years --------					3.5	4.2	-------- Not covered by the series for these years --------					2.2	2.8
Romania	n.a.	3.2	4.5	6.8	6.0	3.9	5.4	n.a.	0.5	0.8	n.a.	n.a.	0.6	1.5
Russia	n.a.	n.a.	n.a.	6.0	4.1	3.9	3.5	n.a.	n.a.	n.a.	1.7	0.9	0.9	1.1
Saudi Arabia	n.a.	n.a.	n.a.	n.a.	n.a.	n.a.	n.a.	n.a.	n.a.	n.a.	n.a.	n.a.	13.6	16.8
Singapore	0.6	0.5	0.7	0.9	0.8	0.7	0.7	n.a.	n.a.	n.a.	n.a.	n.a.	n.a.	n.a.
South Africa	3.1	n.a.	n.a.	n.a.	2.1	1.7	2.6	n.a.	n.a.	n.a.	n.a.	n.a.	< 0.1	< 0.1
Thailand	-------- Not covered by the series for these years --------					0.9	1.0	-------- Not covered by the series for these years --------					n.a.	n.a.

For notes indicated by "/ (number)", see Notes to Tables section at the end of the chapter, p. 237.
Source: Tax Administration 2015 survey responses.

Table 6.10. **Verification actions: Number completed for all taxpayer categories**

	Number of completed verification actions (nearest 000s) /1						
Country	2007	2008	2009	2010	2011	2012	2013
OECD countries							
Australia	805	847	1 041	808	898	1 268 /2	749 /2
Austria	75	78	81	84	85	89	88
Belgium	4 000 /2	4 026 /2	5 505 /2	4 996 /2	4 537 /2	146 /2	142 /2
Canada /2	2 669	2 856	3 070	2 729	2 857	3 503	3 884
Chile	250	326	388	549	601	512	457
Czech Republic	22	129	139	98	68	66	51
Denmark	n.a.	n.a.	n.a.	74	61	56	50
Estonia	n.a.	2	2	3	3	8	8
Finland	n.a.	n.a.	n.a.	143	131	118 /2	113 /2
France	52	52	52	1 052 /2	1 051 /2	1 434 /2	1 390 /2
Germany	453	448	434	426	411	n.a.	n.a.
Greece	14	13	10	15	22	38	28
Hungary	246	60	60	188	206	176	163
Iceland	n.a.	637	693	n.a.	n.a.	n.a.	n.a.
Ireland	266	361	374	466	558	474	465
Israel /2	n.a.	n.a.	n.a	29	28	70	62
Italy	1 486	1 511	1 309	1 183	1 154	252 /2	246 /2
Japan	1 393	1 417	1 323	1 270	1 216	1 310	1 095
Korea /2	19	15	15	18	18	18	n.a.
Luxembourg	28	29 /2	26 /2	32 /2	37 /2	39 /2	38 /2
Mexico	96	93	88	90	102	114	101
Netherlands	1 446	1 158	1 049	691	559	966	1 190
New Zealand	10	8	8	8	8	7	7
Norway	n.a.	n.a.	78	68	55	70	46
Poland	2 833	2 964	3 058	3 294	3 323	3 450	3 527
Portugal /2	128	138	143	113	91	88	80
Slovak Republic /2	25	53	58	63	61	53	57
Slovenia	6	73	85	100	103	117	140
Spain /2	4 244	4 948	5 386	6 180	7 031	1 405	1 464
Sweden	578	511	375	455	489	495	435
Switzerland	9	10	10	8	8	10 /1	10 /1
Turkey	136	58	68	n.a.	n.a.	47	71
United Kingdom	220	n.a.	n.a.	804	679	677	795
United States	6 310	6 371	6 584	7 246	7 822	7 281	6 756
Non-OECD countries							
Argentina	43	162	146	196	193	153	342
Brazil	n.a.	n.a.	n.a.	24	21	18 /2	20 /2
Bulgaria	243	283	168	n.a.	n.a.	99	99
China	540	440	313	n.a.	n.a.	191	177
Colombia	n.a.	n.a.	n.a.	58	55	66	52
Costa Rica			------ Not covered by the series for these years ------			7 /2	15 /2
Croatia /2			------ Not covered by the series for these years ------			8	39
Cyprus /2	21	18	21	52	30	33	34
Hong Kong, China	n.a.	n.a.	n.a.	81	92	104	120
India	n.a.	380	553	331	355	n.a.	n.a.
Indonesia	68	21	69	65	61	35	51
Latvia	21	28	21	10	9	8	9
Lithuania /2	37	32	33	29	39	87	120
Malaysia	289	1 086	1 390	1 732	1 911	1 935	1 758
Malta /2	1	3	2	0.3	0.3	1	1
Morocco /2			------ Not covered by the series for these years ------			2	1
Romania	54	61	60	71	62	99	87
Russia	2 347	3 030	2 816	2 342	2 171	n.a.	n.a.
Saudi Arabia	n.a.	n.a.	n.a.	n.a.	n.a.	n.a.	n.a.
Singapore	6	7	8	8	10	12	11
South Africa	74	n.a.	n.a.	n.a.	1 169	1 056	1 258
Thailand			------ Not covered by the series for these years ------			64	67

For notes indicated by "/ (number)", see Notes to Tables section at the end of the chapter, p. 237.
Source: Tax Administration 2015 survey responses.

Table 6.11. **Verification actions: Number completed for large taxpayers**

	Number of completed verification actions /1						
Country	2007	2008	2009	2010	2011	2012	2013
OECD countries							
Australia	19 227	15 837	20 752	11 519	12 369	12 405	8 425
Austria	7 209	7 177	5 373	5 143	5 331	4 907	4 535
Belgium	n.a.	n.a.	n.a.	n.a.	n.a.	n.a.	n.a.
Canada /2	1 773	1 719	1 865	1 994	1 932	2 125	2 761
Chile	2 377	561	515	719	829	833	790
Czech Republic	n.a.	n.a.	n.a.	n.a.	n.a.	n.a.	174
Denmark	n.a.	n.a.	n.a.	175	227	563	383
Estonia	n.a.	n.a.	n.a.	n.a.	n.a.	n.a.	n.a.
Finland /2	n.a.	n.a.	n.a.	364	276	205	163
France	1 466	1 589	1 551	6 038	5 738	5 539 /2	5 849 /2
Germany	38 662	39 885	38 988	40 502	41 764	41 365	41 746
Greece	4 827	1 066	1 250	n.a.	n.a.	551	914
Hungary	3 889	1 457	1 477	2 792	3 044	3 077	2 994
Iceland	n.a.	n.a.	n.a.	n.a.	n.a.	n.a.	n.a.
Ireland	7 972	9 002	12 942	12 552	10 200	1 528 /1	1 994
Israel	n.a.	11 341	11 341	n.a.	n.a.	n.a.	n.a.
Italy	2 362	729	866	1 994	1 351	382 /1	361 /1
Japan	5 000	4 000	4 000	3 809	3 447	3 357	2 910
Korea	n.a.	n.a.	n.a.	n.a.	n.a.	n.a.	n.a.
Luxembourg	n.a.	n.a.	n.a.	n.a.	n.a.	n.a.	n.a.
Mexico	1 871	1 296	1 427	1 154	1 166	1 152	988
Netherlands	n.a.	9 900	10 700	26 100	16 000	13 200	10 300
New Zealand	928	583	547	582	491	586	593
Norway	n.a.	n.a.	n.a.	n.a.	n.a.	n.a.	n.a.
Poland	89 810	106 132	113 471	174 818	194 063	208 344	196 161
Portugal	743	1 761	2 256	2 303	2 892	2 037	2 320
Slovak Republic /2	89	562	718	399	398	521	1 028 /3
Slovenia	559	637	422	213	271	248	500
Spain	n.a.	n.a.	n.a.	n.a.	n.a.	n.a.	n.a.
Sweden	n.a.	n.a.	n.a.	n.a.	n.a.	n.a.	n.a.
Switzerland	n.a.	n.a.	n.a.	n.a.	n.a.	n.a.	n.a.
Turkey	6 808	1 545	2 277	n.a.	n.a.	2 038	3 676
United Kingdom	6 968	n.a.	n.a.	2 231	4 477	1 759	1 352
United States	13 551	13 449	13 803	14 833	15 293	16 652	15 449
Non-OECD countries							
Argentina	n.a.	36 924	31 504	37 724	33 496	15 870	20 500
Brazil	n.a.	n.a.	n.a.	2 568	2 532	2 168	2 647
Bulgaria	2 338	2 040	1 875	n.a.	n.a.	1 450	1 113
China	n.a.	n.a.	n.a.	n.a.	n.a.	13	17
Colombia	n.a.	n.a.	n.a.	5 519	7 167	6 120	2 397
Costa Rica		------ Not covered by the series for these years ------				664	631
Croatia /2		------ Not covered by the series for these years ------				n.a.	96
Cyprus	n.a.	n.a.	n.a.	n.a.	n.a.	15	19
Hong Kong, China	n.a.	n.a.	n.a.	n.a.	n.a.	n.a.	n.a.
India	n.a.	n.a.	n.a.	n.a.	n.a.	n.a.	n.a.
Indonesia	n.a.	n.a.	657	n.a.	n.a.	730	2 130
Latvia	252	302	636	n.a.	499	536	687
Lithuania /2	n.a.	107 /2	104 /2	108 /2	2 306	1 107	667
Malaysia	200	n.a.	n.a.	n.a.	n.a.	n.a.	n.a.
Malta	n.a.	n.a.	n.a.	n.a.	n.a.	n.a.	n.a.
Morocco /2		------ Not covered by the series for these years ------				199	127
Romania	775	1 049	1 067	1 975	3 000	1 336	1 073
Russia	n.a.	n.a.	15 565	12 182	11 078	n.a.	n.a.
Saudi Arabia	n.a.	n.a.	n.a.	150	180	269	258
Singapore	n.a.	n.a.	n.a.	n.a.	n.a.	n.a.	n.a.
South Africa	4 387	n.a.	n.a.	n.a.	n.a.	75	187
Thailand		------ Not covered by the series for these years ------				n.a.	n.a.

For notes indicated by "/ (number)", see Notes to Tables section at the end of the chapter, p. 237.
Source: Tax Administration 2015 survey responses.

Tax disputes

Table 6.12 sets out the data provided by some surveyed countries on the numbers and values of tax disputes finalised for years 2008 to 2013, while Table 6.13 provides corresponding information on the numbers and value of work unfinalised at year-end covering the same period. As will be apparent, many countries were unable to report complete data for this category of work while for some of those countries where data are available there are significant variations in the respective volumes and values reported, having regard to factors such as taxpayer population. In the circumstances, only limited observations are possible:

Finalised cases

- Countries reporting exceptionally large numbers of tax dispute cases (e.g. France and Germany) administer systems based on return assessment principles, as opposed to more modern self-assessment systems seen in the majority of countries; over the years, high levels of disputation have been a feature of assessment regimes in many countries and for some have contributed to the decision to introduce systems of self-assessment.
- A trend of increased disputation, albeit generally fairly moderate, can be seen in a few countries (e.g. Australia, Chile, Denmark, Italy and United States) while a downwards trend can be observed in Korea, Russia, and Sweden.

Unfinalised dispute cases

- Relatively large volumes of unfinalised cases at end 2013 (vis-à-vis cases completed in 2013) appear in a number of countries (e.g. Argentina, Belgium (2012), Brazil, Canada, Germany (2012), Indonesia, Japan, Latvia, South Africa, and Thailand).

Chapter 9 provides further details on the framework within which administrative reviews are conducted by the revenue bodies surveyed.

Table 6.12. **Tax disputes in administrative review: Finalised cases**

Country	Number of cases finalised in year						Tax amount of cases finalised in year (in millions in local currency)					
	2008	2009	2010	2011	2012	2013	2008	2009	2010	2011	2012	2013
OECD countries												
Australia	16 788 /1	18 638 /1	21 807 /1	24 513 /1	33 272 /1	32 642 /1	n.a.	n.a.	n.a.	n.a.	n.a.	n.a.
Austria	133 924	136 361	145 539	145 440	135 449	131 865	n.a.	n.a.	n.a.	n.a.	n.a.	n.a.
Belgium	n.a.	n.a.	4 118	3 534	75 124	n.a.	n.a.	n.a.	n.a.	n.a.	n.a.	n.a.
Canada	65 663	66 637	46 354	50 485	57 590	55 885	3 550	3 270	5 315	4 216	3 837	4 308
Chile	2 144	2 154	1 867	2 738	4 008	3 004	n.a.	n.a.	167 886	181 128	746 388	349 852
Czech Republic	24 371	23 152	21 008	5 235	5 491	4 481	2 660	3 015	1 925	377	533	5 202
Denmark	n.a.	n.a.	67 615	93 448	65 460	128 747	n.a.	n.a.	n.a.	n.a.	n.a.	n.a.
Estonia	n.a.	n.a.	n.a.	n.a.	475	629	n.a.	n.a.	n.a.	n.a.	13	553
Finland	78 530	73 113	66 406	64 548	80 806	68 394	n.a.	n.a.	n.a.	n.a.	n.a.	n.a.
France	3 770 523	3 822 912	3 615 744	3 580 454	3 552 823	3 501 259	n.a.	n.a.	19 271	10 415	7 890 /1	7 300 /1
Germany	5 536 353	6 105 841	5 252 592	4 149 543	3 648 073	n.a.	n.a.	n.a.	n.a.	n.a.	n.a.	n.a.
Greece /1	n.a.	n.a.	n.a.	n.a.	n.a.	n.a.	n.a.	n.a.	n.a.	n.a.	n.a.	n.a.
Hungary	14 518	1 923	12 318	12 654	14 127	12 973 /1	n.a.	n.a.	39 848	47 941	47 337	51 778 /2
Iceland	n.a.	n.a.	n.a.	n.a.	21 391	20 986	n.a.	n.a.	n.a.	n.a.	n.a.	n.a.
Ireland	59	45	63	74	110	9 /1	n.a.	n.a.	n.a.	n.a.	n.a.	n.a.
Israel	36 102	38 896	n.a.	n.a.	5 477	4 752	n.a.	n.a.	n.a.	n.a.	6 914	6 815
Italy	n.a.	n.a.	223 458	196 135	84 052	101 485	n.a.	n.a.	45 648	40 138	4 464	4 253
Japan	7 360	8 127	7 590	8 463	7 478	6 904	n.a.	n.a.	n.a.	n.a.	n.a.	n.a.
Korea	9 872	9 667	5 940	5 905	5 953	5 443	2 693 205	2 765 277	1 010 502	1 845 262	1 651 203	1 842 192
Luxembourg	488 /1	465 /1	419 /1	294 /1	390 /1	436 /1	n.a.	n.a.	n.a.	n.a.	n.a.	n.a.
Mexico	33 294	33 709	28 829	31 990	32 663	20 757	62 333	70 459	69 696	117 546	100 775	184 519
Netherlands	352 000	342 000	400 009	439 033	473 000	412 000	n.a.	n.a.	n.a.	n.a.	n.a.	n.a.
New Zealand /1	66	61	86	90	75	66	79	214	234	38	124	358
Norway	64 527	64 902	64 572	82 270	97 926	87 292	n.a.	n.a.	n.a.	n.a.	n.a.	n.a.
Poland	n.a.	n.a.	n.a.	n.a.	n.a.	n.a.	n.a.	n.a.	n.a.	n.a.	n.a.	n.a.
Portugal	61 541	66 522	52 684	49 756	44 001	52 099	n.a.	n.a.	n.a.	n.a.	1 041	257
Slovak Republic	4 478	5 455	4 737	5 590	4 555	5 696	n.a.	n.a.	n.a.	n.a.	n.a.	n.a.
Slovenia	15 025	27 230	13 618	11 999	12 558	14 662	n.a.	n.a.	n.a.	n.a.	n.a.	n.a.

Country	Number of cases finalised in year						Tax amount of cases finalised in year (in millions in local currency)					
	2008	2009	2010	2011	2012	2013	2008	2009	2010	2011	2012	2013
Spain /1	153 478	171 323	164 000	184 670	190 374	n.a.	n.a.	n.a.	n.a.	n.a.	n.a.	n.a.
Sweden	11 500	10 100	9 300	8 900	9 900	9 800	n.a.	n.a.	n.a.	n.a.	n.a.	n.a.
Switzerland	n.a.	n.a.	171	196	471 /1	520 /1	n.a.	n.a.	n.a.	n.a.	n.a.	n.a.
Turkey	n.a.	n.a.	n.a.	n.a.	n.a.	n.a.	n.a.	n.a.	n.a.	n.a.	n.a.	n.a.
United Kingdom	n.a.	n.a.	46 045	56 228	n.a.	n.a.	n.a.	n.a.	n.a.	n.a.	n.a.	n.a.
United States	106 722	112 886	133 090	142 553	144 453	131 176	26 475	25 286	25 827	23 691	29 761	32 989
Non-OECD countries												
Argentina	n.a.	n.a.	1 142	929	1 868	1 755	n.a.	n.a.	342	412	478	797
Brazil	n.a.	n.a.	85 597	93 404	71 439	93 963	n.a.	n.a.	94 000	104 000	86 975	126 023
Bulgaria	2 891	3 728	4 185	4 858	4 479	4 152	331	633	823	1 017	947	704
China	n.a.	n.a.	n.a.	n.a.	n.a.	n.a.	n.a.	n.a.	n.a.	n.a.	n.a.	n.a.
Colombia	n.a.	n.a.	2 334	3 019	n.a.	n.a.	n.a.	n.a.	946 342	961 012	727 881	1 351 845
Costa Rica	------ Not covered by the series for these years ------				511 /1	469 /1	------ Not covered by the series for these years ------				29 785	28 422
Croatia	------ Not covered by the series for these years ------				n.a.	n.a.	------ Not covered by the series for these years ------				n.a.	n.a.
Cyprus	88	95	47	53	12 /1	0 /1	6	3	1	51	9 /1	0 /1
Hong Kong, China	n.a.	n.a.	68 525	66 186	70 365	70 120	n.a.	n.a.	n.a.	n.a.	n.a.	n.a.
India	n.a.	n.a.	n.a.	n.a.	n.a.	n.a.	n.a.	n.a.	n.a.	n.a.	2 595 566	2 874 438
Indonesia	15 904	18 613	12 524	16 130	15 790	14 286	8 246 169	15 108 704	n.a.	n.a.	14 307 558	14 720 173
Latvia	309	265	311	274	386	758	36	n.a.	13	11	31	40
Lithuania	492	614	474	381	122	99	139	277	175	124	26	27
Malaysia	n.a.	n.a.	113	101	215	265	n.a.	n.a.	n.a.	n.a.	n.a.	n.a.
Malta	2 561	1 866	n.a.	113	135	61	n.a.	n.a.	151	n.a.	n.a.	n.a.
Morocco	------ Not covered by the series for these years ------				136 906	74 988	------ Not covered by the series for these years ------				n.a.	n.a.
Romania	473	467	401	493	19 039 /1	11 489 /1	2 013	1 641	3 088	6 031	8 117	5 705
Russia /1	45 765	59 037	52 913	48 706	43 771	39 623	161 418	281 114	346 954	322 489	349 646	353 263
Saudi Arabia	118	136	238	288	530	800	n.a.	n.a.	n.a.	n.a.	367	539
Singapore	n.a.	n.a.	n.a.	n.a.	n.a.	n.a.	n.a.	n.a.	n.a.	n.a.	n.a.	n.a.
South Africa /1	410	427	438	459	393	453	n.a.	n.a.	4 567	4 679	5 792	6 937
Thailand	------ Not covered by the series for these years ------				1 019	644	------ Not covered by the series for these years ------				2 034	952

For notes indicated by "/ (number)", see Notes to Tables section at the end of the chapter, p. 238.
Source: Tax Administration 2015 survey responses.

Table 6.13. **Tax disputes in administrative review: Unfinalised cases at year-end**

Country	Number of cases not finalised at year-end						Tax amount of cases not finalised in year (in millions in local currency)					
	2008	2009	2010	2011	2012	2013	2008	2009	2010	2011	2012	2013
OECD countries												
Australia	2 714 /1	3 458 /1	4 450 /1	4 693 /1	5 565 /1	4 430 /1	n.a.	n.a.	n.a.	n.a.	n.a.	n.a.
Austria	n.a.	n.a.	18 065	15 638	15 122	11 743	n.a.	n.a.	n.a.	n.a.	n.a.	n.a.
Belgium	n.a.	n.a.	19 932	21 139	89 261	n.a.	n.a.	n.a.	n.a.	n.a.	n.a.	n.a.
Canada	80 551	109 264	158 454	191 168	203 751	215 668	10 600	14 780	12 553	13 849	19 708	21 740
Chile	178	169	131	459	1 012	1 518	n.a.	n.a.	35 673	104 069	186 856	25 378
Czech Republic	5 724	4 160	3 818	3 662	3 772	3 274	4 675	2 538	937	4 076	990	4 239
Denmark	n.a.	n.a.	n.a.	8 661	n.a.	n.a.	n.a.	n.a.	n.a.	n.a.	n.a.	n.a.
Estonia	n.a.	n.a.	n.a.	n.a.	19	22	n.a.	n.a.	n.a.	n.a.	<1	<1
Finland	37 043	32 345	32 406	39 089	25 938	24 932	n.a.	n.a.	n.a.	n.a.	n.a.	n.a.
France	n.a.	n.a.	162 850	166 125	197 759	208 843	n.a.	n.a.	n.a.	n.a.	n.a.	n.a.
Germany	6 681 448	5 795 332	4 308 249	3 648 705	4 024 325	n.a.	n.a.	n.a.	n.a.	n.a.	n.a.	n.a.
Greece /1	n.a.	n.a.	n.a.	155 831	n.a.	n.a.	n.a.	n.a.	n.a.	n.a.	n.a.	n.a.
Hungary	15 990	2 292	1 649	1 966	2 301	2 219 /1	n.a.	n.a.	64 364	52 075	60 168	85 206 /2
Iceland	n.a.	n.a.	n.a.	n.a.	2 396	3 265	n.a.	n.a.	n.a.	n.a.	n.a.	n.a.
Ireland	6	7	8	11	6	4 /1	n.a.	n.a.	n.a.	n.a.	n.a.	n.a.
Israel	721	673	n.a.	n.a.	266	358	n.a.	n.a.	n.a.	n.a.	n.a.	n.a.
Italy	10 769	9 388	528 730	561 240	n.a.	n.a.	n.a.	n.a.	88 006	108 652	n.a.	n.a.
Japan	3 330	3 397	3 856	3 580	3 486	3 604	n.a.	n.a.	n.a.	n.a.	n.a.	n.a.
Korea	1 911	2 018	653	534	592	544	2 977 247	2 900 129	299 481	173 588	311 376	205 132
Luxembourg	n.a.	312 /1	280 /1	196 /1	18 /1	12 /1	n.a.	n.a.	n.a.	n.a.	n.a.	n.a.
Mexico	2 006	3 403	3 735	5 018	3 576	3 422	38 008	13 613	64 683	86 917	310 983	87 111
Netherlands	n.a.	n.a.	n.a.	n.a.	n.a.	n.a.	n.a.	n.a.	n.a.	n.a.	n.a.	n.a.
New Zealand /1	24	18	21	16	8	3	100	163	5	23	2	14
Norway	n.a.	n.a.	21 921	13 909	11 195	11 834	n.a.	n.a.	n.a.	n.a.	n.a.	n.a.
Poland	n.a.	n.a.	n.a.	n.a.	n.a.	n.a.	n.a.	n.a.	n.a.	n.a.	n.a.	n.a.
Portugal	16 724	6 165	3 815	3 561	2 360	3 291	n.a.	n.a.	n.a.	n.a.	261	198
Slovak Republic	981	725	975	1 271	896	985	n.a.	n.a.	n.a.	n.a.	n.a.	n.a.
Slovenia	3 660	3 221	2 337	1 800	2 695	4 123	n.a.	n.a.	n.a.	n.a.	n.a.	n.a.

Country	Number of cases not finalised at year-end						Tax amount of cases not finalised in year (in millions in local currency)					
	2008	2009	2010	2011	2012	2013	2008	2009	2010	2011	2012	2013
Spain /1	n.a.	n.a.	186 969	220 484	n.a.	n.a.	n.a.	n.a.	n.a.	n.a.	n.a.	n.a.
Sweden	1 800	1 700	1 200	1 000	1 000	1 000	n.a.	n.a.	n.a.	n.a.	n.a.	n.a.
Switzerland	n.a.	n.a.	258	220	465 /1	557 /1	n.a.	n.a.	n.a.	n.a.	n.a.	n.a.
Turkey	n.a.	n.a.	n.a.	n.a.	n.a.	n.a.	n.a.	n.a.	n.a.	n.a.	n.a.	n.a.
United Kingdom	n.a.	n.a.	n.a.	n.a.	n.a.	n.a.	n.a.	n.a.	n.a.	n.a.	n.a.	n.a.
United States	59 899	72 002	72 779	76 633	66 293	59 346	61 693	64 623	66 183	67 836	66 827	57 868
Non-OECD countries												
Argentina	n.a.	n.a.	1 898	1 891	1 831	2 363	n.a.	n.a.	1 425	2 068	1 983	3 055
Brazil	n.a.	n.a.	178 081	174 849	201 077	209 777	n.a.	n.a.	53 000	51 000	82 360	118 005
Bulgaria	624	769	929	1 590	1 781	1 722	167	179	237	n.a.	378	334
China	n.a.	n.a.	n.a.	n.a.	n.a.	n.a.	n.a.	n.a.	n.a.	n.a.	n.a.	n.a.
Colombia	n.a.	n.a.	2 940	2 064	n.a.	n.a.	n.a.	n.a.	1 733 099	1 355 463	789 981	1 383 055
Costa Rica	------ Not covered by the series for these years ------				161 /1	219 /1	------ Not covered by the series for these years ------				98 573	105 917
Croatia	------ Not covered by the series for these years ------				n.a.	n.a.	------ Not covered by the series for these years ------				n.a.	n.a.
Cyprus	142	87	25	31	3 /1	7 /1	133	55	35	9	2 /1	3 /1
Hong Kong, China	n.a.	n.a.	25 826	26 689	28 986	31 165	n.a.	n.a.	n.a.	n.a.	n.a.	n.a.
India	n.a.	n.a.	n.a.	n.a.	n.a.	n.a.	n.a.	n.a.	n.a.	n.a.	n.a.	n.a.
Indonesia	6 284	7 326	9 580	9 384	8 569	9 161	16 370 897	16 134 468	26 315 903	13 420 196	14 682 748	29 065 595
Latvia	355	312	409	421	618	587	49	n.a.	n.a.	n.a.	n.a.	n.a.
Lithuania	77	51	17	24	92	88	n.a.	n.a.	n.a.	n.a.	n.a.	n.a.
Malaysia	n.a.	n.a.	24	19	51	125	n.a.	n.a.	n.a.	n.a.	n.a.	n.a.
Malta	n.a.	n.a.	n.a.	n.a.	211	120	n.a.	n.a.	n.a.	n.a.	n.a.	n.a.
Morocco	------ Not covered by the series for these years ------				25 920	32 104	------ Not covered by the series for these years ------				n.a.	n.a.
Romania	104	217	307	268	2 109 /1	2 363 /1	282	977	3 158	2 952	1 507	3 304
Russia	4 586	5 058	5 031	3 777	2 965	2 510	n.a.	5 031	3 777	3 252	n.a.	n.a.
Saudi Arabia	n.a.	44	n.a.	391	302	1098	n.a.	n.a.	n.a.	n.a.	499	346
Singapore	n.a.	n.a.	n.a.	n.a.	n.a.	n.a.	n.a.	n.a.	n.a.	n.a.	n.a.	n.a.
South Africa /1	n.a.	n.a.	569	505	612	688	n.a.	n.a.	7 895	10 373	12 807	13 148
Thailand	------ Not covered by the series for these years ------				289	433	------ Not covered by the series for these years ------				6 787	7 983

For notes indicated by "/ (number)", see Notes to Tables section at the end of the chapter, p. 238.
Source: Tax Administration 2015 survey responses.

Tax debts and their collection

The collection of tax debts is another important responsibility of almost all revenue bodies. As noted in Chapter 2, Table 2.1, revenue bodies typically operate with a dedicated tax debt collection function to pursue the non-payment of tax debts. In many countries, significant staff resources are devoted to taking action to secure the payment of overdue tax debts, as discussed in Chapter 5. And as described in Chapter 9, most revenue bodies have been given an extensive range of powers to pursue enforced debt collection action in a cost effective way.

Good practice in tax debt collection

In 2013/14, the FTA undertook a study into the tax debt collection practices and experiences of revenue bodies in 14 countries. The study report, published in October 2014, provides a wealth of practical examples, making it a unique and valuable source of reference to revenue bodies. Box 6.3 sets out a summary of essential features identified from the practices and experiences of participating revenue bodies.

Box 6.3. **Essential features of a modern tax debt collection capability**

The report provides a comprehensive overview of the modern tax debt collection function, describing the following essential features:

- **Advanced Analytics**. In the past revenue bodies may have focused on managing debts, rather than debtors. Debts would all be treated the same, which meant, for example, that reminders were sent to every late payer, even when experience shows that many debtors just ignore these letters. The application of advanced analytics makes it possible to use all the information revenue bodies have about taxpayers to accurately target debtors with the right intervention at the right time. This eliminates the cost of ineffective interventions and improves revenue flow. Advanced analytic techniques also make it possible to experiment with different interventions and rapidly assess their effectiveness. As a result some countries have been able to achieve dramatic positive results at very low cost.
- **Treatment Strategies**. The tax debt collection function needs to be able to choose from a wide range of interventions, ranging from soft measures, designed to prevent people from falling into debt in the first place, through to tough enforcement measures. The report describes a large number of different collection and recovery techniques currently being employed by FTA member countries.
- **Call Centres**. Outbound call centres are commonly used in private sector debt collection operations because they make it possible to pursue a large number of debts very efficiently. Revenue bodies are making increasing use of outbound call centres too. The report describes the way in which a debt collection call centre is commonly structured and how to manage the workflow. It discusses the capabilities outbound call centres need to have in terms of technology and in terms of the staff who work there. The report also outlines common approaches to the measurement and management of performance within the call centre.
- **Organisation**. Debt collection is a specialist function and is usually organised as such. It makes sense to group some specific types of taxpayer together, for example large businesses. For the very large number of debtors in the small and mid-sized business segment, it is more important to use analytics to choose the correct intervention.

Box 6.3. **Essential features of a modern tax debt collection capability** *(continued)*

The debt collection function can then be organised around key disciplines, such as call centre management, liquidation, and face-to-face interventions. Choosing the correct key performance indicators is essential if the day to day operations of the collection function are to remain correctly aligned with the desired outcomes. Debtor behaviour is dynamic and so a commitment to continuous improvement will ensure that the organisation is responsive to those changes.

- **Debtors Who Have Gone Abroad**. As people and businesses move around the world more frequently the number of tax debtors who have left the country in which the debt was incurred is growing. One of the keys to addressing these challenges is international assistance and co-operation, particularly in the form of Assistance in Collection Articles in agreements between countries. The report describes the challenges facing revenue bodies and the tools and techniques that are available to tackle these challenges.

Source: Working smarter in tax debt management, Forum on Tax Administration, OECD, October 2014.

Tax debt collection performance

For survey and comparative analysis purposes, outstanding tax debts are defined as the total amount of tax (including any interest and penalties) that is overdue for payment at the end of each fiscal period. By virtue of this definition, the level of "outstanding tax debts" is intended to include tax debts whose collection has been deferred (e.g. as a result of an agreed extension of time to pay or a payment arrangement).

For this edition of the series, data for year-end tax debt were sought in respect of both aggregate tax debt (that *includes* the amount of debt attributable to disputes) and aggregate tax debt (that *excludes* the amount of debts that are the subject of a dispute), sometimes referred to as "collectible tax debt". *(NB: In previous editions of this series, only tax debts excluding disputed tax debt were surveyed and reported).* This aspect of the latest survey caused a number of complications for both revenue bodies and when compiling and analysing the latest reported data on debt collection for this series:

1. Some revenue bodies only measure and are able to report aggregate tax debt (*including* disputed debt).
2. In light of 1), it became apparent that data and related ratios reported in previous editions of the series for some countries were incorrect, overstating their debt position and distorting the ratios reported etc. and related analyses.

Aggregate Tables A.7 to A.9 located in the Annex A of this series set out aggregates over an extended period (generally 2005 to 2013) of: *(1)* year-end tax outstanding (Table A.7); *(2)* tax debt written off (Table A.8), taxes collected from enforced collection action (Table A.9), and numbers of year-end tax debt cases (Table A.9) reported for this and prior series.

Tables 6.14 to 6.16 present these data using various ratios to place the data in a relative and comparative context. Cross-country comparisons of case volume data need to be interpreted with care because, for some revenue bodies, the volumes reported relate to "number of taxpayers" (i.e. for those revenue bodies with integrated accounting systems) while for others the volumes reported are on an individual "tax type" basis (i.e. for those revenue bodies without integrated accounting systems).

Included in Table 6.14 is the ratio of aggregate year-end tax debts (i.e. all unpaid taxes), both *inclusive* and *exclusive* of disputed tax debts, as a proportion of net revenue collections for the year concerned. Also shown for those countries where all data were available are corresponding computations of "non-collectible year-end tax debt/total year-end tax debt" to reflect the incidence of disputation within the overall inventory of tax debts.

Drawing on the data in Tables 6.14 to 6.16 a number of observations can be made:

Aggregate tax debt (including disputed tax debts)

- The overall incidence of aggregate tax debts in OECD countries rose marginally in the years 2011 to 2013-from around 22% to just over 24% – although the computed ratios are significantly impacted by two abnormal "outlier" results (see next point).
- There are significant variations in the incidence of year-end aggregate tax debt as a share of net revenue collections across all countries, including two large "outlier" results (i.e. Brazil and Greece) and one "extreme" outlier result (i.e. Italy). The precise reasons for these "outlier" results have not been identified, although as observed in respect of data reported in Table 6.9 both Brazil and Italy have significant amounts of tax revenue associated with their verification activities.
- For the 19 OECD countries where data are provided the incidence of disputed debt as a share of the overall debt inventory (see columns eight to ten of Table 6.14), while averaging around one-third, also varies to a fair degree, with seven countries reporting ratios in excess of 40%.

Aggregate tax debt (excluding disputed tax debts)

- The incidence of tax debts (undisputed), as reflected in the relative value of debt inventories, varies enormously across surveyed revenue bodies, suggesting significant variations in the levels of payment compliance; applying the benchmark ratio "undisputed tax debt as a share of net revenue collections" for 2013 as a broad indicator of the relative magnitude of the collectible debt inventory:
  - Ten revenue bodies had a ratio < 5% (i.e. Austria, Denmark, Estonia, Hong Kong (China), Ireland, Netherlands, Norway, Singapore, Thailand and United Kingdom);
  - Thirteen revenue bodies had a ratio between 5 and 10%;
  - Six revenue bodies had a ratio between 10-20%;
  - Eight revenue bodies had a ratio over 20% (the highest over 190%); and
  - Twenty revenue bodies, including twelve in OECD countries, were unable to report data for tax debts (excluding disputed debt).
- Viewed over the three years (2011 to 2013), the overall incidence of tax debts/ net revenue collections in OECD countries was fairly stable at around 21 percent, although the computed ratios are significantly impacted by the two "outlier" results.
- Acknowledging that the observation is confined to three years only (2011 to 2013), the data shows a clear downwards trend (reflecting improved payment compliance and/or collection effectiveness) in 15 countries (i.e. Bulgaria, Hong Kong (China), India, Ireland, Lithuania, Malaysia, Malta, Mexico, New Zealand, Portugal, Singapore, Slovak Republic, Slovenia, United Kingdom and United States). On the other hand, an upwards trend is observed for five countries (i.e. Belgium, Cyprus, Czech Republic, Italy and Poland).

  There were insufficient data for 19 countries to determine this ratio and its movement over the period reviewed.

Table 6.14. **Tax debt – year-end aggregates**

Country	Total year-end tax debt (**including** disputed debt) / net revenue collections for fiscal year (%)			Total year-end tax debt (**excluding** disputed debt)/net revenue collections for fiscal year (%)			Non-collectible year-end tax debt/ total year-end tax debt (%)		
	2011	2012	2013	2011	2012	2013	2011	2012	2013
OECD countries									
Australia /1	10.1	10.5	10.7	5.2	5.5	5.7	48.9	47.6	46.7
Austria	8.5	8.5	9.0	2.5	2.4	2.4	70.9	72.1	73.1
Belgium	24.6	24.1	23.4	9.2	15.9	16.3	62.3	33.9	30.1
Canada	12.7	12.3	12.5	9.2	8.9	9.1	27.7	27.7	27.4
Chile	n.a.	n.a.	n.a.	60.6	62.4	68.6	n.a.	n.a.	n.a.
Czech Republic	n.a.	n.a.	n.a.	14.7	16.8	18.1	n.a.	n.a.	n.a.
Denmark	7.4	7.2	6.5	n.a.	n.a.	4.9	n.a.	n.a.	24.9
Estonia	7.5	5.8	4.4	n.a.	n.a.	n.a.	n.a.	n.a.	n.a.
Finland	8.0	8.2	7.4	n.a.	n.a.	n.a.	n.a.	n.a.	n.a.
France	9.6	11.1	10.9	6.8	8.0	7.7	28.8	28.0	29.1
Germany	3.3	3.2	n.a.	1.8	1.7	n.a.	45.8	46.3	n.a.
Greece	103.5	115.7	132.7	n.a.	n.a.	n.a.	n.a.	n.a.	n.a.
Hungary	23.0	21.7	21.8	21.4	21.0	21.1	7.0	3.5	3.3
Iceland	24.2	n.a.	n.a.	n.a.	n.a.	n.a.	n.a.	n.a.	n.a.
Ireland	5.8	4.6	4.0	3.8	2.7	2.2	33.7	41.2	45.2
Israel	14.3	10.1	9.0	3.5	6.8	5.8	75.7	32.8	35.5
Italy	207.8	229.5	257.0	154.4	169.6	190.8	25.7	26.1	25.8
Japan	3.7	3.5	3.1	n.a.	n.a.	n.a.	n.a.	n.a.	n.a.
Korea	3.0	3.1	3.4	n.a.	n.a.	n.a.	n.a.	n.a.	n.a.
Luxembourg	14.6	15.8	15.0	n.a.	n.a.	n.a.	n.a.	n.a.	n.a.
Mexico	52.5	44.3	31.5	20.9	17.1	12.3	60.3	61.3	60.9
Netherlands	7.7	6.9	6.6	3.9	3.8	3.8	49.4	44.9	42.2
New Zealand /1	10.3	10.3	9.2	9.4	9.1	8.2	8.6	11.9	11.1
Norway	3.7	3.0	3.1	2.9	2.3	2.4	20.2	23.6	22.0
Poland	n.a.	13.2	16.4	11.5	12.5	15.6	n.a.	5.7	4.4
Portugal	39.0	35.7	31.7	27.9	26.0	24.2	28.5	27.2	23.7
Slovak Republic	n.a.	n.a.	n.a.	67.4	36.1	33.0	n.a.	n.a.	n.a.
Slovenia	13.3	14.7	14.0	10.7	9.9	8.6	20.0	32.8	38.8
Spain	11.7	13.2	13.9	n.a.	n.a.	n.a.	n.a.	n.a.	n.a.
Sweden	2.2	2.3	2.5	n.a.	n.a.	n.a.	n.a.	n.a.	n.a.
Switzerland	2.5	1.9	1.8	n.a.	n.a.	n.a.	n.a.	n.a.	n.a.
Turkey	n.a.	n.a.	n.a.	n.a.	n.a.	n.a.	n.a.	n.a.	n.a.
United Kingdom	7.4	6.7	6.5	3.5	2.8	2.6	53.4	57.9	59.9
United States	14.4	13.0	11.0	11.0	9.9	8.7	23.5	23.9	21.0
OECD av. (unw.)	22.6	22.8	24.2	21.0	20.5	21.5	38.4	34.1	32.9
Non-OECD countries									
Argentina	6.0	5.9	8.4	n.a.	n.a.	n.a.	n.a.	n.a.	n.a.
Brazil	108.7	117.7	117.8	21.1	34.2	27.9	80.6	71.0	76.3
Bulgaria	14.0	24.4	16.1	27.3	22.9	15.3	n.a.	6.0	4.5
China	n.a.	n.a.	n.a.	n.a.	n.a.	n.a.	n.a.	n.a.	n.a.
Colombia	n.a.	n.a.	n.a.	16.2	n.a.	n.a.	n.a.	n.a.	n.a.
Costa Rica		0.1	0.2		n.a.	n.a.		n.a.	n.a.
Croatia		36.3	35.3		n.a.	n.a.		n.a.	n.a.
Cyprus	44.3	46.7	52.2	34.0	35.5	47.6	23.3	23.9	8.8
Hong Kong, China	40.8	32.4	29.1	4.9	4.2	4.0	87.9	87.1	86.1
India	68.9	82.7	87.0	26.0	24.9	19.1	62.2	69.9	78.1
Indonesia	13.0	8.5	8.4	6.0	0.8	1.2	53.5	91.0	86.3
Latvia	32.6	32.0	29.5	22.9	n.a.	n.a.	29.7	n.a.	n.a.
Lithuania	11.3	9.7	7.3	9.6	8.9	6.4	14.7	8.7	13.3
Malaysia	15.0	12.8	11.4	10.3	7.6	7.1	31.5	40.6	37.7
Malta	39.8	46.3	52.8	25.2	23.9	23.2	36.6	48.4	56.1
Morocco		11.8	11.9		n.a.	n.a.		n.a.	n.a.
Romania	47.7	42.3	42.2	n.a.	10.7	8.6	n.a.	74.8	79.6
Russia	13.1	10.3	10.2	11.0	9.7	9.7	16.6	5.2	4.7
Saudi Arabia	n.a.	n.a.	n.a.	n.a.	n.a.	n.a.	n.a.	n.a.	n.a.
Singapore	n.a.	n.a.	n.a.	1.7	1.3	0.9	n.a.	n.a.	n.a.
South Africa	12.8	11.7	9.9	10.7	10.2	8.5	16.4	13.5	14.1
Thailand	n.a	n.a.	n.a.	n.a.	0.9	1.0	n.a.	n.a.	n.a.

For notes indicated by "/ (number)", see Notes to Tables section at the end of the chapter, p. 239.

Source: Tax Administration 2015 survey responses.

Table 6.15. **Tax debts: Debt written off as a share of debt inventory**

	Debt written off /value of tax debt inventory at year beginning (excluding disputed debt) (%)									
Country	2005	2006	2007	2008	2009	2010	2011	2012	2013	Average: 2005-13
OECD countries										
Australia	32.5	11.1	15.3	16.9	20.4	14.1	26.2	18.6	27.7	19.9
Austria	26.8	25.1	28.7	36.4	32.4	29.1	27.1	24.8	29.3	29.7
Belgium	n.a.	n.a.	n.a.	n.a.	n.a.	15.5	22.8	12.3	10.2	15.2
Canada	14.6	10.3	9.3	9.9	9.1	8.7	8.9	9.6	9.6	9.3
Chile	n.a.	n.a.	n.a.	2.4	1.7	3.4	8.4	3.6	4.4	4.0
Czech Republic	9.3	10.7	13.6	n.a.	13.7	6.6	12.5	23.5	24.8	15.8
Denmark	n.a.	n.a.	n.a.	n.a.	n.a.	n.a.	n.a.	n.a.	n.a.	n.a.
Estonia	n.a.	n.a.	n.a.	n.a.	n.a.	n.a.	n.a.	n.a.	n.a.	n.a.
Finland	n.a.	n.a.	n.a.	n.a.	n.a.	n.a.	n.a.	n.a.	n.a.	n.a.
France	16.2	17.4	19.8	18.5	15.1	14.5	11.3	11.9	11.4	14.6
Germany	69.1	75.7	56.8	52.6	69.7	58.3	46.3	47.8	n.a.	55.3
Greece	n.a.	n.a.	n.a.	n.a.	n.a.	n.a.	n.a.	n.a.	n.a.	n.a.
Hungary	33.2	32.6	34.7	30.4	32.2	30.1	45.0	36.0	35.8	34.9
Iceland	n.a.	n.a.	n.a.	n.a.	n.a.	n.a.	n.a.	n.a.	n.a.	n.a.
Ireland	15.2	14.4	14.9	14.4	18.0	23.1	21.7	21.8	22.3	19.5
Israel	n.a.	n.a.	n.a.	6.1	5.8	n.a.	n.a.	1.2	2.1	3.8
Italy	n.a.	n.a.	n.a.	n.a.	n.a.	n.a.	n.a.	1.3	1.5	1.4
Japan	n.a.	n.a.	n.a.	n.a.	n.a.	n.a.	n.a.	n.a.	n.a.	n.a.
Korea /1	n.a.	n.a.	n.a.	n.a.	n.a.	n.a.	n.a.	n.a.	n.a.	n.a.
Luxembourg	n.a.	n.a.	n.a.	n.a.	n.a.	n.a.	n.a.	n.a.	n.a.	n.a.
Mexico	20.3	32.0	53.4	56.5	77.7	37.9	50.5	20.0	44.3	48.6
Netherlands	32.7	24.5	41.7	37.1	22.4	25.4	32.4	32.2	30.7	31.7
New Zealand	n.a.	n.a.	n.a.	n.a.	n.a.	15.1	17.6	19.2	20.7	18.1
Norway	13.6	6.6	2.5	4.8	7.9	6.5	7.2	7.5	8.6	6.4
Poland	2.2	1.1	0.9	0.5	0.4	0.7	0.4	n.a.	0.4	0.6
Portugal	n.a.	n.a.	n.a.	n.a.	n.a.	n.a.	7.8	5.4	6.4	6.5
Slovak Republic	34.1	22.2	9.2	16.7	18.0	23.1	18.0	6.9	21.1	16.2
Slovenia	4.2	3.5	2.0	1.0	0.4	16.0	10.8	2.5	7.1	5.7
Spain	n.a.	n.a.	n.a.	n.a.	n.a.	n.a.	n.a.	n.a.	n.a.	n.a.
Sweden	n.a.	n.a.	n.a.	n.a.	n.a.	n.a.	n.a.	n.a.	n.a.	n.a.
Switzerland	n.a.	n.a.	n.a.	n.a.	n.a.	n.a.	n.a.	n.a.	n.a.	n.a.
Turkey	n.a.	n.a.	n.a.	n.a.	n.a.	n.a.	n.a.	n.a.	n.a.	n.a.
United Kingdom	24.1	32.7	31.5	22.2	16.6	21.4	18.0	28.1	32.9	24.4
United States	30.2	18.1	16.4	12.1	10.4	8.1	8.1	7.2	8.4	10.1
OECD av. (unw.)	23.6	21.1	21.9	19.9	20.7	18.8	20.1	16.3	17.1	17.8
Non-OECD countries										
Argentina	n.a.	n.a.	n.a.	5.3	3.5	4.9	2.1	n.a.	n.a.	4.0
Brazil	n.a.	n.a.	n.a.	n.a.	n.a.	n.a.	n.a.	n.a.	n.a.	n.a.
Bulgaria	n.a.	n.a.	n.a.	n.a.	n.a.	n.a.	n.a.	n.a.	n.a.	n.a.
China	n.a.	n.a.	n.a.	n.a.	n.a.	n.a.	0.7	n.a.	n.a.	0.7
Colombia	n.a.	n.a.	n.a.	n.a.	n.a.	54.4	51.6	n.a.	n.a.	53.0
Costa Rica	---------------- Not covered by the series for these years ------------------							n.a.	n.a.	n.a.
Croatia	---------------- Not covered by the series for these years ------------------							n.a.	n.a.	n.a.
Cyprus	n.a.	n.a.	n.a.	0	0	0.02	0.05	6.9	2.3	2.3
Hong Kong, China	n.a.	n.a.	n.a.	n.a.	n.a.	n.a.	7.0	7.0	7.0	7.0
India	n.a.	n.a.	n.a.	n.a.	n.a.	n.a.	n.a.	< 0.01	< 0.01	< 0.01
Indonesia	n.a.	n.a.	n.a.	n.a.	n.a.	0.1	n.a.	289.1 /1	n.a.	144.6
Latvia	50.3	39.1	48.2	38.9	40.3	15.3	15.7	n.a.	n.a.	31.7
Lithuania	n.a.	n.a.	n.a.	27.1	21.6	11.6	9.1	18.3	19.7	17.9
Malaysia	0.2	2.7	5.7	3.2	1.5	8.7	7.8	8.7	6.0	5.9
Malta /1	n.a.	n.a.	n.a.	n.a.	n.a.	0.05	0.04	0.3	< 0.01	0.1
Morocco	---------------- Not covered by the series for these years ------------------							n.a.	n.a.	n.a.
Romania	n.a.	n.a.	n.a.	n.a.	n.a.	n.a.	n.a.	n.a.	n.a.	n.a.
Russia	n.a.	6.8	11.9	19.8	15.6	11.6	25.5	23.9	19.4	18.2
Saudi Arabia	n.a.	n.a.	n.a.	n.a.	n.a.	n.a.	n.a.	n.a.	n.a.	n.a.
Singapore	n.a.	n.a.	n.a.	n.a.	n.a.	n.a.	n.a.	n.a.	n.a.	n.a.
South Africa	3.9	16.7	11.3	11.1	11.4	7.5	6.2	11.2	20.2	11.3
Thailand	---------------- Not covered by the series for these years ------------------							46.9	13.5	30.2

For notes indicated by "/ (number)", see Notes to Tables section at the end of the chapter, p. 239.

Source: Tax Administration 2015 survey responses.

Table 6.16. **Tax debts: Movement in tax debt case numbers**

Country	Number of year-end tax debt cases/Number of tax debt cases at year beginning (%)/1									Movement in year-end tax debt cases: 2007-13 (%)
	2005	2006	2007	2008	2009	2010	2011	2012	2013	
OECD countries										
Australia	104.5	103.0	103.1	84.8	102.3	110.6	98.8	110.2	103.1	7.8
Austria	103.3	101.9	101.9	99.1	100.9	94.5	98.1	99.0	104.0	-4.6
Belgium	132.4	95.4	91.3	n.a.	n.a.	n.a.	89.4	89.3	99.5	238.3
Canada	108.1	97.5	94.4	103.3	106.3	101.9	102.9	102.8	102.4	21.4
Chile	80.1	105.4	101.9	104.7	102.0	102.5	102.9	101.9	99.7	14.4
Czech Republic	n.a.	108.9	103.4	94.7	130.8	178.1	87.0	93.4	105.4	88.8
Denmark	n.a.	450.0	111.1	40.3	132.4	81.8	101.3	116.7	107.3	-44.7
Estonia	97.7	100.6	103.4	104.9	65.1	150.4	31.9	86.7	86.5	-75.4
Finland	114.1	102.9	96.8	101.3	100.3	106.5	106.1	111.8	105.1	14.4
France	93.3	102.5	98.1	98.4	101.3	97.8	99.0	103.9	104.2	4.4
Germany	97.5	94.1	104.2	94.6	91.8	94.6	122.5	105.6	n.a.	n.a.
Greece	n.a.	n.a.	n.a.	104.1	117.0	112.9	157.3	132.9	123.2	254.1
Hungary	101.0	99.0	111.5	112.6	115.4	106.1	111.2	101.8	106.6	66.4
Iceland	n.a.	n.a.	n.a.	n.a.	n.a.	n.a.	n.a.	n.a.	n.a.	n.a.
Ireland	n.a.	n.a.	n.a.	n.a.	n.a.	n.a.	n.a.	n.a.	n.a.	n.a.
Israel	n.a.	n.a.	n.a.	102.5	96.9	n.a.	n.a.	93.5	94.0	-34.6
Italy	n.a.	n.a.	n.a.	n.a.	n.a.	n.a.	n.a.	108.7	108.4	n.a.
Japan	96.9	98.3	98.8	98.5	98.9	99.4	98.1	99.7	95.9	-9.1
Korea	96.8	99.3	99.7	117.5	98.9	94.9	108.2	99.1	105.1	24.1
Luxembourg /2	n.a.	n.a.	n.a.	n.a.	n.a.	94.8	95.6	101.0	103.5	n.a.
Mexico	94.0	90.7	65.9	112.6	119.6	204.2	107.3	117.2	82.7	185.7
Netherlands	n.a.	85.7	100.0	100.0	100.0	108.3	107.7	107.1	93.3	16.7
New Zealand /2	108.3	100.4	101.1	129.5	97.0	72.8	102.7	106.1	104.6	4.3
Norway	n.a.	n.a.	n.a.	n.a.	n.a.	n.a.	n.a.	n.a.	n.a.	n.a.
Poland	99.6	110.9	86.1	105.4	96.8	91.9	110.0	n.a.	102.5	9.8
Portugal	115.5	105.8	106.3	112.6	102.0	104.8	107.1	99.8	124.5	-4.7
Slovak Republic	112.9	112.2	73.9	95.5	107.4	97.5	100.0	105.1	87.8	-7.7
Slovenia	n.a.	124.4	70.4	49.3	98.7	112.3	118.2	49.0	169.2	-46.5
Spain	n.a.	n.a.	n.a.	n.a.	n.a.	n.a.	n.a.	n.a.	n.a.	n.a.
Sweden /2	96.8	94.0	94.0	98.8	314.8	98.3	100.6	99.4	99.6	170.8
Switzerland	n.a.	n.a.	n.a.	n.a.	n.a.	n.a.	95.9	n.a.	n.a.	n.a.
Turkey	n.a.	n.a.	n.a.	n.a.	n.a.	n.a.	n.a.	n.a.	n.a.	n.a.
United Kingdom	n.a.	99.9	95.6	n.a.	n.a.	n.a.	n.a.	n.a.	n.a.	n.a.
United States	101.7	104.5	106.9	100.9	110.9	110.4	107.3	101.6	103.8	39.7
Non-OECD countries										
Argentina	127.6	143.4	95.4	53.0 /2	95.3	105.3	97.2	n.a.	n.a.	n.a.
Brazil	n.a.	n.a.	n.a.	n.a.	n.a.	n.a.	118.7	105.6	111.1	n.a.
Bulgaria	101.6	51.4	95.0	171.1	138.3	106.3	112.0	34.5	140.7	36.8
China	n.a.	n.a.	n.a.	n.a.	n.a.	n.a.	n.a.	n.a.	n.a.	n.a.
Colombia	n.a.	n.a.	n.a.	n.a.	n.a.	102.8	98.7	n.a.	n.a.	n.a.
Costa Rica	----------- Not covered by the series for these years ----------------							230.9	n.a.	n.a.
Croatia	----------- Not covered by the series for these years ----------------							n.a.	n.a.	n.a.
Cyprus	n.a.	n.a.	n.a.	n.a.	101.4	98.6	101.9	101.5	113.5	n.a.
Hong Kong, China	n.a.	n.a.	n.a.	n.a.	n.a.	n.a.	n.a.	n.a.	n.a.	n.a.
India	n.a.	n.a.	n.a.	n.a.	n.a.	n.a.	n.a.	n.a.	n.a.	n.a.
Indonesia	n.a.	n.a.	n.a.	n.a.	n.a.	n.a.	n.a.	n.a.	n.a.	n.a.
Latvia	100.6	101.2	104.9	112.8	111.3	102.8	102.7	111.5	100.8	47.7
Lithuania	n.a.	n.a.	129.5	81.4	109.2	127.1	112.1	94.0	120.5	41.7
Malaysia	n.a.	n.a.	103.9	128.8	77.6	49.2	92.0	96.3	92.7	-55.8
Malta /2	n.a.	n.a.	n.a.	n.a.	n.a.	n.a.	103.3	69.5	104.5	n.a.
Morocco	----------- Not covered by the series for these years ----------------							n.a.	n.a.	n.a.
Romania	n.a.	n.a.	n.a.	n.a.	n.a.	n.a.	n.a.	n.a.	n.a.	n.a.
Russia	n.a.	n.a.	n.a.	n.a.	n.a.	87.0	96.8	n.a.	n.a.	n.a.
Saudi Arabia	n.a.	n.a.	n.a.	n.a.	n.a.	n.a.	n.a.	n.a.	n.a.	n.a.
Singapore	n.a.	n.a.	n.a.	n.a.	n.a.	n.a.	n.a.	n.a.	n.a.	n.a.
South Africa	n.a.	n.a.	107.1	147.9	90.1	n.a.	n.a.	127.7	102.5	39.3
Thailand	----------- Not covered by the series for these years ----------------							111.6	98.1	n.a.

For notes indicated by "/ (number)", see Notes to Tables section at the end of the chapter, p. 239.
Source: Tax Administration 2015 survey responses.

Tax debt case volumes

- Looking at movements in year-end case volumes over the period 2007 to 2013:
  - Ten revenue bodies (i.e. Austria, Denmark, Estonia, Germany, Israel, Japan, Malaysia, Portugal, Slovak Republic, and Slovenia) show *a net overall decline in absolute case numbers*; however, this observation needs to be treated with caution as it is possible that for some countries where the reduction is statistically large (e.g. Denmark, Estonia, and Malaysia) the basis for counting "number of tax debt cases" has changed from one based on "numbers of tax debts by individual tax type" to one of "numbers of taxpayers with tax debts" as revenue bodies have adopted more modern debt case management systems.
  - Seven revenue bodies show fairly low growth over the period (i.e. 0-20%) and include Australia, Chile, Finland, France, Netherlands, New Zealand and Poland);
  - Seven show growth in the range 20-50%;
  - Six revenue bodies show growth exceeding 50% (i.e. Belgium, Czech Republic, Greece, Hungary, Mexico, and Sweden); and
  - There were insufficient data for most years for 26 revenue bodies to make this calculation, including for seven OECD countries.

Tax debts written off

- Applying the ratio "tax debts written off/value of year-end tax debt (excluding disputed debt)" over nine years to gauge the relative magnitude of tax debts written off, on average, reveals a wide spread of results:
  - Fourteen revenue bodies generally had a ratio less than 10%;
  - Twelve revenue bodies generally had a ratio in the range 10-20%;
  - Six revenue bodies generally had a ratio in the range 20-40%;
  - Three revenue bodies generally had a ratio over 40% (i.e. Colombia, Germany and Mexico); and
  - There were insufficient data for 22 revenue bodies (including 12 OECD), to compute this ratio and its trend.
- Observed across OECD countries where data are available, the incidence of tax debt written offs averages around 20% and, if anything, is trending slightly downwards.

Tax debt collected from enforcement actions

- Gaps in survey responses for later years (especially 2012 and 2011) suggest weaknesses in the management information systems used for debt collection for many revenue bodies; for example, almost one-third of revenue bodies were unable to report the amount of tax collected resulting from enforced debt collection activities

The data and related ratios reported in the tables give a sense of the magnitude of the tax debt collection problem across surveyed countries along with indications of individual revenue body performance. However, as noted earlier in this report, such information should be used as a pointer for further inquiry before drawing well-founded conclusions. A particular concern in this area of tax administration is that a fair number of revenue bodies did not report basic programme performance information suggesting possible major weaknesses in their systems of performance measurement and monitoring.

Approaches likely to be contributing to low levels of overall tax debt

While there are no doubt many cultural, economic and social factors that influence the overall level of tax debts and tax payment compliance at an individual country level, it is possible to discern from the information collected for this series some fairly common characteristics of the tax administration arrangements in place that may have contributed to the good outcomes being achieved by some revenue bodies.

Based on survey responses, there were 13 revenue bodies with relatively low debt inventories (i.e. year-end tax debt (excluding disputed debt) below 7.5% of aggregate net revenue collections) over each of the years covered by the series – Australia, Austria, Denmark, Hong Kong (China), Ireland, Japan, Korea, Netherlands, Norway, Singapore, Slovenia, Sweden and the United Kingdom (see Table 6.17). While it is beyond the scope of this series to reach definitive conclusions as to all of the factors that may have contributed to the relatively low level of tax debt in these countries, other information from the series provides insights as to possible influencing factors:

- *Extensive powers of enforcement*: It is noted that nine of the thirteen revenue bodies generally have what might be described as a broad range of legislative powers for enforced debt collection purposes (e.g. powers to collect taxes from third parties, obtain liens over assets, require tax clearance for the granting of government contracts, withhold government payments to debtors, and to impose tax debts on company directors) (see Table 9.12, Chapter 9).
- *Extensive use of tax withholding at source arrangements:* In addition to employment income, eight of thirteen countries generally require tax withholding at source in respect of dividend and/or interest income paid to resident PIT taxpayers (see Table 9.6, Chapter 9);

Table 6.17. **Aspects of tax debt collection performance in selected countries**

Country	Tax system design and administrative approaches likely to be contributing to good performance				
	Wide set of collection powers (Table 9.12)	Wide use of withholding for PIT (Table 9.6)	Debt collection resources % (Table 5.6)	Fully electronic payment % (Table 7.6)	IT expenditure/ total expenditure % (Table 5.3)
Australia	✓		9.8	73	21.2
Austria	✓	✓	10.4	70	26.8
Denmark	✓		8.2	n.a.	16.9
Hong Kong, China			17.2	39	10.0
Ireland	✓	✓	14.3	87	12.7
Israel	✓	✓	16.6	17	2.9
Japan		✓	21.2	17	6.9
Korea	✓	✓	n.a.*	35	6.6
Netherlands	✓	✓	7.4	99	15.5
Norway	✓		12.4	99	27.0
Singapore			11.1	72	39.6
Sweden	✓	✓	**	99	19.5
United Kingdom		✓	12.0	60	21.3

* Korea reported there is no separate debt collection function.

** Debt collection carried out by separate body.

- *Well-staffed enforced debt collection organisation*: Nine of eleven reported that around 10% or more of their resources are devoted to enforced debt collection activities within a dedicated organisation unit (see Table 5.6, Chapter 5).
- *Wide use of electronic payment methods*: These methods, in particular the use of direct debiting, are used widely: Eight of twelve revenue bodies reported usage in excess of 50% (see Table 7.4).
- *Extensive investment in information technology for tax administration*: Eight revenue bodies reported annual IT expenditure in excess of 15%.

Notes to Tables

Table 6.3. Revenue collections and refunds (relative shares)

/1. **Luxembourg:** Refunds of tax only refer to VAT.

Table 6.4. Taxpayer services: Service demand ratios

/1. **IVR**: Refers to Interactive Voice Recognition technology providing automated answers to inquiries.

/2. **Austria and Belgium:** Data available only for certain regions/infocentres, and insufficiently complete for comparison purposes. **Costa Rica**: Phone inquiries answered by local offices. **Denmark**: Generally, there were less in-person inquiries in 2013. In addition, in November 2013, a system with personal assistance by appointment was introduced. As a result the number of in-person inquiries in November and December 2013 was almost zero. **France**: Figures only include inquiries made during the 6 weeks devoted to PIT returns. **Israel**: Service is only available to limited subjects. **Latvia**: Decrease due to the development of the Electronic Declaration System and activities directed to taxpayers to receive information by telephone or electronically. **Lithuania**: Since October 2011, only general information can be received at tax offices. **Netherlands**: In 2013, NTCA (gradually) introduced personal inquiries by appointment only which has reduced the number of in-person inquiries. **Portugal**: In-person inquiries are estimated based on data available in local tax and customs offices which have an electronic register of the personal inquiries (number of inquiries by subject, waiting time and attending time) and which represented about 71% of total volume of work, both in 2012 and 2013. The payment of taxes by taxpayers in local offices represented about 43% of all visits in 2013. Other reasons for taxpayers' visits were inquiries (and deliver of tax returns) related to income taxes (23%) and to real estate taxes (20%), and also inquiries associated to tax enforcement proceedings (10%) and to administrative and judicial litigation (4%). **United Kingdom**: Figures for visits to face to face centres.

Table 6.5. Service standards and performance in 2013: PIT returns and complaints

/1. **Chile**: Returns filed between April 1 and 19: refunds by deposit are due on May 11 and refunds by sending a cheque are due on May 30; returns filed between April 20 and 27: refunds by deposit are due on May 17 and refunds by sending a cheque are due on May 30; returns filed between April 28 and May 9: refunds by deposit are due on May 28 and refunds by sending a cheque are due on May 30. **France**: Standard relates to complaints concerning PIT, and contribution to public broadcasting and occupation tax. **Israel**: The standard and performance are for registered taxpayers filing regular annual returns. The legal requirement for employees who are generally not required to file an annual return but file a request for refund is a year from assessment or two years from payment. However, even for those the administrative standard is 90 days. The performance for non-filing individuals requesting a refund is 66%. **United States**: The standard is for Individual paper returns only. A separate standard for electronically filed returns is not applicable. For returns e-filed, the goal is to issue refunds within 5 to 21 days, which the IRS achieves for most returns filed electronically.

/2. **United States**: Follow-up actions should occur within five workdays of the documented follow-up date (93.1%), while a case should only be closed when all necessary actions have been taken to resolve the taxpayer's problem with the IRS (93.8%).

Table 6.6. Service standards and performance in 2013: VAT refunds and correspondence

/1. **Canada**: All returns and not only returns with refunds. **Chile**: Periods by industry: Cattle – 5 working days, Meat – 10 working days, Building industry – 12 working days, Small Agricultural Producers – 60 days, Other – 30 days. **France**: Standard for email correspondence: answer 90% of emails within 5 business days, actual performance: 97.2%. **Norway**: Provided that the business is not subject to audit. **Poland**: Separate standards of 25 days (where special conditions satisfied) and 180 days (where no sales made in fiscal year). **South Africa**: High refund turnaround time is a result of SARS waiting for supporting documents from taxpayers or SARS investigating the submission. An average of 69.6% of VAT refunds was paid within 14 days and 75.1% within 21 days.

Table 6.7. Service standards and performance in 2013: In-person and phone inquiries

/1. **Austria**: Taxpayers do not have to apply for a personal contact in advance they can come to the tax office during the opening hours without any prior arrangement. There is a waiting time only if there is a queue. **Canada**: CRA payment and enquiry counters were closed in two phases – October 2012 and October 2013. **Ireland**: Achievements reported as PAYE: 20% within 30 secs, 44% within 3 mins, and 59% within 5 mins and other categories – 59% within 30 secs, 83% within 3 mins, 89% within 5 mins. **Luxembourg**: Written question is requested in the case of a complex question/answer in the legal delay for written questions.

/2. **Canada**: Separate standards and performance for phone inquiries from charities and in respect of GST/HST and Canada Child Tax Benefit.

Table 6.9. Verification actions: Value of assessments/total net revenue collections

/1. **Luxembourg**: Value of completed actions refers only to VAT.

Table 6.10. Verification actions: Number completed for all taxpayer categories

/1. Comparisons across countries of data on numbers of verification actions need to be treated with caution owing to differences in how revenue bodies interpret the term "verification activities" in practice, and the approach adopted for quantifying results (e.g. by numbers of taxpayers, numbers of cases involving different taxes etc.).

/2. **Australia:** Total amount is the number of audits, reviews and other compliance checks as published in "Your Case Matters" (i.e. excluding letters). **Belgium:** Belgium's reported verification activities for 2007 to 2011 cover three programmes: *(1)* management control; *(2)* comprehensive audits; and *(3)* simple checks regarding the issues affecting the amount of tax that taxpayers are required to pay such as family status, child birth, company mergers, disability situation etc. on taxpayer declarations. Results for 2012 and 2013 appear to have been prepared on a different basis that could not be resolved before publication. **Brazil:** Figures include only the results of tax inspections. **Canada, Cyprus and Slovak Republic**: Volumes represent verification activities, not taxpayers. **Costa Rica**: These amounts refer to verification actions regarding monitoring and extensive control. The amount provided for 2013 does not include extensive control actions from plans that started on 2013 but ended during the first quarter of 2014. The amount of taxpayers subject to verification actions related to default of payment are not included in the given amounts because the records are computed according to the quantity of verified or managed debts. **Croatia**: Information refers to external audit and tax offenses. **Finland**: Income tax (PIT and CIT) only. **France**: Since 2010, reported data includes desk audits that were not reported in prior year information. For 2012 and 2013, the numbers of desk audits were 1.38 million and 1.34 million, respectively. **Korea:** Korea's verification figures do not take desk audits or third party reporting. This is the reason that Korean verification figures may not be comparable with other countries. **Israel**: Data does not include criminal investigations. **Italy**: Only audits carried out by Revenue Agency. **Lithuania**: Data for the year 2005-10 refers to control actions taken by tax administration. Data for 2011 refers to control actions taken by tax administration; also contacts by tax administration with taxpayers regarding their tax obligations are included. Data for 2012/2013 includes tax verifications carried out, tax investigations, letters, interviews and contacts with taxpayers concerning submitted declarations. **Luxembourg**: VAT only. **Malta**: Statistics refer only to authority in charge of Direct Taxation. **Morocco**: Figures relate to field audits. **Portugal**: Total number of verification actions. **Spain**: Number of actions performed. These figures include every type of verification (automated filters, massive control, desk controls, field audits, investigation etc.) homogenised to make them comparable. **Switzerland**: Indications only for VAT

Table 6.11. Verification actions: Number completed for large taxpayers

/1. Comparisons across countries of data on numbers of verification actions need to be treated with caution owing to differences in how revenue bodies interpret the term "verification activities" in practice, and the approach adopted for quantifying results (e.g. by numbers of taxpayers, numbers of cases involving different taxes etc.).

/2. **Canada and Slovak Republic**: Volumes represent verification activities, not taxpayers. **Croatia**: Information refers to external audit and tax offenses. **Finland**: Data relate only to PIT and CIT; **France and Morocco**: Figures relate to field audits. **Ireland**: Only for period May-December 2012. **Italy**: Only audits carried out by Revenue Agency. **Lithuania**: Data for these years to control actions taken by tax administration. Data for 2011 refers to control actions taken by tax administration; also contacts by tax administration with taxpayers regarding their tax obligations are included. Data for 2012/2013 includes tax verifications carried out, tax investigations, letters, interviews and contacts with taxpayers concerning submitted declarations.

/3. **Slovak Republic**: Since 2013, the Tax Office for Selected Taxpayers administers the large taxpayers on the whole territory of the Slovak Republic. Until 2012, it only administered large taxpayers in Bratislava and surrounding areas.

Table 6.12. Tax disputes in administrative review: Finalised cases

/1. **Australia**: 2008-11: Figures include objections against rulings; 2012-13: Figures relate to all head objections, reviews against rulings, extension of time and shortfall interest charge remission requests. **Costa Rica**: The number of cases refers to disputes being analysed by the Administrative Tax Court (Tribunal Fiscal Administrativo). These cases are not finished since they have to undergo assessment and collection phases. Regarding the 511 cases reviewed in 2012 and the 469 cases for 2013, the amounts include cases from previous years. **Cyprus**: Only for direct taxes. **France**: Figures correspond to the tax relief that has been granted. **Greece**: The dispute resolution directorate started operating in September 2013. Data for an entire year will be available from 2014 on. **Hungary**: The number of appeals and requests of supervisory measures are included. **Ireland**: Revised procedures were introduced on 1st January 2013. The new procedures introduced *(i)* a new Local Review stage, *(ii)* maintained the option for an Internal Review and *(iii)* replaced the option for a Joint Review (by an Internal and External Reviewer) with the option of a review solely by an External Reviewer. The figures for 2013 only relate to disputes that were dealt with at the Internal and External Review stage. **Luxembourg**: VAT only. **New Zealand**: *(1)* All data is for disputed cases in administrative review carried out by Inland Revenues' own internal (but independent) Disputes Review Unit. *(2)* Value of tax in dispute: gross amount subject to tax, rather than the amount of tax itself. However the figures have been calculated by using 33% as a proxy for the rate of income tax for the income tax disputes, and the GST rate of 12.5% for the GST disputes. *(3)* The value of disputed tax includes the amounts of tax shortfall penalties that were also in dispute and formed part of the administrative reviews. **Romania:** Results for 2012 and 2013 may have been reported on different basis to prior years; not resolved at time of publication. **Russia**: Amounts include taxes, tax penalties and fees. **South Africa**: Figures reflect head office only. **Spain**: The number of cases refers to disputes being analysed by the Economic Administrative Courts which are administrative bodies within the MOF but independent from the Tax Agency. **Switzerland**: Only indirect taxes.

/2. **Hungary**: Given that exact numbers of cases affected by appeals and supervisory measures is not available, the numbers of court actions are included.

Table 6.13. Tax disputes in administrative review: Unfinalised cases at year-end

/1. **Australia**: 2008-11: Figures include objections against rulings; 2012-13: Figures relate to all head objections, reviews against rulings, extension of time and shortfall interest charge remission requests. **Costa Rica**: The numbers provided refer to cases not yet decided by the Administrative Tax Court. For 2012, apart from the 161 cases that have not been analysed, there are other 1.209 pending cases from previous years. For 2013, the amount of pending cases for previous years is 1.589. **Cyprus:** Only for direct taxes. **Greece**: The dispute resolution directorate started operating in September 2013. Data for an entire year will be available from 2014 on. **Hungary**: The number of appeals and requests of supervisory measures are included. **Ireland**: Revised procedures were introduced on 1st January 2013. The new procedures introduced *(i)* a new Local Review stage, *(ii)* maintained the option for an Internal Review and *(iii)* replaced the option for a Joint Review (by an Internal and External Reviewer) with the option of a review solely by an External Reviewer. The figures for 2013 only relate to disputes that were dealt with at the Internal and External Review stage. **Luxembourg**: VAT only. **New Zealand**: *(1)* All data is for disputed cases in administrative review carried out by Inland Revenues' own internal (but independent) Disputes Review Unit. *(2)* Value of tax in dispute: gross amount subject to tax, rather than the amount of tax itself. However the figures have been calculated by using 33% as a proxy for the rate of income tax for the income tax disputes, and the GST rate of 12.5% for the GST disputes. *(3)* The value of disputed tax includes the amounts of tax shortfall penalties that were also in dispute and formed part of the administrative reviews. **Romania:** Results for 2012 and 2013 may have been reported on different basis to prior years; not resolved at time of publication. **South Africa**: Figures reflect head office only. **Spain**: The number of cases refers to disputes being analysed by the Economic Administrative Courts which are administrative bodies within the MOF but independent from the Tax Agency. **Switzerland**: Only indirect taxes.

/2. **Hungary**: Given that exact numbers of cases affected by appeals and supervisory measures is not available, the numbers of court actions are included.

Table 6.14. Tax debt – year-end aggregates

/1. **Australia**: "Total year-end tax debt (excluding disputed debt)" is collectable debt only. "Non-collectible year-end tax debt" includes both disputed debt and debt where the taxpayer is subject to some form of insolvency administration. **New Zealand**: Tax debt that is disputed is defined as cases under the deferred action code and cases under the objection action code from the debt reporting data. Social policy debt (child support, working for families and student loan) data is excluded from the tax debt data. However, due to system constraints there will be some social policy debt included in tax debt cases for taxpayers who have a tax debt as well as social policy debt.

Table 6.15. Tax debts: Debt written off as a share of debt inventory

/1. **Indonesia:** Underlying data may be unreliable and could not be validated by time of publication. **Korea**: The debt at commencement of 2011 was KRW 4 925 700 and the newly incurred debt during the fiscal year was KRW 18 412 900. On this account, the total amount of debt available for write-off equals KRW 23 338 600. During 2011, KRW 7 880 400 was written off. That explains why the ratio might seem high compared to other countries' relevant ratios. **Malta**: 2010-11 – Statistics refer only to authority in charge of Direct Taxation. 2012-13 – debt written off refers to direct and indirect taxes, and debt at year beginning only to direct taxes.

Table 6.16. Tax debts: Movement in tax debt case numbers

/1. Comparisons of data on case numbers and related ratios need to be treated with caution owing to differences in how revenue bodies count the number of debt cases (e.g. by numbers of taxpayers or by numbers of tax debts for each tax).

/2. **Argentina**: the revenue body has advised that during this year a new computer system was implemented that brings together the various tax debts of taxpayers, resulting in debts being reported on a taxpayer basis; as a result the numbers of cases reported is significantly less than reported in prior years. **Luxembourg:** Only indirect taxes. **New Zealand**: Tax debt that is disputed is defined as the aggregate debt of cases under the deferred action code and cases under the objection action code from debt reporting data. Social policy debt (child support, working for families and student loan) data is excluded from the tax debt data. However, due to system constraints we are unable to separate student loan and working for families from tax debt cases, tax debt collected and tax debt formally written off data. **Malta**: 2011 – Statistics refer only to authority in charge of Direct Taxation. 2012-13 – covers both direct and indirect cases. **Sweden**: Case numbers are computed on the basis of debts for each tax, not the numbers of taxpayers with debts.

Bibliography

IMF (2005), *VAT Refunds: A Review of Country Experience,* IMF Working Paper WP/05/218, International Monetary Fund, Washington.

OECD (2014a), *Revenue Statistics 2014*, OECD Publishing, Paris, http://dx.doi.org/10.1787/rev_stats-2014-en-fr.

OECD (2014b), *Consumption Tax Trends 2014: VAT/GST and excise rates, trends and policy issues*, OECD Publishing, Paris, http://dx.doi.org/10.1787/ctt-2014-en.

OECD (2014c), *Working Smarter in Tax Debt Management*, OECD Publishing, Paris, http://dx.doi.org/10.1787/9789264223257-en.

OECD (2012a), *Consumption Tax Trends 2012: VAT/GST and Excise Rates, Trends and Administration Issues*, OECD Publishing, Paris, http://dx.doi.org/10.1787/ctt-2012-en.

OECD (2012b), *Working smarter in tax administration – Using demand management strategies to meet service delivery goals,* Forum on Tax Administration, Centre for Tax Policy and Administration, Paris.

Chapter 7

The use of online services in tax administration

This chapter provides an overview of developments with, and plans for, the use of modern online services in tax administration, along with performance and trend-related information on taxpayers' take-up of revenue bodies' e-filing and e-payment capabilities.

Key points

Medium term priorities for delivering enhanced online services

- With minor exceptions, all revenue bodies reported having a formal plan to improve the range and quality of online services provided to taxpayers and their representatives over the medium term.
- The most commonly reported priority areas for development were online filing (major taxes), other new online applications (e.g. to access taxpayers accounts), website enhancements, online payments, and enhanced third party data capture. Priorities for the planned use of digital mail products and integrated taxpayer accounts were also reported by the majority of revenue bodies.

Electronic filing of tax returns

- The provision of modern e-filing services for the major taxes administered is just about universal, with well around 95% of surveyed revenue bodies offering such a service.
- Over two-thirds of revenue bodies in OECD countries achieved e-filing usage for over three-quarters of their PIT, CIT, and VAT client taxpayers in 2013.
- Many revenue bodies can point to substantial increases in e-filing usage over the last ten years for one or more of their major taxes, using administrative initiatives and/or mandatory e-filing requirements, the latter particularly for VAT administration.
- Despite the progress made, there is potential for substantially greater usage (i.e. +75%) by fair number of revenue bodies – 13 for the PIT, nine for the CIT, and six for VAT.

The provision of prefilled tax returns to taxpayers

- Pre-filling has become a significant (and for some, transformational) element of revenue bodies' e-services strategy, particularly for the PIT, with around 40% of revenue bodies reporting some use of such a service.
- In its most advanced form (e.g. as seen in Denmark and Sweden), pre-filling services have just about fully automated return preparation and assessment; some eight revenue bodies reported using a prefilling capability that generates fully completed tax returns for the majority of their PIT clients.

Automation of collecting tax payments

- Revenue bodies (able to report payment volume data) appear to have made substantial progress over the last 4-5 years in fully automating tax payment collection. Of concern, however, well over a third of revenue bodies were unable to report payment volume data by type of payment method suggesting that insufficient attention is being given to fully automating this aspect of service delivery.
- Over 45% of revenue bodies continue to provide costly "in-person" payment methods via their office networks. In five countries, these payments exceeded 40% of all payments; in many other countries, the volumes reported were relatively low raising doubts as to the "cost/benefit" arguments for their use.
- Notwithstanding the overall progress observed, there appears to be potential for substantially greater use of fully electronic e-payment capabilities by many surveyed revenue bodies.

Provision and use of modern online services in tax administration

Over the last two decades, many revenue bodies have taken steps to exploit the use of modern computing technologies to transform their operations, in particular those concerned with mainstream tax collection and assessment processes and the provision of services to taxpayers and their representatives. The reasons for this are fairly obvious. The use of technology by citizens and businesses has grown exponentially over the last decade or so and revenue bodies can leverage off this by offering an increased array of online self-service capabilities that are both easy and attractive for taxpayers to use. In addition to making it easier for taxpayers to comply with the law and providing higher standards of services, revenue bodies also benefit from lower costs and greater efficiency. A win: win situation for all!

As reported in previous editions, the main types of online services now being used by large and growing numbers of taxpayers are:

- Provision of a comprehensive range of tax and other information, forms and calculators on websites.
- Electronic filing of tax returns for the major taxes.
- The provision of fully and/or partially completed pre-filled tax returns for personal income tax.
- A range of electronic payment options for all taxes.
- Access to secure detailed personal taxpayer information via online portals.
- Call centres using modern telephony facilities (including IVR technologies) to provide more accessible phone inquiry services.

While considerable progress has been made by many revenue bodies, demands for greater efficiency and improved services are now driving many to attain even higher standards of service capability, taking advantage of technological advances and innovative thinking on how technology can be deployed to deliver improved services to taxpayers and increase organisational efficiency, as reflected in the corporate strategy documents of many revenue bodies, for example:

> People expect convenient and accessible service in their dealings with a contemporary service organisation. (ATO, 2014)
>
> We are aiming to make it easier for people to deal with us, to offer new ways to reach us. We aim to get away from paper, to get more people managing their own tax affairs, preferably online or using mobile technology or through third party service providers. (New Zealand Inland Revenue, 2014)

This edition gives particular attention to reporting on revenue bodies' priorities for enhancing their online services over the medium term.

Enhancing online services: Considerable progress has been made but much more can be done

The use of modern technology to deliver enhanced services to taxpayers and other revenue body clients has been a permanent feature of the work of the FTA since its creation in 2002. The Forum's Taxpayer Services Sub-group exists to provide a forum for members to share experiences and knowledge of approaches to taxpayer service delivery, in particular through the use of modern technology. To achieve this objective, the Subgroup monitors and reports on key developments and trends in taxpayer service delivery, with a particular focus on the application of modern electronic services, and examines ways to promote the uptake and use of electronic services by revenue bodies, and provides practical guidance for revenue bodies, based on observed good practices. Participation in the Sub-group's work is open to all FTA member revenue bodies.

In 2011, the FTA's Taxpayer Services Sub-Group completed a report of a study examining the approaches of revenue bodies for managing service demand (OECD, 2012). A key finding of the study was that despite having implemented multi-channel service models and setting service objectives to move taxpayers to online channels and self-service, many revenue bodies continued to experience high demand for services in their more expensive channels, such as in-person and in-bound call channels. The study also noted that while most revenue bodies were measuring service demand using a variety of methods which provided information on volumes, trends and demand topics, these methods were not effective in determining the root causes of the demand for services.

These findings led the FTA to commissioning further work in 2012 that aimed to provide practical guidance for revenue bodies to help them meet taxpayers' service expectations (OECD, 2013). The guide produced, which was based on observed best practice, provided a whole-of-revenue-body approach to managing service demand and set out a possible model for governance arrangements and practical steps to support revenue bodies identify, analyse, and address the root causes of service demand – see Figure 7.1.

Following publication of the guide the Forum's Bureau commissioned further work in mid-2013 to support revenue bodies' efforts in encouraging taxpayers to use more cost effective online channels. The report of this work, which drew on the experiences of a broad cross section of FTA member countries, provides a rich account of developments and steps being taken to drive the take up of e-services (OECD, 2014). Drawing on the

Figure 7.1. **The demand management framework**

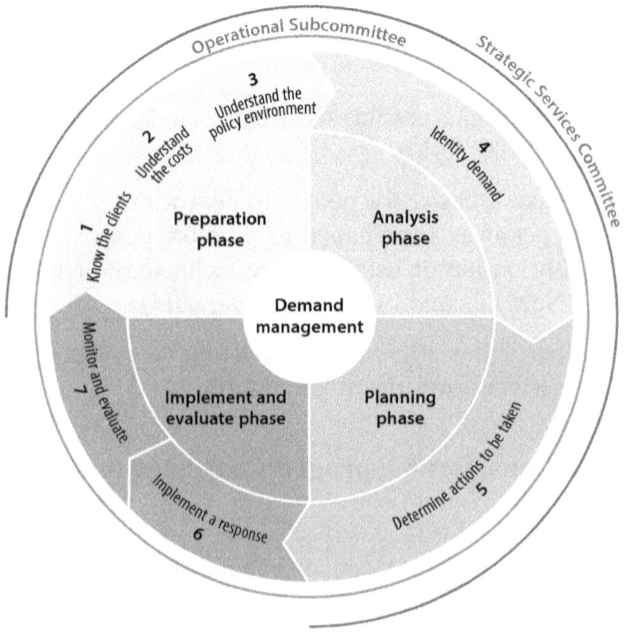

Source: Managing Service Demand: A Practical Guide to Help Revenue Bodies Better Meet Taxpayers' Service Expectations, OECD, 2013.

approaches observed, it emphasises the following imperatives for increasing taxpayers' use of self-service channels:

1. Identify and target opportunities to offer self-services by using effective monitoring and data analytics that support understanding of service demand.
2. Take a user-centred design approach in creating new services or shifting existing services to digital channels.
3. Promote take up, either by mandating or offering incentives and leveraging tax intermediaries and third party providers in assisting taxpayers to take up self-service channels.
4. Consistently direct taxpayers to the preferred channel through communication and education, eliminating channels or leveraging tax intermediaries and third party providers. To retain taxpayers in the preferred channels, consider providing a range of tailored in-channel support tools.
5. To ensure sustainable and progressive use of self-service channels, the report recommends that revenue bodies develop metrics for self-service channels to measure the impact of self-service offerings on service demand and identify and target further opportunities to increase taxpayers' self-service.

For this series, revenue bodies were asked to indicate whether they had a formalised plan or strategy to improve their online services over the coming years and, if so, to identify the five most important areas of proposed development from a menu of online self-service capabilities. Table 7.1 sets out the menu of capabilities used to identify revenue bodies' priorities, while Table 7.2 summarises their responses. In addition, research was undertaken of a range of

Table 7.1. **Menu of possible self-service capabilities for enhancing taxpayer services**

Functionality	Description and potential benefits
Online electronic tax return filing	Initiatives that increase the use of e-filing for the major taxes, making it easier for taxpayers to file returns, reducing the revenue bodies' costs in processing returns, and potentially expediting refunds to taxpayers.
Use of prefilled tax returns	Using third party and other information already held by the revenue body to prefill taxpayers' tax returns, reducing their information requirements and reducing the potential for taxpayer error.
Online electronic payment services	Increasing use of fully electronic e-payment services, making it easier for taxpayers to pay and enabling revenue bodies to reduce and ideally eliminate more costly payment channels (e.g. in-person, by cheque, or through agents).
Increased information on website	Providing forms, guidance and answers to taxpayers' questions as and when they need it, and reducing the costs to revenue bodies of providing corresponding paper or oral responses via costlier service channels.
Integrated taxpayer accounts/ records	Traditionally, taxes were administered on a "tax by tax" basis. For taxpayers (e.g. businesses) with multiple tax responsibilities, this "tax by tax" approach makes it difficult to readily obtain a complete view of their overall tax accounting position, making it complicated for both taxpayers and revenue bodies. The introduction of tax accounting systems that permit a "whole of taxpayer" view across major taxes facilitates overall tax accounting and helps taxpayers understand their full tax position.
New online applications for taxpayers	Providing an increased array of transactions to taxpayers and their representatives to help them meet their tax obligations (e.g. to update records, access accounts and/or taxpayer history, to file requests for amendments, request arrangements to pay, adjust PAYE withholdings)
VAT e-invoicing	System to support businesses and the revenue body's administration in operation of the VAT.
Data capture from third parties	Automating the capture of third party data (e.g. from employers and financial bodies) that are required for routine tax administration processes (e.g. verification and prefilling of tax returns)
Digital mailbox	Reducing large volumes of paper mail (e.g. notices of assessment, taxpayer accounts) that are sent to taxpayers using costly postal services through use of a digital mailbox capability that enables such information to be made available to taxpayers electronically via a secure portal.
New online applications for tax intermediaries	Tax intermediaries play a significant role in tax administration in many countries, handling the tax affairs of many revenue body clients. As described briefly in this chapter and in Chapter 8, there are numerous ways of adapting service delivery approaches and offerings to assist them perform their role, and at the same time help revenue bodies carry out their responsibilities.

published revenue body documents to gather further insights on key developments recently introduced or planned.

The key observations from the information gathered are as set out hereunder:

- With minor exceptions, all revenue bodies reported having a formal plan for improving the range and quality of electronic services provided to taxpayers and their representatives over the medium term.
- From a menu of ten service categories, the five most frequently reported by revenue bodies as priority areas of development were:
  - Enhanced online filing services for the major taxes (49).
  - New online applications (e.g. to access accounts/ taxpayer history) (37).
  - Increased functionality and information on websites (33).
  - Enhanced online payment services for the major taxes (32).
  - Enhanced data capture from third parties (32).

  Priorities for the planned use of digital mail products and integrated taxpayer accounts were also reported by many (29 and 28 revenue bodies respectively).

Box 7.1 describes a variety of website tools developed by Argentina's AFIP to assist taxpayers and help it manage its phone inquiry demand, while Boxes 7.2 and 7.3 outline a variety of new services recently implemented or planned by revenue bodies in the United Kingdom, Canada, and South Africa.

Box 7.1. Argentina's (AFIP) website tools to assist taxpayers

In addition to answering inquiries through its Telephone Information Service, Argentina's tax and customs body (AFIP) provides a large variety of tools on its website to assist taxpayers and reduce the need for phone inquiries. Some of these tools are outlined below along with related data pointing to their wide usage:

- ***ABC inquiries and FAQ:*** This is a service that contains FAQ on tax, customs and social security issues. Inquiries are organised according to their main topic and divided into categories and subcategories. The tool is updated daily by staff of the Telephone Information Center. Each question shows its corresponding response and if applicable, the legal source that supports it. At present, this tool has 8411 consultations available. Over 7.5 million inquiries were received in 2013.
- ***Procedures and Services:*** This service is available on the main page and redirects the citizen to an alphabetically ordered list, where they can access to manuals, useful information, guidelines and other support tools. Over 3.5 million inquiries were received in 2013.
- ***Guideline for procedures:*** This is a service that explains in an accessible and detailed way the procedure to be followed by a taxpayer to complete a procedure before AFIP. It contains a list of the main procedures, providing complete information on each one, such as: objective, persons obliged proceeding, forms, and regulations, among others. Over 3.7 million inquiries were received in 2013.
- ***My guidance:*** This tool allows citizens to perform online simulations, requesting only some information of the activity, and as a result, it details the taxpayer obligations and how to fulfill them. It is a voluntary system that requires no identification and contains 5 modules: *(1)* Registration as new taxpayer; *(2)* Re-categorisation in *Monotributo; (3)* Categorisation/Re-categorisation for self-employed workers; *(4)* Income Tax and Personal Property Tax; *(5)* Luggage Regime; and *(6)* Payment Facilities Plans in force. Around 440 000 inquiries were received in 2013.
- ***Have you received a communication from AFIP?*** This tool details the means of contact used by AFIP and the informative campaigns carried out. A reference number is shown in all campaigns. Thus, those citizens who received a communication from AFIP, may access this service and be informed, inter alia, about the date of the campaign beginning, reason for contact and how to proceed. Just over 450 000 inquiries were received in 2013.

Source: AFIP survey response.

Table 7.2. **Strategic priorities for increasing use of online services**

		Strategic focus for improving electronic services – five key areas of development reported for the medium term									
Country	Formal plan	Online filing	Prefilled returns	Online payment	Website service/ tools	Integrated taxpayer accounts	Other online services	VAT e-invoices	Enhanced data capture	Digital mailbox	Apps for tax agents
OECD countries											
Australia	✓	✓	✓	✓	✓	✓	✓		✓	✓	
Austria	✓	✓	✓		✓				✓	✓	
Belgium	✓	✓	✓	✓	✓	✓	✓	✓	✓	✓	✓
Canada	✓	✓ /1		✓			✓			✓	
Chile	✓	✓	✓					✓	✓	✓	
Czech Republic	x	✓			✓	✓		✓		✓	
Denmark	✓	✓			✓				✓	✓	
Estonia	✓	✓	✓	✓	✓	✓			✓	✓	
Finland	✓	✓	✓	✓			✓		✓		
France	✓	✓			✓	✓	✓			✓	
Germany	-	-	-	-	-	-	-	-	-	-	-
Greece	✓	✓	✓	✓		✓	✓	✓	✓	✓	
Hungary	✓	✓	✓	✓	✓	✓	✓	✓	✓	✓	
Iceland	✓	✓			✓		✓		✓	✓	
Ireland	✓	✓	✓				✓		✓	✓	
Israel	✓	✓					✓		✓	✓	✓
Italy	x	-	-	-	-	-	-	-	-	-	-
Japan	✓	✓		✓	✓						
Korea	✓	✓		✓		✓	✓			✓	
Luxembourg	✓	✓		✓ /1	✓ /2	✓ /1	✓ /1	✓ /1			
Mexico	✓	✓	✓		✓	✓				✓	
Netherlands	✓	✓	✓				✓		✓	✓	
New Zealand	✓	✓	✓	✓	✓	✓	✓		✓		
Norway	✓	✓	✓	✓	✓	✓	✓		✓	✓	
Poland	✓	✓	✓	✓	✓	✓					
Portugal	✓ /1		✓	✓	✓		✓				
Slovak Republic	✓	✓			✓		✓		✓	✓	
Slovenia	✓	✓	✓	✓	✓	✓		✓	✓	✓	
Spain	✓	✓	✓	✓	✓	✓	✓	✓	✓	✓	✓
Sweden	✓	✓		✓	✓				✓	✓	
Switzerland	✓	✓ /1	✓ /1	✓ /1	✓ /1	✓ /1	✓ /1		✓ /1	✓ /1	✓ /1
Turkey	✓	✓		✓	✓		✓				✓
United Kingdom	✓	✓				✓	✓		✓		✓
United States	✓	✓		✓		✓	✓			✓	✓
Non-OECD countries											
Argentina	✓	✓				✓	✓	✓	✓		
Brazil	✓	✓	✓	✓	✓	✓	✓				✓
Bulgaria	x	-	-	-	-	-	-	-	-	-	-
China	✓	---------- No specific key areas for development identified ----------									
Colombia	✓	✓		✓	✓		✓	✓			
Costa Rica	✓	✓		✓	✓	✓	✓	✓	✓	✓	
Croatia	✓	✓			✓	✓	✓	✓			
Cyprus	✓	✓		✓	✓	✓	✓				
Hong Kong	✓	✓	✓		✓		✓				
India	✓	✓	✓	✓	✓	✓	✓		✓		
Indonesia	✓	✓	✓	✓			✓	✓	✓		✓
Latvia	✓	✓				✓	✓		✓	✓	
Lithuania	✓	✓	✓			✓			✓	✓	
Malaysia	✓	✓	✓	✓	✓		✓				
Malta	✓	✓		✓			✓		✓		✓
Morocco	✓	✓		✓	✓	✓	✓				✓
Romania	✓	✓		✓	✓	✓	✓		✓	✓	✓
Russia	✓	✓		✓	✓	✓	✓	✓	✓	✓	
Saudi Arabia	✓	✓		✓	✓				✓		
Singapore	✓	✓	✓				✓		✓	✓	
South Africa	✓	✓	✓	✓	✓	✓	✓		✓	✓	✓
Thailand	✓	✓		✓	✓	✓			✓		

For notes indicated by "/ (number)", see Notes to Tables section at the end of the chapter, p. 259.

Source: Tax Administration 2015 survey responses.

Box 7.2. United Kingdom: Building better services for taxpayers

As an agency under significant pressure to reduce costs and improve performance, the United Kingdom's HMRC has established a challenging plan of developments over the medium term to enhance the services it provides to its customers (HMRC, 2014). The importance being placed on this aspect of tax administration is reflected in the plan's introductory comments provided by its Chief Executive (p.3).

> One of the ways we will meet the rising expectations of our customers is by offering them first class online services – like they experience with online banking and shopping – and this business plan explains how we will start to do this, by setting out how digital technology will change the way we all work.
>
> In elaborating the priority areas for attention over the medium term HMRC's business plan notes (p. 11):
>
> How we serve our customers is critical to how we maximise our revenues and sustainably reduce our costs. It is about more than improving their experience of our services, but making a fundamental shift in the services we provide, making it simpler and more convenient for customers to get their taxes and entitlements right and thereby improve voluntary compliance.
>
> An important part of this is our work to move away from designing services around the taxes customers pay towards operating in real time. We will use the up-to-date information we hold to reassure customers and simplify their dealings with us, minimising the need for us to intervene.
>
> We are building digital services that will enable most of our customers to manage their tax affairs and payments online, while reshaping our products, processes and services around their needs.
>
> We also know that there will always be customers who need to contact us for support, and we will make improvements to the services they receive over the phone, through the post and face-to-face.
>
> Our move towards the new digital service has already begun with HMRC piloting a number of "exemplars" that include:
>
> - ***PAYE Online:*** When fully launched, this will allow our 41 million PAYE customers to use tax calculators, access guidance and report online changes to their circumstances affecting their tax code. Our contact centres currently receive 4.7 million calls a year about tax codes and we estimate that this online service will remove the need for around 1.8 million of these calls. The new service began in February with a limited private beta – a trial run carried out among a small group of customers – and will be progressively scaled up over the next two years.
> - ***Digital Self-Assessment:*** More than eight and a half million (or about 85 per cent) of Self-Assessment customers already file online, but we then communicate with them by letter, sending out 40 million pieces of paper every year. We are piloting paperless services so that customers who opt in will get email alerts to direct them to their online account, with a limited private beta launched in February. In due course Self-Assessment customers will also be able to have queries answered by a new "web chat" facility.
> - ***Your Tax Account:*** This will make it simpler for the UK's 4.9 million small and medium-sized businesses to manage their tax affairs in a single place through a personalised homepage. They will be able to register, file and pay what they owe across Self-Assessment, Corporation Tax, VAT and PAYE for employers. They will also be able to see their liabilities for these taxes, and have links through to relevant guidance. We launched a limited private beta of this service in February 2014.
> - ***Agents Online Self-Serve:*** We will design services to enable agents to act on their clients' behalf. We will introduce a new, single and more secure process for agents to register with HMRC and deal with us across a range of taxes on behalf of their clients. A significant number of businesses and individuals pay tax agents to do part or all of their tax compliance – and this is something that will continue in the future. We plan to start on a small scale from late 2014 and increase the services for wider use in 2015

Source: HM Revenue and Customs Business Plan 2014-16.

Box 7.3. Canada and South Africa: New service offerings

Canada

- In February 2014, the new electronic pre-authorised debit payment service was launched for individuals. This service was expanded to businesses in October 2014. In addition, the CRA plans to implement Visa debit in the future and is exploring the use of credit cards as another payment option.
- In 2014, the CRA released its first mobile app which can provide businesses with reminders for their instalments, payments, returns and remittance due dates. Another mobile app is being developed for 2015 that will allow individuals to access refund and benefit information.
- The Manage Online Mail service was launched in April 2013 for businesses. This service allows the CRA to advise taxpayers by electronic notification that they have new correspondence or an action request to view in a secure portal. The service was expanded to discounters in February 2014 and to representatives in October 2014. The service will also be made available to individuals for Notices of Assessments in February 2015.
- The Submit Document service provides taxpayers and their representatives with the opportunity to submit documents electronically when requested by a CRA programme. To date, the following programmes are using this service: Corporate Assessing Review Programme; T1 Process Review; Benefits Eligibility/Entitlement Programme; and Office Audit Programme. There are plans to expand the service to over 130 other programmes across the CRA.
- In February 2015, the Tax Data Delivery (TDD) service was launched. Authorised representatives, using EFILE certified software, are now able to request the secure electronic transmission of tax information that the CRA has available to complete portions of an individual's tax return. The TDD service electronically transfers tax information that is available and applicable to a taxpayer's account at the time of the service request.

South Africa

- ***Mobisite and MobiAPP:*** SARS enhanced its online service channel for the 2013 PIT season. The e-filing Mobisite, a web site for mobile devises, was upgraded to enable taxpayers to use the service to complete and submit income tax returns. The MobiApp application for mobile devises has been enhanced to allow tax practitioners to use this facility to submit clients' returns.
- ***Help-you-e-file (HYEF):*** SARS has upgraded its HYEF online service, via its call centre, to better support taxpayers completing their tax returns. The system now has the ability to detect when callers are on an active e-filing session. This enables a HYEF session to be automatically launched. "Help" prompts have been added to the e-filing service to assist taxpayers complete and submit their returns. A survey of HYEF users found that more than 90% of callers would use the service again if they needed assistance.

Source: Tax Administration 2015 survey responses.

Electronic filing of tax returns ("e-filing")

Previous editions of this series have given a fair deal of attention to the automation of tax return filing arrangements for the major taxes given their potential to deliver significant benefits to both revenue bodies and taxpayers. In particular, prior editions noted that that there had been substantial progress in the number of revenue bodies offering e-filing capabilities for their major taxes. However, they also noted that there were significant variations across both revenue bodies and the major taxes administered in terms of the level of take-up being achieved, resulting in considerable variability in the benefits across countries.

In the main, most progress had been made with e-filing for the personal income tax (PIT). Also apparent was the fact that an increasing number of revenue bodies had introduced mandatory e-filing requirements on some/all businesses to achieve major progress over a relatively short time frame. For this edition, an update is provided on the progress being made with e-filing for the major taxes – see Tables 7.3, 7.4 and 7.5. The key observations are as follows:

All major taxes

- Over two-thirds of revenue bodies in OECD countries achieved e-filing usage for over three-quarters (75%) of their PIT, CIT, and VAT taxpayers in 2013.

Personal income tax

- The provision of e-filing services for the PIT is now just about universal across the countries surveyed, with all countries where the national revenue body administers a PIT reporting the availability of this service for fiscal year 2013.
- Almost 60% of revenue bodies reported that the majority of their personal taxpayers filing returns used e-filing (either by themselves or via tax professionals) for the 2013 year:
  - Twenty-nine of fifty reported usage rates in excess of 75%;
  - Four of fifty reported usage rates between 50-75%;
  - Four of fifty reported usage rates between 25-50%;
  - Thirteen of fifty reported usage rates less than 25%; and
  - For six countries relevant data were not available.
- A number of countries have made substantial progress (i.e. +75% in absolute terms) over the last 10 years in increasing their e-filing usage-Argentina (+82%), Israel (+95%), Lithuania (+82%), Slovenia (+100%), South Africa (+95%).
- Drawing on the information in Table 9.8, revenue bodies generally have not relied on the use of mandated e-filing requirements to achieve high rates of e-filing take up for PIT taxpayers.
- There is potential for substantially greater use (i.e. +75% in absolute terms) of e-filing in 25% of countries surveyed, including in four OECD member countries-Czech Republic, Hungary, Luxembourg and Slovak Republic

Corporate income tax

- The provision of e-filing services is now just about universal across the countries surveyed (with 48 of 52 surveyed revenue bodies reporting the availability of this service for fiscal year 2013).
- Almost 80% of surveyed revenue bodies reported that returns for the majority of their corporate taxpayers were e-filed for the 2013 fiscal year:
  - Thirty-five reported usage rates in excess of 75%;
  - Seven reported usage rates between 50-75%;
  - One reported usage rates between 25-50%;
  - Nine reported usage rates less than 25%; and
  - For four countries relevant data were not available.

Table 7.3. **Personal income tax returns: Use of electronic filing and pre-filling**

Country	Year e-filing introduced	% of all returns e-filed during this fiscal year				Variation: 2013-2004 (total %)	% returns partially pre-filled in 2013	% returns fully prefilled in 2013
		2004	2009	2011	2013			
OECD countries								
Australia	1990	80	92	92	93	13	84	0
Austria	2003	10	79	79	80	70	n.a.	n.a.ppl.
Belgium	2002	3	40	54	70	67	100	29
Canada	1993	49	58	64	76	27	n.a.ppl	n.a.ppl.
Chile	1999	81	98	99	99	18	n.a.	68
Czech Republic	2004	< 1	1	1	3	3	0	0
Denmark	1994	68	96	98	98	30	100	74
Estonia	2000	59	92	94	95	36	100	n.a.
Finland	2006	0	23	33	45	45	100	73
France	2001	4	27	33	34	30	73	17
Germany	1999	7	30	32	51	44	0	0
Greece	2001	4	13	49	n.a.	n.a.	n.a.	n.a.
Hungary	2003	3	30	17	20	17	6	0
Iceland	1999	86	92	92	96	10	100	28
Ireland	2001	62	67	81	91	29	n.a.	0
Israel	2009	0	79	95	95	95	n.a.	0
Italy	1998	100	100	100	100	0	0	0
Japan	2004	0	31	44	50	50	n.a.	n.a.
Korea	2004	43	80	87	91	48	82	9
Luxembourg	2009	0	< 1	1	1	1	n.a.	n.a.
Mexico	1998	48	96	99	99	51	28	0
Netherlands	1996	69	95	95	96	27	50	0
New Zealand	1992	56	63	71	83	27	7	0
Norway	1999	37	82	86	91	54	100	63
Poland	2008	0	1.4	11	25	25	0	0
Portugal	2000	24	80	83	87	63	87	n.a.
Slovak Republic	2005	0	n.a.	< 1	2	2	0	0
Slovenia	2004	0	77	n.a.	100	100	(see text)	(see text)
Spain	1999	23	36	74	99 /1	76	19	53
Sweden	2002	15	55	63	77	62	100	75
Switzerland	--------------------Personal tax is administered at the sub-national (cantonal level); some cantons use e-filing--------------							
Turkey	2005	30	99	99	99	69	0	0
United Kingdom	2000	17	73	77	85	68	0	0
United States	1986	47	65	76	83	36	0	0
OECD ave. (unw.)		31	59	65	72	41	-	-
Non-OECD countries								
Argentina	1999	18	100	100	100	82	n.a.	n.a.
Brazil	1996	n.a.	n.a.	100	100	n.a.	0	0
Bulgaria	2005	< 1	3	5	11	11	0	0
China	2005	0	n.a.	n.a.	n.a.	n.a.	-	-
Colombia	n.a.	n.a.	n.a.	6	4	n.a.	0	0
Costa Rica	-	-	-	-	-	-	-	-
Croatia	-	-	-	-	-	-	-	-
Cyprus	2004	< 1	6	22	23	23	0	0
Hong Kong, China	n.a.	n.a.	n.a.	14	15	n.a.	100	0
India	n.a.	n.a.	17	(13.1 m)	80	n.a.	10	0
Indonesia	n.a.	n.a.	n.a.	n.a.	< 1	< 1	0	0
Latvia	2008	0	10	15	18	18	0	0
Lithuania	2004	14	71	87	96	82	34	66
Malaysia	2004	33	56	69	83	50	100	0
Malta	2006	1	2	1	1	0	28	73
Morocco	n.a.	n.a.	n.a.	n.a.	n.a.	n.a.	0	0
Romania	2007	0	< 1	n.a.	1	1	0	0
Russia	2006	0	9	3	7	7	7	0
Saudi Arabia	--Not applicable--							
Singapore	1998	67	91	96	97	31	99	49
South Africa	2001	4	46	99	99	95	n.a.	34
Thailand	n.a.	n.a.	n.a.	n.a.	34	n.a.	0	0

Source: Survey responses and prior series' editions.

Table 7.4. **Corporate income tax returns: Use of electronic filing and pre-filling**

Country	Year e-filing introduced	% all returns e-filed during this fiscal year				Variation : 2013-2004 (total %)	% returns partially pre-filled in 2013
		2004	2009	2011	2013		
OECD countries							
Australia	1990s	95	92	92	88	-9	0
Austria	2004	30	96	95	97	67	n.a
Belgium	2006	1	32	73	82	81	0
Canada	2002	2	21	46	70	68	n.appl.
Chile	1999	65	94	95	96	31	0
Czech Republic	2004	1	3	6	21	20	0
Denmark	2005	0	18	25	100	100	0
Estonia	2000	59	95	98	99	40	0
Finland	2000	1	19	32	58	57	0
France	1991	26	77	81	96	70	0
Germany	n.a.	0	0	n.a.	n.a.	0	0
Greece	n.a.	0	0	0	0	0	0
Hungary	2003	3	99	99	99	96	0
Iceland	1997	99	99	66	99	0	0
Ireland	2001	18	85	96	99	81	0
Israel	2009	0	62	74	77	77	n.a.
Italy	1998	100	100	100	100	0	0
Japan	2004	0	38	58	64	64	n.a.
Korea	2004	92	96	97	98	6	0
Luxembourg	n.a.	0	0	0	0	0	0
Mexico	1998	100	100	100	100	0	0
Netherlands	2005	0	100	100	100	100	0
New Zealand	1992	67	75	80	87	20	0
Norway	2000	47	75	86	87	40	0
Poland	2006	0	1	11	10	10	0
Portugal	2000	100	100	100	100	0	100
Slovak Republic	2005	0	n.a.	2	15	15	0
Slovenia	2004	0	100	100	99	99	0
Spain	1999	23	99	99	99	76	0
Sweden	2009	65 /1	68 /1	68 /1	75 /1	10	n.a
Switzerland	-------- Corporate income tax is administered at the sub-national (cantonal level); some cantons use e-filing --------						
Turkey	2005	72	99	99	98	26	0
United Kingdom	2004	1	16	42	98	97	0
United States	2004	1	25	44	40	39	0
OECD ave. (unw.)		31	64	68	81	50	-
Non-OECD countries							
Argentina	1999	34	100	100	100	66	n.a.
Brazil	n.a.	n.a.	n.a.	100	100	n.a	0
Bulgaria	2006	0	21	38	52	52	0
China	2001	n.a.	n.a.	n.a	n.a	n.a	0
Colombia	n.a.			23	8	n.a.	0
Costa Rica	-	-	-	-	-	-	-
Croatia	n.a.	n.a.	n.a.	n.a.	76	n.a	0
Cyprus	2004	0	n.a.	34	97	97	0
Hong Kong, China	2010	n.a	n.a	< 1	<1	<1	0
India	n.a.	0	n.a.	(1.25 m)	100	n.a	0
Indonesia	n.a	n.a	n.a	n.a	5	5	0
Latvia	2008	0	92	75	91	91	0
Lithuania	2004	34	67	73	82	48	0
Malaysia	2001	n.a.	18	49	76	n.a	n.a
Malta	2001	82	99	92	95	13	n.a
Morocco	2009	n.a.	0.4	1.3	2	2	0
Romania	2004	0	2	n.a.	74	74	0
Russia	n.a.	0	12	57	68	68	0
Saudi Arabia	n.a.	0	0	n.a	77	77	0
Singapore	2000	84	67	63	69	-15	0
South Africa	2006	0	36	94	95	95	26
Thailand	n.a.	n.a.	n.a.	n.a.	75	n.a.	0

For notes indicated by "/ (number)", see Notes to Tables section at the end of the chapter, p. 259.
Source: Survey responses and prior series' editions.

Table 7.5. **Value added tax (VAT) returns: Use of electronic filing and pre-filling**

Country	Year e-filing introduced	% all returns e-filed during this fiscal year				Variation: 2013-2004 (total %)	% returns partially pre-filled in 2013
		2004	2009	2011	2013		
OECD countries							
Australia	2001	36	49	54	59	23	0
Austria	2003	80	86	87	89	9	n.a.
Belgium	2001	9	90	97	97	88	0
Canada	2002	11	22	41	64	53	n.a.ppl.
Chile	1999	37	64	71	94	57	0
Czech Republic	2004	1	5	10	17	16	0
Denmark	1999	60	95	98	99	39	0
Estonia	2000	74	96	99	99	25	0
Finland	1997	35	65	80	85	50	0
France	2001	2	28	39	82	80	0
Germany	2000	19	25	28	80	61	0
Greece	2000	51	70	83	n.a.	n.a.	n.a.
Hungary	2000	6	99	99	99	93	0
Iceland	2004	16	65	74	99	83	0
Ireland	2000	13	45	63	98	85	0
Israel	n.a.	n.a.	n.a.	n.a.	23	n.a.	0
Italy	1998	100	100	100	100	0	0
Japan	2004	0	29 /1	40 /1	63 /1	n.a.	n.a.
Korea	2000	50	74	79	83	33	83
Luxembourg	2003	0	26	54	50	50	0
Mexico	2002	55	100	100	100	45	0
Netherlands	2005	0	100	100	100	100	0
New Zealand	1992	9	21	28	48	39	16
Norway	2001	38	88	92	99	61	0
Poland	2006	0	2	11	33	33	0
Portugal	2000	83	100	100	100	17	0
Slovak Republic	2005	0	n.a.	9	49	49	0
Slovenia	2004	0	100	100	99	99	0
Spain	1999	23	75	80	96	73	0
Sweden	2001	3	35	55	75	72	0
Switzerland	2010	0	0	< 1	<1	<1	0
Turkey	2004	70	99	99	99	29	0
United Kingdom	2003	0	20	67	99	99	0
United States	---------- No national VAT ----------						
OECD ave. (unw.)		28	62	67	77	52	
Non-OECD countries							
Argentina	1999	30	100	100	100	70	n.a.
Brazil	---------- No national VAT ----------						
Bulgaria	2004	5	68	82	94	89	0
China	n.a.	n.a.	n.a.	n.a.	n.a.	n.a.	0
Colombia	n.a.	n.a.	n.a.	24	16	n.a.	0
Costa Rica	n.a.	n.a.	n.a.	n.a.	100	n.a.	0
Croatia	n.a.	n.a.	n.a.	n.a.	98	n.a.	0
Cyprus	2004	1	1	2	4	3	0
Hong Kong, China	---------- No national VAT ----------						
India	---------- No national VAT ----------						
Indonesia	n.a.	n.a.	n.a.	n.a.	57	57	0
Latvia	2008	0	64	85	99	99	0
Lithuania	2004	35	87	93	97	62	0
Malaysia	---------- No national VAT ----------						
Malta	2009	0	< 1	2	3	3	n.a.
Morocco	2007	n.a.	0.5	1.3	2	2	0
Romania	2004	0	5	n.a.	86	86	0
Russia	n.a.	0	26	51	64	64	0
Saudi Arabia	---------- No national VAT ----------						
Singapore	2005	0	99	100	100	100	0
South Africa	2001	7	47	92	95	88	0
Thailand	n.a.	n.a.	n.a.	n.a.	69	n.a.	0

For notes indicated by "/ (number)", see Notes to Tables section at the end of the chapter, p. 259.

Source: Survey responses and prior series' editions.

- A number of revenue bodies have made substantial progress (i.e. +75% in absolute terms) over the last 10 years in increasing e-filing usage-Belgium, Cyprus, Denmark, Estonia, Hungary, Ireland, Israel, Latvia, Netherlands, Saudi Arabia, Slovenia, South Africa, Spain, and United Kingdom.
- Drawing on Table 9.9, the use of mandated e-filing requirements appears to have figured fairly prominently in the increased e-filing usage reported.
- There is potential for substantially greater use of e-filing (i.e. +75% in absolute terms) in nine surveyed countries, including in four OECD member countries – Czech Republic, Luxembourg, Poland, and the Slovak Republic.

Value added tax (VAT)

- The provision of e-filing services in those countries administering a VAT is now universal with 50 of 50 revenue bodies administering a VAT reporting the availability of this service for fiscal year 2013.
- There has been a considerable increase in the proportion of surveyed revenue bodies reporting that the majority of VAT returns are now filed electronically, rising from just over 23% for fiscal year 2009 to almost 38% for 2013:
  - Thirty-one reported usage rates in excess of 75%;
  - Seven reported usage rates between 50-75%;
  - Four reported usage rates between 25-50%;
  - Six reported usage rates less than 25%; and
  - For two bodies, no data were available.
- Many revenue bodies have made substantial progress (i.e. +75% in absolute terms) over the last 10 years in increasing the level e-filing usage-Belgium, Bulgaria, France, Hungary, Iceland, Ireland, Latvia, Netherlands, Romania, Singapore, Slovenia, South Africa and United Kingdom.
- Compared with the CIT, far greater use is being made of mandated e-filing requirements for VAT returns (see Table 9.10); for fiscal year 2013, 34 revenue bodies reported actual or intended use of such requirements for some/all of their taxpayers.
- There is potential for substantially greater use of e-filing (i.e. +75% in absolute terms) in at least six surveyed countries, including in three OECD member countries-Czech Republic, Israel and Switzerland.

The provision of pre-filled tax returns to taxpayers

One of the more significant developments in tax return process design and the use of technology by revenue bodies over the last 10-15 years concerns the emergence of systems of pre-filled tax returns for the PIT.

Pre-filling entails the use by revenue bodies of information held by them (e.g. taxpayer identity information, elements of taxpayer history, and third party reports of income and deductions etc.) to populate fields within tax returns etc. that are made available to taxpayers for their examination. Depending on the degree of sophistication of the service (and the legislative framework in place), fully or partially-completed tax returns can be made available to taxpayers in electronic and/or paper form. In their most advanced form, tax return preparation has been fully automated for the vast majority of the taxpayer population. This is particularly the case for Nordic region countries where revenue bodies offer this form of assistance for the vast majority of their taxpayers, with a large proportion of such returns being fully completed for the taxpayers concerned (e.g. Denmark, Finland, and Sweden).

Pre-filling can be carried out with varying degrees of sophistication. To explain this further, the capability/maturity model depicted in Figure 7.2, extracted from a prior FTA study (OECD, 2010), describes the varying degrees of capability (and related enhancements) observed from revenue body experience. Critical to this progress has been the existence of a compatible legislative framework – one that makes provision for extensive third party reporting of relevant taxpayer information and with relatively few deductions and credits that cannot be verified with the use of third party information sources. The model provides a means of classifying the nature of the service being provided by revenue bodies from the viewpoint of potential benefits.

Figure 7.2. **Maturity model of pre-filling capabilities**

LEVEL OF PREFILLING	CAPABILITY DESCRIPTION	LEVEL OF BENEFITS
Minimal	1. A paper form pre-filled with limited taxpayer identity &/or history information	Minor
↓	2. An electronic form pre-filled with limited taxpayer identity &/or history information	↓
	3. A paper form pre-filled with taxpayer identity &/or history information and limited income/deduction and credits information	
	4. An electronic form pre-filled with taxpayer identity &/or history information and limited income/deduction/credits information	
	5. A paper form pre-filled with taxpayer identity &/or history information and most/all income/deduction and credits information	
Maximum (fully completed tax return)	6. An electronic form pre-filled with taxpayer identity &/or history information and most/all income/deduction/credits information	
	7. Full automation (enabling elimination of original process)	Significant

Source: OECD CTPA Secretariat.

For this series, revenue bodies were surveyed on the extent to which pre-filling approaches were being used for the major taxes and, where this was the case for the personal income tax, the proportion of tax returns that were fully pre-filled for 2013. Drawing on the information provided in Table 7.3, the key findings are as follows:

- Many revenue bodies are making substantial use of pre-filling to modernise (and for some, transform) the operation of their PIT system:
  - Eight revenue bodies (i.e. Chile, Denmark, Finland, Lithuania, Malta, Norway, Spain and Sweden) provide a capability that is able to generate a fully completed annual tax return (or its equivalent) online and/or in paper form ***for the majority of taxpayers required to file tax returns in 2013***, while four bodies (i.e. Belgium, Iceland, Singapore, and South Africa) achieved this outcome in 2013 for between 25-50% of their personal taxpayers.
  - While not quantifying the numbers concerned, Slovenia reported that persons liable for personal income tax receive informative calculations of their liability that must be checked by them – if they agree they do not need to do anything

and 15 days later such informative calculations become personal income tax decisions (with the same data deposited on the personal web portal of the e-tax system).

  - Substantial use of pre-filling to partially complete tax returns was reported by 14 revenue bodies-Australia, Belgium, Estonia, Finland, France, Hong Kong, Iceland, Korea, Malaysia, Netherlands, Portugal, Singapore, and Sweden.
  - Overall, almost half of revenue bodies reported use of pre-filling.

- For other taxes, use of pre-filling is much more limited and generally confined to basic taxpayer identification and demographic information.

Electronic payments of tax ("e-payments")

Payments of taxes constitute one of the most common forms of interaction between taxpayers, their agents, and revenue bodies. This is especially the case for businesses that are typically required to regularly remit a variety of payments during each fiscal year (covering both their own tax liabilities and those of their employees). More generally, citizens and businesses are required to make significant numbers of payments for bills they receive each year (e.g. for utilities, and credit card debts). The sheer number of payment transactions that must be effected in a normally-functioning economy has led to significant developments over the last decade in the range of electronic payment methods made available to citizens and businesses at large, all aimed at making the "payment experience" easier and less costly.

Prior editions of this series observed that revenue bodies were making reasonable progress in increasing the range of fully electronic payment methods available to taxpayers. The main examples cited were the use of direct debit, direct credit (i.e. on-line payments by taxpayers), and phone banking. However, it was also noted that manual (more costly) payment methods – for example, mailed cheques, cash, or "in-person" payments by taxpayers at revenue bodies and/or at third party agencies (using cash or cheques) – were still the predominant method of payment in many surveyed revenue bodies. As a result, many were still incurring significant administrative costs for the processing of tax payments. A related concern noted, however, was the fact that many revenue bodies were unable to report volume usage data for their payment method, suggesting that they had little knowledge of the costs being incurred, both by themselves and taxpayers.

As for other types of electronic services, the methods of e-payment available vary in their level of "maturity" (or degree of related automation), and the resulting benefits they can deliver for taxpayers, revenue bodies and third parties. To promote further thinking about this matter an FTA study (OECD, 2010) set out an "e-payment maturity model" depicting the methods of payment available to revenue bodies to collect taxes, a description of the costs typically involved with each method and a judgment as to the associated degree of automation and overall costs involved – see Figure 7.3.

As suggested by the model, costs are reduced significantly when moving from fully manual methods that require the use of cheques and/or personal visits by taxpayers to the revenue body or its agents, to the use of fully electronic payment methods such as Internet banking (direct credit) and "direct debit". Accordingly, in countries where use of fully electronic payment methods is relatively low, there would seem to be potential for significant benefits from substantially increasing their use.

Figure 7.3. **Maturity model of payment methods**

DEGREE OF AUTOMATION	CAPABILITY DESCRIPTION		LEVEL OF COSTS
	DESCRIPTION	COSTS INCURRED	
Low (limited)	1. In-person payment at revenue body; data captured electronically on receipt	Taxpayers' time to pay; revenue bodies' processing costs	High
↓	2. In-person payment at agency (e.g. bank); data captured electronically	Taxpayers' time to pay; agency transaction fee	↓
	3. Mailed cheque to revenue body; automated payment data capture	Postage, banks' and revenue bodies' processing costs	
	4. Taxpayers' use of phone banking	Taxpayers' time and phone call	
	5. Taxpayers' use of Internet payment method (via bank/revenue body)	Taxpayers' time	
	6. Taxpayers use of direct debit authority for payment (on liability-by-liability basis)	Taxpayers' time re renewal of each authorisation	
High (fully electronic – categories 5, 6 and 7)	7. Taxpayers use of direct debit authority for payment of all taxes	Taxpayers' time in providing direct debit authorisation	Very low

Source: OECD CTPA Secretariat.

For this series, revenue bodies were surveyed on the nature of the payment methods available for collecting taxes and their relative usage (in % terms) for the 2013 fiscal year (see Table 7.6). A fair number of revenue bodies were unable to provide volume-related data the findings and the observations are, as a result, limited to just over 60% of surveyed revenue bodies:

- Taken as a whole, and drawing on data from prior series, revenue bodies appear to have made substantial of progress over the last 4-5 years in automating tax payment collection for the majority of taxpayers:

Status of tax payment collection methods	2009	2011	2013
Number of revenue bodies reporting fully electronic payment methods for the majority of tax payments	6 of 22 (27%)	12 of 28 (43%)	20 of 32 (62%)
Number of revenue bodies reporting partially electronic payment methods for the majority of tax payments	6 of 22 (27%)	11 of 28 (39%)	8 of 26 (31%)
Number of revenue bodies reporting non-electronic payment methods for the majority of tax payments	3 of 22 (14%)	5 of 28 (18%)	3 of 22 (14%)
Number of revenue bodies reporting the use of in-person/ in-office payment collection method	27 of 49 (55%)	25 of 52 (48%)	25 of 56 (45%)

- Twenty revenue bodies reported that the majority of payments were made by fully electronic methods, including 11 where the aggregate proportion exceeded 75% (i.e. Chile, Finland, Hungary, India, Ireland, Netherlands, Norway, Singapore, Sweden and United Kingdom).
- Partially electronic payment methods – these typically entail the collection of payments made in-person to a third party agent (e.g. a bank or post office) that transmits the relevant payment data electronically to the revenue body – were the predominant payment method in eight countries.
- Over 45% of revenue bodies continue to provide costly "in-person" payment facilities via their office networks; in many cases, the volumes reported were relatively low raising doubts as to "cost/benefit" arguments for their retention.

Table 7.6. **Tax payment methods available and volume usage (%) in 2013**

	Non-electronic		Partially electronic		Fully electronic: Complete self-service by taxpayers			
Country	Mailed cheques	In-person at office	Agency payment	Phone banking	Internet	Direct debit	Payment kiosk	Others
OECD countries								
Australia	✓ (8)		✓ (19)	✓	✓ (71)	✓ (2)		
Austria	✓ (<1)	✓ (2)	✓ (27)		✓ (70)			
Belgium			✓	✓	✓ (70)	✓		
Canada	✓ (32)	✓ (<1)	✓ (30)	--------------	✓ (38)	--------------		
Chile			✓ (5)		--------------	✓ (95) /1	--------------	--------------
Czech Republic		✓	✓	✓	✓	✓		
Denmark			✓		✓			
Estonia			✓		✓	✓		
Finland			✓ (5)		✓ (92)	✓ (3)		
France	✓ (21)	✓ (6)			✓ (7)	✓ (66)		
Germany	✓		✓	✓	✓	✓		
Greece			✓		✓	✓		
Hungary	✓ (15)	✓ (<1)			------- ✓ (85)	-------	✓ (<1)	
Iceland	✓	✓	✓		✓	✓		
Ireland	✓ (3)	✓ (<1)	✓ (10)		✓ (77)	✓ (10)		✓ (<1)
Israel	✓ (<1)	✓ (2)	✓ (73)		------- ✓ (17)	-------		
Italy			✓ (40)		✓ (36)	✓ (24)		
Japan			✓ (75)		✓ (2)	✓ (15)		
Korea		✓ (5)	✓ (60)	✓ (<1)	✓ (25)	✓ (4)	✓ (6)	
Luxembourg	✓ /1	✓ /2	✓		✓ /2	✓ /1		
Mexico			✓ (51)		✓ (49)	✓		✓ (<1)
Netherlands			✓ (<1)		✓ (44)	✓ (55)		
New Zealand	✓ (26)		✓ (4)	--------------	✓ (70)	--------------		
Norway	✓ (<1)	✓ (<1)	✓	✓	✓ (99)			
Poland	✓	✓	✓		✓	✓		
Portugal		✓ (45)	✓ (15)		✓ (40)			
Slovak Republic			✓		✓			
Slovenia			✓ (100)					
Spain			✓	✓	✓	✓		
Sweden			✓ (1)	✓	✓ (90)	✓ (9)		
Switzerland			✓		✓	✓		
Turkey	✓	✓	✓	✓	✓	✓		
United Kingdom	✓ (9)	✓ (<1)	✓ (8)	✓ (2)	✓ (29)	✓ (52)		
United States	✓ (36 est.)	✓ (<1 est.)	✓ (<1 est.)	✓ (3 est.)	✓ (25 est.)	✓ (10 est.)		✓ (25 est.)
Non-OECD countries								
Argentina			✓ (32)	✓ (<1)	✓ (10)	✓ (8)	✓ (50)	
Brazil			✓ (49)	✓ (<1)	✓ (51)			
Bulgaria			✓	✓	✓		✓	
China	✓	✓	✓	✓	✓	✓		
Colombia			✓ (90)		✓ (10)			
Costa Rica			✓		✓	✓		
Croatia			✓		✓			
Cyprus	✓ (<1)	✓ (40)	✓ (50)		✓ (6)			✓ (4)
Hong Kong, China	✓ (6)		✓ (38)	✓ (17)	✓ (31)	✓ (8)		
India			✓ (14)		✓ (86)			
Indonesia			✓		✓			
Latvia			✓		✓			
Lithuania			✓		✓		✓	
Malaysia	✓	✓ (51)	✓ (43)	✓	✓ (6)	✓	✓	
Malta	✓ (47)	✓ (7)			✓ (9)	✓ (14)		✓ (23)
Morocco		✓ (98) /1			✓ (2) /1			
Romania		✓	✓		✓	✓		
Russia			✓		✓			
Saudi Arabia			✓ (100)					
Singapore	✓ (12)	✓ (7)		------- 10	-------	✓ (50)	✓ (17)	✓ (5)
South Africa		✓ (2)			------- ✓ (65)	-------		
Thailand		✓ (70)	✓ (<1)		✓ (29)			

For notes indicated by "/ (number)", see Notes to Tables section at the end of the chapter, p. 259.
Source: Tax Administration 2015 survey responses.

- Four revenue bodies reported reasonably significant volumes (25% or more) of mailed cheques that require internal processing by them (i.e. Canada, Malta, New Zealand, and United States); all four countries reported that increased use of e-payments was a priority for them in 2014 and beyond (see Table 7.2).
- Payments made in person at the revenue body were relatively significant (i.e. representing over 40% of all payments) in five countries (Cyprus, Malaysia, Morocco, Portugal, and Thailand); all five reported that increased use of e-payments was a strategic priority for them in their plans (see Table 7.2).
- Well over a third of revenue bodies were unable to report payment volume data by type of payment method suggesting that insufficient attention is being given to fully automating this aspect of service delivery.
- The overall rate of fully electronic e-payments in 2013 appears well below e-filing rates for the major taxes; while not researched as part of this survey, factors possibly contributing to this outcome include: *(1)* taxpayers' perceptions of security weaknesses in the banking system; *(2)* taxpayers' general reluctance to use direct debit facilities; *(3)* the failure of revenue bodies to adequately promote e-payment methods; and *(4)* lack of Internet access.

The lack of comprehensive data on payment volumes and the methods used complicates the drawing of any firm conclusions across the full population of surveyed revenue bodies; that said, there appears potential for substantially greater use of e-payment capabilities in many surveyed countries.

Notes to Tables

Table 7.2. Strategic priorities for increasing use of online services

/1. **Canada:** The CRA implemented a secure online method in 2012 for taxpayers and their representatives to submit supporting documentation and receipts to the CRA. This service is currently offered for four programmes, with consideration being given to further expansion. **Luxembourg:** Indirect taxes only. **Portugal:** Reported that its plans also include the use of "big data" tools to provide statistical information (by sectors and geographical areas) on VAT and income tax for market research and new investments, and applications for Smartphones. **Switzerland:** The use of e-services for PIT and CIT administered by the 26 sub-national cantons varies significantly. The answers reflect the perspectives of those cantons that are generally more advanced in their use of e-services, including use of apps for mobile devices.

/2. **Luxembourg:** Direct taxes only.

Table 7.4. Corporate income tax returns: Use of electronic filing and pre-filling

/1. **Sweden:** Volumes represent file transfers of profit and loss account, balance sheet and tax adjustments, not tax returns per se.

Table 7.5. VAT income tax returns: Use of electronic filing and pre-filling

/1. **Japan**: Take up rates reported relate only to the proportion of incorporated taxpayers filing VAT returns.

Table 7.6. Tax payment methods available and volume usage (%) (where known) in 2013

/1. **Chile:** Includes Internet, direct debit and others (e.g. credit card payments). **Luxembourg:** Direct taxes only. **Morocco:** Results reported are for VAT and CIT only.

/2. **Luxembourg:** Indirect taxes only.

Bibliography

ATO (2014), *ATO Strategic Intent – Reinventing the ATO*, Australian Taxation Office, Canberra, p.9.

HMRC (2014), *Business Plan 2014-16*, United Kingdom Her Majesty's Revenue and Customs, London.

New Zealand Inland Revenue (2014), *Statement of Intent 2014-18,* New Zealand Inland Revenue, Wellington, p.7.

OECD (2014), *Increasing Taxpayers' Use of Self-service Channels*, OECD Publishing, available at: http://dx.doi.org/10.1787/9789264223288-en.

OECD (2013), *Managing Service Demand: A Practical Guide to Help Revenue Bodies Better Meet Taxpayers' Service Expectations*, OECD Publishing, available at: http://dx.doi.org/10.1787/9789264200821-en.

OECD (2012), *Working Smarter in Revenue Administration – Using demand management strategies to meet service delivery goals*, OECD, Paris, available at: www.oecd.org/dataoecd/53/8/49428187.pdf.

OECD (2010), *Survey of Trends and Developments in the Use of Electronic Services,* OECD, Paris, available at: www.oecd.org/tax/administration/45035933.pdf.

Chapter 8

Tax administration and tax intermediaries

This chapter outlines aspects concerned with revenue bodies' administration of tax intermediaries, and provides examples of specific approaches and initiatives used by revenue bodies to leverage improvements to taxpayers' compliance and the general functioning on the tax system.

Key points

- Many surveyed revenue bodies may be missing substantial opportunities for leveraging improved compliance and easing taxpayers' compliance burden through the use of tax intermediaries, as evidenced by the following survey findings:
  - Around 40% of revenue bodies reported that there were no specific laws/regulations governing the tax-related operations of tax intermediaries; the absence of laws/ regulations was particularly prevalent among many advanced European economies.
  - Just over half of revenue bodies were unable to report (or even estimate) the volumes of tax returns prepared by tax intermediaries, suggesting limited focus by them on the role tax intermediaries play in this critical aspect of tax administration.
  - Over 60% of revenue bodies do not regularly survey tax intermediaries (or their representatives) on service delivery and other aspects of the tax administration.
  - Almost 40% of revenue bodies do not have formal consultative arrangements for engaging with representatives of tax intermediaries.
  - From a menu of five potential specialised services for tax intermediaries observed in some countries, only around 25% of revenue bodies appear to offer a "comprehensive" range (i.e. four or more) of such services; just over 60% reported offering two or less.
- There appear opportunities for at least 75% of surveyed revenue bodies to enhance the range of services offered to tax intermediaries.
- The chapter includes useful examples from selected countries dealing with the regulation and registration of tax intermediaries, consultation and engagement, information services, relationship/ account managers, and online services.

This chapter provides a fairly brief description of revenue bodies' approaches for administering and supporting the work of tax agents/tax preparers/tax professionals, etc., hereafter referred to as "tax intermediaries".

Introduction and context

Tax intermediaries play a significant role in the operation of the tax system of many countries, carrying out a range of tasks essential to its smooth functioning (e.g. preparing tax returns, providing advice to taxpayers on the application of the tax laws, and representing them in their dealings with the revenue body). While tax intermediaries are engaged principally by taxpayers to assist them in meeting their tax obligations, their high usage in many countries means that they can play a significant role in achieving high levels of compliance, in essence assisting the revenue body, and the community at large, achieve its overall revenue collection goals. For example:

- ***Tax law complexity:*** With few exceptions, tax laws (and often the administrative procedures related to those laws) are complex. Most taxpayers, particularly those in business, have neither the time nor the knowledge to fully understand and deal with all aspects of their taxation responsibilities.

  Tax intermediaries operate as conduits, advising taxpayers of the requirements of the law that apply to their affairs, what actions are required of them to meet those obligations, preparing relevant tax returns and other tax documents, and representing them when issues arise (e.g. an audit inquiry). For those taxpayers who do business globally, the assistance sought by them on tax matters often extends to the tax laws of other countries, thus increasing the degree of reliance on the services they provide.

- ***Tax law changes:*** Tax laws change frequently and many taxpayers may not be aware of such changes and the implications for their own financial and business affairs. Timely provision of comprehensive and accurate tax information by revenue bodies to tax intermediaries can assist greatly in the dissemination of changed laws and their implications for taxpayers.
- ***Tax compliance:*** Tax intermediaries can directly assist taxpayers comply with their tax obligations in a number of ways: *(1)* Provide advice on the nature and quality of books and records to be kept to properly comply; *(2)* Remind them when specific obligations fall due (e.g. return filing and payment); *(3)* Correct taxpayers' misunderstandings of specific areas of law and administrative requirements; *(4)* Advise them of common compliance risk issues (that may result in deliberate or inadvertent non-compliance); and *(5)* Represent them in compliance-related dealings with the revenue body (e.g. seeking extensions of time to file or pay tax, and assisting with voluntary disclosures and tax audits).

It was largely in the context of the positive contribution that tax intermediaries could play in achieving tax compliance and contributing to the smooth functioning of the tax system that the FTA's 2008 study (OECD, 2008) into the role of tax intermediaries conceived and recommended the idea of an "enhanced relationship" involving tax intermediaries, taxpayers and the revenue body. While the focus of the study was on aggressive tax planning and the tax affairs of large taxpayers, the general principles underpinning the "enhanced relationship" apply across all segments of taxpayers and their representatives. The essence of what the study recommended is set out in Box 8.1. In early 2012, the FTA Bureau commissioned an evaluation

Box 8.1. Study into the role of tax intermediaries: The enhanced relationship

The study's key finding is that revenue bodies could achieve a more effective and efficient relationship in their dealings with taxpayers and tax intermediaries if their actions are based upon the following attributes:

- Understanding based on commercial awareness;
- Impartiality
- Proportionality
- Openness
- Responsiveness

An explanation of the characteristics of these attributes and what it means for revenue bodies and their approach to tax administration is set out in the study report – see www.oecd.org/dataoecd/28/34/39882938.pdf. The report emphasises that these attributes are fundamental for any revenue body and should underpin all their dealings with all taxpayers. If revenue bodies demonstrate these five attributes and have effective risk-management processes in place taxpayers, especially large corporate taxpayers, would be more likely to engage in a relationship with revenue bodies based on co-operation and trust, what is described in the report as an "enhanced relationship".

An enhanced relationship offers benefits for revenue bodies as well as taxpayers. The report notes that taxpayers who behave transparently and who provide a high level of disclosure of relevant information can expect greater certainty and an earlier resolution of tax issues with less extensive audits and lower compliance costs. An enhanced relationship between revenue bodies and tax intermediaries would also yield significant benefits.

Source: Study into the Role of Tax Intermediaries (OECD, 2008).

of the progress made in the application of the concept as it applies to large taxpayers. This matter is addressed in Chapter 3 of this series under the heading of "co-operative compliance".

The population and work volumes of tax intermediaries

Comprehensive data on the population of tax intermediaries in surveyed countries are not readily available but the following information, some a little dated, gives a sense of the degree of their involvement in the operation of the tax system in the countries concerned:

- ***Australia:*** In 2011-12, there were around 23 000 active registered tax agents and over 6 000 active registered business activity statements agents (source: ATO Compliance Programme 2012-13); as noted in the ATO's survey response, these tax intermediaries were responsible for preparing tax returns for over 70% of personal taxpayers and 90% of corporate tax returns in 2013.
- ***New Zealand:*** In 2012, around 5 200 tax agents were registered with Inland Revenue, and were responsible for handling the tax affairs of nearly two million clients, filing 83% of all income tax returns. (Source: IR website)
- ***United Kingdom:*** In 2010, HMRC estimated that there were around 43 000 tax agent firms representing around eight million clients. (Source: The report *Engaging with tax agents* (United Kingdom National Audit Office (October 2010); as noted in HMRC's survey response, these tax intermediaries were responsible for preparing tax returns for 66% of personal self-assessment taxpayers and an estimated 93% of corporate tax returns in 2013.
- ***United States:*** As part of the Paid Preparer Initiative launched in 2010, around 750 000 tax preparers had been registered by 2011. As noted in the IRS's survey response, these tax intermediaries were responsible for preparing tax returns for an estimated 63% of personal tax returns and an estimated 97% of corporate tax returns in 2013.

Certainly for the countries highlighted, tax intermediaries are major stakeholders for both personal and corporate taxpayers, and thus present significant potential to assist the revenue body in achieving taxpayers' compliance with the laws.

Regulation of tax intermediaries

The role of regulation and registration

The report of the study into the role of tax intermediaries (OECD, 2008) made special reference to the role and value of regulation and registration of tax intermediaries:

> An ability to identify tax intermediaries is generally seen as being an important step in understanding and effectively managing their role within the tax system. However, the level of revenue body involvement in the registration and regulation of tax intermediaries varies considerably among FTA countries. In some FTA countries, tax advisers are entirely self-registered and regulated; generally, within the framework provided by professional bodies. This framework can be very strict as some tax intermediary businesses are tightly regulated and operate under a number of professional and ethical codes.
>
> The United Kingdom is an example of a country that, to some extent, relies on self-regulation by professional bodies. The five main principles of one such body, the

Institute of Chartered Accountants in England and Wales (ICAEW), are integrity, objectivity, professional competence and due care, confidentiality and professional behaviour.

In other countries, the revenue body is more active and this may involve some form of regulation by it. This will typically involve a registration process that allocates a unique number to individual tax intermediary businesses or professionals within the business. The number must then be included on any contact with the revenue body and on any submission made by their clients to the revenue body. In order to become "registered", tax advisers must sign up to a minimum standard of behaviour or meet a minimum standard of qualification as set out in relevant legislation. These standards are then monitored by the revenue body. For example, in Japan, the National Tax Agency (NTA) provides guidance and supervision for certified public tax accountants (CPTAs) or "Zeirishi". The NTA is currently making efforts to collect information on cases of professional misconduct and dealing strictly with those in breach of the CPTA Law.

Since the study report was released, both Australia and the United States have introduced new regulatory requirements for tax intermediaries, which were described in some detail in TA2013. In brief:

- ***Australia:*** Modernised laws governing the registration and operation of "tax agents" came into effect in March 2009. The new laws were introduced after extensive consultation with the tax and accounting profession to modernise an outdated legislative and administrative framework. These laws are known as the: *(1) Tax Agent Services Act 2009 (TASA 2009); (2) Tax Agent Services Regulations 2009 (TAS Regulations 2009);* and *(3) Tax Transitional Act.*
- ***United States:*** The IRS launched a return preparer review in 2009 to strengthen partnerships with tax return preparers and tax practitioners and ensure that all preparers and practitioners adhere to professional standards. After an extensive review that included significant public input, the IRS announced in January 2010 a fundamental change in how the agency will regulate the tax return preparation industry. Under this change, the IRS will implement new regulations and procedures that will better serve taxpayers, tax administration and the tax professional industry.

Other examples drawn from survey responses for this series include:

- ***Croatia:*** The Tax Consultancy Act prescribes the establishment of the Croatian Chamber of Tax Advisers, which administers a register of persons who have passed the tax consultancy exam and a register of public companies which can perform tax consultancy services, including those who are actually providing tax consultancy services. The Chamber also maintains a record of foreign tax consultants (tax intermediaries) performing tax consultancy services in Croatia. (Source: Survey response).
- ***South Africa:*** Persons who provide advice on tax matters, including assistance with tax return preparation, must register with SARS, as required in the Tax Administration Act of 2011. To register as a tax practitioner, they must meet the following requirements: *(1)* they must belong to or fall under the jurisdiction of a Recognised Controlling Body as referred to in s 240A of the Tax Administration Act; *(2)* Have the minimum qualifications and experience set by their respective recognised Controlling Body; *(3)* have no criminal convictions for the offences described in s 240(3) of the Tax Administration Act; *(4)* Participate in continuous

professional development programmes set by your Recognised Controlling Body; and *(5)* Be tax compliant as monitored by your Recognised Controlling Body. (Source: SARS website, October 2014)

There have also been some developments identified from Secretariat research. In January 2014, Canada's Minister of National Revenue launched a national consultation on a proposed "Registration of Tax Preparers Programme" (RTPP). Under the proposed programme, all tax preparers who prepare an individual or corporate income tax return for a fee would be required to register. The programme's goal is to allow the CRA to link errors to the tax preparer who prepared the return thus enabling the CRA to work with that tax preparer to prevent errors from occurring in the future. The proposed programme envisions a tailored strategic compliance approach that commences with education and moves to more progressive sanctions up to and including deregistration. The proposed RTPP would have a redress process to ensure fair and consistent administration of sanctions. The CRA received extensive feedback throughout the consultation process, which it continues to consider.

Country survey findings

For this series, revenue bodies were asked to indicate whether there were any laws prescribing the registration and/or operation of tax intermediaries in relation to their dealings with revenue bodies, the proportion of PIT and CIT returns prepared by tax intermediaries, and whether they regularly survey tax intermediaries (or their representative bodies) on their views and perceptions on aspects of service delivery and administration of the laws.

A summary of the information provided by revenue bodies is set out in Table 8.1 and the key observations are as follows:

- Just over half of revenue bodies reported the existence of laws/regulations prescribing the registration and/or operations of tax intermediaries; however, it was not entirely clear from some responses whether the laws referred to were specific to tax intermediaries or more generic in nature.
- The absence of regulations concerning tax intermediaries was particularly prevalent among many advanced European economies (e.g. Finland, France, Ireland, Luxembourg, Netherlands, Norway, Switzerland and United Kingdom).
- Just over half of revenue bodies were unable to report, or even estimate, the proportion of PIT and CIT returns prepared by tax intermediaries, suggesting limited focus by the revenue body on the their operations; of the 20 revenue bodies that did report, 11 indicated volumes of over 40% of all PIT returns and 17 reported volumes of over 60% of all CIT tax returns.
- Just over one-third (20) reported that they regularly survey tax intermediaries (or their representative bodies) on their views/perceptions of the revenue body's service delivery and overall tax administration.

The services and support provided to tax intermediaries

With responsibilities for a fair proportion of taxpayers' affairs in many countries tax intermediaries can be viewed as a special type of "client" through which, as explained earlier in the chapter, there are likely to be many opportunities for revenue bodies to leverage improved compliance with the tax laws. In recognition of this, some revenue bodies have taken steps to devise an overarching strategy for supporting tax intermediaries and to develop capabilities (e.g. consultation and tailored services) to foster the overall

Table 8.1. **Tax intermediaries: Laws and regulations, returns prepared, surveys**

Country	Name(s) of any laws regulating the tax responsibilities of tax intermediaries	Tax returns in 2013 (%)		Regular surveys on service, etc.
		Personal income tax	Corporate income tax	
OECD countries				
Australia	Tax Agent Services Act (2009)	74	90	✓
Austria	Tax Procedure Code and Law on the Profession of Tax Advisers and Public Accountants	81	95	✓ /1
Belgium	Income Tax Code 1992 – Article 305	17	n.a.	✓
Canada	Income Tax Act	55	n.a.	✓
Chile	Tax Code (e.g. Arts. 34 and 100).	n.a.	n.a.	x
Czech Republic	Act on Tax Consulting and Chamber of Tax Advisers	n.a	n.a.	x
Denmark	Professional Accountant s Law	5	85-90	✓
Estonia	Taxation Act	n.a.	n.a.	x
Finland	x	n.a.	n.a.	✓
France	x	n.a.	n.a.	x
Germany	Tax advisory law	n.a.	n.a.	✓
Greece	x	n.a.	n.a.	x
Hungary	Act XCII of 2003 on the Rules of Taxation	n.a.	n.a.	x
Iceland	x	24	72	x
Ireland	x	n.a.	n.a.	x
Israel	Law for Regulating the Activity of Tax Consultants, 2005, etc.	n.a.	n.a.	✓ /1
Italy	Various legislative decrees	99	98.3	x
Japan	Certified Public Tax Accountant Act	n.a.	n.a.	✓
Korea	Certified Tax Accountant Act	50	95	x
Luxembourg	-	40 (est.)	70 (est.)	x
Mexico	Federal Tax Code and Customs Law	n.a.	n.a.	✓
Netherlands	x	25	85	✓
New Zealand	Tax Administration Act 1994, s34B	67 /1	75 /1	✓
Norway	Law of Authorisation for Accountants. Auditing and Auditors' Act of 1999	n.a	n.a.	x
Poland	Tax Adviser Law	n.a	n.a.	x
Portugal	General Tax Law	2	100	✓
Slovak Republic	Act 78 /1992 Coll. on Tax Advisers and Slovak Chamber of Tax Advisers	40	70	x
Slovenia	x	n.a.	n.a.	✓
Spain	✓	n.a.	n.a.	✓
Sweden	Tax Law Procedure	n.a.	n.a.	x
Switzerland	-	n.a.	n.a.	x
Turkey	✓ /1	n.a	n.a	x
United Kingdom	x	66	93 (est.)	✓
United States	✓ /1	63 (est.)	97 (est.)	✓
Non-OECD countries				
Argentina	x	n.a.	100	x
Brazil	x	0	n.a.	x /1
Bulgaria	x	46	46	✓
China	x	n.a.	n.a.	x
Colombia	x	n.a.	n.a.	x
Costa Rica	x	n.a.	n.a.	n.a.
Croatia	The Tax Consultancy Act etc.	n.a.	n.a	✓
Cyprus	Assessment and Collection of Taxes Law	21	100	x
Hong Kong, China	x (Subject to regulations of their respective professional bodies)	n.a.	75	x
India	Income Tax Act, 1961 and Income Tax Rules, 1962 /1	3	n.a.	x
Indonesia	✓	n.a	n.a	x
Latvia	x	n.a.	n.a.	x
Lithuania	x	n.a.	n.a.	x
Malaysia	Malaysian Income Tax Act 1967, Section 153	n.a.	n.a.	x
Malta	Electronic Communications (Income Tax) Regulations S.L. 372.23 /1	1	99	x
Morocco	x	0	0	x
Romania	Ordinance on the organisation and exercise of fiscal consultancy activity	n.a.	n.a.	x
Russia	x	n.a.	n.a.	x
Saudi Arabia	x	-	-	x
Singapore	Accountants Act (Cap 2)(Singapore Statutes)	2	n.a.	✓
South Africa	The amended Tax Administration Act 28 of 2011	n.a.	n.a.	x
Thailand	x	n.a.	n.a.	x

For notes indicated by "/ (number)", see Notes to Tables section at the end of the chapter, p. 276.
Source: Tax Administration 2015 survey responses.

relationship. A few examples to these strategies and capability elements reported by a number of revenue bodies and/or identified by research are set out in the following section.

An overall strategy for providing service and support

The Netherlands

The Netherlands Tax and Customs Administration's (NTCA) approach to supporting tax intermediaries is based largely on its strategy for improving compliance with tax law. The NTCA strategy is to get to know this group and to be more receptive to their needs and ways of working. For this purpose, the NTCA applies a strategy termed "horizontal monitoring" (the Dutch term for "co-operative compliance") in the SME segment and for those tax intermediaries who are not eligible for horizontal monitoring the focus is on compiled signals per tax intermediary, as described in the report prepared by the Forum on Tax Administration (OECD, 2012). More background to the NTCA's horizontal monitoring approach is set out in Box 8.2.

Box 8.2. **The Netherlands: Horizontal monitoring and tax intermediaries**

The State Secretary's letter of 8 April 2005 to the House of Representatives of the States-General explained horizontal monitoring as follows:

Horizontal monitoring refers to mutual trust between the taxpayer and the Netherlands Tax and Customs Administration, the more precise specification of each other's responsibilities and options available to enforce the law and the setting out and fulfilment of mutual agreements. In so doing, the mutual relationships and communications between citizens and the government shift towards a more equal position. Horizontal monitoring is also compatible with social developments in which the citizen's personal responsibility is accompanied by the feeling that the enforcement of the law is of great value. In addition, the horizontal monitoring concept also implies that enforcement is feasible in today's complex and rapidly changing society solely when use is made of society's knowledge.

The relationship of trust in the SME segment is not directly with the taxpayers, but rather with the tax intermediaries. Considering the size of the SME segment the NTCA is aiming in this segment for co-operation with tax intermediaries. The objective of the co-operation is to provide assurance that the quality of the tax returns the tax intermediary files is acceptable (i.e. the returns comply with legislation and regulations and are free of material errors). SMEs wishing to participate in horizontal monitoring are required to sign a statement of affiliation together with the tax intermediary. Tax intermediaries verify the identity of the SMEs participating in horizontal monitoring and they assess their integrity.

An important principle of horizontal monitoring is not to duplicate work carried out by others. The NTCA relies on the work the tax intermediaries carry out for their clients. Supervision is shifted to the tax intermediary's internal quality system, in particular to the acceptance policy governing the admission of clients and the work processes. By adopting this approach the NTCA can reduce the supervisory burden for entrepreneurs who file acceptable tax returns and devote more attention to higher-risk returns.

The NTCA justifies the relationship of trust with the tax intermediary by meta-monitoring which makes use of information that includes the results from the tax intermediary's quality assurance system.

Sources: Tax Supervision – Made to Measure – Flexible when possible, strict where necessary, Committee for Horizontal Monitoring Tax and Customs Administration (http://download.belastingdienst.nl/belastingdienst/docs/tax_supervision_made_to_measure_tz0151z1fdeng.pdf), and *Guide to horizontal monitoring within the SME segment; Tax service providers, NTCA* (http://download.belastingdienst.nl/belastingdienst/docs/guide_horiz_monit_dv4071z1pleng.pdf).

The United Kingdom

In August 2010 HMRC's Board considered a new strategy for engaging with tax agents. The strategy acknowledges that the Department can do more to reduce the costs of engaging with tax agents, increase compliance of represented taxpayers and improve agent satisfaction. It sets a direction which could allow the Department to work more effectively with tax agents. Further information is set out in Box 8.3.

Box 8.3. United Kingdom: HMRC's strategy for administering tax agents

HMRC's review

HMRC conducted a review in 2010 on how it worked with paid agents and intermediaries. The purpose was to help develop the way it would work with agents in the future as part of a new Agents Strategy. The review found that changes in the commercial market and the growth of software and virtual products would provide new opportunities for working together in the digital environment. Key points from the review:

- For many reasons, not all about tax, a significant number of HMRC's customers will continue to employ a paid tax agent.
- Evolving expectations and advances in IT, increasing competition from software developers and other professional service providers, are driving innovation in paid agent business models.
- HMRC should design all future digital services with agents in mind. (An initiative known as "Agent Online Self-Serve" will lay the foundations for this).
- HMRC should work with agents to promote voluntary compliance.
- HMRC should work with software developers and service providers to determine the role they should play in supporting compliance.

HMRC is working closely with representative bodies to take this work forward and plans to talk to as many of agents as possible to obtain their views.

The strategy

HMRC's Agents Strategy aims to transform the relationship between it and agents by:

- Gaining a better understanding of them and their clients to help HMRC target the right services and communications;
- Aligning HMRC and agent processes where possible, and enabling agents to carry out more transactions with minimal HMRC involvement;
- Eliminating duplication and reworking to make it easier for agents to do business with HMRC and reduce their costs;
- Supporting them in improving services for their clients, including tackling the small minority of agents with poor performance more effectively;
- Working closely with agents' representative bodies on the development of Agent and Client Statistics.

HMRC is working with the Government Digital Service to develop new digital services and will consult regularly with agents' representative bodies as the work progresses.

Source: UK HMRC website (accessed October 2014).

Special services for tax intermediaries

As for the prior series, the survey of revenue bodies set out a menu of possible "services" for supporting tax intermediaries, drawing on the observed approaches and experiences of a number of revenue bodies. The menu is described briefly in Table 8.2, while specific examples drawn from a variety of revenue bodies are set out thereafter:

Table 8.2. **Menu of possible services to assist tax intermediaries**

Service	Description
Consultative forum	A forum organised by the revenue body for regularly engaging with representatives of tax intermediaries on important/ topical technical and administrative issues.
Flexible returns filing policy	A policy that permits tax intermediaries satisfying specified criteria to have longer return filing periods (beyond legislated due dates), recognising their large workloads.
Dedicated phone service	A phone service offered by the revenue body that is dedicated to dealing with the inquiries of tax intermediaries.
Access to technical experts	Access to revenue body technical experts on specific aspects of tax law, with inquiries raising complex issues.
Relationship managers	Nominated officials within the revenue body to be the point of contact for inquiries of, and support to, tax intermediaries.
Dedicated website	A portion of the revenue bodies website that is devoted to providing information specifically dealing with matters of interest to tax intermediaries
News information bulletins	Regular communications with tax intermediaries on topical and important matters affecting operation of tax system.

Consultation and engagement

- ***Canada:*** The CRA has established a Framework Agreement with the Chartered Professional Accountants of Canada (CPA Canada) to strengthen collaboration on priority issues. The Framework Agreement is a key element in the CRA's efforts to build strong relationships with the Canadian accounting community and tax service providers. It recognises the important relationship between the CRA and CPA Canada in the successful administration of Canada's tax system, and promotes regular dialogue between the two organisations on tax-related matters of common interest. It will also ensure that input from Canada's accounting professionals is considered as the CRA moves forward with its change agenda. A central part of the Framework Agreement includes the creation of seven committees, each co-chaired by a senior representative from both the CRA and CPA Canada, to focus on seven priority areas: service; compliance; tax administration; scientific research and experimental development; commodity tax; red tape reduction; and training. (More information can be found on the CRA's website.

- ***Hong Kong:*** As part of the process to maintain good communication with the accounting profession on taxation matters, the Inland Revenue Department (IRD) holds annual meetings with the Hong Kong Institute of Certified Public Accountants (the Institute) to exchange views and discuss issues of common interest. This arrangement has been in place for many years. The agreed minutes of the meeting are published in the form of an electronic tax bulletin on the Institute's homepage, and are also accessible from IRD's website. Minutes from the 2013 meeting reveal that the discussions held encompass a broad array of technical and administrative issues, initiated by both tax professionals and the IRD. (Source: IRD website, October 2014).

- ***Ireland:*** Revenue places very high importance on achieving a high degree of engagement with tax practitioners, and works closely with practitioners and business representative bodies through structured and regular contacts such as the Tax Administration Liaison Committee (TALC). TALC is a forum for Revenue and tax practitioner representative groups to meet and discuss issues relating to the administration of the tax system. The work of TALC is supported by sub-committees, discussing items such as reduction in administrative burden, modernisation of the administration of Taxes and the Self-Assessment systems, mandatory e-filing and payment, and administrative and interpretative issues arising from Finance Acts and Budgets. (Source: Revenue's survey response.)
- ***Spain:*** The Forum for Tax Professionals' Associations was created in March 2011 on the initiative of the revenue body. The aim of the Forum of Associations and Colleges of tax professionals is to improve the relationship between the State Tax Administration Agency and taxpayers by promoting a co-operative relationship between Tax Agency and tax professionals based on transparency and mutual trust. The Forum meets periodically to discuss matters that can be introduced by either the tax agency or professional associations. Details of matters discussed are made public. The initial feedback from participants has been very positive, since it is a major qualitative change in the pattern of relationship between government tax and representatives of taxpayers, aiming at establishing a transparent and trusted relationship to promote compliance voluntary and prevent fiscal risk. (Agencia Tributaria, 2014)

Flexible returns filing policy

- ***Australia:*** Tax intermediaries are generally permitted to adopt a staggered programme for filing tax returns of their clients subject to them meeting a number of specified performance criteria.

Information services

- ***Canada:*** CRA has a formal licensing agreement with several commercial tax publishers to publish a severed version of its advance income tax rulings and technical interpretations. These publishers provide up-to-date content from the CRA to tax professionals (and other interested taxpayers) generally on a subscription basis. In addition, the CRA freely provides technical information in a variety of online publications, including through its new technical publication product: income tax folios. The CRA also has a Tax Professionals webpage which provides a public portal to common areas of interest to Tax Professionals and highlights general news from the CRA.
- ***Hungary:*** The revenue body and the Hungarian Association of Certified Tax Experts (MOKLASZ) have concluded a Memorandum of Understanding (MOU) for the conduct of the professional relations concerning tax experts' activities. Based on the MOU, the NTCA provides the MOKLASZ with its taxation-related guidelines and information sheets free of charge (except materials issued only for internal use).

A dedicated organisational unit

- ***United States:*** The IRS's Office of Professional Responsibility (OPR) is organised to oversee the administration of tax practice standards for all federal tax professionals. Its functions include education and outreach; proposing and negotiating appropriate levels of discipline; initiating disciplinary proceedings in un-agreed cases; and bringing or responding to appeals in disciplinary cases. OPR's vision and commitment are for OPR to be the standard bearer for integrity in tax practice. OPR's mission is to apply the standards of practice to all tax professionals in a fair, equitable, and effective manner.

  In its latest survey response, the IRS advised that the organisational changes, including substantial staff increases, that were specifically reported in the previous edition of this series (TA2013) in connection with regulatory "expansion of its [OPR's] authority and jurisdiction" have not been implemented (and have been at least delayed) because of litigation successfully disputing the validity of the particular regulatory provisions involved. However, these developments have not affected OPR's general operations. OPR continues to hire attorney-advisers capable of handling sophisticated projects and cases. OPR's needs in this regard are due to the organisation's on-going reorientation and further focusing of its investigative and legal resources on the more complex, egregious cases of misconduct with the most potential to impair the tax system. The makeup of OPR's cases accordingly reflects this trend – with a shrinking percentage of cases involving small, simple violations of the practice rules, and a larger share involving more serious and elaborate violations."

Relationship/account managers

- ***New Zealand:*** As described on IR's website (November 2014), every listed tax agent has an Inland Revenue account manager. The account manager can provide support and assistance, along with services such as monitoring extension of time agreements. Specifically:
  - **Relationship management:** *(1)* a centralised point of contact for specific issues; *(2)* to facilitate resolution on exceptional issues; *(3)* for management of complaints as directed by Complaints Management; and *(4)* to negotiate and update status.
  - **Education and information:** *(1)* to actively provide support and increase awareness of the self-service tools IRD provides; *(2)* to keep tax agents informed with information updates; and *(3)* to provide reports which cannot be accessed through self-service.
  - **Compliance and monitoring:** *(1)* to register new tax agents, ensuring they meet the legislative definition of a tax agent and monitoring this on an on-going basis; *(2)* to monitor overall tax agent compliance with legislation and our policies; *(3)* to monitor outstanding debt and returns for tax agents and associated entities; *(4)* to ensure all guideline dates are met by tax agents filing income tax returns and monitor tax agents who don't meet the required guidelines; *(5)* to withdraw tax agents' extension of time (EOT) if they don't meet their obligations and negotiate with them on the early reinstatement of a client's EOT; and *(6)* to remove tax agent status where they are in breach of legislative requirements.

Online services

A number of country examples identified from survey responses or Secretariat research are set out in Table 8.3. Generally speaking, the range and nature of the services offered align with or exceed those provided to individual taxpayers.

Table 8.3. **Examples of on-line services to assist tax intermediaries**

Country	Description
Canada	***Canada's "Represent a Client" portal:*** "Represent a Client" is a service that provides registered representatives with secure, controlled online access to tax information on behalf of individuals and businesses, including their employees. Users of the service can range from tax advisory or payroll businesses to individuals representing family members and friends. Access for representatives can vary based on the client's authorisation, with the ability to restrict access to view only, view and make changes, or to a limited number of accounts. Representatives are able to access most of the same features available to business owners via "My Business Account" and to individuals via "My Account". The "Represent a Client" service also provides representatives with tools to view their client lists, and associated authorisations including expiry dates. Detailed transaction records are made available to administrators and owners of tax businesses providing them with the tools to monitor the activities of their employees. The same tool is made available to business owners via "My Business Account" and to individuals via "My Account", allowing them to view transactions that their representatives have made on their behalf. The CRA introduced the Manage Online Mail service in October 2014 for registered electronic filer representatives receiving Pre-assessment and Processing Review letters on behalf of their clients.
Ireland	***Ireland's online service:*** Revenue's Online Service (**ROS**) is the primary method by which Revenue is delivering its interactive services electronically to the customer. This service is an internet facility which provides customers with a quick and secure facility to file tax returns, pay tax liabilities and access their tax details, 24 hours a day, 7 days a week, 365 days a year. In July 2003 Revenue received an e-Government label from the European Commission for this service which was found to be one of the best practices of its type. The main features of **ROS** include facilities to: *(1)* File returns online; *(2)* Make payments by debit/credit card, debit instruction or by online banking for Income Tax only; *(3)* Obtain online details of personal/clients Revenue Accounts; *(4)* Calculate tax liability; *(5)* Conduct business electronically; and *(6)* Claim repayments. ROS has a specially designed access control system which allows a tax agent or "administrator" in the accounting/tax firm (the Senior Partner or Financial Controller, for example) to provide the appropriate access to ROS for staff within the business or practice. This control system is hosted on ROS but is maintained by the administrator using his or her digital certificate for identification and access. In many tax practices and in larger businesses staff have different levels of authorisation in relation to certain clients or in relation to filing certain returns. Some may get permission to view certain details on ROS solely. Others may be enabled to file VAT returns while others may be enabled to file all returns on behalf of certain clients. A Senior Partner might reserve certain clients to him or herself exclusively. (Source: Ireland: Survey response and web-site.)
Russia	Taxpayers can give tax advisers access to their private information by means of the "taxpayer's personal office" on the website of FTS of Russia.
United Kingdom	HMRC's Digital Strategy sets out its ambition to deliver a transparent tax system by encouraging voluntary compliance through customer-focused digital services that are easy to use. As part of HMRC's strategy, Agent Online Self-serve will provide: *(1)* a new digital agents' registration service enabling them to deal with HMRC across a range of taxes; *(2)* a more secure process that will help to protect agents, their your clients and HMRC from fraudulent activity; *(3)* a new and improved authorisation process allowing agents to quickly identify themselves and tell HMRC when they take on a new client; *(4)* information about agents' clients and services in one place; *(5)* the ability for agents to tailor the information they see about their clients; *(6)* a single access point for services for a client, even if agents act for them for more than one type of tax; and *(7)* access to other digital services as they are introduced (once agents have successfully registered for Agent Online Self-Serve). HMRC is aiming to deliver an early version of the service to some users by December 2014. This will offer access to a limited range of digital services, including agent registration and authorisation. The service will then be enhanced and made available to more agents from 2015 onwards.
United States	IRS e-services online tools for tax professionals provide multiple online electronic products and services to tax professionals. Eligible tax professionals may use e-Services to: *(1)* request and receive tax account transcripts, wage and income documents, tax return transcripts, and verification of non-filing letters for both individual and business taxpayers and *(2)* match payee taxpayer identification number and name combinations against IRS records prior to submitting an information return – all online.

Sources: Canada-E-facilitation of compliance: Taxpayer Services via the Internet, Canada Revenue Agency, CIAT 46th Assembly, April 2012 and survey responses.

Table 8.4. **Tax administration: Supporting and interacting with tax intermediaries**

Country	Formal consultative forum exists	Flexible returns filing policy	Specialised services offered to tax intermediaries: Dedicated phones (**P**); Access to technical experts (**E**); Relationship managers (**R**); Dedicated website section (**I**); News/ information bulletins (**N**)	Specialised services offered to tax intermediaries: Online access to clients' records	Dedicated division to administer tax intermediaries	Compliance treatment is differentiated for tax intermediaries
OECD countries						
Australia	✓	✓	P, E, R /1, I, N	✓	✓ /2	✓
Austria	✓	✓	E, N	✓	x	x
Belgium	✓	✓	P, E, R, I, N	✓	x	x
Canada	✓	x	E, I, N	✓	x	x
Chile	✓	x	-	✓	x	x
Czech Republic	✓	✓	-	x	✓	✓
Denmark	✓	✓	P, E, R	✓	x	x
Estonia	x	x	-	✓	x	x
Finland	✓	x	P, E, R, I, N	x	x	x
France	x /1	x	E /2, R /3, N /3	✓	x	x
Germany	x	✓	N	✓	x	x
Greece	x	x	-	✓	x	x
Hungary	✓	x	E, N	✓	x	✓
Iceland	x	✓	P, E, R, I, N	✓	✓	x
Ireland	✓	x	P, E, I, N	✓	x	x
Israel	✓	✓	P /1, E, I, N	✓	✓	x
Italy	x	x	P, E, R, I, N	✓	✓	x
Japan	✓	x	-	x	✓	x
Korea	✓	✓	I	✓	✓	✓
Luxembourg	✓ /1	✓	N	x	x	x
Mexico	✓	x		✓	x	x
Netherlands	✓	✓	P, E, R, I, N	✓	x	✓ /1
New Zealand	✓	✓	P, R, I, N	✓	x	x
Norway	✓	✓	P, E, R, I, N	✓	x	✓
Poland	x	x	-	x	x	x
Portugal	x	x	I	✓	x	x
Slovak Republic	✓ /1	x	-	x	x	x
Slovenia	x	x.	E, N	✓	x	x
Spain	✓	x	I	✓	x	x
Sweden	✓	✓	-	✓	x	x
Switzerland	✓ /1	✓	-	x	x	x
Turkey	✓	✓	N	✓	✓	x
United Kingdom	✓	x	P, E, R, I, N	✓	✓	x
United States	✓	✓	P, E, R, I, N	✓	✓	x
Non-OECD countries						
Argentina	✓	x	I, N	x	✓	x
Brazil	x	x	E, I, N	✓	x	x
Bulgaria	✓	x	E, I, N	✓	x	x
China	x	x	-	x	✓	x
Colombia	x	x	N	x	x	x
Costa Roca	x	x	-	x	x	x
Croatia	x	x	E	✓	x	x
Cyprus	✓	✓	E, R, I, N	✓	✓	x
Hong Kong, China	✓	✓	E, I, N	x	x	x
India	✓	x	P /1, E /1, R /1, I, N	x	x	x
Indonesia	x	x	-	x	x	x
Latvia	x	x	E, N	x	x	x
Lithuania	✓	x	R	x	x	x
Malaysia	✓	x	-	x	x	x
Malta	x	✓	E, R, I	✓	x	x
Morocco	x /1	x	x	✓	x	x
Romania	x	x	-	✓	x	x
Russia	x	x	I, N /1	✓	x	x
Saudi Arabia	x	x	-	x	x	x
Singapore	✓	x	I, N	✓	x	x
South Africa	✓	x	E, R, I, N	✓	x	✓
Thailand	x	x	-	x	x	x

For notes indicated by "/ (number)", see Notes to Tables section at the end of the chapter, p. 276.
Source: Tax Administration 2015 survey responses.

Information reported by revenue bodies

For this survey revenue bodies were asked a number of basic questions related to the nature of services and other support provided to tax intermediaries. A summary of their responses is set out in Table 8.4. The key observations are as follows:

- Only just over 60% (35) of revenue bodies (including for 25 of the 34 OECD countries) reported the operation of a formal consultative forum for exchanges with tax intermediaries (and/or their representative bodies).
- Just over half (18) of revenue bodies in OECD countries reported having a flexible returns filing policy for tax intermediaries, but use of such a policy was largely absent in most non-OECD countries (i.e. only three of 22).
- For the specific range of services defined in the survey it can be seen that:
  - Only 25% (14) of revenue bodies appear to offer a "comprehensive" range of services (i.e. four or more of the five services specified), although it must be emphasised that little is known of the individual services in place.
  - Around 12% (7) of revenue bodies offer a "reasonable" range of services (i.e. three of the five services specified).
  - Just over 60% (34) of revenue bodies reported two or less service offerings, including 18 revenue bodies that offer none of the specified services.
- Around one-third (11) of revenue bodies in OECD countries reported having a dedicated organisational division to oversee the administration of their dealings with tax intermediaries, but this practice was noticeably absent in most non-OECD countries with only three reporting such an arrangement.
- Just over half of revenue bodies reported they provide the capability for authorised tax intermediaries to be given online access via the Internet/dedicated portal to clients' personal information – Box 8.9 set out examples of such services.
- The practice of differentiating the compliance treatment afforded to particular tax intermediaries (based on risk) appears largely ignored by revenue bodies, and very few examples can be identified of existing or proposed practice.

  In their survey response ***Australia*** reported that its risk modelling is able to identify tax intermediaries who have a significant level of risk in their client base with respect to various individual tax risks such as cash economy participation, personal income tax deductions, filing of returns or payment of debt. Differentiated treatments are applied according to the risk profile of the client base.

  The CRA's Registration of Tax Preparers Programme (RTPP) described earlier in this chapter would, when implemented, allow the CRA to tailor its activities to the needs of the tax preparer and the risk of non-compliance.

Conclusion

The wide variation in the nature and range of services provided to tax intermediaries, as implied by the survey data, have not been studied in detail by the FTA. However, in light of the FTA's prior work it would seem that there is likely to be considerable potential for many revenue bodies to strengthen this aspect of their administration.

Notes to Tables

Table 8.1. Tax intermediaries: Laws and regulations, returns prepared and surveys

/1. **Austria:** Integrated part of regular customer surveys. **Brazil:** Project underway to implement permanent channels of direct contact with representation councils, focusing on the development of improvements in the RFB Service. **India:** Unemployed and partially employed graduates from select disciplines have been trained as Tax Return Preparers (TRPs) to assist individual and Hindu Undivided Family (HUF) taxpayers to file their returns of income and also to e-file TDS Statements. TRP Scheme has a Help Desk and a Toll Free Call Centre which TRPs can contact for seeking clarifications on legal issues from tax experts. **Israel:** Joint survey with CPA Bureau carried out in 2012 and 2014. **Malta:** Applies to Direct Tax Authority only. **New Zealand:** This percentage has been based on the number of returns filed via a channel only available to tax agents, divided by the total number of tax returns filed. **Turkey:** Public Accountant, Certified Public Accountant, and Sworn-in Certified Public Accountant (Law No: 3568).**United States:** Relevant laws and regulations include United Stated Code Title 26 (Internal Revenue Code) Section 6109(a) (4); Title 5 U.S.C. Section 500; Title 31 U.S.C. Section 330; Title 31 Code of Federal Regulations, Subtitle A, Part 10 (also known as Treasury Department Circular No. 230).

Table 8.4. Tax administration: Supporting and interacting with tax intermediaries

/1. **Australia:** There is no dedicated relationship manager programme for all tax intermediaries. However, there is a programme to support those tax intermediaries which ATO systems identify as struggling to ensure the compliance of their clients, a key agent programme to support the most significant tax intermediaries and a dedicated e-mail linked service to deal with tax intermediary issues that are unable to be solved through other methods. **France:** No formal consultative forum but there are some national and local user committees where certified accountants' and the federation of certified bodies' representatives serve. **India:** For Tax Return Preparers (TRPs), there is a Help Desk and a Toll Free Call Centre which TRPs can contact for seeking clarifications on legal issues from tax experts. This "Online Tax Help" is also open to taxpayers on the website www.trpscheme.com. **Israel:** Service is only for technical support for online services. **Luxembourg:** For direct taxes only. **Morocco:** There is an informal consultative forum for regular exchanges with tax intermediaries. **Netherlands:** Part of the NTCA's co-operative compliance strategy for the SME segment is that tax intermediaries' associations conclude agreements with NTCA re aspects of compliance; clients who sign up to such an agreement are part of NTCAs co-operative compliance strategy. **Russia:** Monthly magazine "Tax police and practice". **Slovak Republic:** The revenue body organises meetings with the Chamber of the Tax Professionals to assure unified implementation of tax regulations. **Switzerland:** For VAT matters only.

/2. **Australia:** The Tax Practitioners Board (TPB) that registers and regulates the conduct of tax practitioners in Australia has its own Consultative Forum with recognised not-for-profit tax intermediary associations; TPB maintains its own separate web site (www.tpb.gov.au) and provides information to practitioners and the public about tax agent registration, conduct and professional practice matters. **France:** The French tax administration allows certified bodies to be connected with experts when questions are complex/raise unusual issues. Entry point is the correspondent of the certified body who has a territorial responsibility.

/3. **France:** Certified bodies have a dedicated correspondent within each departmental or regional tax administration. Professionals can subscribe to news bulletins by selecting themes that are sent through an information flow received in mail boxes.

Bibliography

Agencia Tributaria (2014), *The Forum for Tax Professionals' Associations,* Description of the Forum and its rules of operations as per Spanish revenue body's website, www.agenciatributaria.es/AEAT.internet/en_gb/Inicio_en_GB/_Segmentos_/Colaboradores/Foro_de_Asociaciones_y_Colegios_de_Profesionales_Tributarios/Foro_de_Asociaciones_y_Colegios_de_Profesionales_Tributarios.shtml (accessed November 2014).

ATO (2012a), *Compliance Programme 2012-13*, Australian Taxation Office, Canberra.

ATO (2012b), *Tax Practitioner Programme,* Australian Taxation Office, Canberra.

CRA (2012), *E-facilitation of Compliance: Taxpayer Services via the Internet*, Paper presented at CIAT 46th Assembly, Canada Revenue Agency, Ottawa.

Committee on Horizontal Monitoring by the Netherlands Tax and Customs Administration (2012), *Tax Supervision – Made to Measure – Flexible when possible, strict where necessary, Ministry of Finance*, The Hague, http://download.belastingdienst.nl/belastingdienst/docs/tax_supervision_made_to_measure_tz0151z1fdeng.pdf.

Comptroller and Auditor General (2010), *Engaging with Tax Agents*, UK Comptroller and Auditor General, The Stationery Office, London.

Hong Kong Inland Revenue (2014), Revenue body website (accessed October 2014).

Netherlands Tax and Customs Administration (2007), *Guide to horizontal monitoring within the SME segment; Tax service providers,* The Hague, http://download.belastingdienst.nl/belastingdienst/docs/guide_horiz_monit_dv4071z1pleng.pdf.

New Zealand Inland Revenue (2012), *Mechanisms implemented for assisting taxpayers in remote geographical areas*, Paper presented at CIAT 46th Assembly, New Zealand Inland Revenue Department, Wellington.

OECD (2012), *Working Smarter in Structuring the Administration, in Compliance, and Through Legislation*, OECD, Paris, www.oecd.org/site/ctpfta/49428209.pdf.

OECD (2008), *Study into the Role of Tax Intermediaries,* OECD Publishing, Paris, http://dx.doi.org/10.1787/9789264041813-en.

Chapter 9

Legislated administrative frameworks for tax administration

This chapter provides an overview of the legislated administrative frameworks for the conduct of tax administration in surveyed countries, including matters such as: (1) *taxpayers' rights and obligations;* (2) *access to rulings;* (3) *taxpayer registration and identification systems;* (4) *withholding and third party information reporting regimes;* (5) *return filing and payment regimes;* (6) *administrative review;* (7) *enforced collection of unpaid taxes;* (8) *information and access powers; and* (9) *tax offences (including use of voluntary disclosure policies and approaches). A number of selected country examples are also included to elaborate particular recommended approaches and/or describe recent developments.*

Key points

Taxpayers' rights and charters

- With minor exceptions, all revenue bodies operate with a formal set of taxpayers' rights set out in law or other statutes, and/or in administrative documents. (A number of related recent developments are described for revenue bodies in Ireland and the United States.)

Access to rulings

- Over 90% of revenue bodies reported they provide public and, at taxpayer's request, private rulings.
- Concerning private rulings, time limits are applied for their provision in over two-thirds of surveyed revenue bodies while over a third impose fees for such rulings for some/all taxes.

Taxpayer registration and identification numbering systems

- The most commonly used types of identifier for PIT purposes are a unique taxpayer identifier and a citizen ID number; a very small number use the identifier established for social insurance purposes.
- Reflecting quite different systems of personal tax administration and registration, there are significant variations between countries in the relative size of their respective taxpayer registration databases.
- The majority of revenue bodies use unique identification and numbering systems for CIT and VAT.

Collection of Personal Income Tax

- With a few exceptions all revenue bodies administer "withholding at source" arrangements for the collection of PIT (and in most countries where applicable, SSC) on employment income.
- Withholding regimes for employment income fall into two categories (i.e. non-cumulative and cumulative), with the latter most commonly observed.
- Employers are generally required to withhold and remit payments on a monthly basis although there are some noteworthy exceptions observed. Significant variations are also observed in the frequency of employers' reporting obligations.
- Withholding regimes for the collection of income tax – as a final or creditable tax – for both interest income and dividend income of resident taxpayers are in place in over two-thirds of revenue bodies.
- Withholding and/or mandatory reporting arrangements are also used to varying degrees in many countries for payments made by businesses to certain categories of self-employed/contractors/small medium enterprises, rents, royalties and patents, and sales of shares and real property.
- With minor exceptions, all countries provide for the graduated collection of PIT (on income not subject to withholding of tax at source) and CIT with a regime of advance/instalment payments. The requirements of these arrangements vary substantially (e.g. numbers of payments and mandatory use of e-payment) with implications for taxpayers and revenue body workloads.

Collection of Corporate Income Tax

- With minor exceptions, all countries provide for the graduated collection of CIT with a regime of advance payments. Most countries aim to maximise the amount of tax collected by advance payment regimes *within the year the relevant income is derived.* Typically, this is achieved with a regime of monthly advance payments for large taxpayers (just over 40% of countries) and quarterly for small/medium sized taxpayers (just under 30%).
- While there is no "optimal" approach, over 40% of countries have what appears to be a relatively rigid "one size fits all" approach to the frequency of advance payments. For some, this may present opportunities to advance the collection of taxes from larger taxpayers and/or reduce payment frequency for smaller taxpayers, taking account of compliance costs and other considerations.
- Many countries (almost half) have mandated the use of e-filing and e-payment for their largest corporate taxpayers, while a significant number have also extended the requirement to smaller corporations.

Key points *(continued)*

Collection of Value Added Tax

- Most countries aim to align the collection of VAT with underlying economic activity, in practice using a regime of monthly or quarterly returns and payments. Some countries differentiate between large and SME taxpayers, requiring returns and payments less frequently from SME and very small taxpayers. A small number of countries administer what appear to be relatively rigid "one size fits all" requirements for VAT return filing and payments, suggesting opportunities for reform to produce a variety of benefits.
- Around two-thirds of surveyed countries have mandated use of e-filing and e-payment obligations for their largest and SME taxpayers, while over half have extended this obligation to their smallest VAT payers. This factor accounts for the very high overall rates of e-filing observed (see Table 7.5) and, in particular, for the rapid growth seen in many countries over the last 4 to 5 years.

Enforced debt collection

- The vast majority of surveyed bodies have the more traditional forms of powers to enforce the payment of tax debts (e.g. payment arrangements, collection of debts from third parties, and tax clearances for government contracts); the less commonly-observed powers included imposing liability for certain tax debts on company directors, closure of businesses/loss of license to operate, and use of publicity).
- The series observes that just under one-fifth of revenue bodies have, in comparison with others, what appears to be a more limited range of powers for enforced debt collection purposes.

Information and access powers

- With minor exceptions, revenue bodies have powers to obtain relevant information and in virtually all countries these powers extend to third parties; the circumstances in which entry of dwellings and business premises and search powers can be used vary between countries, as do the use of warrants and the extent of the involvement of other government agencies.

Tax offences, interest, penalties and enforcement

- The vast majority (almost 90%) of revenue bodies reported they have a common administrative penalty framework for the major taxes administered by them.
- The use of voluntarily disclosure policies and programmes appears to be an under-utilised strategy for many revenue bodies. Results from selected countries indicate they can be an effective tool for encouraging taxpayers to report past acts of non-compliance, in particular concerning that concerning the concealment of assets and income in offshore bank accounts. (A number of related recent developments are described for revenue bodies in Australia, Chile and Israel.)

Introduction

This chapter outlines key elements of the legislated administrative frameworks of tax systems in the countries surveyed, identifying common features as well as some of the more unique practices and recent developments. The specific topics covered are: *(1)* taxpayers rights and obligations; *(2)* access to rulings; *(3)* taxpayer registration and identification systems; *(4)* withholding and third party information reporting regimes; *(5)* return filing and payment regimes; *(6)* administrative review; *(7)* enforced collection of unpaid taxes; *(8)* information and access powers; and *(9)* tax offences (including use of voluntary disclosure policies and approaches).

Taxpayers' rights and obligations

In any democratic society taxpayers/citizens will have a number of basic rights as well as obligations in relation to their government and its agencies. Revenue bodies are no exception and most countries have legislation governing taxpayer's rights and obligations in relation to taxation.

As would be expected, given the diversity of environments in which revenue bodies around the world exist, the specific details of taxpayers' rights and obligations vary somewhat by country. There are, however, a number of common threads that can be identified. In 1990, the OECD's Committee of Fiscal Affairs completed a report (unpublished) of its study examining the legal and administrative frameworks in place in OECD countries concerning taxpayers' rights and obligations. The survey found that, while most countries at that time did not have an explicit "taxpayers' charter", the following basic taxpayer rights were present in all systems:

- The right to be informed, assisted, and heard.
- The right of appeal.
- The right to pay no more than the correct amount of tax.
- The right to certainty.
- The right to privacy.
- The right to confidentiality and secrecy.

These basic taxpayers' rights also imply obligations on the part of taxpayers. There is a set of behavioural norms expected of taxpayers by Governments to underpin smooth functioning of the tax system. These expected behaviours are so fundamental to the successful operation of taxation systems that they are legal requirements in many, if not most, countries. These taxpayer obligations are:

- The obligation to be honest.
- The obligation to be co-operative.
- The obligation to provide accurate information and documents on time.
- The obligation to keep records.
- The obligation to pay taxes on time.

Without this balance of taxpayers' rights *and* obligations taxation systems could not function effectively and efficiently.

Over recent decades, many countries have elaborated these basic rights and obligations into a "taxpayer/customer" or "service" charter. These documents often include statements about behaviours expected from officials and taxpayers. Some countries have chosen to consolidate the measures taken to protect taxpayers into a "taxpayers' charter" or "declaration", and to publish these widely. In some countries, they have taken the form of a general statement of the broad principles which should govern the relationship between the revenue body and taxpayers. In other countries, these documents provide a more detailed guide to the rights of taxpayers at each stage in the assessment process. Yet other countries have taken the approach of including statements about behaviours expected from officials and taxpayers in documents such as their mission statements. Accordingly, it should be stressed that even countries without a taxpayer charter may, nevertheless, attach equal importance to taxpayers' rights and that in practice taxpayers in such countries have rights similar to those found in formal taxpayers' charter statements.

As set out in Table 9.1, as of early 2014 just about all revenue bodies conduct tax operations that are underpinned with a formal set of taxpayers' rights set out in either legislative and/or administrative form. Of these, 45 countries have codified them (partly or in full) in tax law or other statutes, while 43 revenue bodies operate with a set of rights and obligations that are elaborated in administrative documents, sometimes referred to as "taxpayer" or "service" charters. These figures suggest an increasing trend towards the codification of taxpayers' rights and obligations since 2003 when further OECD work found that only two-thirds of member countries had some form of formal statements of taxpayers' rights (OECD, 2003).

The decision whether to take a codified or administrative approach appears to be based on a range of different factors, in addition to cultural and legal issues. Reasons advanced in support of relying on an administrative approach include:

1. It is likely to be quicker to develop and implement than a legislative document.
2. Administrative documents can be drafted in a "reader-friendly" and readily disseminated, which may not be easily duplicated with a legislated approach.
3. It allows for the inclusion of "service" and other broader rights that may be less suitable for a legislative approach.
4. Administrative documents can be easily adapted to address changing taxpayer requirements.
5. Administrative redress mechanisms tend to be cheaper and quicker than statutory processes.

On the other hand, there is some attraction to adopting a codified approach. First, such an approach may strengthen taxpayers' perceptions that the rights set out in law are indeed are genuine and will be respected in practice. Second, revenue body staff may be more responsive, aware that the rights have the force of law. Third, there may be less scope for interference as a result of political interests. Finally, taxpayers' rights will be subject to established mechanisms of redress and challenge that are seen as independent.

The form and content of these sets of rights varies between countries. There are, however, some common themes and elements. Drawing on the experiences of revenue bodies in a number of OECD countries, the CFA's 2003 note described the elements, including both "taxpayers' rights" and "taxpayers' obligations", of an illustrative taxpayers' charter (see Box 9.1) and encouraged revenue bodies to develop a taxpayers' charter covering the basic rights and obligations identified, if they had not already done so.

The promotion of taxpayers' rights and the objective making them highly transparent is also evident in the guidance provided by other international bodies, for example:

- The IMF's *Manual on Fiscal Transparency* gives explicit recognition to the importance of taxpayers' rights and provides some specific guidance (IMF, 2007):

  > […] The constitutional framework of almost all countries embodies the principle that no tax may be levied unless it has a clear legal basis (although there are some differences in the application of this principle). It is fundamental to fiscal transparency that taxation be under the authority of law and that the administrative application of tax laws be subject to procedural safe-guards, such as taxpayer rights and tax dispute procedures […]

Box 9.1. Illustrative Taxpayers' Charter: Description of taxpayers' rights and obligations

Taxpayers' Rights

Your right to be informed, assisted and heard:

We will treat you with courtesy and consideration at all times and will, in normal circumstances, strive to help you to understand and meet your tax obligations; explain to you the reasons for decisions made by us concerning your affairs; finalise refund requests within ... days/[as quickly as possible] and, where the law allows, pay you interest on the amount; answer written enquiries within ... days/[as quickly as possible]; deal with urgent requests as quickly as possible; answer your telephone call promptly and without unnecessary transfer; return your telephone call as quickly as possible; keep your costs in complying with the law to a minimum; give you the opportunity to have your certified legal or taxation adviser present during any investigation; send you, within ... days/[as quickly as possible] of the completion of an investigation, written advice of the result of that investigation including the reasons for any decision and, where an assessment has been issued, details of how the assessment was calculated.

Your right of appeal

We will, in normal circumstances, strive to fully explain your rights of review, objection and appeal if you are unsure of them or need clarification; review your case if you believe that we have misinterpreted the facts, applied the law incorrectly or not handled your affairs properly; ensure that the review is completed in a comprehensive, professional and impartial manner by a representative who has not been involved in the original decision; determine your objection within ... days/[as quickly as possible], unless we require more information to do so, or the issues are unusually complex; give you reasons if your objection has been completely or partially disallowed; and request further information from you only where it is necessary to resolve the issues in dispute.

Your right to pay no more than the correct amount of tax:

We will act with integrity and impartiality in all our dealings with you, so that you pay only the tax legally due and that all credits, benefits, refunds and other entitlements are properly applied.

Your right to certainty

We will, in normal circumstances, strive to provide you with advice about the tax implications of your actions; let you know at least ... days/[as quickly as possible] before the conduct of an interview; advise you of the scope of an interview and our requirements; and arrange a suitable time and place for the interview and allow you time to prepare your records.

Your right to privacy

We will only make enquiries about you when required to check that you have complied with your tax obligations; only seek access to information relevant to our enquiries; and treat any information obtained, received or held by us as private.

Your right to confidentiality and secrecy

We will not use or divulge any personal or financial information about you unless you have authorised us in writing to do so or in situations where permitted by law; and only permit those employees within the administration who are authorised by law and require your personal or financial information to administer our programmes and legislation, to access your information.

Taxpayers' Obligations

Your obligation to be honest

We expect you to provide complete and accurate information as and when required; declare all your assessable income in your income tax return; claim only deductions, rebates and credits to which you are entitled; answer questions completely, accurately and honestly; explain the full facts and circumstances when you seek tax advice or when you request a private ruling.

Your obligation to be co-operative

We expect you to co-operate with tax administrators and treat them with courtesy, consideration and respect, as we do in our dealings with you.

Your obligation to provide accurate information and documents on time:

We expect you to file correct returns and documents within time limits specified; provide complete and accurate information by certain dates; take reasonable care in preparing your tax returns, documents and information; inform us of relevant events such as incorporation, opening a business, correspondence address changes, moving the place of business, ceasing business, with required taxpayer identifiers in a timely manner so that we can administer tax legislation properly, efficiently and effectively.

Your obligation to keep records

We expect you to keep sufficient records and books to enable you to meet your tax obligations; keep sufficient records and books for the required retention period; take reasonable care in preparing your records and books; allow us access to records and books so that we can check your tax obligations.

Your obligation to pay taxes on time

We expect you to pay the full amount of your taxes by the due dates; pay the full amount of any balance outstanding resulting from assessment or reassessment; help us develop a mutually acceptable payment arrangement if you cannot pay any outstanding balance in full and have exhausted all reasonable possibilities of obtaining the necessary funds by borrowing or re-arranging your financial affairs; withhold and remit by due dates all taxes withheld or collected on behalf of others; advise us as soon as practical if some event beyond your control has affected your ability to pay your taxes on time so that appropriate arrangements can be put into place to assist you.

Source: Practice note: Taxpayers' Rights and Obligations (OECD CFA, July 2003).

Tax laws should provide taxpayers with the following rights or safeguards: *(i)* confidentiality – the right to have personal information accorded the greatest possible confidentiality with the tax authorities; *(ii)* notice – the right to be notified of an assessment, a decision on adjudication, or any collection action against the taxpayer's assets; *(iii)* explanation – the right to an explanation of why a tax is being assessed in the way it is and to an explanation of the reasons for a decision by adjudication; *(iv)* appeal – the right to an independent administrative appeal and a final judgment appeal; and *(v)* representation – the right to be represented by a qualified professional (attorney, accountant, etc.) in any dealings with the tax authority.

These rights should be established in law and can also be incorporated in a taxpayers' charter or equivalent that is used to communicate taxpayer rights and to hold agencies accountable for their performance, including administrative discretion, etc.

- The European Commission's (EC) set of Fiscal Blueprints, the background to which is described in Chapter 1 of this series, includes a blueprint concerning "Taxpayer Services" which emphasises the importance of defining and publicising taxpayers' rights and obligations so that taxpayers have confidence in the fairness and equity of the tax system but are also aware of the implication of non-compliance (EC, 2007).

Country developments with the development of taxpayers' or service charters

Previous editions of this series highlighted developments in the codification of taxpayers' rights and the introduction of taxpayer and/or service charters. CIS 2008 outlined examples from Canada and Slovenia, CIS 2010 drew attention to the approaches of revenue bodies in Australia, Denmark, and the United Kingdom, while the 2013 series looked outside the OECD and outlined developments in Hong Kong and Lithuania. For this series, the opportunity is being taken to again provide other examples – see Boxes 9.2 and 9.3.

Ireland

Ireland's Revenue has also developed and published a customer service charter, and, like a few other countries, its charter also includes a set of its expectations of its customers – see Box 9.2 (Revenue, 2014). That distinction aside, the principles underpinning Revenue's charter broadly align with those in the OECD model although, in addition, Revenue gives explicit recognition to the issue of taxpayers' compliance costs. Revenue also complements its charter with a comprehensive statement on service standards that set out the levels/rates of performance customers can expect in relation to the more common categories of services, and publishes the level of performance achieved in its annual performance report.

United States

The Internal Revenue Service (IRS) published a "Taxpayer Bill of Rights" in June 2014. As reported by the IRS's National Taxpayer Advocate, the Taxpayer Bill of Rights takes the multiple existing rights embedded in the tax code and groups them into 10 broad categories, making them more visible and easier for taxpayers to locate:

> Congress has passed multiple pieces of legislation with the title of "Taxpayer Bill of Rights". However, taxpayer surveys conducted by my office have found that most taxpayers do not believe they have rights before the IRS and even fewer can name their rights. I believe the list of core taxpayer rights the IRS is announcing today will help taxpayers better understand their rights in dealing with the tax system. (IRS, 2014)

Box 9.2. Ireland: Revenue's Customer Service Charter

Revenue collects taxes and duties which fund the provision of public services for the benefit of all citizens. Revenue protects society through its Customs Service working on frontier control. The effective and fair administration of tax and customs law requires Revenue and citizens to recognise certain basic rights and responsibilities. This Customer Charter sets out mutual expectations in this context.

Consistency, Equity and Confidentiality

- Revenue will administer the law fairly, reasonably and consistently and will seek to collect no more than the correct amount of tax or duty.
- Revenue will treat the information you give us in confidence and ensure that it will not be used or disclosed except as provided for by law.

Courtesy and Consideration

- You can expect to be treated courteously, with consideration and in a non-discriminatory way in your dealings with Revenue.
- We expect you to treat Revenue officials with courtesy and to give them all reasonable co-operation.

Information and Assistance

- You can expect to be given the necessary information and all reasonable assistance to enable you to clearly understand and meet your tax and customs obligations and to claim your entitlements and credits.
- We expect you to provide true and correct information in all your contacts with Revenue and to advise Revenue in a timely manner of developments (such as change of address, commencement or cessation of business) that are relevant to your tax and customs affairs.

Presumption of Honesty

- You can expect to be treated as honest in your dealings with Revenue unless there is clear reason to believe otherwise and subject to Revenue's responsibility for ensuring compliance with tax and customs law.
- We expect you to deal in an honest way with Revenue by returning the tax and duty which you are due to pay and seeking only those entitlements and credits to which you are due.

Compliance Costs

- You can expect that Revenue will administer the tax and duty regimes in a way that will minimise, as far as possible, compliance costs.
- We expect you to maintain proper records and accounts and to ensure that your returns and declarations are completed fully, accurately and in a timely manner.

Complaints, Review and Appeal

There are comprehensive complaints and appeal procedures open to all customers of Revenue and we encourage you to avail of these if you are in any way dissatisfied with the service you receive from us. You can expect:

- That if you make a complaint, Revenue will deal with it promptly, impartially and in confidence.
- That availing of Revenue's own complaints procedures will never prejudice your rights to raise issues with the Ombudsman or lodge, within the statutory time limits, a formal appeal to the Office of the Appeal Commissioners against an assessment raised by Revenue or against certain determinations made by Revenue officials.

Source: Revenue website (September 2014).

Box 9.3. United States: Taxpayer Bill of Rights

The Right to Be Informed

Taxpayers have the right to know what they need to do to comply with the tax laws. They are entitled to clear explanations of the laws and IRS procedures in all tax forms, instructions, publications, notices, and correspondence. They have the right to be informed of IRS decisions about their tax accounts and to receive clear explanations of the outcomes.

The Right to Quality Service

Taxpayers have the right to receive prompt, courteous, and professional assistance in their dealings with the IRS, to be spoken to in a way they can easily understand, to receive clear and easily understandable communications from the IRS, and to speak to a supervisor about inadequate service.

The Right to Pay No More than the Correct Amount of Tax

Taxpayers have the right to pay only the amount of tax legally due, including interest and penalties, and to have the IRS apply all tax payments properly.

The Right to Challenge the IRS's Position and Be Heard

Taxpayers have the right to raise objections and provide additional documentation in response to formal IRS actions or proposed actions, to expect that the IRS will consider their timely objections and documentation promptly and fairly, and to receive a response if the IRS does not agree with their position.

The Right to Appeal an IRS Decision in an Independent Forum

Taxpayers are entitled to a fair and impartial administrative appeal of most IRS decisions, including many penalties, and have the right to receive a written response regarding the Office of Appeals' decision. Taxpayers generally have the right to take their cases to court.

The Right to Finality

Taxpayers have the right to know the maximum amount of time they have to challenge the IRS's position as well as the maximum amount of time the IRS has to audit a particular tax year or collect a tax debt. Taxpayers have the right to know when the IRS has finished an audit.

The Right to Privacy

Taxpayers have the right to expect that any IRS inquiry, examination, or enforcement action will comply with the law and be no more intrusive than necessary, and will respect all due process rights, including search and seizure protections and will provide, where applicable, a collection due process hearing.

The Right to Confidentiality

Taxpayers have the right to expect that any information they provide to the IRS will not be disclosed unless authorised by the taxpayer or by law. Taxpayers have the right to expect appropriate action will be taken against employees, return preparers, and others who wrongfully use or disclose taxpayer return information.

The Right to Retain Representation

Taxpayers have the right to retain an authorised representative of their choice to represent them in their dealings with the IRS. Taxpayers have the right to seek assistance from a Low Income Taxpayer Clinic if they cannot afford representation.

The Right to a Fair and Just Tax System

Taxpayers have the right to expect the tax system to consider facts and circumstances that might affect their underlying liabilities, ability to pay, or ability to provide information timely. Taxpayers have the right to receive assistance from the Taxpayer Advocate Service if they are experiencing financial difficulty or if the IRS has not resolved their tax issues properly and timely through its normal channels.

Source: United States IRS website (September 2014).

The IRS released the Taxpayer Bill of Rights publication after extensive discussions with the Taxpayer Advocate Service, an independent office inside the IRS that represents the interests of US taxpayers. Since 2007, the development of a Taxpayer Bill of Rights has been a goal of National Taxpayer Advocate, Nina Olson, and it was listed as the Advocate's top priority in her most recent Annual Report to Congress. The Taxpayer Bill of Rights contains 10 provisions that are set out in Box 9.3 and aligns closely with the set of rights recommended in the OECD's model charter (Box 9.1).

The IRS is attaching high priority to ensuring taxpayers are aware of the new provisions and have a clear understanding of their rights. As recently stated by the IRS's tax commissioner (IRS, 2014):

> This information is critically important for taxpayers to read and understand [...] We encourage people to take a moment to read the Taxpayer Bill of Rights, especially when they are interacting with the IRS. While these rights have always been there for taxpayers, we think the time is right to highlight and showcase these rights for people to plainly see.

To help disseminate the provisions, the IRS has created a publication that is being sent routinely with IRS correspondence to taxpayers. The publication was initially available in English and Spanish and updated versions have subsequently been made available in Chinese, Korean, Russian and Vietnamese. The IRS has also created a special section on its website to highlight the 10 rights (see www.irs.gov/Taxpayer-Bill-of-Rights. The IRS internal website for employees has added a special section so people working in the IRS have easy access as well. As part of its ongoing efforts to disseminate the new Bill of Rights, the IRS has added posters and signs to its public offices so taxpayers visiting the IRS can easily see and read the information, and in September 2014, it released a new YouTube video encouraging taxpayers to learn about the Taxpayer Bill of Rights.

Access to tax rulings

In line with taxpayers' rights to be informed, assisted and provided with certainty, it has become a matter of practice for revenue bodies to provide services in the form of advice on how they will interpret the laws they administer. This section provides an overview of the regimes operated by revenue bodies that provide rulings on important aspects of tax law (that are made public) and allow taxpayers to seek advanced rulings in respect of certain transactions being considered by them or already undertaken.

A public ruling is a published statement of how a revenue body will interpret provisions of the tax law in particular situations. They are generally published to clarify the application of the law, especially in situations where large numbers of taxpayers may be impacted by particular provisions of the law and/or where a particular provision has been found to be causing confusion and/or uncertainty – in other words, a taxation issue or question of public importance. Typically, a public ruling is binding on the revenue body if the ruling applies to the taxpayer and the taxpayer relies on the ruling.

A private ruling relates to a specific request from a taxpayer (or their tax representative) seeking clarification of how the law would be applied by the revenue body in relation to a particular proposed or completed transaction/s. The objective of private ruling systems is to provide additional support and early certainty to taxpayers on the tax consequences of certain, often complex or high-risk transactions.

Table 9.1. Taxpayers' rights and selected features of the revenue rulings system

	Rights are formally defined in		Public rulings are		Private rulings are			
Country	Tax or other laws	Administrative documents	Issued	Binding	Issued	Binding	Subject to time limits (time limit)	Subject to fees
OECD Countries								
Australia	✓	✓	✓	✓	✓	✓	✓ (28 days) /1	x
Austria	✓	✓	✓	✓	✓	✓ /1	✓	✓ /1
Belgium	✓	✓	✓	✓	✓	✓	✓ (3 months)	x
Canada	✓	✓	✓	x	✓	✓	✓ (varies by tax) /1	✓ /2
Chile	✓	✓	✓	✓	✓	✓	x	x
Czech Republic	✓	x	✓	✓	✓	✓	✓	x
Denmark	✓	✓	✓	✓	✓	✓	✓	✓
Estonia	✓	x	✓	✓	✓	✓	(60 days) /1	✓
Finland	✓	✓	✓	✓	✓	✓	✓	✓
France	✓	✓	✓	✓	✓	✓	✓ (3 months)	x
Germany	✓	x	✓	✓	✓	✓	x	✓
Greece	✓	✓	✓	✓	✓ /1	✓ /1	✓ (120 days)	✓
Hungary	✓	✓	✓	✓	✓	x	✓ (30 days)	x
Iceland	✓	x	✓	✓	✓	✓ /1	✓	✓
Ireland	x	✓	✓	✓	✓	✓	✓	x
Israel	✓	✓	✓	✓	✓	✓	✓	x /1
Italy	✓	✓	✓	✓ /1	✓	✓ /1	✓	x
Japan	✓	x	✓	✓	✓	x	x	x
Korea	✓	✓	✓	✓	✓	✓	✓ (1 month)	x
Luxembourg /1	✓	✓	✓	✓	✓	✓	x	x
Mexico	✓	✓	✓	✓	✓	✓	✓ (3 months)	x
Netherlands	✓	✓	✓	✓	✓	✓	x	x
New Zealand	x	✓	✓	✓	✓	✓	✓ (3 months)	✓
Norway	✓	✓	✓	✓	✓	✓	✓	✓
Poland	✓	x	✓	✓	✓	✓	✓ (3 months)	✓
Portugal	✓	✓	✓	✓	✓	✓	✓ (150 days) /1	✓
Slovak Republic	✓	x	✓	✓	✓	✓ /1	✓ /1	✓ /1
Slovenia	✓	x	✓	✓	✓	✓	✓	✓
Spain	✓	✓	✓	✓	✓	✓	✓	x
Sweden	✓	✓	✓	✓	x	n.a.	n.a.	n.a.
Switzerland	✓	x	✓	✓	✓	✓	x	x
Turkey	x	✓	✓	✓	✓	✓	x	x
United Kingdom	✓	✓	✓	✓	✓	✓	✓	x
United States	✓	✓ /1	✓	✓	✓	✓	x	✓
Non-OECD countries								
Argentina	x	x	✓	✓	✓	✓	✓ (90 days)	x
Brazil	✓	✓	✓	✓	✓	✓	✓ (360 days)	x
Bulgaria	✓	✓	✓	✓	✓	x	x	x
China	✓	✓	x	x	x	x	x	x
Colombia	x	✓	✓	✓	x	x	x	x
Costa Rica	✓	x	✓	✓	✓	✓	✓ (2 months)	x
Croatia	✓	✓	✓	✓	✓	✓	x	x
Cyprus	✓	✓	✓	✓	✓	✓	✓ (30 days)	x
Hong Kong, China	✓	✓	✓	x	✓	✓	✓ (6 weeks)	✓
India	✓	✓	✓ /1	✓	✓ /2	x	x	✓
Indonesia	✓	x	✓	✓	x	x	x	x
Latvia	✓	✓	✓	✓	✓	✓	✓ (1 month) /1	x
Lithuania	✓	✓	✓	✓	✓	✓	✓ (60 days) /1	x
Malaysia	✓	✓	✓	✓	✓	✓	✓ (60 days)	✓ /1
Malta	✓	✓	✓	✓	✓	x	x	x
Morocco	✓	✓	✓	✓	✓	✓	x	x
Romania	✓	✓	✓	✓	✓	✓	✓	✓
Russia	✓	x	✓	✓	✓	✓	✓ (1 month)	x
Saudi Arabia	✓	✓	✓	✓	✓	✓	x	x
Singapore	✓	✓	✓	✓	✓	✓	✓ (varies by tax) /1	✓ /1
South Africa	x	✓	✓	✓	✓	✓	✓ (varies) /1	✓
Thailand	✓	x	✓	✓	✓	✓	3 months	x

For notes indicated by "/ (number)", see Notes to Tables section at the end of the chapter, p. 332.

Source: Tax Administration 2015 survey responses.

Table 9.1 identifies some important features of the systems in place for obtaining public and private tax rulings. The key observations are as follows:

- With one exception (i.e. China) all revenue bodies reported the operation of a public rulings system. Most revenue bodies (53 of 55) reported that such rulings are generally binding on them.
- Most revenue bodies (51 of 56) reported the operation of a private rulings service, although around 10% reported that such rulings are generally not binding on the revenue body. In Sweden, there is a council independent of the revenue body that provides advance private rulings that, in some cases, are subject to a charge (but there are no time limits).
- Over two-thirds of revenue bodies providing private rulings reported the existence of time limits (either imposed under the law or applied administratively) for making rulings, with some indicating additional time requirements for complex cases or where further information is required from taxpayers. As will be evident from Table 9.1, the time limits applied in practice vary widely, ranging from 28 days up to a year.
- Just over a third of revenue bodies also reported that provisions exist for imposing a fee for the provision of a ruling, for some/all of the taxes administered by them.

Taxpayer registration and identification numbering systems

Comprehensive systems of taxpayer registration and numbering are a critical feature of the tax administration arrangements in most countries, supporting most tax administration processes and underpinning all return filing, collection, assessment and verification activities.

For some revenue bodies, registration involves the maintenance of basic taxpayer identifying information (e.g. for individuals, full name and address, date of birth, and for businesses, full name, business and postal addresses) using a citizen or business identification number that is used generally across government and which, for tax administration purposes, permits the routine identification of taxpayers for a range of administrative functions (e.g. issue of notices, detection of non-filers and follow-up enforcement actions). For others, the registration system involves the operation of a system of unique taxpayer identification numbers (TINs) which similarly facilitates general administration of the tax laws. Regardless of whether the identification and numbering of taxpayers is based on a citizen number or a unique TIN, many revenue bodies also use the number to match information reports received from third parties with tax records to detect instances of potential non-compliance, to exchange information between government agencies (where permitted under the law), and for numerous other applications. Japan is an example of a country that has recently taken steps to adopt a new numbering system for tax and social security administration purposes – see Box 9.4 (NTA, 2014).

Box 9.4. Japan. New numbering system for tax and social security administration

In May 2013, the Act on Use of Numbers to Identify Particular Individuals in Administrative Procedures and other bills related to Act were promulgated, thereby introducing a new social security and tax number system. The social security and tax number system is to be the base of a more fair social security and tax system, and will contribute to the people's convenience and a higher efficiency of administration as infrastructure of information society. Personal numbers will first be introduced in limited areas such as the social security and tax fields.

Box 9.4. **Japan. New numbering system for tax and social security administration** *(continued)*

On the other hand, corporate numbers will be used widely and generally disclosed. Both the public and private sectors shall be able to make various uses of them.

Introduction schedule: At present, introduction of the number system is scheduled as follows: *(1)* Personal numbers and Corporate numbers will be notified around the autumn of 2015: *(2)* The numbers will start to be used from January 2016 in the fields of social security, taxes and disaster measures. As a result, in accordance with the Act for Introduction of the Number Act, the numbers in the tax area will start to be used from the tax returns of the year 2016 for income tax, from the tax returns of the business year starting in or after January 2016 for corporate tax, from statutory statements for the payment of money, etc. made in or after January 2016, from applications, etc. that should be submitted in or after January 2016.

Outline of the number system: In the tax field, the NTA expects that use of the numbers on tax-related documents (such as final tax returns and statutory statements, etc.) will facilitate name-based aggregation of statutory statements and matching with tax returns. This is expected to improve the accurate verification of income and thus, contribute to proper and fair taxation.

Introduction of the numbers is also expected to be more convenient for taxpayers, for example, attachment of certificates of residence can be omitted in final tax return procedures by utilising the Basic Resident Registration network system, and electric filings can be submitted to only one address for the payment records and withholding records of salary/pension which the taxpayers are required to submit with the same entries to both the national and the local governments.

Source: NTA's Annual Report, 2014.

Information concerning the registered taxpayer populations of surveyed revenue bodies, the system of taxpayer identifiers used, and the use of such identifiers is set out in Tables 9.2, 9.3 and 9.4. The key observations are as follows:

Personal Income Tax

- Around half (27) of surveyed revenue bodies utilise a unique taxpayer identifier for personal taxation purposes, while just under half (22) use a citizen ID number, with the balance (including Canada, Finland, United Kingdom and United States) employing the identifier originating for social insurance purposes.
- For around 75% of the countries surveyed, the identifiers used are all numeric although, of some concern, six countries (including China, Switzerland, and the United States) reported using an identifier that does not incorporate a check digit that can be used for point-of-entry data validation purposes; where a citizen ID number is used, the identifier often includes digits that are taxpayer specific (e.g. age, nationality or residence) as is the case in Spain.
- Taxpayer identifiers, regardless of their specific nature, are used widely in the reporting of employment income, pension, interest and dividend income (all in over 80% of countries, but less so for asset sales and payments to prescribed contractors, which is around two-thirds).

- Using country labour force data as a benchmark, the proportion of personal taxpayers who are registered with the revenue body varies substantially across revenue bodies. For around one-third of revenue bodies (18), the proportion was less than 80%, and for many well below this figure; in the vast majority of these countries employees are generally not required to file annual tax returns, being either under the income threshold for personal income tax or dealt with under the cumulative form of employee withholding that is used in these countries (see further comments later in this chapter).
- Revenue bodies with relatively low rates of registration (i.e. less than 60% of the labour force population or 20% citizen population) were Brazil, Colombia, Costa Rica, Croatia, Czech Republic, India, Indonesia, Japan, Korea, Malaysia, Mexico, Morocco, Romania, Slovak Republic, Thailand, and Turkey); all of these revenue bodies administer withholding regimes for their PIT taxpayers that free the majority of them from the requirement to file annual tax returns.
- Revenue bodies with relatively high rates of personal taxpayer registration (i.e. over 180% of their respective labour forces or over 90% of their respective citizen populations) such as Australia, Finland, Greece, Israel, Luxembourg, and the United States) typically have some other unique features attaching to their systems of personal tax administration (e.g. use of a social security or citizen identity number as the taxpayer identifier and/or non-cumulative withholding regimes that require an end-of-year tax return/reconciliation).

Corporate Income Tax and Value Added Tax

- Similar arrangements apply for CIT and VAT, with unique identification and numbering systems used by 40 revenue bodies (for CIT) and 37 revenue bodies (for VAT) respectively.

Table 9.2. System of taxpayer identifiers used and numbers of registrations – PIT

	Nature of identifier			Features of identifier				Number	Registrations as % of	
Country	Unique TIN	Citizen ID number*	SSC number	N or AN	No. of digits	Check digit	Taxpayer specifics	registered end 2013 (millions)	Labour force	Citizen population
OECD countries										
Australia	✓			N	9	✓	x	27.2	223	118
Austria	✓			N	9	✓	x	6.9	157	81
Belgium		✓		N	11	✓	✓	6.83	138	61
Canada			✓	N	9	✓	x	28.8 /1	150	82
Chile		✓		N	8	✓	x	8.88	106	51
Czech Republic		✓		AN	10	✓	✓	2.92	55	28
Denmark		✓		N	10	✓	✓	5.00	173	89
Estonia		✓		N	11	✓	✓	0.55 /1	81	42
Finland			✓	AN	10	✓	✓	5.4	201	99
France	✓			N	13	✓	✓	36.5 /1	128	56
Germany	✓			N	11	✓	x	62.92	147	77
Greece	✓			N	9	x	x	11.85	238	107
Hungary	✓			N	10	✓	✓	5.19	118	52
Iceland		✓		N	10	✓	✓	0.26	144	81
Ireland		✓		AN	9	✓	x	2.72	126	59
Israel		✓ /1		N	9	✓	x	7.22 /1	196	90
Italy	✓			AN	16	✓	✓	41.41 /1	162	68
Japan	-	-	-	-	-	-	-	22.0 /1	33	17
Korea		✓		N	13	✓	✓	21.4 /1	83	43
Luxembourg		✓		N	11	✓	✓	1.10	440	204
Mexico	✓			AN	13	✓	✓	9.76	19	8
Netherlands		✓		N	9	✓	x	7.85	88	47
New Zealand	✓			N	9	✓	x	3.70	153	83
Norway		✓		N	11	-	✓	3.4	126	67
Poland		✓		N	10 /1	✓	✓	17.27	99	45
Portugal	✓			N	9	✓	x	7.0	130	65
Slovak Republic	✓			N	10	✓	x	0.66 /1	24	12
Slovenia	✓			N	8	✓	x	1.01	100	49
Spain		✓		AN	9	✓	✓	19.4 /1	84	42
Sweden		✓		N	12	✓	✓	7.5	146	78
Switzerland			✓	N	Vary	x	x	4.8 /1	103	60
Turkey	✓			N	11	✓	x	1.79	6	2
United Kingdom			✓	N	10	✓	x	39.0	121	62
United States			✓	N	9	x	x	283.1 /1	181	90
Non-OECD countries										
Argentina	✓			N	11	✓	✓	4.4	23	11
Brazil	✓			N	11	✓	x	25.6	25	13
Bulgaria	✓			N	10	✓	✓	2.6	77	36
China	✓			AN	18	x	✓	n.a.	n.a.	n.a.
Colombia	✓			AN	9	✓	x	1.56	n.a.	3
Costa Rica		✓		N	12	✓	x	0.33*	15	7
Croatia		✓		N	11	✓	x	0.10 /1	6	2
Cyprus	✓			AN	9	✓	✓	0.36	84	41
Hong Kong, China	✓			AN	7	✓	x	3.30	85	46
India	✓			AN	10	✓	✓	32.50	n.a.	3
Indonesia	✓			N	15	✓	x	25.06	21	10
Latvia		✓		N	11	✓	✓	0.91	90	45
Lithuania	✓			N	9-11	✓	✓	1.40	95	47
Malaysia	✓			AN	11	✓	x	6.79	51	23
Malta		✓		AN	Vary	x	✓	0.28	147	67
Morocco	✓			N	8	x	x	4.5	n.a.	14
Romania		✓		N	13	✓	✓	0.56 /1	6	3
Russia	✓			N	10	✓	x	145.3 /1	192	101
Saudi Arabia	-			-	-	-	-	/1	n.a.	n.a.
Singapore		✓		AN	7	✓	x	2.0 /1	93	37
South Africa	✓			N	10	✓	x	15.7 /1	79	30
Thailand		✓		N	13	✓	x	16.76	42	25

* Citizen ID number = national personal/individual identity card number (or equivalent ID used across Government).

For notes indicated by "/ (number)", see Notes to Tables section at the end of the chapter, p. 333.

Source: Tax Administration 2015 survey responses.

Table 9.3. **System of taxpayer identifiers used and number of registrations – CIT and VAT**

Country	Corporate income tax (CIT)						Value added tax (VAT)					
	Characteristics of identifier					Number registered end FY2013 (millions)	Characteristics of identifier					Number registered end FY2013 (millions)
	Unique TIN	N or AN	No. of digits	Check digit	Taxpayer specifics		Unique TIN	N or AN	No. of digits	Check digit	Taxpayer specifics	
OECD countries												
Australia	✓	N	9	✓	x	3.1	✓	N	11	✓	x	2.7
Austria	✓	N	9	✓	x	0.15	✓	AN	11	✓	x	0.83
Belgium	x /1	N	10	✓	x	0.56	✓	AN	12 /1	✓	x	0.84
Canada	✓	AN	15	✓	x	2.98 /1	✓	AN	15	✓	x	2.56 /1
Chile	✓	N	8	✓	x	0.94 /1	✓	N	8	✓	x	0.83 /1
Czech Republic	✓	AN	10	✓	x	0.53	✓	AN	10	✓	x	0.53
Denmark	✓	N	8	✓	x	0.25	✓	N	8	✓	x	0.47
Estonia	x /1	N	8	✓	x	0.20	✓	AN	11	✓	x	0.07
Finland	x	N	8	✓	x	0.41	✓	AN	10	✓	x	0.31
France	x /1	N	9	✓	x	1.88	✓	N, AN /1	13	✓	x	3.77
Germany	✓	N	11	✓	x	1.02	✓	N	11	✓	x	5.75
Greece	✓	N	9	x	x	0.43	x	N	9	x	x	1.12
Hungary	✓	N	11	✓	✓	0.58	✓	N, AN /1	10 or 11	✓	✓	0.62*
Iceland	x	N	10	✓	x	0.04	✓	N	6	x	x	0.03
Ireland	✓	AN	9	✓	x	0.16	✓	AN	9	✓	x	0.25
Israel	x /1	N	9	✓	x	0.22 /2	x /1	N	9	✓	x	0.51 /2
Italy	✓	N	11	✓	x	1.24 /1	✓	N	11	✓	x	5.06 /1
Japan	-	-	-	-	-	3.0 /1	-	-	-	-	-	3.0 /1
Korea	✓	N	10	✓	✓	0.57	✓	N	10	✓	✓	5.9 /1
Luxembourg	x	N	11	✓	✓	0.09	✓	AN	10	✓	x	0.06
Mexico	✓	AN	12	✓	✓	1.52	✓	AN	12 or 13 /1	✓	✓	5.31
Netherlands	✓	N	9	✓	x	0.89	✓	N	9	✓	x	1.64
New Zealand	✓	N	9	✓	x	0.45	✓	N	9	✓	x	0.63
Norway	x /1	N	9	✓	x	0.26	x /1	AN	9	✓	x	0.35
Poland	✓	N	10	✓	x	0.46	✓	N	10	✓	x	2.44
Portugal	✓	N	9	✓	x	0.42	✓	N	9	✓	x	1.36
Slovak Republic	✓	N	10	✓	x	0.29	✓	N	10	✓	x	0.23
Slovenia	✓	N	8	✓	x	0.10	✓	AN	10	✓	x	0.1
Spain	✓	AN	9	✓	✓	2.53	✓	AN	9	✓	✓	3.25
Sweden	x	N	12	✓	✓	0.65	x	N	12	✓	✓	1.0

Table 9.3. **System of taxpayer identifiers used and number of registrations – CIT and VAT** *(continued)*

	Corporate income tax (CIT)						Value added tax (VAT)					
	Characteristics of identifier					Number	Characteristics of identifier					Number
Country	Unique TIN	N or AN	No. of digits	Check digit	Taxpayer specifics	registered end FY2013 (millions)	Unique TIN	N or AN	No. of digits	Check digit	Taxpayer specifics	registered end FY2013 (millions)
Switzerland	x	N	Varies	x	x	0.3 /1	✓	N	9	x	x	0.3 /1
Turkey	✓	N	10	✓	x	0.67	✓	N	10 or 11	✓	x	2.37
United Kingdom	✓	N	10	✓	x	1.8	✓	N	9	✓	x	1.97
United States	✓	N	9	x	x	22.8 /1	No national VAT in place					
Non-OECD countries												
Argentina	✓	N	11	✓	✓	0.36	✓	N	11	✓	✓	1.52
Brazil	✓	N	14	✓	x	0.9	No national VAT in place					
Bulgaria	✓	N	9	✓	x	0.4	✓	AN	11 or 12	✓	x	0.2
China	✓	AN	15	x	x	7.71	✓	AN	15	x	x	24.24
Colombia	✓	AN	9	✓	x	0.78	✓	AN	9	✓	x	0.93
Costa Rica	x	N	12	✓	x	0.16	x	N	12	✓	x	0.1
Croatia	✓	N	11	✓	x	0.13	✓	N	11	✓	x	0.15
Cyprus	✓	AN	9	✓	✓	0.20	✓	AN	9	✓	✓	0.09
Hong Kong, China	✓	N	Up to 8	✓	x	0.96	No national VAT in place					
India	✓	AN	10	✓	✓	0.60	No national VAT in place					
Indonesia	✓	N	15	✓	x	2.32	✓	N	15	✓	x	0.51
Latvia	x /1	N	11	✓	x	0.08	x /1	AN	11	✓	✓ /1	0.09
Lithuania	✓	N	9-10	✓	✓	0.11	✓	AN	9 or 12	✓	✓	0.08
Malaysia	✓	AN	10	✓	x	0.77	No national VAT in place					
Malta	✓	N	9	✓	✓	0.05	✓	N	8	✓	x	0.05
Morocco	✓	N	8	x	x	0.2	✓	N	8	x	x	0.3
Romania	✓	N	12	✓	x	0.66	✓	AN	2-12	✓	x	0.38
Russia	✓	N	12	✓	x	4.7 /1	✓	N	12	✓	x	2.7
Saudi Arabia	✓	N	10	✓	x	/1	No national VAT in place					
Singapore	x	AN	10	✓	x	0.18 /1	x /1	AN	9 or 10	✓	x	0.09
South Africa	✓	N	10	✓	x	2.2	✓	N	10	✓	x	0.7
Thailand	x /1	N	13	✓	x	0.72	x /1	N	13	✓	x	0.49

TIN: Taxpayer Identification Number, **AN**: Alpha-Number, **N**: Number

For notes indicated by "/ (number)", see Notes to Tables section at the end of the chapter, p. 333.

Source: Tax Administration 2015 survey responses.

Table 9.4. **Use of taxpayer identifiers for information reporting and matching**

Country	Use of taxpayer identifiers (or some other number) for information reporting and matching					
	Wages	Pensions and benefits	Interest	Dividends	Asset sales and purchases	Payments to sub-contractors
OECD countries						
Australia	✓	✓	✓	✓	x	✓
Austria	✓	✓	x	x	x	x
Belgium	✓	✓	✓	x	x	x
Canada	✓	✓	✓	✓	✓ (some)	✓
Chile	✓	✓	✓	✓	✓	✓
Czech Republic	✓	✓	✓	✓	✓	✓
Denmark	✓	✓	✓	✓	✓	x
Estonia	✓	✓	✓	✓	✓	x
Finland	✓	✓	✓	✓	✓	✓
France	x	x	x	x	x	✓
Germany	✓	✓ /1	x	x	x	x
Greece	✓	✓	✓	✓	✓	✓
Hungary	✓	✓	✓	✓	✓	✓
Iceland	✓	✓	✓	✓	✓	✓
Ireland	✓	✓	✓	x	x	✓
Israel	✓	✓	✓	✓	✓	✓
Italy	✓	✓	✓	✓	✓	✓
Japan	x	x	x	x	x	x
Korea	✓	✓	✓	✓	✓	✓
Luxembourg /1	✓	✓	x	✓	✓	✓
Mexico	✓	✓	✓	✓	x	✓
Netherlands	✓	✓	✓	✓	✓	✓
New Zealand	✓	✓	✓	✓	x	✓
Norway	✓	✓	✓	✓	✓	✓
Poland	✓	✓	✓	✓	✓	✓
Portugal	✓	✓	✓ /1	✓	✓	✓
Slovak Republic	x	x	x	x	x	x
Slovenia	✓	✓	✓	✓	n.a.	n.a.
Spain	✓	✓	✓	✓	✓	✓
Sweden	✓	✓	✓	✓	✓	x
Switzerland	✓	x	x	x	x	x
Turkey	x	x	x	x	x	x
United Kingdom	✓	✓	✓	x	✓	✓
United States	✓	✓	✓	✓	x	✓
Non-OECD countries						
Argentina	✓	✓	✓	✓	✓	✓
Brazil	✓	✓	✓	✓	✓	✓
Bulgaria	✓	✓	✓	✓	✓	✓
China	✓	✓	✓	✓	✓	✓
Colombia	✓	✓	✓	✓	✓	✓
Costa Rica	✓	✓	✓	✓	x	x
Croatia	✓	✓	✓	✓	✓	✓
Cyprus	✓	✓	x	✓	✓	x
Hong Kong, China	✓	✓	n.a.	n.a.	n.a.	n.a.
India	✓	✓	✓	✓	✓	✓
Indonesia	✓	✓	✓	✓	✓	✓
Latvia	✓	✓	✓	✓	n.a.	n.a.
Lithuania	✓	✓	✓	✓	✓	✓
Malaysia	✓	✓	x	x	x	x
Malta	✓	✓	✓	✓	✓	✓
Morocco	✓ /1	✓ /1	✓ /1	✓ /1	✓ /1	✓ /1
Romania	✓	✓	✓	✓	✓	✓
Russia	✓	✓	✓	✓	✓	x
Saudi Arabia	x	x	✓	✓	✓	✓
Singapore	✓	✓	x	x	x	✓
South Africa	✓	✓	✓	✓	✓	x
Thailand	✓	✓	✓	✓	x	x

For notes indicated by "/ (number)", see Notes to Tables section at the end of the chapter, p. 334.

Source: Tax Administration 2015 survey responses.

Collection and assessment of taxes

The policy decisions that shape the frameworks for collecting and assessing taxes are often influenced by decisions made outside a revenue body's control. However, these decisions can have significant implications for the compliance burden imposed on taxpayers, how the tax system is to be administered and the resulting workload for the revenue body, as well as general efficiency and effectiveness considerations. This section focuses on arrangements for the collection and assessment of income taxes.

Overview – income tax withholding regimes

Withholding at source arrangements are generally regarded as the cornerstone of an effective income tax system. Imposing the obligation on independent third parties such as employers and financial institutions to withhold an amount of tax from payments of income to taxpayers: *(1)* significantly reduces, if not eliminates, their ability to understate such income for tax assessment purposes; *(2)* is a more cost efficient way for both taxpayers and the revenue body to transact the payment of taxes; and *(3)* reduces the incidence of unpaid taxes that might otherwise arise where taxpayers correctly report their income but are unable to pay all of the tax assessed.

Published research findings of selected revenue bodies (Swedish Tax Agency, 2008, United Kingdom HMRC, 2014; United States IRS, 2012) provide strong evidence of the substantial compliance benefits from withholding. Furthermore, the timely remittance of amounts withheld by employers to the revenue body ensures a regular flow of revenue to Government, thereby assisting budgetary management.

In practice, withholding is applied almost universally to employment income – of the 55 countries covered by this series that administer a PIT only four (i.e. France, Hong Kong, Singapore and Switzerland) generally do not use withholding regimes for the collection of personal income tax from employment income, although in the case of France, withholding is applied for the collection of SSC from employment income, while Switzerland requires withholding in respect of employment income paid to non-residents. In all four countries, reporting regimes ensure that the revenue body has a record of each employee's annual employment income, facilitating the checking of tax returns, while taxpayers are generally required to make advance payments of tax.

Withholding regimes for employment income

As already noted, withholding regimes are almost universally applied for the collection of personal income tax on employment income. However, there are some significant differences in the design of these regimes, with implications for how they operate in practice and the responsibilities and costs they impose on employers, taxpayers and revenue bodies. This series applies the terms "cumulative withholding" and "non-cumulative withholding" to distinguish the two basic approaches.

1) Cumulative withholding regimes

The objective of the cumulative approach to employee withholding is to ensure that for the majority of employees the total amount of taxes withheld over the course of a fiscal year matches their full-year tax liability. To the extent this is achieved, employees are freed of the obligation to prepare and file an annual tax return, the primary benefit frequently attributed to the cumulative approach. Under this approach, employees are required to provide employers with details of relevant entitlements to assist them determine the amount of tax to be deducted from their earnings. In some countries (e.g. Ireland and United Kingdom), employees provide this information to the revenue body which in turn advises the employer of a code that determines the amount of tax to be deducted from earnings. Employers withhold tax from income paid, as required, determining amounts to be withheld on a progressive/cumulative basis over the course of the fiscal year. Employees changing jobs during the course of a fiscal year must inform their new employer of their tax position and, in some countries, the revenue body as well.

Under the cumulative approach, employees tend to have few entitlements (that reduce tax payable) as this enables greater accuracy in calculating the amount of taxes withheld over the course of a fiscal year vis-à-vis their end-of-year tax liabilities. However, in two countries (i.e. Japan and Korea), employee taxpayers can present details of certain deductions/entitlements to their employers towards the end of the fiscal year for an adjustment to their overall withholdings for the year.

Employers report annually or more regularly in some countries, to revenue bodies on incomes paid and taxes withheld in respect of individual employees. Increasingly, this reporting is being done using electronic reporting methods. For some countries, this reporting facilitates checks that are carried out to ensure that the correct amount of tax has been paid and/or to determine whether taxpayers are required to file a tax return. In practice, the operation of withholding regimes for other categories of income (e.g. for interest income) complement the employment cumulative withholding arrangements and together ensure that most employees are not required to file an end-of-year tax return.

The United Kingdom's PAYE system, administered by HMRC, is based on the cumulative approach. In 2013/14, HMRC introduced a system known as "real-time information (RTI)", *moving from an annual system of employers' reporting wage income to one where wage income is reported contemporaneously (and electronically) with the payment of wages* – see Box 9.5 (UK NAO, 2014). RTI reporting has been introduced to improve the efficiency and effectiveness of withholding administration and, while

Box 9.5. **United Kingdom. Collecting employees' PAYE data in real time**

In 2013-14, HMRC changed PAYE so it could collect more timely data from employers through the Real Time Information system (RTI). RTI offers HMRC the prospect of tracking changes in income and employment in year, helping to keep people on the correct tax code when their employments change and thereby reducing the levels of under and overpayments of tax. RTI also allows HMRC to identify PAYE debt in year rather than at the end-of-year reconciliation.

HMRC piloted RTI in 2012-13 before introducing it for all employers in 2013-14. As at 31 March 2014, 1.6 million employer schemes (94 per cent) are filing through RTI, comprising 47.7 million employments (over 99 per cent). Data quality has improved and HMRC's own evaluation suggests that RTI is helping to change employer behaviour by encouraging them to tell HMRC of changes in employee circumstances earlier.

HMRC's employer survey suggests that, for most employers, changing to RTI has not been unduly burdensome. HMRC has nevertheless recognised that some smaller employers struggled to adapt their internal processes and systems in time. For example, in December 2013, it allowed employers with nine or fewer employees to report PAYE information on or before the last payday in the tax month until April 2016.

Source: Report by the Comptroller and Auditor General, HMRC Resource Accounts 2014.

at first glance may appear to be overly burdensome on employers, the UK experience to date tends to suggest this impact is marginal, particularly given advances with the automation of payrolls, and is significantly outweighed by the overall benefits. A number of other countries have already adopted similar arrangements or are planning to do so (e.g. Denmark, and Norway from January 2015).

2) Non-cumulative withholding

The alternate approach to withholding on employment income is described as "non-cumulative". By way of contrast, the non-cumulative withholding approach operates on a "pay period" basis for each employee. Under this approach, employers withhold taxes for each pay period having regard to their gross income, known entitlements (that may reduce the amount to be withheld) and the rate of withholding to be applied. Where an employee changes jobs, the new employer simply commences the withholding process on the employee's future income without regard to his/her previous employment withholdings. However, as this approach involves a less precise form of withholding, the amount deducted for each employee over the course of a fiscal year represents only an approximation of their full-year tax liability. In these circumstances, employees are normally required to file annual tax returns to ensure that the correct overall amount of tax is paid (and to obtain a refund of any overpaid tax), taking account of all categories of assessable income and entitlements (e.g. tax deductions and credits), as well as any other responsibilities administered by the revenue body that may be linked to the personal tax system (e.g. collection of student loans).

Information on the regimes of employers' withholding, payment and reporting obligations of surveyed revenue bodies is set out in Table 9.5. Among other things, this table reveals that of the 51 revenue bodies administering employer withholding regimes, approximately two-thirds administer "cumulative" type regimes. These include countries such as Austria, Bulgaria, Ireland, Japan, Korea, Mexico, New Zealand, South Africa, Spain, and the United Kingdom. Use of the non-cumulative withholding approach is limited to around one-third of surveyed countries, including Canada, Finland, Malaysia, Netherlands, Norway, Portugal, and the United States.

3) The pros and cons of cumulative and non-cumulative regimes

Providing an exhaustive account of the advantages and disadvantages of both the cumulative and non-cumulative approaches is beyond the scope of this series, particularly given the many differences in the personal tax legislative framework applying from country to country. However, it is possible to make some general observations drawing on various published reports and other FTA work.

Concerning the cumulative approach, the view is sometimes expressed that it is highly attractive (and beneficial) because it eliminates the requirement for annual tax returns from most employees, which would otherwise have to be processed by the revenue body. In other words, applying this approach frees large numbers of employees of a significant compliance burden while the revenue body avoids the cost of processing tax returns. These arguments are particularly relevant and persuasive in countries with relatively new tax systems, where the level of awareness and understanding of the tax system is likely to be very low, and/or where the costs of having most employees prepare tax returns which must be processed by the revenue body are likely to be significant. However, the administration of cumulative regimes presents some additional costs which may be significant depending on a range of factors (e.g. the degree of automation and complexity of tax law). Such regimes, with their objective of achieving an exact amount of withholding pay-by-pay, can be costly for employers to administer and their operation can entail considerable in-year administrative action by the revenue body (e.g. dealing with adjustments to entitlements and changes of employment that affect an employee's withholding) to achieve withholding precision. The extent of these costs will depend on a variety of factors, including the degree of employment mobility and technological support from the revenue body and tax law complexity.

In countries where employees are generally required to prepare and file end-of-year tax returns to finalise their overall tax situation, including those using non-cumulative PAYE regimes, significant costs potentially arise for taxpayers and the revenue body from the requirement to prepare and process tax returns. However, over the last two decades technology has been used increasingly to automate and streamline these processes and to reduce their attendant costs. These developments include, as described in Chapter 7 of the series, electronic filing and the use of fully or partially completed pre-filled tax returns that can be accessed electronically by taxpayers and their representatives.

At the end of the day, these quite different approaches to personal tax administration for employee taxpayers turn largely on whether absolute precision in pay-by-pay withholdings is an objective worth pursuing for the majority of employees, or whether a simpler approach entailing approximate in-year withholdings and an end-of-year reconciliation (largely automated) is to be preferred. Factors such as the complexity of the tax law and demographic factors (e.g. ageing populations with a more diverse range of incomes) are likely to be quite relevant to these considerations and may have quite different applicability across the 51 countries covered by this series that apply withholding regimes to employment income.

Employers' obligations on payment and reporting

Regardless of whether a country's withholding regime operates on a cumulative or non-cumulative basis, an important consideration in their design concerns the frequency of payment and reporting obligations, given the compliance burden these may impose on SME and very small businesses. With this perspective in mind, the survey sought to identify the frequency of payment and reporting and whether countries differentiated between large, medium and very small employers to take account of compliance burden considerations. This and related information concerning the mandatory use of e-payment and e-reporting obligations are set out in Table 9.5. The key observations are as follows:

- All but four countries (i.e. France, Hong Kong, Singapore, and Switzerland) apply "withholding at source" requirements for the collection of personal income taxes (and in most countries where applicable, social security contributions) on employment income.
- Employers are generally required to withhold tax from wages and remit withheld amounts to the revenue body on a *monthly* basis. However, in four countries (i.e. Australia, Canada, New Zealand, and the United States) the relevant tax laws provide for the accelerated collection of wage withholdings from the largest employers (e.g. on a weekly or fortnightly basis).
- To reduce the administrative burden on smaller businesses, around eleven countries (including Australia, Canada, Czech Republic, Greece, Ireland, Romania, Spain, Turkey, and United Kingdom) permit less frequent remittance of withheld taxes. Examples of such regimes are set out in Table 9.10.
- A number of countries reported the use of mandatory e-payment and/or e-reporting obligations for some of their employer size categories (e.g. by amount

of withholdings or business turnover). Just under a quarter indicated that larger employers must pay electronically while the use of mandatory reporting obligations was far more extensive, with almost two-thirds reporting such an approach, including Japan which requires electronic reporting from employers with over one thousand employees.

- The frequency of employers' income reporting obligation varies significantly across surveyed revenue bodies. In the majority of cases, employers must report details of individual employees' income etc., on an annual basis, while in other countries employers are required to report more regularly (often monthly but for others bi-monthly or quarterly). Variations in the frequency of reporting requirements may imply substantial differences in the compliance burden imposed on employers and the associated workload of revenue bodies, although it is known that some revenue bodies have taken steps to automate much of this regular reporting obligation, for example:

  > We are committed to improving our work efficiency and reducing taxpayers' compliance cost. Targeted at the small and medium enterprises, we strengthened the functions of electronic filing of employer's return during the year. Now, employers can upload and submit the details of employee's remuneration via the Internet using the approved Employer's Software. In addition, the maximum number of forms for filing of employees' remuneration under eTAX has been increased to cater for the need of more employers. The electronic data so provided will be transmitted to our computer system for direct processing. The data will be pre-filled onto the respective employees' electronic tax returns on the next day. It brings convenience to the employers, employees and the Department. Besides, we have upgraded our system server and workstation infrastructure during the year to achieve greater efficiency. (Hong Kong Inland Revenue, 2014)

Withholding regimes for other categories of income

In addition to employment income, many countries apply withholding at source arrangements to other categories of income – see Table 9.5. The key observations from the information reported are as follows:

- Well over two-thirds of revenue bodies administer withholding regimes to collect income tax – either as a final or creditable tax – for payments of interest income (39 revenue bodies) and dividend income (42 revenue bodies) made to *resident* taxpayers; relative high use is also seen for payments of royalties while almost 50% of revenue bodies apply withholding to prescribed categories of business and self-employment income. (Box 9.6 sets out some examples.)
- OECD countries that make fairly limited use of withholding for incomes of resident taxpayers, other than for employment-related income, are Australia, France, Norway, and the United States. However, for both Australia and the United States, the law requires application of withholding to payments made where taxpayers have not provided a valid taxpayer identifier to a prescribed payer (e.g. a financial institution).
- For payments made to *non-residents*, even higher rates of withholding usage were reported for interest income (45), dividends (47) and payments of prescribed business income (35).

Table 9.5. **Personal income tax: Employer withholding, payment and income reporting obligations**

Country	Type of withholding regime[a]	Large[b]				Small/medium[b]				Very small[b]			
		Frequency of obligation[c]		Mandatory electronic[d]		Frequency of obligation[c]		Mandatory electronic[d]		Frequency of obligation[c]		Mandatory electronic[d]	
		Payment	Reporting	Payment	Reporting	Payment	Reporting	Payment	Reporting	Payment	Reporting	Payment	Reporting
OECD countries													
Australia	NC	W	A	✓	x	M	A	✓	x	Q	A	✓	x
Austria	C	M	M, A	x	✓	M	M, A	x	✓	M	M, A	x	✓
Belgium	NC	M	A	✓	✓	M	A	✓	✓	M	A	✓	✓
Canada	NC	I	A	✓	✓ /1	M	A	x	✓ /1	Q	A	x	x
Chile	C	M	A	✓ /1	✓ /1	M	A	✓ /1	✓ /1	M	A	✓	✓
Czech Republic	C	Q	M	x	x	SA	M	x	x	A	M	x	x
Denmark	C	M	M	✓	x /1	M	M	✓	x	M	M	✓	x
Estonia	NC	M	M	x	x	M	M	x	x	M	M	x	x
Finland	C	M	A	x	x	M /1	A	x	x	Q	A	x	x
France	n.appl. /1	n.appl.	A	n.appl.	x	n.appl.	A	n.appl	x	n.appl.	A	n.appl.	x
Germany	C	M	M	x	✓	M	Q	x	✓	M	A	x	✓
Greece	NC	M	A	✓	✓	BM	A	x	✓	BM	A	x	✓
Hungary	NC	M	M	✓	✓	M	M	✓	✓	M	M	✓	✓
Iceland	NC	M	M	x	x	M	M	x	x	M	M	x	x
Ireland	C	M	A	✓	✓	M	A	✓	✓	M	A	✓	✓
Israel	C	M	A	x	✓	M	A	x	✓	BM	A	x	✓
Italy	C	M	A	x	✓	M	A	x	✓	M	A	x	✓
Japan	C	M	A	x	✓	M	A	x	x	SA	A	x	x
Korea	C	M	A	x	x	M	A	x	x	SA	A	x	x
Luxembourg	C	M	A	x	x	M	A	x	x	M	A	x	x
Mexico	C	M	M	x	✓	M	M	x	✓	M	M	x	✓
Netherlands	NC	M	A	x	✓	M	A	x	✓	M	A	x	✓
New Zealand	C	I	I	✓	✓	M	M	x	x	M	M	x	x
Norway	NC	BM	BM	x	✓	BM	BM	x	✓	BM	BM	x	✓
Poland	C	M	A	x	x	M	A	x	x	M	A	x	x
Portugal	NC	M	M	x	✓	M	M	x	✓	M	M	x	✓
Slovak Republic	C	M	M	x	✓ /1	M	M	x	✓ /1	M	M	x	✓ /1
Slovenia	C	I	I	✓	✓	I	I	✓	✓	I	I	✓	✓
Spain	C	M	A	✓	✓ /1	Q	A	✓	✓ /1	Q	A	✓	✓ /1
Sweden	NC	M	A	x	x	M	A	x	x	M	A	x	x
Switzerland		PIT is administered at the sub-national (i.e. canton) level and generally does not provide for tax withholdings on employment income of resident taxpayers /1											
Turkey	C	M	n.a	x	n.a	M, Q	n.a.	x	n.a.	Q	n.a.	x	n.a.

Table 9.5. **Personal income tax: Employer withholding, payment and income reporting obligations** *(continued)*

Country	Type of withholding regime[a]	Large[b]				Small/medium[b]				Very small[b]			
		Frequency of obligation[c]		Mandatory electronic[d]		Frequency of obligation[c]		Mandatory electronic[d]		Frequency of obligation[c]		Mandatory electronic[d]	
		Payment	Reporting	Payment	Reporting	Payment	Reporting	Payment	Reporting	Payment	Reporting	Payment	Reporting
United Kingdom	C	M	M	x	✓	M, Q	M	x	✓	Q, A	Q, A	x	✓
United States	NC	I /1	Q	✓	x	I	Q	x	x	I	A	x	x
Non-OECD countries													
Argentina	NC	M	M	✓	x	M	M	✓	x	M	M	✓	x
Brazil	NC	M	A	x	✓	M	A	x	✓	M	A	x	✓
Bulgaria	C	M	M	x	✓	M	M	x	✓	M	M	x	✓
China	C	M	I	x	x	M	I	x	x	M	I	x	x
Colombia	C	M	A	x	✓	M	A	x	✓	M	A	x	✓
Costa Rica	C	M	A	✓	x	M	A	✓	x	M	A	✓	x
Croatia	C	I /1	I /1	✓	✓	I /1	I /1	✓	x	I /1	I /1	x	x
Cyprus	C	M	A	x	✓	M	A	x	✓	M	A	x	✓
Hong Kong, China	n.a	n.a	A	n.a	x	n.a	A	n.a	x	n.a	A	n.a	x
India	C	M	A	✓ /1	✓	M	A	✓ /1	✓	M	A	✓ /1	x
Indonesia	NC	M	A	x	✓	M	A	x	x	M	A	x	x
Latvia	C	M	M	x	✓	M	M	x	✓	M	M	x	✓
Lithuania	NC	M	A, M	x	x	M	A, M	x	x	M	A, M	x	x
Malaysia	C	M	A	x	x	M	A	x	x	M	A	x	x
Malta	NC	M	A	x	✓	M	A	x	✓	M	A	x	✓
Morocco	C	M	A	✓	✓	M	A	x /1	x /1	M	A	x	x
Romania	C	M	A	x	✓	Q	M, Q, A	x	✓	Q	M, Q, A	x	✓
Russia	C	M	A	x	✓	M	A	x	✓	M	A	x	x
Saudi Arabia	There is no system of withholding on personal income tax												
Singapore	n.a	n.a /1	A	n.a	✓ /1	n.a /1	A	n.a	✓ /1	n.a /1	A	n.a	✓ /1
South Africa	C	M	SA	✓	-	M	SA	✓	-	M	SA	✓	-
Thailand	NC	M	M	x	x	M	M	x	x	M	M	x	x

Legend: a. **C**: cumulative; **NC**: Non-cumulative.

b. Size criteria (e.g. annual amount of liability or turnover) for large, SME and very small employers as defined by individual countries in their law for employer income tax withholding payment and reporting purposes.

c. Legend: **W**: weekly; **M**: monthly; **BM**: bi-monthly; **Q**: quarterly; **SA**: semi-annually; **A**: annually; **I**: irregular (number of payments).

d. Mandatory e-payment and e-reporting may apply to some or all taxpayers in this size category.

For notes indicated by "/ (number)", see Notes to Tables section at the end of the chapter, p. 334.

Source: Tax Administration 2015 survey responses.

Box 9.6. **Withholding regimes and self-employment/business income**

Ireland's Professional Services Withholding Tax: This is a withholding and reporting regime covering prescribed professional services: *(1)* medical, dental, pharmaceutical, optical, veterinary; *(2)* architectural, engineering, surveying and related services; *(3)* accounting, auditing, finance, advertising, marketing; *(4)* legal services; and *(5)* geological services.

Ireland's Relevant Contracts Tax: The regime applies to payments by principal contactors for construction, forestry and meat processing operations. Since 2012, all contracts entered into and payments made must be notified to Irish Revenue in real time using Revenue's Online Service (ROS). Revenue responds to payment notifications in real time advising the principal contractor of the rate of tax to be deducted from the payment to the subcontractor. For compliant subcontractors the rate of tax to be applied is 0%. For substantially compliant subcontractors, the rate of tax to be applied is 20%. Where the subcontractor is unknown to Revenue, or has serious compliance issues that are not being addressed, the rate of tax to be applied is 20%. The subcontractor will automatically be credited with the deducted tax for offset against any other tax liabilities they may have. Any excess tax can only be refunded once the annual Income Tax or Corporation Tax return for the period has been filed.

The return filing frequency for the principal contractor is either monthly or quarterly, depending on size. Revenue pre-populates a summary based on the payment notifications made by the principal during the return period and make this summary available through ROS. The principal has the opportunity to make amendments to the summary and sign and submit an amended return. Otherwise, the summary automatically becomes the return on the return filing date. As all information is now supplied either monthly or quarterly, there is no annual return.

United Kingdom's Construction Industry Scheme (CIS): The CIS is a withholding and reporting regime for contractors in the construction industry. A contractor may be a construction company and building firm, as well as a Government department or local authority and other businesses known in the industry as "clients". Non-construction businesses or other concerns are treated as contractors if their average annual expenditure on construction operations over a period of 3 years is GBP 1 million or more. Contractors must withhold tax at varying rates from payments to subcontractors unless the subcontractor is entitled to exemption from withholding. Sub-contractors who can pass a business test, a turnover test, and a good compliance test administered by the revenue body can be paid "gross" (i.e. no withholding).

Sources: Previous OECD publications (OECD, 2009; and OECD 2013).

Use of third party information reporting requirements

In practice, most withholding regimes are complemented by the reporting of information to the revenue body on individual payees (e.g. name of payee, their identification number, amount paid, and amount of taxes withheld). In the absence of a withholding requirement, systems of information reporting in their own right are an important compliance tool for the administration of income tax systems in many countries. As evidenced from the cited US research, considerably higher rates of compliance are achievable where income is subject to systematic reporting and matching with tax records, compared to where this is not the case. For the purpose of this series, the term "*third party information reporting*" refers to a mandatory requirement on prescribed third parties (e.g. businesses, financial institutions, and government agencies) to report payments of income (and other tax-related transactions) and payee details (generally with a taxpayer identifying number) to the revenue body. Traditionally, these reports have been used to verify the information reported by taxpayers in their returns. However, a more recent development has seen use of these reports to pre-fill tax returns, as discussed in chapter 7.

Table 9.6. **Withholding and reporting regimes for income of resident taxpayers**

Country	Type of income normally subject to withholding (**W**) and/or reporting (**R**) where paid to resident taxpayer								
	Wages/ salaries	Dividends	Interest	Rents	Prescribed business income	Royalties/ patents	Share sales	Real estate sales	Other income
OECD countries									
Australia	W, R	R	R	-	-	-	-	-	-
Austria	W, R	W	W	-	R	-	W /1	W, R /2	-
Belgium	W, R	W	W	-	W, R /1	W	-	R	W, R
Canada	W, R	R	R	-	R	R	R	R /1	W, R
Chile	W, R	R	W /1, R	R	W, R	-	R	R	W, R /1
Czech Republic	W	W	W	-	R	-	-	-	W
Denmark	W, R	R	R	R	-	W, R	-	-	W, R /1
Estonia	W, R	- /1	-	W, R	-	W, R	R	-	W, R
Finland	W, R	W, R	W, R	R	W, R	W, R	R /1	R /1	W /1, R /1
France	R	R /1	R /1	-	-	R	-	-	-
Germany	W, R	W	W	-	-	-	W	R	R
Greece	W, R	W, R	W, R	-	W, R	W, R	-	W, R	-
Hungary	W, R	W, R	W, R	-	-	W, R	-	-	W, R
Iceland	W, R	W, R	W, R	R	W, R	R	R	-	W, R
Ireland	W, R	W, R	W, R	-	W, R	W, R	-	R	-
Israel	W, R	W, R	W, R	W, R	W, R	W, R	W, R	W, R	W, R
Italy	W, R	W, R /1	W, R	-	W, R	W, R	W, R /1	-	W /2
Japan	W, R	W, R	W, R	R	W, R	W, R	W, R	R	W, R /1
Korea	W, R	W, R	W, R	R	W, R	W, R	-	-	W, R /1
Luxembourg /1	W, R	W	W	W, R	-	-	-	-	-
Mexico	W, R	R	W, R	W, R	W, R	W, R	W, R	W, R	W, R
Netherlands	W, R	W	R /1	-	-	-	-	/2	-
New Zealand	W, R	W /1, R	W, R	-	W, R	-	-	-	-
Norway	W, R	R	R	-	-	-	R /1	R	-
Poland	W, R	W	W	-	-	W, R	R	-	-
Portugal	W, R	W, R	W, R	W, R	W, R	W, R	R	R /1	-
Slovak Republic	R /1	-	W, R	R	R	W, R	R	R	W, R
Slovenia	W, R	W, R	W, R /1	W, R	R	W, R	R	R	W, R
Spain	W, R	W, R	W, R	W, R	W /1, R	W, R	R	R	W /1, R
Sweden	W, R	W, R	W, R	R	-	R	R	R	R
Switzerland	W, R /1	W	W	-	R	-	-	-	-
Turkey	W, R	W, R	W, R	W, R	W, R	W, R	W, R	R	R
United Kingdom	W, R	-	W, R /1	-	W, R /2	W, R	W, R	R	-
United States	W, R	R /1	R /1	R /1	R /1	R /1	R /1	R	R /1
Non-OECD countries									
Argentina	W, R	W, R	W, R	W, R	W, R	W, R	R	W, R	W, R
Brazil	W, R	R	W, R	R	W, R	W, R	W, R	R	R
Bulgaria	W, R	W, R	W /1	R	R	W, R	R	R	-
China	W	W	W	-	-	-	-	-	-
Colombia	W, R	W, R	W, R	W, R	W, R	W, R	W, R	W, R	W, R
Costa Rica	W, R	W, R	W, R	-	n.a.	W, R	-	W, R /1	-
Croatia	W, R	W, R	W, R	R	W, R	W, R	W, R	R	W, R
Cyprus	W, R	W, R	W	W, R /3	-	-	R /1	R /2	-
Hong Kong, China	R	- /1	- /1	-	R	-	- /1	- /1	-
India	W, R		W, R	W, R	-	-	-	W	-
Indonesia	W, R	W, R	W, R	W, R	W, R	W, R	R	R	W, R
Latvia	W, R	W, R	W, R	W, R /1	/2, R	W, R	R	R	W, R
Lithuania	W, R	W, R	R	W, R	R	W, R	R	R	R
Malaysia	W, R	-	-	-	R	-	-	W, R	-
Malta	W, R	W, R	W, R	-	-	-	W, R	W, R	-
Morocco	W, R	W, R	W, R	R	W, R	R	/1, R	R	-
Romania	W, R	W, R	W, R	R	W, R /1	W, R	W, R /1	W	W, R
Russia	W, R	W, R	W, R	W /1, R	-	W, R	W, R	W, R	W, R
Saudi Arabia	-	-	-	-	-	-	-	-	-
Singapore	R	-	-	-	-	-	-	-	-
South Africa	W, R	W, R	R	-	-	-	R /1	-	-
Thailand /1	W, R	W, R	W, R	W, R	W, R	W, R	W, R	W, R	-

For notes indicated by "/ (number)", see Notes to Tables section at the end of the chapter, p. 334.
Source: Tax Administration 2015 survey responses.

Table 9.7. **Withholding and reporting regimes for income of non-resident taxpayers**

	Type of income normally subject to withholding (**W**) and/or reporting (**R**) where paid to non-resident taxpayer								
Country	Wages/ salaries	Dividends	Interest	Rents	Prescribed business income	Royalties/ patents	Share sales	Real estate sales	Other income
OECD countries									
Australia	W, R	W, R	W, R	-	W, R	W, R	-	-	-
Austria	W, R /1	W	W /1	-	W, R	W	W /1	W, R /1	-
Belgium	W, R	W	W	-	W, R	W	-	R	W, R
Canada	W, R	W, R	W, R	W, R	R	W, R	R	R	W, R
Chile	W, R	W, R	W, R	W, R	W, R	W, R	W /1, R /1	W /1, R /1	W, R
Czech Republic	W, R	W, R	W, R	-	R	W, R	-	-	W, R
Denmark	W, R	R	R	R	-	W, R	-	-	W, R
Estonia									
Finland	W, R	W, R	W, R	R	W, R	W, R	R	R	W, R /1
France	W, R /1	W /2, R	W /3, R	-	-	W, R	-	-	-
Germany	W, R	W /1	W /1	R	W /1	W, R	W	R	R /1
Greece	W, R	W, R	W, R	-	W, R	W, R	-	W, R	
Hungary	W, R	W, R	W, R	-	-	W, R	-	-	-
Iceland	W, R	W, R	W, R	R	W, R	W, R	W, R	-	W, R
Ireland	W, R	R	W, R	/1	W, R	W, R	-	R	-
Israel	W, R	W, R	W, R	W, R	W, R	W, R	W, R	W, R	W, R
Italy	W, R	W, R /1	W, R	-	W, R	W, R	W, R	-	W, R /2
Japan	W, R	W, R	W, R	W, R	W, R	W, R	W, R	W, R	W, R /1
Korea	W, R	W, R	W, R	R	W, R	W, R	W /1, R	W /1, R	W, R /1
Luxembourg	W, R	W		W, R	W /1				
Mexico	W, R	-	W, R	W, R	W, R	W, R	W, R	W, R	W, R
Netherlands	W, R	W	R /1	-	-	-	-	/2	-
New Zealand	W, R	W, R /1	W, R	-	W, R	W	-	-	-
Norway	W, R	W, R	R	-	R	-	R	R	-
Poland	W, R	W, R /1	W, R /1	-	-	W, R	-	-	-
Portugal	W	W	W, R	W, R	W	W, R	R	R	-
Slovak Republic	R /1	-	W, R	W /1, R	R	W, R	R	R	W, R
Slovenia	W, R	W	W	W, R	W, R	W, R	R /1	R	W, R
Spain	W, R	W, R	W, R	W, R	W, R	W, R	R	W, R	W, R
Sweden	W, R	W, R	R	R	-	R	R	R	R
Switzerland	W, R	W	W	-	W, R /1	-	-	-	-
Turkey	W, R	W, R	W, R	W, R	W, R	W, R	W, R	R	R
United Kingdom	R	-	W, R	W, R	-	W, R	R	R	W
United States /1	W, R	W, R	W, R	W, R	W, R	W, R	-	W, R	W, R
Non-OECD countries									
Argentina	W, R	W, R	W, R	W, R	W, R	W, R	W, R	W, R	W, R
Brazil	W, R	R	W, R	W, R	W, R	W, R	R	W, R	W, R
Bulgaria	W, R	W, R	W, R	R	R	W, R	W, R	W, R	-
China	W	W	W	-	-	-	-	-	-
Colombia	W, R	W, R	W, R	W, R	W, R	W, R	W, R	W, R	W, R
Costa Rica	W, R	W, R	W, R	-	-	W, R	-	W, R /1	-
Croatia /1	W, R	W, R	W, R	R	W, R	W, R	W, R	R	W, R
Cyprus	W, R /1	R	R /1		W /1	W /1	R /1	R /1	W /1
Hong Kong, China	R	- /1	- /1	-	W, R	W, R	- /1	- /1	-
India	W, R	W, R	W, R	W, R	R	W, R	R	W, R	R
Indonesia	W	W	W	W	W	W	R	W	W
Latvia	W, R	W, R	W, R	W /1, R	R	W, R	W, R	W, R	W, R
Lithuania	W, R	W, R	W, R	W, R	R	W, R	R	W, R	R
Malaysia	W, R	-	W, R	W, R /1	W, R	W, R	-	W, R	W, R
Malta	W, R	W, R	R	-	-	-	W, R	W, R	-
Morocco	W, R	W, R	W, R	R	W, R	W, R	/1, R	R	-
Romania	W, R	W, R	W, R	R	W, R	W, R	W, R	W	W, R
Russia	W, R	W, R	W, R /1	W, R /1	-	W, R /1	W, R /1	W, R /1	W, R /1
Saudi Arabia	W, R	W, R	W, R	W, R	W, R	W, R	-	-	W, R
Singapore	W, R	-	W, R	W, R	W, R	W, R	-	W, R	W, R
South Africa	W, R	W, R	R /1	-	-	W, R	R /2	W /3, R	-
Thailand /1	W, R	W, R	W, R	W, R	W, R	W, R	W, R	W, R	-

For notes indicated by "/ (number)", see Notes to Tables section at the end of the chapter, p. 335.
Source: Tax Administration 2015 survey responses.

In contrast to the high cost and low audit coverage that can be achieved with traditional audit processes, comprehensive programmes of information reporting and matching can provide an extremely effective tool to screen relatively large populations of taxpayers' records, to both detect non-compliance and to encourage the correct reporting of tax liabilities. However, there are two pre-conditions for such arrangements to be sufficiently efficient to make them attractive to revenue bodies: *(1)* electronic reporting by third parties of information reports; and *(2)* the use of a high integrity taxpayer identifier to enable accurate matching of information reports with revenue body records.

As indicated in Table 9.5, many countries require the mandatory reporting of payments in respect of salaries and wages, dividend and interest income (much of which is also subject to withholding). However, beyond these categories of payments, use of mandatory third party reporting varies substantially. Other examples include:

- ***Australia's reporting system for the building and construction industry:*** An annual reporting regime introduced from July 2012 that requires details of payments made to sub-contractors in prescribed industries to be reported to the ATO on an annual basis.
- ***Canada's Contract Payments Reporting System*:** This is an annual reporting regime introduced in 1999 for payments in the building and construction sector and payments by Government for services provided by business.
- ***Ireland's system of third party returns:*** Traders (incl. farmers), professionals and others carrying on a business (incl. non-profit bodies and Government bodies) are required to automatically make third party returns. Broadly, the following payment categories are included: *(1)* payments for services rendered in connection with the trade, profession, business, etc., whether paid on their own behalf or on behalf of someone else; *(2)* payments for services rendered in connection with the formation, acquisition, development or disposal of the trade or business; and *(3)* periodical or lump sum payments made in respect of copyright. There is a prescribed list of exclusions to these requirements.
- ***United States' information reporting requirements:*** The US tax code contains information reporting requirements for a very wide variety of transactions that must be reported to the IRS, generally in electronic format, for matching with tax records. In addition to wages and investment incomes, these transactions include agricultural payments, allocated tips, barter exchange income, brokers' transactions, capital gains distributions, non-employee compensation and fees, fishing boat crew member proceeds, fish purchases for cash, prescribed gambling winnings, real estate transactions, rents, and sales of securities.

Income tax payment and return filing obligations

In the absence of withholding, there is a need for an alternate approach to ensure a timely and appropriate flow of revenue to Government. For this purpose, Governments have implemented systems of advance payments for both the PIT and CIT.

The design of advance payment regimes for both the PIT and CIT is not a straightforward issue given a number of competing considerations, including: *(1)* taxpayers should be able to determine their payment obligations and make payment with minimal compliance burden; *(2)* the volume of payments and information to be processed by the revenue body should be minimised to avoid excessive costs; *(3)* excessive lagging of tax payments may jeopardise their ultimate collectability; *(4)* Government requirements for a timely flow of tax revenue to fund expenditure commitments; and *(5)* taxpayers in similar circumstances should be treated equally.

Taking these sorts of factors into account, the vast majority of surveyed countries have evolved systems for the advanced collection of personal income and corporate income taxes, the basic features of which are set out in Tables 9.8 and 9.9. The key observations are set out hereunder:

Personal income tax

- With two exceptions (i.e. Lithuania and Singapore), all countries provide for the graduated collection of PIT on income not subject to withholding with a regime of advance/instalment payments.
- Most countries aim to maximise the amount of tax collected by advance payment regimes *within the year the relevant income is derived.* Typically, this is achieved with a regime of quarterly instalments to be made largely within the year of income, often subject to minimum threshold below which instalments are not generally required. In the case of France where employees themselves are generally required to make advance payments, a number of payment schemes apply: *(1)* three instalments, with payments by 15 February, 15 May and 15 September of the assessment year; or *(2)* a monthly scheme using the banking system.
- Around 30% of revenue bodies appear to require monthly advance payments from all taxpayers, including those with relatively small liabilities, suggesting opportunities for reducing taxpayers' compliance burden and low value administrative workloads.
- A minority of revenue bodies have mandated the use of electronic payment and return filing services, with the vast majority preferring to rely on the attractiveness of the electronic services offered. As indicated in Table 9.8, only nine revenue bodies reported some use of mandated e-payment obligations, while 22 revenue bodies reported the use of mandatory e-filing requirements for some/all PIT taxpayers.
- Just over half of revenue bodies confirmed that their PIT system is designed on based on self-assessment principles. Of the 22 revenue bodies not reporting this to be the case, almost two-thirds were from Europe.

Corporate income tax

- All countries provide for the gradual collection of CIT with a regime of advance payments, although the requirements of these systems vary substantially in terms of the frequency of payments (and as observed in TA2013, in relation to their timing and method of computation).
- Most countries aim to maximise the amount of tax collected by advance payment regimes *within the year the relevant income is derived.* Typically, this is achieved with a regime of monthly advance payments for large taxpayers (just over 40% of countries) and quarterly for small/medium sized taxpayers (just under 30%) to be made largely within the year of income.
- Many countries apply a regime that reduces the frequency of payments for smaller CIT taxpayers to reduce their administrative/compliance burden; some examples reported in survey responses are set out in Table 9.10.

Table 9.8. **Personal income tax: Assessment system and advance payments (excl. withholdings)**

			Mandatory obligations (for some/all taxpayers)	
Country	System of assessment	Frequency of advance payments*	e-payment	e-filing
OECD countries				
Australia	Self-assessment	Q, A	x	x
Austria	Assessment	Q	x	✓
Belgium	Assessment	Q	✓	x
Canada	Self-assessment	Q	x	✓ /1
Chile	Self-assessment	M	x	x
Czech Republic	Assessment	Q, SA, A (depending on liability size)	x	x
Denmark	Assessment	M (for 10 months)	✓	✓
Estonia	Self-assessment	Q	x	x
Finland	Assessment	M	x	x
France	Assessment	I /1	✓	x
Germany	Assessment	Q	✓	✓
Greece	Assessment	BM (3 payments)	x	✓
Hungary	Self-assessment	Q	✓	✓
Iceland	Assessment	A	x	x
Ireland	Self-assessment	M	✓	✓
Israel	Self-assessment	M/BM	x	✓
Italy	Self-assessment	SA /1	x	✓
Japan	Self-assessment	SA	x	x
Korea	Self-assessment	A	x	x
Luxembourg	Assessment	Q	x	x
Mexico	Self-assessment	M	x	✓
Netherlands	Assessment	M	x	x
New Zealand	Self-assessment	I (3)	x	x
Norway	Assessment	Q	x	x
Poland	Self-assessment	M	x	x
Portugal	Assessment	I (3)	x	✓
Slovak Republic	Self-assessment	M, Q	x	✓ /1
Slovenia	Assessment	M, Q	✓	✓
Spain	Self-assessment	Q, A	x	✓ /1
Sweden	Assessment	M	x	x
Switzerland	----------------------------- PIT is administered at the sub-national (i.e. canton) level -----------------------------			
Turkey	Self-assessment	SA	x	✓
United Kingdom	Self-assessment	SA	x	✓
United States	Self-assessment	Q	x	x
Non-OECD countries				
Argentina	Self-assessment	BM	✓	✓
Brazil	Self-assessment	M	x	✓
Bulgaria	Self-assessment	M, Q	x	x
China	Self-assessment	n.a.	x	x
Colombia	Self-assessment	I	x	✓
Costa Rica	Self-assessment	Q	✓	✓
Croatia	Self-assessment	M	x	x
Cyprus	Self-assessment	SA	x	✓
Hong Kong, China	Assessment	I (2) /1	x	x
India	Assessment	M	x	✓
Indonesia	Self-assessment	M	x	x
Latvia	Self-assessment	Q	x	✓
Lithuania	Self-assessment	n.applic.	x	x
Malaysia	Self-assessment	BM	x	x
Malta	Self-assessment	Q	x	x
Morocco	Assessment	A	✓ /1	✓ /1
Romania	Assessment			
Russia	Assessment	Q	x	x
Saudi Arabia	--No personal income tax--			
Singapore	Assessment	---------------------No system for making advance payments applies----------------		
South Africa	Assessment	SA	n.a.	n.a.
Thailand	Assessment	SA	x	x

* Legend: **M**: monthly; **BM**: bi-monthly; **Q**: quarterly; **SA**: semi-annually; **A**: annually; **I**: irregular (number of payments)

For notes indicated by "/ (number)", see Notes to Tables section at the end of the chapter, p. 336.

Source: Survey responses and Secretariat research.

Table 9.9. **Corporate income tax: Advance payment and annual return filing obligations**

	Large*			Small/medium*			Very small*		
	Payment	Mandatory electronic		Payment	Mandatory electronic		Payment	Mandatory electronic	
Country	frequency**	Payment	File return	frequency**	Payment	File return	frequency**	Payment	File return
OECD countries									
Australia	M	✓	x	Q	x	x	A	x	x
Austria	Q	x	✓	Q	x	✓	Q	x	✓
Belgium	Q	✓	✓	Q	✓	✓	Q	✓	✓
Canada	M, Q	x	✓ /1	M, Q	x	✓ /1	M, Q	x	x
Chile	M	✓ /1	✓ /1	M	✓ /1	✓ /1	M	✓ /1	✓ /1
Czech Republic	Q	x	x	SA	x	x	A	x	x
Denmark	SA	✓	x	SA	✓	x	SA	✓	x
Estonia	M /1	x	✓	M /1	x	✓	M /1	x	✓
Finland	M	x	x	M	x	x	M	x	x
France	Q	✓	✓	Q	✓	✓	Q	✓	✓
Germany	Q	✓	✓	Q	✓	✓	Q	✓	✓
Greece	M /1	✓	✓	M /1	✓	✓	M /1	✓	✓
Hungary	M	✓	✓	Q	✓	✓	Q	✓	✓
Iceland	M/ 1	x	x	M/ 1	x	x	M/ 1	x	x
Ireland	SA	✓	✓	A	✓	✓	A	✓	✓
Israel	M	x	x /1	M/BM	x	x	BM	x	x
Italy	SA	✓	✓	SA	✓	✓	/1	/1	/1
Japan	A	x	x	A	x	x	A	x	x
Korea	I (1)	x	x	I (1)	x	x	I (1)	x	x
Luxembourg	Q	x	x	Q	x	x	Q	x	x
Mexico	M	x	✓	M	x	✓	BM	x	✓
Netherlands	M	x	✓	M	x	✓	M	x	✓
New Zealand	I (3)	x	x	I (3)	x	x	I (3)	x	x
Norway	SA	x	x	SA	x	x	SA	x	x
Poland	M	✓	x	M, Q	✓	x	M, Q	✓	x
Portugal	Q	✓	✓	Q	✓	✓	Q	✓	✓
Slovak Republic	M, Q	x	✓ /1	M, Q	x	✓ /1	M, Q	x	✓ /1
Slovenia	M, Q	✓	✓	M, Q	✓	✓	M, Q	✓	✓
Spain	M	✓	✓	Q	✓	✓	Q	✓	✓
Sweden	M	x	x	M	x	x	M	x	x
Switzerland	---------- CIT is administered at the sub-national (i.e. canton) level ----------								
Turkey	Q	✓	✓	Q	✓	✓	Q	✓	✓
United Kingdom	Q	x	✓	n.a	x	✓	n.a	x	✓
United States	Q /1	✓	✓	Q /1	✓	x	Q /1	✓	x
Non-OECD countries									
Argentina	M	✓	✓	M	✓	✓	M	✓	✓
Brazil	M	✓	✓	M	✓	✓	M	✓	✓
Bulgaria	M	x	x	Q	x	x	-	-	-
China	M, Q, A	x	x	M, Q, A	x	x	Q, A	x	x
Colombia /1	BM	x	✓	SA	x	✓	SA	x	✓
Costa Rica	Q	✓	x	Q	✓	x	Q	✓	x
Croatia	M	x	✓	M	x	✓	M	x	✓
Cyprus	SA	x	✓	SA	x	✓	SA	x	✓
Hong Kong, China	I (2) /1	x	x	I (2) /1	x	x	I (2) /1	x	x
India	Q	✓	✓	Q	✓	✓	Q	✓	✓
Indonesia	M	x	x	M	x	x	M	x	x
Latvia	M	x	✓	M	x	✓	M	x	✓
Lithuania	Q	x	x	Q	x	x	A	x	x
Malaysia	M	x	x	M	x	x	M	x	x
Malta	Q	x	x	Q	x	x	Q	x	x
Morocco	Q	✓	✓	Q	✓ /1	✓ /1	Q	x	x
Romania	Q	✓	✓	Q	✓	✓	Q	✓	x
Russia	M	x	✓	M	x	✓	M	x	x
Saudi Arabia	Q	✓	x	A	✓	✓	A	✓	✓
Singapore	I /1	x	x	I /1	x	x	I /1	x	x
South Africa	SA	x	x	SA	x	x	SA	x	x
Thailand	SA	x	x	SA	x	x	SA	x	x

* Size criteria as defined by individual countries in their law for CIT filing and payment purposes.

** Legend: **M**: monthly; **BM**: bi-monthly; **Q**: quarterly; **SA**: semi-annually; **A**: annually; **I**: irregular (no. of payments).

For notes indicated by "/ (number)", see Notes to Tables section at the end of the chapter, p. 337.

Source: Tax Administration 2015 survey responses.

- While there is no "optimal" approach, over 40% of countries have what appears to be a relatively rigid "one size fits all" regime for CIT advance payments. For some, there may be potential to advance the collection of taxes from larger taxpayers, having regard to other countries' approaches; for others, there may be a case for reducing payment frequency for smaller taxpayers, taking account of compliance costs and other factors and other countries' approaches.
- Many countries (almost half) have mandated the use of e-filing and e-payment for their largest corporate taxpayers, while a significant number have also extended the requirement to smaller corporations.

VAT payment and return filing obligations

As evident from the tax revenue data reported in Chapter 6, VAT constitutes a significant source of tax revenue in just about all surveyed countries. Of the 56 countries surveyed, only Hong Kong, India, Malaysia, Saudi Arabia and the United States currently do not administer a VAT as part of their system of indirect taxation.

Given the significant and growing reliance being placed on VAT systems it is not surprising that the compliance burden resulting from their application has come under a fair deal of scrutiny by Governments, revenue bodies and the business community at large. Over the last decade, many studies have been conducted pointing to the nature and scale of the compliance burden that can result from the policy and administrative design features of a country's VAT system.

A report prepared for the FTA in 2008 observed that, based on a number of country studies of the compliance burden resulting from their major taxes (e.g. Canada, Germany, Sweden and United Kingdom), the VAT was clearly the most burdensome on business of all taxes (OECD, 2008). Among other things, it pointed to data from a study carried out for the United Kingdom's HMRC which had found that invoice requirements and return filing obligations were the most burdensome responsibilities of the VAT system in place and particularly impacted the population of smaller businesses. The FTA's report noted that to address such concerns, some countries had taken steps to reduce the compliance burden by modifying the design of their VAT (e.g. by raising the threshold for registration and collection of VAT, by adjusting the frequency of return filing and payment obligations, and/or by adopting simplified liability calculation rules). (Similar action had been taken by some in respect of other taxes.) In addition, it pointed to increased use by some revenue bodies of modern technology to ease the burden, including electronic filing of returns and electronic tax payments. For Chile, the report highlighted an initiative to largely automate the production of VAT invoices and related record-keeping for SME taxpayers, as briefly described in Chapter 3.

For this series, data were captured on the return filing and payment obligations of VAT systems in surveyed countries, including the use of electronic filing and payment – see Table 9.11. The key observations are:

- Most countries aim to align the collection of VAT with the underlying economic activity; typically, this is achieved with a regime of monthly or quarterly returns and tax payments. Some countries differentiate between large and SME taxpayers, requiring returns and payments less frequently from SME and very small taxpayers – see Table 9.10.

- A small number of countries (e.g. Australia, Canada, Finland and Luxembourg) permit very small remitters of VAT and/or those taxpayers with irregular transactions to file returns/make payments less frequently (e.g. annually).
- A small number of countries administer what appear to be relatively rigid "one size fits all" requirements for VAT return filing and payments, including Argentina, Bulgaria, Chile, Costa Rica, Estonia, Lithuania and Thailand.
- Around two-thirds of surveyed countries have mandated use of e-filing and e-payment obligations for their largest and SME taxpayers, while over half have extended this obligation to their smallest VAT payers. This factor accounts for the very high overall rates of e-filing reported, and in particular for the rapid growth seen in many countries over the last 4 to 5 years – see Table 7.5.

Table 9.10. **Country examples of differentiated tax filing and/or payment regimes**

Tax	Country	Taxpayer category and size criteria	Filing/payment frequency
Employees' income tax withholdings	Australia	Large: Withholdings over AUD 1 million/year	Weekly
		Medium: Withholdings over AUD 25 000-1 million/year	Monthly
		Small: Withholdings less than AUD 25 000/year	Quarterly
	Canada	Large: Average monthly withholding amount (AMWA) – over CAD 50 000	Weekly (must be paid electronically)
		Medium: AMWA – CAD 15 000 to 49 999	Monthly
		Small: AMWA below CAD 3 000	Quarterly
Corporate income tax	Czech Republic	Large: Tax liability over CZK 150 000	Quarterly
		Small/ medium: Tax liability of CZK 30 000-150 000	Semi-annually
		Very small: Tax liability below CZK 30 000	Annually
	Ireland	Large: Tax in prior year over EUR 200 000	In 6th and 11th month of accounting period.
		Other: Tax in prior year less than EUR 200 000	31 days before end of accounting period.
VAT	Japan	Where consumption exceeded JPY 48 million during the last taxation period	Monthly
		Where consumption exceeded JPY 4 million but was less than JPY 48 million during last taxation period	Quarterly
		Where consumption exceeded JPY 480 000 but was less than JPY 4 million	Annually
	New Zealand	Large: Taxable supplies exceed NZD 24 million in a 12 month period	Monthly
		Small Medium Enterprise: Taxable supplies between NZD 500 000 and NZD 24 million in a 12 month period	Bi-monthly
		Very Small: Taxable supplies up to NZD 500 000 in a 12 month period.	Semi-annually
	South Africa	Large: Taxable supplies exceed ZAR 30 million in 12 month period	Monthly
		Medium: Taxable supplies less than ZAR 30 million	Bi-monthly
		Small: Where taxable supplies do not exceed ZAR 1.5 million in a 12 month period, vendor can request longer period	Four monthly
		Persons in agriculture and farming etc., where taxable income is below ZAR 1.5 million and taxable supplies less than ZAR 30 million	Six-monthly

Source: Tax Administration 2015 survey responses.

Administrative review

Administrative review is an important part of tax administration in just about all surveyed revenue bodies. It is the process by which a taxpayer can challenge a revenue body's decision without or prior to entering the legal system, to safeguard their rights and aiming to have the laws administered correctly. Also relevant in some countries are the operation of oversight bodies and Ombudsman, as mentioned in Chapter 1. Based on survey responses, an administrative review is generally compulsory in just over three-quarters of surveyed countries before a taxpayer can seek legal recourse. In the vast majority of countries, the process is undertaken by the revenue body itself, although for a small number of revenue bodies further assistance is provided by another government body such as the MOF. An exception is Austria where the process was the responsibility of an independent tribunal until the end of 2013, and the Federal Financial Court from 1 January 2014.

Table 9.12 sets out selected features of the tax dispute systems in the surveyed countries. The following observations can be made:

- The time period in which taxpayers have to appeal for administrative review varies considerably between countries. The minimum time reported was 14 days while the maximum extend out to five years; periods of 30-60 days were frequently reported.
- Despite being an integral part of the tax assessment and collection mechanism, the use of performance standards for reviews was only reported by just over half of revenue bodies.
- Around two-thirds of revenue bodies reported (some with qualifications) that they can collect disputed tax where a case is under administrative review. This can be compared with cases under court review where almost 80% of revenue bodies reported that disputed tax can be collected, albeit in some cases only in certain circumstances.
- Specialised tax courts exist in just under half of surveyed revenue bodies.

Performance data on tax disputes in administrative review are set out in Tables 6.14 and 6.15, with brief analysis in Chapter 6. As noted earlier, there were many gaps in survey responses limiting any comprehensive analysis and observations.

Enforced collection of unpaid taxes

The efficiency and effectiveness of a revenue body's enforced debt collection activities relies to a large degree on the nature and scope of the remedies that can be applied under the laws to enforce the payment of tax debts, including the provision of an appropriate regime of sanctions (e.g. interest and/or penalties) to deter and penalise non-compliance. In practice, the legal framework for the enforced collection of taxes is set out separately in the laws governing each tax administered or, ideally, in a single comprehensive law on tax administration that provides a common set of provisions covering all taxes.

The survey undertaken set out a menu of 14 specific powers that are known to exist to varying degrees across revenue bodies and sought an indication as to whether the powers indicated were available to the revenue body. (Performance data and selected ratios on tax debt are described in Chapter 6).

Table 9.11. **VAT: Payment and return filing obligations**

	Large[a]				Small/medium[a]				Very small[a]			
	Frequency of obligation[b]		Mandatory electronic[c]		Frequency of obligation[b]		Mandatory electronic[c]		Frequency of obligation[b]		Mandatory electronic[c]	
Country	Payment	File return	Payment	File return	Payment	File return	Payment	File return	Payment	File return	Payment	File return
OECD countries												
Australia	M	M	✓	✓	Q	Q	✓	x	A	A	x	x
Austria	M	M, A	x	✓	M	M, A	x	✓	M	M, A	x	✓
Belgium	M	M	x	✓	Q	Q	x	✓	-	-	-	-
Canada	M	M	✓ /1	✓	Q	Q	✓ /1	✓	A	A	x	x
Chile	M	M	✓ /1	✓ /1	M	M	✓ /1	✓ /1	M, Q /2	M, Q /2	✓	✓
Czech Republic	M	M	x	✓ /1	Q	Q	x	✓ /1	Q	Q	x	✓ /1
Denmark	M	M	✓	✓	Q	Q	✓	✓	SA	SA	✓	✓
Estonia	M	M	x	x	M	M	x	x	M	M	x	X
Finland	M	M	x	x /1	M	M	x	x /1	A/Q	A/Q	x	x /1
France	M	M	✓ /1	✓	M	M, Q	✓ /1	✓	I	A	✓ /1	✓
Germany	M/Q/A /1	M/Q/A /1	x	✓	M/Q/A /1	M/Q/A /1	x	✓	M/Q/A/ 1	M/Q/A /1	x	✓
Greece	M	M	✓	✓	Q	Q	✓	✓	Q	Q	x	✓
Hungary	M	M	✓	✓	Q	Q	✓	✓	A	A	✓	✓
Iceland	BM	BM	x	✓	BM	BM	x	✓	BM	BM	x	✓
Ireland	BM	BM	✓	✓	BM/Q	BM/Q	✓	✓	BM/Q/SA/A	BM/Q/SA/A	✓	✓
Israel	M	M	x	✓	M/BM	BM	x	✓ /1	BM	BM	x	✓ /1
Italy	M	A	✓	✓	Q	A	✓	✓	- /1	-	-	-
Japan	M	M	x	x	Q	Q	x	x	Q	Q	x	x
Korea	Q	Q	x	x	SA	SA	x	x	A	A	x	x
Luxembourg	M	M	x	✓	Q	Q	x	✓	A	A	x	x
Mexico	M	M	x	✓	M	M	x	✓	BM	BM	x	✓
Netherlands	M	M	x	✓	Q	Q	x	✓	A	A	x	✓
New Zealand	M	M	x	x	BM	BM	x	x	SA	SA	x	x
Norway	BM	BM	x	x	BM	BM	x	x	A	A	x	x
Poland	M	M, Q	x	x	Q, M	M, Q	x	x	Q, M	M, Q	x	x
Portugal	M	M	✓	✓	Q	Q	✓	✓	Q	Q	✓	✓
Slovak Republic	M, Q /1	M, Q /1	x	✓ /2	M, Q /1	M, Q /1	x	✓ /2	M, Q /1	M, Q /1	x	✓ /2
Slovenia	M	M	✓	✓	M	M	✓	✓	M, Q	M, Q	✓	✓
Spain	M	M, A	✓	✓	M, Q	M, Q, A	✓	✓	M, Q	M, Q, A	✓	✓
Sweden	M	M	x	x	M, BM, Q	M, BM, Q	x	x	A	A	x	x
Switzerland	M, Q /1	M, Q /1	x	x	Q, SA /2	Q, SA /2	x	x	Q, SA /2	Q, SA /2	x	x

Table 9.11. **VAT: Payment and return filing obligations** *(continued)*

	Large[a]				Small/medium[a]				Very small[a]			
	Frequency of obligation[b]		Mandatory electronic[c]		Frequency of obligation[b]		Mandatory electronic[c]		Frequency of obligation[b]		Mandatory electronic[c]	
Country	Payment	File return	Payment	File return	Payment	File return	Payment	File return	Payment	File return	Payment	File return
Turkey	BM	I	x	✓	BM	I	x	✓	BM	I	x	✓
United Kingdom	Q	Q	x	✓	Q	Q	x	✓	Q	Q	x	✓
United States	No national VAT											
Non-OECD countries												
Argentina	M	M	✓	✓	M	M	✓	✓	M	M	✓	✓
Brazil	No national VAT (see footnote 1 for Table 1.1)											
Bulgaria	M	M	x	✓	M	M	x	✓	M	M	x	✓ /1
China	/1	/1	x	x	/1	/1	x	x	/1	/1	x	x
Colombia	BM	BM	✓	✓	Q	Q	✓	✓	Q	A	✓	✓
Costa Rica	M	M	✓	✓	M	M	✓	✓	M	M	✓	✓
Croatia	M, Q	M, Q, A	x	✓	M, Q	M, Q, A	x	✓	M, Q	M, Q, A	x	✓
Cyprus	Q	Q	x	x	Q	Q	x	x	Q	Q	x	x
Hong Kong, China	No national VAT											
India	No national VAT											
Indonesia	M	M	x	✓	M	M	x	✓	M	M	x	✓
Latvia	M	M	x	x	M	M	x	x	M, Q, SA	M, Q, SA	x	x
Lithuania	M	A, SA, M	x	x	M	A, SA, M	x	x	M	A, SA, M	x	x
Malaysia	No national VAT											
Malta	M	M	x	x	Q	Q	x	x	A	A	x	x
Morocco	M	Q, M	✓	✓	Q, M /1	Q, M /1	✓ /2	✓ /2	Q	Q	x	x
Romania	M	M, Q, SA, A /1	x	x	Q	M, Q, SA, A /1	x	x	SA, A	M, Q, SA, A /1	x	x
Russia	M	Q	x	✓	M	Q	x	✓	M	Q	x	✓
Saudi Arabia	No national VAT											
Singapore	M, Q, SA	M, Q, SA	x	✓	M, Q, SA	M, Q, SA	x	✓	n.a	n.a	n.a	n.a
South Africa	M	M	x	x	BM	BM	x	x	(4 monthly)	(4 monthly)	x	x
Thailand	M	M	x	x	M	M	x	x	M	M	x	x

a. Size criteria as defined as defined by individual countries in their law for VAT filing and payment purposes.

b. Legend: **M**: monthly; **BM**: bi-monthly; **Q**: quarterly; **SA**: semi-annually; **A**: annually; **I**: irregular (number of payments).

c. Mandatory e-payment and e-payment may apply to some or all taxpayers in this size category.

For notes indicated by "/ (number)", see Notes to Tables section at the end of the chapter, p. 337.

Source: Tax Administration 2015 survey responses.

Table 9.12. **Selected features of tax disputes of assessment or rulings**

	Administrative review						Revenue body can make a risk-based settlement	There is a court specialised in tax	Collection of disputed tax	
Country	Availability	Compulsory before court review	Organisation(s) in charge	Time limit in law to request review after assessment/ ruling	Time limit in law for revenue body to resolve dispute	Performance standard in place			Possible during administrative review	Possible during court review
OECD countries										
Australia	✓ /1	✓ /2	Revenue	/3	/4	✓ (70% in 56 days)	✓	x	✓	✓
Austria	✓	✓	Federal Financial Court /1	1 month	6 months	x	x	✓	✓ /2	✓ /2
Belgium	✓	✓	Revenue	6 months	6 months	✓(6 months)	x	x	x	x
Canada	✓	✓	Revenue /1	✓ /2	90-180 days	✓ /3	x /4	✓	In certain cases	
Chile	✓	x	Revenue	x	50 days	✓	x	✓	x	✓
Czech Republic	✓	✓	Revenue	30 days	6 months	x	x	x	✓	✓
Denmark	✓	✓	Revenue	3 months	1-11 months	✓	✓	x	✓	✓
Estonia	✓	x	Revenue	30 days	30 days /1	x	x	x	✓	✓
Finland	✓	✓	Revenue +	Within reasonable time	5 years	✓ /1	x	x	✓	✓
France	✓	✓	Revenue + /1	/2	6 months	✓ /3	✓ /4	x	✓ /5	/6
Germany	✓	✓	Revenue	1 month	No time limit	x	x	✓ /1	✓ /1	✓ /1
Greece	✓	✓ /1	Revenue	30 days	90 days	✓	x	✓	✓ /1	✓
Hungary	✓	✓	Revenue+ MONE	15 or 30 days /1	30 days /2	✓	✓	x	x /3	✓ /4
Iceland	✓	x	Revenue Board	3 months	None	✓	x	x	✓	✓
Ireland	✓	x	Revenue+ /1	None	None	✓ /1	✓	x /1	x	✓
Israel	✓	✓	Revenue	30 days	1 years	x	✓	x	x	x
Italy	✓	✓ /1	Revenue	60 days	90 days	x	✓	✓	✓	✓
Japan	✓	✓	Revenue	2 months /1	n.a.	✓	x	x	✓	✓
Korea	✓	✓	Revenue+ /1	90 days	90 days	x	x	x	✓	✓
Luxembourg	✓	✓	Revenue	3 months	6 months	x	x	x /1	✓	✓
Mexico	✓	x	Revenue	30 business days	3 months	✓	x	✓	x	x
Netherlands	✓	✓	Revenue	6 weeks	6 weeks	✓	✓	✓	✓ /1	✓ /1
New Zealand	✓	✓ /1	Revenue /2	2 months /3	None /4	✓ /5	✓ /6	✓ /7	x	x
Norway	✓	x	Revenue	3-6 weeks	Within reasonable time	x	x	x	✓	✓
Poland	✓	✓	Revenue	14 days	2 months	x	x	✓	x	x
Portugal	✓	x	Revenue	120 days	4 months	✓ (0.76 months)	x	✓	✓	✓
Slovak Republic	✓	✓	Revenue+ MOF	15 days	Various /1	x	x	x	x	✓
Slovenia	✓	✓	Revenue+ MOF /1	15 and 30 days /2	2 months	x /3	x	x	✓	✓
Spain	✓	✓	Revenue+	1 month	1 month	x	x	✓	x	x
Sweden	✓	✓	Revenue	2 months – 5 years	None	✓	x	x	✓	✓

Table 9.12. **Selected features of tax disputes of assessment or rulings** *(continued)*

Country	Administrative review						Revenue body can make a risk-based settlement	There is a court specialised in tax	Collection of disputed tax	
	Availability	Compulsory before court review	Organisation(s) in charge	Time limit in law to request review after assessment/ ruling	Time limit in law for revenue body to resolve dispute	Performance standard in place			Possible during administrative review	Possible during court review
Switzerland	✓	✓	Revenue	30 days	None	✓(all in 6 months)	✓	✓	x	x
Turkey	✓	x	Revenue	30 days	30 days	x	x	✓	✓	✓
United Kingdom	✓	x	Revenue+ /1	30 days	45 days (extended by agreement)	Statutory time limit	✓	✓	✓	✓ /2
United States	✓	✓	Revenue	30 days	/1	/1	✓	✓	✓ /1	✓ /1
Non-OECD countries										
Argentina	✓	✓	Revenue	15 days	60 days	x	x	✓	x	✓
Brazil	✓	x	Revenue	30 days	n.a.	✓	x	x	x	x
Bulgaria	✓	✓	Revenue	14 days	60 days	✓	x	x /1	✓	✓
China	✓	✓	Revenue	60 days	60 days	✓	x	x	✓	✓
Colombia	✓	x	Revenue	2 months	1 year	✓	x	✓	x	x
Costa Rica	✓	x	Revenue +	30 business days	30 business days	x	✓	x	✓	✓
Croatia	✓	✓	Revenue + /1	30 days	2 months	x	x	x	✓ /2	✓ /3
Cyprus	✓	✓	Revenue+		3 years	x	✓	x	✓	x
Hong Kong, China	✓	✓	Revenue	1 month/6 years /1	None	✓(98% in 4 months)	✓	x	✓	✓
India	✓	✓	Revenue	30 days	1 year	✓	x	✓	x	x
Indonesia	✓	✓	Revenue	3 months	12 months	✓	x	✓	x	x
Latvia	✓	✓	Revenue+	1 month	1-3 months	x	✓	x	x	✓
Lithuania	✓	✓	Revenue+ /1	20 days	30/60 days	✓	x	x	x	x
Malaysia	✓	✓	Revenue	30 days	12 months	✓	✓	✓	✓	✓
Malta	✓	✓	Revenue	30 days – 6 months	n.a.	x	✓	x	x	x
Morocco	✓	✓	Revenue + /1	60 days	6 months	x	-	x	✓	✓
Romania	✓	✓	Revenue	30 days	45 days	✓	x	x	✓	✓
Russia	✓	✓ /1	Revenue	1 month /2	1 month /3	✓	x	x	✓ /4	✓ /5
Saudi Arabia	✓	✓	Revenue+	60 days	60 days	x	x	✓	✓	✓
Singapore	✓	✓	Revenue+ /1	30 (21) days	None	✓ /1	✓	x	✓	✓
South Africa	✓	✓	Revenue	30 days /1	90 days	✓ /1	✓	✓	✓	✓
Thailand	✓	✓	Revenue /1	30 days	90 days	x	x	✓	✓	✓

For notes indicated by "/ (number)", see Notes to Tables section at the end of the chapter, p. 337.

Source: Tax Administration 2015 survey responses.

Powers to enforce the collection of unpaid taxes

As set out in Table 9.13, most of the 56 surveyed revenue bodies have been given the more traditional types of powers to enforce (and encourage) the collection of unpaid taxes:

1. To grant taxpayer further time to pay (50 revenue bodies);
2. To make payment arrangements (52 revenue bodies);
3. To collect from third parties that have liabilities to taxpayers (50 revenue bodies), for some with limitations/qualifications;
4. To obtain a lien over taxpayers' assets (48 revenue bodies), with a few requiring a court order;
5. To arrange seizure of taxpayer's asset (49 revenue bodies), although in a few a court order is required);
6. To require a tax clearance for government contracts (41 revenue bodies);
7. To offset taxpayer's liabilities to his/her tax credits (51 revenue bodies); and
8. To initiate bankruptcy action (48 revenue bodies), although some require a court order.

Other powers available but reported less frequently included: *(1)* to withhold government payments to debtor taxpayers (34 revenue bodies); *(2)* to close a business/ cancel a license to operate (22 countries); and *(3)* to impose tax liabilities on company directors when certain conditions are satisfied (38 revenue bodies), with a court order required by some. Only 20 of 52 revenue bodies reported that they are permitted to publically disclose details of individual taxpayers' tax debts.

Looking across the population of surveyed countries and having regard to the menu of 14 powers used for survey purposes, revenue bodies in Belgium, Brazil, Chile, China, Colombia, Costa Rica, Hong Kong, Indonesia, Japan, New Zealand, Romania and Thailand appeared to have a fairly limited range of powers. However, in the case of Chile it must be acknowledged that the enforced collection of taxes is primarily the responsibility of the Treasury, not the revenue body.

While more information is required to be conclusive, the data reported suggests that there may be opportunities for revenue bodies' wishing to improve tax payment compliance and their collection effectiveness to examine the approaches of others.

Information and access powers

The ability of authorised revenue body staff to readily obtain information from taxpayers and other parties is critical to the smooth and efficient functioning of the tax system. For this reason, the legislative framework in place for conducting tax administration generally includes provisions that enable tax officials to acquire information required for tax purposes from taxpayers and other parties and to have adequate access to books and records. At the same time, there is a need for safeguards to ensure that such powers are not abused.

Table 9.14 provides an overview of the information and access powers that are used by revenue bodies in OECD and selected non-OECD countries to administer the tax system. The key points are as follows:

- With one exception, all surveyed revenue bodies have powers to obtain relevant information and for virtually all these revenue bodies (except Slovak Republic and Slovenia) these powers extend to requests to third parties.
- Without exception, taxpayers are required to produce all records on request from revenue bodies.
- Revenue bodies' access powers are a little more limited with regard to taxpayers' private dwellings. A search warrant is required in over half of surveyed bodies to enter taxpayers' dwellings for any purposes and in two countries these can only be for fraud or criminal cases. There are exceptions in a few countries (e.g. Ireland and Hungary) that apply where parts of the dwelling are used for business purposes.
- Just over half of surveyed revenue bodies require a warrant to seize taxpayers' documents.
- In just over half of OECD countries tax officials can request a search warrant without the help of other government agencies. This is less prevalent in non-OECD countries surveyed (less than half reported having this power).

Table 9.13. **Enforced tax debt collection powers**

Country	Powers provided for enforced payment of taxes and filing of tax returns (* denotes court order required)													
	Grant further time to pay	Make payment arrange-ments	Collect from third parties	Restrict overseas travel by debtor	Arrange seizure of debtors' assets	Close business/ cancel licence	Offset debits on tax credits	Obtain lien over assets	Withhold government payments to debtors	Tax clearance needed for government contracts	Deny access to certain government services	Impose tax debts on company directors	Publish names of debtors	Initiate bankruptcy
OECD countries														
Australia	✓	✓	✓	✓	✓	x	✓	✓	✓	x /1	x	✓	x /1	✓
Austria	✓	✓	✓	x	✓	x	✓	✓	✓	✓	x	✓	x	✓
Belgium	-	x	x /1	-	x	x	x	x	x /2	x	-	x	-	x /3
Canada	✓	✓	✓	x	✓ /1	x	✓	✓ /1	✓	x /2	x	✓ /1	x	✓ /1
Chile	x /1	x /1	✓	x /1	x /1	✓	✓	✓	x	x /1	x	x	x	✓
Czech Republic	✓	✓	✓	x	✓	✓	✓	✓	x	✓	x	x	✓	✓
Denmark	✓	✓	✓	✓	✓	✓	✓	✓	✓	✓	x	✓	x	✓
Estonia	x	✓	✓	x	✓	x	✓	✓	✓	✓	x	✓	✓	✓
Finland	✓	✓	✓	x	✓	✓ /1	✓	✓	✓	✓	x	✓	✓	✓
France	✓	✓	✓	x	✓	x	✓	✓	✓	✓	x	✓	x	✓
Germany	✓	✓	✓	✓ /1	✓	✓ /1	✓	✓	✓	✓	x	✓	x	✓
Greece	✓	✓	✓	x	✓	✓	✓	✓	✓	✓	✓	✓	✓	✓
Hungary	✓	✓	✓	x	✓	✓	✓	✓	✓	✓	✓	✓	✓ /1	✓
Iceland	x	✓	✓	x	✓	✓	✓	✓	x	✓	x	✓	x	✓
Ireland	✓	✓	✓	✓	✓	✓	✓	x	x	✓	x	✓	✓	✓
Israel	✓	✓	✓	✓	✓	x	✓	✓	x	✓	x	✓	x	✓
Italy	✓	✓	✓	x	✓ /1	✓	✓ /1	✓ /1	✓	✓	x	✓ /1	x	✓ /1
Japan	✓	✓	✓	x	✓	x	✓	✓	x	✓	x	x	x	x
Korea	✓	✓	✓	✓	✓	✓	✓	✓	✓	✓	✓	✓	✓	x
Luxembourg	✓	✓	✓	x	✓	x	✓ /1	✓	✓	✓	x	✓ /2	x	✓
Mexico	✓	✓	✓	x	✓	✓	✓	✓	✓	✓	x	✓	✓	✓
Netherlands	✓	✓	✓	✓	✓	x	✓	✓	x	✓	x	✓	x	✓
New Zealand	✓	✓	✓	x	✓	x	✓	✓	x	x	x	✓	x	✓
Norway	✓	✓	✓	x	✓	x	✓	✓	✓ /1	✓	x	✓	x	✓
Poland	✓	✓	✓	x	✓	x	✓	✓	x	✓	x	✓	x	✓
Portugal	✓	✓	✓	x	✓	x	✓	✓	✓	✓	x	✓	✓	✓
Slovak Republic	✓	✓ /1	✓	x	✓	x /1	✓	✓	x	✓	x	x	✓	✓
Slovenia	✓	✓	✓	x	✓	x	✓	✓	✓	✓	x	x	✓	✓
Spain	✓	✓	✓	x	✓	x	✓	✓	✓	✓	x	✓	x	✓

Table 9.13. **Enforced tax debt collection powers** *(continued)*

Country	Powers provided for enforced payment of taxes and filing of tax returns (* denotes court order required)													
	Grant further time to pay	Make payment arrange-ments	Collect from third parties	Restrict overseas travel by debtor	Arrange seizure of debtors' assets	Close business/ cancel licence	Offset debits on tax credits	Obtain lien over assets	Withhold government payments to debtors	Tax clearance needed for government contracts	Deny access to certain government services	Impose tax debts on company directors	Publish names of debtors	Initiate bankruptcy
Sweden	✓	✓	✓	x	✓	✓ /1	✓	✓	✓ /2	x	x	x /3	x	✓
Switzerland	✓	✓	✓	x	✓	x	✓ /1	x	✓ /1	✓	x	x	x	x
Turkey	✓	✓	✓	x	✓	x	✓	✓	✓	✓	x	✓	✓ /1	✓
United Kingdom	✓	✓	✓ /1	x	✓	x	✓	✓ /1	x	x	x	✓	x /1	✓ /1
United States	✓	✓	✓	x	✓	x	✓	✓	✓	✓ /1	x	✓	x	✓ /2
Non-OECD countries														
Argentina	✓	✓	✓	x	✓	✓	✓	✓	✓	✓	✓	✓	✓	✓
Brazil	x	x	x	x	✓	x	✓	x	x	✓	✓	✓	✓	✓
Bulgaria	✓	✓	✓	x	x	✓ /1	✓	✓	✓	✓	x	✓	✓ /2	✓
China	✓	x	✓	✓	✓	x	✓	x	x	✓	x	x	✓	x
Colombia /1	✓	✓	✓	x	✓	✓	x	✓	✓	x	x	✓	x	x
Costa Rica	✓	✓	x	x	x /1	✓	✓	x	x	x /2	x	x /3	✓	x
Croatia	✓ /1	✓	✓	x	✓	✓	✓	✓	✓	✓	✓	x	✓	✓
Cyprus	✓	✓	✓	✓	✓	x	✓	✓	x	✓	✓	x/✓	x	✓
Hong Kong, China	✓	✓	✓	✓ /1	✓	x	✓	x	x	x	x	x	x	✓
India	✓	✓	✓	x	✓	x	✓	✓	✓	x	x	x	✓	✓
Indonesia	✓	✓	x	✓	✓	x	✓	✓	x	✓	x	✓	x	x
Latvia	✓	✓	✓	x	✓	✓	✓	✓	✓	✓	✓	x	✓	✓
Lithuania	✓	✓	x	x	x	✓	✓	✓	x	✓ /1	x	✓	✓	✓
Malaysia	✓	✓	✓	✓	✓	x	✓	✓	x	x	x	✓	x	✓
Malta	✓ /1	✓ /1	✓ /1	x	✓ /1	✓ /2	✓ /3	✓ /4	✓ /5	✓	✓ /2	✓	x	✓ /3
Morocco	✓ /1	✓	✓	✓	✓	x	✓	✓	✓	✓	x	✓ /2	x	✓
Romania	x	✓	✓	x	✓	x	x	✓	x	✓	x	✓	✓	✓
Russia	✓	✓	✓	✓	✓	✓ /1	✓	✓	✓	x	✓	✓ /2	✓ /3	✓
Saudi Arabia	✓	✓	✓	x	✓	x	✓	✓	✓	✓	✓	x	x	✓
Singapore	✓	✓	✓	✓	✓	x /1	✓	x	✓	x	x	x	x	✓
South Africa	✓	✓	✓	✓ /1	✓	x	✓	✓	x	✓	x	✓	✓ /2	✓
Thailand	✓	✓	x	x	✓	x	x	✓	✓	x	x	x	x	✓

For notes indicated by "/ (number)", see Notes to Tables section at the end of the chapter, p. 340.

Sources: Survey responses.

Table 9.14. **Verification of taxpayers' liabilities: information access and search powers of tax officials**

Country	Nature of powers available to authorised/delegated tax officials								
	Obtain all relevant information	Powers extend to third parties	Taxpayers must produce records on request	Obtain information from other government departments	Enter business premises without taxpayer's consent and search warrant	Enter taxpayers' dwellings without consent and search warrant	Seize taxpayers' documents without consent and search warrant	Request a search warrant without help of other government agencies	Serve a search warrant without help of other government agencies
OECD countries									
Australia	✓	✓	✓	✓	✓	✓ /1	x	x	x
Austria	✓ /1	✓	✓	✓	✓ /2	✓ /2	✓ /3	✓ /4	x
Belgium	✓	✓	✓	✓	✓	x	✓	✓	x
Canada	✓ /1	✓ /1	✓ /1	limited	✓ /1	x	x	✓	✓ /2
Chile	✓	✓	✓	✓	✓ /1	✓ /1	✓ /1	✓	✓
Czech Republic	✓	✓	✓	✓	✓	✓ /1	✓	✓	✓
Denmark	✓	✓	✓	✓	✓	x	✓	x	x
Estonia	✓	✓	✓	✓	x	x	x	✓	✓
Finland	✓	✓	✓	✓	✓	✓ /1	✓	x /1	x /1
France	✓	✓	✓	✓	✓	x	x	x	x
Germany	✓	✓	✓	✓ (limited)	✓ (in work hours)	x	x /1	✓	✓
Greece	✓	✓	✓	✓	✓	x	✓	✓	✓
Hungary	✓	✓	✓	✓	x /1	x /1	x /1	x /1	x
Iceland	✓	✓	✓	✓	✓	x	✓	✓	x
Ireland /1	✓	✓ /1	✓	✓	✓	x /1	✓	✓	✓
Israel	✓	✓	✓	✓	x	x	x	✓	✓
Italy	✓	✓	✓	✓	✓	x	x	x	x
Japan	✓	✓	✓	✓	x	x	x	✓	✓
Korea	✓	✓	✓	✓	x	x	x	x	✓
Luxembourg	✓	✓	✓	✓	x	x	x	x	x
Mexico	✓	✓	✓	✓	x	x	x	x	✓
Netherlands	✓	✓	✓	✓	✓ (in work hours)	x /1	x /2	✓	✓
New Zealand	✓	✓	✓	✓	✓	x	x /1	✓	✓
Norway	✓	✓	✓	✓	✓	x	✓	x	x
Poland	✓	✓	✓	✓	x	x	x	x	x
Portugal	✓	✓	✓	✓	x /1	x /1	x	✓	x
Slovak Republic	✓	x	✓	✓	x /1	x /1	✓	x	✓
Slovenia	✓	x	✓	✓	✓ /1	x	✓	-	-
Spain	✓	✓	✓	✓	x	x	x	✓	x
Sweden	✓	✓	✓	✓	x /1	x /1	x /1	x	x

Table 9.14. **Verification of taxpayers' liabilities: information access and search powers of tax officials** *(continued)*

Country	Nature of powers available to authorised/delegated tax officials								
	Obtain all relevant information	Powers extend to third parties	Taxpayers must produce records on request	Obtain information from other government departments	Enter business premises without taxpayer's consent and search warrant	Enter taxpayers' dwellings without consent and search warrant	Seize taxpayers' documents without consent and search warrant	Request a search warrant without help of other government agencies	Serve a search warrant without help of other government agencies
Switzerland	✓	✓	✓	✓	x	x	x	✓	✓
Turkey	✓	✓	✓	✓	x	x	x	✓	x
United Kingdom	✓	✓	✓	✓	✓	x	x	✓	✓
United States	✓	✓	✓	✓	x	x	x	x	✓
Non-OECD countries									
Argentina	✓	✓	✓	✓	x	x	x	✓	✓
Brazil	✓	✓	✓	✓	x /1	x	✓	x	✓
Bulgaria	✓	✓	✓	✓	x	x	x	x	x
China	x	x	✓	✓	✓	x	x	x	x
Colombia	✓	✓	✓	✓	✓	x	✓	x	✓
Costa Rica	✓	✓	✓	✓	x	x	x	✓	x
Croatia	✓	✓	✓	✓	x	x	x	x	x
Cyprus	✓	✓	✓	✓	x (VAT, ✓)	x	x	✓	x (VAT, ✓)
Hong Kong, China	✓	✓	✓	✓	x	x	x	✓	✓
India	✓	✓	✓	✓	✓ /1	x	x	n.a. /2	✓
Indonesia	✓	✓	✓	✓	x	x	x	✓	x
Latvia	✓	✓	✓	✓	✓	x	x	x	x
Lithuania	✓	✓	✓	✓	✓	x	✓	x	x
Malaysia	✓	✓ /1	✓	✓ /2	✓ /3	✓ /3	✓ /3	x	x
Malta	✓	✓ /1	✓	✓	x	x	x	✓ /2	✓ /3
Morocco	✓	✓	✓	✓	x	x	x	n.a.	n.a.
Romania	✓	✓	✓	✓	x	x	✓ /1	x	x
Russia	✓	✓ /1	✓	✓	✓ /2	x	✓ /2	x	x
Saudi Arabia	✓	✓	✓	✓	✓	x	✓	✓	✓
Singapore	✓	✓ /1	✓	✓	✓	✓	✓	✓ /1	✓ /1
South Africa	✓	✓	✓	✓	✓ /1	✓ /1	✓ /1	✓	✓
Thailand	✓	✓	✓	✓	✓	✓	✓	x	✓

For notes indicated by "/ (number)", see Notes to Tables section at the end of the chapter, p. 340.

Source: Tax Administration 2015 survey responses.Just over half of surveyed revenue bodies have powers of access to taxpayers' business premises and dwellings for the purpose of obtaining information required to verify or establish tax liabilities without the need for taxpayers' consent or search warrants. For a few, such access is permitted only in business hours. A search warrant is required to enter business premises in 23 countries for any purpose and in 2 countries only in criminal cases.

Tax offences (including policies to encourage voluntary disclosures)

Revenue bodies typically have resorted to a range of sanctions under the laws they administer for various offences that arise in the day to day operation of the tax system. Sanctions are intended to serve three fundamental purposes: *(1)* to act as a deterrent to non-compliant behaviour; *(2)* to punish those who offend; and *(3)* to enforce compliance with a specific provision of the law (e.g. the filing of a tax return and the payment of taxes). The most commonly-observed acts of non-compliance in practice tend to be: *(1)* the failure to file tax returns on time; *(2)* the failure to pay taxes on time; and *(3)* the failure to correctly declare all tax liabilities.

For this edition, revenue bodies were asked a range of questions concerning the offence of taxpayers failing to correctly declare all their tax liabilities, including the use of voluntary disclosure policies and the results achieved from such policies.

Survey responses concerning the questions posed are set out in Table 9.15, while details of recent developments reported by some revenue bodies are briefly outlined towards the end of the chapter. The key findings and observations are as follows:

- Six revenue bodies reported the absence of a common administrative penalty framework for the major taxes administered, suggesting the possibility of taxpayers being penalised inconsistently across taxes for identical acts of non-compliance.
- Nine revenue bodies reported that taxpayers' culpability is not a consideration in the imposition of these penalties, raising the prospect of taxpayers being penalised inconsistently for identical acts of non-compliance.
- Relatively few revenue bodies are empowered to publish details of individual taxpayers who are penalised for this offence.
- Only around 40% of survey revenue bodies reported they were empowered to offer reduced penalties as an incentive to taxpayers to voluntarily disclose past understatements of declared tax liabilities.

Voluntary disclosure policies

With reduced resources available for compliance programmes and greater expectations of improved revenue collection performance, revenue bodies are generally looking for effective "quick win" strategies. The deployment of "voluntary disclosure" policies is a proven (low cost) strategy which a number of revenue bodies have used successfully for many years as an integral feature of their approach to encouraging voluntary compliance. Furthermore, the imminent introduction of a new global standard for automatic exchanges of information between treaty partners – the OECD's Common Reporting Standard (CRS) – and the commitments already made to its adoption by individual countries presents a powerful incentive for revenue bodies to make use of this tool to achieve improved compliance and increased tax revenues (OECD, 2014).

What is a voluntary disclosure policy?

In general terms, voluntary disclosure programmes are opportunities offered by revenue bodies to allow previously non-compliant taxpayers to correct their tax affairs under specified terms. When drafted carefully, voluntary disclosure programmes benefit everyone involved – taxpayers making the disclosure, compliant taxpayers and governments.

Table 9.15. **Incorrect reporting of tax liabilities – framework for sanctions**

Country	Common administrative framework for PIT, CIT and VAT penalties	Revenue body is authorised to: Consider taxpayers' culpability in raising penalty	Remit penalties in appropriate circumstances	Publish details of taxpayers penalised	Offer reduced penalties for voluntary disclosures	Policy in place to encourage voluntary disclosures
OECD countries						
Australia	✓	✓	✓	x	✓	✓
Austria	✓	✓	✓	x	✓	✓
Belgium	-	✓	-	x	✓	x
Canada	x	x /1	✓	x	✓ /2	✓ /2
Chile /1	✓	✓	✓	✓ /2	✓	✓
Czech Republic	✓	x	x	x	x	x
Denmark	x	✓	✓	x	x	x
Estonia	✓	✓	x	✓	x	x
Finland	✓	✓	✓	✓ /1	x	x
France	✓	✓	✓	x	✓	✓ /1
Germany	✓	✓	✓	x	x	x
Greece	✓	✓	x	x	x	x
Hungary	✓	✓	✓	✓	x	x
Iceland	✓	✓	✓	x	x	x
Ireland	✓	✓	✓	✓	✓	✓
Israel	✓	x /1	✓	x /2	✓	✓
Italy	✓	✓	✓	x	✓	✓
Japan	✓	x	✓	x	✓	x
Korea	✓	✓	✓	✓	x	x
Luxembourg	x	✓	✓	x	x	x
Mexico	✓	✓	✓	✓ /1	✓	✓
Netherlands	✓	✓	✓	x	✓	✓
New Zealand	✓	✓	✓	x	✓	✓
Norway	✓	✓	✓	x	✓	✓
Poland	✓	✓	✓	x	✓	x
Portugal	✓	✓	✓	✓	✓	✓
Slovak Republic	✓ /1	x	✓	x	x	x
Slovenia	✓	✓	x	x	✓	✓
Spain	✓	✓	✓	x	✓ /1	✓
Sweden	✓	x	✓	x	x	x
Switzerland	✓	✓	✓	x	✓ /1	x
Turkey	✓	✓	✓	✓	✓	✓
United Kingdom	✓	✓	✓	✓	✓	✓
United States	✓	✓	✓	x	✓	✓
Non-OECD countries						
Argentina	✓	✓	✓	✓	x	✓
Brazil	x	x	✓	x /1	✓	x
Bulgaria	x	✓	✓	x	x	x
China	✓	✓	x	✓	x	x
Colombia	✓	x	x	x	x	x
Costa Rica	✓	✓	✓	✓ /1	✓ /2	x
Croatia	✓ /1	✓	x	x	x	x
Cyprus	PIT and CIT only	✓	✓	x	✓	x
Hong Kong, China	✓ /1	✓	x /1	x	✓	✓
India	✓ (No VAT)	✓	✓	x /1	x	x
Indonesia	✓	✓	✓	x	x	x
Latvia	✓	✓	✓	x	✓ /1	x
Lithuania	✓	✓	✓	✓	x	x
Malaysia	✓ (No VAT)	✓	✓	x	✓	✓
Malta	PIT and CIT only	✓	✓	x	✓	✓
Morocco	✓	✓	✓	x	✓	✓
Romania	✓	x	x	x	x	x
Russia	✓	✓	✓	✓	✓	x
Saudi Arabia	✓ (No VAT)	x	x	x	x	x
Singapore	✓	✓	✓	x	✓ /1	✓
South Africa	✓	✓	✓	x	✓	✓
Thailand	PIT and CIT only	✓	✓	x	✓	✓

Source: Tax Administration 2015 survey responses.

Many countries have features in their general law or administrative practice that encourage voluntary disclosures and thus provide certain incentives to taxpayers who have not complied with their tax obligations to come forward. In addition, several countries have put in place a temporary voluntary disclosure programme in order to take advantage of the momentum given by, for example, the availability of information about financial accounts held offshore and increased co-operation between revenue bodies. These programmes generally offer incentives, such as reduced penalties and interest charges, together with some form of protection from prosecution. Generally, programmes run for a short defined period, with a deadline for disclosure being set at the outset and the incentives, or incentives that are superior to those offered under existing general provisions, only being available during that period. Voluntary disclosure programmes, whether part of general law or designed as special programmes, can offer revenue bodies the chance of increased revenues at reduced cost, e.g. through fewer audits, litigation and criminal proceedings and increased voluntary compliance in future years by taxpayers that have come forward through the programme.

A critical consideration in the design of a voluntary disclosure programme is the set of incentives offered to encourage taxpayers to come forward voluntarily (e.g. concessions regarding penalties and/or interest). Typically, countries do *not* waive tax as part of their voluntary disclosure programme. Waiving tax would represent some form of a tax amnesty. According to IMF research, tax amnesty programmes are unlikely to deliver benefits that exceed their true costs. In fact, the IMF suggests that repeated stand-alone amnesties can lead to an erosion of the gross revenue collected from each successive amnesty, and may negatively affect overall tax compliance (IMF, 2008). This particular point highlights the fundamental difference between a "tax amnesty" and a "tax voluntary disclosure" policy, a distinction often not appreciated by commentators and particularly by the media where the terms are frequently used interchangeably.

Principles for successful voluntary disclosure programmes

In 2010, the OECD published the report of a study examining revenue bodies' approaches to, and experiences with, the use of voluntary disclosure policies and programmes (OECD, 2010). The report, drawing on a comprehensive survey of member countries and advice received from external parties, identified a set of principles on which a successful voluntary disclosure programme should be based, as part of a wider tax compliance strategy. Specifically, a successful programme will:

a) be clear about its aims and terms;

b) deliver demonstrable and cost-effective increases in current revenues;

c) be consistent with the generally applicable compliance and enforcement regimes;

d) help to deter non-compliance;

e) improve levels of compliance among the population eligible for the programme; and

f) complement the immediate yield from disclosures with measures that improve compliance in the longer-term.

The report concluded that how these principles are to be implemented is a matter for each country, taking into account its particular circumstances and including its tax law and practice.

For this series, revenue bodies were asked whether their tax law permitted the use of such policies and, if so, were the policies being employed as part of their compliance strategy and what results were being achieved. Drawing on survey responses and limited research, the key findings and observations are as follows, while Table 9.16 sets out details of the value of adjustments and/or assessments reported in respect of these programmes, where data were available:

- Around 40% of revenue bodies have a policy to encourage voluntary disclosures; however, less than three-quarters of these revenue bodies were able to provide details concerning the scale of these programmes and the results achieved in practice.
- A number of revenue bodies (e.g. ATO, HMRC and IRS) have a policy of promoting/targeting such programmes to specific areas of non-compliance (e.g. assets concealed in offshore bank accounts).
- Results achieved by a number of revenue bodies suggest that voluntary disclosure programmes can be an effective means of encouraging taxpayers to come forward and make disclosures and a reasonable source of revenue.

Table 9.16. **Revenue bodies' use of voluntary disclosure**

	Numbers of cases processed				Taxes, penalties and interest (millions in local currency)			
Country	2010	2011	2012	2013	2010	2011	2012	2013
OECD countries								
Australia	9 776	13 742	10 945	11 216	582 /1	764 /1	838 /1	836 /1
Austria	n.a.	2 589	6 965	12 947	n.a.	n.a	n.a	n.a
Canada	12 506	13 009	13 633	15 133	/1	/1	/1	/1
Israel	-	-	1 079	255	-	-		
Italy /1	-	-	2	59	-	-	7	413
Mexico	-	-	-	-	-	-	-	170 538 /1
Netherlands /1	1 035	353	/1	/1	98	60	/1	/1
New Zealand	1 301	1 120	2 527	3 077	188	265	407	489
Portugal	1 033 534	2 679 891	1 956 346	2 041 435	45 /1	70 /1	58 /1	52 /1
Slovenia	21 315	13 887	14 491	17 522	14	10	14	10
Sweden	998	5 641			115	452		
Turkey	17 600	1 198 000			3.3	2 455		
United Kingdom	19 000	22 000	595	1 295	400	275		
United States	15 000 /1	18 000 /1	4 800	4 200	360 /1	3 040 /1	1 500	1 600
Non-OECD countries								
Malta	1 374	1 117	2 946	1 783	41	16	11	16
Morocco	n.a	n.a	5 961	29 254	n.a	n.a	n.a	1. 360
Russia	333 592	202 907	n.a	n.a	75 248	50 063	n.a	n.a
Singapore /1	818	745	13 209	13 851	68	36	17	20
South Africa	-	3 140 /1	814 /1	1 622 /1	-	1 700 /1	1 670 /1	1 490 /1
	-	-	-	28 /2	-	-	-	230 /1

For notes indicated by "/ (number)", see Notes to Tables section at the end of the chapter, p. 342.

Source: Tax Administration 2015 survey responses.

Table 9.17 provides examples from revenue bodies that routinely offer voluntary disclosure programmes as part of their normal on-going compliance activities.

Table 9.17. **Examples of voluntary disclosure regimes**

Country	Brief outline
Australia	The ATO has for many years promoted a policy of voluntary disclosure to encourage compliance with the tax laws. When a taxpayer tells the ATO about a false or misleading statement they have made or a mistake that increases their tax or reduces their credits – and they do so without prompting, persuasion or direct compulsion on the ATO's part, it is referred to it as a "voluntary disclosure". A voluntary disclosure generally opens the way to concessional treatment both for any administrative penalties that apply and any interest charges. (Administrative penalties are those the ATO may impose without taking court action. They apply uniformly across most tax laws. That is, the penalty imposed for a particular type of mistake is the same regardless of the law involved, except for excise. (Excise law has its own penalties regime.) More information can be found at ATO website (ATO, 2014).
Canada	The CRA's Voluntary Disclosures Programme (VDP) allows taxpayers to come forward and correct inaccurate or incomplete information or to disclose information they have not reported during previous dealings with the CRA. Taxpayers may avoid being penalised or prosecuted, if they make a valid disclosure. A disclosure may be made for Income Tax and Goods and Services Tax/Harmonised Sales Tax (GST/HST) purposes. A valid disclosure must meet **all** of the following four conditions: *(1)* The disclosure is voluntary (made before the taxpayer becomes aware of any compliance action taken by the CRA against him/her); *(2)* a penalty applies to it; *(3)* the information is at least one year overdue; and *(4)* the information is complete. If the CRA accepts the disclosure as valid, the taxpayer may only have to pay the taxes or charges owing, plus interest. The VDP does not assess penalties, but rather relieves them. More information can be found at CRA website (CRA, 2014).
New Zealand	New Zealand IR's voluntary disclosure rules provide an incentive to taxpayers to determine their correct tax liability. By making a full voluntary disclosure, a taxpayer will attain the advantage of either a full or partial reduction of any "shortfall penalty" for which they are liable and may also avoid prosecution action. A taxpayer can make a full voluntary disclosure for the purpose of a shortfall penalty reduction, either: *(1)* before the taxpayer is first notified that a tax audit is pending ("pre-notification disclosure"), or *(2)* after the taxpayer is first notified of a pending audit but before the audit starts ("post-notification disclosure"). The relevant provisions of the law do not apply unless the taxpayer makes a full voluntary disclosure. It allows the Commissioner to specify what information must be provided by the taxpayer to be a full disclosure and the form in which the disclosure must be provided. Where a taxpayer makes a full voluntary disclosure a full or partial reduction will be allowed in the shortfall penalty rate, depending on the circumstances of the case (e.g. taking account of the degree of culpability, and the point in time when the voluntary disclosure is made in the course of the administrative process). When a taxpayer makes a pre-notification disclosure, the Commissioner's practice is not to consider subsequent prosecution action against them in respect of the tax shortfall that they have voluntarily disclosed. However, Inland Revenue may consider prosecution action when a taxpayer makes a post-notification disclosure that involves evasion or similar offending. (New Zealand Inland Revenue, 2014)
Singapore	IRAS introduced a Voluntary Disclosure Programme (VDP) in 2009 to encourage taxpayers to come forward voluntarily to disclose past errors made in tax declarations in exchange for no or reduced penalties; the VDP is applicable to Income Tax (including withholding tax) as well as, Goods and Services Tax. Further details of the VDP can be found in the IRAS e-tax guide "IRAS Voluntary Disclosure Programme" (IRAS, 2014).

Use of voluntary disclosure policies concerning off-shore non-compliance

In recent years, a number of revenue bodies have introduced more targeted voluntary disclosure programmes aimed at specific types or forms of non-compliance, in particular, non-compliance involving the concealment of income and assets in offshore accounts. These programmes have generally coincided with work of the OECD's co-ordinated effort to counter and eliminate offshore tax evasion practices through initiatives to eliminate bank secrecy, and expand and modernise the arrangements for automatic exchanges of information between treaty partners, as acknowledged in the following example provided by Australia's Commissioner of Taxation:

> The G20 work on increasing tax transparency across borders is having an impact – people are realising they need to come forward and clean up their affairs. Over 500 taxpayers have already made disclosures under the ATO's Project DO IT, totalling more than AUD 100 million in income and AUD 450 million in previously unreported assets. (ATO, 2014)

Examples of a few of these more targeted forms of voluntary disclosure campaigns are set out below:

- In March 2014, ***Australian*** tax authorities announced an initiative (Project DO IT) to allow eligible taxpayers to come forward and voluntarily disclose unreported foreign income and assets. In announcing the initiative, the ATO Commissioner urged taxpayers with offshore assets to declare their interests ahead of a global crackdown on people using international tax havens. The initiative covers amounts not reported or incorrectly reported in tax returns, including foreign income or a transaction with an offshore structure; deductions relating to foreign income that have been claimed incorrectly; capital gains in respect of foreign assets or Australian assets transferred offshore; income from an offshore entity that is taxable in your hands; and offshore deductions relating to domestic income.

  The initiative closed on 19 December 2014, with more than 5 600 taxpayers coming forward. More background can be found on the ATO website – see www.ato.gov.au/projectdoit.

- ***Chile*** reported that a special voluntary disclosure programme for declaration of assets and incomes held abroad is in effect between 1 January 2015 and 31 December 2015 (provisional Art. 24 Tax Reform). Taxpayers that choose to come forward under the programme are subject to a tax of 8% on the value of the assets and incomes declared. This tax replaces all other taxes that would otherwise be applicable to such assets and incomes. No further interest and monetary penalties are applicable. Taxpayers that comply with the requirements provided for in the law to declare assets and related income held abroad and pay the corresponding 8% tax, are exempted from further administrative, civil or criminal penalties applicable under tax, companies limited by shares, foreign exchange and securities laws. However, criminal prosecution is possible under anti-money laundering law.

- ***Israel*** reported that it implemented an offshore voluntary disclosure initiative between November 2012 and September 2013; the tax involved is established only after approval of the voluntary report and, as of May 2014, 600 cases had been approved, with tax of ILS 348 688 for cases reported in 2012-13.

Tax sanctions – recent legislative developments

Reforms concerning the sanctions regime administered were reported by a number of surveyed revenue bodies. The reforms reported are described briefly hereunder:

- ***Canada's*** CRA reported a number of developments:

  - *New Sanctions for Income Tax and GST/HST – Electronic Suppression of Sales Software:* Budget 2013 introduced new administrative monetary penalties and criminal offences for both GST/HST and income taxes to specifically address the underreporting of revenues through the use of electronic suppression of sales software. These measures strengthen existing penalties and offences for making false statements or omissions under each of the Excise Tax Act and the Income Tax Act, as well as existing sanctions under the Criminal Code. The provisions came into effect on January 1, 2014 and are in relation to the use, possession, acquisition, manufacture, development, sale, possession for sale, offer for sale or otherwise making available electronic sales suppression software.

- *False statements in Excise Tax Returns:* Budget 2014 standardided sanctions related to false statements in Excise Tax Returns to make them consistent with GST/HST sanctions. This included adding a new monetary penalty and amending the existing criminal offence.
- *Scientific Research and Experimental Development (SR&ED)*: The CRA revised Form T661, *SR&ED Expenditures Claim*, to include new prescribed information "Part 9 – Claim preparer information". A penalty of CAD1 000 may be assessed in respect of each SR&ED claim for which the prescribed information about the claim preparer(s) is missing, incomplete or inaccurate. If a claim preparer has prepared or assisted in the preparation of the claim, the claim preparer will be jointly and severally, or solidarily, liable with the taxpayer for the penalty. The penalty applies in respect of claims filed on or after 1 January 2014.
- *Gifting Tax Shelters:* Budget 2012 increased the penalties for unregistered charitable donation tax shelters and unreported tax shelter sales. Starting with the 2013 tax year, the CRA will not assess taxes owed or provide a refund to taxpayers who claim a tax credit under a gifting tax shelter scheme until the CRA has audited the tax shelter. Further, legislation introduced in Budget 2013 allows the CRA to collect 50% of the amount in dispute or to withhold 50% of the refund of an amount in dispute, when these amounts are related to a gifting tax shelter, starting with amounts assessed for the 2013 tax year.

- ***Chile*** reported that in November 2012 a tax reform bill was approved introducing Transfer Pricing regulations including sanctions for non-compliers in filing sworn affidavits informing on their operations with cross-border related entities.
- ***Costa Rica*** noted that changes to the General Tax Code in 2013 (Law No. 9069 of 28 September 2013) provided for increased penalties for failure to provide information as requested or in a timely manner, for the provision of wrongful and inaccurate information, and for the failure to comply with the duty to keep records of shareholders of corporate entities.
- ***Croatia*** reported that new legislation introduced in January 2013 for regulating the procedure of fiscalisation of cash payments, taxpayers subject to fiscalisation, contents of fiscalised receipts, recordkeeping on taxpayers subject to cash payment fiscalisation, the implementation of fiscalisation procedures, cash payments between taxpayers subject to fiscalisation, and the supervision of the implementation of this Act. The Act also includes a comprehensive set of sanctions, with fines up to HRK 500 000 for non-compliance, including by customers.
- In ***Denmark***, small/medium-sized corporations are now subject to an administrative fine of DKK 5 000-80 000 (depending on size of size of company) in case of (significant) monthly non-reporting, delay or faulty statement of tax liabilities of PAYE for employees to the e-Income register. Under separate "hidden economy" legislation in 2012 there is now a risk of liability for payment of tax for contracted works when transactions above EUR 1 200 are paid for in cash.

- ***Hungary*** reported that the penalty for under-declaration of tax liabilities (previously set at 75%) has been increased to a maximum 200% from January 2012, if it relates to the concealment of revenues or the falsification or destruction of documents, books or records.
- ***Ireland*** reported a number of developments: *(1)* Security for certain fiduciary taxes (i.e. Employers Tax, VAT, Relevant Contracts Tax, Universal Social Charge) where the person, in relation to a business that has ceased to trade, was involved in the management of the business and tax arose while the business was trading which has not been paid in full – if security is not provided and they continue to trade, they may be prosecuted; *(2)* New powers to request documentation and information for the purposes of investigation of a relevant offence; *(3)* Power to require certain persons to provide return of property; *(4)* New anti-avoidance measures; *(5)* Publication of the details of any excise licences revoked; *(6)* Extended provisions for penalties for failure to make an excise return; and *(7)* New provisions to authorise the forfeiture of alcohol products held for sale in unlicensed premises.
- ***Israel*** advised a number of developments were reported concerning new or revised sanctions. Major businesses are obliged to submit an expanded VAT annual report (a report that notes every invoice digitally). From January 2012, those taxpayers who fail to file an expanded report are subject to imprisonment of one year. In addition, proposed regulations for an administrative fine of ILS 2 000 for this offence are under way. The extended VAT filing requirement has been expanded from 2014. In 2012 and 2013, the requirement applied to businesses with a turnover exceeding 2.5 million NIS. From March 2014, the amended law was enforced so this requirement now includes businesses with turnover exceeding ILS 2 million. From January 2015, the turnover threshold will fall to ILS 1.5 million.
- ***Japan*** reported two developments: *(1) Penalties for a person who submits a request form for reassessment that includes falsified descriptions:* A person who submits a request form for reassessment that includes falsified descriptions to the district director of the tax office shall be punished by imprisonment with work for one year or less or by a fine of JPY 500 000 or less; and *(2) Penalties for intentional failure to file a foreign assets statement:* If a person submits a foreign assets statement that includes falsified descriptions, or fails to file the statement by the due date without reasonable reasons, the person shall be punished by imprisonment with work for one year or less or by a fine of JPY 500 000 or less. Provided, however, that if a person fails to file the statement by the due date, the person may be exculpated from the punishment in light of the circumstances.
- ***New Zealand*** advised that new penalties are being introduced to domestic legislation in order for New Zealand to be able to remedy "significant non-compliance" in accordance with the proposed inter-governmental agreement (IGA) with the United States in respect of FATCA. The specific change is the introduction of new offences for failing to register with a foreign government agency when required to by an agreement such as the proposed IGA. (Further information can be found under the heading "penalties" at the bottom of page 59 of the commentary to the relevant tax bill, http://taxpolicy.ird.govt.nz/sites/default/files/2013-commentary-arearm.pdf.
- ***Singapore*** reported a range of developments:
  - *New sanctions under the Anti-Money Laundering Legislation for tax offences:* The Corruption, Drug Trafficking and other Serious Crimes (Confiscation of Benefits) Act (*CDSA*) is the principal anti-money laundering legislation in

Singapore that criminalises laundering of benefits derived from drug trafficking and other serious offences. Certain tax offences relating to fraud and evasion have been newly included as serious, and therefore predicate offences under the CDSA, and the laundering of proceeds of such crimes has been criminalised.

- *New sanctions relating to the Productivity and Innovation Credit (PIC) Scheme*: The PIC scheme was introduced in 2010 to encourage businesses to invest in productivity and innovation activities. Tax benefits include tax deductions/ allowances and cash payouts. Criminal sanctions have been introduced in respect of fraudulent claims for such benefits.

- *New sanctions relating to exchange of information:* Criminal sanctions have been introduced in respect of failure to provide information as required, providing false or misleading information in response to the revenue body's notice, as well as contravening the confidential nature of such notice (anti-tipping).

- ***Slovenia*** reported that new sanctions have been implemented for taxpayers who possess or use computer software or other electronic devices, which allow adaptation, hiding, deletion or any other kind of change to specific records, saved in the device or other media, with no possibility to trace such changes. The same sanctions apply to developers who supply such software to taxpayers.

Notes to Tables

Table 9.1. Taxpayers' rights and selected features of the revenue rulings system

/1. **Australia:** Where the taxpayer's request raises particularly complex matters that will take more than 28 days to resolve after receiving all the required information, an extended reply date is negotiated. **Austria:** From 2011 only private rulings on group taxation, business restructuring or transfer pricing are binding on the revenue body and fees will be charged. **Canada:** Income Tax – within 90 business days of receipt of all essential information from the client; GST/HST – within 45 working days of receipt in the CRA. This excludes highly technical and precedent and/or policy-setting GST/HST rulings and interpretations. **Estonia:** With provision to extend by 30 days. **Greece:** Private rulings only apply as regards to Advance Pricing Agreements (APAs). **India:** Central Board of Direct Taxes issues Circulars, which are in the nature of public guidance. **Israel:** Fees are required only for rulings on mergers and acquisitions. **Latvia:** 1 month is norm but may be extended for objective reasons up to 4 months, subject to notification of this to applicant. **Italy:** Rulings are binding only on the Revenue Agency. **Lithuania:** 60 days is norm but further 60 days may be added where additional examination required. **Luxembourg:** Direct taxes only. **Malaysia:** Fees are charged only for Advanced Private Rulings. **Portugal:** 150 days is norm but can be 90 days if a request to justify its urgency is made by the taxpayer and accepted by the tax administration. **Singapore:** 8 weeks for income tax and 4 weeks for GST; expedited rulings can be made for an additional fee. **Slovak Republic:** There is no general period within which the revenue body (SFA) is obliged to issue a private ruling following a taxpayer's request. The SFA will issue (on the basis of the written request of the taxpayer) the binding statements (defined by the Tax Procedure Code) to the tax regulations application from 1 September 2014. In such cases, the issuing period is to be defined 60 days from the day of the written request delivery (max. 6 calendar months – after consultation with the taxpayer). Required fee is 1% (at minimum EUR 4 000), 2% (at minimum EUR 5 000) or 3% (at minimum EUR 6 000) of the assumed business case value. These binding statements are binding for the revenue body and the second-instance (appellate) authority. **South Africa:** Depends on complexity of ruling. **United States:** IRS has not adopted a separate Taxpayer Bill of Rights that sets forth basic rights of taxpayers, nor has Congress codified that. However, Congress has enacted various specific protections of taxpayers' rights over the years, and the IRS has published a publication "Your Rights as Taxpayer" which spells out some of those statutory and other rights.

/2. **Canada:** Only private rulings on income tax matters are subject to a fee. **India:** Tax administration does not give private rulings. There is the institution of the Authority of Advance Rulings which the taxpayers may approach for a ruling on specific facts applicable to their case.

Table 9.2. System of taxpayer identifiers used and number of registrations – PIT

/1. **Canada:** Number of taxpayers who were alive on 31 December 2012 and who filed at least one return in the last five years. **Croatia:** The number represents individuals/natural persons who are conducting self-employment activities reported to the revenue body, as well as of craft and freelance business activities. **Estonia:** Number of natural persons who submitted PIT return for 2013. **France:** Number of "fiscal households", which are made up of one person (single, widow, divorced), two persons (married or partners) children, even adult children under certain conditions for the latter. **Israel:** A special number is given for combined businesses and a unique identifier is issued for withholding files. Concerning the registered population, only active taxpayers are counted, thereby excluding closed files such as terminated businesses that are not required to file and businesses in the process of closing files. **Italy:** Data for 2013 are not available because the terms of submission of returns are currently open. Figure refers to 2012. **Japan:** The number of people who filed a final tax return for 2013. **Korea:** Number of registered taxpayers subject to 2012 Global Income Tax (5.6 million) and number of wages and salary earners subject to year-end settlement (15.8 million). **Poland:** Two numbering systems exists, and each has different features. PESEL (Powszechny Elektroniczny System Ewidencji Ludności), the personal identification number is the tax identifier for the selected taxpayer groups (i.e. individuals who do not lead the business or they are not registered as VAT taxpayers; others have a NIP (Numer Identyfikacji Podatkowej), tax identification number. PESEL has 11 digits including some that are taxpayer specific, while the NIP has ten digits, none of which are taxpayer specific. **Romania:** Registered taxpayers are those who are recorded on the taxpayer master files that are under regular administration by the revenue body; the number shown does not include those employee taxpayers who are generally not required to file an income tax return because their income tax liabilities are finalised by employers' withholding. **Russia:** FTS have no statistics of PIT taxpayers. The number shown is all registered individuals payers of due taxes. **Saudi Arabia:** The revenue body administers a tax on income/profits and a tax unique to SA known as the ZAKAT. There are around 11 000 individuals and companies registered for the tax on income/profits and 250 000 registered for the ZAKAT. **Singapore:** The number of individual tax filing packages issued for 2014 year of assessment to taxable individuals as at end of February 2014. **Slovak Republic:** The number recorded on the taxpayer master files that are under regular administration of the revenue body. **South Africa:** The number registered at the end of the 2013 financial year (i.e. end of March 2013) and includes individuals and trusts (totalling 0.3 million in 2012/13). In 2010/11, SARS changed its policy and stipulated that all individuals who are formally employed must register as taxpayers, rather than only those taxpayers above the tax threshold, resulting in the number of individuals on register increasing from 5.9 million in 2009/10 to 15.4 million in 2012/13. **Spain:** Number of registered personal taxpayers is the number of annual PIT returns (with including several taxpayers as it is possible a joint PIT return with spouses or children under 18). **Switzerland:** Last precise figures available for PIT are for 2010. **United States:** These include all taxpayers on the IRS Master File, including spouses as of the close of cycle 2013, and it includes all taxpayers for which activity has taken place within the last four years, and within ten years for those with outstanding tax liabilities.

Table 9.3. System of taxpayer identifiers and number of registrations – CIT and VAT

/1. **Belgium:** The CIT number is the official registered enterprise number that can be used across Government. The VAT number is the enterprise number plus the code "BE". **Canada:** Figure for CIT represents the number of registered corporations in the Business Number system as of end of March. The figure for VAT represents the total number of CRA administered GST/HST programme accounts as of end of March 2013 and excludes GST/HST programme accounts administered by the Province of Quebec (Federal/Provincial Administrative Agreement). **Chile:** Figure for CIT registrants represents number who filed return in 2014; figure for VAT registrants is number who filed returns in 2013. **Estonia:** The CIT number is the registered entity number for government purposes, recorded in the Business Register. **France:** Business identification (SIREN) is a unique company registration number. It is allocated for each company by the national statistics office and is made by 9 numbers (8 numbers and 1 check number). For public entities, this number starts automatically with "1" or "2". For VAT, the identification number consists of 3 elements: the country code (FR), the numeric or alphanumeric key of 2 characters and the unique company registration number of 9 characters. **Hungary:** For VAT registration and identification purposes, taxpayers are identified using either their PIT number where a natural person or their CIT number where a legal entity. Thus the client identifier used for VAT will reflect the individual features of the respective numbering systems. **Israel:** CIT number is the registered company number. A special number is given for combined businesses and a unique identifier is issued for withholding files. The number for VAT purposes is either the registered company number or the citizen identity number for a sole trader or self-employer. **Italy:** Data for 2013 are not available because the terms of submission of returns are currently open. Figure refers to 2011 for CIT and VAT. **Japan:** The CIT amount is the number of declared cases for 2012, and the VAT figure is the number of declared cases (payments and refunds) for 2012. **Korea:** Amount is the number of registered taxpayers at the end of 2012. **Latvia:** For CIT identification, a joint registration number is granted by the Enterprise Register; where such a code has not been granted to the legal entity, it is granted an 11-digit taxpayer registration code. For VAT payer identification, one applies the taxpayer registration code which is the same as the PIT or the CIT identifier, if such an identifier has not been granted, the VAT liable person is granted an 11-digit VAT registration number. **Mexico:** The number of digits of the identifier for VAT can be 12 (where a corporate taxpayer) or 13 where an individual (and registered for PIT). **Norway:** CIT is the same number as the registration number in the Company House. The VAT number is the same number as CIT plus MVA (abbreviation for VAT). **Russia:** The expressed figure is the number of all registered legal entities payers of CIT and special regimes taxpayers. **Saudi Arabia:** Revenue body administers a tax on income/profits and a tax unique to SA known as the ZAKAT. There are around 11 000 individuals and companies registered for the tax on income/profits and 250 000 registered for the ZAKAT. **Singapore:** For CIT, figures represent the number of active companies that were issued a tax return for the 2014 year of assessment 2014 as at 23 March 2014. **Switzerland:** Latest precise figures available are CIT (2010) and VAT (2011). **Thailand:** Number as per Certificate of Juristic Person Registration. **United States:** The corporation figure includes all active and inactive corporations that file Form 1120. Inactive corporations remain on the master file for four years and up to 10 years if there are outstanding tax judgments.

/2. **Israel:** Only active taxpayers are counted for CIT and VAT. Closed files (such as terminated businesses that are not required to file and businesses in the process of closing files) are not included.

Table 9.4. Use of taxpayer identifiers for information reporting and matching

/1. **Germany:** Legislation enacted with technical implementation underway. **Luxembourg:** Direct Taxes only. **Morocco:** Individuals are not obliged to have a fiscal identifier so the revenue body uses the national identifier. **Portugal:** Interest income is generally subject to final withholding tax. Taxpayer identification is reported only in case of global income taxation.

Table 9.5. PIT: Employer withholding, payment and reporting obligations

/1. **Canada:** Mandatory electronic filing obligations apply to employers that file more than 50 information returns for a calendar year. Generally this would exclude very small businesses. **Chile:** Mandatory e-payment and e-filing applies to taxpayers authorised to keep electronic accounting records. **Croatia:** Employers generally are required to remit tax withholdings and report income details to the revenue body when wage payments are made to employees. **Denmark:** Although reporting electronically is not mandatory 99.7% of reports are received this way; it is planned to introduce mandatory reporting requirements in 2015. **Finland:** Small employers can apply to make their payments quarterly. **France:** There is no regime for the collection of PIT by withholding at source, although such requirements exist for social security contributions. **India:** All corporates and persons who are required to have their books of account audited are required to use e-payment for their withholdings. **Morocco:** The requirements for e-payment and the e-filing for tax returns are optional for taxpayers who have a turnover between 10 and 50 million MAD. **Singapore:** No tax withholding on employment income where paid to taxpayers who are citizens of Singapore; reporting of wage income must be made electronically by employers participating in the auto-inclusion (i.e. prefilling service) system used by IRAS. **Slovak Republic:** Mandatory from 2014 where taxpayer is also a VAT payer or uses the services of tax agents. **Spain:** From January 2014, all reporting must be made electronically, or by using special Tax Help Programme that produces reports that can be processed using scanners. **Switzerland:** Requirements vary across cantons. However, all foreign employees who do not hold a long term residence permit but who nevertheless have their tax domicile or residence in Switzerland shall be subject to tax withholding on employment income. **United States:** Frequency of payments depends on the employer's payment schedule as determined by prior liabilities and how often employees are paid.

Table 9.6. Withholding and reporting regimes for income of resident taxpayers

/1. **Austria:** From 1 April 2012. **Belgium:** Specified business income (e.g. commissions, broker fees, etc.) **Bulgaria:** Some bank interest is subject to withholding taxation. **Canada:** Only if property is other than primary residence. **Chile:** Re interest, withholding on certain public debt instruments; other payments include directors' fees and rents when paid to real estate agents. **Costa Rica:** Tax Administration is in charge of collecting the tax derived from transfer of immovable property. This tax is collected by bank entities as a requirement for filing the correspondent public deed before the Public Registry. Real estate tax is collected by each local government. **Finland:** Sale/purchase of shares: No withholding when shares are sold or purchased. Sale/purchase of real estate: No withholding when real estates are sold or purchased; Other types of income:

Pensions, social benefits etc. are all mainly subject to withholding **France:** dividends and interests are subject to general rate of income tax since incomes earned in 2013. **Hong Kong:** Capital gains, dividends or interest are not subject to tax in Hong Kong. **Italy:** withholding only for non-qualified shares and reporting only for qualified shares; **Japan:** Distribution of profits based on contracts of specified anonymous association etc. **Korea:** Retirement income, Pension, Other income. **Latvia:** If one has registered economic activity, the tax shall be paid upon submission of the annual income return. **Luxembourg:** For individuals only. **Morocco:** Tax for sales/purchases of shares is withheld at source only if shares are quoted in Casablanca Stock Exchange. **Netherlands:** Banks and insurance companies provide the values at the beginning and end of fiscal year of accounts and capital insurance policies. **New Zealand:** New Zealand operates an imputation credits system. **Norway:** (if listed). **Portugal:** 50% of this income is taxed but can be exempted provided that the sale value is reinvested in real estate for private residence purposes. **Romania:** For certain activities/transactions tax is not withheld. **Russia:** No, if rent income of the individual (physical person) is received from the legal entity, the tax is withheld at source of income. If rent income of the individual (physical person) is received from another individual, then income should be declared and tax should be paid by recipient of income. **Slovak Republic:** Employer (payer of the tax) shall deduct or withheld the tax advances (monthly) from the taxable income (wage and salary) of employee and employee shall ask employer for annual tax assessment. If employee (resident or non-resident) does not ask employer for annual tax assessment he has to report it in the tax return. (The taxpayer reports incomes from dependent activity (salary and wage) not withheld in the tax return.) **Slovenia:** Interest withholding is not valid for all types of interest. **South Africa:** Shares listed on the Johannesburg Stock Exchange and participatory interests in regulated Collective Investment Schemes. **Switzerland:** Requirements vary across cantons. However, all foreign employees who do not hold a long term residence permit but who nevertheless have their tax domicile or residence in Switzerland shall be subject to tax withholding on employment income. **Thailand:** Non-residents may not be subject to tax according to relevant double tax treaties. **United Kingdom:** No interest withholding if taxpayer make claims, as below income tax charge. **United States:** Backup withholding may be required under certain circumstances.

/2. **Austria:** From 1 April 2012. **Italy:** a special regime is applied on gambling income sourced on Italian territory. **Latvia:** If one has not registered economic activity, the tax shall be withheld by the income payer at the moment of payment. **The Netherlands:** For the transfer of real estate a notarial act is obligatory and these are registered at the tax administration. **United Kingdom:** Withholding and reporting is in place for certain workers in the construction industry

Table 9.7. Withholding and reporting regimes for income of non-resident taxpayers

/1. **Austria:** *Wages:* Only if employee is employed by a permanent establishment (for wage tax proposes) in Austria; *Interest:* Within EU: withholding tax according to council directive 2003//48/EC; outside the EU; normally no. limited tax liability in Austria. *Share sales:* Only for those activities listed in Income Tax Act. *Real estate sales*: from 1 April 2012. **Chile**: Withholding must be applied over the capital gain obtained in a transaction. **Costa Rica:** The Tax Administration is in charge of collecting tax derived from the transfer of immovable property. This tax is collected by bank entities as a requirement for filing the correspondent public deed before the Public Registry. **Croatia:** Agreed provisions of concluded Agreements on avoidance of double taxation apply. Depending on whether there is full documentation submitted (e.g. residency certificate) the tax on specific income can be withheld at source; otherwise it cannot be withheld at the source and national tax procedures apply. **Cyprus:** *(1) Employment income*: where employment is exercised in Republic or if directors' fees paid by a resident company; *(2) Interest income*: If subject to EU savings directive; *(3) Professional income:* All types of such income of an individual; *(4) Income from royalties/patents:* Exempt if royalties/patents used abroad and non-resident was not engaged in business in Cyprus or per interest and royalties directive; *(5) Shares:* By seller: For CGT purposes, if there is a sale of shares of companies not registered on a recognised stock exchange with immovable property in Cyprus; *(6) Real estate*: By seller: Before any transfer of immovable property situated in Cyprus. Any CGT due needs to be settled before the transfer; *(7) Other income:* Technical assistance, cinematography film, entertainer group including football clubs and athletic missions. **Finland:** Other types of income such as pensions, social benefits etc. are all mainly subject to withholding and reporting. **France:** Yes, by taxpayers using tax returns. **Germany:** From 2009, interest, dividends, fund distributions and capital gains from capital investments (e.g. shares or units) are subject to a uniform final flat-rate withholding tax of 25%. The investment income of non-residents is only liable to tax in a few exceptional cases, e.g. where the principal is secured through domestic real property or where over-the-counter transactions are involved. Tax deduction is only provided for in the case of the latter. Dividend payments are, however, reported in case of an application for refund of the withholding tax. Interest payments are reported in the cases falling under the Interest Information Regulation (implementation of the Savings Taxation Directive). No deduction of tax in the case of renting out domestic real property, dwellings and office space etc. Business income withholding for certain types of income, e.g. income of artistes, professional sportsmen, authors and journalists applies. Upon deduction of the tax for business income, the remuneration debtor must submit a self-assessed tax return, in which it is, however, generally only necessary to enter the entire remuneration amount subject to the tax deduction. It is not normally necessary to state what the total figure comprises. Other incomes are recurring benefits and pensions. In case of pension payments, the amount of the benefits has been communicated using a pension payment notification for assessment periods since 2005. **Hong Kong:** Capital gains, dividends or interest are not subject to tax in Hong Kong. **Ireland:** Payments of rent to non-residents of the state are paid gross if the payments are made to a resident agent who is acting on behalf of the non-resident property owner. Revenue may request third-party returns from letting agents and managers of premises. Payments of rent to non-residents are subject to withholding tax by the tenant at the standard rate (currently 20%) where the rent is paid directly to the non-resident into his/her bank account. In this situation, the tenant must account for the tax to the Revenue Commissioners. **Italy:** Under certain circumstances, a reduced withholding of 1.375% is applied for UE and EEA companies. **Japan:** Distribution of profits based on contracts of specified anonymous association etc. **Korea**: Withheld only when selling shares or real estate, Retirement income, Pension, Other income. **Latvia:** If one has registered economic activity, the tax shall be paid upon submission of the annual income return. **Luxembourg:** Artists and sportsmen only. **Malaysia:** Income from rents of immovable property and other income type are subject to withholding and reporting by the payer. **Morocco:** Tax for sales/purchases of shares is withheld at source only if shares are quoted in Casablanca Stock Exchange. **The Netherlands:** Banks and insurance companies provide the values at the beginning and end of fiscal year of accounts and capital insurance policies. **New Zealand:** New Zealand operates an imputation credit scheme. **Poland:** (CIT) Remitters are obliged withhold withholding tax on dividends, interests, royalties and patents on the day of making the payment. Taxpayers shall transfer the amounts of tax, no later than the 7th day of the month following the month in the course of which the tax was withheld to the account of the tax office headed by the Head of the tax office relevant for matters of taxation of foreign persons (non-resident taxpayers). Remitters are obliged to send the non-resident taxpayers and the tax office information about the payments made and the withheld tax prepared in compliance with the set template. **Russia:** In relation to legal entity – when a non-resident carries out business activities by creating a permanent establishment for the purposes of taxation. **Slovak Republic:** Employer (payer of the tax) shall deduct or withheld the tax advances (monthly) from the taxable income (wage and salary) of employee and employee shall ask employer for annual tax assessment. If employee (resident or non-resident) does not ask employer for annual tax assessment he has to report it in the tax return. (The taxpayer reports incomes from dependent activity (salary and wage) not withheld in the tax return.). **Slovenia:** If non-residents alienate Slovenian source financial capital they are not required to pay the tax on capital gains earned by this alienation, unless the alienated security or equity share represented a majority share in an entity (defined in the Slovenian Personal Income Tax Act as 10% of voting rights or 10% share in a capital or in a particular class of securities that a legal entity issued directly or indirectly through an associated enterprise) in the period of 5 years before the alienation. **South Africa:** A withholding tax on interest paid to non-residents is to be introduced with effect from 1 January 2015. **Switzerland:** Only applicable if performance of artists, musicians, sportspersons and contributors is in Switzerland. Also applies for income paid by a Swiss-company to members of a governing board. **United States:** The requirements for withholding and reporting vary depending on the source of the income (US or foreign), provisions of tax treaties, amount and type of payments, etc. **Thailand:** Non-residents may not be subject to tax according to DTA.

/2. **France:** Only if incomes are taxable in France according to a tax convention. **Italy:** A special regime is applied on gambling income sourced on Italian territory. **Netherlands:** For transfer of real estate a notarial act is obligatory and these are registered at the tax administration. **South Africa:** Shares listed on the Johannesburg Stock Exchange and participatory interests in regulated Collective Investment Schemes.

/3. **France:** Yes, by taxpayers using tax returns. **South Africa:** Withholding tax on payments to non-resident sellers of immovable property.

Table 9.8. PIT: Assessment system and advance payments (excl. withholdings)

/1. **Canada:** Tax agents filing more than 10 returns must e-file returns. **France:** There are a number of schemes: *(1)* Three instalments, with payments by 15 February, 15 May and 15 September of assessment year; or *(2)* monthly scheme using banking system. **Hong Kong**: A person who is chargeable to salaries tax (or PIT) is required to pay provisional salaries tax. Provisional salaries tax is normally payable in two instalments of 75% in January and 25% in April. **Italy:** Special regime for individual entrepreneurs (without employees) with yearly income under EUR 30 000; they pay a cumulative/substitutive tax of 5% and must file annual return of their income. **Morocco:** Mandatory requirements for e-payment and the e-filing for tax returns depend on the turnover. **Slovak Republic:** Mandatory from 2014 where taxpayer is also a VAT payer or uses the services of tax agents. **Spain:** From January 2014, paper returns are no longer allowed and all returns must be e-filed or filed using a Tax Help Programme designed by the Tax Agency that enables the production of a return in PDF format that can be easily read by scanners.

Table 9.9. Corporate income tax: Return filing and advance payment obligations

/1. **Canada:** Most corporations with annual gross revenue over CAD 1 million are required to file CIT returns via Internet. **Chile:** Taxpayers authorised to keep electronic ledgers with annual turnover over 50 million pesos are required to file electronically the annual income tax return. Re monthly advance payments, taxpayers authorised to keep electronic accounting books are required to file and pay electronically. **Colombia:** Data sourced from IBFD database. **Estonia:** Data relates to Estonia's flat rate distribution tax on distributed profits; there is no CIT per se. **Greece:** Eight monthly advance payments are required. **Hong Kong:** CIT taxpayers (regardless of their size) are required to pay provisional profits tax (or CIT). Depending on the accounting year-end date of the companies and time of issue of the profits tax assessments, provisional profits tax is in general payable in two instalments-75% in November/January and 25% in January/April. **Iceland:** 10 monthly payments. **Israel:** Legislation process initiated to mandate CIT e-filing. **Italy:** Special regime for individual entrepreneurs (without employees) with yearly income under EUR 30 000. They pay a cumulative/substitutive tax of 5% and must file annual return of their income. **Morocco:** Mandatory requirements for e-payment and e-filing for tax returns depend on the turnover. **Singapore:** Advance payment of CIT is applicable only if a company is winding down (e.g. striking off, liquidation). **Slovak Republic:** Mandatory from 2014 where taxpayer is also a VAT payer or uses the services of a tax agent. **United States:** Corporations must make instalment payments of estimated taxes if expected tax for a year is USD 500 or more. Certain corporations (or a group of related corporate entities) with total assets of USD 10 million or more that file at least 250 returns during the calendar year of any type (including income tax returns, information returns, payroll returns, etc.) are required to e-file (unless a waiver is received).

Table 9.11. VAT: Payment and return filing obligations

/1. **Bulgaria:** VAT return and sales and purchases registers must be reported electronically where there are more than five records in any register. **Canada:** Payments of CAD 50 000 must be made electronically or at the taxpayers' financial institution. **Chile:** Enterprises authorised to keep electronic accounting records are required to file and pay through the Internet. **China:** According to VAT law, the frequency of file return and payment obligation is as follows: The VAT assessable period shall be one day, three days, five days, ten days, fifteen days or one month. The actual assessable period of the taxpayer's shall be determined by the competent tax authorities according to the magnitude of the tax payable of the taxpayer; tax that cannot be assessed in regular periods may be assessed on a transaction-by-transaction basis. Taxpayers that adopt one month as an assessable period shall report and pay tax within ten days following the end of the period. If an assessable period of one day, three days, five days, ten days or fifteen days is adopted, the tax shall be prepaid within five days following the end of the period and a monthly return shall be filled with any balance of tax due settled within ten days from the first day of the following month. **Czech Republic:** Mandated e-filing obligations commenced from January 2014. **Finland:** There are no mandatory requirements; however, those filing electronically are given an additional 5 days to file (and pay). **France:** e-payments are mandatory for all sizes of taxpayer from 1 October 2014. **Germany**: Frequency of payments of VAT and return filing obligations does not depend on the taxpayer segment but in general on the amount of previous year's tax. Return filing: quarterly (generally), annually if previous year's tax does not exceed EUR 1 000; monthly if previous year's tax does exceed EUR 7 500. Taxable persons starting their business have to file monthly in the first and the following calendar year. In addition, annual return filing is required from all taxable persons (monthly or quarterly fillings are provisional advance returns). **Israel:** Only mandatory for a tax refund request. **Italy:** Special regime for individual entrepreneurs with yearly income below EUR 30 000; a VAT exemption regime is granted. **Morocco:** The frequency of payments and return filing of VAT depends on the turnover. **Romania:** filing frequency depends on taxpayer turnover and whether there are intra-community procurements; **Slovak Republic:** Thresholds apply to determine filing frequency (i.e. monthly (large) and quarterly (others); all taxpayers have choice to file monthly if they wish. **Switzerland:** Large enterprises can choose between monthly or quarterly if they are regular creditors (over CHF 50 000 per month).

/2. **Chile:** Taxpayers who participate in the Simplified VAT regime file and pay quarterly. **Morocco:** Mandatory requirements for e-payment and e-filing of tax returns depend on turnover. **Slovak Republic:** All businesses must e-file VAT returns from January 2014. **Switzerland:** SME and very small enterprises can choose either quarterly or semi-annual filing if annual turnover is below CHF 5 million.

Table 9.12. Selected features of tax disputes of assessment or rulings

/1. **Australia:** In large disputes, ATO attempts to use alternative dispute resolutions processes to solve the matter before the need for a judicial hearing. **Austria:** Financial Tribunal has become a court from the 1 January 2014. **Bulgaria:** There is no specialised court, but the administrative courts and the Supreme Administrative Court have judicial panels that are dealing primarily with tax disputes. **Canada:** Province of Québec resolves GST (VAT) objections on behalf of Canada for registrants within the province of Québec.

Croatia: Independent Sector for Second-Instance Administrative Procedure, Service for Second-Instance Tax Procedure formed within the Ministry of Finance. **Estonia:** 30 day (may extend by 10 days). **Finland:** Complete 40% in 3 months, 80% in 6 months, and 100% in 12 months. **France:** Taxpayers dissatisfied with a decision that has been made about their disagreement can ask the departmental tax conciliator (i.e.: a senior tax officer of the local tax services) for a review, or the ombudsman of the financial and economic ministries located in the tax administration's headquarters for a further review. **Germany:** With limitations. **Greece:** Taxpayers who submit an objection have to pay 50% of the tax assessed in order to get a clearance and not pay the balance until a decision by the Dispute Resolution Unit or courts is made. **Hong Kong:** Applicable to an assessment which is excessive by reason of an error or omission in respect of any return or statement submitted. **Hungary:** In the case of dissolution proceedings, the time limit is 8 days. **Ireland:** Generally, there is no time limit, but after appeal to the Appeal Commissioners no administrative review is available; Ombudsman can also conduct administrative review of disputed tax cases. Performance standard is 4-6 weeks from receipt of complete information. The Appeal Commissioners are the persons appointed under statute for hearing appeals by taxpayers against decision of the Revenue Commissioners concerning taxes and duties. Appeals to the courts may be made against their determinations. **Italy:** Legislative Decree n. 98/2011, amending the regulations on tax disputes, introduced a mandatory mediation for the assessments less than EUR 20 000. Taxpayers are obliged to lodge a complaint procedure with the Revenue Agency, seeking to solve the dispute before requiring the Court decision. Initial appeal period of 60 days and legal decision period of 90 day apply to the abovementioned mediation. **Japan:** Requests for re-investigation: within 3 months. Requests for reconsideration: within 1 year. **Korea:** Tax Tribunal and the Board of Audit and Inspection of Korea. **Lithuania:** Central tax administration is a compulsory pre-trial institution, decisions of which may be appealed to the Commission on Tax Disputes (a voluntary pre-trial. institution) or courts. General time limit for legal decision of central tax administration (30 days) may be extended by a decision of the central tax administration for a period up to 60 days. Decision of Commission on Tax Disputes shall be made within 60 days from receipt of an appeal. **Luxembourg:** For Indirect Taxes. **Morocco:** Regional and national tax commissions have authority to conduct administrative review of disputed tax cases. **The Netherlands:** Tax law allows for the full amount to be collected but NTCA's policy is that payment of the disputed tax liability is deferred on the taxpayer's request and collection is suspended pending the outcome of the dispute. **New Zealand:** There is provision for the taxpayer and Inland Revenue to agree that a dispute proceed straight to a review by an external judicial body without first going through an administrative review, if the dispute would be resolved more efficiently by doing so. **Russia:** The procedure of compulsory pre-court review is applied to cases when the rulings rendered in the results of tax audits. In addition, if the tax administration has failed to make a decision on appeal in due term the taxpayer will be entitled to appeal in court. **Singapore:** Once an objection is raised by taxpayer, IRAS will have 6 months (from the date of receipt of complete information) to review and convey our decision to taxpayer. For complex cases, IRAS will inform the taxpayer the estimated time needed for review. **Slovak Republic:** The first instance appeal body (level) – a Customs office – decides on review of a tax dispute case in 30 days period. The second instance (level) body – the Financial Directorate of the Slovak Republic – decides on review of a tax dispute case in 60 days period, which can be extended by the Ministry of Finance of the SR (no time limit for it). **Slovenia:** 1. Ministry of Finance as second instance according to State Administration Act, conducts the administrative review of disputed tax cases. The Revenue body conducts the administrative review of disputed tax cases only in means of testing the grounds stated in appeals. If the Revenue body finds the statements grounded, can by itself substitute the existing decision. If not, the appeal must be sent to the MOF. **South Africa:** Aim to resolve within 90 days. **Thailand:** The Commission of Appeal comprises of Director-General of the Revenue Department or representative, representative of the Office of the Attorney General in Thailand and representative of the Department of Provincial Administration. **United Kingdom:** Also the Adjudicator and Parliamentary Ombudsman. **United States:** Appeals officers are urged to consider tax disputes in a timely manner. IRC 6501 requires a tax assessment within the statute of limitations. Appeals consideration is finalised before the expiration of the statute of limitations, which is generally 3 years from the due date of the tax return. IRC 7122 provide review of rejected Offer in Compromise. IRC 7429 provides for a 16 day time frame to consider the jeopardy or levy assessment. IRC 6404 provides for interest abatement due to unreasonable errors or delay by the IRS. Whether the IRS unreasonably delayed a tax dispute may be brought before the Tax Court. Appeals Quality Measurement System (AQMS) is Appeals' quality review organisation. Appeals looks to AQMS to measure how well it communicates with its customers, resolves cases, and treats customers. The AQMS review data is used to assess the performance of Appeals as an organisation. The review data is compiled, analysed, and explained in an AQMS Annual Report. It's also used to identify trends, procedural concerns, and training needs. In this way, closed case reviews provide information and benefits to Customers, Appeals Management, and Appeals employees. Collection during appeal process is generally not possible, except for jeopardy and termination assessments under IRC sections 6851, 6852, 6861, and 6862.

/2. **Australia:** The administrative reviews of disputed tax cases are conducted by independent officers. **Austria:** Under certain circumstances deferral of payment can be applied and will be granted. **Brazil:** There is not any time limit set up in law. Nevertheless, Article 27, of Decree nº 70.235/72, states that decisions shall be delivered attending to order and time limit established in an Act issued by the RFB. Except for first instance tax dispute cases addressing high amounts of tax credit or having criminal consequences, which shall be ruled. **Canada:** For PIT, the time limit for filing an objection is the later of: *(1)* one year after the filing due date of the return; and *(2)* 90 days after date of notice of assessment. **Croatia:** In accordance with the tax decision disputed – only when an appeal does not postpones the execution of the tax decision. **France:** General rule: until December 31st of the second year following this of collection or payment. This time is reduced of one year for direct local taxes. **Hungary:** Exceptions: In case of posteriori tax assessment the deadline for adopting a resolution is 60 days, or in the event of dissolution proceedings the time limit is 15 days and it may be extended by up to 30 days. **India:** Yes, subject to stay granted by Authority. **Malaysia:** Appeal on tax matters is handled by Special Commissioners of Income Tax, an independent body under MOF. **New Zealand:** Review is conducted by a separate impartial unit (the Disputes Review Unit) within Inland Revenue. **Russia:** Rulings, rendered upon the results of tax audit, which have not yet come into force can be reviewed within a month (in order of appeal) Rulings, rendered in the results of tax audit, that have come into force and which were not reviewed in order of appeal can be reviewed within a year. Other rulings and actions of tax authorities can be reviewed within a year. **Slovenia:** An appeal may be filed within 15 days after the serving of a decision, an appeal against an assessment decision issued under a tax inspection may be filed within 30 days after the serving of the decision. **United Kingdom:** HMRC can collect disputed debt where a court has previously found for HMRC, even if the taxpayer files a further appeal.

/3. **Australia:** The large corporate taxpayers that are eligible for an independent review of proposed audit adjustments must request the independent review within 10 days of receiving the Statement of Audit Position. **Canada:** Published service standards for all dispute programmes require taxpayers to be provided with an initial contact letter within 30 days of receipt of the objection or appeal to the Minister. **Croatia:** Generally, lawsuit before a court does not postpone execution of the tax decision disputed. **France:** Performance standard: rate of disputed cases in terms of tax basis for PIT, residence tax and television fee should be answered within 30 days by local tax services. **Hungary:** In exceptional cases (e.g. taxpayers may be fined for non-compliance with the obligation of notification or for the pursuit of taxable activities without a tax number) the resolution of the tax authority shall be executable, irrespective of any appeal. In the absence of a final appellate decision precautionary measures may be ordered, which ensures the enforcement of a claim at a later date only. **India:** Yes, subject to stay granted by any Authority/Court. **New Zealand:** Any assessment required in respect of the adjustment that the taxpayer disputes is made at the completion of the administrative review. The overall disputes process, which includes the administrative review, contains a number of steps and is commenced by a taxpayer filing a notice in response to the notice of proposed adjustment ("NOPA") within a time limit of 2 months after the NOPA. The NOPA outlines the adjustment proposed to the taxpayer's return. Many of the other steps in the process also have their own 2 month time limits within which they have to be completed. **Russia:** Time limit for finalising a review of a tax dispute case in the revenue body can be extended but not more than for a month in special circumstances. When rulings, rendered in the results of tax audit, that have come into force, are reviewed (in order of appeal) the recovery of tax is not imposed. Upon the taxpayer's motion for suspense execution of the ruling under review can be suspended. **Slovenia:** Performance standards are set in the General Administrative Procedure Act, Decree on Education and Proficiency Exam to Head and Decide in the Framework of Administrative Procedure, and in Tax Administration Act. An official person conducting proceedings or deciding in administrative matters in a public law authority should have the appropriate degree of education, the necessary work experience and shall have passed the state professional exam.

/4. **Australia:** All independent reviews will be completed within 60 days of the request being received. **Canada:** CRA does not have ability to negotiate a settlement to tax disputes based on the likelihood of litigation success or amounts at issue or a taxpayer's ability to pay, and is bound to apply the law to the particular facts of a case. **France:** DGFIP can reach a compromise with the taxpayer but only penalties can be deducted in that case. **Hungary:** Except the suspension of enforcement by the court. **New Zealand:** There are time limits set in the law for some other steps in the disputes process but no overall time limit for completion of the administrative review stage. However, although not specifically related to these reviews, there is a general 4 year limit (statute bar) in the law on reassessments to increase a taxpayer's liability. **Russia:** Where the disputed decision has come into force and the motion for suspense of enforced actions has not been filed, or filed but not granted by court.

/5. **France:** The dispute has no payment suspension effect in itself but the taxpayer can ask for the suspension of payment concerning the contested tax. **New Zealand:** Standard: Minimum % of adjudication cases completed within three months of receipt: 2012 – target 90%, actual 94.7%; 2013 – target 90%, actual 94.7%. **Russia:** If the motion for suspense of enforced actions has not been filed, or filed but not granted by court.

/6. **France:** Taxpayers who ask for the suspension of payment can benefit from it until the Court of first instance's judgement. Each taxpayer has the right to benefit from the suspension of payment if he provides warranties to the tax officer that is in charge of recovery when the contested amount exceeds EUR 4 500. **New Zealand:** Ability to settle applies most often at a later stage than the administrative review, i.e. after the taxpayer has filed challenge proceedings with an external appellate body, but on occasion a case may be settled at an earlier stage than the administrative review.

/7. **New Zealand:** A tribunal – Yes; An appellate court – No. Taxpayers can only be required to pay tax in dispute if there is a significant risk that the tax will not be paid if they are unsuccessful in their dispute.

Table 9.13. Enforced tax debt collection powers

/1. **Australia:** Currently under consideration **Belgium:** By garnishment order. **Brazil:** Through a judicial proceeding conducted by the National Treasury Attorney's Office (PGFN). **Bulgaria:** NRA can only request licenser for a license withdrawal. **Canada:** Court order required. **Chile:** The revenue body has very limited responsibility in enforced tax debt collection as this function is the primary responsibility of the Treasury. **Costa Rica:** Compulsory tax debt collection is in charge of the General Direction of Fiscal Matters. The Ministry of Finance does not have the powers required to seize assets, but it can request a judge to proceed accordingly. **Croatia:** Under the provisions of the Law on the collection of the tax debt of natural persons (Official Gazette no. 55/2013) and of legal persons (Official Gazette no. 45/2011). **Finland:** Can cancel certain registrations (e.g. pre-assessment registry).**Germany:** Actions of other authorities if needed can be initiated/requested by tax administration, vehicle registration may be denied if vehicle tax is not paid. **Hong Kong:** A departure prevention direction can only be sought from a District Judge to prevent a delinquent taxpayer from leaving Hong Kong without paying his taxes. **Hungary:** Details can be published if the tax arrears exceed 100 million HUF, 10 million HUF in case of natural persons. **Italy:** Only Revenue Agency has this power. **Lithuania:** The revenue body issues tax clearance certificate by law. **Luxembourg:** Only for VAT. **Malta:** Applies only to Direct Tax Authority and Customs Department; **Morocco:** To grant extensions of time to pay tax debts requires guaranties. **Norway:** Can only be done according to set-off rules, not against payments according to social security legislation. **Russia:** Collection from third parties is possible in cases of imposition of joint liability in bankruptcy procedures. **Singapore:** Certain recovery or prosecutorial actions taken by the revenue body will likely give effect to the closure of a taxpayer's business/withdrawal of his license. E.g. Application for winding-up, criminal conviction for tax evasion results in revocation of professional licence **Slovak Republic:** See previous notes. **South Africa:** Only by order of court for purposes of compulsory repatriation of foreign assets to satisfy local debts. **Sweden:** Neither the Swedish Enforcement Agency, which collects tax debts, or the revenue body can close a business but the revenue body can recall a tax license. **Switzerland:** Only for VAT. **Turkey:** The names of debtor taxpayers are published for 2 months per year. **United Kingdom:** Court order required. **United States:** While a "certificate" per se is not issued, federal contractors are required to be compliant with Federal tax obligations.

/2. **Belgium:** By garnishment order or through offsetting. **Bulgaria:** NRA publishes a list of debtors whose liabilities exceed BGN 5000. **Canada:** Quebec Province requires any business wishing to bid on a call for tenders or to obtain a negotiated contract of CAD 25 000 or more, to provide a Certificate of Compliance from the province. **Costa Rica:** A sworn statement is requested to entities. **Luxembourg:** Not for limited liability companies or public limited companies. **Malta:** Applies only to Customs Department. **Morocco:** Liability on company directors depends on the legal form of the company. **Russia:** Indirectly, by virtue of initiation a criminal case or making a requesting to court by initiating a procedure of subsidiary liability. **South Africa:** May publish names in respect of criminal offences. **Sweden:** Requires a court order e.g. from sequestration. **United States:** Forced asset liquidation action is done through the seizure process.

/3. **Belgium:** Tax body can close business after repeated non-payment of taxes due. **Costa Rica:** Regarding liability on company directors, it is questioned only in cases where negligence or intent in the related actions performed by directors can be demonstrated. **Malta:** Direct Tax Authority only. **Russia:** Debtors' names can only be published when the bankruptcy procedure is pending towards the taxpayer. **Sweden:** Revenue body is liable.

/4. **Malta:** VAT and Direct Tax Authority only.

/5. **Malta:** Direct Tax Authority in case of court decision.

Table 9.14. Verification of taxpayers' liabilities: information access and search powers of tax officials

/1. **Australia:** ATO uses search powers in very limited cases. **Austria:** Except information covered by bank secrecy. **Brazil:** Provision of National Tax Code prevents any legislation to exclude or limit tax administrations to examine taxpayers merchandise, records or documents. However, Brazilian Supreme Court has been of the opinion that Article 5, XI, of Federal Constitutional Act, represents a Constitutional guarantee that should be extended to businesses premises. Article 5, XI – Federal Constitutional Act: "The home is inviolable refuge of the individual, and no one may enter therein without the consent of the dweller, except in the event of flagrante delicto or disaster, or to give help, or, during the day, by court order." **Canada:** Civil matters only. **Chile:**

Seizure can only be made where the SII is compiling information in order to decide on the presentation of a lawsuit to prosecute a tax crime. **Czech Republic:** Only if dwelling is business place. **Finland:** With police only. **Germany:** Limited to criminal cases. **Hungary:** Where it is reasonably presumed that the taxpayer is concealing any physical evidence of importance or is attempting to cover up the true circumstances of his operations, a tax inspector is entitled to search and inspect any site, premises or motor vehicle that may be presumed to be involved in the business operations as well as the cargo of any such vehicle. This provision may be applied in respect of the search of a residential property if any part of the property is used for business activities. The search must be approved by the public prosecutor in advance, unless there is reason to believe that any delay is likely to result in detrimental consequences in terms of the objective of the search. The tax authority must subsequently notify the competent public prosecutor of any search conducted without prior approval, with the search warrant and a copy of the report made on the search attached. **India:** Tax officials can enter a taxpayer's premises without his/her consent on the basis of a warrant that is issued by the administrative head of the Investigation Wing. If the premises do not include a residence, a search warrant is not required. In such cases, an authorisation for entering the business premises will suffice, which can be issued by an official above a specified rank. **Ireland:** Excluding confidential information between professional and client; except parts of a dwelling where a business is being carried on. **Malaysia:** Relevant tax law extends to "any person" for purposes of the Tax Act. **Malta:** Applies to Direct Tax Administration and to Customs Department. **Netherlands:** Warrant needed. **New Zealand:** Warrant now required to seize documents. **Portugal:** To enter taxpayer's premises without their consent and execute a search warrant is only possible with the co-operation of police bodies. To enter taxpayer's dwellings without consent and execute a search warrant and to seize documents is only possible with the authorisation of a Public Prosecutor or a judge. **Romania:** In conformity with the Fiscal Procedure Code the fiscal body can withhold documents for a period for up to 30 days, which can be extended to 90 days with the approval of the manager of the fiscal body. **Russia:** With regard to taxpayer to which an audit has been carried out **Singapore:** In light of the revenue body's power to enter taxpayer's business premises/dwellings and seize taxpayer's documents without requiring taxpayer's consent and a search warrant, there is accordingly no need for the revenue body to request a court to issue a search warrant or serve search warrants with the help of other government agencies. **Slovak Republic:** The Financial Administration has competence according to the Tax Code to serve a search and to enter the taxpayer's business premises and dwellings; there is not the need to get any warrant of other government agencies or the court. Entry to the taxpayer's business premises and dwellings depends on taxpayer's consent. There is one exemption only, if the entry is realised during the tax recovery proceeding when taxpayer's consent is not needed; in this case the tax authorities can realise the entry also by force with the police assistance. **Slovenia:** Tax officials can enter and search business premises without taxpayer's consent and search warrant, therefore requesting a court to issue a search warrant is not intended in law. **South Africa:** Search and seizure without a warrant under special circumstances and only part of dwelling used for business purposes may be entered without consent and search warrant. **Sweden:** If a taxpayer does not comply, coercive measures can be taken according to the relevant law. A court must approve the actions to be taken.

/2. **Austria:** Inspections only under the Tax Procedure Code (no right to search). **Canada:** When conducting a criminal investigation the CRA uses search warrants to enter a taxpayer's dwelling or place of business. To ensure safety of its officers, the CRA will normally be accompanied by police. **India:** Revenue bodies do not have to approach the courts for a warrant; it can be issued by the administrative head. **Malaysia:** Does not extend to a public officer who is under statutory obligation to observe secrecy to provide the particular. **Malta:** Applies to VAT and Customs only. **Netherlands:** Only in criminal cases. **Russia:** Only in case of field tax audit.

/3. **Austria:** As per the Fiscal Penal Code, only if delay is dangerous to secure evidence related to criminal investigations. **Malaysia:** These powers are only exercised in conducting investigation cases. **Malta:** Applies to Customs only.

/4. **Austria:** Only in case of criminal investigations.

Table 9.15. Incorrect reporting of tax liabilities: Framework for sanctions

/1. **Brazil:** Cases where taxpayers' registration numbers have been cancelled or exclusion from the small or medium size businesses programme (SIMPLES) has occurred are published in the Official Journal. **Canada:** There is a civil penalty of 10% of unreported income for repeated omissions within 3 prior years for income taxes (PIT and CIT) for which there is no consideration of culpability. There are also civil penalties for false statement or omission (either knowingly or through gross negligence) for income taxes (50% of understated tax) and VAT (25% of net tax advantage). Additionally, criminal charges can result in fines which vary for income taxes (from 50% to 200% of understated tax and prison up to 5 years) and for VAT (from 50% to 200% of amount evaded, or CAD1 000-25 000 if amount cannot be verified, and prison up to 2 years). The CRA accepts that in cases where the CRA determines that a person has exercised due diligence, certain penalties may be either not charged by the CRA, or if already charged, cancelled by the CRA. The acceptance of a due diligence defence is limited to the cancellation of the penalties, and will not result in the cancellation of interest payable. The onus is on the person who claims to have been duly diligent to demonstrate to the CRA that due diligence has been exercised. **Chile:** Tax Code establishes that Regional Directors have the authority to write-off all or part of penal interest for late payment of taxes in cases expressly authorised by the Law and to reduce or forgive administrative sanctions. **Costa Rica:** Under the General Tax Code, the only lists that may be published are the ones concerning taxpayers who are defaulters, hidden or neglectful. The Constitutional Chamber has established that this article applies only to taxpayers not having an ongoing judicial case. **Croatia:** There is a common administrative violation sanctions and similar measures framework (not penalty/criminal measures framework). **Finland:** Tax liability register from year 2014. **France:** Yes, for some rare situations (voluntary disclosure campaign). **Hong Kong:** Penalty can only be imposed if the taxpayer has without reasonable excuse filed incorrect returns. The taxpayer may appeal to a tax tribunal against the imposition of administrative penalties, or that the administrative penalties imposed are excessive in the circumstances of the cases. **India**: The revenue body does not make any specific taxpayer information public. Information on tax debts is also confidential. Judicial decisions are reported through the normal channels of case law reporting. The tax information of taxpayers is held by the Income Tax Department in a fiduciary capacity and is treated as confidential. **Israel:** Except for penalties for shortfall which vary for "careless" and "deliberate" cases. **Latvia:** For penalties but not for interest rate. **Mexico:** With the 2013 tax reform, the Tax Administration can now make public details of taxpayers that simulate operations. **Singapore:** The penalties imposed depend on the section the taxpayer is charged under. The discretion of imposing the penalty is left to the court when the taxpayer has been charged with an offence. **Slovak Republic:** Relevant laws stipulate for the tax administrator a duty to always levy a fine (penalty) if the taxpayer commits a tax offence. The legislation allows the tax administrator to levy a fine in a minimal amount. In this regard the tax administrator considers the relevance, consequences and duration of the illicit state. **Spain:** A temporary law entered into force in 2012 designed to encourage the voluntary reporting of unreported tax liabilities at low rates. Deadline for the submission of the Special Tax Return (Form 750) was 30 November 2012. **Switzerland:** Direct tax only at cantonal level and varies between cantons.

/2. **Canada:** Relief from penalty and prosecution with respect to tax liabilities including the late filing of tax and information returns. **Chile**: However, Law No. 19 628, on Protection of Personal Information, indicates that personal data about criminal convictions and administrative or disciplinary offenses cannot be communicated -if they are requested by anyone except a Court of Justice or any other Public Entity in the exercise of their functions – once the statute of limitations about criminal or administrative action, penalty or punishment has expired, or once the penalty or punishment has been carried out. **Costa Rica:** The current legislation includes provisions for offering reduced penalties, but not for reduced interest or tax payment. **Israel:** Public details are published only of some persons who paid a penalty in lieu of criminal (not administrative) procedures.

Table 9.16. Revenue bodies' use of voluntary disclosure policies

/1. **Australia**: The figures shown on taxes etc., raised do not include penalties or interest amounts because it is not possible to derive those amounts separately from the impact of other audit outcomes. **Canada**: Total amounts of unreported income related to the number of disclosures reported are CAD 1.8 billion (2010), CAD773 million (2011), CAD 863 million (2012), and CAD 1.2 billion (2013). **Italy**: Numbers reported relate to results of provisional law concerning voluntary disclosure of individuals owning unreported and undetected assets abroad, in force from 2012 until early 2014. **Mexico:** In 2013, the programme "Catch Up" was implemented; programme was part of Revenue Act for 2013 and ran for the period January to May of 2013. **Netherlands**: Since 2010 about 3 500 taxpayers have come forward to voluntarily disclose their offshore capital with a total value of EUR 1 500 million. Over half of these taxpayers have come forward in 2013 (the voluntary disclosure arrangement was expanded in September 2013). For the 3 500 taxpayers, tax assessments have been imposed with a total (tax, interest, fines) value of EUR 235 million. For those taxpayers who came forward in 2013 the amount assessed was EUR 72 million. **Portugal:** Only penalties. **Singapore:** IRAS has a Voluntary Disclosure Programme ("VDP"), introduced in 2009, to encourage voluntary disclosure of past errors made in tax declarations by taxpayers in exchange for no or reduced penalties. Arising from a review of the programme, VDP treatment is now extended to past actions involving wilful intent to evade taxes. Taxpayers who voluntarily disclose their actions face reduced penalties instead of criminal prosecution, subject to the meeting of conditions stipulated under the VDP. **South Africa**: These results arise from temporary legislation where the applications window period ended October 2011. **United States:** The reported case numbers represent the number of submissions received and not the number of cases processed. The IRS commissioner recently testified that the offshore voluntary disclosure programme has resulted in more than 43 000 disclosures and the collection of about USD 6.5 billion in taxes, penalties and interest since its introduction in 2009.

/2. **South Africa:** These results arise from current permanent legislation (Tax Administration Act, Act 28 of 2011).

Bibliography

ATO (2014), *Correct a mistake or amend a return: Make a voluntary disclosure*, Australian Taxation Office, www.ato.gov.au/general/correct-a-mistake-or-amend-a-return/make-a-voluntary-disclosure/ (accessed December 2014).

Baer, K and Le Borgne, E (2008), *Tax Amnesties: Theory, Trends, and Some Alternatives*, International Monetary Fund, Washington.

EC (2007), *Fiscal Blueprints – A Path to a Robust, Modern and Efficient Tax Administration*, Luxembourg: Office for Official Publications of the European Commission, pp. 13-20.

HMRC (2014), *Measuring Tax Gaps 2014,* United Kingdom Her Majesty's Revenue and Customs, London.

Hong Kong Inland Revenue (2014), *2013-14 Annual Report,* Hong Kong.

International Bureau of Fiscal Documentation (2014), *Tax Database (various countries).*

IMF (2007), *Manual on Fiscal Transparency,* International Monetary Fund, Washington, DC.

IRAS (2014*), IRAS Voluntary Disclosure Program,* Inland Revenue Authority of Singapore, https://www.iras.gov.sg/irashome/About-Us/Taxes-in-Singapore/Helping-and-Encouraging-Compliance/IRAS--Voluntary-Disclosure-Programme/ (accessed July 2014).

IRS (2014), *IRS media release IR-2014-72,* United States Internal Revenue Service, Washington, DC.

IRS (2012), *Tax Gap Estimates for Tax Year 2006*, United States Internal Revenue Service, www.irs.gov/uac/The-Tax-Gap (accessed September 2014).

New Zealand Inland Revenue (2014), *Voluntary Disclosure Policy*, Inland Revenue, http://www.ird.govt.nz/income-tax-individual/filing-your-return/making-disclosures/running-puttingtaxaffairsright.html#incentives (accessed August 2014).

NTA (2014), *Annual Report 2013-14,* National Tax Agency of Japan, Tokyo.

OECD (2014), *Standard for Automatic Exchange of Financial Account Information in Tax Matters*, OECD Publishing, Paris, http://dx.doi.org/10.1787/9789264216525-en.

OECD (2013), *Tax Administration 2013: Comparative Information on OECD and Other Advanced and Emerging Economies*, OECD Publishing, Paris, http://dx.doi.org/10.1787/9789264200814-en.

OECD (2010), *Offshore Voluntary Disclosure Comparative Analysis, Guidance and Policy Advice,* OECD, Paris, available at: www.oecd.org/ctp/exchange-of-tax-information/46244704.pdf.

OECD (2009), W*ithholding and Information Reporting Regimes for Small/Medium-sized Businesses and Self-employed Taxpayers,* OECD, Paris, available at: www.oecd.org/tax/administration/48449751.pdf.

OECD (2008), *Programmes to reduce the administrative burden of tax regulations in selected countries,* OECD, Paris, www.oecd.org/ctp/administration/39947998.pdf.

OECD (2003), *Taxpayers Rights and Obligations,* Centre for Tax Policy and Administration, OECD, Paris.

Revenue (2014), *Customer Service Charter*, Irish Tax and Customs, available at www.revenue.ie/en/about/custservice/customer-charter.html (accessed September 2014).

UK NAO (2012), *HM Revenue and Customs Annual Report and Accounts 2011-12*, Comptroller and National Audit Office, London.

Annex A

Aggregate Tables

Table A.1. **Revenue aggregates: Gross revenue collections for all taxes administered**

(For some countries the historical data has been modified as a result of country revisions of previously reported data)

Country	Gross revenue collections for all taxes administered by revenue body (in millions in local currency)								
	2005	2006	2007	2008	2009	2010	2011	2012	2013
OECD countries									
Australia	263 649	288 650	313 619	341 793	348 808	337 780	361 297	393 518	409 175
Austria	n.a.	n.a.	n.a.	n.a.	n.a.	n.a.	n.a.	87 127	89 589
Belgium	n.a.	n.a.	n.a.	117 689	110 892	n.a.	n.a.	123 870	126 891
Canada	307 019	325 245	344 135	371 482	366 258	360 011	387 997	419 782	437 911
Chile (a)	13 860 847	16 886 122	22 430 852	21 821 541	20 681 059	22 071 864	25 771 202	29 712 878	29 872 542
Czech Republic	685 229	723 834	n.a.	868 291	739 264	785 147	824 360	855 559	879 826
Denmark	n.a.	n.a.	n.a.	n.a.	n.a.	n.a.	n.a.	1 106 336	1 173 339
Estonia	66 048	78 690	96 851	97 930	91 586	88 157	6 139 (b)	7 180	7 559
Finland	52 658	55 424	59 522	63 630	57 491	58 513	63 040	64 817	67 152
France	456 250	382 080	510 742	442 958	418 792	431 369	447 543	427 529	439 634
Germany	n.a.	n.a.	n.a.	n.a.	n.a.	n.a.	n.a.	n.a.	n.a.
Greece	42 093	44 991	48 405	51 085	49 725	48 517	48 611	51 722	51 619
Hungary	8 141 223	8 676 256	10 393 139	10 711 185	10 161 926	11 394 882	11 676 561	12 669 750	13 118 253
Iceland	n.a.	n.a.	n.a.	389 850	361 237	n.a.	n.a.	486 281	503 119
Ireland	54 152	62 325	66 143	60 061	50 744	47 559	48 444	50 176	51 858
Israel	n.a.	n.a.	n.a.	213 775	206 662	202 548	221 686	223 929	248 310
Italy	n.a.	n.a.	n.a.	321 972	302 906	309 517	315 097	324 474	329 262
Japan	47 523 796	51 466 586	53 533 371	55 120 938	48 877 807	44 372 729	44 939 222	45 262 168	46 917 960
Korea	152 232 557	163 587 621	191 644 776	206 269 066	200 280 805	216 275 154	239 912 911	252 385 885	253 474 577
Luxembourg	n.a.	n.a.	n.a.	9 421	9 086	11 572	12 313	11 618	12 396
Mexico	1 023 855	1 272 481	1 356 768	1 584 840	1 536 993	1 768 066	2 005 511	2 186 432	2 483 639
Netherlands	n.a.	n.a.	n.a.	n.a	n.a.	n.a	n.a.	n.a	n.a
New Zealand	50 291	56 057	58 273	62 483	60 110	56 127	58 496	61 728	65 483
Norway	n.a.	n.a.	n.a.	n.a.	n.a.	n.a.	n.a.	n.a.	n.a.
Poland	n.a.	n.a.	n.a.	261 278	249 904	276 108	308 920	316 021	313 798
Portugal	35 602	39 333	42 152	40 727	36 661	37 291	39 879	43 800	47 162
Slovak Republic	302 704	307 831	343 057	12 756 (b)	11 624	10 659	12 093	16 658	16 932
Slovenia	n.a.	n.a.	n.a.	n.a.	n.a.	n.a.	n.a.	n.a.	n.a.
Spain	197 329	222 385	250 589	227 589	205 320	209 076	209 909	212 741	219 761

Table A.1. **Revenue aggregates: Gross revenue collections for all taxes administered** *(continued)*

Country	Gross revenue collections for all taxes administered by revenue body (in millions in local currency)								
	2005	2006	2007	2008	2009	2010	2011	2012	2013
Sweden	n.a.	n.a.	n.a.	n.a.	n.a.	n.a.	n.a.	n.a.	n.a.
Switzerland	n.a.	n.a.	n.a.	69 198	63 196	66 139	64 763	75 295	76 822
Turkey	131 949	151 272	171 098	189 981	196 313	235 715	284 490	317 218	367 473
United Kingdom	437 924	476 441	495 536	532 000	526 500	486 800	532 800	560 913	564 361
United States	2 260 396	2 499 053	2 682 242	2 742 520	2 345 337	2 345 056	2 414 952	2 524 320	2 855 059
Non-OECD countries									
Argentina	124 670	151 326	202 107	290 395	313 057	361 637	482 657	744 098	948 670
Brazil	n.a.	n.a.	n.a.	n.a.	n.a.	799 760	938 915	992 089	1 100 178
Bulgaria	7 910	11 495	15 912	18 983	17 917	16 726	17 962	19 253	19 870
China	n.a.	n.a.	n.a.	57 862 000	63 104 000	n.a.	n.a.	n.a.	n.a
Colombia	n.a.	n.a.	n.a.	n.a.	n.a.	47 566 125	59 843 244	99 226 458	105 309 455
Costa Rica	---------- Not covered by the series for these years ----------							n.a.	n.a.
Croatia	---------- Not covered by the series for these years ----------							122 132	118 796
Cyprus	2 122	2 472	3 037	4 124 (b)	3 609	3 618	3 760	3 662	3 501
Hong Kong, China	n.a.	n.a.	n.a.	n.a.	n.a.	132 051	152 148	184 459	191 992
India	n.a.	n.a.	n.a.	3 479 500	4 341 630	5 138 729	5 789 808	5 881 080	6 393 870
Indonesia	n.a.	n.a.	n.a.	526 451 316	546 724 428	585 614 322	714 235 181	888 917 502	989 217 116
Latvia	3 013	3 800	5 122	5 820	4 667	4 268	4 832	5 337	5 625
Lithuania	15 952	19 802	24 318	27 237	19 086	18 098	19 863	21 649	23 441
Malaysia	56 748	65 739	74 762	90 651	88 402	86 499	109 610	124 892	128 933
Malta	n.a.	n.a.	n.a.	2 230	2 245	2 337	2 441	2 469	2 662
Morocco	---------- Not covered by the series for these years ----------							126 802	124 901
Romania	n.a.	n.a.	n.a.	154 555	144 335	141 288	157 503	178 829	186 257
Russia	n.a.	n.a.	n.a.	n.a.	n.a.	n.a.	n.a.	n.a.	n.a.
Saudi Arabia	n.a.	n.a.	n.a.	15 332	14 103	n.a.	n.a.	23 717	25 045
Singapore	n.a.	n.a.	n.a.	n.a.	n.a.	n.a.	n.a.	n.a.	n.a.
South Africa	427 517	500 142	596 085	694 283	779 368	752 344	818 291	919 237	1 000 540
Thailand	---------- Not covered by the series for these years ----------							1 617 283	1 764 603

Notes: (a) Does not include taxes paid by CODELCO (Corporación Nacional del Cobre) which are also administered by the revenue body.
(b) In euros from this year.

Source: Survey responses for current and prior series.

Table A.2. **Revenue aggregates: Total refunds of taxes administered, and gross VAT collections and refunds**

(For some countries the historical data has been modified as a result of country revisions of previously reported data)

Country	Total refunds of all taxes administered (millions in local currency)									Gross VAT collections (mln)		VAT refunds (mln)	
	2005	2006	2007	2008	2009	2010	2011	2012	2013	2012	2013	2012	2013
OECD countries													
Australia	50 093	56 287	63 037	70 931	84 274	84 591	88 321	92 565	97 372	99 953	104 966	53 748	56 695
Austria	n.a.	n.a.	n.a.	n.a.	n.a.	n.a.	n.a.	14 347	14 054	36 351	36 726	11 749	11 860
Belgium	n.a.	n.a.	n.a.	23 884	24 916	n.a.	n.a.	24 503	24 289	42 532	41 855	13 770	13 311
Canada	67 397	73 828	74 340	73 988	86 110	84 038	89 028	93 381	96 667	86 139	90 198	45 972	48 917
Chile	3 001 080	3 992 420	6 571 444	5 665 074	7 499 059	4 753 918	4 973 168	7 253 236	7 221 296	16 194 957	17 169 437	5 768 155	6 006 663
Czech Republic	171 307	210 636	n.a.	261 626	216 779	230 865	257 250	266 359	263 426	544 411	571 726	266 359	263 426
Denmark	n.a.	n.a.	n.a.	n.a.	n.a.	n.a.	n.a.	275 087	286 485	425 096	440 430	245 573	257 266
Estonia	19 088	22 427	27 990	17 876	26 007	15 708	1 178 (a)	1 306	1 313	2 650	2 746	1 156	1 195
Finland	10 532	11 861	12 916	15 241	13 047	13 128	14 547	15 055	14 471	24 060	24 802	11 063	10 774
France	35 588	30 184	42 392	61 442	78 179	72 781	71 293	79 100	74 570	195 353	194 773	51 265	49 232
Germany	n.a.	n.a.	n.a.	n.a.	n.a.	n.a.	n.a.	n.a.	n.a.	194 353	197 326	n.a	n.a
Greece	2 535	2 375	2 606	3 633	4 927	5 292	5 224	3 484	3 747	14 955	13 856	1 441	1 916
Hungary	1 489 844	1 509 669	1 766 834	1 774 018	1 687 266	2 072 744	2 352 715	2 451 799	2 395 615	4 542 002	4 721 792	1 794 593	1 912 217
Iceland	n.a.	n.a.	n.a.	n.a.	n.a.	n.a.	n.a.	n.a.	n.a.	263 500	272 100	113 500	110 400
Ireland	7 096	8 320	9 212	9 178	8 146	15 641	14 207	6 370	5 857	13 015	13 219	2 849	2 895
Israel	n.a.	n.a.	n.a.	34 704	33 674	36 989	35 088	43 935	47 015	43 800	42 700	32 500	33 000
Italy	n.a.	n.a.	n.a.	42 049	42 986	43 420	40 110	44 423	51 018	97 939	97 688	21 465	25 100
Japan	5 085 046	5 712 791	6 745 205	7 542 349	7 898 700	8 544 292	6 598 481	6 249 782	6 180 157	12 404 239	12 408 441	3 183 620	3 104 650
Korea	30 294 279	32 717 524	36 220 863	48 740 475	45 950 266	50 260 280	59 759 738	60 293 290	63 239 298	106 352 391	108 702 729	50 684 757	52 740 176
Luxembourg (b)	n.a.	n.a.	n.a.	987	1 018	985	1 108	1 161	1 116	4 221	4 559	1 161	1 116
Mexico	251 024	364 619	334 223	402 213	435 124	476 550	589 131	677 630	846 376	886 713	922 222	306 725	365 419
Netherlands	n.a.	n.a.	n.a.	n.a.	n.a.	n.a.	n.a.	n.a.	n.a.	42 071	41 879	n.a.	n.a.
New Zealand	8 288	8 887	9 701	11 228	11 066	10 090	11 651	12 564	11 714	23 746	23 927	10 627	9 920
Norway	n.a.	n.a.	n.a.	n.a.	n.a.	n.a.	n.a.	n.a.	n.a.	219 935	233 045	118 637	120 945
Poland	n.a.	n.a.	n.a.	71 273	71 682	74 483	85 363	91 928	95 890	197 506	194 854	76 349	80 247
Portugal	6 058	6 446	6 792	6 957	7 618	7 365	7 979	8 187	8 249	18 702	18 510	4 887	5 139
Slovak Republic	158 920	179 465	210 980	8 031 (a)	7 074	6 865	7 987	8 195	7 796	10 723	10 706	6 416	5 971
Slovenia	n.a.	n.a.	n.a.	n.a.	n.a.	n.a.	n.a.	n.a.	n.a.	3 934	3 969	1 822	1 733
Spain	36 111	38 028	45 357	53 983	61 048	49 540	48 149	44 174	50 914	74 174	78 050	23 710	26 119

Table A.2. **Revenue aggregates: Total refunds of taxes administered, and gross VAT collections and refunds** *(continued)*

Country	Total refunds of all taxes administered (millions in local currency)									Gross VAT collections (mln)		VAT refunds (mln)	
	2005	2006	2007	2008	2009	2010	2011	2012	2013	2012	2013	2012	2013
Sweden	n.a.	n.a.	n.a.	n.a.	n.a.	n.a.	n.a.	n.a.	n.a.	492 900	n.a.	214 000	n.a.
Switzerland	n.a.	n.a.	n.a.	33 529	27 871	30 330	28 625	27 798	27 272	32 348	33 039	10 013	10 239
Turkey	12 322	13 791	18 263	21 872	23 873	25 154	30 681	38 438	41 348	50 201	57 231	n.a.	n.a.
United Kingdom	57 368	64 319	65 906	77 100	81 200	83 200	99 300	92 674	93 346	168 444	173 345	70 152	72 772
United States	268 987	277 395	295 047	425 773	437 686	467 303	415 880	373 429	364 354	No national VAT			
Non-OECD countries													
Argentina	6 732	7 264	8 691	8 780	6 182	6 721	8 519	4 558	8 131	193 067	251 743	2 571	2 737
Brazil	n.a.	n.a.	n.a.	n.a.	n.a.	35 775	41 540	57 280	45 805	292 002	259 390	9 053	13 929
Bulgaria	3 151	3 966	4 463	5 877	4 465	4 737	5 295	6 012	6 271	9 311	9 674	5 902	6 074
China	n.a.	n.a.	n.a.	5 866 000	6 487 000	n.a.	n.a.	n.a.	n.a.	4 044 822	4 217 486	n.a.	n.a.
Colombia	n.a.	n.a.	n.a.	n.a.	n.a.	4 995 200	4 865 500	5 787 331	4 884 618	46 252 329	41 384 630	3 008 561	2 134 689
Costa Rica	Not covered by the series for these years							n.a.	n.a.	n.a.	n.a.	n.a.	n.a.
Croatia	Not covered by the series for these years							14 595	13 309	53 909	52 300	13 257	12 047
Cyprus	121	126	176	168	219	184	185	203	253	1 716	1 628	170	220
Hong Kong, China	n.a.	n.a.	n.a.	n.a.	n.a.	8 867	9 141	7 637	9 550	No national VAT			
India	n.a.	n.a.	n.a.	411 220	573 970	751 690	952 780	941 610	807 290	No national VAT			
Indonesia	n.a.	n.a.	n.a.	32 366 772	30 778 476	36 144 802	41 916 093	53 083 544	67 819 134	351 565 694	403 483 387	32 916 721	37 709 267
Latvia	n.a.	n.a.	n.a.	681	733	625	772	787	825	1 791	1 870	674	699
Lithuania	1 986	3 061	4 425	4 038	2 659	2 595	2 957	3 354	3 513	9 514	11 438	2 946	3 119
Malaysia	3 291	4 339	5 383	8 560	10 758	7 000	7 000	8 003	8 500	No national VAT			
Malta	n.a.	n.a.	n.a.	160	140	155	181	195	196	698	726	123	121
Morocco	Not covered by the series for these years							6 868	6 036	33 171	33 874	5 208	5 082
Romania	n.a.	n.a.	n.a.	11 728	10 552	10 826	13 960	11 026	12 704	64 946	67 474	8 343	9 450
Russia	n.a.	n.a.	n.a.	n.a.	n.a.	n.a.	n.a.	n.a.	n.a.	3 392 607	3 595 098	1 506 472	1 726 889
Saudi Arabia	n.a.	n.a.	n.a.	0	0	n.a.	n.a.			No national VAT			
Singapore	n.a.	n.a.	n.a.	n.a.	n.a.	n.a.	n.a.	n.a.	n.a.	n.a.	n.a.	n.a.	n.a.
South Africa	66 628	76 232	92 682	112 514	144 171	143 101	133 009	164 403	173 332	322 028	353 843	131 008	138 820
Thailand	Not covered by the series for these years							265 995	289 334	659 806	698 025	221 632	234 804

Notes: (a) In euros from this year.
(b) Refunds of tax only refer to VAT.

Source: Survey responses for current and prior series.

Table A.3. Net revenue collections for all taxes administered by revenue body

(For some countries the historical data has been modified as a result of country revisions of previously reported data)

Country	Net revenue collections for all taxes administered by revenue body (in millions in local currency)								
	2005	2006	2007	2008	2009	2010	2011	2012	2013
OECD countries									
Australia	213 556	232 364	250 581	270 862	264 534	253 189	272 976	300 953	311 803
Austria	55 353	57 935	62 630	68 762	63 685	65 491	69 852	72 780	75 535
Belgium	81 518	83 962	82 471	93 805	85 976	91 113	93 597	99 367	102 602
Canada	239 622	251 417	269 795	297 494	280 148	275 973	298 969	326 401	341 244
Chile	10 859 767	12 893 702	15 859 408	16 156 467	13 182 001	17 317 946	20 798 034	22 459 643	22 651 246
Czech Republic	513 922	513 198	n.a.	606 665	522 485	554 282	567 110	589 200	616 400
Denmark	825 250	n.a.	817 727	805 552	767 419	741 019	793 487	831 250	886 853
Estonia	46 960	56 263	68 861	80 054	65 579	72 449	4 961(a)	5 874	6 246
Finland	42 127	43 563	46 606	48 389	44 444	45 385	48 493	49 762	52 681
France	420 662	351 895	468 350	381 516	340 613	358 588	376 250	348 429	365 064
Germany	403 569	443 237	492 946	508 700	479 000	485 100	524 800	554 004	573 044
Greece	39 558	42 616	45 799	47 452	44 798	43 225	43 387	48 238	47 872
Hungary	6 651 379	7 166 587	8 626 305	8 937 167	8 474 660	9 322 138	9 323 846	10 217 952	10 722 639
Iceland	n.a.	n.a.	n.a.	n.a.	n.a.	402 639	428 328	n.a.	n.a.
Ireland	47 056	54 005	56 931	50 883	42 598	31 918	34 237	43 806	46 001
Israel	n.a.	n.a.	n.a.	179 071	172 988	165 559	186 598	179 994	201 295
Italy	n.a.	n.a.	n.a.	279 923	259 920	266 097	274 987	280 051	278 244
Japan	42 438 750	45 753 795	46 788 167	47 578 589	40 979 107	35 828 437	38 340 741	39 012 386	40 737 803
Korea	121 938 278	130 870 097	155 423 913	157 528 591	154 330 539	166 014 874	180 153 173	192 092 595	190 235 279
Luxembourg	n.a.	n.a.	6 898	8 433	8 068	10 586	11 205	10 457	11 280
Mexico	772 832	907 861	1 022 544	1 182 627	1 101 870	1 291 515	1 416 380	1 508 802	1 637 263
Netherlands	157 238	193 433	200 576	209 283	188 518	202 249	204 247	210 286	217 038
New Zealand	42 003	47 170	48 572	51 255	49 045	46 035	46 846	49 164	53 769
Norway	n.a.	666 600	737 900	748 300	846 000	773 200	804 400	917 095	969 151
Poland	155 393	175 571	229 254	190 005	178 222	201625	223557	224 093	217 908
Portugal	29 544	32 887	35 360	33 770	29 043	29 926	31 900	35 613	38 913
Slovak Republic	143 784	128 365	132 077	4 725 (a)	4 550	3 794	4 106	8 463	9 136
Slovenia	9 457	10 479	10 989	12 114	11 191	10 925	11 179	10 976	10 541
Spain	161 217	184 357	205 233	173 606	144 272	159 536	161 760	168 567	168 847

Table A.3. **Net revenue collections for all taxes administered by revenue body** *(continued)*

Country	Net revenue collections for all taxes administered by revenue body (in millions in local currency)								
	2005	2006	2007	2008	2009	2010	2011	2012	2013
Sweden	n.a.	n.a.	n.a.	1 491 024	1 440 134	1 416 430	1 493 815	1 502 871	1 536 121
Switzerland	n.a.	n.a.	n.a.	35 669	35 325	35 809	36 139	47 497	49 550
Turkey	119 627	137 481	152 835	168 109	172 440	210 560	253 809	278 780	326 125
United Kingdom	380 556	412 121	429 630	454 900	445 300	403 600	433 500	468 238	471 016
United States	1 998 851	2 238 287	2 396 291	2 316 747	1 907 651	1 877 753	1 999 072	2 150 891	2 490 706
Non-OECD countries									
Argentina	117 938	144 063	193 417	281 615	306 875	354 916	474 138	739 540	940 539
Brazil	n.a.	n.a.	n.a.	n.a.	n.a.	763 985	897 375	934 809	1 054 373
Bulgaria	4 759	7 529	11 449	13 106	13 452	11 988	12 667	13 240	13 599
China	n.a.	n.a.	n.a.	51 996 000	56 617 000	n.a.	n.a.	n.a.	n.a.
Colombia	n.a.	n.a.	n.a.	n.a.	n.a.	42 570 925	54 977 744	93 439 127	100 424 837
Costa Rica	Not covered by the series for these years							1 927 477	2 184 216
Croatia	Not covered by the series for these years							107 537	105 487
Cyprus	2 001	2 346	2 861	3 956 (a)	3 390	3 433	3 575	3 459	3 248
Hong Kong, China	n.a.	n.a.	n.a.	n.a.	n.a.	123 184	143 007	176 822	182 442
India	n.a.	n.a.	n.a.	3 068 280	3 767 660	4 387 039	4 837 028	4 939 470	5 589 580
Indonesia	n.a.	n.a.	n.a.	494 084 544	515 945 952	549 469 520	672 319 088	835 833 958	921 397 982
Latvia	2 663	3 428	4 609	5 139	3 934	3 642	4 059	4 550	4 800
Lithuania	13 966	16 741	19 893	23 199	16 427	15 503	16 906	18 295	19 928
Malaysia	53 457	61 400	69 379	82 091	77 644	79 499	102 609	116 889	120 433
Malta	n.a.	n.a.	n.a.	2 070	2 105	2 182	2 259	2 274	2 466
Morocco	Not covered by the series for these years							119 934	118 865
Romania	n.a.	n.a.	n.a.	142 827	133 783	130 462	143 543	167 803	173 553
Russia	4 627 000	5 432 000	6 955 000	7 949 000	6 288 000	7 695 792	9 719 960	10 960 265	11 327 496
Saudi Arabia	n.a.	n.a.	n.a.	15 333	14 103	15 962	20 006	23 712	25 045
Singapore	17 948	19 861	22 863	29 113	29 801	29 871	34 731	38 440	41 361
South Africa	360 889	423 911	503 403	581 769	635 197	609 243	685 282	754 834	827 208
Thailand	Not covered by the series for these years							1 351 288	1 475 269

Note: (a) In euros from this year.

Source: Survey responses for current and prior series.

Table A.4. **Aggregate expenditure for all revenue body functions and total expenditure for information technology operations**

(For some countries the historical data has been modified as a result of country revisions of previously reported data)

Country	Aggregate expenditure for all revenue body functions and related overheads (in millions in local currency)									Total expenditure for information technology operations (in millions in local currency)				
	2005	2006	2007	2008	2009	2010	2011	2012	2013	2009	2010	2011	2012	2013
OECD countries														
Australia	2 578	2 531	2 604	3 003	3 025	3 045	3 230	3 444	3 458	692	662	695	725	733
Austria	n.a.	n.a.	n.a.	709	712	563	579	605	612	74	76	89	167	164
Belgium	1 615	1 826	1 590	1 677	1 717	1 768	1 965	1 849	1 920	134	114	119	98	87
Canada	3 520	3 856	3 874	4 030	4 423	4 441	4 606	4 758	4 575	557	500	483	499	506
Chile	74 921	81 693	94 553	108 427	120 510	133 109	141 902	151 203	150 295	6 314	7 439	8 070	11 259	8 035
Czech Republic	6 977	7 240	7 666	7 553	8 056	7 424	7 972	8 335	8 491	1 102	251	1 623	1 366	1 265
Denmark	n.a.	5 721	5 714	5 760	5 703	5 591	5 604	5 636	5 147	923	813	831	930	870
Estonia	n.a.	n.a.	n.a.	695	591	583	38 (a)	38	40	68	67	6 (a)	0	0
Finland	330	343	359	387	390	381	389	395	395	78	n.a.	107	110	106
France	7 831	7 786	7 781	7 573	7 438	7 448	7 497	7 678	7 471	311	266	271	244	220
Germany	6 709	6 850	6 817	6 914	6 973	7 279	7 360	7 400	7 733	446	471	480	514	527
Greece	n.a.	n.a.	n.a.	n.a.	n.a.	n.a.	n.a.	n.a.	n.a.	n.a.	n.a.	n.a.	n.a.	n.a.
Hungary	65 789	79 204	99 231	120 676	117 823	112 181	141 800	150 766	161 754	14 175	5 387	7 369	9 184	10 467
Iceland	n.a.	n.a.	n.a.	1 092	1 149	2 503	2 557	2 586	2 649	349.3	410	430	416	442
Ireland	386	420	448	485	460	402	392	381	393	n.a.	54	40	45	50
Israel	n.a.	n.a.	n.a.	1 488	1 534	1 578	1 601	1 900	2 100	135	79	83	45	60
Italy	n.a.	n.a.	4 615	3 785	3 752	2 870	2 744	2 839	3 385	185	131	143	136	167
Japan	699 866	697 430	702 595	706 688	700 809	692 179	669 768	718 541	709 325	57 901	59 066	57 721	51 240	48 796
Korea	979 476	1 076 391	1 239 950	1 298 159	1 076 391	1 341 751	1 370 933	1 346 300	1 407 206	81 784	117 744	97 251	104 168	92 895
Luxembourg	72	76	81	85	91	90	95	99	105	5 (b)	2 (b)	4 (b)	3.3 (b)	5 (b)
Mexico	9 058	9 552	9 660	10 467	11 670	11 350	12 274	12 965	13 971	450	471	507	523	553
Netherlands	2 666	2 760	2 796	2 881	2 904	2 911	2 775	2 824	2 945	527	472	394	421	457
New Zealand	427	480	529	608	663	601	640	672	654	127	147	144	126	120
Norway	3 813	4 010	4 064	4 093	4 300	4 614	4 654	4 838	4 950	904	1 012	968	1 204	1 338
Poland	3 964	3 982	4 176	3 020	3 107	3 861	3 776	3 990	4 035	87	54	62	35	39
Portugal	441	445	464	477	508	517	484	528	600	12	7	6	8	12
Slovak Republic	3 256	3 669	3 284	n.a.	n.a.	116 (a)	129	197	224	n.a.	10 (a)	20	23	40
Slovenia	n.a.	n.a.	95	98	101	n.a.	n.a.	100	94	n.a.	n.a.	n.a.	13	10
Spain	n.a.	n.a.	n.a.	1 649	1 653	1 410	1 387	1 291	1 313	76	81	78	145	142
Sweden	6 095	6 520	6 899	6 413	6 297	6 895	7 290	7 393	7 464	1 226	1 155	1 292	1 256	1 453

Table A.4. **Aggregate expenditure for all revenue body functions and total expenditure for information technology operations** *(continued)*

Country	Aggregate expenditure for all revenue body functions and related overheads (in millions in local currency)									Total expenditure for information technology operations (in millions in local currency)				
	2005	2006	2007	2008	2009	2010	2011	2012	2013	2009	2010	2011	2012	2013
Switzerland	n.a.	n.a.	n.a.	170	169	151	151	152	153	15	3	4	2	5
Turkey	1 043	1 153	1 274	1 421	1 607	1 638	1 936	2 496	2 429	58	13	43	47	87
United Kingdom	n.a.	n.a.	n.a.	4 073	4 241	4 105	3 764	3 632	3 590	899	832	858	725	764
United States	10 398	10 606	10 765	11 307	11 709	12 353	12 359	12 059	11 598	1 743	1 902	1 851	1 836	2 018
Non-OECD countries														
Argentina	n.a.	n.a.	n.a.	5 363	7 143	9 555	11 592	14 157	17 279	50	57	88	119	186
Brazil	n.a.	n.a.	n.a.	n.a.	n.a.	7 755	8 134	8 249	8 473	n.a.	1 260	1 260	1 279	1 355
Bulgaria	152	127	129	154	161	168	170	174	170	n.a.	1	4	5	5
China	n.a.	n.a.	n.a.	n.a.	n.a.	n.a.	n.a.	81 516	81 761	n.a.	n.a.	n.a.	1 529	1 540
Colombia	n.a.	n.a.	n.a.	n.a.	n.a.	723 261	680 539	794 723	981 777	n.a.	24 798	23 836	53 166	51 544
Costa Rica	---------- Not covered by the series for these years ----------							25 924	25 988	----------			730	1 014
Croatia	---------- Not covered by the series for these years ----------							859	845	----------			111	135
Cyprus	n.a.	n.a.	n.a.	31 (a)	32	43	44	40	38	n.a.	1 (a)	1.3	1.7	3
Hong Kong, China	n.a.	n.a.	n.a.	n.a.	n.a.	1 148	1 188	1 265	1 332	n.a.	104	114	122	133
India	n.a.	n.a.	n.a.	n.a.	n.a.	27 258	26 979	29 789	32 847	n.a.	1 910	1 922	3 071	3 943
Indonesia	n.a.	n.a.	n.a.	n.a.	n.a.	n.a.	n.a.	4 997 444	5 203 785	748 772	n.a.	n.a.	141 293	142 054
Latvia	n.a.	n.a.	n.a.	74	54	60	61	89	94	8	8	6	12	15
Lithuania	196	206	226	245	194	164	166	164	162	13	12	13	16	15
Malaysia	n.a.	n.a.	n.a.	1 065	1 216	1 009	1 118	1 583	1 906	334	60	27	48	37
Malta (c)	n.a.	n.a.	n.a.	11	12	25	24	23	24	0.95	0.04	0.04	0.03	0.04
Morocco	---------- Not covered by the series for these years ----------							n/a	n/a	----------			48	45
Romania	n.a.	n.a.	n.a.	1 152	965	803	1 464	2 086	2 097	n.a.	n.a.	40	183	58
Russia	n.a.	n.a.	n.a.	108 078	103 009	97 519	102 041	101 756	107 928	5 822	5 802	7 003	7 542	8 025
Saudi Arabia	n.a.	n.a.	n.a.	162	178	220	314	370	406	12	n.a.	n.a.	n.a.	n.a.
Singapore	183	184	189	224	240	267	302	298	328	81	108	119	109	130
South Africa (d)	4 312	5 135	5 156	5 615	6 511	7 032	7 426	8 221	8 696	341	n.a.	n.a.	n/a	n/a
Thailand	---------- Not covered by the series for these years ----------							9 883	10 403	----------			130	27

Notes: (a) In euros from this year.

(b) Major part of IT-related costs not quantified as shared with other parts of MOF in separate IT-department.

(c) Aggregates: Data prior to 2010 does not include customs department which collects excise; IT expenditure only for direct tax authority.

(d) Aggregates include costs of custom administration which cannot be separately quantified.

Source: Survey responses for current and prior series.

Table A.5. **Aggregate expenditure for tax functions and related overheads and human resource management expenditure**

(For some countries the historical data has been modified as a result of country revisions of previously reported data)

Country	Aggregate expenditure for tax functions and related overheads (in millions in local currency)									HRM expenditure (in millions in local currency)			
	2005	2006	2007	2008	2009	2010	2011	2012	2013	2010	2011	2012	2013
OECD countries													
Australia	2 217	2 303	2 318	2 560	2 656	2 664	2 710	2 935	2 901	160	193	163	146
Austria	364	381	399	546	541	459	463	495	507	28	29	30	32
Belgium	1 163	1 315	1 145	1 191	1 202	1 178	1 275	1 218	1 201	n.a.	n.a.	41	40
Canada	3 159	3 316	3 290	3 372	3 681	3 744	3 903	4 039	3 927	86	86	73	72
Chile	74 921	81 693	94 553	108 427	120 510	133 109	141 902	151 203	150 295	4 260	4 862	6 203	5 540
Czech Republic	6 628	7 095	7 206	7 175	7 653	7 062	7 593	7 919	8 062	40	42	46	51
Denmark	5 686 /1	4 977	4 971	5 184	5 133	n.a.	n.a.	4 621	4 272	116	104	131	126
Estonia	481	494	590	306	260	255	17 (a)	22	25	9	1 (a)	0.5	0.4
Finland	330	343	359	387	390	381	389	395	395	n.a.	n.a.	n.a.	n.a.
France	4 542	4 516	4 513	4 468	4 463	4 468	4 513	4 133	4 039	n.a.	n.a.	190	184
Germany	6 709	6 850	6 817	6 914	6 973	7 279	7 360	7 400	7 738	95	99	107	121
Greece	n.a.	n.a.	n.a.	n.a.	n.a.	n.a.	n.a.	n.a.	n.a.	n.a.	n.a.	n.a.	n.a.
Hungary	65 789	79 204	99 231	104 151	102 015	111 727	104 606	114 996	122 909	1 754	4 167	3 045	3 252
Iceland	n.a.	n.a.	n.a.	1 092	1 149	2 503	2 557	2 586	2 649	n.a.	n.a.	n.a.	n.a.
Ireland	386	420	448	485	460	402	392	381	393	5.26	5.66	5.48	4.98
Israel	n.a.	n.a.	n.a.	1 324	1 365	1 242	1 263	1 684	1 884	21	20	30	30
Italy	4 571	4 582	4 573	3 028	3 114	2 363	2 270	2 482	2 930	109	106	108	144
Japan	699 866	697 430	702 595	706 688	700 809	692 179	669 768	718 541	709 325	280	317	340	336
Korea	979 476	1 024 000	1 082 000	1 240 000	1 301 000	1 341 751	1 370 933	1 346 300	1 407 206	9 527	9 813	8 939	10 157
Luxembourg	72	76	81	85	91	90	95	99	105	n.a.	n.a.	n.a.	n.a.
Mexico	7 790	8 119	8 308	8 897	9 219	9 165	9 877	10 533	11 343	131	128	118	112
Netherlands	2 133	2 208	2 237	2 074	2 091	2 069	1 984	1 969	2 069	74	54	60	65
New Zealand	320	336	365	389	431	372	417	452	458	9	10	10	12
Norway	3 660	3 850	3 901	4 011	4 214	4 321	4 464	3 917	3 969	103	106	58	61
Poland	3 013	3 066	3 257	3 012	3 062	3 861	3 776	3 472	3 487	2	14	11	10
Portugal	397	401	418	429	457	465	436	334	386	n.a.	n.a.	2.5	2.8
Slovak Republic	3 158	3 192	3 185	n.a.	n.a.	116 (a)	125	115	131	1 (a)	1	3.4	3.7
Slovenia	90	102	92	98	101	105	104	100	94	n.a.	n.a.	n.a.	n.a.
Spain	1 195	1 247	1 323	1 418	1 405	1 410	1 387	1 114	1 130	n.a.	n.a.	111	111
Sweden	5 059	5 412	5 864	5 836	5 730	5 850	6 046	5 933	5 961	n.a.	n.a.	n.a.	n.a.

Table A.5. **Aggregate expenditure for tax functions and related overheads and human resource management expenditure** *(continued)*

Country	Aggregate expenditure for tax functions and related overheads (in millions in local currency)									HRM expenditure (in millions in local currency)			
	2005	2006	2007	2008	2009	2010	2011	2012	2013	2010	2011	2012	2013
Switzerland	143	145	149	160	161	134	136	144	144	1.2	1.3	1.5	1.5
Turkey	1 043	1 153	1 274	1 421	1 607	1 638	1 936	2 180	2 096	n.a.	n.a.	n.a.	n.a.
United Kingdom	4 202	4 509	4 773	4 073	4 068	3 937	3 600	3 479	3 433	69	61	51	43
United States	10 398	10 606	10 765	11 307	11 709	12 353	12 359	12 059	11 598	242	225	200	176
Non-OECD countries													
Argentina	1 047	1 458	2 092	2 628	3 500	4 701	5 911	7 178	8 974	4.1	6.6	6.7	8.8
Brazil	n.a.	n.a.	n.a.	n.a.	n.a.	7 755	8 134	8 249	8 473	n.a.	n.a.	n.a.	n.a.
Bulgaria	152	127	129	154	161	169	170	174	170	1.7	1.8	0.6	1.6
China	n.a.	n.a.	n.a.	n.a.	n.a.	n.a.	n.a.	67 473	68 875	n.a.	n.a.	n.a.	n.a.
Colombia	n.a.	n.a.	n.a.	n.a.	n.a.	394 437	371 138	458 222	566 073	8 178	8 847	n.a.	n.a.
Costa Rica	Not covered by the series for these years							25 924	25 988			n.a.	n.a.
Croatia	Not covered by the series for these years							859	845			3.8	3.78
Cyprus	n.a.	n.a.	n.a.	31 (a)	32	43	44	40	38	0.3	0.5	0.27	0.34
Hong Kong, China	n.a.	n.a.	n.a.	n.a.	n.a.	1 042	1 075	1 147	1 202	14	16	14	15
India	n.a.	n.a.	n.a.	23 319	28 404	26 701	26 456	29 218	32 099	31	87	169	337
Indonesia	n.a.	n.a.	n.a.	3 179 000	2 991 000	2 654 038	3 725 257	4 997 444	5 203 785	n.a.	n.a.	28 230	19 600
Latvia	33	41	52	58	45	29	32	47	51	3.2	2.9	1.3	1.1
Lithuania	196	206	226	245	194	164	166	164	162	1.8	1.5	1.5	1.5
Malaysia	640	701	895	852	1 094	624	716	956	1 200	27	33	60	67
Malta (b)	10	10	9	9	10	25	23	22	23	0.14	0.14	0.19	0.19
Morocco	Not covered by the series for these years							n.a.	n.a.			n.a.	n.a.
Romania	500	690	1 044	1 152	965	646	1 244	2 086	2 097	n.a.	n.a.	0.26	0.08
Russia	n.a.	n.a.	n.a.	92 299	87 667	84 432	87 519	86 690	92 063	1 723	1 865	1 968	2 159
Saudi Arabia	109	136	157	162	178	220	314	370	406	n.a.	n.a.	n.a.	n.a.
Singapore	183	184	189	224	240	267	302	298	328	4.3	5.3	5.3	5.7
South Africa (c)	4 312	5 135	5 156	5 615	6 511	7 032	7 426	8 221	8 696	n.a.	n.a.	n.a.	n.a.
Thailand	Not covered by the series for these years							9 883	10 403			223	229

Notes: (a) In euros from this year.
(b) Aggregates: Statistics prior to 2010, not including customs department; HRM expenditure: Not including customs department.
(c) Aggregates include costs of custom administration which cannot be separately quantified.

Source: Survey responses for current and prior series.

Table A.6. **Total staff usage in 2013 by functional groupings (FTEs) and total salary costs for tax functions and related overheads**

Country	Total staff usage in 2013 on tax administration by functional groupings (FTEs)							Total staff usage for all roles etc.	Total salary costs for tax functions and related overheads (in millions in local currency)						
	Account Management	Verification	Tax Debt Collection	Other Tax Operations	Support: HRM	Support: Other	Total		2007	2008	2009	2010	2011	2012	2013
OECD countries															
Australia	3 065	6 120	1 708	2 879	1 047	2 658	17 477	20 248	1 652	1 526	1 654	1 655	1 711	1 903	1 814
Austria	851	4 765	780	649	0	439	7 484	7 521	328	345	365	367	372	410	425
Belgium	n.a.	n.a.	n.a.	n.a.	n.a.	n.a.	19 485	22 232	935	976	982	977	1 038	976	956
Canada	9 669	11 042	7 620	2 928	1 321	5 592	38 172	39 521	2 534	2 602	2 906	2 870	3 036	3 137	2 998
Chile	836	1 693	0	60	146	1 460	4 195	4 195	73 818	84 966	96 780	108 853	118 247	125 981	129 712
Czech Republic	8 585	2 713	824	2 150	0	0	14 272	15 031	5 669	4 330	4 573	5 768	5 474	n.a.	n.a.
Denmark	1 564	2 386	480	133	136	1 162	5 861	6 802	3 404	n.a.	n.a.	2 889	2 816	2 905	2 602
Estonia	10	659	99	99	6	110	983	1 549	448	234	201	200	13 (a)	17	19
Finland	1 941	1 974	481	125	102	449	5 072	5 072	234	251	251	250	251	253	256
France	29 019	10 268	6 756	8 250	12 671	0	66 964	114 417	3 571	3 633	3 619	3 640	3 645	3 279	3 228
Germany	43 685	43 800	7 560	10 479	4 021	948	110 494	110 494	5 676	5 787	5 740	5 917	6 006	6 016	6 132
Greece	4 500	2 000	800	300	200	200	8 000	11 500	n.a.	n.a.	n.a.	n.a.	n.a.	n.a.	n.a.
Hungary	4 296	6 482	2 727	198	277	3 890	17 870	22 482	79 368	64 187	72 838	54 133	54 121	66 552	64 462
Iceland	16	157	0	24	2	41	240	240	n.a.	585	606	1 643	1 775	1 773	1 826
Ireland	1 545	1 765	822	496	49	1 068	5 745	5 745	321	332	330	292	294	283	288
Israel	657	2 058	847	182	215	1 145	5 104	6 035	n.a.	1 159	1 200	847	863	1 005	1 148
Italy	11 343	12 186	900	2 833	1 468	1 890	31 706 (b)	39 814	3 178	1 712	1 756	1 286	1 261	1 417	1 714
Japan	0	35 591	11 940	1 300	369	6 994	56 194	56 194	569 504	570 580	566 034	557 126	540 341	585 027	574 326
Korea	10 927	4 519	196	1 744	117	1 338	18 841	18 841	719 319	793 095	827 185	830 700	883 464	916 641	959 292
Luxembourg (c)	218	414	168	121	23	39	984	984	66	68	74	75	78	82	85
Mexico	4 054	8 970	5 952	2 009	1 287	3 185	25 457	36 410	6 850	7 331	7 665	8 149	8 419	8 643	8 858
Netherlands	5 515	8 726	1 542	425	1 379	3 286	20 873	28 313	1 431	1 359	1 403	1 460	1 428	1 473	1 515
New Zealand	1 284	768	322	220	68	771	3 433	5 282	230	243	277	223	247	250	252
Norway	418	2 799	833	734	133	1 815	6 733	6 962	2 460	2 567	2 748	2 871	3 057	2 634	2 670
Poland	8 875	11 819	5 779	8 454	398	12 268	47 593	48 821	2 340	2 159	2 230	3 103	3 086	2 393	2 394
Portugal	5 338	1 695	1 890	256	214	673	10 066	11 341	332	339	370	381	350	288	320
Slovak Republic	2 744	1 558	289	603	120	1 499	6 813	9 296	1 581	n.a.	n.a.	59 (a)	56	83	90
Slovenia	146	1 362	437	82	33	305	2 365	2 365	63	67	69	69	69	64	61
Spain	7 195	5 057	4 421	0	1 750	3 979	22 402	26 231	888	971	1 027	1 011	1 001	795	823
Sweden	0	2 557	0	2 842	0	2 478	7 877	9 705	4 084	3 810	3 951	4 067	4 138	4 180	4 180

Table A.6. **Total staff usage in 2013 by functional groupings (FTEs) and total salary costs for tax functions and related overheads** *(continued)*

Country	Total staff usage in 2013 on tax administration by functional groupings (FTEs)							Total staff usage for all roles etc.	Total salary costs for tax functions and related overheads (in millions in local currency)						
	Account Management	Verification	Tax Debt Collection	Other Tax Operations	Support: HRM	Support: Other	Total		2007	2008	2009	2010	2011	2012	2013
Switzerland	85	235	73	522	10	0	925	965	135	145	144	126	126	118	118
Turkey	30 677	10 134	4 113	134	1 713	4 275	51 046	51 369	872	960	1 062	1 167	1 389	1 469	1 432
United Kingdom	17 745	22 715	6 409	1 916	945	3 475	53 205	63 843	2 923	2 396	2 245	2 140	2 057	2 045	1 990
United States	28 910	29 612	12 560	1 356	1 348	13 191	86 977	86 977	7 702	7 960	8 371	8 846	9 007	8 838	8 550
Non-OECD countries															
Argentina	3 342	6 098	1 221	2 043	362	3 835	16 901	22 157	1 970	2 488	3 337	4 504	5 727	6 886	8 546
Brazil	4 985	4 840	5 112	6 237	542	2 909	24 625	24 625	n.a.	n.a.	n.a.	4 658	4 861	5 713	5 872
Bulgaria	1 941	3 224	755	725	100	927	7 672	7 680	98	118	137	138	137	145	141
China	n.a.	n.a.	n.a.	n.a.	n.a.	n.a.	n.a.	756 000	n.a.	n.a.	n.a.	n.a.	n.a.	n.a.	n.a.
Colombia	469	1 469	898	1 050	146	1 212	5 244	9 095	n.a.	n.a.	n.a.	301 229	281 300	340 357	393 868
Costa Rica	n.a.	n.a.	n.a.	n.a.	n.a.	n.a.	961	961	------- Not covered by the series for these years -------					17 835	19 300
Croatia	2 345	827	362	357	197	99	4 187	4 212	------- Not covered by the series for these years -------					492	483
Cyprus	180	284	91	98	8	113	774	782	18	22 (a)	25	35	36	33	31
Hong Kong, China	1 523	240	446	52	3	324	2 588	2 826	n.a.	n.a.	n.a.	902	956	1 009	1 038
India	n.a.	n.a.	n.a.	n.a.	n.a.	n.a.	n.a.	41 357	n.a.	13 400	18 594	17 612	16 216	16 865	18 814
Indonesia	6 710	4 522	640	683	2 961	16 757	32 273	32 273	n.a.	1 009 000	1 115 000	1 725 835	1 882 068	1 552 002	1 636 817
Latvia	1 438	801	250	63	41	498	3 091	4 312	32	42	31	17	21	32	35
Lithuania	1 350	998	233	498	32	365	3 476	3 476	155	179	151	131	131	126	128
Malaysia	823	3 415	2 125	1 357	183	1 102	9 005	11 049	602	436	429	494	590	721	941
Malta	105	95	36	448	11	45	736	750	n.a.	16	16	16	18	16	16
Morocco	2 808	507	601	0	110	709	4 735	4 735	------- Not covered by the series for these years -------					n.a.	n.a.
Romania	3 929	4 955	7 513	2 486	188	2 972	22 043	24 481	799	990	937	n.a.	n.a.	1 566	1 779
Russia	9 559	60 705	11 220	21 836	2 600	23 057	128 977	128 977	n.a.	61 337	59 806	62 776	62 865	57 772	63 781
Saudi Arabia	264	571	162	198	292	102	1 589	n.a.	130	131	141	n.a.	n.a.	n.a.	n.a.
Singapore	165	990	210	184	30	319	1 898	1 898	110	132	132	141	167	169	177
South Africa (d)	5 846	1 966	1 102	1 024	301	1 625	11 864	14 701	3 125	3 472	3 755	n.a.	n.a.	5 503	5 821
Thailand	n.a.	n.a.	n.a.	n.a.	n.a.	n.a.	23 129	23 129	------- Not covered by the series for these years -------					6 275	6 538

Notes: (a) In euros from this year.

(b) Total does not match the total of all sub-categories as not all the associated processes have been linked to all staff.

(c) Staff usage figures not expressed in FTE.

(d) Aggregates include costs of custom administration which cannot be separately quantified.

Source: Survey responses for current and prior series.

Table A.7. **Value of tax debt outstanding at the year-end: excluding disputed tax debt vs. including disputed tax debt**

(For some countries the historical data has been modified as a result of country revisions of previously reported data)

Country	Value of tax debt outstanding (**not disputed**, i.e. excluding disputed tax debt) at the year-end (in millions in local currency)									Value of total tax debt outstanding (**including disputed**) at the year-end (in millions in local currency)		
	2005	2006	2007	2008	2009	2010	2011	2012	2013	2011	2012	2013
OECD countries												
Australia (a)	9 611	10 225	10 776	10 887	12 148	14 700	14 083	16 629	17 708	27 548	31 721	33 240
Austria	1 882	1 796	1 691	1 808	1 816	1 664	1 724	1 735	1 822	5 926	6 214	6 784
Belgium	4 565	4 450	4 206	12 311	12 195	9 445	8 654	15 833	16 763	22 981	23 945	23 971
Canada	18 026	18 488	20 027	23 200	24 400	25 000	27 400	29 000	31 000	37 900	40 100	42 700
Chile	n.a.	7 738 000	8 080 000	9 536 000	10 202 000	11 140 000	12 610 000	14 020 000	15 550 000	n.a.	n.a.	n.a.
Czech Republic	105 354	101 100	n.a.	100 500	98 400	71 166	83 367	98 734	111 390	n.a.	n.a.	n.a.
Denmark	n.a.	n.a.	n.a.	n.a.	n.a.	n.a.	n.a.	n.a.	43 211	58 776	59 670	57 511
Estonia	n.a.	n.a.	n.a.	n.a.	n.a.	n.a.	n.a.	n.a.	n.a.	372	343	275
Finland	n.a.	n.a.	n.a.	n.a.	n.a.	n.a.	n.a.	n.a.	n.a.	3 898	4 084	3 921
France	32 391	30 263	28 101	26 290	23 592	24 215	25 682	27 803	28 261	36 073	38 626	39 833
Germany	7 922	7 313	8 237	8 068	8 162	11 125	9 368	9 587	n.a.	17 287	17 838	n.a.
Greece	n.a.	n.a.	n.a.	n.a.	n.a.	n.a.	n.a.	n.a.	n.a.	44 895	55 791	63 517
Hungary	964 450	1 024 822	1 328 451	1 684 992	2 029 973	2 295 517	1 998 129	2 140 855	2 259 412	2 147 811	2 219 382	2 335 838
Iceland	n.a.	n.a.	n.a.	n.a.	n.a.	n.a.	n.a.	n.a.	n.a.	103 656	114 274	111 156
Ireland	832	792	895	1 233	1 443	1 389	1 317	1 180	1 009	1 986	2 006	1 840
Israel	n.a.	n.a.	15 782	19 447	21 699	6 316	6 474	12 161	11 630	26 673	18 092	18 035
Italy	n.a.	n.a.	n.a.	n.a.	n.a.	n.a.	424 566	475 096	530 958	571 552	642 591	715 183
Japan	n.a.	n.a.	n.a.	n.a.	n.a.	n.a.	n.a.	n.a.	n.a.	1 420 104	1 361 737	1 270 177
Korea	n.a.	n.a.	n.a.	n.a.	n.a.	n.a.	n.a.	n.a.	n.a.	5 460 070	5 908 940	6 540 049
Luxembourg	n.a.	n.a.	n.a.	n.a.	n.a.	n.a.	n.a.	n.a.	n.a.	1 637	1 649	1 687
Mexico	296 076	302 870	282 767	258 826	219 454	252 485	295 397	258 584	201 748	743 783	668 543	516 504
Netherlands	6 604	5 803	7 616	7 873	7 582	8 096	8 001	8 012	8 239	15 804	14 535	14 245
New Zealand	2 312	2 776	2 906	3 657	4 097	4 186	4 418	4 477	4 417	4 835	5 083	4 970
Norway	15 840	16 081	16 643	19 273	21 267	25 553	23 543	20 974	23 543	29 501	27 435	30 173
Poland	13 053	13 519	17 284	19 667	20 276	22 772	25 775	27 902	34 090	n.a.	29 595	35 660
Portugal (c)	12 965	13 224	12 890	8 214	7 338	6 740	8 890	9 254	9 426	12 428	12 714	12 349
Slovak Republic	62 690	58 663	65 114	2 291 (b)	2 387	2 423	2 768	3 057	3 014	n.a.	n.a.	n.a.
Slovenia	350	356	397	465	482	573	1 191	1 086	902	1 489	1 616	1 473
Spain	n.a.	n.a.	n.a.	n.a.	n.a.	n.a.	n.a.	n.a.	n.a.	18 891	22 325	23 401
Sweden	n.a.	n.a.	n.a.	n.a.	n.a.	n.a.	n.a.	n.a.	n.a.	32 858	35 302	38 130
Switzerland	n.a.	n.a.	n.a.	n.a.	n.a.	n.a.	n.a.	n.a.	n.a.	896	923	906

Table A.7. **Value of tax debt outstanding at the year-end: excluding disputed tax debt vs. including disputed tax debt** *(continued)*

Country	Value of tax debt outstanding (**not disputed**, i.e. excluding disputed tax debt) at the year-end (in millions in local currency)									Value of total tax debt outstanding (**including disputed**) at the year-end (in millions in local currency)		
	2005	2006	2007	2008	2009	2010	2011	2012	2013	2011	2012	2013
Turkey	n.a.	n.a.	n.a.	n.a.	n.a.	n.a.	n.a.	n.a.	n.a.	n.a.	n.a.	n.a.
United Kingdom	n.a.	n.a.	n.a.	17 324	21 345	17 916	15 010	13 294	12 238	32 178	31 561	30 544
United States	127 056	139 478	153 558	162 025	180 318	207 136	220 430	213 305	217 231	288 266	280 132	275 099
Non-OECD countries												
Argentina	1 887 (d)	2 305 (d)	2 321 (d)	5 523 (d)	5 477 (d)	18 338	n.a.	n.a.	n.a.	28 654	43 463	79 355
Brazil	n.a.	n.a.	n.a.	n.a.	n.a.	265 707	189 427	319 558	294 064	975 803	1 100 640	1 242 228
Bulgaria	1 891	1 647	1 460	1 476	2 103	2 916	3 452	3 032	2 084	n.a.	3 226	2 183
China	n.a.	n.a.	n.a.	n.a.	n.a.	83 000	92 000	n.a.	n.a.	n.a.	n.a.	n.a.
Colombia	n.a.	n.a.	n.a.	n.a.	8 582 523	9 477 229	8 881 709	n.a.	n.a.	n.a.	n.a.	n.a.
Costa Rica	Not covered by the series for these years							n.a.	n.a.	1 405	2 014	3 512
Croatia	Not covered by the series for these years							n.a.	n.a.	44 213	39 038	37 247
Cyprus	950	938	1 104	1 098 (b)	1 212	1 228	1 215	1 228	1 546	1 584	1 614	1 696
Hong Kong, China	n.a.	n.a.	n.a.	n.a.	n.a.	7 895	7 064	7 416	7 362	58 315	57 289	53 001
India	n.a.	n.a.	179 770	137 010	759 030	1 049 680	1 259 450	1 227 710	1 066 100	3 330 790	4 084 180	4 861 800
Indonesia	n.a.	n.a.	19 524 282	29 081 881	45 173 000	40 628 000	40 595 000	6 372 608	10 623 800	87 225 216	70 721 181	77 366 561
Latvia	365	415	406	730	721	794	929	n.a.	n.a.	1 322	1 457	1 416
Lithuania	848	748	690	876	1 447	1 547	1 630	1 627	1 268	1 911	1 783	1 462
Malaysia	11 119	13 815	12 627	9 799	9 250	10 091	10 568	8 864	8 539	15 425	14 929	13 703
Malta (e)	n.a.	n.a.	n.a.	n.a.	620	675	570	543	572	899	1 052	1 302
Morocco	Not covered by the series for these years							n.a.	n.a.	12 600	14 100	14 170
Romania	n.a.	n.a.	11 862	13 005	17 231	n.a.	n.a.	17 909	14 942	68 425	71 019	73 309
Russia	1 804 267	1 778 315	1 232 657	1 092 784	1 393 372	1 190 524	1 064 397	1 066 972	1 100 965	1 276 100	1 125 800	1 155 239
Saudi Arabia	n.a.	n.a.	n.a.	n.a.	n.a.	n.a.	n.a.	n.a.	n.a.	n.a.	n.a.	n.a.
Singapore	1 098	925	1 064	893	767	669	604	483	374	n.a.	n.a.	n.a.
South Africa	56 200	48 000	42 900	37 719	55 674	74 673	73 173	76 625	70 667	87 534	88 608	82 250
Thailand	Not covered by the series for these years							12 455	14 108	n.a.	n.a.	n.a.

Notes: (a) "Value of tax debt outstanding (not disputed)" is collectable debt only.
(b) In euros from this year.
(c) Data until end of 2010 includes non-tax debt.
(d) The amounts reported (and related ratios) do not take account of tax debts subject to repayment plans.
(e) Statistics refer only to authority in charge of Direct Taxation and VAT.

Source: Survey responses for current and prior series.

Table A.8. Value of tax debt written off

(For some countries the historical data has been modified as a result of country revisions of previously reported data)

Country	Value of tax written off (in millions in local currency)						
	2007	2008	2009	2010	2011	2012	2013
OECD countries							
Australia	1 568	1 826	2 221	1 714	3 849	2 617	4 600
Austria	516	616	585	528	451	428	509
Belgium	n.a.	n.a.	n.a.	1 896	2 155	1 881	1 615
Canada	1 721	1 982	2 122	2 123	2 222	2 632	2 778
Chile	n.a.	196 115	159 449	349 811	931 971	457 600	614 859
Czech Republic	13 734	16 211	13 786	6 500	8 900	19 600	24 500
Denmark	3 572	2 215	3 096	3 353	5 009	5 311	4 817
Estonia	333	595	498	1 205	56 (a)	65	90
Finland	280	257	216	212	208	198	262
France	6 002	5 203	3 960	3 416	2 738	3 048	3 174
Germany	4 157	4 333	5 626	4 756	5 148	4 480	n.a.
Greece	n.a.	276	280	520	n.a.	n.a.	n.a.
Hungary	355 966	404 303	542 876	610 911	1 034 106	737 653	766 923
Iceland	n.a.	10 776	13 844	12 810	14 590	17 461	18 978
Ireland	118	129	222	334	302	287	263
Israel	n.a.	960	1 130	n.a.	n.a.	155	257
Italy	n.a.	n.a.	n.a.	n.a.	n.a.	5 520	7 358
Japan	166 014	176 238	188 437	n.a.	n.a.	n.a.	n.a.
Korea	n.a.	n.a.	n.a.	n.a.	n.a.	n.a.	n.a.
Luxembourg	n.a.	46	64	81	98	112	122
Mexico	161 670	159 871	201 195	83 072	127 424	58 977	114 621
Netherlands	2 421	2 827	1 762	1 926	2 627	2 580	2 457
New Zealand	n.a.	n.a.	n.a.	619	737	849	925
Norway	396	806	1 530	1 379	1 834	1 766	1 794
Poland	118	90	85	134	101	96	110
Portugal	n.a.	n.a.	n.a.	n.a.	529	476	590
Slovak Republic	5 410	10 884	413	552	436	192	644
Slovenia	7	4	2	77	62	30	77
Spain	n.a.	n.a.	n.a.	n.a.	n.a.	n.a.	n.a.

Table A.8. **Value of tax debt written off** *(continued)*

Country	Value of tax written off (in millions in local currency)						
	2007	2008	2009	2010	2011	2012	2013
Sweden	n.a.	n.a.	n.a.	6 268	5 083	5 320	7 695
Switzerland	n.a.	n.a.	n.a.	172	197	178	184
Turkey	n.a.	n.a.	n.a.	n.a.	n.a.	n.a.	n.a.
United Kingdom	4 285	5 462	4 148	5 928	4 695	4 214	4 378
United States	22 924	18 519	16 831	14 580	16 730	15 894	17 922
Non-OECD countries							
Argentina	n.a.	124	194	269	385	n.a.	n.a.
Brazil	n.a.	n.a.	n.a.	n.a.	n.a.	n.a.	n.a.
Bulgaria	n.a.	n.a.	n.a.	n.a.	n.a.	n.a.	n.a.
China	n.a.	n.a.	n.a.	324	545	n.a.	n.a.
Colombia	n.a.	n.a.	n.a.	4 672 678	4 887 299	n.a.	n.a.
Costa Rica	Not covered by the series for these years					n.a.	n.a.
Croatia	Not covered by the series for these years					n.a.	n.a.
Cyprus	n.a.	0	0	0.3	0.6	84	28
Hong Kong, China	n.a.	n.a.	n.a.	557	554	497	518
India	n.a.	n.a.	n.a.	n.a.	n.a.	33	77
Indonesia	n.a.	n.a.	n.a.	45 800	n.a.	28 075 791	n.a.
Latvia	200	158	294	110	125	312	311
Lithuania	n.a.	187	189	168	141	324	321
Malaysia	781	399	149	801	791	921	530
Malta (b)	n.a.	n.a.	n.a.	0.31	0.26	1.8	0.004
Morocco	Not covered by the series for these years					n.a.	n.a.
Romania	n.a.	n.a.	n.a.	n.a.	n.a.	n.a.	n.a.
Russia	211 822	243 707	169 995	160 981	303 684	254 434	206 888
Saudi Arabia	n.a.	n.a.	n.a.	n.a.	n.a.	0.2	1.3
Singapore	n.a.	n.a.	n.a.	n.a.	n.a.	n.a.	n.a.
South Africa	5 400	4 744	4 305	4 152	4 623	8 184	15 494
Thailand	Not covered by the series for these years					3 988	1 684

Notes: (a) In euros from this year.
(b) Statistics refer only to authority in charge of Direct Taxation and VAT.

Source: Survey responses for current and prior series.

Table A.9. **Total amount of debt collected from enforcement actions during the fiscal year and number of year-end debt cases**

(For some countries the historical data has been modified as a result of country revisions of previously reported data)

Country	Total amount of debt collected during the fiscal year (in millions in local currency)									Number of year-end debt cases (thousands)								
	2005	2006	2007	2008	2009	2010	2011	2012	2013	2005	2006	2007	2008	2009	2010	2011	2012	2013
OECD countries																		
Australia	n.a.	n.a.	n.a.	n.a.	n.a.	12 140	14 948	17 500	20 200	1 458	1 502	1 549	1 314	1 344	1 487	1 469	1 620	1 670
Austria	n.a.	n.a.	n.a.	n.a.	n.a.	n.a.	n.a.	n.a.	n.a.	105	107	109	108	109	103	101	100	104
Belgium	n.a.	n.a.	n.a.	n.a.	n.a.	6 915	9 005	1 241	1 603	495	472	431	n.a.	n.a.	746	667	1 465	1 458
Canada	19 130	21 514	22 185	30 500	35 200	29 600	34 100	40 000	37 300	3 255	3 172	2 995	3 095	3 291	3 354	3 452	3 550	3 636
Chile	n.a.	n.a.	n.a.	409 589	498 316	446 184	511 579	559 438	561 339	391	412	420	440	449	460	473	482	481
Czech Republic	68 205	68 505	68 477	6 334	5 999	7 012	5 754	7 941	7 525	1 608	1 751	1 811	1 715	2 244	3 997	3 476	3 245	3 420
Denmark	n.a.	2 946	3 474	4 714	5 076	n.a.	n.a.	n.a.	n.a.	144	648	720	290	384	314	318	371	398
Estonia	1 090	771	844	0	1.302	2 616	237 (a)	232	491	176	177	183	192	125	188	60	52	45
Finland	1 261	1 298	1 401	1 569	1 476	1 300	1 400	1 513	1 583	306	315	305	309	310	330	350	397	349
France	24 089	22 934	24 535	26 686	19 794	21 113	21 672	21 868	23 343	4 025	4 127	4 050	3 984	4 035	3 945	3 905	4 059	4 229
Germany	n.a.	n.a.	n.a.	n.a.	n.a.	n.a.	n.a.	n.a.	n.a.	3 016	2 839	2 959	2 798	2 569	2 430	2 976	2 746	n.a.
Greece	n.a.	n.a.	n.a.	n.a.	n.a.	n.a.	n.a.	2 495	3 264	n.a.	n.a.	772	804	941	1 062	1 671	2 220	2 734
Hungary	204 253	213 765	251 279	292 195	282 171	300 366	327 792	342 997	362 595	194	192	214	241	278	295	328	334	356
Iceland	n.a.	n.a.	n.a.	445 277	414 734	442 467	463 471	508 892	n.a.	n.a.	n.a.	n.a.	n.a.	n.a.	n.a.	n.a.	n.a.	n.a.
Ireland	226	347	352	323	261	217	207	186	189	n.a.	n.a.	n.a.	n.a.	n.a.	n.a.	n.a.	n.a.	620
Israel	n.a.	n.a.	n.a.	n.a.	n.a.	n.a.	n.a.	5 138	7 577	n.a.	n.a.	477	489	474	n.a.	n.a.	332	312
Italy	1 295	2 022	3 461	n.a.	n.a.	n.a.	n.a.	975	1 038	n.a.	n.a.	n.a.	n.a.	n.a.	n.a.	n.a.	64 566	70 015
Japan	1055007	1012757	999824	951747	960079	806050	759066	665676	685046	4 370	4 296	4 243	4 181	4 135	4 111	4 034	4 021	3 857
Korea	6268723	6535800	6930104	7106042	8022710	8146900	8 151 100	8513363	8900054	682	677	675	793	784	744	805	798	838
Luxembourg (b)	n.a.	n.a.	n.a.	n.a.	n.a.	n.a.	n.a.	n.a.	n.a.	n.a.	n.a.	n.a.	n.a.	25	24	23	23	24
Mexico	4 305	4 595	34 464	8 944	11 238	17 137	21 227	2 055	10 694	796	722	476	536	641	1 309	1 404	1 645	1 360
Netherlands	n.a.	n.a.	n.a.	2 055	2 027	1 781	1 647	1 623	1 625	1 400	1 200	1 200	1 200	1 200	1 300	1 400	1 500	1 400
New Zealand	1 492	1 774	1 850	2 208	2 428	2 085	1 566	2 398	2 036	277	278	281	364	353	257	264	280	293
Norway	2 440	2 929	1 668	2 439	4 861	n.a.	n.a.	n.a.	n.a.	n.a.	n.a.	n.a.	n.a.	n.a.	n.a.	n.a.	n.a.	n.a.
Poland	2 054	2 213	2 248	2 078	2 299	2 781	3 024	3 271	3 287	770	854	735	775	750	689	758	787	807
Portugal	1 420	1 546	1 633	1 548	1 326	1 240	1 230	1 218	1 923	2 856	3 021	3 211	3 615	3 689	3 866	4 140	2 459	3 061
Slovak Republic	15 167	13 564	14 664	513 (a)	604	581	589	174	277	188	211	156	149	160	156	156	164	144
Slovenia	292	403	409	501	608	693	520	544	580	516	642	452	223	220	247	292	143	242
Spain	4 287	4 512	4 887	6 949	9 074	6 810	7 019	n.a.	n.a.	n.a.	n.a.	n.a.	n.a.	n.a.	n.a.	n.a.	n.a.	n.a.
Sweden	4 700	4 300	n.a.	4 690	5 581	4 291	4 683	4 564	4 583	188	182	171	169	532 /1	523	526	465	463

Table A.9. **Total amount of debt collected from enforcement actions during the fiscal year and number of year-end debt cases** *(continued)*

Country	Total amount of debt collected during the fiscal year (in millions in local currency)									Number of year-end debt cases (thousands)								
	2005	2006	2007	2008	2009	2010	2011	2012	2013	2005	2006	2007	2008	2009	2010	2011	2012	2013
Switzerland	n.a.	n.a.	n.a.	n.a.	n.a.	1 780	1 873	n.a.	n.a.	n.a.	n.a.	n.a.	n.a.	n.a.	49	47	n.a.	n.a.
Turkey	n.a.	n.a.	n.a.	n.a.	n.a.	n.a.	n.a.	n.a.	n.a.	n.a.	n.a.	n.a.	n.a.	n.a.	n.a.	n.a.	n.a.	n.a.
United Kingdom	n.a.	n.a.	n.a.	n.a.	n.a.	n.a.	n.a.	n.a.	n.a.	10 553	10 544	10 076	n.a.	n.a.	n.a.	n.a.	n.a.	n.a.
United States	47 347	48 716	59 210	56 436	48 886	57 592	55 229	50 189	53 345	15 546	16 243	17 367	17 516	19 422	21 436	23 008	23 368	24 256
Non-OECD countries																		
Argentina	470	572	550	16 729	25 347	45 024	62 290	n.a.	n.a.	4 113	5 900	5 629	2 984	2 845	2 997	2 914	n.a.	n.a.
Brazil	n.a.	n.a.	n.a.	n.a.	n.a.	2 892	3 904	n.a.	n.a.	n.a.	n.a.	n.a.	n.a.	n.a.	6 220	7 382	7 682	8 531
Bulgaria	579	491	821	1 394	1 470	1 165	1 354	2 339	3 273	1 118	575	546	934	1 292	1 374	1 539	531	747
China	n.a.	n.a.	n.a.	n.a.	n.a.	16 000	20 000	n.a.	n.a.	n.a.	n.a.	n.a.	n.a.	n.a.	n.a.	n.a.	n.a.	n.a.
Colombia	n.a.	n.a.	n.a.	n.a.	n.a.	2 138 194	3 037 621	n.a.	n.a.	n.a.	n.a.	n.a.	n.a.	n.a.	315	311	n.a.	n.a.
Costa Rica	--------------- Not covered by the series for these years ---------------							2 770	4 250	------------- Not covered by the series for these years -------------							926	n/a
Croatia	--------------- Not covered by the series for these years ---------------							n.a.	n.a.	------------- Not covered by the series for these years -------------							n.a.	n.a.
Cyprus	n.a.	n.a.	n.a.	n.a.	n.a.	n.a.	n.a.	67	84	n.a.	n.a.	n.a.	207(c)	210(c)	207(c)	211(c)	214(c)	243(c)
Hong Kong, China	n.a.	n.a.	n.a.	n.a.	n.a.	n.a.	n.a.	n.a.	n.a.	n.a.	n.a.	n.a.	n.a.	n.a.	n.a.	n.a.	n.a.	n.a.
India	n.a.	n.a.	n.a.	100 160	n.a.	537 150	550 200	550 200	638 120	n.a.	n.a.	n.a.	n.a.	n.a.	n.a.	n.a.	n.a.	n.a.
Indonesia	n.a.	n.a.	n.a.	12612341	18365095	22684000	12407000	12240472	13472389	n.a.	n.a.	n.a.	n.a.	n.a.	n.a.	n.a.	n.a.	n.a.
Latvia	146	183	249	324	222	216	210	335	416	81	82	86	97	108	111	114	126	127
Lithuania	715	n.a.	n.a.	1 066	854	756	686	494	724	n.a.	237	307	250	273	347	389	361	435
Malaysia	1 722	2 070	3 899	2 778	3 256	5 636	6 402	2 161	2 312	n.a.	2 119	2 201	2 835	2 201	1 083	996	1 050	973
Malta (d)	n.a.	n.a.	n.a.	n.a.	n.a.	47	18	37	46	n.a.	n.a.	n.a.	n.a.	n.a.	92	95	66	69
Morocco	--------------- Not covered by the series for these years ---------------							2 500	2 900	------------- Not covered by the series for these years -------------							n.a.	n.a.
Romania	n.a.	n.a.	n.a.	12 826	11 240	n.a.	n.a.	17 680	16 420	n.a.	n.a.	396	n.a.	n.a.	n.a.	n.a.	n.a.	n.a.
Russia	305 577	302 922	319 073	425 231	584 032	428 357	407 418	354 698	368 356	n.a.	n.a.	n.a.	n.a.	n.a.	11 762	11 384	n.a.	n.a.
Saudi Arabia	n.a.	n.a.	n.a.	n.a.	n.a.	n.a.	n.a.	7	167	n.a.	n.a.	n.a.	n.a.	n.a.	n.a.	n.a.	8 090	7 353
Singapore	n.a.	n.a.	n.a.	n.a.	n.a.	n.a.	n.a.	n.a.	n.a.	n.a.	n.a.	n.a.	n.a.	n.a.	n.a.	n.a.	n.a.	n.a.
South Africa	21 900	20 500	17 700	12 279	13 584	n.a.	n.a.	14 734	23 468	n.a.	1 400	1 500	2 219	2 000	n.a.	2 131	2 038	2 089
Thailand	--------------- Not covered by the series for these years ---------------							34	32	------------- Not covered by the series for these years -------------							0.1	0.1

Notes: (a) In euros from this year.
(b) VAT only.
(c) Number of assessments not taxpayers.
(d) Statistics refer only to authority in charge of Direct Taxation and VAT.

Source: Survey responses for current and prior series.

Table A.10. **Value of verification actions: For all taxpayers and large taxpayers**

(For some countries the historical data has been modified as a result of country revisions of previously reported data)

Country	Value of completed actions for all taxpayers (in millions in local currency)									Value of completed actions for large taxpayers (in millions in local currency)								
	2005	2006	2007	2008	2009	2010	2011	2012	2013	2005	2006	2007	2008	2009	2010	2011	2012	2013
OECD countries																		
Australia	6 779	6 899	6 960	8 206	8 308	9 320	10 268	11 369	12 200	3 201	2 495	2 557	3 325	2 136	3 342	2 343	2 391	2 353
Austria	1 517	2 077	2 038	2 177	1 453	1 567	2 147	2 165	1 882	880	1 189	1 193	1 358	546	648	1 218	1 279	823
Belgium	n.a.	n.a.	n.a.	n.a.	6 825	8 104	8 841	n.a.	n.a.	n.a.	n.a.	n.a.	n.a.	n.a.	n.a.	n.a.	n.a.	n.a.
Canada	6 566	6 295	8 671	9 311	8 891	10 883	9 934	9 791	10 534	2 214	2 125	3 169	4 627	3 482	4 269	3 560	3 687	4 210
Chile	250 324	216 039	179 189	289 835	284 398	623 000	799 378	976 102	905 072	46 408	29 289	37 507	38 008	18 204	117 043	167 177	275 251	104 178
Czech Republic	2 177	5 336	2 858	10 114	9.520	14 008	14 004	15 120	11 232	n.a.	n.a.	n.a.	n.a.	n.a.	n.a.	n.a.	n.a.	3 462
Denmark	n.a.	n.a.	n.a.	n.a.	n.a.	21 521	15 268	27 114	28 982	n.a.	n.a.	n.a.	n.a.	n.a.	3 260	3 521	17 765	22 915
Estonia	n.a.	n.a.	n.a.	729	1 325	955	50 (a)	45	50	n.a.	n.a.	n.a.	n.a.	n.a.	n.a.	n.a.	n.a.	n.a.
Finland	295	244	266	2 129	2 298	465 /2	400 /2	402	372	n.a.	n.a.	n.a.	n.a.	n.a.	n.a.	n.a.	44	45
France	9 803	9 944	10 518	9 563	9 935	16 002	16 407	19 096	18 000	2 137	2 444	2 743	3 117	3 317	5 737	6 020	7 206	6 258
Germany	15 845	18 178	18 544	19 374	20 938	17 760	18 423	n.a.	n.a.	10 922	12 952	13 196	13 974	15 292	11 916	12 527	14 643	13 430
Greece	1 808	3 685	2 553	2 657	2 822	3 681	2 960	2 315	1 660	1 355	2 836	1 857	1 693	1 280	2 160	2 091	299	312
Hungary	328 730	480 812	569 063	768 639	751 751	813 685	707 799	821 474	979 631	11 210	13 367	55 996	83 453	87 522	109 653	98 126	112 305	140 495
Iceland	n.a.	n.a.	n.a.	3 086	3 075	n.a.	n.a.	n.a.	n.a.	n.a.	n.a.	n.a.	n.a.	n.a.	n.a.	n.a.	n.a.	n.a.
Ireland	575	692	734	632	670	493	522	492	548	97	108	208	140	191	84	112	83	111
Israel	n.a.	n.a.	n.a.	6 114	7 218	5 616	6 443	12 251	15 797	n.a.	n.a.	n.a.	695	1 069	n.a.	n.a.	n.a.	n.a.
Italy	29 282	25 807	31 540	37 500	44 300	54 100	63 600	57 382	49 163	3 762	3 324	4 523	2 800	5 400	9 600	12 400	10 818	7 649
Japan	686 700	731 200	819 700	768 100	671 200	728 900	574 700	513 400	467 900	184 100	201 100	236 500	203 600	142 100	223 156	111 024	94 108	101 086
Korea	4 316 901	3 905 041	5 538 000	n.a.	n.a.	n.a.	n.a.	7 010 800	n.a.	n.a.	n.a.	n.a.	n.a.	n.a.	n.a.	n.a.	n.a.	n.a.
Luxembourg	137	161	118	50 (b)	70 (b)	62 (b)	72 (b)	64 (b)	83 (b)	n.a.	n.a.	n.a.	n.a.	n.a.	n.a.	n.a.	n.a.	n.a.
Mexico	42 181	64 794	52 289	62 980	74 413	97 966	102 622	96 940	145 351	18 326	32 435	29 221	37 636	44 835	59 646	60 388	59 963	80 858
Netherlands	n.a.	n.a.	n.a.	n.a.	n.a.	n.a.	n.a.	n.a.	n.a.	n.a.	n.a.	n.a.	n.a.	n.a.	n.a.	n.a.	n.a.	n.a.
New Zealand	763	980	996	1 449	1 269	2 865	1 451	1 204	1 222	268	357	359	723	583	2 095	756	340	638
Norway	10 635	15 999	5 351	n.a.	n.a.	n.a.	n.a.	28 900	19 200	n.a.	n.a.	n.a.	n.a.	n.a.	n.a.	n.a.	n.a.	n.a.
Poland	422	426	402	1 257	1 344	1 903	2 138	2 494	3 294	84	115	54	426	382	610	703	913	1 142
Portugal	1 141	1 352	1 769	1 660	2 606	2 049	1 749	2 009	1 583	237	344	561	396	739	502	455	677	353
Slovak Republic	7 955	8 751	8 424	382 (a)	436	556	707	528	586	158	487	166	58	6	17	2	11	8
Slovenia	85	69	87	150	174	264	286	275	346	n.a.	n.a.	n.a.	7.6	4.5	n.a.	n.a.	23	15
Spain	4 583	5 310	5 954	6 500	7 010	8 500	9 200	11 517	10 950	n.a.	n.a.	n.a.	n.a.	1 080	n.a.	n.a.	n.a.	n.a.
Sweden	n.a.	11 856	12 504	8 556	5 493	7 671	4 352	n.a.	n.a.	n.a.	n.a.	n.a.	n.a.	n.a.	n.a.	n.a.	n.a.	n.a.
Switzerland	343	249	135	95	163	89	82	103	97	n.a.	n.a.	n.a.	n.a.	n.a.	n.a.	n.a.	n.a.	n.a.

Table A.10. **Value of verification actions: For all taxpayers and large taxpayers** *(continued)*

	Value of completed actions for all taxpayers (in millions in local currency)									Value of completed actions for large taxpayers (in millions in local currency)								
Country	2005	2006	2007	2008	2009	2010	2011	2012	2013	2005	2006	2007	2008	2009	2010	2011	2012	2013
Turkey	5 142	5 167	11 865	11 252	14 043	n.a.	n.a.	13 311	27 648	3 802	3 080	6 872	6 021	7 973	n.a.	n.a.	n.a.	n.a.
United Kingdom	5 200	5 600	9 200	n.a.	n.a.	16 487	14 086	18 600	20 700	4 160	3 400	4 300	n.a.	n.a.	7 179	7 886	5 000	5 300
United States	38 379	38 531	53 049	57 940	58 249	58 799	61 405	48 164	50 297	11 079	8 079	8 876	16 403	11 060	15 811	13 186	9 705	13 230
Non-OECD countries																		
Argentina	4 202	5 802	4 789	6 829	8 211	8 955	12 060	10 307	12 006	n.a.	n.a.	n.a.	5 272	5 760	6 223	8 761	5 590	6 015
Brazil	n.a.	n.a.	n.a.	n.a.	n.a.	87 468	103 421	108 969	181 604	n.a.	n.a.	n.a.	n.a.	n.a.	55 350	74 496	86 626	152 508
Bulgaria	240	163	235	263	295	189	275	355	177	60	27	90	58	87	41	85	65	22
China	36 700	38 600	43 000	44 000	119 200	n.a.	n.a.	12 500 474	12 836 733	n.a.	n.a.	n.a.	n.a.	n.a.	n.a.	n.a.	203 000	171 718
Colombia	n.a.	n.a.	n.a.	n.a.	n.a.	475 555	476 409	663 542	733 314	n.a.	n.a.	n.a.	n.a.	n.a.	201 685	252 259	379 693	310 416
Costa Rica	---- Not covered by the series for these years ----							n.a.	n.a.	---- Not covered by the series for these years ----							16 728	5 909
Croatia	---- Not covered by the series for these years ----							1 663	1 519	---- Not covered by the series for these years ----							n.a.	464
Cyprus	194	145	201	38 (a)	44	213	227	259	206	n.a.	n.a.	n.a.	n.a.	n.a.	n.a.	n.a.	19(b)	4(b)
Hong Kong, China	n.a.	n.a.	n.a.	n.a.	n.a.	2 634	3 873	6 056	3 503	n.a.	n.a.	n.a.	n.a.	n.a.	n.a.	n.a.	n.a.	n.a.
India	n.a.	n.a.	n.a.	n.a.	n.a.	1 826	3 092	n.a.	n.a.	n.a.	n.a.	n.a.	n.a.	n.a.	n.a.	n.a.	n.a.	n.a.
Indonesia	n.a.	n.a.	n.a.	10345000	12179000	16480000	15911000	25548000	39015000	n.a.	n.a.	n.a.	n.a.	1 028 666	n.a.	n.a.	11 147000	10242000
Latvia	147	191	94	147	160	166	228	189	202	2	3	2	0.9	10	n.avail.	51	25	76
Lithuania	220	204	186	262	478	311	267	323	311	n.a.	n.a.	n.a.	15	45	0.9	38	22	38
Malaysia	1 631	3 715	3 230	1 754	3 055	2 871	2 673	1 759	3 732	n.a.	212	261	n.a.	n.a.	n.a.	n.a.	n.a.	n.a.
Malta (c)	n.a.	n.a.	n.a.	n.a.	n.a.	25	16	28	41	n.a.	n.a.	n.a.	n.a.	n.a.	n.a.	n.a.	n.a.	n.a.
Morocco	---- Not covered by the series for these years ----							4 179	5 047	---- Not covered by the series for these years ----							2 679	3 374
Romania	2 990	2 293	2 587	4 587	6 081	8 906	8 593	6 547	9 309	0.074	568	245	735	1 017	n.a.	n.a.	944	2 559
Russia	n.a.	n.a.	n.a.	n.a.	n.a.	464 904	397 992	429 552	397 849	n.a.	n.a.	n.a.	n.a.	n.a.	129 684	91 089	95 918	119 288
Saudi Arabia	n.a.	n.a.	n.a.	n.a.	n.a.	n.a.	n.a.	n.a.	n.a.	n.a.	n.a.	n.a.	n.a.	n.a.	n.a.	n.a.	3 213	4 198
Singapore	255	170	135	151	199	256	295	273	275	n.a.	n.a.	n.a.	n.a.	n.a.	n.a.	n.a.	n.a.	n.a.
South Africa	12 200	21 800	15 700	n.a.	n.a.	n.a.	14 669	12 686	21 820	n.a.	n.a.	n.a.	n.a.	n.a.	n.a.	n.a.	43	316
Thailand	---- Not covered by the series for these years ----							12 769	14 447	---- Not covered by the series for these years ----							n.a.	n.a.

Notes: (a) In euros from this year.
(b) VAT only
(c) Statistics refer only to authority in charge of Direct Taxation.

Source: Survey responses for current and prior series.

Table A.11. **Service demand volumes for selected services**

(For some countries the historical data has been modified as a result of country revisions of previously reported data)

Country	In-person inquiries (millions)				Written correspondence from taxpayers (millions)							
					Paper				E-mail			
	2010	2011	2012	2013	2010	2011	2012	2013	2010	2011	2012	2013
OECD countries												
Australia	0.66	0.54	0.49	0.44	3.11	5.01	5.50	5.80	0.02	0.02	n.a.	n.a.
Austria	n.a.	n.a.	n.a.	n.a.	n.a.	n.a.	n.a.	n.a.	0.13	0.13	0.23	0.24
Belgium	n.a.	n.a.	n.a.	n.a.	n.a.	n.a.	in email	in email	n.a.	n.a.	0.02	0.05
Canada	0.24	0.23	0.26	0.16	0.41	0.36	0.31	0.22	n.a. (a)	n.a. (a)	n.a. (a)	n.a. (a)
Chile	2.34	2.44	2.73	2.69	n.a.	0.14	0.17	0.19	0.02	0.03	0.03	0.04
Czech Republic	n.a.	n.a.	n.a.	n.a.	n.a.	n.a.	< 0.01	< 0.01	n.a.	n.a.	in paper	in paper
Denmark	0.40	0.39	0.39	0.26	n.a.	n.a.	n.a.	n.a.	0.38	0.35	0.40	0.44
Estonia	0.31	0.29	0.20	0.16	n.a.	n.a.	n.a.	n.a.	n.a.	n.a.	0.02 (b)	0.03 (b)
Finland	n.a.	n.a.	1.29	1.07	n.a.	n.a.	n.a.	n.a.	0.02	0.02	0.02	0.02
France	15.15	17.86	17.93	17.94	> 4.50	n.a.	n.a.	n.a.	3.38	4.15	0.59	0.71
Germany	n.a.	n.a.	n.a.	n.a.	n.a.	n.a.	n.a.	n.a.	n.a.	n.a.	n.a.	n.a.
Greece	n.a.	n.a.	n.a.	n.a.	n.a.	n.a.	n.a.	n.a.	n.a.	n.a.	n.a.	n.a.
Hungary	2.35	2.50	2.58	2.37	0.01	0.01	0.01	0.01	0.03	0.27	0.03 (c)	0.02 (c)
Iceland	0.04	0.07	n.a.	n.a.	n.a.	0.06	n.a.	n.a.	0.01	0.02	n.a.	n.a.
Ireland	0.87	0.81	0.77	0.67	2.89	2.72	2.01	1.95	in paper	in paper	in paper	in paper
Israel	n.a.	n.a.	n.a.	n.a.	n.a.	n.a.	0.07 (d)	0.08 (d)	n.a.	n.a.	0.02 (d)	0.03 (d)
Italy	9.70	10.30	9.47	9.65	n.a.	n.a.	n.a.	n.a.	0.08	0.11	0.07	0.09
Japan	4.20	3.76	3.88	3.91	n.a.	n.a.	< 0.01	< 0.01	n.a.	n.a.	n.a.	n.a.
Korea	n.a.	n.a.	n.a.	n.a.	n.a.	n.a.	n.a.	n.a.	n.a.	n.a.	n.a.	n.a.
Luxembourg	n.a.	n.a.	n.a.	n.a.	n.a.	n.a.	n.a.	n.a.	n.a.	n.a.	n.a.	n.a.
Mexico	8.97	10.33	10.25	8.39	n.a.	n.a.	n.a.	n.a.	1.20	1.60	1.90	1.70
Netherlands	0.88	0.98	0.81	0.49	n.a.	n.a.	n.a.	n.a.	0	0	n.a.	n.a.
New Zealand	0.20	0.20	0.20	0.20	0.90	0.80	0.80	0.70	0.70	0.70	0.80	0.80
Norway	n.a.	n.a.	n.a.	n.a.	n.a.	n.a.	0.80	0.76	n.a.	n.a.	0.04 (e)	0.04 (e)
Poland	n.a.	n.a.	n.a.	n.a.	n.a.	n.a.	n.a.	n.a.	n.a.	n.a.	n.a.	n.a.
Portugal	14.99	12.98	16.00	17.50	n.a.	n.a.	n.a.	n.a.	n.a.	n.a.	n.a.	n.a.
Slovak Republic	n.a.	n.a.	n.a.	n.a.	< 0.01	< 0.01	< 0.01	< 0.01	0.01	0.01	0.01	0.01
Slovenia	n.a.	n.a.	n.a.	n.a.	n.a.	n.a.	0.03	0.03	n.a.	n.a.	0.02	0.02
Spain	n.a.	n.a.	13.37	19.28	n.a.	n.a.	n.a.	n.a.	n.a.	n.a.	n.a.	n.a.
Sweden	1.40	1.50	1.91	2.20	n.a.	n.a.	n.a.	n.a.	0.30	0.40	0.38	0.37
Switzerland	0	0	n.a.	n.a.	0.20	0.20	n.a.	n.a.	0.10	0.10	n.a.	n.a.

Table A.11. **Service demand volumes for selected services** *(continued)*

Country	In-person inquiries (millions)				Written correspondence from taxpayers (millions)							
					Paper				E-mail			
	2010	2011	2012	2013	2010	2011	2012	2013	2010	2011	2012	2013
Turkey	n.a.	n.a.	n.a.	n.a.	n.a.	n.a.	n.a.	n.a.	< 0.01	< 0.01	< 0.01	n.a.
United Kingdom	3.09	3.20	2.70	2.00	11.39	9.69	23.60	18.30	n.a.	n.a.	n.a.	n.a.
United States	6.38	6.39	6.85	6.52	20.79	19.83	20.90	20.80	0.05	0.05	6.16	5.76
Non-OECD countries												
Argentina	n.a.	n.a.	n.a.	n.a.	n.a.	n.a.	n.a.	n.a.	0.33	0.34	0.37	0.39
Brazil	20.30	20.10	20.22	20.01	n.a.	n.a.	n.a.	n.a.	0.12	0.15	0.16	0.18
Bulgaria	n.a.	n.a.	n.a.	n.a.	n.a.	n.a.	n.a.	n.a.	0.01	0.01	0.02	0.02
China	n.a.	n.a.	n.a.	n.a.	n.a.	n.a.	n.a.	n.a.	n.a.	n.a.	n.a.	n.a.
Colombia	3.27	3.14	n.a.	n.a.	1.45	0.92	0.01	0.01	0.12	0.10	0.00	0.00
Costa Rica	-----	-----	0.06	0.07	-----	-----	0.01	0.01	-----	-----	0.02	0.02
Croatia	-----	-----	n.a.	n.a.	-----	-----	n.a.	n.a.	-----	-----	n.a.	n.a.
Cyprus	n.a.	n.a.	n.a.	n.a.	< 0.01	< 0.01	< 0.01	< 0.01	< 0.01	< 0.01	< 0.01	< 0.01
Hong Kong, China	0.23	0.21	0.22	0.23	0.43	0.44	0.55	0.64	0.10	0.11	0.17	0.14
India	n.a.	n.a.	n.a.	n.a.	n.a.	n.a.	n.a.	n.a.	n.a.	n.a.	0.62	2.56
Indonesia	-----	-----	n.a.	n.a.	-----	-----	n.a.	n.a.	-----	-----	n.a.	n.a.
Latvia	0.47	0.56	0.42	0.20	0.01	0.17	< 0.01	< 0.01	0.10	0.13	0.05	0.05
Lithuania	0.19	0.11	n.a.	n.a.	< 0.01	< 0.01	< 0.01	< 0.01	0.02	0.01	0.02	0.03
Malaysia	0.08	0.09	2.49	2.71	0.01	< 0.01	0.74	0.77	0.12	0.10	0.10	0.07
Malta	0.05	0.04	0.05	0.04	0.02	0.02	0.04	0.04	< 0.01	< 0.01	0.02	0.02
Morocco	-----	-----	n.a.	n.a.	-----	-----	0.09	0.08	-----	-----	n.a.	n.a.
Romania	n.a.	n.a.	n.a.	n.a.	< 0.01	0.05	0.05	0.02	0.02	0.02	0.02	0.02
Russia	n.a.	n.a.	n.a.	n.a.	0.17	0.16	n.a.	n.a.	0.02	0.05	n.a.	n.a.
Saudi Arabia	n.a.	n.a.	0.21	0.25	n.a.	n.a.	n.a.	n.a.	n.a.	n.a.	n.a.	n.a.
Singapore	0.19	0.14	0.10	0.10	0.45	0.28	0.25	0.21	0.26	0.22	0.23	0.23
South Africa	n.a.	n.a.	6.36	8.37	n.a.	n.a.	n.a.	n.a.	n.a.	n.a.	n.a.	n.a.
Thailand	-----	-----	n.a.	n.a.	-----	-----	n.a.	n.a.	-----	-----	n.a.	n.a.

Notes: (a) CRA does not track incoming email volumes and for security reasons does not encourage email communication with taxpayers.
(b) Does not include emails sent directly to officials.
(c) Only incoming inquiries through the email system located on the official website of NTCA.
(d) Only for mail received by service centres, not including items received by regional offices or HQ.
(e) Number of emails between July and December.

Source: Survey responses for current and prior series.

Table A.12. **Service demand volumes for selected services**

(For some countries the historical data has been modified as a result of country revisions of previously reported data)

Country	Phone inquiries received (millions)								Other phone calls answered (excl. IVR-handed calls) (millions)			
	Handled by IVR				Other calls							
	2010	2011	2012	2013	2010	2011	2012	2013	2010	2011	2012	2013
OECD countries												
Australia (a)	1.09	1.78	1.50	1.10	10.12	10.98	11.70	10.90	8.89	9.35	10.10	9.50
Austria	n.a.	n.a.	n.a.	n.a.	n.a.	3.54	5.40	5.90	n.a.	3.54	4.60	4.90
Belgium			n.a.	n.a.	1.01	1.26	1.05	0.96	0.70	0.63	0.68	0.63
Canada	7.15	7.02	6.72	6.61	17.04	18.10	17.97	17.12	16.39	17.39	17.19	16.54
Chile	n.a.	n.a.	n.a.	n.a.	0.99	1.01	0.87	0.79	0.84	0.84	0.86	0.78
Czech Republic	n.a.	n.a.	n.a.	n.a.	n.a.	n.a.	n.a.	n.a.	n.a.	n.a.	n.a.	n.a.
Denmark	3.39	3.35	n.a.	n.a.	4.32	4.28	3.52	3.55	n.a.	n.a.	2.71	2.77
Estonia	n.a.	n.a.	n.a.	n.a.	0.25	0.28	0.24	0.24	0.24	0.25	0.23	0.22
Finland	n.a.	n.a.	n.a.	n.a.	1.41	1.71	2.44	2.70	0.94	1.07	1.78	2.08
France	n.a.	n.a.	n.a.	n.a.	3.14	4.34	2.87	2.53	3.25	3.07	n.a.	n.a.
Germany	n.a.	n.a.	n.a.	n.a.	n.a.	n.a.	n.a.	n.a.	n.a.	n.a.	n.a.	n.a.
Greece	n.a.	n.a.	n.a.	n.a.	n.a.	n.a.	n.a.	n.a.	n.a.	n.a.	n.a.	0.68
Hungary	1.26	1.23	1.40	1.35	0.81	0.77	n.a.	n.a.	0.78	0.75	n.a.	n.a.
Iceland	n.a.	n.a.	n.a.	n.a.	0.26	0.26	n.a.	n.a.	0.13	0.13	n.a.	n.a.
Ireland	3.93	3.96	1.51	1.36	1.91	1.94	0.74	1.54	1.71	1.74	1.50	2.44
Israel	n.a.	n.a.	n.a.	n.a.	n.a.	n.a.	n.a.	n.a.	n.a.	n.a	0.60	0.64
Italy	0.08	0.09	0.08	0.13	2.61	3.63	3.09	2.67	2.00	2.00	n.a.	n.a.
Japan	0.03	n.a.	n.a.	n.a.	n.a.	n.a.	n.a.	n.a.	5.14	5.04	5.30	5.01
Korea	5.01	4.78	n.a.	n.a.	n.a.	n.a.	n.a.	n.a.	n.a.	n.a.	1.50	1.50
Luxembourg	n.a.	n.a.	n.a.	n.a.	n.a.	n.a.	n.a.	n.a.	n.a.	n.a.	n.a.	n.a.
Mexico	5.76	5.75	4.57	3.74	5.39	4.87	4.57	3.74	4.77	4.45	4.19	3.60
Netherlands	n.a.	n.a.	n.a.	n.a.	15.09	15.81	15.40	16.8	13.73	14.02	14.20	14.50
New Zealand	0.60	0.70	0.70	0.90	5.40	5.10	4.10	4.70	4.00	3.70	3.50	3.30
Norway	n.a.	n.a.	n.a.	n.a.	2.62	2.66	2.19	2.15	2.18	1.99	1.76	1.80
Poland	0.27	0.27	2.23	2.67	0.21	0.22	2.44	2.96	n.a.	n.a.	1.61	1.69
Portugal	1.13	1.16	1.60	2.30	n.a	n.a	n.a	n.a	0.71	0.98	1.20	1.70
Slovak Republic	n.a.	0.02	n.a.	n.a.	n.a.	n.a.	n.a.	n.a.	n.a.	n.a.	n.a.	0.06
Slovenia	n.a.	n.a.	0.02	n.a.	n.a.	n.a.	1.08	1.22	n.a.	n.a.	n.a.	n.a.
Spain	4.20	5.48	3.71	3.38	6.72	6.18	10.95	10.27	5.99	5.70	6.24	5.85
Sweden	8.30	8.30	n.a.	n.a.	n.a	n.a	7.59	7.50	4.50	4.40	1.62	1.36
Switzerland	n.a.	n.a.	n.a.	n.a.	0.20	0.20	n.a.	n.a.	0.20	0.20	n.a.	n.a.

Table A.12. **Service demand volumes for selected services** *(continued)*

Country	Phone inquiries received (millions) – Handled by IVR 2010	2011	2012	2013	Phone inquiries received (millions) – Other calls 2010	2011	2012	2013	Other phone calls answered (excl. IVR-handed calls) (millions) 2010	2011	2012	2013
Turkey	n.a.	n.a.	n.a.	n.a.	0.25	0.48	n.a.	n.a.	0.25	0.47	n.a.	n.a.
United Kingdom	3.11	6.51	8.65	8.15	41.34	50.64	33.52	29.37	26.92	23.43	21.87	21.62
United States	35.11	42.29	59.21	54.50	48.40 (b)	47.60 (b)	44.62 (b)	43.94 (b)	36.67	34.24	30.79	30.12
Non-OECD countries												
Argentina	0.388	0.436	0.48	0.58	5.5	3.5	2.59	3.09	0.20	0.26	0.32	0.41
Brazil	n.a.	n.a.	n.a.	n.a.	10.16	9.71	9.2	11.19	2.10	2.50	2.01	0.85
Bulgaria	0.125	0.095	0.10	0.09	0.218	0.211	0.24	0.28	0.21	0.20	0.23	0.27
China	n.a.	n.a.	11.6	10.4	n.a.	n.a.	18.1	20.2	n.a.	n.a.	14.30	16.30
Colombia	0.54	0.54	1.19	1.65	n.a.	n.a.	0.97	1.48	n.a.	n.a.	0.73	1.16
Costa Rica	---	---	n.a.	n.a.	---	---	n.a.	n.a.	---	---	0.09	0.09
Croatia	---	---	0.07	0.08	---	---	n.a.	n.a.	---	---	0.07	0.08
Cyprus	n.a.	n.a.	n.a.	n.a.	n.a.	n.a.	n.a.	n.a.	n.a.	n.a.	n.a.	n.a.
Hong Kong, China	1.24	1.17	1.38	1.41	0.04	0.04	0.04	0.04	0.03	0.03	0.04	0.03
India	n.a.	n.a.	0.22	0.21	n.a.	n.a.	1.37	2.33	n.a.	n.a.	1.12	2.11
Indonesia	---	---	0.91	0.34	---	---	1.22	0.80	---	---	0.32	0.46
Latvia	n.a.	n.a.	0.46	0.43	n.a.	n.a.	0.44	0.48	0.12	0.22	0.40	0.40
Lithuania	n.a.	n.a.	n.a.	n.a.	0.94	0.76	0.82	0.94	0.77	0.70	0.65	0.67
Malaysia	0.07	0.09	0.08	0.02	0.43	0.47	0.54	0.41	0.49	0.53	0.43	0.27
Malta	n.a.	n.a.	n.a.	n.a.	0.18	0.15	0.12	0.09	0.10	0.07	0.07	0.07
Morocco	---	---	0	0	---	---	0	< 0.01	---	---	0	< 0.01
Romania	n.a.	n.a.	n.a.	n.a.	0.98	1.00	n.a.	n.a.	n.a.	n.a.	1.15	0.98
Russia	n.a	n.a	n.a.	n.a.	n.a	n.a	n.a.	n.a.	n.a	0.48	n.a.	n.a.
Saudi Arabia	n.a.	n.a.	n.a.	n.a.	n.a.	n.a.	0.10	0.14	n.a.	n.a.	n.a.	n.a.
Singapore	0.54	0.47	n.a.	n.a.	1.07	1.05	n.a.	n.a.	1.00	1.00	0.99	0.98
South Africa	n.a.	n.a.	n.a.	n.a.	5.66	6.16	6.16	5.49	5.04	5.58	5.58	5.11
Thailand	---	---	n.a.	n.a.	---	---	n.a.	n.a.	---	---	0.62	0.66

Notes: (a) *(1)* Phone inquiries handled by IVR: Total call volumes are all inbound calls offered via the IVR which were either ultimately answered or abandoned; *(2)* Other phone enquiries include Self Help calls and calls blocked before they enter the system. Self Help calls usually do not require call centre staff intervention. Blocking of calls is used at times of high demand to manage the flow of calls to call centres so that the majority of calls are answered within a reasonable time. Call blocking data for 2011/12 is only available from January 2012; *(3)* Other phone enquires answered are internally escalated or transferred calls.

(b) The number of phone inquiries received includes the number of calls answered by an assister and the number of calls abandoned by the taxpayer.

Source: Survey responses for current and prior series.

Table A.13. **General country statistical information: GDP, citizen and labour force populations**

(For some countries the historical data has been modified as a result of country revisions of previously reported data)

	Gross domestic product (in billions in local currency)							Citizen population (millions)		Labour force population (millions)	
Country	2007	2008	2009	2010	2011	2012	2013	2012	2013	2012	2013
OECD countries											
Australia	1 088	1 179	1 259	1 296	1 407	1 486	1 521	22.72	23.13	12.03	12.21
Austria	282	292	286	294	309	317	323	8.43	8.47	4.37	4.39
Belgium	345	355	350	366	380	388	395	11.13	11.16	4.89	4.95
Canada	1 566	1 646	1 567	1 663	1 760	1 820	1 881	34.88	35.16	18.94	19.14
Chile	90 429	93 848	96 444	111 008	121 403	129 601	137 212	17.40	17.56	8.20	8.38
Czech Republic	3 832	4 015	3 922	3 954	4 022	4 048	4 086	10.51	10.51	5.26	5.31
Denmark	1 739	1 798	1 714	1 799	1 833	1 863	1 891	5.59	5.60	2.91	2.89
Estonia	251	254	219	225	16 (a)	17	18	1.33	1.32	0.70	0.68
Finland	187	194	181	187	197	199	201	5.41	5.43	2.71	2.68
France	1 946	1 996	1 939	1 998	2 059	2 091	2 114	63.52	65.58	29.14	28.57
Germany	2 510	2 558	2 457	2 576	2 699	2 750	2 809	81.91	82.11	42.38	42.71
Greece	223	233	231	222	209	193	182	11.09	11.06	4.97	4.97
Hungary	24 990	26 543	25 626	26 513	27 635	28 048	29 078	9.92	9.91	4.35	4.39
Iceland	1 309	1 480	1 498	1 536	1 628	1 699	1 786	0.32	0.32	0.18	0.18
Ireland	190	180	162	158	163	164	164	4.59	4.59	2.16	2.16
Israel	726	768	812	871	925	992	1 049	7.91	8.06	3.61	3.68
Italy	1 610	1 633	1 574	1 606	1 639	1 628	1 560	60.51	60.67	25.64	25.53
Japan	512 975	501 209	471 139	482 384	471 311	473 777	478 368	127.52	127.30	65.55	65.77
Korea	1 043 258	1 104 492	1 151 708	1 265 308	1 332 681	1 377 457	1 428 295	50.00	50.22	25.50	25.87
Luxembourg	37	37	36	39	42	43	45	0.53	0.54	0.25	0.25
Mexico	11 399	12 257	12 073	13 267	14 509	15 561	16 104	117.05	118.40	51.48	51.87
Netherlands	609	636	618	632	643	641	643	16.76	16.78	8.89	8.96
New Zealand	184	186	190	199	207	212	227	4.43	4.47	2.39	2.42
Norway	2 306	2 560	2 382	2 544	2 751	2 909	3 011	5.02	5.08	2.68	2.70
Poland	1 177	1 276	1 345	1 417	1 528	1 596	1 636	38.53	38.50	17.34	17.36
Portugal	175	179	175	180	176	170	171	10.51	10.72	5.49	5.39
Slovak Republic	1 851	67 (a)	63	66	69	71	72	5.41	5.42	2.71	2.72
Slovenia	35	37	35	35	36	35	35	2.06	2.06	1.01	1.01
Spain	1 053	1 088	1 047	1 046	1 046	1 029	1 023	46.77	46.61	23.44	23.19

Table A.13. **General country statistical information: GDP, citizen and labour force populations** *(continued)*

Country	Gross domestic product (in billions in local currency)							Citizen population (millions)		Labour force population (millions)	
	2007	2008	2009	2010	2011	2012	2013	2012	2013	2012	2013
Sweden	3 126	3 204	3 106	3 338	3 481	3 550	3 641	9.52	9.56	5.06	5.12
Switzerland	541	568	554	573	585	592	603	8.00	8.04	4.60	4.67
Turkey	843	951	953	1 099	1 298	1 417	1 565	75.18	76.06	27.02	27.96
United Kingdom	1 428	1 462	1 417	1 486	1 537	1 558	1 613	63.71	62.57	31.93	32.18
United States	14 480	14 720	14 418	14 958	15 534	16 245	16 800	313.87	316.13	156.37	156.76
Non-OECD countries											
Argentina	1 027	1 284	1 412	1 810	2 303	2 745	3 340	41.09	41.45	18.85	19.09
Brazil	2 661	3 032	3 239	3 770	4 143	4 392	4 845	196.53	200.36	100.07	102.52
Bulgaria	60	69	68	71	75	78	78	7.33	7.28	3.34	3.37
China	26 581	31 405	34 090	40 151	47 310	51 894	56 885	1 350.70	1 357.38	787.63	793.00
Colombia	431 072	480 087	504 647	544 924	619 894	665 441	706 677	46.58	48.32	23.11	23.55
Costa Rica	------------------- Not covered by the series for these years -------------------					22 819	24 799	4.81	4.87	2.18	2.21
Croatia	------------------- Not covered by the series for these years -------------------					327	327	4.28	4.26	1.72	1.68
Cyprus	9	17 (a)	17	17	18	18	17	0.86	0.87	0.44	0.43
Hong Kong, China	1 651	1 707	1 659	1 776	1 934	2 037	2 125	7.18	7.22	3.79	3.86
India	49 864	55 826	65 503	77 841	90 097	101 133	113 551	1 236.69	1 252.14	472.13	481.24
Indonesia	3 950 893	4 948 688	5 603 871	6 422 918	7 419 187	8 229 439	9 083 972	246.86	249.87	118.38	120.17
Latvia	16	17	13	13	14	15	16	2.04	2.02	1.03	1.01
Lithuania	99	112	92	96	107	114	120	3.00	2.97	1.47	1.47
Malaysia	665	770	713	797	884	941	984	29.34	29.71	13.21	13.40
Malta	2	6 (a)	6	6	7	7	7	0.42	0.42	0.18	0.19
Morocco	------------------- Not covered by the series for these years -------------------					828	873	32.52	33.01	11.55	12.03
Romania	416	515	501	524	557	587	629	20.10	20.02	9.96	9.98
Russia	33 248	41 277	38 807	46 309	55 967	62 218	66 755	143.21	143.50	76.87	75.53
Saudi Arabia	1 559	1 949	1 609	1 976	2 511	2 752	2 795	28.29	28.83	11.00	11.36
Singapore	271	272	280	322	345	359	373	5.31	5.40	2.09	2.14
South Africa	2 016	2 256	2 408	2 674	2 933	3 139	3 385	52.27	52.98	18.06	19.75
Thailand	------------------- Not covered by the series for these years -------------------					11 375	11 899	66.79	67.01	39.84	39.47

Note: (a) In euros from this year.

Source: OECD Statistics, World Bank Statistics, International Labour Organization Statistics, and EC.

Annex B

Description of formulae used for computation of ratios

Table B.1. **Description of formulae used for computation of ratios**

Table		Formulae
Chapter 4		
4.5	Staff attrition	Number of staff departures / average staffing level (where the average staffing level equals opening staff numbers + year-end staff numbers / 2) x 100
4.5	Churn	Total recruits in 2013 + Total Resignations in 2013 / Average staff (where Average staff = Staff at beginning of 2013+ Staff at end of 2013 / 2)
Chapter 5		
5.2	Salary expenditure/total expenditure for tax administration and support functions	Salary expenditure all tax administration-related functions (Table A.6) / total expenditure for all tax administration-related functions (Table A.5)
5.3	IT and human resource management expenditure	Total information technology-related expenditure for all revenue body functions (Table A.4) / total expenditure for all revenue body functions (Table A.4)
		Total human resource management-related expenditure for all revenue body functions (Table A.5) / total expenditure for all revenue body functions (Table A.4)
5.4	Cost of collection ratios (administrative costs/net revenue collections)	Total expenditure for all tax administration-related functions (Table A.5) / net revenue collections (Table A.3)
5.5	Tax administration expenditure/ gross domestic product	Total expenditure for all tax administration-related functions (Table A.5) / Gross domestic product (Table A.13)
5.6	Revenue body staff usage for fiscal year 2013 and related ratios	Total staff usage for all tax administration-related functions (Table A.6) / total staff usage for all revenue body functions (Table A.6)
		Total citizen population (Table A.13) / total staff usage for all tax administration-related functions (Table A.6)
		Total labour force population (Table A.13) / total staff usage for all tax administration-related functions (Table A.6)
5.7	Staff usage (2013) by major tax functional groupings	Each separate tax function (Table A.6) / total staff usage for all tax administration-related functions (Table A.6)
5.9	Expenditure on non-tax roles	(Total expenditure for all revenue body functions (Table A.4) – total expenditure for all tax administration-related functions [Table A.5]) / total expenditure for all revenue body functions (Table A.4)
Chapter 6		
6.3	Revenue collections and refunds (relative shares)	Refunds for all taxes (Table A.2) / gross revenue collections (Table A.1)
		VAT refunds (Table A.2) / gross VAT collection (Table A.2)
		VAT refunds (Table A.2) / refunds for all taxes (Table A.2)
6.4	Taxpayer services: Service demand ratios	In-person inquiries (Table A.11) / total citizen population (Table A.13) * 100
		Phone inquiries (excl. IVR) (Table A.12) / total citizen population (Table A.13) * 100
6.8	Verification actions: Value of assessments/total net revenue collections	Value of completed actions for all taxpayers (Table A.10) / net revenue collections (Table A.3)
		Value of completed actions for large taxpayers (Table A.10) / net revenue collections (Table A.3)
6.13	Tax debt – year-end aggregates	Total tax debt (**including** disputed debt) outstanding at year-end (Table A.7) / net revenue collections (Table A.3)
		Total tax debt (**excluding** disputed debt) outstanding at year-end (Table A.7) / net revenue collections (Table A.3)
		[Total tax debt (**including** disputed debt) outstanding at year-end (Table A.7) – total tax debt (**excluding** disputed debt) outstanding at year-end (Table A.7)] / total tax debt (**including** disputed debt) outstanding at year-end (Table A.7)

Table		Formulae
6.14	Tax debts: Debt written off as a share of debt inventory	Tax debt written off (Table A.8) / total tax debt (**excluding** disputed debt) outstanding at year beginning
6.15	Tax debts: Movement in tax debt case numbers	Total number of tax debt cases at year-end (Table A.8) / total number of tax debt cases at year beginning
		Movement in year-end tax debt cases = (number of cases 2013 – number of cases 2007) (Table A.9) / number of cases 2007 (Table A.9)
Chapter 9		
9.2	Registrations as a % of labour force	Total number of PIT registrations / total labour force population (Table A.13)
9.2	Registrations as a % of citizen population	Total number of PIT registrations / total citizen population (Table A.13)

Annex C

Participating revenue bodies

Table C.1. **Country details of participating revenue bodies**

Country	Revenue body name	Website address	Monetary unit (symbol)	Fiscal year
OECD countries				
Australia	Australian Taxation Office	www.ato.gov.au	Dollar (AUD)	1 July-30 June
Austria	Federal Ministry of Finance	https://english.bmf.gv.at/	Euro (EUR)	Calendar Year
Belgium	Federal Public Service Finance	minfin.fgov.be	Euro (EUR)	Calendar Year
Canada	Canada Revenue Agency	www.cra-arc.gc.ca	Dollar (CAD)	1 April-31 March
Chile	Servicio de Impuestos Internos	www.sii.cl	Chilean Pesos	Calendar Year
Czech Republic	Financial Administration of the Czech Republic	www.financnisprava.cz	Czech Koruna (CZK)	Calendar Year
Denmark	Danish Ministry of Taxation (Skat)	www.skat.dk	Krone (DKK)	Calendar Year
Estonia	Tax and Customs Board	www.emta.ee	Estonian Kroon (EEK), EUR (from 2011)	Calendar Year
Finland	Finnish Tax Administration	www.tax.fi	Euro (EUR)	Calendar Year
France	Direction générale des finances publiques (General Directorate of Public Finances)	www.impots.gouv.fr	Euro (EUR)	Calendar Year
Germany	Federal Ministry of Finance – Tax Administration of The "Länder" (Federal States)	www.bundesfinanzministerium.de	Euro (EUR)	Calendar Year
Greece	General Secretariat for Public Revenue, Ministry of Finance	www.publicrevenue.gr/kpi/	Euro (EUR)	Calendar Year
Hungary	National Tax and Customs Administration	www.nav.gov.hu	Forint (HUF)	Calendar Year
Iceland	Directorate of Internal Revenue (Rikisskattstjóri)	www.rsk.is	Krona (ISK)	Calendar Year
Ireland	Office of the Revenue Commissioners	www.revenue.ie	Euro (EUR)	Calendar Year
Israel	Israel Tax Authority	http://ozar.mof.gov.il/taxes	New Israeli sheqels (ILS)	Calendar Year
Italy	Revenue Agency	www.agenziaentrate.it	Euro (EUR)	Calendar Year
Japan	National Tax Agency	www.nta.go.jp	Yen (JPY)	1 April-31 March
Korea	National Tax Service	www.nts.go.kr	Won (KRW)	Calendar Year
Luxembourg	Administration des contributions directes (Acd) – Direct Tax Administration Administration de l'enregistrement et des domaines (Aed)-Indirect Tax Administration	www.impotsdirects.public.lu www.aed.public.lu	Euro (EUR)	Calendar Year
Mexico	Tax Administration Service (Servicio de administración tributaria)	www.sat.gob.mx	Peso (MXN)	Calendar Year
Netherlands	Netherlands Tax and Customs Administration	www.belastingdienst.nl	Euro (EUR)	Calendar Year
New Zealand	Inland Revenue Department – Te Taari Taake	www.ird.govt.nz	Dollar (NZD)	1 April-31 March
Norway	Skatteetaten (Tax Norway)	www.skatteetaten.no	Norwegian Kroner	Calendar Year
Poland	Ministry Of Finance	www.mf.gov.pl	Zloty (PLN)	Calendar Year
Portugal	Autoridade Tributária e Aduaneira (Since 1st January 2012)	www.portaldasfinancas.gov.pt	Euro (EUR)	Calendar Year

Country	Revenue body name	Website address	Monetary unit (symbol)	Fiscal year
Slovak Republic	Financial Directorate of the Slovak Republic (Since 1st January 2012)	www.financnasprava.sk	Euro (EUR)	Calendar Year
Slovenia	Tax Administration of the Republic of Slovenia	www.durs.gov.si	Euro (EUR)	Calendar Year
Spain	Agencia estatal de administración tributaria – State Tax Administration Agency	www.agenciatributaria.es	Euro (EUR)	Calendar Year
Sweden	Swedish Tax Agency (Skatteverket)	www.skatteverket.se	Krona (SEK)	Calendar Year
Switzerland	Federal Tax Administration	www.estv.admin.ch	Franc (CHF)	Calendar Year
Turkey	Gelir İdaresi Başkanlığı (Turkish Revenue Administration)	www.gib.gov.tr	Lira (TRY)	Calendar Year
United Kingdom	Her Majesty's Revenue and Customs	www.hmrc.gov.uk	Pound (GBP)	1 April-31 March
United States	Internal Revenue Service	www.irs.gov	Dollar (USD)	1 October-30 September
Non-OECD countries				
Argentina	Federal Administration of Public Revenues	www.afip.gov.ar	Peso (ARS)	Calendar Year
Brazil	Secretariat of Federal Revenue of Brazil	www.receita.fazenda.gov.br	Real BRL)	Calendar Year
Bulgaria	National Revenue Agency (NRA)	www.nap.bg	Lev (BGN)	Calendar Year
China	State Administration of Taxation	www.chinatax.gov.cn	Yuan (RMB)	Calendar Year
Colombia	National Tax and Customs Administration	www.dian.gov.co	Pesos (COP)	Calendar Year
Costa Rica	Directorate of Taxation, Ministry of Finance	dgt.hacienda.go.cr	Colon (CRC)	Calendar Year
Croatia	Tax Administration, Ministry of Finance	www.porezna-uprava.hr	Kuna (HRK)	Calendar Year
Cyprus	Department of Inland Revenue, VAT Service	www.mof.gov.cy/ird www.mof.gov.cy/vat	Euro (EUR)	Calendar Year
Hong Kong, China	Inland Revenue Department	www.ird.gov.hk/	Dollar (HKD)	1 April-31 March
India	Central Board of Direct Taxes	www.incometaxindia.gov.in	Rupee (INR)	Calendar Year
Indonesia	Directorate General of Taxes	www.pajak.go.id/?lang=en	Rupiah (IDR)	Calendar Year
Latvia	State Revenue Service	www.vid.gov.lv	Lat (LVL)	Calendar Year
Lithuania	State Tax Inspectorate under the Ministry of Finance	www.vmi.lt	Litai (LTL)	Calendar Year
Malaysia	Inland Revenue Board	www.hasil.gov.my	Ringgit Malaysia (RM)	Calendar Year
Malta	Inland Revenue Department (Direct Taxes), VAT Department	www.ird.gov.mt www.vat.gov.mt	Euro (EUR)	Calendar Year
Morocco	Geeral Administration of Taxes	www.tax.gov.ma	Dirham (MAD)	Calendar Year
Romania	National Agency for Fiscal Administration	www.anaf.ro	Leu (RON)	Calendar Year
Russia	Federal Tax Service (FTS of Russia)	www.nalog.ru	Rouble (RUB)	Calendar Year
Saudi Arabia	Department of Zakat and Income Tax (DZIT)	www.dzit.gov.sa	Riyal (SAR)	Calendar Year
Singapore	Inland Revenue Authority of Singapore	www.iras.gov.sg	Dollar (SGD)	1 April-31 March
South Africa	South African Revenue Service (SARS)	www.sars.gov.za	Rand (ZAR)	1 April-31 March
Thailand	Revenue Department	www.rd.go.th	Baht (THB)	1 October-30 September

ORGANISATION FOR ECONOMIC CO-OPERATION AND DEVELOPMENT

The OECD is a unique forum where governments work together to address the economic, social and environmental challenges of globalisation. The OECD is also at the forefront of efforts to understand and to help governments respond to new developments and concerns, such as corporate governance, the information economy and the challenges of an ageing population. The Organisation provides a setting where governments can compare policy experiences, seek answers to common problems, identify good practice and work to co-ordinate domestic and international policies.

The OECD member countries are: Australia, Austria, Belgium, Canada, Chile, the Czech Republic, Denmark, Estonia, Finland, France, Germany, Greece, Hungary, Iceland, Ireland, Israel, Italy, Japan, Korea, Luxembourg, Mexico, the Netherlands, New Zealand, Norway, Poland, Portugal, the Slovak Republic, Slovenia, Spain, Sweden, Switzerland, Turkey, the United Kingdom and the United States. The European Union takes part in the work of the OECD.

OECD Publishing disseminates widely the results of the Organisation's statistics gathering and research on economic, social and environmental issues, as well as the conventions, guidelines and standards agreed by its members.

OECD PUBLISHING, 2, rue André-Pascal, 75775 PARIS CEDEX 16
(23 2015 11 1 P) ISBN 978-92-64-23231-0 – 2015-02

www.ingramcontent.com/pod-product-compliance
Lightning Source LLC
Chambersburg PA
CBHW061156240926
51846CB00006B/1026
9789264232310